Canadian Federalism

Performance, Effectiveness, and Legitimacy

Second Edition

Edited by
Herman Bakvis & Grace Skogstad

OXFORD
UNIVERSITY PRESS

OXFORD
UNIVERSITY PRESS

70 Wynford Drive, Don Mills, Ontario M3C 1J9
www.oup.com/ca

Oxford University Press is a department of the University of Oxford.
It furthers the University's objective of excellence in research, scholarship,
and education by publishing worldwide in

Oxford New York

Auckland   Cape Town   Dar es Salaam   Hong Kong   Karachi
Kuala Lumpur   Madrid   Melbourne   Mexico City   Nairobi
New Delhi   Shanghai   Taipei   Toronto

With offices in

Argentina   Austria   Brazil   Chile   Czech Republic   France   Greece
Guatemala   Hungary   Italy   Japan   Poland   Portugal   Singapore
South Korea   Switzerland   Thailand   Turkey   Ukraine   Vietnam

Oxford is a trade mark of Oxford University Press
in the UK and in certain other countries

Published in Canada
by Oxford University Press

Copyright © Oxford University Press Canada 2008

The moral rights of the author have been asserted

Database right Oxford University Press (maker)

First published 2008

Library and Archives Canada Cataloguing in Publication

Canadian federalism: performance, effectiveness and legitimacy/edited by
Herman Bakvis and Grace Skogstad. — 2nd ed.

Includes bibliographical references and index.

ISBN 978-0-19-542512-3

1. Federal government—Canada—Textbooks. 2. Federal-provincial relations—
Canada—Textbooks. 3. Canada—Politics and government—1993–2006—Textbooks.

I. Bakvis, Herman, 1948– II. Skogstad, Grace, 1948–

JL27.C3493 2007   320.471   C2007-903289-3

Cover design: Sherill Chapman
Cover image: Fred Dimmick/istockphoto

This book is printed on permanent (acid-free) paper ∞.
Printed in Canada

Contents

Contributors

GERALD BAIER
Department of Political Science
University of British Columbia

HERMAN BAKVIS
School of Public Administration
University of Victoria

KEITH G. BANTING
School of Policy Studies
Queen's University

DOUGLAS M. BROWN
Department of Political Science
St Francis Xavier University

MARTHA FRIENDLY
Childcare Resource and Research Unit
University of Toronto

ALAIN-G. GAGNON
Department of Political Science
University of Quebec at Montreal

RODNEY HADDOW
Department of Political Science
University of Toronto

RAFFAELE IACOVINO
Department of Political Science
McGill University

JAMES B. KELLY
Department of Political Science
Concordia University

DOUGLAS MACDONALD
Centre for the Environment
University of Toronto

ANTONIA MAIONI
McGill Institute for the Study of Canada
McGill University

AMY NUGENT
Department of Political Science
University of Toronto

MARTIN PAPILLON
School of Political Studies
University of Ottawa

ANDREW SANCTON
Department of Political Science
University of Western Ontario

RICHARD SIMEON
Department of Political Science
University of Toronto

JULIE SIMMONS
Department of Political Science
University of Guelph

GRACE SKOGSTAD
Department of Political Science
University of Toronto

A. BRIAN TANGUAY
Department of Political Science
Wilfrid Laurier University

LINDA A. WHITE
Department of Political Science
University of Toronto

MARK WINFIELD
Faculty of Environmental Studies
York University

Preface

This second edition of *Canadian Federalism: Performance, Effectiveness and Legitimacy* asks the same three questions posed in the first edition. How well are the institutions and processes of Canadian federalism *performing*? Are they *effective* in addressing substantive problems? And are they seen as *legitimate* by the various communities and constituencies that make up Canada? The policy sectors and institutions under scrutiny likewise remain largely unchanged. Even so, this new edition offers considerably more than an updated look at the policies and institutions documented in the earlier edition. There are eight new authors and seven new chapter themes, as well as a new concluding chapter. Like Canadian federalism itself, this volume represents both continuity and change.

This new edition would not have been possible without the collaboration and assistance of many people. Above all, we thank our contributors. Some are well-known scholars in the area of federalism, some are specialists in particular policy domains, and some are just beginning their academic careers, but all have been highly professional. Most of the chapters began as papers presented at a conference in the Department of Political Science at the University of Toronto in May 2006, and they have benefited from the thoughtful comments of several people at various stages: Steven Bernstein (Toronto), Steve Dupré (Toronto), Ian Greene (York), John Kirton (Toronto), Ronald Manzer (Toronto), Patricia Reilly (Ryerson), Peter Russell (Toronto), Lorne Sossin (Toronto), Michael Stein (McMaster), Garth Stevenson (Brock), Neil Thomlinson (Ryerson), and Carolyn Tuohy (Toronto). We thank them as well as the two anonymous reviewers for Oxford University Press whose detailed comments helped at the final revision stage. We also appreciate the financial assistance of the Department of Political Science in hosting the May conference. Herman Bakvis, Gerald Baier, and Douglas Brown would like to acknowledge the financial assistance of the Social Sciences and Humanities Research Council of Canada in making possible the research on which their chapters are based. We are also grateful for the editing and formatting assistance of Stephen Gillies, then an MA student in Political Science at the University of Toronto. Finally, we thank Sally Livingston and Richard Tallman for their careful copy editing, and Paula Druzga and her colleagues at Oxford University Press for steering this collection through to publication.

Herman Bakvis
(hbakvis@uvic.ca)

Grace Skogstad
(skogstad@chass.utoronto.ca)

Part One

The Institutions and Processes of Canadian Federalism

Chapter 1

Canadian Federalism: Performance, Effectiveness, and Legitimacy

Herman Bakvis and Grace Skogstad

Since the latter half of the nineteenth century, Canada has sought to unite a linguistically and regionally diverse citizen body within the confines of a single nation-state. The chosen formula has been federalism: a combination of shared rule, through a central government, on matters common to all citizens, and local self-rule, through provincial governments, on matters involving regionally distinctive identities, within a balanced structure designed to ensure that neither order of government is subordinate to the other (Watts, 1999: 1). From most perspectives, the Canadian federal arrangement has succeeded in striking the requisite balance between unity and diversity. It has also proven to be both flexible and resilient, allowing Canada to adjust its public policies to changing circumstances over time.

Even so, there have always been critics of the way Canadian federalism performs. Some observers have claimed that the federal 'balance' is actually lopsided, skewed by a tendency to either centralization or decentralization; others, that effective policy-making is hampered by either intergovernmental conflict or elite collusion. And, of course, the legitimacy of the Canadian federal system has been tested by groups with a strong sense of their own national identity, notably francophone Quebecers and indigenous peoples.

The purpose of this text is to investigate the state of contemporary Canadian federalism. It does so by asking three questions. How are the institutions of Canadian federalism performing? How do existing patterns of intergovernmental relations help or hinder effective policy-making? And how do Canadians evaluate the legitimacy of the institutions, processes, and outcomes of intergovernmental relations?

The investigation that follows has three dimensions: descriptive, evaluative, and explanatory. To explain the performance, effectiveness, and legitimacy of Canadian federalism it is necessary to look at a number of factors besides the structures of federalism itself. The Canadian federal system, like federal systems elsewhere, is embedded in a broader social, economic, institutional and political context. In other words, the institutions and processes of federalism can be seen as both responding to and shaped by:

1. structural cleavages in Canadian society, of which the most important historically have been ethno-linguistic and territorial differences in identities, values, and material/economic base;
2. the interests and ideas of authoritative political leaders in provincial and national capitals; and
3. extra-federal institutions including, most prominently, the Constitution and the parliamentary system.

These contextual factors, together with others originating in the international political economy, shape the performance of Canadian federalism. Some of them, like the Westminster parliamentary system, are relatively stable over time, and so their effects tend to be stable as well. Others, like the ideas and interests of first ministers, may vary quite widely: as the individuals who hold the highest government offices change, so (to a greater or lesser degree) does the functioning of Canadian federalism. A major objective of this text is to highlight how these institutional and contextual features interact with the structures and processes of federalism to shape the latter's performance, effectiveness, and legitimacy.

Performance: Institutions and Processes

Assessing the performance of the Canadian federal system means focusing on the functioning of the institutions and processes of Canadian federalism. These institutions and processes are first, the constitutional division of powers between the two orders of government, along with the process of judicial review to which it is subject; second, the institutions of intrastate federalism that provide for the representation of constituent units within the central government and the management of conflicts between the two orders of government; and, third, the institutions and processes of interstate federalism through which the two orders relate directly to one another. Throughout this book, three criteria are used to assess performance: the consistency of governing arrangements with federal principles; the 'workability' of the institutions in question, both formal and informal; and the capacity of federal institutions to produce results in the form of agreements.

Consistency with Federal Principles

The foremost principle of federalism is that each order of government is autonomous within its sphere of authority: its jurisdictional powers may be altered only in conformity with constitutional provisions, never through unilateral action by the other order of government. Two questions are relevant here. Are the component units recognized by the centre as full members of the federation, with their own powers and the authority to act on them? And do the constituent units recognize the central government as having its own proper and autonomous role? To answer these questions we begin by examining the formal division of powers laid out in the Canadian Constitution (Chapter 2, by Gerry Baier) and the judicial review process (Chapter 3, by James Kelly). Still, the formal Constitution is not a reliable guide to the actual performance of Canadian federalism.

The second principle of federalism follows from the first and is the purpose that federal systems are created to serve: to provide a balance between unity and diversity. The relevant 'performance' question here is whether the mechanisms of interstate and intrastate federalism in fact secure the balance needed to ensure that the system does not slide into either a confederal arrangement (with the central government subordinate to the constituent units) or a unitary system (with the constituent units subordinate to the central government). Generally, the federal balance is a function of both the pattern of intergovernmental relations (interstate federalism) and the representation of constituent units in the central government (intrastate federalism).

Intrastate federalism is weak in Canada because, unlike most other federations, Canada lacks an effective second chamber of Parliament. The German upper house (Bundesrat), for example, is composed of representatives of the state (Länder) governments, while the Australian and American senates provide direct representation for citizens of the various constituent states. But the Canadian Senate offers no such representation to the provinces. With limited opportunity for formal representation of provincial interests in federal policy-making institutions, provincial governments acquire greater authority to speak on behalf of the people within their borders. One consequence is that in Canada the task of securing the federal balance falls mainly to interstate federalism, since most intergovernmental activity takes places *between* governments rather than *within* an intrastate body such as a senate.

'Workability'
We adopt Dupré's (1985) definition of well-performing federal institutions and processes as providing forums 'conducive to negotiation, consultation, or simply an exchange of information'. Given a changing policy environment and continually shifting agendas, governments need to interact with each other in order to address mutual problems and manage interdependencies; at a minimum, they need to communicate with one another in order to make adjustments in their respective roles. As policy interdependence increases, so does the need for co-ordination and collaboration.

Capacity to produce results
In a federal system, producing results means reaching agreement on issues. Conflict is inherent in federal systems. Thus a crucial test of their performance is

their ability to manage intergovernmental conflict. Simply agreeing to disagree may be one way of managing conflict. However, citizens will normally expect the two orders of government to set aside their differences and deal with the issues on which citizens' well-being and the integrity of the political community as a whole depend.

In brief, to perform well a federal system must respect federal principles, sustain the balance between unity and diversity, provide a setting for discussion and negotiation between governments, and facilitate agreement, or at least understanding, on major issues in a manner that respects the positions of both levels of government. Given the centrality of interstate federalism to the performance of the Canadian federal system, patterns of intergovernmental relations are a frequent theme in this book.

The chapters that follow make it abundantly clear that there is no single way to describe intergovernmental relations in Canada. Patterns shift not only over time but across issues within a single period, and scholars have used a variety of labels to describe them. Figure 1.1, for example, locates several models of federalism along a continuum from independence to interdependence of the two orders of government.

At one end of the continuum, central and provincial/territorial governments are independent of one another. This is the classical form of federalism: the 'watertight compartments' model in which each order of government has exclusive authority in its sphere of jurisdiction, and no attempt is made to consult or co-ordinate activities with the other order (Wheare, 1951). But exclusivity of jurisdiction in itself does not ensure respect for the federal balance. Much depends as well on the distribution of legal authority across the two orders of government: each must have sufficient authority to maintain the unity–diversity balance. Striking that balance in the Constitution Act of 1867 (formerly the British North America Act, 1867) was crucial to the formation of a political and economic union that included Quebec.

Scholars have generally situated the Canadian federal Constitution in the nineteenth century at the 'watertight compartments' end of the continuum. In contrast to some other federal constitutions, the 1867 Act assigned almost all subject matters to either the federal or the provincial order of government, giving that order the exclusive authority both to make laws in that area and to implement them. The one exception is criminal law: what constitutes criminal activity is defined by the federal government in the Criminal Code, but the provinces are responsible for enforcing that legislation. There are also three areas of shared or concurrent jurisdiction: immigration and agriculture have been shared jurisdictions since 1867, and pensions joined them in the mid-twentieth century.

Thus the federal system created in 1867 was situated near the left-hand end of the continuum—but at the same time it was not entirely consistent with the watertight compartments model. In fact the compartments were far from impermeable (Stevenson, 1993; Watts, 2003), and the central government had various instruments it could use in areas of provincial jurisdiction: the power to appoint

Figure 1.1 Models of Canadian Federalism

Independent governments	Consultation	Co-ordination	Collaboration	Joint decision-making

lieutenant-governors with the right to reserve provincial legislation, the declaratory power that allowed the federal government to take over provincial undertakings in the national interest, and the power of the governor general to disallow provincial legislation. Federal challenges to provincial legislative authority through these 'quasi-federal' mechanisms were infrequent by the late nineteenth century, but it was not until 1943 that Ottawa used the power of disallowance for the last time.

Since the 1930s Canadian federalism has moved towards the other end of the continuum. As governments at both levels expanded the range of their activities, jurisdictional overlap and policy interdependence intensified. So did the need for consultation and, eventually, co-ordination. 'Consultation' as a model of intergovernmental relations means that governments exchange information and views before acting independently, leaving the other order to make its own arrangements (Watts, 2003). Co-ordination means going beyond consultation to develop mutually acceptable policies and objectives, which each order of government then applies in its own jurisdiction.

Successful intergovernmental co-operation around taxation policies during the Second World War continued after 1945 as the Canadian social welfare state was constructed. A period of federal dominance during the Second World War and lasting into the early 1960s gave way to an era of 'co-operative federalism' (Simeon and Robinson, 1990: ch. 6, 8, and 9). Together, fiscally and politically strong provincial governments and a national government armed with a potent spending power create social programs in areas of provincial jurisdiction like health care, post-secondary education, and social assistance. (For a more detailed discussion of 'shared-cost federalism', see Keith Banting in Chapter 7 below.) At least one of these social programs, the Canada Pension Plan, led to a joint-decision model of federalism: not only did the two orders of government work closely to construct the pension plan, but under its decision-making rules any changes to the plan required the agreement of a certain number of provincial governments as well as Ottawa.

Co-operative federalism coexisted with competitive federalism. The competitive dynamic is virtually inherent in Canadian federalism, rooted in ideological diversity, genuine differences of interests arising from differences in material/economic base and societal demands, and the electoral imperative to gain credit and avoid blame (Simeon, 1972). Led by different political parties, fighting elections at different times, over different issues, provincial and national governments inevitably butt heads as each seeks to maximize its autonomy, jurisdiction, and standing with voters. Intergovernmental competition reached a zenith during the 1970s and early 1980s, when province-building ambitions clashed with the unilateral nation-building initiatives of Prime Minister Trudeau, including the 1980 National Energy Program and constitutional patriation and reform. Competition receded somewhat during the Mulroney era (1984–93).

Whether in its co-operative or its competitive form, the pattern of intergovernmental relations that took shape in the 1960s brings elected and appointed officials of the two orders of government into repeated interaction. Labelled 'executive federalism' (Smiley, 1976: 54), this is the defining feature of Canadian federalism. The predominant role of governmental executives (ministers and their officials) in intergovernmental relations is a uniquely Canadian phenomenon that originated in the combination of Canada's jurisdictional federalism and Westminster parliamentary system.

As we noted earlier, Canada's weak intrastate federalism gives provincial governments both the opportunity and the incentive to claim an exclusive right to represent the interests of Canadians within their borders. In Chapter 5 Richard Simeon and Amy Nugent elaborate on how the logics of the parliamentary and federal systems combine to create this effect. The national government lacks effective forums for the representation of 'provincial' interests. At the same time, political authority is concentrated in the executive: the prime minister/premier and cabinet (Savoie, 1999, White, 2005). Executives at both levels thus have considerable latitude to strike bargains on behalf of their governments. And because these executives are relatively few in number—fourteen with the inclusion of territorial governments—the federal–provincial bargaining characteristic of executive federalism is, at least in theory, logistically manageable in a way that it would not be in the United States, for example. Accordingly, interprovincial disputes are generally resolved through direct negotiations between ministers or senior officials rather than submitted to the upper chamber of the central government (as in Germany or even the United States) for resolution by elected representatives of the people.

As we suggested above, executive federalism is also a response to policy interdependence: the overlap and duplication that are inevitable with two activist orders of government. Since the rise of the modern state in the mid-twentieth century, there have been very few policy areas in which either Ottawa or the provinces can operate without bumping into the jurisdiction of another government. Thus finding an effective solution to a policy dilemma, even one that lies entirely within the jurisdiction of a single order of government, invariably requires collaboration with the other order. At the very least, the government with the authority to make a decision must take into account its implications for other governments. Executive federalism, with its dual logic of co-operation and competition, is therefore central to any discussion of the performance of Canadian federalism, as well as its effectiveness and legitimacy.

The most important forums of intergovernmental consultation and co-ordination are

1. first ministers' conferences (FMCs) and first ministers' meetings (FMMs) of premiers and the prime minister;
2. ministerial meetings (i.e., meetings of the various ministers holding a particular portfolio, such as health or the environment);
3. meetings of public servants (officials); and
4. interprovincial meetings of the provinces and the territories, in which the federal government does not take part.

FMCs were particularly frequent during the constitutional negotiations of the early 1990s, after which they declined in number and were replaced by less formal FMMs. At the same time, the numbers of ministerial and, especially, officials' meetings began to increase, and they have grown steadily ever since.

These forums of executive federalism have often provided opportunities for intergovernmental co-operation, allowing politicians to circumvent constitutional rigidities and respond more directly to societal demands and problems. Co-operation is most likely when the stakes are relatively low and the participants share the same values, typically in a substantive policy domain. When the stakes are higher, political elites may not be so willing to compromise, and the forums of executive federalism can become venues for intergovernmental competition. This dysfunctional feature of executive federalism, J.S. Dupré (1985) has argued, has been promoted by the centralization of intergovernmental relations within first ministers' offices and specialized agencies. It manifests itself in particular at the upper levels: at FMCs or meetings of finance ministers, where the stakes tend to be very high.

Since the mid- to late 1990s, some analysts have identified a new variant that they call 'collaborative federalism'. For Cameron and Simeon (2002: 49) the distinguishing feature of collaborative federalism is 'co-determination of broad national policies'. This collaboration takes one of two forms: federal and provincial/territorial governments 'working together as equals', or provincial and territorial governments working together to formulate national policy themselves, without the federal government. For Lazar (1997) collaborative federalism is less hierarchical than the co-operative federalism of the Pearson and Trudeau years (the 1960s and 1970s), when Ottawa alone initiated shared-cost programs and the provinces followed its lead. In some respects collaborative federalism reflects Canada's evolution, since the era of co-operative federalism, into one of the world's most decentralized federations, with federal and provincial governments relatively evenly balanced in their power and status and at the same time highly interdependent (Watts, 1996: 111).

Collaborative federalism represents an effort to formalize the increasingly informal, rules-free relationship that had developed between the two orders of government under executive federalism. Agreements like the 1995 Agreement on Internal Trade (AIT), the 1998 Canada-Wide Accord on Environmental Harmonization, and the 1999 Social Union Framework Agreement (SUFA) sought to clarify and streamline government responsibilities in order to minimize the negative spillover effects for other governments and/or industry. These agreements are not legally binding ('justiciable'), but they do include dispute settlement mechanisms. Whether this rule-based federalism is effective in managing the conflict inherent in federal systems is a question taken up by Gerry Baier in Chapter 2.

Collaborative federalism emerged in response to the circumstances in which Ottawa and the provinces found themselves in the 1990s. Formal efforts to reverse the decline in perceptions of the performance and legitimacy of the federal arrangement through constitutional reform—specifically the Meech Lake Accord (1987–90) and the Charlottetown Agreement (1992)—had failed. When the Liberal government of Jean Chrétien took power in 1993, it turned its back on constitutional reform as a way of correcting perceived deficiencies in the Canadian federal system. The need to demonstrate that the federal system could be renewed and reformed to work in the interests both of Quebec and of the other provinces was only heightened following the razor-thin defeat of the separatist forces in the 1995 Quebec referendum (Lazar, 1997). Collaboration was not the only game in town, however. The referendum result stiffened Ottawa's resolve vis-à-vis Quebec separatists, as well as its determination to demonstrate that the government of Canada was a power to be reckoned with. The *Reference re Quebec Secession* and the subsequent Clarity Bill were two indications of this 'tough love' strategy.

Three other circumstances also promoted collaborative federalism. First was the *internationalization* of the Canadian political economy in the 1990s, which took three forms: increasing integration into the North American region, increasing exposure to foreign competition, and increasing sharing of Canadian sovereignty with international institutions, such as the World Trade Organization. These developments highlighted the interdependence of governments, and responding effectively to them, it is argued, demanded greater policy coordination and collaboration between governments within Canada. A second factor was the increasing *regionalization* of Canada's national political parties after 1993 with the rise of the Reform and Bloc Québécois parties. As the governing Liberal party became increasingly vulnerable to charges that it did not represent all parts of the country, provincial governments increasingly became the champions of interests and ideas not represented in Ottawa. A third factor was the ascendancy of *neo-liberalism* and the companion philosophy known as *new public management*. While the former called for governments to play a smaller role in society and the market, the latter called for governments to work more closely with one another in the interest of greater administrative efficiency and clarity. Proponents of New Public Management and collaborative federalism espouse similar values and tenets: decentralization, less emphasis on formal rules, and more flexible and informal arrangements (Simeon, 1997).

At the same time, internationalization and the new public management philosophy were creating pressures for extension of the collaborative model to embrace non-state actors. And a shift in the *political culture*, away from elitist and non-transparent executive federalism towards more direct citizen input into decision-making, had a similar effect (Nevitte, 1996). Among the societal cultural changes that were particularly consequential, as Martin Papillon explains in Chapter 14, was the growing determination of Canada's First Nations to move beyond the legacy of colonialism and take more direct control over their own affairs in many areas.

A number of contextual factors ensured that the competitive dynamic never disappeared from intergovernmental relations in this period, despite the rhetoric of collaborative federalism. *Fiscal deficits* at both levels of government put the two starkly at odds over who would fund costly social programs like health care. And in other policy domains, as the first edition of *Canadian Federalism* (2002) showed, initiatives such as the National Child Benefit (1998) demonstrated that the Chrétien government never entirely abandoned the 'independent governments' model.

As the chapters that follow will make clear, Canadian federalism has taken a variety of forms, sometimes simultaneously: co-operative and competitive, collaborative and independent. Figure 1.1 (p. 7) captured neither the competitive dynamic nor the element of unilateralism in intergovernmental relations. Lazar (2006), in a recent typology of intergovernmental relations in the area of social policy, subdivides the 'independent governments' model into classical federalism and unilateral federalism. In the former, governments act independently and each remains within its own constitutionally assigned jurisdiction; in the latter, one order of government (usually the federal) imposes its views and priorities on the other, usually by attaching conditions to its fiscal transfers. Lazar differentiates unilateral federalism, which he reserves for cases of policy interdependence, from 'beggar-thy-partner federalism', in which governments act independently but the actions of one impose substantial obligations on the other (2006: 29).

Classical federalism, independent governments, collaborative federalism, joint-decision federalism, unilateral federalism, competitive federalism, shared-cost federalism: is there reason to see one or more of these patterns as dominant in the latter half of the first decade of the twenty-first century? More specifically, has the collaborative federalism of the late 1990s and early 2000s moved to the fore, as many observers predicted it would?

To answer that question, it is helpful to reflect on some features of the contemporary context that are likely to shape the ideas and interests of pivotal actors (in particular, first ministers and their cabinets). The current situation is in some ways similar to the one that gave rise to collaborative federalism in the 1990s; internationalization, particularly the integration of the Canadian and American economies, remains as important as ever. But the implications for federalism are unclear. In an examination of several federal states, Lazar et al. (2003) find no evidence that the federal bargain is being undermined or that the basic political equilibrium between self- and shared-rule is being altered by regional and global integration. Nor does Simeon (2003) believe that regional and global integration have had a discernible impact on Canadian federalism and intergovernmental relations. Those who are concerned that agreements made by the federal government could be altered as a result of internationalization note that central governments in many federal systems have the exclusive authority to sign, ratify, and implement international treaties. As Grace Skogstad observes in Chapter 11, however, this is not the case in Canada, where the provinces have the authority to implement provisions that fall within their jurisdiction.

Continuity can also be seen in the central institutions of intrastate and interstate federalism, if only because the various logics of parliamentary government, federalism, and intergovernmental relations tend to encourage certain patterns of behaviour (see Chapter 5). Still, the individual actors have changed. So have some of the circumstances in which they find themselves. The national government has been beset by instability since 2004, when the Liberal government moved into a minority situation. Although the Conservative government elected in January 2006 also lacked a majority in Parliament, it did secure representation in every province but Prince Edward Island. This suggests that the trend towards regionalization in the party system may be ending, putting the national government in a much better position to claim that it speaks for Canadians in all provinces and linguistic/cultural communities.

The fiscal situation, which generated so much intergovernmental conflict in the 1990s, has improved not only for the national government but for most provincial governments as well. The federal budgetary surplus has given the Conservatives at least two options in their quest to transform their minority into a majority. One vote-garnering strategy is to demonstrate the importance of the national government by expanding the scope of its activity to include spheres of provincial jurisdiction like health, child care, and cities. This strategy would increase the interdependence of the two orders of government and their need for collaboration. A second option is to direct the federal surplus principally to matters within federal jurisdiction and to increase unconditional fiscal transfers to provincial governments. This strategy would send the federal system in a different direction, back towards the 'independent governments' model. As different governments (Chrétien, Martin, and Harper) make different choices among these options, fiscal federalism remains central to the politics of Canadian federalism as well as its performance, effectiveness, and legitimacy, as Doug Brown explains in Chapter 4.

Effectiveness: Policy Outcomes

'Effectiveness' refers explicitly to policy outcomes: the public policies and programs made within and resulting from the web of intergovernmental interactions. How effective are they in dealing with the substantive problems that occasioned intergovernmental bargaining and conflict resolution in the first place? How efficient are the resulting programs in marshalling resources? Do policies allow for asymmetry where it is desired and appears warranted? Do policy outcomes allow international commitments to be met? The fact that two or more governments reach agreement on a particular issue does not necessarily mean that the underlying social or economic issues have been effectively resolved. Focusing on substantive policy typically requires the use of benchmarks or standards to see how policy outcomes measure up. But assessment is easier in some policy areas than in others. In the case of the environment, it is possible to measure quantities of emissions and effluents. In other areas, however, one has to depend on more qualitative assessments. The quality of policy outcomes often lies in the eyes of the beholder. It is also useful to remember that there may be a distinction between 'policy outcomes' and 'policy outputs'. Policy outputs—the decisions made regarding programs and policies—may have unintended consequences, and as a result their actual outcomes may look quite different from the original plan. It is often only with hindsight that the distinction between outputs and outcomes becomes clear.

It *is* difficult to determine exactly how federalism and intergovernmental relations affect public policy outcomes. First, developments in any policy area are contingent on several factors, of which federalism is only one—though it may be the most important. Studies of federal systems have found no discernible effects of federalism on policy outcomes and have had difficulty identifying any differences between federal and decentralized unitary states in this respect (Braun, 2000; Norris, 2005). Second—and a reason why those studies have yielded few results—the effects of federalism on policy-making are likely to depend on the prevailing model of federalism: independent governments, unilateralism, competitive, collaborative, or joint-decision (McRoberts, 1993).

Any discussion of how different models of federalism shape public policy outcomes in Canada must begin with a discussion of the spending power: the power that allows the Parliament of Canada to make payments to individual Canadians, institutions, or provincial governments for purposes outside its constitutional jurisdiction. Although the spending power can be used in a way consistent with the independent governments model (for example, when the federal government makes payments directly to individual Canadians for child care, or to post-secondary educational institutions), it is more often used as an instrument to increase interdependence across the two orders of government.

The federal spending power has important implications for the performance, effectiveness, and legitimacy of the federation. It breaches the federal principle of exclusive jurisdictions and (as will be discussed further in the next section) undermines the legitimacy of the federal system in the eyes of many Quebecers in particular. The chapters on social policy in this volume suggest that its impact on the effectiveness of the federation may be more positive. But the impact of its use has generally been judged differently, depending on whether it is used unilaterally (in a model of unilateral federalism, to use Lazar's 2006 term) or constrained by collaborative or joint-decision federalism.

The arm's length or 'independent governments' model of classical federalism preserves autonomy and freedom of action at both levels. It gives each government the opportunity and flexibility to experiment and innovate in devising solutions to policy problems (Banting, 1995). Indeed, citizens beyond the borders of an innovative state or province may eventually benefit from its experiments. The classic Canadian example is the adoption of universally available and publicly funded hospital and clinical care, following Saskatchewan's pioneering example (see Chapter 8 by Antonia Maioni). A more recent example is child care; Quebec's innovative low-cost, universally available program has provided an attractive model for child-care advocates in other provinces.

Some analysts argue that the 'independent governments' model is likely to be particularly efficacious in addressing citizens' demands when the competitive dynamic is uppermost (Breton, 1996; Harrison, 1996; Young, 2003). Competition across provinces can create 'a race to the top' when voters press their provincial governments to emulate policies and standards developed somewhere else (Harrison, 2005). In a period of buoyant finances, the competition for voters' support can lead both orders of government to expand public services and take on new state activities, as Banting demonstrates in Chapter 7.

The 'independent governments' model can also work to the advantage of non-state actors with the resources to organize on both federal and provincial fronts. Having two access points, federal and provincial, gives non-state actors two kicks at the can, allowing them to play one order of government off against the other in pursuit of their policy objectives.

There are, of course, downsides when governments act independently of one another and fail to co-ordinate their activities. The risks of policy incoherence and program incompatibility increase. Problems are more likely to be ignored when blame can be shifted to the other order of government. This dynamic is especially likely when it is unclear which level of government should be responsible for addressing a problem, or when resolving it will entail significant financial or political costs. Even when intergovernmental competition promotes the development of new programs, the results may not be entirely beneficial. Policies may be designed with more concern for the interests of the sponsoring government than for efficacy in dealing with the problem at hand. A tax benefit or direct payment to parents to help cover child-care costs, for instance, may serve the interests of a government seeking to improve its image among voters; but such a policy will do nothing to create the new day-care spaces that working parents need.

The joint decision-making model is typically associated with ineffective policy-making and poor outcomes (Scharpf, 1988; Pierson, 1995). This model requires joint action of governments at both levels, by virtue of either unanimous or super-majority agreement. Governments lose their autonomy and flexibility, but they do retain the power of veto. With multiple points at which change can be rejected, joint decision-making typically leads to a number of 'traps'. Existing programs become difficult if not impossible to modify. When agreement is reached, the outcome is often less than optimal—a 'lowest common denominator' solution, designed to satisfy the most recalcitrant party.

As with any collaborative model, resolving substantive problems in the most effective and efficient way is likely to take second place to the political and institutional concerns of state actors, the desire for status and recognition, to gain credit and avoid blame. From the perspective of non-state actors, the multiple 'veto points' offered by a joint-decision model present both opportunities and obstacles. As Banting explains in Chapter 7, those who favour the status quo are likely to welcome the high threshold of agreement for policy change, while those who seek change will be frustrated.

Co-operative and collaborative models fit somewhere between the 'independent governments' and joint-decision models, depending on how formalized they are and how much scope they leave for independent action by governments. Social safety-net programs are a case in point. At first the government of Canada contributed half the costs of hospital care, post-secondary education, and social assistance. Then it reduced its financial contribution for these programs, leaving the provincial level to pay a larger share of the tab, although the shift to block funding gave the provinces more scope to direct the money as they saw fit. More recent forms of collaborative federalism have limited the participating governments' scope for action; SUFA, for example, constrains the federal spending power even while recognizing its legitimacy. The more rule-bound the collaborative model, the greater the likelihood that intergovernmental relations will be hampered by these joint-decision traps.

The ability of Canadian federalism to tackle major policy challenges has varied over time. The Depression of the 1930s is widely seen as a low-water mark, when the Judicial Committee of the Privy Council insisted on a classic interpretation of federalism that prevented the national government from playing a broader role in social and economic programs to address the needs of Canadians. Federalism scored higher points after the Second World War, as governments variously recognized their interdependence, co-operated, and competed with one another for the political affections of Canadians (Simeon, 1972, 2006). If international indices measuring physical and social well-being and overall quality of life are a reliable guide, it appears that federalism has not impeded Canadian federal and provincial governments in their pursuit of effective and coherent policies, either jointly or separately.

Still, the effectiveness of Canadian federalism depends on both the policy area or substantive issue in question and the model of federalism at work. The following chapters cover a wide array of policy areas: from social policy, health care, child care, and post-secondary education to the environment, economic development, skills training, and international trade. They also investigate some subjects that involve multiple policy issues: cities, Aboriginal governance, recognition of Quebec's distinct needs, and the role of non-governmental actors in intergovernmental relations. These policy areas have been chosen for three reasons.

First, they are essential to the integrity of the Canadian social and economic union. In the field of social policy, for example, programs such as child and health care represent principles central to Canadian identity and citizenship: all Canadians, regardless of where they live, share both the obligation to finance these programs and the right to benefit from them. It is the sense of mutual obligations and rights that underpins Canada as a social union (Courchene, 1994). Policies in areas such as post-secondary education (Chapter 10 by Herman Bakvis), the regulation of international trade (Chapter 11 by Grace Skogstad), economic development and skills training (Chapter 12 by Rodney Haddow), and environmental sustainability (Chapter 13 by Doug Macdonald and Mark Winfield) have more to do with the productivity and competitiveness of the economic union. At the same time, distinctive provincial needs and tastes in these policy areas reinforce claims for provincial jurisdiction and policy diversity. This policy array therefore provides insight into the balance struck between the rights and duties of membership in the social and economic union, on the one hand, and recognition of the diverse needs and circumstances of the constituent provincial units and communities, on the other.

Second, the policy areas chosen for examination are ones that allow us to assess the resilience and adaptability of Canadian federalism in response to different kinds of challenges. The contextual shift from a period of government deficits to one of fiscal surpluses, for instance, has significant implications for social policies (health, child care, and post-secondary education); it also tests the capacity of fiscal federalism to continue playing the role of an east–west 'social railway' ascribed it by Courchene (1994). Canadians' commitment to income redistribution appears to be threatened as we increasingly trade more with non-Canadians than with each other. Canada's participation in international environmental treaties and protocols tests the capacity of the two orders of government to devise a coherent response to evolving international environmental norms and to implement effective international agreements at home. Similarly, Canada's integration into the North American political economy tests the collaborative capacities of Canadian governments, in this case to develop coherent trade and economic development strategies.

Third, the policy areas and issues examined in this book contain a mix of high- and low-profile issues on which the dynamics of intergovernmental relations, and potentially the models as well, can be expected to differ (Dupré, 1985). To some extent this is also a distinction between 'old' and 'new' issues. Some issues, like economic development strategies, post-secondary education funding, fiscal federalism, and international trade are of interest to specialized policy communities. Others, like health care, attract the attention of all Canadians. Some fall somewhere in between, engaging the attention of the general public only intermittently. Intergovernmental competition is expected to be greater on high-profile issues, particularly when the issue is an old one with a history of intergovernmental acrimony (e.g., health care), while co-operative or collaborative models are more likely to come to the fore on issues of interest mainly to those citizens with a direct stake in the policy. International trade and post-secondary education are examples here. Issues that touch deeply on provincial areas of jurisdiction, or are associated with a history of intergovernmental acrimony, are likely to prove especially difficult tests. Policy interdependence itself is not necessarily a barrier to effective policy-making; whether it becomes a problem will depend on the public salience of the policy area and the historic legacy of intergovernmental relations attached to it.

Even though the focus of this text is on the role of federalism in policy development, it is important not to exaggerate federalism's impact. Developments in any one policy area are contingent on a number of factors, and (as we observed earlier) federalism's impact in that area may be minimal at a particular point in time. At other times federalism may well be the crucial factor determining success or failure. Furthermore, neither competition nor co-operation should be automatically equated with positive outcomes. Competition can be associated with either innovation or stalemate, co-operation with either problem resolution or elite collusion.

Legitimacy

Governments must be perceived as legitimate if they are to count on the unequivocal support of citizens. Legitimacy is a reflection of the public's perceptions of the appropriateness of governing arrangements and their outcomes. In federal systems, the cleavages of region, culture, language, and the division between first peoples and immigrant settlers (to name the most obvious case), raise the real possibility that some citizens may view the governing arrangements associated with federalism as legitimate and others may not. To appraise the legitimacy of Canadian federalism, therefore, we view it through the separate lenses of the various communities and constituencies that make up Canada.

One highly relevant question for appraising the legitimacy of Canadian federalism is whether the governing federal arrangements incorporate the various constituent units' understandings of their own roles and status in federal system. For most of Canada's history, Quebec's political elite (if not most of its population) has had a different understanding of federalism from its counterparts in other provincial capitals and in Ottawa. For Quebec's political elite, the federal union represents the union of two political communities, 'peoples', or 'nations': one English-speaking and located mostly outside Quebec; the other overwhelmingly francophone and based in Quebec. In the words of Claude Ryan (2003), 'Quebec is the seat of a national community. Its legislature and government are national institutions, at least in their jurisdictions.' English-speaking Canada, by contrast, sees the country as a union of territorial units (provinces), all of which are equal in legal status. In other words, the distinction is between Canada as a multinational federation (of which Quebec is one of two or more constituent nations) versus Canada as a territorial federation (Tully, 1995).

The understanding that Quebec constitutes a distinct political community within Canada has led Quebec's political elite to demand two things of the federal system: (1) formal recognition of Quebec's distinct status within the federation and, consistent with such recognition, (2) preservation and expansion of the province's legal authority and autonomy so as to safeguard the unique cultural and linguistic character of the Quebec national community. For Quebec's political elite, the legitimacy of the federal system depends overwhelmingly on the degree to which it provides for asymmetry between Quebec's status in the federation and that of the other provinces (Gagnon, 2001).

There has always been some asymmetry in the autonomy and power of different provinces within the Canadian federation (Watts, 2005). Some asymmetrical features were embedded in the Constitution Act of 1867; others have been introduced over time—for example, the administrative arrangement under which Quebec runs its own pension plan (all the provinces were offered this option, but only Quebec took it up). Even so, Quebec wanted formal recognition of its distinct status within the federation, and in this respect the Constitution Act 1982 represented an outright rejection of its aspirations.

The failure of subsequent efforts at constitutional reform (the Meech Lake Accord and the Charlottetown Agreement) almost proved deadly for Canadian federalism. The 1995 referendum on Quebec's secession from Canada was defeated by the slimmest of margins. Alain-G. Gagnon and Raffaele Iacovino argue in Chapter 16 that initiatives since 1995 (the Chrétien government's Clarity Bill, the premiers' Calgary Declaration, and so on), continue to fall short of recognizing Quebec's distinct place and needs in Canada. In their view, the federal government's support for official bilingualism, multiculturalism, and the Charter of Rights and Freedoms detracts from Canada's character as a multinational democracy and undermines the legitimacy of Canadian federalism in Quebec. Their view is not shared by James Kelly, however, at least when it comes to the Charter (see Chapter 3).

Quebec is not the only political community to question the legitimacy of Canada's federal Constitution: so do Canada's Aboriginal peoples. Martin Papillon (Chapter 14) reminds us that Aboriginal peoples also seek recognition and greater control over their own communities, often through a third order of self-governing communities. Papillon explores the progress that has been made towards Aboriginal self-government and the obstacles that still lie in the way of reconciling the federal system and Aboriginal self-government.

A different sort of pressure on the federal system comes from the order of government that has been excluded from the federal arrangement. Advocates for the municipal level argue that changes in the global economy have put cities at the heart of provincial and national competitiveness strategies, and therefore that cities urgently need greater political autonomy and more fiscal resources. Andrew Sancton weighs the case for city-states against that for better co-ordination of federal and provincial policies with respect to cities in Chapter 15.

For many Canadians, including executives of most of the English-speaking provinces, assessing the legitimacy of the Canadian federal system means examining the appropriateness of the procedures and processes followed in policy-making and the substantive features of policy outcomes. Are the rules of the game by which governments interact and negotiate to arrive at policy decisions accepted by governments themselves? How well do existing federal institutions and intergovernmental processes conform to citizens' expectations regarding their own roles as participants in decision-making? Are these processes consistent with norms of accountability and transparency? Do they meet the expectations of the relevant policy community? Do the outcomes of intergovernmental policy-making reflect the distinct values and preferences of the communities concerned? Are they consistent with those communities' standards of effectiveness, efficiency, and fairness?

The three criteria—performance, effectiveness and legitimacy—are closely linked. Weak performance, in the form of gridlock in executive federalism, for instance, will normally lead to policy ineffectiveness. Problems will go unresolved where effective action requires intergovernmental co-operation. Yet intergovernmental consensus in itself does not necessarily yield effective policies. It may simply mean that the two orders of government have agreed to ignore politically difficult issues. Repeated over time, policy ineffectiveness will only lead citizens to give failing marks to the system as a whole. Similarly, a federal system that underperforms by failing to provide sufficient scope for the expression of regional particularities will also undermine the legitimacy of the system. Because legitimacy is appraised in both substantive and procedural terms, the links between effectiveness and legitimacy are somewhat complex. One would ordinarily expect citizens to support federal practices that yield effective policies by addressing problems in a timely and efficient manner. If the political culture places a high priority on democratic processes, however, policies arrived at through closed, non-transparent, and unaccountable processes may still be viewed as illegitimate, even if they are highly effective in delivering certain outcomes.

When individual Canadians are asked to appraise the legitimacy of Canadian federalism, they appear to be much more interested in outcomes than in respect for federal principles. Cutler and Mendelsohn (2001a) found that Canadians outside Quebec show little concern for whether governments respect the constitutional division of powers. In their words:

> Canadians have no deep commitment to the principle of federalism, have little knowledge of the existing division of powers, and care little about which government exercises which power. In important policy areas, they care about results, and they see co-operation between governments as best able to achieve this (Cutler and Mendelsohn, 2001b).

Even so, individual Canadians' perceptions of the legitimacy of Canadian federalism are likely to be based on both the results of executive federalism (output legitimacy) and its procedures (input legitimacy). Certainly, Jennifer Smith (2004) argues that Canadian federalism falls short when it comes to promoting democratic participation in the policy-making process.

Two chapters in this collection focus directly on the democratic quality of intergovernmental processes. First, in Chapter 5, Richard Simeon and Amy Nugent examine how three different models of democracy—representative, consultative, and deliberative participatory—operate. Later, in Chapter 17, Julie Simmons takes a careful look at the roles played by non-state actors in a variety of intergovernmental policy initiatives. Several other chapters also examine the roles of non-state actors in policies related to the social and economic union.

In the early twenty-first century federalism continues to provide the framework for governing in Canada. How effectively and legitimately it does so, and how it is changing as political elites within both orders of government grapple with contemporary challenges, is the subject of the chapters that follow.

References

Banting, K. 1995. 'The Welfare State as Statecraft: Territorial Politics and Canadian Social Policy'. In *European Social Policy*, ed. S. Leibfried and P. Pierson. Washington: Brookings Institution.

Breton, A. 1996. *Competitive Governments: An Economic Theory of Politics and Public Finance*. New York: Cambridge University Press.

Braun, D. 2000. 'Territorial Division of Power and Public Policy-Making: An Overview'. In *Public Policy and Federalism*, ed. D. Braun. Aldershot: Ashgate.

Cameron, D., and R. Simeon. 2002. 'Intergovernmental Relations in Canada: The Emergence of Collaborative Federalism', *Publius* 32, 2: 49–71.

Courchene, T.J. 1994. *Social Canada in the Millennium: Reform Imperatives and Restructuring Principles*. Toronto: C.D. Howe Institute.

Cutler, F., and M. Mendelsohn. 2001a. 'What Kind of Federalism Do Canadians (outside Quebec) Want?' *Policy Options* 22, 8: 23–9.

——— and ———. 2001b. Op-Ed. *Globe and Mail*, 31 Jul.: A11.

Dupré, J.S. 1985. 'Reflections on the Workability of Executive Federalism'. In *Intergovernmental Relations*, ed. R. Simeon. Toronto: University of Toronto Press.

Gagnon, A.-G. 2001. 'The Moral Foundations of Asymmetrical Federalism'. In *Multinational Democracies*, ed. A.-G. Gagnon and J. Tully. Cambridge: Cambridge University Press.

Harrison, K. 1996. *Passing the Buck: Federalism and Canadian Environmental Policy*. Vancouver: University of British Columbia Press.

———, ed. 2005. *Racing to the Bottom? Provincial Interdependence in the Canadian Federation*. Vancouver: University of British Columbia Press.

Lazar, H. 1997. 'Non-Constitutional Renewal: Toward a New Equilibrium in the Federation'. In *The State of the Federation 1997: Non-Constitutional Renewal*, ed. H. Lazar. Kingston: Institute of Intergovernmental Relations, Queen's University.

———. 2006. 'The Intergovernmental Dimensions of the Social Union: A Sectoral Analysis', *Canadian Public Administration* 49, 1: 23–45.

———, H. Telford, and R.L. Watts. 2003. 'Diverse Trajectories: The Impact of Global and Regional Integration on Federal Systems'. In *The Impact of Global and Regional Integration on Federal Systems: A Comparative Analysis*, ed. H. Lazar, H. Telford, and R.L. Watts. Kingston and Montreal: McGill–Queen's University Press.

McRoberts, K. 1993. 'Federal Structures and the Policy Process'. In *Governing Canada: Institutions and Public Policy*, ed. M.M. Atkinson. Toronto: Harcourt Brace Janovich.

Nevitte, N. 1996. *The Decline of Deference: Canadian Value Change in Cross-national Perspective.* Peterborough, Ont.: Broadview.

Norris, P. 2005. 'Stable Democracy and Good Governance in Divided Societies: Do Powersharing Institutions Work?' Faculty Research Working Paper RWP05-014. John F. Kennedy School of Government, Harvard University.

Pierson, P. 1995. 'Fragmented Welfare States: Federal Institutions and the Development of Social Policy', *Governance* 8, 4: 449–78.

Rice, J.J. and M.J. Prince. 2000. *Changing Politics of Canadian Social Policy.* Toronto: University of Toronto Press.

Ryan, C. 2005. 'Quebec and Interprovincial Discussion and Consultation'. Kingston: Queen's Institute of Intergovernmental Relations. Available online at: <www.iigr.ca/iigr.php/site/pdf/publications/316QuebecandInterprovinci.pdf>.

Savoie, D.J. 1999. *Governing from the Centre: The Concentration of Power in Canadian Politics.* Toronto: University of Toronto Press.

Scharpf, F. 1988. 'The Joint-Decision Trap: Lessons from German Federalism and European Integration', *Public Administration* 66, 3: 239–78.

———. 1999. *Governing in Europe: Effective and Democratic?* Oxford: Oxford University Press.

Simeon, R. 1972. *Federal–Provincial Diplomacy: The Making of Recent Policy in Canada.* Toronto: University of Toronto Press.

———. 1997. 'Rethinking Government, Rethinking Federalism'. In *The New Public Management and Public Administration in Canada*, ed. M. Charih and A. Daniels. Toronto: Institute of Public Administration.

———. 2003. 'Important? Yes. Transformative? No. North American Integration and Canadian Federalism'. In *The Impact of Global and Regional Integration on Federal Systems: A Comparative Analysis*, ed. H. Lazar, H. Telford, and R.L. Watts. Kingston and Montreal: McGill–Queen's University Press.

———. 2006. *Federal–Provincial Diplomacy: The Making of Recent Policy in Canada.* Toronto: University of Toronto Press. (With a new preface and post-script.)

——— and Ian Robinson. 1990. *State, Society, and the Development of Canadian Federalism.* Toronto: University of Toronto Press.

Smiley, D.V. 1976. *Canada in Question: Federalism in the Seventies.* 2nd edn. Toronto: McGraw Hill-Ryerson.

Smith, J. 2004. *Federalism.* Vancouver: University of British Columbia Press.

Stevenson, G. 1993. *Ex Uno Plures: Federal–Provincial Relations 1867–1896.* Montreal and Kingston: McGill–Queen's University Press.

Tully, J. 1995. *Strange Multiplicity: Constitutionalism in an Age of Diversity.* Cambridge: Cambridge University Press.

Watts, R.L. 1996. *Comparing Federalism in the 1990s.* Kingston: Institute of Intergovernmental Relations, Queen's University.

———. 1999. *The Spending Power in Federal Systems: A Comparative Study.* Kingston: Institute of Intergovernmental Relations, Queen's University.

————. 2003. 'Managing Interdependence in a Federal Political System'. In *The Art of the State: Governance in a World Without Frontiers*, ed. T.J. Courchene and D.J. Savoie. Montreal: Institute for Research on Public Policy.

————. 2005. 'A Comparative Perspective on Asymmetry in Federations'. Kingston: Institute of Intergovernmental Relations. Available at: <www.iigr. ca/pdf/publications/359_A_Comparative_Perspectiv.pdf>.

Wheare, K.C. 1951. *Federal Government*. London: Oxford University Press.

White, G. 2005. *Cabinets and First Ministers*. Vancouver: University of British Columbia Press.

Young, R. 2003. 'Managing Interdependence in a Federal Political System: Comments'. In *The Art of the State: Governance in a World Without Frontiers*, ed. T.J. Courchene and D.J. Savoie. Montreal: Institute for Research on Public Policy.

Chapter 2

The Courts, the Division of Powers, and Dispute Resolution

Gerald Baier

Canada's federal system is characterized by a growing gap between the jurisdictional model set out in the written Constitution and the actual operations of governments. Overlapping jurisdictional responsibilities and the concentration of financial powers at the federal level make the formal division of powers an increasingly poor guide to 'who does what' in Canadian federalism. As the other chapters in this volume show, since major constitutional reform was last attempted in 1992, intergovernmental negotiations have replaced the courts as the primary venue of change in the federation.

This trend began decades earlier. Since the 1960s, the mutual priority-setting, negotiation, and co-operation that are hallmarks of intergovernmental relations have committed governments to increasing collaboration and have further blurred the question of 'who does what'. In a more classic federal system, with clear divisions between national and sub-unit jurisdiction, courts would play a central role in patrolling boundaries and keeping governments to their constitutionally assigned tasks. In a federal system characterized by the blurring of responsibilities, the courts' role is less clear, though disputes are no less likely to arise. This chapter examines the role of courts, particularly the Supreme Court of Canada, in a collaborative federation where courts are increasingly not the institutions called on to settle intergovernmental disputes.

One prominent feature of the collaborative model of federalism is increased reliance on sector-specific accords and agreements, often directed by ministerial councils (e.g., the Canadian Council of Ministers of the Environment) and carried out by institutionalized secretariats. Often secretariats are also called on to organize mechanisms for the settlement of intergovernmental disputes related to the specific topics covered by a particular accord or agreement. These councils and secretariats are relatively new additions to the Canadian intergovernmental structure. In many ways they embody the collaborative spirit essential to joint policy-making and information-gathering.

They also represent a response to the critics who decried the ad hoc nature of Canadian intergovernmental relations in the era of co-operative federalism, when provincial governments simply signed on to programs designed at the federal level. The secretariats represent an important shift in that they provide the policy knowledge, or at least the neutral ground, necessary for the provinces to play a more active role in decision-making. At the same time they provide a forum both for consultation to resolve conflicts informally (dispute avoidance) and for alternative dispute resolution, should it be necessary.

The chapter begins with a brief description of how judicial review of the Constitution has historically shaped Canadian federalism. It then looks at two contemporary instances of Supreme Court intervention in issues of intergovernmental import, illustrating the Court's traditional role in such matters. We then turn to two of the institutions that have emerged to replace the Supreme Court as umpire of intergovernmental conflict. These examples, drawn from the post-Charlottetown generation of intergovernmental agreements, are the mechanisms for intergovernmental dispute resolution incorporated in the Agreement on Internal Trade (AIT; 1994) and the Social Union Framework Agreement (SUFA; 1999). The role of judicial power in intergovernmental relations is then discussed and analyzed in the light of these new developments.

These dispute settlement institutions may be a response to the democratic critique of judicial review, but they are not without transparency and legitimacy problems of their own. They disperse and muddy responsibility for unpopular or unwanted government action and leave those seeking to challenge intergovernmental arrangements on constitutional grounds, including the weaker governments within the federation, with few avenues to pursue. In effect, the trend away from the courts in such cases is minimizing their oversight role and giving priority to the sovereignty and manoeuvrability of governments over the guarantees set out in the federal Constitution.

Recent Division-of-Powers Cases

There is something of a chicken-and-egg debate about the origins of Canada's decentralized federalism. Historically, judicial review was often blamed for the expansion of provincial power: if not for the permissive interpretation of provincial powers by the Lords of the Judicial Committee of the Privy Council (JCPC), the argument went, the strong central government envisioned by the Fathers of Confederation would have been realized.

An earlier era of disputes between the provinces and the federal government gave the judiciary a more prominent role as umpire. For nearly a century after Confederation, governments challenged the boundaries of each other's constitutional powers. In particular, the provinces successfully challenged the federal Parliament's power to make laws for the 'peace, order and good government' (POGG) of Canada granted in the preamble to section 91 of the Constitution Act, 1867. At Confederation this clause was generally believed to represent a grant of residual or plenary power to the federal level that—in conjunction with the federal control of what seemed to be the most important legislative and taxing powers, along with the power to reserve or disallow provincial legislation—would ensure that Canadian federalism took a centralized form. However, the scope of the POGG clause was profoundly influenced by those early challenges and the JCPC's interpretation of it.

Rather than read the POGG clause generously, as the centralist framers of Confederation appear to have intended, the JCPC chose to restrict its scope, treating it largely as an emergency provision, to be used only on rare occasions. (Federal advocates argued that the power should also cover matters of national concern, but those arguments were rarely accepted.) Instead the JCPC favoured the enumerated powers of the provinces, especially the power over property and civil rights granted by section 92 (13). Thus portions of the federal Parliament's so-called Bennett New Deal were ruled *ultra vires*, raising considerable ire among legal and political observers in Canada.

The Canadian critics of the JCPC took it as gospel that a Canadian court would not interpret the federal Parliament's POGG power so restrictively (Laskin, 1951). After the abolition of appeals to the JCPC in 1949, the early years of the autonomous Supreme Court seemed to prove the critics right. In one of its last decisions on Canadian federalism, the *Canada Temperance Federation* case, the JCPC offered up the possibility that POGG could be interpreted more generously in areas of national concern. The Supreme Court took full advantage of this possibility and began to define a broader scope for the federal Parliament to exercise its POGG power in cases involving aeronautics (*Johannesson*, 1952), atomic energy (*Pronto Uranium Mines*, 1956), a national capital region (*Munro*, 1966), and seabed natural resources (*Offshore Minerals*, 1967).

This cautious run of centralization was essentially brought to a halt by the *Anti-Inflation Reference* case of 1976, when the Supreme Court, led by one of the most outspoken critics of previous POGG jurisprudence, Chief Justice Bora Laskin, was asked to consider the constitutionality of the federal government's legislation to control inflation. Given the diffuse nature of a problem like inflation, the case created an ideal opportunity to address the POGG question. But the court did not take it up. Leaving the potential of a federal plenary power unresolved, it ushered in a period of 'balanced' federalism that seemed to favour neither level of government (Hogg, 1979; Russell, 1985).

More recently the Supreme Court has opened up some possibilities for the extension of federal power under POGG—one example was *Crown Zellerbach* (1988), in which federal control over the environment was justified on grounds of national concern—but it has generally continued to favour the balanced approach. In *Hydro-Quebec* (1997) and the *Firearms Reference* (2000), for example, it opted for a more generous interpretation of the federal power over criminal law rather than a generous interpretation of the POGG power.

POGG jurisprudence is only one part of the history of how the division of powers has been interpreted by Canada's highest courts. The federal power in the area of trade and commerce has been interpreted in an equally restrictive way, particularly in comparison with the broad interpretation given to its counterpart in the United States. Perhaps because of its limited success in the courts, the federal government has generally chosen to assert itself not through legislation but through use of its spending power and subsequent agreements with the provinces. Judicial review of the division of powers or other federalism issues has become less frequent since the shift to co-operative federalism in the 1960s.

Alan Cairns, in his 1971 assessment of the critics of the Judicial Committee, downplayed the direct role of the court in shaping the nature of the federation. If Canada was decentralized, he argued, there must be some reason apart from the fact that the old men across the pond (the JCPC) gave a generous interpretation to the provincial powers set out in the Constitution. To attribute Canada's decentralization entirely to judicial interpretation is to take too formal and legalistic a view of what a federation is. More recently, Rosenberg (1991) has argued that courts can never be the sole movers of societal changes such as an expansion of civil rights or an increase in government activity. Judicial review is only one of several forces influencing relationships between the two levels of government. The strength of provincial identities and governments, for instance, also contributed to decentralization. Further proof of the limited role played by judicial review could be found in the absence of any significant move towards recentralization once the Supreme Court had begun to favour the federal government in jurisdictional disputes.

Recognizing the strategic role that jurisdiction plays in intergovernmental relations, Peter Russell (1985) discussed the incentives that exist for governments to pursue jurisdictional claims, or to defend jurisdictional ground, as a subset of the broader intergovernmental relations process. If the court upholds a federal claim to jurisdiction in a disputed field, negotiating with the provinces to co-operate in the delivery or provision of services in that field becomes easier. Litigating for jurisdictional resources is not restricted to the division of powers, as the *Patriation*, *Quebec Veto*, and *Secession* references indicate.[1] In these three cases, questions about the process and conventions of constitutional change were put to the Supreme Court for clarification, in the hope that the answers might serve as a road map for future negotiations.

The *Secession* reference, and its impact on the tone of Quebec–Canada relations, was a clear demonstration of the resource game that governments play in constitutional litigation. As part of its response to the 1995 Quebec referendum, the federal government used the constitutional reference procedure to query the Court on the legality of a unilateral declaration of independence. The Court's unanimous ruling found that Quebec lacked the formal power to separate unilaterally from Canada. But it also found that a substantial informal obligation exists in Canada's constitutional culture to address assertions of independence, especially when such assertions have popular support—while conceding that it was not easy to determine what would constitute a popular demonstration of support for sovereignty. The federal Clarity Act, passed in 2000, sought to give the federal Parliament some role in determining what would constitute (a) a clear question for a sovereignty referendum and (b) a clear result. The decision legitimized federal efforts to demand a more formal demonstration of the will of Quebecers to separate and thus raised the hurdle for sovereignist forces in the province.

Although the government of Quebec contested Ottawa's intervention, the ruling in the *Secession* reference provided some justification for the federal government to entertain such questions, particularly if it were to meet the Court's mandated obligation to negotiate either sovereignty or new constitutional arrangements. Dealing as it does with the structure of intergovernmental decision-making on critical constitutional change, the *Secession* reference demonstrates that the judicial role is important, but supplemental to intergovernmental co operation and negotiation. The Court can weigh in on questions that will affect relative resources and standing, but ultimately it is up to the actors within the federal system to work out the specifics. The Supreme Court is not an umpire definitively settling specific disputes so much as it is one setting the stage for intergovernmental compromises to be reached.

In 2005 the Supreme Court weighed in on two matters with less obvious consequences for the intergovernmental relations process. In *Chaoulli*, the Court inserted itself into federal–provincial policy-making on health care by way of interpreting the guarantees of the Quebec Charter of Rights. In the *Employment Insurance Reference*, the Court's ruling on a more traditional division-of-powers question had demonstrable consequences for an eventual intergovernmental agreement on the delivery of maternity and parental benefits.

Chaoulli v. Quebec (Attorney General)

In *Chaoulli v. Quebec (Attorney General)*, Dr Jacques Chaoulli, a physician who had contested regulations in the Quebec health-care system for more than a decade, challenged restrictions in the province's Health Insurance Act and Hospital Insurance Act that prevent residents in the province from purchasing private health insurance or private services in a hospital. He argued that excessive delays, combined with legislative prohibitions preventing patients from seeking private insurance and care, amounted to violations of federal and provincial Charter rights to security of the person. Chaoulli did not challenge the constitutionality of provincial jurisdiction over health care; in that sense the case was not a typical division-of-powers controversy. However, health care has become the principal issue in intergovernmental relations and a battleground for differing visions of federal and provincial roles in service provision, so the court's decision on the case was bound to have an impact on the tone of intergovernmental relations, at the very least.

The Supreme Court of Canada agreed that the undue waiting times experienced in the Quebec public system and the absence of private alternatives amounted to a violation of rights—but only under the Quebec Charter. Thus the decision applied only to the province of Quebec. Had the Court found a violation of guarantees in the federal Charter, similar legislation in other provinces would also have been found unconstitutional.

The main issues in the *Chaoulli* case—waiting times and bans on private insurance and provision of health-care services—have become key debating points in intergovernmental discussions. Although the ruling applied only to Quebec, a number of provinces have made efforts to respond to the general thrust of the *Chaoulli* decision. Prime Minister Stephen Harper has endorsed the basic idea, reflected in Quebec government proposals, that some role for private insurance and provision of services might be necessary for the survival of Canadian medicare.

The other important lesson of the *Chaoulli* case is the opportunity that litigation offers for ordinary citizens to become involved in intergovernmental relations. Dr Chaoulli's activism on health care had taken a variety of forms prior to his constitutional challenge, and he had long petitioned Quebec regulators and policy-makers to change the rules governing the delivery of health care. By challenging the constitutionality of legislation, Chaoulli was able to have an impact in an area otherwise dominated by intergovernmental negotiations. While it has become increasingly fashionable for Canadian politicians to pledge their support for the health-care system or to promise fixes for future generations, there are serious accountability flaws in a policy field so dominated by intergovernmental interaction. The fact that most Canadians are unsure of which level of government is responsible for health care makes it hard for them to influence policy or demand accountability (Cutler, 2004). Mounting a constitutional challenge may be a last resort, but it offers an opportunity nonetheless to infiltrate some of the closed circles of intergovernmental policy-making, and to ensure that governments respond.

Employment Insurance Reference

The agenda-setting role of the Supreme Court in intergovernmental relations is also illustrated in the *Reference Re: Employment Insurance Act*, which forced the Court to revisit questions about unemployment insurance and pension schemes first considered in the 1930s.[2] Ultimately, constitutional amendments were necessary to provide the federal government with adequate constitutional jurisdiction to deliver services in some of those fields. The federal government has since used its assigned heading of employment insurance to design a variety of benefit programs including plans for maternity and parental leave from regular employment.

Quebec has long sought greater control over social and economic policy matters in which the federal government exercises jurisdiction. At Quebec's behest, the Meech Lake and Charlottetown Accords both contemplated limits on federal jurisdiction in provincial labour market development. Since those failed attempts at constitutional change, Quebec has sought more control over areas of social welfare related to employment, including the provision of parental leave. Because parental benefits were not part of the original unemployment insurance program, it seemed there was a case to be made that provinces could provide such programs under their own social welfare jurisdiction. Most provinces have been reluctant to take on the expense. However, the Liberal government of Jean Chrétien reduced federal parental benefits, giving the Quebec government added incentive to implement its own, more generous program. Quebec sought to retain federal transfers for parental leave benefits to Quebecers, but to have them administered by the provincial government rather than the federal.

Negotiations between Quebec and Ottawa through the late 1990s failed to produce an agreement. Then in 1999 the Chrétien government reversed its original policy and increased the federal benefits substantially. It also suspended efforts to negotiate an opt-out version of the parental-leave program with Quebec. Quebec went ahead with its own enhanced program but initiated a challenge to the constitutionality of the federal program, arguing that the employment insurance power was intended only to cover people who were involuntarily unemployed but able to work, and that the parental-leave provisions of the federal program were *ultra vires*. The Quebec Court of Appeal agreed. It offered a fairly narrow reading of the federal power and found that parental benefits more appropriately belonged under the provincial constitutional headings of 'property and civil rights' or 'matters of a merely local nature'.

The federal government appealed this ruling to the Supreme Court on the grounds that it jeopardized not only the parental-leave program delivered by the Employment Insurance legislation, but also programs for sickness and compassionate leave. It also renewed negotiations with Quebec for some share in the delivery of the enhanced Quebec plan. In October 2005 the Supreme Court ruled unanimously that parental benefits were legitimately included in the federal power to provide employment insurance in the amended Section 91(2a) of the Constitution Act, 1867. The ruling was almost moot, as negotiations between Quebec and the federal government had already resolved the issue earlier that year. Nevertheless, the federal ministers involved in the negotiations repeatedly hailed the agreement as evidence that co-operative federalism works. One can only speculate on how the negotiations would have gone if the spectre of an adverse constitutional ruling had not been hanging over both parties.

New Umpires: Intergovernmental Agreements and Dispute Resolution

If federal judicial review is simply a mechanism for resolving intergovernmental disputes, the main candidates to replace it would be the numerous other forms of intergovernmental co-operation and dispute settlement found in the accords, frameworks, and communiqués that are the products of intergovernmental consultation and bargaining. But such intergovernmental agreements have long been notorious for their lack of legal enforceability. As Katherine Swinton notes, 'the method for resolving disputes about obligations between governments tends to lie in the political, rather than the legal, arena. Indeed, some intergovernmental agreements are designed not to be enforceable in any other forum' (1992: 140). This claim is bolstered by the reluctance of the Supreme Court to interfere when disputes have arisen about such agreements.

The leading example is the *Reference Re: Canada Assistance Plan (*CAP; 1991*)*, in which a unanimous Supreme Court refused to limit Parliament's power to unilaterally alter its obligations to the 'have' provinces under long-standing federal–provincial cost-sharing agreements.[3] Parliament was able to limit the increases in CAP grants to the richer provinces, despite a history of 50–50 cost-sharing, and the provinces had no legal recourse to force the continuation of equal cost-sharing, even if departure from this formula would have a negative impact on the delivery of services. The CAP case is generally interpreted as a warning to the provinces about the risks they take in dealing with the federal government in the strictly non-constitutional realm (Barker, 2000; Baier, 2001). But the CAP reference only touches on what might be called the *external enforceability* of intergovernmental agreements. Since the Canada Assistance Plan never took a constitutional form, altering Parliament's obligations was as simple as passing new legislation, and, as the Court ruled, the provinces had few grounds on which to appeal. Any federal or provincial legislation has a duty to abide by constitutional guarantees, whether of jurisdictional boundaries or of rights. These are matters of external enforceability: courts must ensure that legislation, including legislation that enacts intergovernmental agreements, still abides by rules such as the division of powers. When agreements go unaltered but are not implemented, or are not respected by one party or another, there is a dimension of *internal enforceability*. The court essentially argued in the CAP case that no external guarantee existed to stop the federal government from changing the internal terms of its agreement with the provinces.

Doubts about the external enforceability of intergovernmental agreements have always been present (Sossin, 1999),[4] and now the idea that they have some internal enforceability seems headed for the same fate. In the Finlay cases, a recipient of social benefits tried to ensure that the government of Manitoba lived up to what she argued were its obligations under the Canada Assistance Plan. Although her argument was successful at the lower court level, a narrow majority of the Supreme Court in *Finlay* (1993) rejected it and refused to directly patrol the program and its funding levels, leaving the province to achieve 'substantial compliance' with the objectives of the CAP. This ruling dashed hopes that courts would recognize that 'intergovernmental agreements are not the preserve of the signatory governments' and give 'the citizen status to patrol the intergovernmental relations process and to enforce obligations between governments' (Swinton, 1992: 145).

The following sections examine how the Agreement on Internal Trade and the benchmark Social Union Framework Agreement have tried to remedy the enforceability problem. These agreements consciously added internal mechanisms for dispute resolution, essentially replacing the Supreme Court as the arbiter of conflict. Both widely heralded as triumphs of flexible federalism, both favour the informal adjustment typical of contemporary executive federalism over the more rigid and legalistic constitutional model of judicial review. They place a premium on negotiation and compromise. Superficially at least, they appear to represent a giant leap forward in making federalism more responsive, collaborative, and workable.

The Agreement on Internal Trade

Canada's governments were stung by the defeat of the Charlottetown Accord in 1992 and were understandably loath to revisit the wasp's nest of constitutional change any time soon. However, governments (except Quebec) were still eager to make progress on the issues left hanging by the Accord's defeat. The Agreement on Internal Trade, signed in July 1994, was just such a case. The AIT is in many ways a model for post-Charlottetown intergovernmental relations. Its primary goal is the elimination of barriers to trade and economic mobility between the provinces. It commits signatories to the removal of economic barriers in areas such as government procurement, labour mobility, and environmental protection. It also includes provisions for dispute settlement in the event that either a government or person complains that government policies are in conflict with the commitments of the Agreement.

These mechanisms are contained in Chapter 17 of the AIT. From the start, the chapter indicates that co-operation is the overriding principle. It provides for the general mechanism of dispute resolution, but refers all conflicts initially to chapter-specific methods of dispute avoidance. Before a government or person can engage the general mechanism, the relevant governments must first exhaust the negotiation, consultation, and alternative dispute resolution mechanisms embodied in the sector-specific chapters. These processes give the government(s) involved the opportunity to adjust policies or legislation to conform with their commitments under the AIT. In this initial stage, a premium is placed on working out differences with a minimum of conflict and publicity. Thus the sector chapters include fairly rigid deadlines meant to move claims through the process reasonably quickly. If disputes remain unresolved after all the chapter-specific processes have been completed, they may proceed to a more formal Chapter 17 resolution.

Disputes under the AIT are administered by the Internal Trade Secretariat; the actual resolution process is overseen first by the Committee on Internal Trade (made up of ministers from the provinces and federal government) and then by appointed panels drawn from a roster maintained by the governments. Person-to-government disputes face an additional hurdle in the form of a pre-panel screening conducted by a roster-appointed screener who determines whether a claim is simply vexatious or harassing. If the dispute cannot be settled by confidential consultation, a panel is struck. It follows procedures similar to those of a court, hearing briefs from both parties and releasing a written decision. The enforcement of panel rulings is voluntary and in the case of government-to-government conflicts retaliatory action is possible.

The relatively weak enforcement mechanisms and the ad hoc nature of the panel process were necessitated by provincial objections to using either the courts or an independent 'third tier' institution. Doern and Macdonald cite the prevailing belief that the 'provinces were sovereign entities within a system of federalism and that no enforcement mechanism should be ceded' (1999: 140). The dispute resolution mechanism was thus structured to be 'clearly government driven and controlled rather than private-sector-access driven' (ibid.: 141). As of 2005, only ten complaints had proceeded to a formal panel resolution, and only two non-government parties had initiated complaints (Internal Trade Secretariat, 2005), which suggests that private parties wishing to use the dispute resolution mechanisms may face some barriers (Monahan, 1995: 212). Anecdotally, the business press has labelled the dispute resolution mechanisms 'complex, inaccessible, expensive [and] time consuming' and 'frighteningly vulnerable to bureaucratic inertia' (Wahl, 2000: 62).

Given the initial emphasis in the AIT on negotiation and conciliation of disputes—really dispute avoidance—courts are probably not the best institutions to perform such oversight (one provincial official described a mechanism allowing the federal government or the courts to get involved as 'thermonuclear'; Silcoff, 2000: C9). Since interpretation of the agreement is likely to involve trade-offs between permitted 'legitimate objectives' of governments and unduly restrictive barriers, governments are unwilling to trust the courts to make those trade-offs and, according to Swinton, they 'remain reluctant to surrender their sovereignty to such a politically unaccountable body' (1995: 203). Douglas Brown (2002) notes similar hesitation on the part of governments, particularly those of Ontario and Quebec, to surrender too much authority to an independent secretariat or dispute resolution process. Alberta and the federal government, on the other hand, were enthusiastic about the prospect of a more independent arbiter of such disputes and greater external enforceability of the agreement in general. In fact, the government of Alberta has been the AIT's biggest booster, unique among the provinces in publicly touting its benefits (Alberta, 2006). The government claims that a 26–8 winning record of complaints resolved in favour of Albertans is evidence that 'the dispute resolution process under the AIT has been effective in addressing trade-related complaints'. Even so, it is not clear that Alberta is judging the process by the right measures. Not all of the 34 complaints that Alberta counts followed AIT procedures. The Internal Trade Secretariat (2005) reported that 43 disputes had engaged its processes since 1995, 9 of which were still pending—and some of those dated to 1997. It is the unresolved or difficult cases that are the truest test of the AIT's dispute resolution processes. One must look beyond Alberta's seemingly rosy experience to find such cases.

Unilever, a British multinational with Canadian operations based in Ontario, has actively challenged one of the more pernicious trade barriers in Canadian history: the ban on yellow margarine in Quebec. Though justified as providing a way to reduce consumer confusion between margarine and butter, the regulations were largely intended to protect Quebec dairy products from interprovincial competition. The ban on yellow margarine is exactly the kind of discriminatory regulation that the AIT was meant to get rid of. In 1997 Unilever sold several cases of yellow margarine to a Quebec distributor in order to test the legality of Quebec government regulations under the AIT. Under the dispute resolution provisions, the margarine producer must go through its home government to initiate a dispute against another province. While the company received some initial support from Ontario, the province was ultimately unwilling to pursue the case against its neighbour.

When Ontario refused to engage the AIT process, Unilever turned to the regular court system. Challenging the constitutional authority of Quebec's government to enact such regulations and arguing that they were inconsistent with both the AIT and freedom of expression guarantees in the Quebec Charter of Rights, Unilever lost at both the Quebec Court of Appeal and the Supreme Court of Canada. In a terse oral decision delivered within weeks of hearing arguments, the Supreme Court upheld the Quebec regulations as entirely within the legislative authority of the province. Further, it rejected Unilever's argument that the AIT precluded such a regulation, finding that 'provincial and international trade agreements have no effect on the validity of this provision.'

The Unilever case demonstrates the limited internal enforceability of intergovernmental agreements. An interprovincial agreement cannot supersede the authority that a province has under the Constitution. The case also stands as a prime example of the lengths to which companies and individuals may have to go to assert their rights under the AIT, should their provincial government prove a reluctant ally. As a large multinational, Unilever had the resources as well as the incentive to launch such a challenge; for the smaller producer or manufacturer adversely affected by these kinds of barriers, the protections that they might seek are even more illusory under the AIT's structure. Little surprise, then, that the Council of the Federation has identified changes to the dispute resolution process as a priority issue for the future of the AIT (Council of the Federation, 2006).

The Social Union Framework Agreement

The Social Union Framework Agreement (SUFA), signed in 1999, is the benchmark of post-Charlottetown intergovernmental relations. While it already seems passé among dedicated observers, and governments seem less and less committed to its promises, the format and spirit of the agreement are still important indicators of the way intergovernmental negotiations are conducted in Canada. For example, section 6 of the Accord calls for new efforts to avoid and resolve disputes between governments. It commits governments 'to working collaboratively to avoid and resolve intergovernmental disputes' and allows governments to retain 'maximum flexibility' to do so 'in a non-adversarial way'.

Governments have differed strongly about how to implement these commitments (Lazar, 2003), since the SUFA outlines no specific mechanism or approach. Instead section 6 promotes a 'spirit' of dispute resolution marked by intense collaboration and avoidance of formal processes and third parties. Preference is given to quiet consultation and negotiation rather than reference to courts or tribunals. When the Accord underwent an internally mandated three-year review in 2003, stakeholders from the policy community as well as provincial and territorial governments had the opportunity to report on its effectiveness. On dispute avoidance and resolution, the report suggested that the process proposed by the federal government in 2001–2 to deal with disputes under the Canada Health Act should be used as the model for future mechanisms to implement section 6 (Federal/Provincial/Territorial Ministerial Council, 2003).

The Canada Health Act Process

Despite its imperfections, the model of dispute resolution found in the AIT seems to be replicating itself in SUFA processes. In April 2002, then federal Health minister Anne McLellan wrote to her provincial counterpart in Alberta, Gary Mar, outlining a dispute avoidance and resolution process for potential violations of the federal Canada Health Act. The act grants federal transfers to the provinces that abide by its conditions. Provinces that fail to abide by the five principles of universal public health care outlined in the act are meant to face financial penalties in the form of reduced transfer payments. The decision to withhold funds for violations of the Act's principles belongs exclusively to the federal minister.

Minister McLellan's letter outlines a process that is strikingly similar to the one prescribed in the AIT. The initial emphasis is placed on dispute avoidance, facilitating information exchange and discussion in order to avoid formal resolution. If the dispute remains, the more formalized process begins with a letter from either the federal or the provincial minister of Health to his or her counterpart. A panel is then formed of one provincial representative and one federal representative who jointly choose a chairperson and undertake 'fact-finding and provide advice and recommendations' (McLellan, 2002). The final authority for the interpretation of the act and the implementation of penalties for non-compliance remains with the federal minister, who may abide by or ignore the panel's interpretation of the facts, advice, or recommendations. The minister pledges that governments will report publicly on any dispute, including the release of panel reports.

As of spring 2007 no disputes have been reported by Health Canada, so the potential of the dispute settlement procedures recommended for SUFA remains theoretical. Incumbent ministers of health may not feel obliged to abide by the assurances—never put into law—of predecessors who may well have been of a different party. Furthermore, although the panel provisions recommended in the McLellan/Mar correspondence suggest a desire for more 'objective' decision-making in federal–provincial controversies, or for some third party to look at the details of a dispute, ultimately the procedures contemplated in McLellan's promises could undermine that objectivity. Discretion remains with the minister, so panels might provide the political credibility that a federal minister needs to deny funding to provinces under the CHA—but in practice no such penalties have been imposed, despite numerous provincial violations of the act (Flood and Choudry, 2002; Choudry, 1996). The extra ounce of credibility that a panel finding might give to a federal government that wishes to enforce its own legislation seems little justification for the creation of an ad hoc process with minimal procedural guidance or permanent expertise in the resolution of such conflicts.

The Harper Conservative government has expressed some ambivalence about aggressive enforcement of the Canada Health Act. And Ralph Klein, during his last year as Alberta premier, abandoned a very short-lived attempt at 'third way' reform of his province's health system, making it less likely that Alberta's experiments would necessitate the engagement of the dispute settlement process. Nevertheless, the model for future health disputes between a province and the federal government is in place; whether it will prove satisfying is as yet unknown.

Conclusion: The Devil You Know

The judicial review of federalism is a difficult practice to defend. Judicial reasoning is not always as consistent or objective as its practitioners may profess, and judicial power has come under increasing scrutiny since the enactment of the Charter of Rights. The political character of judicial review in Canada is more muted than is generally true in other federations (Baier, 2002), and courts incur much less criticism for their federalism rulings than they do for rulings centred around rights. The Supreme Court's power in Canadian federalism runs up against the incrementalist, pragmatic style favoured in intergovernmental relations. Even if judicial review has a limited direct role in shaping the federation, the resources it assigns are still important to the settlement of intergovernmental issues. Judicial settlement of federalism disputes is by nature largely a zero-sum game: one party generally wins in any given constitutional litigation. While governments can subsequently negotiate with one another to work around the results of judicial decisions, those very decisions can affect the bargaining power that participants have in such negotiations.

Hence it is little surprise that governments have refrained from seeking judicial settlement of disputes over federalism practice. The courts have been reluctant to enforce intergovernmental agreements, so effective intergovernmental negotiation and strategy remains the best tool for individual governments to achieve their goals. Ultimately, though, the creeping informalism of Canadian federalism may not be to the advantage of either governments or democracy. Giving up federalism litigation might not be as wise as governments think.

The fact that the Supreme Court played only a bit role in the outcomes of the *Chaoulli* and *Employment Insurance* cases discussed above suggests that it is no longer the principal arbiter of the division of powers. Even if the Court cannot settle such disputes, however, judicial review still offers procedural advantages over its replacements. Unlike the new mechanisms of intergovernmental dispute resolution, it gives actors other than governments an opportunity to influence the politics of intergovernmental relations. It also reinforces the constitutional character of the federal order, reminding governments that the Constitution is meant to be supreme. If on the contrary intergovernmental agreements are all that holds the federation together, the federal order will begin to be much more confederal, dependent on the goodwill of governments rather than the guarantees provided by the Constitution.

As Richard Simeon and Amy Nugent elaborate in Chapter 5, students of executive federalism today frequently question the accountability and transparency of intergovernmental decision-making. The more collaborative the decision-making process becomes—in the sense that priorities are set and mechanisms designed collectively by first ministers or their representatives—the less democratic executive federalism appears. No doubt co-operation is a noble goal; but the emphasis on settling, avoiding, or amicably resolving disputes in the new collaborative federalism is also about keeping the business of governing and policy-making in the hands of governments. As Harvey Lazar (2003) has noted, 'intergovernmental conflict can be constructive when it exposes competing ideas to public deliberation.' By contrast, collaborative federalism as it has been practised in Canada ensures that the intergovernmental process produces no such benefit. As Winfield and MacDonald note in Chapter 13, on environmental policy-making, successful collaborative federalism can detract from the policy-making roles of the federal Parliament, provincial legislators, and non-governmental stakeholders.

Federalism litigation, we should not forget, is routinely initiated by individuals or societal actors who wish to challenge the constitutional authority of a particular government to pass a particular piece of legislation. Whether or not one agrees with Dr Chaoulli's efforts to break into the closed club of health-care policy-making, they remind us of how hard it is for non-governmental interests to get a hearing in the context of collaborative federalism. Opportunities to avail oneself of the constitutional guarantees that governments cannot legitimately act outside their assigned jurisdiction have all but disappeared, replaced by dispute resolution mechanisms which privilege governments. Certainly the Charter of Rights makes it possible to hold intergovernmental agreements to an individual rights standard, but the courts have proven fairly reluctant, *Chaoulli* notwithstanding, to second-guess the policy choices of legislatures on issues involving intergovernmental co-operation.

Governments seem to prefer this limited oversight. The Agreement on Internal Trade puts numerous hurdles in the way of individuals or interests who want to seek redress. The process is stacked against them, and the agreement works efficiently to stop disputes before they happen. The bulk of the consultation and alteration that takes place stays confidential. How are interested citizens to keep abreast of the sacrifices or commitments made in those negotiations? The dispute resolution procedures laid out in the AIT have simply exaggerated the already negative tendencies of executive federalism.

The SUFA provisions are even less encouraging, lacking both the detail and the relatively institutionalized character of their AIT cousins. Instances of dispute resolution are supposed to be reported yearly, but this goal may be difficult to realize. As a public-service primer on the SUFA notes, 'there is no formula for deciding that a dispute has occurred or been resolved' (CCMD Roundtable, 2002). The same primer tells managers to use prudence to determine when a dispute has been identified and settled and to report accordingly. Reference to third parties is possible but not required, and governments determined to keep conflicts to themselves will be able to do so.

Perhaps even more troubling than the loss of the genuine benefits of judicial review is the resemblance of some of the new dispute resolution mechanisms to courts themselves. The panel decisions of the AIT, for instance, have included dissenting opinions. While, unlike court rulings, these decisions do not set precedents, they do use legalistic language and encourage participants to present their cases in adversarial terms. Essentially, these mechanisms trade on the courts' reputation for objectivity[5] and the public's respect for judges as impartial and independent. The new dispute settlement mechanisms may look like courts, but they are without any of the strictures that condition the judicial mind. Nor are their decisions legally binding on the parties before them.

One of the defining features of a federation is that in it sovereignty is neither wholly national nor wholly regional. The constitution and its judicial umpires are meant to enforce the promises enshrined in the Constitution, even when governments seek to ignore or circumvent them. Both the AIT and the new dispute resolution process under the Canada Health Act make a point of preserving governmental and ministerial discretion, respectively. We have come full circle. Judicial review of federalism is avoided whenever possible because judges are depicted as political and unreliable; yet the institutional replacements seem most legitimate when they look most like courts. The consequences of this paradox for the performance, legitimacy, and effectiveness of Canadian federalism are not yet clear.

Notes

The author thanks the editors for their enormously helpful comments and suggestions; Erin Crandall for research assistance; and the Social Sciences and Humanities Research Council of Canada for financial support.

1. *Reference re: Amendment of the Constitution of Canada* (Patriation Reference) (1981), 125 D.L.R. 3rd; Re: A.G. Quebec and A.G. Canada (Quebec Veto Reference) (1982), 2 S.C.R. 793 and *Reference Re: Secession of Quebec* (1998), 2 S.C.R. 217.
2. *Employment and Social Insurance Reference* (1937), A.C. 355.
3. *Reference Re: Canada Assistance Plan* (1991), 83 D.L.R.(4th).
4. Sossin (1999) includes 'disputes involving intergovernmental relations' among the settings that stand outside the reach of judicial inquiry.

5. The offshore 'boundary' between Newfoundland and Labrador and Nova Scotia for the purposes of oil and gas development was essentially determined by a non-judicial tribunal that, while not a court, conducted a judicial-style proceeding to determine its recommendations to the federal minister of Natural Resources. For a criticism of this process see Baier and Groarke (2003).

References

Alberta. 2006. 'Agreement on Internal Trade: Benefits for Albertans'. Available on-line at: <www.iir.gov.ab.ca/trade_policy/pdfs/5.3.2.1-Benefits_for_Albertans_Resolved_Complaints.pdf>.

Baier, G. 2006. *Courts and Federalism: Judicial Doctrine in the United States, Australia and Canada*. Vancouver: University of British Columbia Press.

———. 2002. 'New Judicial Thinking on Sovereignty and Federalism: American and Canadian Comparisons', *Justice System Journal* 23, 1: 1–24.

———. 2001. 'Judicial Review and Federalism'. In *Canadian Federalism: Performance, Effectiveness and Legitimacy*, ed. H. Bakvis and G. Skogstad. Toronto: Oxford University Press.

——— and P. Groarke. 2003. 'Arbitrating a Fiction: The Nova Scotia/ Newfoundland and Labrador Boundary Dispute and Canadian Federalism', *Canadian Public Administration* 46, 3: 315–38.

Barker, P. 2000. 'Acceptable Law, Questionable Politics: The Canada Assistance Plan Reference'. In *Political Dispute and Judicial Review: Assessing the Work of the Supreme Court of Canada*, ed. H. Mellon and M. Westmacott. Scarborough, Ont.: Nelson.

Brown, D.M. 2002. *Market Rules: Economic Union Reform and Intergovernmental Policy Making in Australia and Canada*. Kingston and Montreal: McGill–Queen's University Press.

Cairns, A. 1971. 'The Judicial Committee and Its Critics', *Canadian Journal of Political Science* 4, 3: 301–45.

Canada. 1994. *Agreement on Internal Trade*. Ottawa: Industry Canada.

———. 1999. *Social Union Framework Agreement*. Available on-line at: <www.socialunion.gc.ca>.

CCMD Roundtable on the Implementation of the Social Union Framework Agreement. 2002. *Implementing the Social Union Framework Agreement: A Learning and Reference Tool*. Ottawa: Canadian Centre for Management Development.

Choudry, S. 1996. 'The Enforcement of the *Canada Health Act*', *McGill Law Journal* 41, 2: 462–509.

Council of the Federation. 2006. *Internal Trade Workplan Progress Report January 2006*. Available on-line at: <http://councilofthefederation.ca>.

Cutler, F. 2004. 'Government Responsibility and Electoral Accountability in Federations', *Publius: The Journal of Federalism* 34, 2: 19–38.

Doern, G.B., and M. MacDonald. 1999. *Free-Trade Federalism: Negotiating the Agreement on Internal Trade*. Toronto: University of Toronto Press.

Federal/Provincial/Territorial Ministerial Council on Social Policy Renewal. 2003. *Three Year Review Social Union Framework Agreement*.

Flood, C. and S. Choudry. 2002. *Strengthening the Foundations: Modernizing the Canada Health Act*. Discussion Paper No. 13, Royal Commission on the Future of Health Care in Canada.

Government of Quebec. 2006. *Guaranteeing Access: Meeting the Challenges of Equity, Efficiency and Equality*.

Hogg, P. 1979. 'Is the Supreme Court of Canada Biased in Constitutional Cases?' *Canadian Bar Review* 57: 721–39.

Internal Trade Secretariat. 2005. *AIT Disputes—Summary Statistics*. Available on-line at http://ait-aci.ca/index_en/dispute.htm.

Laskin, B. 1951. 'The Supreme Court of Canada: A Final Court of and for Canadians?' *Canadian Bar Review* 29: 1038–79.

Lazar, H. 2003. 'Managing Interdependencies in the Canadian Federation: Lessons from the Social Union Framework Agreement'. In *Constructive and Co-operative Federalism?* Kingston and Montreal: IIGR/IRPP.

McLellan, A. 2002. 'Letter to Gary Mar'. 2 Apr. Available on-line at: <www.gov.bc. ca/igrs/down/gary_mar_e.pdf>.

Monahan, P. 1995. '"To the Extent Possible": A Comment on Dispute Settlement in the Agreement on Internal Trade'. In *Getting There: An Assessment of the Agreement on Internal Trade*, ed. M. Trebilcock and D. Schwanen. Toronto: C.D. Howe Institute.

Rosenberg, G. 1991. *The Hollow Hope: Can Courts Bring About Social Change?* Chicago: University of Chicago Press.

Russell, P. 1985. 'The Supreme Court and Federal Provincial Relations: The Political Use of Legal Resources', *Canadian Public Policy* 11, 2: 161–70.

Silcoff, S. 2000. 'Trade Among Provinces Badly Flawed, Official Says: Internal Trade deal. Ottawa Urged to Step in and End Disputes'. *Financial Post* 17 Oct.: C1, C9.

Sossin, L.M. 1999. *Boundaries of Judicial Review: The Law of Justiciability in Canada*. Scarborough: Carswell.

Swinton, K. 1995. 'Law, Politics and the Enforcement of the Agreement on Internal Trade'. In *Getting There: An Assessment of the Agreement on Internal Trade*, ed. M. Trebilcock and D. Schwanen. Toronto: C.D. Howe Institute.

———. 1992. 'Federalism Under Fire: The Role of the Supreme Court of Canada', *Law and Contemporary Problems* 55, 1: 121–45.

Wahl, A. 2000. 'Trade Secrets: Why Is Nothing Being Done about Interprovincial Barriers', *Canadian Business* 73, 10 (29 May): 61–2.

Cases

Chaoulli v. Quebec (Attorney General) (2005), 1 S.C.R. 791.

Employment and Social Insurance Reference (1937), AC 355.
Finlay No. 1 (1986), 2 S.C.R. 633.
Finlay v. Canada (1990), 71 D.L.R. (4th) 422.
Finlay v. Canada (Minister of Finance) (1993) 1 S.C.R. 1080.
Johannesson v. West St. Paul (1952), S.C.R. 292.
Munro v. National Capital Commission (1966), S.C.R. 663.
Pronto Uranium Mines, Ltd. v. O.L.R.B. (1956), 5 D.L.R.(2nd).
R. v. Crown Zellerbach (1988), 49 D.L.R. (4th).
R. v. Hydro-Québec (1997), 151 D.L.R. (4th).
Re: A.G. Quebec and A.G. Canada (Quebec Veto Reference) (1982), 2 S.C.R. 793.
Reference Re: Amendment of the Constitution of Canada (Patriation Reference)
    (1981), 125 D.L.R. (3rd).
Reference Re: Anti-Inflation (1976), 68 D.L.R. (3rd).
Reference Re: Canada Assistance Plan (1991), 83 D.L.R. (4th).
Reference Re: Employment Insurance Act (Can.) (2005), 2 S.C.R. 669.
Reference Re: Firearms Act (Can.), (2000), 1 S.C.R. 783.
Reference Re: Offshore Mineral Rights of B.C (1967), S.C.R. 792.
Reference Re: The Secession of Quebec (1998), 161 D.L.R. (4th).
UL Canada Inc. v. Quebec (Attorney General) (2005), 1 S.C.R. 143.

Websites

The Social Union Framework Agreement: www.socialunion.gc.ca
The Agreement on Internal Trade: www.ait-aci.ca
The Supreme Court of Canada: www.scc-csc.gc.ca

Chapter 3

The Courts, the Charter, and Federalism

James B. Kelly

Judicial review has had a significant impact on Canadian federalism since 1867. The Judicial Committee of the Privy Council played an important role in interpreting the constitutional division of powers and determining the relative positions of the two orders of government (Cairns, 1971). As Gerald Baier argues in Chapter 2, the Supreme Court of Canada continues to serve as umpire in disputes over the division of powers and in the use of residual or plenary powers in areas such as 'peace, order and good government' (POGG) and trade and commerce (Baier, 1998).

However, the effect of judicial review on federalism has changed significantly since the introduction of the Charter of Rights and Freedoms in 1982 because of the remedy powers available to the judiciary when legislation is found to be inconsistent with protected rights and freedoms. A considerable number of issues involving federalism arise in Charter decisions, and criticism of the Supreme Court has intensified since the Charter's introduction because of its implications for federalism and provincial autonomy.

There are important similarities and differences in the two roles of the Supreme Court as the umpire of federalism with respect to the division of powers and as the guardian of the Constitution under the Charter of Rights and Freedoms (Kelly, 2004). As the umpire of federalism, the Supreme Court monitors the boundaries between the two orders of government and ensures that neither encroaches on the jurisdictional authority of the other (Greschner, 2001). In effect, the Court assigns jurisdictional responsibility and ensures that jurisdictional boundaries are respected by both orders of government.

Under the Charter of Rights the Supreme Court's role is more expansive: the

Court determines whether legislation violates protected rights and freedoms, and, when it finds that this is the case, determines whether the violation is reasonable in a free and democratic society under section 1 of the Charter. The Supreme Court is required to determine the substantive qualities of legislation and whether public policy that violates rights should be considered constitutional because it advances important legislative objectives. Further, under section 24(1) of the Charter, if the Court determines that certain legislation does violate the Charter and is not a reasonable limit under section 1, it has the responsibility to introduce remedies that are 'appropriate and just in the circumstances'. This latter responsibility has clearly shifted the role of the Supreme Court to that of an institutional actor with the ability to participate in and to shape policy debates central to the federation.

Criticism of the Supreme Court since the Charter's introduction has taken several forms. Some critics have focused on a particular decision, such as the Court's rejection of the framers' intent as a constraint on judicial review in *Reference re s.94(2) of the Motor Vehicle Act*; others have objected to what they perceive as the Court's recent dominance in areas that were traditionally the domain of elected institutions, such as language, education, labour, social, and health policy, or the absence of a formal provincial role in the selection of the Court's members even though its decisions may play a crucial role in provincial affairs, or the Court's repeated description of the judiciary as the 'guardian of the Constitution', which suggests a dominant, if not domineering, role for the Court in the age of rights (Weinrib, 2001).

There are, however, factors beyond the control of the Supreme Court itself that have generated criticism of it. One is the increasing use of the reference procedure by the national government, which has sought the Court's advice on contentious social and political issues such as same-sex marriage and the constitutionality of Quebec secession. Another is the intense criticism of the Court by political parties such as the Reform Party, the Canadian Alliance, and most recently, the Conservative Party of Canada.

The purpose of this chapter is to assess the performance, effectiveness, and legitimacy of Charter review by the Supreme Court of Canada and its impact on Canadian federalism. Overall, the Court has performed well in regard to the Charter, showing sensitivity to federalist concerns that the Charter would lead to standardization of public policy at the expense of provincial autonomy. Through a balanced jurisprudence that has accepted policy variation as consistent with the Charter, the Court has advanced both its own legitimacy and that of the Charter, particularly among provincial governments, which were initially reluctant to have their statutes evaluated against a national statement of rights and freedoms, and feared that judicial review would increase centralization of the federation. The Charter has also improved the effectiveness of the Canadian federation because of the political response to rights and freedoms. The machinery of government has been reformed at all levels to explicitly reconcile legislative objectives with rights commitments, and this has resulted in public policy with greater legitimacy and effectiveness. The performance, effectiveness, and legitimacy of the Charter might be enhanced if the notwithstanding clause (section 33) were revised to require cross-party agreement to override a judicial decision.

In addition to the Canadian Charter of Rights and Freedoms, this chapter will discuss two significant cases involving the Quebec Charter of Human Rights and Freedoms. In recent years the Supreme Court of Canada has decided a number of important policy issues by reference to the Quebec Charter, which has a quasi-constitutional status that is not accorded to any other provincial human rights code. This can be viewed as a strategic move on the part of the Court, designed to enhance the legitimacy of Charter decisions by demonstrating that the two Charters are compatible. Accordingly, any discussion of the impact of constitutional protections on Quebec must include analysis of the Quebec Charter. In this sense, the status of human rights codes in Canada is asymmetrical, with only the Quebec National Assembly elevating its human rights code to the status of a quasi-constitutional document (Schneiderman, 1998).

This chapter will argue that the Supreme Court has demonstrated sensitivity to federalism in its Charter Jurisprudence and that 25 years of judicial review based on a national statement of rights and freedoms has not led to a more centralized state. Further, the Court's approach to remedies in Charter cases indicates that a Charter dialogue is developing between courts and legislatures. This dialogic approach has enhanced the legitimacy of the Supreme Court as an institution, while safeguarding federalism in Canada (Hogg and Bushell, 1997; Manfredi and Kelly, 1999).

The reconciliation between nation-wide rights and provincial autonomy has been achieved in part as a result of the Supreme Court's sensitivity to its new role under the Charter of Rights but also in part by the efforts of governments to govern in the context of the Charter (Kelly, 2005). Although bureaucratic responses to the Charter are beyond the scope of this chapter, all governments have worked to develop legislation that complies with it, and the resulting changes have helped to safeguard federalism and provincial autonomy. By developing legislation that complies with the Charter or at least constitutes a reasonable limitation that is demonstrably justified, provincial governments can ensure the constitutionality of their laws when these are challenged before the courts. Indeed, the attempt to reconcile legislative objectives and rights through an activist policy process has avoided the possibility of risk-averse governments under the Charter, where provincial autonomy would surely be compromised because of the possibility of judicial nullification that reduced the activity of government. Though the Supreme Court of Canada may consider itself the guardian of the Constitution, this is principally a political responsibility, as the main responsibility for protecting rights and freedoms lies not with the Supreme Court but with Parliament and the provincial legislatures at the stage when legislation is developed.

This chapter is organized in three sections. The first considers the academic debate that has surrounded the Charter and the question of whether judicial review has led to increased centralization. The second section provides an empirical overview of the Supreme Court's Charter jurisprudence and identifies significant trends that reinforce the legitimacy of the Court as a federal actor. Finally, the third section examines three major provincial policy areas that have been the subject of judicial review involving both the Canadian Charter and the Quebec Charter: language and education policy; labour and social policy; and health policy. In short, the relationship between the Supreme Court, the Charter, and federalism is complex, and the legitimacy, performance, and effectiveness of the Charter are the responsibility of both the Supreme Court and the governments that make up the Canadian federation.

The Charter and Federal–Provincial Relations

After the defeat of the 'Non' forces in the May 1980 Quebec referendum on sovereignty-association, the Trudeau government sought to demonstrate its commitment to 'renewed federalism' by calling a series of federal–provincial meetings during the summer of 1980 to amend the Canadian Constitution. But the two orders of government had different reform priorities. While the federal government wanted to establish a Charter of Rights and a domestic amending formula, the provincial premiers wanted to change the division of powers in their favour. Premiers argued that recent constitutional decisions by the Supreme Court had served to centralize the federation by favouring the national government (Kelly, 2005). The result was a political stalemate. The Trudeau government advocated a further round of constitutional reform once the Charter was entrenched, and the premiers argued that the division of powers should be addressed before the Charter was entrenched.

The first ministers' conference (FMC) called to address constitutional reform in September 1980 ended in failure, and it appeared that Trudeau's pledge of 'renewed federalism' would not be fulfilled. Then on 2 October Trudeau informed the premiers that he would bring the Canadian Constitution home from Britain, entrench a Charter of Rights, and introduce a domestic amending formula. The premiers challenged the constitutionality of unilateral patriation, and a year later the Supreme Court decided (in the *Patriation Reference*) that substantial provincial consent was required—by constitutional convention, though not by law—before the federal government could request changes to the Constitution (Russell, 1983). In the meantime the draft Charter of Rights had been significantly strengthened in the course of the proceedings of the Special Joint Committee on the Constitution of Canada. In other words, the substantive content of the Charter was the product not of federal–provincial negotiations but of the Parliament of Canada and the individuals who appeared before the Special Joint Committee on the Constitution of Canada (Kelly, 2005).

The *Patriation Reference* facilitated the FMC in November 1981 at which substantial provincial consent was secured after the federal government agreed to several concessions that satisfied all provinces but Quebec. The most important of these concessions[1] was the addition to the Charter of Rights of section 33 (the notwithstanding clause), under which Parliament or a legislature may override a judicial decision invalidating legislation that violates sections 2 and 7– 15 of the Charter for a renewable period of five years by passing a resolution to this effect. Although the provincial premiers generally opposed entrenchment of a Charter of Rights on the grounds that political actors rather than courts should be responsible for protecting rights, they saw section 33 as a way to preserve the principle of parliamentary supremacy by allowing legislatures to have the final word in the event of fundamental disagreement with judicial decisions involving the Charter.

The demand for the legislative override clearly reflected the premiers' view that the Supreme Court of Canada had not acted as an impartial umpire of federalism since the 1960s, when it consistently ruled in favour of the federal government, strengthening the POGG power in the *Anti-inflation Reference* (Russell, 1977), and its ability to tax the natural resources of provinces (e.g., in *Reference re Offshore Mineral Rights of British Columbia, Canadian Industrial Gas & Oil Ltd.*, and *Central Canada Potash Co. Ltd*). Indeed, the premiers expected the Supreme Court of Canada—a national institution appointed by the national government—to use the Charter of Rights as an additional instrument to promote further centralization. Specifically, there were concerns that the Charter, as a national statement, would not be sensitive to the particular challenges facing individual provinces and the value of diversity that is at the heart of a federal system, and that the Supreme Court, acting as the guardian of the Constitution, would homogenize provincial policies by requiring a single approach to ensure consistency with Charter rights and freedoms (Romanow et al., 1984).

Provincial opposition to the Charter has influenced the scholarly debate on its consequences for Canadian federalism. The scholarly concern that the Charter would standardize policy in provincial areas of responsibility was rooted in Peter Hogg's claim that 'where guaranteed rights exist, there must be a single national rule' (1985: 250). The nation-building objectives of the Charter were considered to be a direct challenge to provincial autonomy. It was argued that national values would be given priority and used to evaluate whether provincial policies were constitutional (Knopff and Morton, 1985).

In Quebec the Canadian Charter was viewed as a direct challenge to provincial control over language and education policy. Section 23, providing minority-language education rights to the children of Canadian citizens educated in either official language in Canada, was designed to override the Charter of the French Language (CFL), which restricted English education to the children of anglophones educated in English in Quebec (Laforest, 1995). After reviewing the invalidation of provisions of the CFL in *Protestant School Boards* as inconsistent with section 23 of the Canadian Charter, Yves de Montigny suggested that 'the Charter has destroyed whole sections of the language regime gradually adopted by the province over the years' (1997: 9–10). The concern that the Charter of Rights, as interpreted by the Supreme Court of Canada, would be detrimental to federalism and provincial autonomy has also been raised by academics outside of Quebec.

F.L. Morton, for example, argues the 'Charter has . . . allowed the federal govern-ment to achieve indirectly what it could not have achieved directly' (1995: 9–10). Specifically, Morton contends that lobby groups funded through the former fed-eral court challenges program, such as Alliance Quebec, successfully challenged the constitutionality of provincial statutes and thereby weakened provincial autonomy.

The Supreme Court and the Charter

Supporters of the centralization thesis contend that provincial autonomy has been weakened through judicial review involving the Charter as national values are prioritized and provincial policies that vary from national values are ruled unconstitutional. This was a dominant view during the initial period of Charter review. Yet it has not been demonstrated empirically or substantively that Charter review has resulted in further centralization of the Canadian federation. Of the 67 provincial statutes that the Supreme Court reviewed in relation to the Charter of Rights between 1982 and 2005, it invalidated only 25 as unconstitutional—an average of just slightly more than one statute per year. Recent analysis suggests that the Supreme Court has demonstrated an appreciation of federal values such as diversity, and that this appreciation has significantly influenced the Court's approach in Charter cases (Gaudreault-DesBiens, 2003). Indeed, the safeguard-ing of provincial autonomy, and by extension federalism, is the result of two developments that are directly attributable to the Supreme Court: first, the Court's approach to sections of the Charter such as reasonable limits (s. 1) and equality rights (s. 15); and, second, its approach to remedies when it determines that legislation does violate the Charter and is not justified as a reasonable limit under section 1.

The reasonable limits clause of the Charter is known as the *Oakes* test, after the case of that name. In order for the limitation of a right or freedom to be con-sidered reasonable, the statute in question must satisfy three criteria: the legisla-tive objective must be pressing and substantial; there must be a rational connec-tion between the legislative means chosen and the objectives sought; and, finally, the infringement must be a minimal impairment of the right or freedom in ques-tion. Section 1 of the Charter has also acted as a safeguard for provincial auton-omy because the Supreme Court has given weight to the federal character of Canada when it determines whether an infringement is reasonable in a free and democratic society. Indeed, the Court has read this provision to accept limita-tions that are demonstrably justified in a free and democratic *federal* society (Hiebert, 1996). For instance, in *R. v. Edwards Books and Arts Ltd* [1986], the Court determined that Ontario's Retail Business Holiday Act was a violation of freedom of religion because it compelled a common day of rest. After comparing other provinces' laws in the same area, however, it concluded that the act in ques-tion did in fact constitute a reasonable limit. According to Justice La Forest in his section 1 reasoning, 'the simple fact is that what may work effectively in one province (or part of it) may simply not work in another without unduly inter-fering with the legislative scheme' (*Edwards*, 1986: 802). In effect, the Supreme Court has altered its approach to section 1 to incorporate federalism as a justifi-cation for limiting rights.

Another example of the Court's use of policy variation to satisfy section 1 of the Charter was *RJR-Macdonald Inc. v. Canada*, a case involving the constitu-tionality of the federal Tobacco Products Control Act. Although the Court did not find that the restrictions on tobacco advertising constituted a reasonable lim-itation, it reinforced the principle that section 1 must be sensitive to the contexts in which particular policies are made. Justice McLachlin articulated the Court's view that a uniform approach to section 1 should be avoided, and acknowledged the difficulty that legislative actors face in reconciling legislative objectives with protected rights:

> The tailoring process seldom admits of perfection and the courts must accord some leeway to the legislator. If the law falls within a range of reasonable alternatives, the courts will not find it overbroad merely because they can conceive of an alternative which might better tailor objective to infringement . . . (*RJR-Macdonald*, 1995: 342).

Indeed, while the Supreme Court has sought to ensure that rights and freedoms are uniformly protected across Canada, federalism and provincial diversity have not suffered because the Court has recognized that different policy contexts, which clearly exist in a federal system, can justify different interpretations of what constitutes a reasonable limit. As we will see in part 3 below, this approach has served to moderate much of the Charter's centralizing potential.

Another early concern was section 15, entrenching equality rights. Peter Russell, for instance, initially suggested that this section would have 'a centraliz-ing effect on social policy' because it was unclear whether the Supreme Court would accept policy variation among provinces as consistent with equality rights (1982: 26). Reflecting on the tenth anniversary of the Charter's introduction, however, Russell concluded that equality rights had not resulted in homogeniza-tion of provincial responsibilities (Russell, 1994: 173). Specifically, the Supreme Court established the principle early on that equality does not require confor-mity and that differential treatment under various provincial legislative schemes can be consistent with section 15 of the Charter. It also determined that the legit-imate use of provincial powers that result in unequal treatment 'cannot be sub-ject to a s.15(1) challenge on the basis that it creates distinctions based on province of residence' because such an approach would 'undermine the value of diversity which is at the foundation of the division of powers' (*R. v. S.(S.)*, 1990: 288). Federalism, therefore, must be balanced with rights. This reasoning too has helped to limit the centralizing potential of the Charter.

Should the Supreme Court of Canada read federalism into section 1? Or is this the role envisioned for section 33, the notwithstanding clause? The provincial insistence on section 33 was based on federalist arguments: if provincial governments fundamentally disagreed with Charter decisions by the Supreme Court, the notwithstanding clause would allow provincial values to trump the national values in the Charter. There are, however, both judicial and political arguments in favour of giving more weight to federalist principles in section 1. One is that the Charter's reasonable limits test is similar to a judicial test developed by the European Court of Human Rights (ECHR). Known as the 'margin of appreciation', this test gives member states some flexibility in honouring their commitments under European Union (EU) law. In effect, both the ECHR 'margin of appreciation' and the Supreme Court of Canada's reasonable limits test recognize federalism as an important variable when evaluating the constitutionality of laws.

A second argument in favour of the Court's interpretation of section 1 is based on the idea that the Supreme Court of Canada ceases to be simply a legal actor and becomes a political actor when it considers the reasonableness of a legislative instrument that limits a freedom. It functions as a political actor when it engages in a section 1 analysis because it is required to decide non-legal questions such as whether the legislative objectives are pressing and substantial, and whether there are alternative policy choices that would restrict the right in question to a lesser degree. Further, the Court must also determine which community standard—federal or provincial—should be applied in considering the reasonableness of a rights violation. Because provincial communities are part of a federal society, it is legitimate for the Supreme Court to consider what is reasonable in a federal society when it evaluates provincial or national policies under section 1 of the Charter.

The legitimacy of section 33 has been questioned ever since Quebec used it in 1988 to override the Supreme Court's invalidation of the sign law. Some argue that this move contributed to the defeat of the Meech Lake Accord because the overruling of a judicial decision protecting rights resulted in a backlash against the 'distinct society' clause outside Quebec. The fundamental question regarding the legitimacy of section 33 is whether any institution should monopolize the interpretation of rights or the determination of reasonableness. To argue that section 33 lacks legitimacy is to support the supremacy of the judiciary over Parliament, the notion that judicial interpretation of the Charter is subjectively preferable to parliamentary interpretation and will result in good policy choices.

One case in which section 33 could have been (but was not) used to override a questionable judicial decision was *RJR-Macdonald* (1995), which (as we have seen) involved the restrictions on tobacco advertising in the federal Tobacco Products Control Act. The federal government justified the restrictions as necessary to protect the health of Canadians and dissuade young smokers, but the Supreme Court ruled that the act violated the freedom of expression of tobacco advertisers and that such restriction was not reasonable in a free and democratic society. In effect, whereas Parliament, in passing the legislation, had given priority to the health of Canadians, the Supreme Court gave priority to the expression rights of a multinational corporation. Would the use of section 33 in *RJR-Macdonald* have been illegitimate if Parliament had decided to overrule that decision in order to advance the pressing and substantial legislative objective of reducing tobacco addiction through restrictions on advertising? This case suggests that the notwithstanding clause can be a legitimate instrument when judicial decisions result in policy distortion.

Christopher Manfredi has suggested that the legitimacy of section 33 would be enhanced if the threshold for a legislature to overrule a judicial decision were raised from a simple majority vote to three-fifths of sitting members (Manfredi, 2001). This threshold would require substantial cross-party support, and as a result use of section 33 would signify a substantial policy disagreement with the courts on the part of the legislature.

The Supreme Court's choice of remedies also has important implications for federalism and can contribute to both the legitimacy of judicial decisions and the performance of the federation. As previously stated, section 24(1) of the Charter requires the Supreme Court to remedy constitutional violations. The Court has employed several remedies to this end: nullification, in which the Court simply declares an act unconstitutional; suspended decision, in which the Court rules that an act is unconstitutional but allows it to continue in force for a specified period of time; declaration of rights, in which the Court simply determines that a constitutional right exists; and, finally, reading-in (or reading-down) a legislative scheme or definition to ensure its constitutionality. The best example is *Vriend v. Alberta* where the Supreme Court of Canada, having ruled that the provincial human rights code violated the Charter of Rights because it did not extend the protection against discrimination to gays and lesbians, read sexual orientation into Alberta's human rights code to establish its constitutionality. It is in using this remedy that the Supreme Court is a policy actor, since reading-in amends the legislation through section 24(1) of the Charter of Rights.

The judicial remedy of suspended decision is one that demonstrates recognition of the distinct roles performed by courts and legislatures in our parliamentary democracy: the judiciary simply rules on the constitutionality of legislation and leaves it to the discretion of the responsible legislature to introduce amendments to ensure the continued functioning of an act within a specified period. This remedy has been used in 36 per cent (9/25) of the cases in which the Supreme Court has invalidated provincial statutes since 1982, and has been the remedy used most frequently since 1990, accounting for 64 per cent (9/14) of remedial orders issued by the Supreme Court under section 24(1) of the Charter (see Table 3.1). Since a suspended decision respects the distinct institutional roles of courts and legislatures, this remedy can improve the legitimacy of judicial review because the determination of constitutionality is an appropriate judicial function and the development of policy responses is a legislative function. Suspended decisions can also improve the effectiveness of federalism because they require the government in question to reflect on the judicial decision and to decide autonomously on the policy response required to re-establish the constitutionality of a law determined by the Supreme Court to violate the Charter.

Table 3.1   Judicial Remedies Involving Provincial Statutes, 1982–2005

Remedy	1982–9	%[1]	1990–2005	%[2]	Total	%[3]
Nullification	9	81.82	1	7.14	10	40
Suspended	0	0	9	64.29	9	36
Read-in or down	0	0	3	21.43	3	12
Declaration of rights	2	18.18	1	7.14	3	12
Total	11	100	14	100	25	100

1 as percentage of remedies used, 1982–9
2 as percentage of remedies used, 1990–2005
3 as percentage of remedies used, 1982–2005

Provincial Policy and the Charter of Rights

In order to evaluate the effect of Charter review, this final section will focus on three significant areas of provincial jurisdiction that have been reviewed by the Supreme Court of Canada: language and education policy; labour and social policy; and health policy. This survey is far from exhaustive, but it highlights two aspects of Supreme Court jurisprudence that have strengthened the performance, effectiveness, and legitimacy both of the Charter itself and of federalism: acceptance of provincial variation to satisfy section 1 of the Charter and, perhaps more important, the limited policy impact of declarations of unconstitutionality through suspended remedies. Indeed, both activist decisions, where the Supreme Court invalidates provincial legislation, and decisions where the Supreme Court is deferential to the policy choices of provincial governments and upholds the constitutionality of challenged provincial acts will be used to demonstrate how federalism structures the Supreme Court's approach to the Charter of Rights. Particular attention will be devoted to the province of Quebec. The Charter of Rights has not been endorsed by the National Assembly or prominent Québécois intellectuals (Dumont, 1993),[2] and therefore the legitimacy of the Supreme Court and the Charter rests on weaker foundations amongst the political elite, but, surprisingly, not among the general public (Fletcher and Howe 2000).

Language and Education Policy

The first test of the Canadian Charter of Rights and its relationship to provincial autonomy and federalism occurred in *Attorney General (Quebec) v. Protestant School Boards* (1984). The Supreme Court determined that sections of the Charter of the French Language (CFL), or Bill 101, which restricted English-language instruction to the children of anglophones educated in Quebec, infringed the minority-language education rights set out in section 23 of the Charter. The government of Quebec readily admitted that aspects of the CFL violated section 23, but contended that this limitation was reasonable because of its legislative objectives: specifically, to help ensure the survival of the French language by channelling immigrants into the French-language education system. Quebec reasoned that the limitations would be upheld through section 1 of the Charter (*Protestant School Boards*, 1984). While the Supreme Court was sensitive to the policy objectives underlying Bill 101, however, it determined that denying English-language instruction to the children of Canadian citizens educated in English outside Quebec was not a limitation but a denial of their rights.

This decision was taken as early evidence that the nation-building objectives of the Trudeau government were being implemented through the Charter of Rights and its interpretation by the Supreme Court (Laforest, 1995). However, this analysis assumed that an activist decision would have a policy impact leading to a loss of provincial control of essential jurisdictional responsibilities. In fact, the *Protestant School Boards* decision has had no substantive impact on provincial control of education. Nor has the Supreme Court's validation of national values undermined the CFL, because the only people it privileged were Canadian citizens educated outside Quebec who later moved there. The children of new migrants to Quebec who are not Canadian citizens and were not educated in English in Canada are not entitled to an English education. Given that the demographic strength of francophones is not threatened by interprovincial migration (there is a net outflow of anglophones from Quebec),[3] but rather bolstered by French-speaking migrants from La Francophonie, the partial invalidation of Bill 101 has had no practical impact beyond providing a strong rhetorical tool for critics of the 1982 constitutional settlement (Laforest, 1995). Beyond the requirement to provide educational services to a restricted part of a declining anglophone population, the Quebec National Assembly retains nearly complete autonomy in education policy.

Even the Supreme Court's invalidation of the sign law in *Ford v. Quebec* (1988) has had limited policy impact in Quebec. In that case the Supreme Court invalidated sections 58 and 69 of the CFL, which prohibited languages other than French on public signs, as a violation of both the Canadian Charter and the Quebec Charter (Gaudreault-DesBiens, 2003). In its analysis of section 1, the Supreme Court did not consider the challenged provisions of the sign law to constitute a reasonable limitation on either the Canadian or the Quebec Charter: 'requiring the predominant display of the French language, even its marked predominance, would be proportional to the goal of promoting and maintaining a French "visage linguistique" but a total restriction could not be justified' (Ford, 1988: para. 74). In response to this decision, the Quebec National Assembly invoked the Charter's notwithstanding clause, setting aside the Supreme Court's decision and allowing the sign law to continue functioning for five years.

This exchange between the Supreme Court and the National Assembly was an example of the dialogue that takes place between legislatures and the courts when acts are found to violate rights (Hogg and Bushell, 1997). A legitimate disagreement existed between the Supreme Court and the Quebec National Assembly on whether the sign law constituted a reasonable limit on freedom of expression. After a public debate framed by the Court, the National Assembly decided to use section 33 of the Charter. The use of section 33, however, was not the only legislative response or example of Charter dialogue involving *Ford*. When the five years expired in December 1993, the National Assembly did not reinvoke the notwithstanding clause even though it could have done so. Instead it amended the CFL to establish conditions under which languages other than French would be permitted on public signs. Though these amendments were consistent with the changes suggested by the Court in its section 1 analysis, this did not mean any loss of policy autonomy for Quebec, since the National Assembly retained the right to decide how it would respond. In the end, it decided that minor revisions to the bill would be sufficient to advance its policy objectives and allow Quebec to retain control over its linguistic destiny and survival. Otherwise the National Assembly would surely have reinvoked the notwithstanding clause with the broad support of the Quebec population (Binnette, 2003).

In two important cases involving challenges to the CFL in 2005, *Gosselin v. Quebec* and *Solski v. Quebec*, the Supreme Court upheld the CFL 's constitutionality. It did, however, argue that provisions of the CFL were not properly administered in *Solski*. Previous challenges to Bill 101 had originated within the anglophone community, but the complainants in *Gosselin* were francophone parents who argued that the prohibition against sending their children to English schools was a violation of the equality provisions in both the Canadian and the Quebec Charters. The Court rejected this claim, arguing that section 23 of the Canadian Charter provides specific rights only to minority-language education communities. It also ruled that there cannot be a hierarchy of constitutional rights, and the equality rights provisions of the Canadian Charter cannot be used to expand section 23 to provide equal access to English education in the province of Quebec (*Gosselin*, 2005). In effect, federalism came to the aid of the CFL, since the Court ruled that the 'appellants are members of the French Language majority in Quebec, and, as such, their objective in having their children educated in English simply does not fall within the purpose of section 23' (ibid., para. 30). In reaching this conclusion, the Court was sensitive to the loss of control over education policy that free access to minority language education would mean for Quebec: 'the problem has the added dimension that what are intended as schools for the minority language community should not operate to undermine the desire of the majority to protect and enhance French as the majority language in Quebec, knowing that it will remain the minority language in the broader context of Canada as a whole' (para. 31).

In *Solski* the Supreme Court upheld section 73(2) of the CFL, which limited English education in Quebec to children who have received 'the major part of [their] elementary or secondary instruction . . . in Canada' (*Solski*, 2005: para.

25). However, the Court ruled that the interpretation of the 'major part' requirement used by the Administrative Tribunal of Quebec—the body to which parents apply for approval to have their children educated in English—was inconsistent with section 23 of the Charter. It ruled that a purely quantitative approach to section 73(2) violated the purpose of section 23, as only a significant part and not the majority of a child's education would have to be in English to qualify for minority language education in Quebec (*Solski*, 2005). In reaching this conclusion, the Supreme Court recognized that the provision of minority language education rights varies between provinces and that, in the case of Quebec, the 'latitude given to the provincial government in drafting legislation regarding education must be broad enough to ensure the protection of the French language while satisfying the purposes of section 23' (para. 34).

The very narrow basis of this decision did not affect provincial control over education policy. Although the Court upheld the constitutionality of section 72(3) of the CFL, the decision simply required that the Administrative Tribunal of Quebec adopt a more contextual, less rigid test when determining whether a child qualifies for English education.

The impact of section 23 has been strongest outside Quebec, even though it was drafted to directly challenge provisions of the CFL that restricted access to English education (Riddell, 2003). At issue in *Arsenault-Cameron v. Prince Edward Island* was the decision of the province's minister of Education to overrule a decision made by the French Language Board to offer French language instruction in Summerside. The Supreme Court ruled that this use of ministerial discretion was 'unconstitutional because the offer of classes or facility came within the exclusive right of management of the minority and met with all provincial and constitutional requirements' (*Arsenault-Cameron*, 2000: para. 55). The Court reaffirmed that, once numbers warranted the provision of minority language instruction and a minority language education board was established, the minority community was constitutionally empowered to manage the provision of education: 'The Minister had no power to impose his own criteria as a substitute. Nor could the Minister substitute his decision for that of the Board simply because he was of the view that the decision of the Board was not a good one' (para. 55). Without challenging provincial control over education, the Court found that the discretion of the minister of Education did not extend to interpreting the School Act in such a way as to infringe the responsibilities of minority communities provided under the act.

Labour and Social Policy

Respect for policy variation in a federal system has also been reflected in cases involving provincial labour relations and social policy. In *Dunmore v. Ontario* (2001), the Supreme Court determined that the Ontario Labour Relations Act (LRA) violated freedom of association and did not represent a reasonable limitation because it excluded agricultural workers. In its section 1 analysis, the Court pointed out that comparable legislation in New Brunswick, Quebec, and Alberta excluded only agricultural workers who actually worked on family farms; therefore it rejected the Ontario Cabinet's claim that the categorization of agricultural workers was impossible (*Dunmore v. Ontario*, 2001: para. 64). The only national standard established by the Supreme Court in this case was that provincial acts governing labour relations must not exclude all agricultural workers. Otherwise, the Court accepted the need for provincial variation in labour relations.

A significant discussion of federalism occurred in *R. v. Advance Cutting & Coring Ltd* (2001): a constitutional challenge of the requirement in Quebec's construction legislation that workers be members of one of five listed union groups to obtain competency certificates. In a majority decision (5/4), the Court dismissed the argument that the requirement of membership violated freedom of association. Speaking for three members of the majority, Justice LeBel accepted the policy rationale because of the history of conflict in the construction industry and the unique structure of the labour industry in Quebec.

The majority of the Court found that Quebec's legislation did not violate section 2(d) of the Charter. However, the decision included a section 1 analysis by Justice LeBel that highlighted the importance of federalism in determining whether a limitation on freedom of association would be reasonable, since 'provincial differences must be factored into any proper analysis of the concept of minimal impairment, when assessing the validity of provincial legislation' (*Advance Cutting & Coring Ltd*, 2001: para. 275). LeBel's reasoning articulated the significance of diversity when the Supreme Court evaluates whether provincial statutes satisfy section 1 of Charter: 'the principle of federalism means that the application of the Charter in fields of provincial jurisdiction does not amount to a call for legislative conformity. It expresses shared values, which may be achieved differently, in different settings' (para. 275). The deferential nature of this judgment is important. The Court accepted that provincial governments were best positioned to manage labour relations because of the complex policy context in each jurisdiction. Federalism and the institutional capacity of provincial governments, therefore, directly influenced the Court's finding of constitutionality.

The Court's acceptance of provincial variation demonstrates that Charter review does not necessarily ensure uniformity, even when provincial statutes are found to violate the Charter. In *Nova Scotia (Workers' Compensation Board) v. Martin* (2003) the Court found section 10(b) of the Workers' Compensation Act and the Functional Restoration Program Regulations unconstitutional because their exclusion of chronic pain coverage infringed the equality rights of disabled workers. On the question of whether the Act's blanket exclusion of chronic disability was a reasonable limitation on equality rights, the court found that the only defensible legislative objective for such a measure was to avoid fraudulent claims, and determined that this objective could be advanced without excluding all sufferers of chronic pain (2003: para. 113).

This decision was reached following comparative analysis of chronic-pain regimes in Alberta, British Columbia, Quebec, and Ontario that provided for coverage by changing the method of assessment to accurately determine each claimant's degree of disability. Justice Gonthier acknowledged that the Nova Scotia Cabinet had the authority to choose its own approach to a chronic-pain regime but maintained that it was 'impossible to conclude that the blanket exclusion it enacted was necessary to achieve a principled response to chronic pain and avoid fraudulent claims' (para. 113). Therefore provincial, not national, standards determined that Nova Scotia had infringed the equality rights of disabled workers in an unreasonable manner. Federalism is a significant element of Charter review, as the Supreme Court considers how different provincial cabinets approach shared problems and recognizes that distinct policy contexts and historical experiences weigh against uniformity in public policy. This approach has been a significant part of the Charter jurisprudence that has balanced individual rights and provincial autonomy.

Perhaps the decision most attuned to federalism and the need to balance rights with the reality of government is *Newfoundland v. N.A.P.E.* (2004), in which the Court considered the constitutionality of legislation (the Public Sector Restraint Act) that suspended a pay-equity agreement between the provincial government and female employees in the health sector that awarded $24 million to members of the Newfoundland Association of Public and Private Employees (NAPE). The Supreme Court found that the Public Service Restraint Act did violate equality rights because it resulted in gender discrimination against female employees. In this case, however—in contrast to *Singh v. Canada* (1985), in which it had ruled that budgetary considerations can never justify limiting a right—the Court determined that the province was facing a severe financial crisis, and that the need for spending cuts to preserve the province's credit rating and maintain existing government services constituted a pressing and substantial legislative objective that justified limiting equality rights. As it explained: 'The government in 1991 was not just debating rights versus dollars but rights versus hospital beds, rights versus layoffs, rights versus jobs, rights versus education and rights versus social welfare. The requirement to reduce expenditures, and the allocation of the necessary cuts, *was* undertaken to promote other values of a free and democratic society' (*Newfoundland v. N.A.P.E.*, 2005: para. 75).

In accepting the cancellation of the pay-equity agreement as reasonable, the Court recognized that the province had reviewed all budgetary expenditures in consultation with the groups affected and determined that this was the most responsible course of action. Two considerations saved the Public Service Restraint Act: first, the implications of fiscal federalism and the difficulty the province faced when $130 million in federal transfers were unilaterally cut in 1991; and second, the need to preserve provincial fiscal autonomy by preventing a reduction in the province's credit rating that would have jeopardized the delivery of government services in key areas of provincial responsibility such as health and education.

The Court's acceptance of reduced fiscal capacity as justifying limitation of a Charter right is clearly controversial. Is it appropriate for the Court to consider such factors in a section 1 analysis? Should fiscal constraints be recognized as part of the justification when a government invokes the notwithstanding clause to overrule a judicial decision? In this case the Supreme Court showed unprecedented deference in a section 1 analysis, accepting statements made by the President of the Treasury Board before the House of Assembly as proof of the province's fiscal situation. I believe that the Court erred in this instance: a more acceptable solution would have been to rule the Public Service Restraint Act unconstitutional and not a reasonable limitation on section 15 and suspend the decision for two years. In this way the Court could have upheld equality rights under the Charter while recognizing the province's difficult financial situation and the need to preserve existing public services. The financial situation might have improved over 24 months to the point where the pay-equity agreement could be honoured and the province's credit rating maintained. Alternatively, the provincial government could have negotiated with the federal government to restore a portion of the cut transfer payments so that it could honour the pay-equity agreement. If, having had a reasonable opportunity to rectify the situation, the province still had not done so, then the Court's declaration that the Public Service Restraint Act was unconstitutional should have taken effect.

Health-care Policy

As Antonia Maioni argues in Chapter 8, health care is central to Canadian federalism. Health care has also become a judicialized policy area involving both the Canadian and the Quebec Charter and has increased the involvement of the Supreme Court in essential areas of provincial responsibility (Manfredi and Maioni, 2002). At the same time, however, the Supreme Court has shown a high degree of deference to provincial governments. Indeed, health-care policy clearly demonstrates the tension between the Charter and federalism: the Charter focuses on the rights of individuals whereas federalism is concerned with the jurisdictional autonomy of governments. In an attempt to reconcile rights and federalism, there are necessary tradeoffs that weaken the rights of individuals. Further, the way in which the Supreme Court of Canada frames a judicial decision also limits the impact on federalism. This outcome is demonstrated in *Chaoulli v. Québec* (2005), a case involving the constitutionality of the prohibition on private health insurance that was decided on the basis of the Quebec Charter of Human Rights and Freedoms.

The judicialization of health-care policy has produced victories for rights claimants in cases such as *Eldridge v. British Columbia* (1997), a defeat in *Auton v. British Columbia* (2004), and a partial victory for residents of Quebec (*Chaoulli*). In *Eldridge* the Supreme Court determined that the absence of sign-language interpreters in emergency rooms violated section 15 of the Charter, denying the hearing-impaired equal benefit of the law and equal access to health-care services (*Eldridge*, 1997). Even though this activist decision created a constitutional obligation to provide sign-language interpreters in hospital settings, the Court still upheld the constitutionality of the province's Hospital Insurance and Health Care Services legislation and did not challenge provincial control over health care. The policy response to *Eldridge* was left completely to the discretion of British Columbia, and the Supreme Court suspended its decision for six months, to give the BC government time to introduce the necessary legislation, During that time British Columbia introduced an interim measure that created a 24-hour toll-free line with special provisions to accommodate the hearing-impaired and made a commitment to provide sign-language interpreters for doctor and hospital visits within 10 months (Roach, 2002). In effect, a minor policy change on the part of the BC government itself both satisfied the Court and protected provincial autonomy. At issue in *Auton v. British Columbia* was the failure of the provincial government to provide applied behavioural therapy (ABAS/IBI) for autistic children between the ages of 3 and 6, which was challenged as a violation of equality rights protected by the Charter. The basis of this claim was the argument that ABA/IBI therapy is a medically necessary treatment for autism comparable to other medically necessary treatments provided under the Medicare Protection Act. Because autistic children were treated differently from comparable groups who were provided with publicly funded medical services, their equality rights were violated when this discriminatory treatment resulted in a denial of a benefit (*Auton*, 2004). While the Supreme Court expressed sympathy for the plaintiffs, it dismissed the constitutional challenge against the Medicare Protection Act on the grounds that the province was not required to provide all medical services and retained the discretion, under the Canada Health Act, to decide which ones would be considered core services, to be funded by the province, and which would be designated non-core services, to be provided only at the discretion of a Medical Services Commission (*Auton*, 2004). As ABA/IBI therapy was designated a non-core service, the Court ruled that equality rights were not violated.

In this case the Supreme Court protected provincial autonomy at the expense of rights by requiring only that, once a medical procedure or therapy has been designated a core service, the province provide equal access to it. Beyond this narrow constitutional requirement, each province retains the discretion to decide which services will be funded under its health-care act. This ruling could undermine health care in the long run, as provinces may be reluctant to designate new treatments as core services.

One final decision illustrates how activist decisions, if framed by the Supreme Court of Canada and responded to by the relevant legislature in a particular way, can have minimal implications for federalism and provincial autonomy (Sossin, 2005). In *Chaoulli* the Supreme Court, in a majority decision (4/3), determined that the prohibition on private medical insurance in Quebec's Health Insurance Act and Hospital Insurance Act violated section 1 of the Quebec Charter (right to life and to personal security) and did not constitute a reasonable limit under section 9.1—the equivalent of the Canadian Charter's reasonable limits clause. A minority of the judges also determined that this prohibition violated section 7 of the Canadian Charter (right to life, liberty and security of the person), but the majority decision was limited to the Quebec Charter. As a result, the constitutional significance of the *Chaoulli* decision was limited to the Quebec health-care system, although several other provinces responded to it by addressing waiting times in their own jurisdictions, in order to prevent future constitutional challenges involving the Canadian Charter.

Thus the provincial reaction to *Chaoulli* had implications for federalism, but the decision in itself did not. As Peter Russell argues, the decision was very narrow: 'it neither changed the face of medicare nor established a Charter right to timely health care—nor ushered in a two-tier system of health care' (Russell, 2005: 6). The decision delivered by Justice Deschamps ruled that the waiting periods in the present health-care system violated security of the person; the delays in receiving essential services significantly increased the possibility of death, and in non-essential surgeries, such as knee and hip replacement, resulted in chronic pain and reduced quality of life (*Chaoulli*, 2005). Since several other provinces already allowed their residents to purchase private health care, the majority of the judges rejected the argument that a total prohibition on private health insurance was essential to ensure the integrity of the public system (*Chaoulli*, 2005). The prohibition on private health insurance was declared a violation of section 1 of the Quebec Charter and declared unconstitutional, as it did not constitute a reasonable limit.

The policy impact of this decision was limited by two factors. First, the decision was suspended for 12 months, to give the National Assembly the opportunity to make the legislative changes necessary to ensure the constitutionality of the Health Insurance Act and the Hospital Insurance Act. The changes, introduced in February 2006, were in many respects minimal. The legislation allows access to private health care for a limited numbers of services. Based on the Court's ruling that waiting times had violated section 1 of the provincial Charter, the Quebec government decided that private insurance can be purchased to cover three services for which the waiting periods are often excessive: hip and knee replacement and cataract surgery. However, to discourage the purchase of private health care and preserve the integrity of the public service, the Quebec government will pay for the listed services in a private facility if they cannot be provided in a public setting within 6 months of being recommended by a physician (Séguin, 2006). This legislative response suggests that many activist decisions by the Supreme Court can have minimal policy implications for provincial autonomy. Indeed, as long as a provincial government is willing to address a constitutional violation using existing policy instruments, as Quebec did, it can retain nearly complete autonomy in a policy field. Thus parliamentary supremacy can be maintained as long as governments are sensitive to the necessity of ensuring that their legislative and executive actions take full account of the rights guaranteed by the Charter.

Conclusion

The performance, effectiveness, and legitimacy of the Charter of Rights as it relates to federalism are generally quite good. The legitimacy of Charter review has clearly been strengthened by the Supreme Court's preference for a balanced approach that allows federalism and rights to co-exist within a national Charter. Charter review has not impaired provincial autonomy, and by using a balanced approach the Supreme Court has enhanced its own legitimacy as an institution.

Although this chapter has focused exclusively on the Supreme Court and its interpretation of the Charter, other factors also help to shape the effect of the Charter on Canadian federalism and its performance. As Parliament and the provincial legislatures continue reforming their policy processes to conform to a rights-based policy context, contradictions between federalist principles and citizens' rights are being reconciled (Kelly, 2003). The institutionalization of 'Charter vetting' within the bureaucracy before legislation is introduced into Parliament or the provincial legislatures has meant that fewer statutes are now invalidated as inconsistent with the Charter. New bureaucratic procedures have been implemented to advance Charter values, and the machinery of government has improved as a result. The effort to ensure that new legislation conforms to the Charter before the possibility of constitutional challenges arises makes for more effective policy outcomes. Reconciling federalist and Charter principles safeguards both federalism and individual rights.

There is still a risk, however, that the legitimacy of judicial review will be undermined among those who believe that the courts should compel governments to reform essential policy areas such as health care and education. Similarly, the Court's acceptance that rights may be limited if demonstrably justified in a free and democratic *federal* society clearly challenges the national unity function of the Charter. For instance, a federalist approach to section 1 implies asymmetrical application of the Charter of Rights, so that the level of rights protection available to individual Canadians depends on which province they live in. This federalizing of rights may enhance the legitimacy of the Supreme Court for provincialists while undermining the legitimacy of the Charter for those who believe in nation-wide rights in a federal system.

Notes

I thank Lorne Sossin for his valuable feedback on this chapter. I would also like to acknowledge the financial support provided by the Social Sciences and Humanities Research Council of Canada and the Fonds de recherche sur la société et la culture.

1. Among the other concessions were changes to the Charter's mobility rights, allowing provincial governments to restrict labour mobility if the provincial unemployment rate was above the national rate; an amending formula requiring that provincial legislatures pass resolutions accepting future constitutional changes; and section 92A, an amendment giving provincial governments a role in international trade involving non-renewable natural resources.

2. Fernand Dumont views the nation-building objective of the Canadian Charter as a project in 'anglo-conformité' that undermines the distinctiveness of Quebec and is likely to erode the civil law tradition that exists in this province.
3. Between 1991 and 2001 a net outflow of 53,750 Quebec anglophones moved to other provinces, reducing this community to 8 per cent of the Quebec population. In the same period the allophone community increased to 10 per cent of Quebec's population. Statistics Canada, cited at: www12.stat can.ca/english/census01/Products/Analytic.

References

Baier, G. 1998. 'Tempering Peace, Order and Good Government: Provincial Inability and Canadian Federalism', *National Journal of Constitutional Law* 9: 277–305.

Binette, A. 2003. 'Le pouvoir dérogatoire de l'article 33 de la *Charte canadienne des droits et libertés* et la structure de la Constitution du Canada', *Revue du Barreau*: 107–50.

Cairns, A.C. 1971. 'The Judicial Committee and its Critics,' *Canadian Journal of Political Science* 3: 301–45.

de Montigny, Y. 1997. 'The Impact (Real or Apprehended) of the Canadian Charter of Rights and Freedoms on the Legislative Authority of Quebec'. In *Charting the Consequences*, ed D. Schneiderman and K. Sutherland. Toronto: University of Toronto Press.

Dumont, F. 1995. *Raisons communes*. Montréal: Boréal.

———. 1993. *Genèse de la société québécoise*. Montréal: Boréal.

Fletcher, J.F., and P. Howe. 2000. 'Canadian Attitudes toward the Charter and the Courts in Comparative Perspective', *Choices* 6: 4–29.

Gaudreault-DesBiens, J.-F. 2003. 'La Charte canadienne des droits et libertés et le fédéralisme: quelque remarques sur les vingt premières années d'une relation ambiguë', *Revue du Barreau*: 271–310.

Greschner, D. 2001. 'The Supreme Court, Federalism and Metaphors of Moderation', *Canadian Bar Review* 79: 47–76.

Hiebert, J.L. 1996. *Limiting Rights: The Dilemma of Judicial Review*. Montreal: McGill–Queen's University Press, 1996.

Hogg, P. 1989. 'Federalism Fights the Charter'. In *Federalism and Political Community*, ed. D. Shugarman and R. Whitaker. Peterborough: Broadview Press.

——— and A. Bushell. 1997. 'The Charter Dialogue Between Courts and Legislatures (Or Perhaps the Charter Isn't Such a Bad Thing After All?)', *Osgoode Hall Law Journal* 35: 75–125.

Kelly, J.B. 2005. *Governing with the Charter: Legislative and Judicial Activism and Framers' Intent*. Vancouver: University of British Columbia Press.

———. 2004. 'Guarding the Constitution: Parliamentary and Judicial Roles under the Charter.' In *Canada: The State of the Federation 2004*, ed. J.P. Meekison, H. Telford, and H. Lazar. Montreal: McGill–Queen's University Press.

————. 2003. 'Governing with the Charter of Rights and Freedoms', *Supreme Court Law Review* 2d 21: 299–337.

Knopff, R., and F.L. Morton. 1985. 'Nation Building and the Canadian Charter of Rights and Freedoms'. In *Constitutionalism, Citizenship and Society in Canada*, ed. A. Cairns and C. Williams. Toronto: University of Toronto Press.

Laforest, G. 1995. *Trudeau and the End of the Canadian Dream*. Montreal: McGill–Queen's University Press.

Manfredi, C.P. 2001. *Judicial Power and the Charter: Canada and the Paradox of Liberal Constitutionalism*, 2nd edn. Toronto: Oxford University Press.

———— and J.B. Kelly. 1999. 'Six Degrees of Dialogue: A Response to Hogg and Bushell', *Osgoode Hall Law Journal* 37: 513–27.

———— and A. Maioni. 2002. 'Courts and Health Policy: Judicial Policy Making and Publicly Funded Health Care in Canada', *Journal of Health Politics, Policy and Law*, 27: 213–40.

Morton, F. L. 1995. 'The Effects of the Charter of Rights on Canadian Federalism', *Publius* 25: 173–89.

Riddell, T.Q. 2003. 'Official Minority-Language Education Policy outside of Quebec: The Impact of Section 23 of the Charter and Judicial Decisions', *Canadian Public Administration* 46: 27–49.

Roach, K. 2002. 'Remedial Consensus and Dialogue under the *Charter*: General Declarations and Delayed Declarations of Invalidity', *UBC Law Review* 35: 211–69.

Romanow, R., J. Whyte, and H. Leeson. 1984. *Canada . . . Notwithstanding: The Making of the Constitution 1976–1982*. Toronto: Carswell.

Russell, P.H. 2005. '*Chaoulli*: The Political versus the Legal Life of a Judicial Decision'. In *Access to Care, Access to Justice*, ed. C.M. Flood, K. Roach, and L. Sossin. Toronto: University of Toronto Press.

————. 1994. 'Canadian Constraints on Judicialization from Without', *International Political Science Review* 15: 165–75.

————. 1983. 'Bold Statescraft, Questionable Jurisprudence'. In *And No One Cheered*, ed. K. Banting and R. Simeon. Toronto: Metheun.

————. 1982. 'The Effect of a Charter of Rights on the Policy-making Role of Canadian Courts', *Canadian Public Administration* 25: 1–33.

————. 1977. 'The *Anti-Inflation Case*: The Anatomy of a Constitutional Decision', *Canadian Public Administration* 20: 632–65.

Scheiderman, D. 1998. 'Human Rights, Fundamental Differences? Multiple Charters in a Partnership Frame'. In *Beyond the Impasse – Toward Recognition*, ed. R. Gibbins and G. Laforest. Montreal: IRPP.

Séguin, R. 2006. 'Quebec Opens Door to Private Health Care', *Globe and Mail*. 17 Feb., A1.

Sossin, L. 2005. 'Towards a Two-Tier Constitution? The Poverty of Health Rights'.

In *Access to Care, Access to Justice*, ed. C.M. Flood, K. Roach, and L. Sossin. Toronto: University of Toronto Press.

Weinrib, L.E. 2001. 'The Supreme Court of Canada in the Age of Rights: Constitutional Democracy, the Rule of Law and Fundamental Rights under Canada's Constitution', *Canadian Bar Review* 80: 699–748.

Cases

Arsenault-Cameron v. Prince Edward Island (2000), 1 S.C.R. 3.

Attorney General (Quebec) v. Protestant School Boards (1984), 2 S.C.R. 66.

Auton v. British Columbia (2004), 3 S.C.R. 657.

Canadian Industrial Gas & Oil Ltd. v. Government of Saskatchewan (1978), 2 S.C.R. 545.

Central Canada Potash Company Ltd. and Attorney General of Canada v. Government of Saskatchewan (1979), 1 S.C.R. 42.

Chaoulli v. Quebec (2005), 1 S.C.R. 791.

Dunmore v. Ontario (2001), 3 S.C.R. 1016.

Eldridge v. British Columbia (1997), S.C.R. 624.

Ford v. Quebec (1988), 1 S.C.R. 712.

Gosselin v. Quebec (2005), 1 S.C.R. 238.

Newfoundland v. N.A.P.E. (2004), 3 S.C.R. 381.

Nova Scotia (Workers' Compensation Board) v. Martin (2003), 2 S.C.R. 504.

Reference re s.94(2) of the Motor Vehicle Act, (1985) 2 S.C.R. 486.

Reference re Offshore Mineral Rights of British Columbia (1966), S.C.R. 663.

RJR-Macdonald Inc. v. Canada (1995), 3 S.C.R. 199.

R. v. Advance Cutting & Coring Ltd. (2001), 3 S.C.R. 209.

R. v. Edwards Books and Art Ltd. (1986), 2 S.C.R. 713.

Singh v. Minister of Employment and Immigration (1985), 1 S.C.R. 177.

Solski v. Quebec (2005), 1 S.C.R. 201.

Websites

Supreme Court of Canada Decisions: http://scc.lexum.umontreal.ca/en/index.html

Canadian Charter of Rights and Freedoms: http://lois.justice.gc.ca/en/charter/index.html

Institute of Intergovernmental Relations: www.iigr.ca/iigr.php/

Mapleleafweb: Supreme Court of Canada decision: www.mapleleafweb.com/scc/public3/faq.html

Chapter 4

Fiscal Federalism: Searching for Balance

Douglas M. Brown

In 2006 and 2007 Ontario Premier Dalton McGuinty claimed that Canada's largest provincial government is chronically short of cash and gets $23 billion less than it should every year from the federal government. Jean Charest has staked his federalist vision for Quebec on resolving the long-standing 'fiscal imbalance' in the federation. Ralph Klein warned other Canadians to keep their hands off Alberta's burgeoning oil and gas revenues, while Danny Williams of Newfoundland and Labrador defended his province's special arrangement to keep more of its oil revenue while also receiving equalization payments designed for poorer provinces. Conservative Prime Minister Stephen Harper, in turn, made it clear that he wanted to fix the fiscal imbalance. But his solution could involve considerable political controversy.

Existing alongside the formal Constitution, 'fiscal federalism' is the evolving system of financial arrangements between the federal and provincial orders of government, and it is an essential part of the discussion of how Canada's federal system works. This chapter begins by outlining the structure of Canadian fiscal federalism: constitutional powers, tax structure and harmonization, intergovernmental transfers, and the fiscal relations process. Then it surveys the evolution of fiscal federalism over the past fifty years, emphasizing the important role played by fiscal relations in building Canada's welfare state, and how the balance—both between the two orders of government and between the values of equity and efficiency—has shifted in the past fifteen years. The chapter concludes with a review of the issues that have emerged in the current decade, as federalism seeks a new balance.

Fiscal federalism has a role to play in all three of the areas that are the focus of this book: the performance of the federation, policy effectiveness, and political legitimacy. First, since flexibility is essential to the federation's ability to adapt over time, the federation's performance depends in no small part on the nature of any strings attached to federal transfers. The equalization program is the key to maintaining autonomy and equality for all provinces under the Constitution. At the same time, negotiations over fiscal policy provide forums for federal–provincial competition and co-operation.

Second, the contribution of fiscal federalism to policy effectiveness depends on the observer's point of view (federal or provincial). This chapter examines two classic policy criteria that can be applied to fiscal relations as a whole: equity and efficiency. A historical overview shows that the balance shifted significantly towards efficiency in the 1900s and, despite a brief move back to the equity side in the early 2000s, still emphasizes efficiency values. However, fiscal relations are usually a means to a more specific policy end, and can have a substantial effect on the outcomes in many policy fields, from health care, post-secondary education, and social assistance to labour mobility and regional economic development.

The third point of evaluation, political legitimacy, reveals long-standing problems in executive federalism, including excessive secrecy and complexity and muddled accountability. But even if the technical discussions involved in fiscal federalism continue to take place behind closed doors, the underlying issues (funding for health care, fair shares among regions, fiscal off-loading) are well aired and cannot be confined to private discussions. And pressure is building for greater simplicity, transparency, and accountability for individual governments.

The Structure of Canadian Fiscal Federalism

Fiscal relations among governments in Canada are shaped by the documents and conventional practices that together make up the Canadian Constitution. The allocation of expenditure and revenue functions is among the more important constitutional features. In this respect, it is fiscal federalism that gives shape to the Constitution, not vice versa. Formal constitutional powers would have little relevance if revenues could not be collected and expenditures made. Canada's Constitution would have been obsolete long ago if not for the flexible instruments of fiscal federalism. For example, governments used intergovernmental fiscal arrangements to respond to the rise of the modern welfare state—and more recently to its partial retrenchment and adaptation to global economic integration. Federal constitutions are notoriously difficult to amend, and ours is no exception. However, fiscal arrangements change frequently and thus can provide opportunities for system-wide adaptation.

Four features of the structure of Canadian fiscal federalism should be well understood, even if they can be sketched only briefly here. These are (1) the constitutional division of legislative, taxation, and expenditure powers; (2) the evolved pattern of tax allocation, sharing, and harmonization; (3) the system of intergovernmental transfers to bridge the gap between revenue and expenditure responsibilities; and (4) the process through which fiscal arrangements are made by the federal and provincial governments.

Constitutional Powers

The constitutional allocation of powers affects fiscal relations in the Canadian federation in three ways. First, the Canadian Constitution emphasizes exclusive fields of jurisdiction, as opposed to the scheme of concurrent, or legally shared, powers typical of other federations such as Australia, Germany, and the United States. Exclusivity of jurisdiction, the hallmark of what Keith Banting in Chapter 7 calls the classic model of federalism, means that the central government has relatively little opportunity to legislate specific conditions and funding formulae for programs to be delivered by the provinces (Watts, 1999). In Canada fiscal mechanisms must respect the jurisdictional autonomy of the provinces in major expenditure fields. This characteristic has taken on greater significance since the mid-twentieth century because most of the fields central to the welfare state (e.g., social assistance, health care, and education) are under provincial jurisdiction. Moreover, the arrangements for equalization in these areas are designed to ensure that all provinces have a similar fiscal capacity to exercise their autonomy, and thus reinforce the continuation of jurisdictional exclusivity. The second important feature of this country's constitutional arrangements is that, unlike other federations, Canada gives the two senior levels of government full access to the most important and most broadly based sources of taxation. Both orders of government can levy not only income taxes (personal and corporate) but general sales or consumption taxes, as well as payroll taxes for specific purposes such as unemployment insurance, health care, and pensions. The constituent parts of other federal systems are more restricted in their ability to pay for their expenditure responsibilities from their own revenue sources. Thus the vertical fiscal gap (defined more fully below) has been considerably less in Canada than in Germany or Australia, for example. On the other hand, governments at both levels must pay attention to tax harmonization to ensure that taxpayers are not subjected to conflicting demands and overwhelming tax burdens.

The third important feature is the constitutional allocation of what is known as 'the spending power'. Although this is not spelled out in detail, it is recognized that the federal Parliament has a constitutional right to spend in any field, as it sees fit. This power has been controversial, particularly among those Canadians, especially in Quebec, who insist on strict adherence to the principle of the provinces' autonomy in their exclusive jurisdictions. Nonetheless, the spending power has been the means by which the federal government has promoted a national (pan-Canadian) approach to social programs, including direct payments to individuals and to organizations for redistributive purposes. The courts have upheld the spending power, so long as the granting of money does not constitute regulation by other means. And in 1999 the federal government and nine provinces (all but Quebec) signed the Social Union Framework Agreement, establishing some general principles for the use of the federal spending power where provincial jurisdiction is concerned. Finally, although there is no provincial 'spending power' per se, the provinces have a residual power to spend wherever they see fit, including in areas outside their formal field of legislative power, such as the funding of international trade offices (Hogg, 1996: 151–2), so long as such spending is not a backdoor attempt to regulate a federal area of jurisdiction.

These three sets of constitutional powers—in the areas of regulation, taxation, and expenditure—have interacted over the course of Canada's history to produce dramatically different responses to the needs of the day.

Tax Structure and Harmonization

As we have just noted, Ottawa and the provinces share the most important and broadly based sources of revenue, including income taxes; in 2005 the federal government took 63 per cent of personal income tax (PIT) and 65 per cent of corporate income tax (CIT) (Treff and Perry, 2005: Table A1). In addition, all provinces except Alberta collect a retail sales tax, and the federal government levies the Goods and Services Tax (GST), a general consumption tax that is harmonized with the sales tax in some provinces (Newfoundland and Labrador, Nova Scotia, and New Brunswick), and nearly so in Quebec (see Bird, 2001). Overall, the federal and provincial shares from these general sales taxes in 2005 were 51 per cent and 49 per cent respectively (Treff and Perry, 2005). The federal and provincial governments also share revenues from taxes on gasoline and other motive fuels, as well as taxes on alcohol and tobacco.

The remaining tax sources of the federal and provincial governments are more exclusive. Only the federal government can impose customs and excise duties; and since the provinces own almost all the natural resources, they levy almost all of the resource royalties and related rents. Resource revenues have been especially important to Alberta because of the exceptional value and volume of petroleum, but are also important to a number of other provinces.

The past sixty years have seen a steady trend towards decentralization in the overall revenue split between the federal and provincial governments. In 1950, when Ottawa exercised strong central control over revenue generation, the federal government levied about 65 per cent of total taxes. By 2005 this figure had declined by about one-third to 44 per cent. The main reason for this change was the provinces' need for a greater share of tax revenues to meet their spending responsibilities in areas (e.g., health) where costs were rising much more quickly than they were in areas of federal responsibility (e.g., defence). To help meet provinces' revenue needs, the federal government ceded considerable 'tax room' (see the glossary on pp. 87–8) on corporate and personal income to the provinces in the 1950s, 1960s and 1970s. At the same time, tax sources both big and small have proliferated at the provincial level.

In any federal system, tax decentralization has the potential to erode the goals of economic integration (i.e., the creation of a common market). Moreover, decentralized revenue generation creates a gap between provinces with lucrative sources of tax revenues and provinces whose yield from tax sources is far less. It is to address this type of fiscal imbalance or inequity, resulting from such decentralization, that equalization programs (see p. 69) become necessary. Harmonization of taxes is also important, to ensure that similarly situated taxpayers are treated similarly, and to facilitate the movement between provinces of capital, labour, goods, and services. One of the most successful means of ensuring harmonization has been the Tax Collection Agreements (TCAs), under which the federal government agrees to collect taxes on behalf of any province or territory. TCAs are in place for federal PIT collection in all provinces and territories except Quebec, and for CIT in all except Ontario, Alberta, and Quebec. Under these arrangements the federal government absorbs the collection costs, and in return the provinces agree to a common definition of the tax base and a common approach to tax enforcement and allocation. Harmonization through unified collection is less advanced for consumption taxes. In Quebec the GST is collected by the province on behalf of the federal government, not vice versa.

Intergovernmental Transfers

Public-finance analysts refer to two kinds of fiscal relationships: vertical and horizontal (Boadway, 2005; Bird and Tarasov, 2002). Vertical relations are those between different levels or orders of government: not only federal–provincial or federal–territorial, but also provincial–local, federal–Aboriginal, even federal–local. In all federations there is a natural gap between the central or federal government and the constituent governments or provinces. Central governments, by virtue of their authority over the entire country, are able to tax economic resources—wealth, profits, income, consumption—wherever they occur. Thus from an efficiency perspective it makes sense that the federal government has a greater fiscal capacity, either legally or practically, than the federation's constituent parts. States or provinces usually have neither the full legal power nor the practical means to tax national wealth in order to fund their expenditures.

The result is a gap between federal revenues and provincial expenditures that needs to be closed. The most common method is for the federal government to transfer cash to the provinces on an annual basis. Another way is to reallocate or transfer a share of the federal government's tax room to the provinces, enabling them to levy new taxes. Yet another way is to shift an entire tax field to the provinces, permanently reducing the federal government's fiscal capacity. And a fourth way is simply to transfer the spending responsibility upwards from the provincial to the federal level. All four methods have been used in Canada at one time or another.

A vertical fiscal imbalance (as opposed to a gap) is said to exist when a province's revenues are still not sufficient to meet its needs, even after federal transfers are taken into account. How does one determine what those expenditure needs are, whether provincial revenues (or the ability to raise revenues) are in fact inadequate, and exactly how insufficient federal transfers are? The answers to these questions involve significant differences in interpretation and not a small amount of political posturing. Suffice it to say that 'vertical fiscal imbalance' (VFI) is a loaded term (Lazar et al., 2004).

The term 'horizontal imbalance' refers to distinctions at the provincial or territorial level: more specifically, the differing fiscal capacities of the various provinces and territories to fund their own expenditure responsibilities. These differences are primarily due to regional economic disparities: differences in economic activity and accrued wealth among the constituent units. In virtually all federations, some way is found to even out these horizontal imbalances, for two reasons. One is a matter of general equity, to ensure a measure of fiscal equality across the country; the other has a constitutional purpose, to ensure that every unit within the federation can manage the responsibilities allocated to it.

In some federations the richer provinces make direct payments to the poorer ones, but more commonly the federal government uses its fiscal capacity to redistribute wealth regionally, through intergovernmental grants and, in some cases, transfers to individual persons through programs such as employment insurance. Since transfers from the federal level are the chief means of bridging horizontal gaps, the federal level would still need to have a larger revenue capacity than the provinces even if, on average, provincial expenditure responsibility and revenue capacity were evenly matched (no VFI).

Intergovernmental transfer payments are also an important means through which the federal government can build national programs while leaving their delivery to the provincial governments. In so doing, the federal government can choose to require that the provinces follow central policy objectives and program design, or it can leave those decisions to the provinces. Thus transfers come in two basic types: conditional and unconditional. Conditional transfers are payments made for specific purposes, often to introduce new social programs with similar entitlements across the country. Unconditional transfers have no strings attached, but are still guided by specific formulae determining which provinces get what proportions of funds.

Transfers from the federal government to the provinces and territories are now largely unconditional, with arguably fewer conditions imposed on federal monies than in any other federal system. The two largest programs, accounting for about 90 per cent of all federal transfers in recent years, are the Equalization Program, funded in 2007–8 at $12.7 billion, and the Canada Health and Social Transfers (CHT and CST), funded in 2007–8 at $31.1 billion (see Table 4.1). The equalization program is wholly unconditional, while the CHT and CST come with only a few general conditions. The conditions on the CST and CHT are discussed in Chapters 7 and 8, respectively. They amount to national principles and leave considerable room for provincial interpretation.

Moreover, both the CHT and CST are block grants, intended to cover a broad range of program expenditures in areas from health to social assistance to post-secondary education. Block grants represent the amalgamation of more specific cost-shared programs. In the former, funds are transferred without reference to explicit provincial expenditures; in the latter, federal funds are matched to actual

Table 4.1   Major Federal Transfers to Provinces and Territories

| | Estimated Cash Transfers, 2007–8 $millions | | | | | |
	CHT	CST	Equalization	TFF	Other	Total
Nfld & Labrador	346	151	477		555.4	1,529
PEI	94	41	294		40.4	470
Nova Scotia	636	277	1,308		219.5	2,441
New Brunswick	510	222	1,477		77	2,286
Quebec	5,225	2,278	7,160		550.8	15,214
Ontario	8,107	3,796			859	12,762
Manitoba	804	350	1,826		104.3	3,084
Saskatchewan	668	291	226		229	1,414
Alberta	1,804	1,009			243	3,056
British Columbia	3,090	1,290			362	4,742
Nunavut	24	9		893	35.6	962
NWT	19	13		788	34	854
Yukon	22	9		540	38.6	609
All Provinces & Territories	21,348	9,737	12,768	2,221	3,349	49,427

SOURCE: Compiled from Department of Finance, Government of Canada, Federal Budget Papers, 2007.

NOTES: Totals may not add because of rounding.

CST funding includes child care transition funding of $250 million in 2007–8 (provided outside the CST for that year only). 'Other' includes Offshore Accord offset payments of $494 million to Newfoundland and Labrador and $130 million to Nova Scotia; transitional CHT and CST protection payments to certain provinces and territories; devolution transfer funds to Yukon; and payments under the Infrastructure and ecoTrust programs. Equalization payments assume that NL and NS both elect to stay with pre-2007 arrangements.

expenditures according to a formula (e.g., 50–50). Canadian governments still maintain some cost-shared programs, including economic and regional development agreements, and federal–provincial–municipal infrastructure agreements (Vaillancourt, 2000). But in dollar terms they are much less important than the two big transfers. Canada is unique among federations in that almost all (about 94 per cent) of its intergovernmental transfers take the form of block payments.

The most unconditional of the transfer programs, equalization, is intended to sustain the provinces' constitutional autonomy by ensuring that each province has the capacity to deliver comparable services at comparable rates of taxation.

Initiated in 1957, equalization brings provinces with a fiscal capacity below the national average up to a national standard. Except indirectly, through the redistributive effects of the federal tax system, equalization does not take funds from the richer provinces. The latter are not equalized *down* to the national level: it is only the poorer provinces that are equalized *up*. The funds for this purpose come wholly from the federal budget. They are collected throughout the country and individual taxpayers in the poorer provinces contribute according to their income, at the same rate as individual taxpayers in the richer provinces. There are no direct transfers between provincial governments.

Provincial fiscal capacity is measured using a national standard based on tax yield from five different categories of revenue sources, an approach referred to as the 'representative tax system'. From 1982 until the March 2007 federal budget, that standard had been the average of the five provinces of British Columbia, Saskatchewan, Manitoba, Ontario, and Quebec (from 2007 on, it will be a ten-province standard). Against this standard each province's actual fiscal capacity was measured to determine the extent of its entitlement. Eight of the ten provinces (all but Ontario and Alberta) were entitled to receive funds to bring them up to the national standard of fiscal capacity. Unlike equalization schemes in some other countries (e.g., Australia, South Africa), the Canadian system is designed only to determine differences in fiscal capacity; it does not attempt to measure differences in the costs of providing provincial services or in the need for specific program expenditures (see Brown, 1996).

For a brief period in 2004–7, following a decision of Paul Martin's Liberal government, this complex system for determining equalization entitlements was essentially abandoned. Instead, the federal government made payments based on the recent past, with an incremental increase each year. That approach came under considerable criticism as departing from rational principles and a transparent formula. In 2007 Stephen Harper's Conservative government restored the program to a principles-based formula.

The federal government also transfers funds to the governments of the Northwest Territories, Yukon, and Nunavut. These territorial governments are responsible for nearly the same range of expenditures as the provinces. Yet their needs and per capita costs are greater because of their huge land mass, northern isolation, and sparse populations; furthermore, they lack the full range of provincial taxing powers (resource revenues are shared with the federal government) and their fiscal capacity is much less than that of even the poorest province. Thus the territorial governments depend on federal transfers for well over half of their revenues; the figures range from roughly 65 per cent to 81 per cent, depending on the territory and yearly fluctuations in economic activity (Canada, 2006b: 1). These transfers are provided mainly by the Territorial Funding Formula (TFF); in addition territorial governments receive the CHT and CST, but these are deducted from their TFF entitlements. From 1985 to 2004, TFF amounts were determined according to an expenditure-based formula, adjusted for population, which reflected the special expenditure needs of the territories. The TFF did not escape fiscal restraint, however; the grants were frozen in 1995–6, and further reduced by 5 per cent in 1996–7. In 1998 a ceiling on future increases was imposed, and in 2004–7 the actual payments were de-linked from the need-based formula. A new formula was introduced in the 2007 federal budget. In 2007–8 the three northern territories will receive a combined total of $2.21 billion from the TFF (see Table 4.1).

Finally, intergovernmental transfers play a crucial role in funding First Nations governments (the more than 600 Indian Band Councils) and other Aboriginal governments and organizations. These governments are not part of the regular fiscal federalism (Federal–Provincial–Territorial) arrangements, and do not receive either equalization or CHT and CST payments. Instead, their funding comes from a specialized federal agency (Indian and Northern Affairs Canada, or INAC) and other specific federal programs. According to federal estimates for 2006–7, the two largest federal sources for funding to Aboriginal people are INAC, which will transfer $4.4 billion to Aboriginal governments and organizations, and Health Canada, which will spend $2 billion on First Nations and Inuit health programs; approximately $1.5 billion of that total consists of transfers to Aboriginal governments and organizations (Canada, 2006b).

Aboriginal governments differ from the other governments in the federation constitutionally, economically, and fiscally (see Chapter 14 below). Some Aboriginal governments have a limited taxing power, but few have much fiscal capacity (i.e., ability to obtain revenues from economic activity as opposed to the legal power to levy taxes), and none have the broad-based fiscal powers of the provinces. Also, the politics and policy discussions surrounding Aboriginal finances tend to take place on a separate track and under the auspices of different executive institutions than discussions at the federal–provincial–territorial level (Prince and Abele, 2005).

Finally, in recent years many First Nations have sought modifications in the funding system, including multi-year and more loosely conditional comprehensive arrangements. In late 2005 the Martin government, together with the provinces and territories, agreed in principle with Aboriginal leaders on the 'Kelowna Accord' (CICS, 2005), which was to provide a $5-billion, 10-year framework for significant increases in program funding to Aboriginal governments. However, shortly after its election in January 2006, the Conservative government of Stephen Harper declared that it was not bound by the Accord.

The Fiscal Relations Process

The preceding structural outline may seem bloodless and technical, but the decision-making process through which Canadian fiscal arrangements are made is anything but. As W.A.C. Bennett, the long-time BC premier, used to tell his fellow first ministers: 'Let's get down to the real business of Canada and divvy up the cash.' Fiscal arrangements are at the heart not only of federal–provincial (and provincial–municipal and federal–Aboriginal) relations, but also the budget-making process in every government. They are among the most hotly contested issue in politics, reflecting real ideological differences and regional interests.

Intergovernmental relations on financial matters suffer from all the defects of other executive federalism processes—and more. Although the fiscal battles between Ottawa and the provinces, and among the provinces themselves, have become highly public, the details of fiscal arrangements are so complex that governments leave them to a handful of technical experts who meet in private. The resulting lack of transparency makes accountability difficult to trace—a characteristic often exploited by governments eager to avoid taking the blame for cutbacks in funding or program entitlements.

Decisions about fiscal arrangements, particularly the final amounts to be transferred to the provinces, are rarely made jointly. Rather, the different levels of government tend to hold frequent meetings, argue their positions, agree on some general approaches and principles, and then leave the final decisions to their own cabinets. The most dramatic changes in fiscal arrangements in recent times, the introduction of the CHST in 1995 and the major reforms announced in the federal budget of 2007, were made by the federal government alone, following consultation with the provinces (Greenspan and Wilson-Smith, 1997). So too were many, if not all, of the major turns in the fiscal road over the past half-century (Burns, 1980). Negotiations with the provinces shape the options facing the federal government, and a decision taken against the wishes of all the provinces can backfire politically. In the end, though, Ottawa's allocation of the cash is a political act, and considerations other than the interests of the provinces can have a big say, particularly when the money is to be directed to social programs.

Finally, the tendency to leave the big budgetary decisions to individual governments is reinforced by two institutional features. Both the federal Parliament and the provincial legislatures want to protect their power to appropriate funds every year (even if budgetary decisions as such are made by the Finance minister or the cabinet). Thus no legislature will consent to be bound to multi-year intergovernmental agreements as such. Second, Canada's intergovernmental machinery does not function well when it comes to taking final, substantive and binding decisions (Painter, 1991; Brown, 2002). Issues of accountability, transparency, and decision-making are all of current concern to Canadian citizens and their governments.

Fiscal Federalism 1950–2005: The Balance Shifts

Fiscal relationships in Canada are subject to frequent change, but the changes themselves are usually incremental. Therefore a long sweep of time is required to understand and evaluate the effect of fiscal federalism in Canada. Before turning to the issues facing fiscal relationships in the current decade, it is vital to see where we have been.

Harvey Lazar wrote in 2000 that

Until the late 1970s or early 1980s, Canadian fiscal federalism had a 'mission statement'. Its sense of purpose mirrored the post-war consensus about the role that the state could play, through programs of redistribution and macroeconomic stabilization, in building a fair and compassionate society and a prosperous and stable economy. The golden age of consensus had eroded badly, however, by the early 1980s. And since then, fiscal federalism has also lacked a strong sense of purpose (Lazar, 2000: 4).

The post-war consensus was that fiscal policy should strike a balance between equity and efficiency. Interpersonal equity was pursued through a progressive income tax system, the social security system, and other universal social programs such as health care and education. Inter-regional equity was pursued through fiscal equalization, unemployment insurance, and regional development programs.

As Banting documents in Chapter 7 below, Canadian governments constructed a welfare state slowly but for the most part co-operatively from 1945 to about 1970. Through constitutional amendments, the federal government took over exclusive jurisdiction for unemployment insurance (1940) and concurrent (shared) jurisdiction for contributory pension plans (1950 and 1961). Quebec opted to retain control of its own pension plan, but in substantial harmony with the federal plan. The federal government also introduced old age security and mother's allowances to be paid directly to Canadian citizens. However, other aspects of the welfare state could be delivered effectively (and constitutionally) only by the provinces. Thus, beginning in the 1950s, the federal government used cost-shared programs to induce provincial spending in the areas of social assistance, vocational training, universities, social services, and hospital and medical insurance plans, among others. And after 1957, Ottawa began making separate payments to poorer provinces for fiscal equalization. This era was the pinnacle of what Banting calls shared-cost federalism.

The era of shared-cost, co-operative federalism came to an end by 1976, as economic growth and thus federal revenues slowed and the federal government entered a period of chronic budgetary deficits that would not end until 1998. In response to its tighter fiscal position, Ottawa decoupled its transfers from provincial spending. In 1977 federal legislation combined transfers for health and post-secondary education into a block grant called the Established Programs Financing (EPF). And in 1990 it put a ceiling on payments to the richer provinces from the Canada Assistance Plan (transfer for social assistance, i.e., welfare). As a result of these and other changes, the provinces were obliged to fund an ever-larger proportion of social programs from their own revenues.

Transfers to the provinces as a share of total government spending peaked around 1982. In that year, as part of the effort to patriate and amend the Constitution, Canadian governments and legislatures made a commitment to the equality of regional economic opportunity and to the principle of equalization payments in Section 36 of the Constitution Act 1982. This constitutional commitment has been crucial in sustaining the political commitment to equalization. Equalization payments were spared the relentless cuts in either the growth rate or the actual cash of intergovernmental transfers after 1981.

The 1990s saw even more dramatic changes as fiscal relations in Canada responded to dramatic changes in the economic and political environments. In this decade of globalization and market liberalization, governments reformed the welfare state to suit the more competitive economic environment. All governments eliminated their budgetary deficits and began to reduce their accumulated debts by introducing balanced budgets, and many were eventually able to accumulate substantial surpluses. Tax reform and tax cuts were responses to a sea-change among Canadian taxpayers, the majority of whom came both to expect less of government and to trust government less when it came to spending their money wisely.

From the perspective of fiscal relations, the most important event was the introduction of the CHST. Announced as part of the 1995 federal budget and its dramatic plan to restore federal fiscal balance, the CHST began as a way of cutting provincial transfers; then, after 1998, it set about restoring those cuts. Since April 2004 the CHST has been treated by the federal government as two programs, the Canada Health Transfer and the Canada Social Transfer (the latter being earmarked for both social assistance and post-secondary education). The CHT and CST inherited two sets of conditions from the CAP and EPF programs (which the original CHST combined): that no province restrict the eligibility for welfare of residents arriving from other provinces, and that all provinces meet the five broad principles of the Canada Health Act in the design and delivery of their health services.

The federal government invited the provinces to work with it to develop shared principles and objectives for the new transfer. But the most important intergovernmental discussions revolved solely around the money: how much there would be and how it would be allocated among the provinces and territories. The question of how much money the provinces should get has been driven by the provinces' claim that the federal government unfairly off-loaded its deficit onto them in the mid-1990s. They claimed that cuts to the funds placed into the 1995 CHST were 35 per cent between 1994–5 and 1998–9, while the federal government's cuts to its own programs were only 7 per cent in the same period (PTFM, 1998: table 1). The primary goal of the provinces, therefore, was to restore the cash to 1994 levels; that is, from the initial CHST allocation of $11.5 billion to $18.5 billion. The federal government argued that Canada's fiscal position could not be improved without cuts to transfers, and some analysts bluntly declared that the provinces must be forced to bring cost efficiencies and other reforms to their expensive social programs (Watson et al., 1994).

The outcomes of this tug of war included increased cash payments to the provinces, especially for health care, announced in the federal budgets of 1996, 1998, and 1999. As Maioni documents in Chapter 8, three health-care 'accords' were also concluded among the first ministers in 2000, 2003, and 2004. With the last of these agreements, the funds cut in 1995 were largely restored (Lazar and St-Hilaire, 2004). What remains at issue is whether increasing provincial health care costs should be met by a still larger federal contribution.

Finally, there is a growing recognition of the need to restore as well a larger and more specific cash transfer for post-secondary education. In all provinces, provincial funding to universities and community colleges remained relatively flat over the past ten years, as provincial budgets squeezed education funding in favour of health care. (See Chapter 10 in this volume, by Herman Bakvis.) However, most provinces compensated the universities for the restriction of grant funding by allowing them to raise tuition rates substantially.

Allocation of CHST funds across provinces has been even more complicated. The CHST inherited from the EPF and CAP differing entitlements per province that were based on historic patterns of cost-sharing under CAP and rooted in the differences in value of the EPF tax points originally transferred in 1977. During the inaugural year of the CHST, 1996–7, per capita entitlement ranged from $825 for Alberta to $993 for Quebec and $1018 for the Northwest Territories. Over the past decade the four provinces with below-average per capita entitlements— British Columbia, Alberta, Saskatchewan, and Ontario—have waged a campaign for equal per capita shares. The 1996 federal budget reduced the disparity by 10 per cent per year, cutting it in half over five years. And in the 1999 budget the rate of reduction was accelerated, with total elimination of differential entitlements scheduled for 2001–2. Yet actual cash payments continued to vary until 2007.

2006 and Beyond: The Search for Balance

The challenge in this decade is to find a new equilibrium between the competing pressures of equity and efficiency, and decentralization and local initiative versus national (federal) objectives and control. Here I assess how the search for balance might continue in three areas of the system: the tax structure, major social program transfers, and equalization.

The Future of the Tax Structure

The Canadian tax system is already considerably decentralized. It has been for at least twenty years, especially in relation to most other federal systems. Even so, the federal government is not short of revenues, although it has signalled a need to reinvest in some purely or primarily federal responsibilities such as defence, border security, immigration, and Aboriginal peoples (Canada, 2006a). Ottawa also significantly reduced its taxation of personal income tax (PIT) in the past decade, and has reduced the GST by a percentage point. These tax changes, combined with new spending commitments, will place some limits on the ability of the federal government to reduce vertical or horizontal imbalances to the extent that some provinces would like.

Tax reform has been important for the provinces as well. Alberta, Saskatchewan, and Ontario have been leaders, although all provinces have been under pressure to follow suit. Provincial taxes have been cut and tax systems redesigned. Alberta introduced its 'single rate' PIT, and other provinces are collapsing rate and bracket structures. Moreover, most provinces increasingly use the tax structure to pursue social policy objectives, including integration of tax treatment with social assistance and related family and social security issues. Quebec, with its additional PIT tax room and its own tax collection system, has enjoyed such policy flexibility for some time (Lachance and Vaillancourt, 2001). The nine provinces with Tax Collection Agreements (TCAs) have been advocating more flexible arrangements to allow the provinces to vary their tax rate and bracket structure. The federal government has agreed in the past decade to accommodate many different tax credit and deduction schemes and in 1998 to allow direct provincial 'tax on income' to replace the existing system in which provincial tax is simply a percentage of federal tax.

These changes do not seem to pose a significant threat to the harmony of the Canadian tax system, although economists and tax experts worry that a more fragmented tax base will erode the benefits of economic union and increase transaction costs (Brown, 2001). Meanwhile, the Harper government has signalled its intention to re-engage the provinces in strengthening the tax collection system by bringing more of them into the harmonized sales tax regime and by encouraging more harmonization of corporate income tax (Canada, 2006c: 70). For example, in October 2006 the federal government reached agreement with the government of Ontario on a single federal–provincial system for the collection of corporate income tax in that province (Canada, 2007a: 44).

The Future of Social Program Transfers

Three broad methods for renewing federal funding suggest themselves. The first is a return to direct federal funding; the second is through co-operative funding with the provinces; and the third is a more dramatic solution to vertical fiscal imbalance. In the 1990s Ottawa largely abandoned the sharing of social policy functions and with it shared-cost federalism (Hobson and St-Hilaire, 2000). Intergovernmental transfers continued to grow faster than direct federal payments to individuals, but Ottawa under Prime Minister Chrétien tended to see new federal–provincial programs as the last resort. The Martin government, by contrast, was willing to renew co-operative funding approaches with the provinces, notably in the 2004 health-care accord and the child-care agreements of 2005.

The Conservative government (2006–) has rejected, in general terms, the direct-delivery approach, but in the long run its commitment to this course will depend on its success in reaching co-operative arrangements with the provinces. While it did not resurrect the Liberals' 2005 child-care agreements (see Chapter 9 in this volume, by Martha Friendly and Linda White), the Harper government has set out an ambitious intergovernmental agenda. It is honouring the 2004 10-year accord on health care; has put equalization and TFF back on a more predictable, formula-driven track; has renewed funding for cities and infrastructure; and is in the process of reaching agreement on 'equitable and predictable' support for post-secondary education and training.

Meanwhile, the terms 'fiscal balance' and 'fiscal imbalance' have clearly entered the Canadian political discourse. Since the late 1990s, the premiers have adopted explicit arguments using the concept of vertical fiscal imbalance. The federal government under Prime Minister Stephen Harper is focusing on 'restoring fiscal balance'. The provinces and territories have maintained for years that a serious imbalance exists, and that the current situation—a strong federal surplus and a weak fiscal position in most provinces—will only get worse unless corrected. Their view was substantiated by an independent panel (Gagné and Stein, 2006: 62–8) and, more significantly, was generally acknowledged by the Harper government.

The solutions proposed included transfer of all proceeds of the GST to the provinces (Séguin, 2002); further transfer of income tax points to the provinces (ibid.); significant increases to the CHST for health care (Romanow, 2002; Gagné and Stein, 2006); and increases in federal equalization and TFF payments, even if these do not benefit all provinces (Senate, 2002; Gagné and Stein, 2006; O'Brien, 2006a; O'Brien, 2006b). Few experts argued for a wholesale realignment of federal and provincial spending responsibilities. Liberal governments in the past decade used direct federal spending to make up gaps in provincial funding adequacy—not a co-operative approach, but one that does address the VFI to some degree. The Conservative government (and its predecessor parties on the right of the political spectrum) have generally opposed this approach as program realignment by stealth, although the 2006 and 2007 federal budgets indicated some minor clarification of roles that might alleviate part of the VFI.

While the provinces as a whole are clearly in favour of reducing the VFI, they have differed sharply on the best solution. The only unambiguous proponent of tax transfers has been Alberta. Quebec supported tax transfers until it became clear that it could not afford them without some form of 'associated equalization': either equalized tax points, as in 1977, or an enhanced general equalization program (see below). The idea of equalized tax points was opposed by the richer provinces. The other provinces have also been open to a combination of tax and cash solutions, and most also shared Quebec's position regarding equalization. Ontario has taken a hard line against enhanced equalization at the expense of correcting its own particular VFI.

Ontario's position is especially noteworthy, since it is the largest province and has historically been seen as the principal beneficiary of the federal union in economic and fiscal terms. Ontario governments have until recently tended to support federal fiscal policy and regional redistribution. Now Ontario increasingly makes a special case for itself alone (MacKinnon, 2005a and 2005b; Ontario, 2006; Canada, 2006C: 118–22). It claims a chronic shortfall of at least $23 billion (in 2005) from the federal government (without accounting for the still enormous net economic advantages it reaps from the Canadian economic union; see Page, 2002). For its part, the federal government has countered that its fiscal position depends on contributions from the largest and wealthiest Canadian provinces. Once again, the point at issue is balance, and the appropriate point of equilibrium is in the eye of the beholder.

The Future of Equalization

Equalization remains the bottom-line component of Canadian fiscal federalism: a residual device for smoothing out the effects of tax allocation and other transfer decisions. Of all the intergovernmental arrangements, it is probably the best understood and the most broadly supported (Gagné and Stein, 2006; O'Brien, 2006a). It is also a constitutional commitment. Equalization makes fiscal and program decentralization possible by ensuring a basic level of comparable services at comparable tax rates across provinces. Without equalization, most provinces could not contemplate the degree of autonomy they enjoy now.

During the 1990s, when vertical redistribution (i.e., from higher-income to lower-income Canadians) was heavily scrutinized, the richer provincial governments and social policy analysts questioned why regional redistribution should remain so relatively generous and why it was needed at all outside the Equalization Program (Courchene, 1995; Boessenkool, 1996; PTMF, 1998; Banting, 1995; Milne, 1998). The influence of such voices was clear in Ottawa's dramatic reduction in employment insurance entitlements and regional development programs, and its move to equal per capita shares in the CHST.

Thus it has been even more important that the equalization program be sustained. Although it fared reasonably well in the 1990s compared with other federal programs, equalization has been to some degree undermined since 2000. Payments became more volatile after 2001. The eight recipient provinces formed a common front on the VFI and have all benefited from increased cash transfers for health care. But provinces like Newfoundland and Labrador, Nova Scotia, and Saskatchewan did not benefit when equalization was clawed back because of their oil and gas revenues. And the benefits to other provinces were limited by the fact that the formula inadequately reflected real revenue differences. Under the 'five province standard' used until 2004, Alberta's petroleum royalties were left out of the formula.

Under the Martin government, bilateral arrangements were made with Nova Scotia and Newfoundland and Labrador to achieve fairer revenue sharing with respect to natural resources. Other provinces, notably Ontario and Quebec, criticized these bilateral arrangements as subverting the logic and purpose of the existing equalization program. Moreover, the richest provinces, led by Ontario and Alberta, have waged a campaign since 1995 for program transfers such as CHST to be determined on a per capita basis across the provinces. A per capita formula would put an end to what they see as the penalty for their relative wealth. These provinces have also opposed any general measure to enhance the equalization program, which essentially has a redistributive or even zero-sum character to it.

Throughout 2006 the provinces were at odds on what to do about equalization (Harding, 2006). The difficulty has been rooted in the necessity (given finite federal resources) of a trade-off between fixing the vertical imbalance and fixing the horizontal one. Common ground was achievable on health care in 2004 because all provinces and territories got the same share of a growing fiscal pie. This increase made more acceptable, in the short term, the Martin government's decision, a few weeks after the health accord, to de-link equalization and TFF payments from any kind of formula. However, governments and observers alike have been concerned about the fairness, predictability, and lack of transparency of the arrangements. In 2006 two major independent panels, one appointed by the provinces, the other by the federal government, proposed ways to return the horizontal equity programs to a firmer foundation. Both reports called for a ten-province standard—that is, one that includes Alberta—and for either all resource revenues (Gagné-Stein, 2006) or 50 per cent of them (O'Brien, 2006a) to be included in equalization. Both also acknowledged that the level of entitlements that such a new formula would create might be more than the federal government could afford. They recommend scaling back the allocations accordingly, while still retaining what they hope would be a more transparent and fairer determination of provincial entitlements. One key difference between the two reports is that the federal expert panel would impose a cap on equalization payments to any province whose per capita fiscal capacity is greater than that of a province not receiving equalization (O'Brien, 2006a). This proposed equalization cap responded to concerns that the offshore resources agreement between the federal government and Newfoundland and Labrador could soon cause that province's per capita fiscal capacity, after equalization, to exceed Ontario's

Conclusion: The Conservatives' 2007 Budget: Restoring the Balance?

Fiscal federalism is both shaping the changing policy agenda and responding to it. Although the 1990s saw a strong shift in the equilibrium within the federation towards relative fiscal decentralization and a greater emphasis on efficiency over equity, the pendulum has since swung back to federal power and a somewhat greater commitment to equity. Paul Martin's Liberal government responded positively to provincial demands for an enhanced and stable contribution to health-care programs through the CHT. In the March 2007 budget tabled by Finance Minister Jim Flaherty, the Conservative government made even greater strides towards fiscal balance. Indeed, it proposes to re-engineer virtually every aspect of intergovernmental fiscal arrangements (except for the 2004 health-care accord, which it has agreed to implement fully). The Conservatives' policy puts the equalization and territorial funding formulas back on a principled, long-term, transparent basis. It responds to concerns about fiscal balance by broadening the standard for equalization, yielding an initial increase of $1 billion in entitlements. It increases social-program spending under the CST and puts that transfer on a long-term legislated basis. It also increases funding for municipalities, extending the gasoline tax program for another four years and providing new funds for infrastructure.

Moreover, the 2007 budget gives further substance to the Harper commitment to 'open federalism'—essentially a more decentralized and classical approach to intergovernmental arrangements. The Conservatives continue in general to support a more limited use of the federal spending power, avoiding the introduction of any new direct federal programs in areas of provincial jurisdiction. On the other hand, new co-operative spending initiatives in labour-market training, infrastructure, and post-secondary education will be subject to measures designed to 'ensure appropriate reporting and accountability to Canadians' (Canada, 2007: 23, 26, 31); these measures have the potential to become intrusive new conditions on provincial programs.

In his 'historic plan' to restore fiscal balance, Finance Minister Flaherty may have hoped to achieve intergovernmental harmony. Yet as always the detailed allocation of funds is guaranteed to be seen in terms of winners and losers, especially since there is no consensus among provinces and territories on how best to reform fiscal arrangements. In other words, while all provinces and territories will be better off financially, some will benefit more than others. Largely by virtue of its population size, Quebec gets the lion's share of total cash in the improved equalization program. Ontario and Alberta benefit the most from the decision to make cash entitlements under the CHST equal per capita, after three decades of differentiation. In this respect, the richer provinces have achieved a significant gain, while the equity scope of fiscal federalism has been narrowed.

Meanwhile, the provinces that are still receiving equalization payments while their revenues from non-renewable resources (oil and gas) continue to rise—Saskatchewan, Nova Scotia, and Newfoundland and Labrador—will lose ground under two new measures, both recommended by the O'Brien report of 2006: the inclusion of 50 per cent of natural-resource revenues in the formula for calculating fiscal capacity, and the capping of entitlements if they exceed the fiscal capacity of a non-recipient province (i.e., Ontario). Also, the new policy claims to respect the Offshore Accords signed in 2005 with the governments of Nova Scotia and Newfoundland and Labrador, but clearly the new rules—which force the two provinces to choose between the pre-2007 regime and the new one—compromise the intended operation of the offshore accords.

The above are only some of the many implications suggested by the new budget, but they are the ones most likely to stand the test of time. It is also important to remember that the Harper government has only a minority in Parliament: should the government change, the Conservatives' fiscal policy will inevitably be revisited. Nonetheless, the budget's move in the direction of fiscal balance constitutes a significant milestone, despite the very real differences that remain over how it has been achieved.

Evaluating Canadian Fiscal Federalism

We may now come to some judgments about fiscal federalism as a whole, as determined by the three criteria set out at the beginning of this chapter. On the *performance of the federation*, fiscal federalism gets good grades. Its flexibility has enabled the system to transform gradually (though not without conflict) from the heavily centralized framework of the 1940s to the markedly decentralized framework of the late 1990s and into the current decade. The transfer of tax points, the removal of conditions on grant programs, and the maintenance of equalization payments have enabled Canada to sustain an emphasis on provincial autonomy that most other federal systems have abandoned. In the 1960s asymmetrical adjustment for Quebec on the pension plan, tax collection, extra tax room, and program delivery helped to accommodate the province's distinct needs. But these developments have not prevented a long-running conflict between Quebec and Ottawa over the federal spending power, a conflict that has been reactivated as the federal surplus has grown (Lazar, 2000).

Since the 1950s fiscal federalism has been generally consistent with federal principles, including respect for unity and diversity and provincial autonomy, although Quebec's concern about the use of the federal spending power remains an important and occasionally serious problem. As noted, the arrangements have shown considerable flexibility, contributing in turn to workable intergovernmental relations. The major exception, even if it is part of the pattern, came with the unilateral cuts of 1995. Some think that these cuts so undermined intergovernmental trust as to make broader intergovernmental co-operation much more difficult in the past decade (Inwood, Johns and O'Reilly, 2004).

The Harper government's move towards long-term, predictable, transparent and principled funding is, in our view, consistent with federal principles and with a more classical view of federal–provincial responsibilities. The working out of those principles could also entail a more co-operative ethos than the unilateral federalism of the 1980s and 1990s.

On *policy effectiveness,* the system's remarkable flexibility is also an asset, although judgment on outcomes depends on the beholder and the specific policy program in question. After all, fiscal relations are usually a means to an end, not an end in themselves. The discussions of social program funding in Chapters 7 to 10 of this volume provide fuller answers on policy effectiveness. Programs such as equalization and territorial financing can be judged on their own merits. While there remains some debate about the economic effects of alleged dependency on such transfers, both programs have worked effectively to achieve their stated purposes of closing the fiscal capacity gap across the provinces and territories:

> Without Equalization payments, the fiscal capacity of the least well-off province was between 58 and 68 per cent of the national average. With Equalization, the fiscal capacity of that province was raised to between 91 and almost 100 per cent of the national average (O'Brien, 2006a: 30).

The Territorial Funding program is also clearly effective in terms of its simple objective to close the gap between expenditure needs and own-source revenues, although the full adequacy of that funding has been debatable (O'Brien, 2006b: 32–3).

The fiscal relations system also has a significant policy impact on the broader macroeconomic functioning of the national economy and economic union. Fiscal and economic policy has strayed far from the initial efficiency–equity balance implied in the post-war consensus. The commitment to efficiency has been greatly increased, primarily through changes in macro and micro economic policies such as the introduction of free trade, adoption of a low-inflation monetary stance, and the accumulation of budgetary surpluses, among others. By the year 2003, the economic results of this commitment to efficiency were impressive: apparently sustainable economic growth in all provinces, continuing low inflation, much lower unemployment than anyone would have predicted, healthy government revenues, and a strong balance of trade (OECD, 2003). But there have been costs. Labour-market income has been polarizing, although not as severely as in the United States. Most universal social programs have been slashed and entitlements clawed back from upper- and sometimes middle-income Canadians. Health-care funding may be inadequate to sustain comprehensive and accessible programs. Higher education is becoming a greater burden on individuals and their families. And most programs to actively promote regional economic development are gone. In sum, the intergovernmental fiscal cuts of the mid-1990s did help to restore Canada's economic and fiscal competitiveness, earning a passing grade for the policy effectiveness of fiscal federalism. However, as other chapters will note in more detail, fiscal federalism has also stood in the way of policy effectiveness rather than enabled it, particularly in health care.

The new focus on correcting the fiscal balance need not have meant abandoning the emphasis on equity considerations introduced in the early 2000s. But the size and distribution of the increased equalization payments announced in the 2007 budget must be measured against other changes such as the relentless move to equal per capita cash shares (and thus less interregional redistribution) in all other federal transfers.

Finally, on the criterion of *political legitimacy*, the most significant trend in the past decade has been the erosion of mutual trust among the governments. As a recent independent report on its fiscal relations with the provinces found, the government of Canada has too often been perceived as a 'rule-breaker, non-negotiator, [and] unapologetic unilateralist' —the very traits that the federal government itself condemns in international contexts (Gagné and Stein, 2006: 90). Thus the provinces and territories have been calling for more formal, deliberate, and predictable fiscal relations.

While it would be unfair to characterize the new federal policy of 2007 as unilateral, it is true that, in the absence of an intergovernmental consensus, the federal government had to impose its own solutions. However, there is potential for mutual trust to be rebuilt in the government's commitment to more stable, predictable, fair, and transparent fiscal arrangements. The 10-year agreement on health-care funding seems already to have reduced conflict.

A second set of legitimacy considerations relates to accountability. Here the focus is more on citizens' expectations than on governments' needs, although the trend in public management towards greater transparency and simpler, more direct and quantifiable accountability structures has clearly permeated government agendas too. Being notoriously complex, fiscal federalism is not particularly transparent. Yet policy effectiveness often requires complex responses to the widely varying circumstances across a diverse federation, and flexible rather than rigid formulas for responding to often rapidly changing economic, social, and fiscal conditions. In other words, good policy in this area probably should be complex. That said, the very complexity of fiscal federalism has made it easy for governments at both levels to avoid direct accountability, each often blaming the other for perceived failings. According to some, including the Harper government, another aspect of the accountability deficit is insufficient clarity regarding government roles and responsibilities, made worse by federal intrusions into areas of provincial responsibility, notably social policy (Canada, 2006a: 22–3).

Issues of legitimacy and accountability turn in part on changing norms of democratic input and deliberation. Some Canadians have asked why momentous fiscal federalism issues should be decided behind closed doors by first ministers, finance ministers, and technocrats when other major intergovernmental policy issues are decided in forums that are open to the media and hence to the public. One partial answer, as noted already, is that they are not. Most of the broad issues surrounding fiscal relations are debated in the media and are matters for question period in the House of Commons and the broader political community. Even when tied into budgetary planning, the discussion of fiscal federalism is becoming more open and transparent. Canadian governments are indeed now leading a broad public debate on the future of fiscal federalism, and public opinion and electoral support will go a long way towards determining what can and cannot be achieved.

Note

The author is grateful to Harvey Lazar for his helpful comments on the 2002 edition of this chapter and to the editors and anonymous referee for their comments on the 2002 and present edition. All remaining errors are mine.

References

Banting, K.G. 1995. 'Who "R" Us?' In *The 1995 Federal Budget: Retrospect and Prospect*, ed. J. Courchene and T.A. Wilson. Kingston: John Deutsch Institute for the Study of Economic Policy, Queen's University.

————, A. Sharpe, and F. St-Hilaire, ed. 2001. *The Review of Economic Performance and Social Progress, Volume 1*. Montreal: Institute for Research on Public Policy.

Bird, R.M. 2001. 'Sales Tax Harmonization Issues'. In *Tax Competition and the Fiscal Union in Canada (Conference Proceedings/Working Paper Series)*, ed. D. Brown. Kingston: Institute of Intergovernmental Relations, Queen's University.

————, and A.V. Tarasov. 2002. *Closing the Gap: Fiscal Imbalances and Intergovernmental Transfers in Developed Countries, Working Paper 02-02*. Atlanta: Andrew Young School of Policy Studies, Georgia State University.

Blomqvist, A. 2002. *Canadian Health Care in Global Context: Diagnoses and Prescriptions, C.D. Howe Institute Benefactors Lecture*. Toronto: C.D. Howe Institute.

Boadway, Robin. 2005. 'The Vertical Fiscal Gap: Conceptions and Misconceptions'. In *Canadian Fiscal Arrangements: What Works, What Might Work Better*, ed. H. Lazar. Kingston: Institute of Intergovernmental Relations, Queen's University.

———, and P. Hobson. 1993. *Intergovernmental Fiscal Relations in Canada*. Toronto: Canadian Tax Foundation.

———, eds. 1998. *Equalization: Its Contribution to Canada's Economic and Fiscal Progress Policy Forum (Series No. 36)*. Kingston: John Deutsch Institute for the Study of Economic Policy, Queen's University.

Boessenkool, K. 1996. *The Illusion of Equality: Provincial Distribution of the Canada Health and Social Transfer*. Toronto: C.D. Howe Institute.

Brown, D.M. 1996. *Equalization on the Basis of Need in Canada (Reflections Series No. 15)*. Kingston: Institute of Intergovernmental Relations, Queen's University.

———, ed. 2001. *Tax Competition and the Fiscal Union in Canada (Conference Proceedings / Working Paper Series)*. Kingston: Institute of Intergovernmental Relations, Queen's University.

———. 2002. *Market Rules: Economic Union Reform and Intergovernmental Policy-Making in Australia and Canada*. Montreal: McGill–Queen's University Press.

Burns, R.M. 1980. *The Acceptable Mean: The Tax Rental Agreements, 1941–62*. Toronto: Canadian Tax Foundation.

Canada. 2007. *Restoring Fiscal Balance for a Stronger Federation, Budget 2007*. Ottawa: Department of Finance.

———. 2006a. *The Budget in Brief 2006*. Ottawa: Department of Finance.

———. 2006b. *The Estimates, 2006–07*. Ottawa: Treasury Board Secretariat.

———. 2006c. *Restoring Fiscal Balance in Canada Budget Paper, 2006*. Ottawa: Department of Finance.

———. Senate. 2002. *The Effectiveness and Possible Improvements to the Present Equalization Policy, Report of the Standing Committee on National Finance*. Ottawa: Senate of Canada.

CICS (Canadian Intergovernmental Conference Secretariat) 2005. 'First Ministers and National Aboriginal Leaders Strengthening Relationships and Closing the Gap', 24–25 November 2005, Kelowna, BC, text at <www.scsis.gc.ca>; accessed 1 June 2006.

Clark, D.G. 1998. 'Canada's Equalization Program: In Principle and in Practice'. In *Equalization: Its Contribution to Canada's Economic and Fiscal Progress Policy Forum (Series No. 36)*, ed. R. Boadway and P. Hobson. Kingston: John Deutsch Institute for the Study of Economic Policy, Queen's University.

Courchene, T.J. 1995. *Redistributing Money and Power: A Guide to the Canada Health and Social Transfer (Observation No. 39)*. Toronto: C.D. Howe Institute.

Dupré, S. 1985. 'Reflections on the Workability of Executive Federalism'. In *Intergovernmental Relations Vol. 63 of the Collected Research of the Royal*

Commission on the Economic Union and the Development Prospects for Canada, ed. R. Simeon. Toronto: University of Toronto Press.

Gagné, R., and J. Stein (co-chairs). 2006. *Reconciling the Irreconcilable: Addressing Canada's Fiscal Imbalance, Report of the Advisory Panel on Fiscal Imbalance*. Ottawa: Council of the Federation.

Greenspan, E., and A. Wilson-Smith. 1997. *Double Vision: The Inside Story of the Liberals in Power*. Toronto: McClelland and Stewart / Seal Books.

Harding, K. 2006. 'Premiers' Bid for Unity Turns to Acrimony: No Deal Achieved on Equalization Plan', *Globe and Mail* 9 Jun.

Hobson, P., and F. St-Hilaire. 2000. 'The Evolution of Federal-Provincial Fiscal Arrangements: Putting Humpty Together Again'. In *Search of A New Mission Statement for Fiscal Federalism: Canada: the State of the Federation, 2000*, ed. H. Lazar. Kingston: Institute of Intergovernmental Relations, Queen's University.

Hogg, P.W. 1996. *Constitutional Law of Canada (Fourth Student Edition)*. Toronto: Carswell.

Inwood, G., C.M. Johns, and P.L. O'Reilly. 2004. 'Intergovernmental Officials in Canada'. In *Reconsidering the Institutions of Canadian Federalism: Canada, the State of the Federation, 2002*, ed. J.P. Meekison, H. Telford and H. Lazar. Kingston: Institute of Intergovernmental Relations, Queen's University.

Kennett, S.A. 1998. *Securing the Social Union: A Commentary on the Decentralized Approach (Research Paper No. 34)*. Kingston: Institute of Intergovernmental Relations, Queen's University.

Lachance, R. and F. Vaillancourt. 2001. 'Quebec's Tax on Income: Evolution, Status and Evaluation'. In *Tax Competition and the Fiscal Union in Canada (Conference Proceedings / Working Paper Series)*, ed. D.M. Brown. Kingston: Institute of Intergovernmental Relations, Queen's University.

Lazar, H., ed. 2000. *In Search of A New Mission Statement for Fiscal Federalism: Canada: The State of the Federation, 2000*. Kingston: Institute of Intergovernmental Relations, Queen's University.

————, 2000. 'In Search of a New Mission Statement for Canadian Fiscal Federalism'. In *Search of A New Mission Statement for Fiscal Federalism: Canada: the State of the Federation, 2000*. Kingston: Institute of Intergovernmental Relations, Queen's University.

————, ed. 2005. *Canadian Fiscal Arrangements: What Works, What Might Work Better*. Kingston: Institute of Intergovernmental Relations, Queen's University.

————, and F. St-Hilaire, ed. 2004. *Money, Politics and Health Care: Reconstructing the Federal–Provincial Partnership*. Montreal: Institute for Research on Public Policy.

————, F. St-Hilaire, and J.-F. Tremblay. 2004. 'Vertical Fiscal Imbalance: Myth or Reality?' In *Money, Politics and Health Care: Reconstructing the Federal-Provincial Partnership*, ed. H. Lazar. Montreal: Institute for Research on Public Policy.

MacKinnon, D. 2005a. *Fairness in Confederation: Fiscal Imbalance, Driving Ontario to 'Have-Not' Status, Phase One Report for the Ontario Chamber of Commerce*. Toronto: Ontario Chamber of Commerce.

————. 2005b. *Fairness in Confederation: Fiscal Imbalance, A Roadmap to Recovery, Phase Two Report for the Ontario Chamber of Commerce*. Toronto: Ontario Chamber of Commerce.

Milne, D. 1998. 'Equalization and the Politics of Restraint'. In *Equalization: Its Contribution to Canada's Economic and Fiscal Progress Policy Forum (Series No. 36)*, ed. R. Boadway and P. Hobson. Kingston: John Deutsch Institute for the Study of Economic Policy, Queen's University.

O'Brien, A. (chair). 2006a. *Achieving a National Purpose: Putting Equalization Back on Track, Report of the Expert Panel on Equalization and Territorial Formula Financing*. Ottawa: Department of Finance.

———— (chair). 2006b. *Achieving a National Purpose: Improving Territorial Formula Financing and Strengthening Canada's Territories, Report of the Expert Panel on Equalization and Territorial Formula Financing*. Ottawa: Department of Finance.

Ontario. 2006. *'Strong Ontario: Seeking Fairness for Canadians Living in Ontario'*. Available on-line at <www.strongontario.ca/english/>; accessed 23 June 2006.

Organization for Economic Co-operation and Development. 2003. *Canada: OECD Economic Surveys, 2002-03*. Paris: OECD.

Page, M. 2002. *Provincial Trade Patterns (Statistics Canada, Agricultural and Rural Working Paper Series No. 58*. Ottawa: Statistics Canada.

Painter, M. 1991. 'Intergovernmental Relations: An Institutional Analysis', *Canadian Journal of Political Science* 24: 269–88.

Prince, M., and F. Abele. 2005. 'Paying for Self-Determination: Aboriginal Peoples, Self-Government and Fiscal Relations in Canada'. In *Reconfiguring Aboriginal-State Relations in Canada (Canada: The State of the Federation, 2003)*, ed. M. Murphy. Kingston: Institute of Intergovernmental Relations, Queen's University.

PTMF—Provincial/Territorial Ministers of Finance. 1998. 'Report to Premiers: Redesigning Fiscal Federalism—Issues and Options' (mimeo).

Romanow, R. 2002. *Final Report of the Commission on the Future of Health Care in Canada*. Ottawa: Health Canada.

Séguin, Y. 2002. *Report: A New Division of Canada's Fiscal Resources, Commission on Fiscal Imbalance*. Quebec: Commission sur le déséquilibre fiscal.

Treff, K., and D.B. Perry. 2005. *Finances of the Nation 2005*. Toronto: Canadian Tax Foundation.

Vaillancourt, F. 2000. 'Federal-Provincial Small Transfer Programs in Canada, 1957–1998: Importance, Composition and Evaluation'. In *Search of A New Mission Statement for Fiscal Federalism: Canada: the State of the Federation, 2000*, ed. H. Lazar. Kingston: Institute of Intergovernmental Relations, Queen's University.

Watson, W., J. Richards, and D. Brown. 1994. *The Case for Change: Reinventing the*

Welfare State. Toronto: C.D. Howe Institute.

Watts, R.L. 1999. *The Spending Power in Federal Systems: A Comparative Study*. Kingston: Institute of Intergovernmental Relations, Queen's University.

Websites

Canadian Intergovernmental Conference Secretariat (for official documents from intergovernmental meetings): www.scics.gc.ca

Canadian Tax Foundation (leading think-tank on taxation and budgetary matters in Canada): www.ctf.ca

Council of the Federation (institution for provincial–territorial co-operation): www.councilofthefederation.ca/

The federal Department of Finance has a site of good general information and description of federal-provincial transfer programs, as well as a very helpful set of 'hotlinks' to topics in public finance, including links to every provincial and territorial finance ministry: www.fin.gc.ca

Intergovernmental Affairs, Government of Canada, for a selection of links to general information on federalism in Canada and abroad, and to SUFA: www.pco-bcp.gc.ca/aia

Glossary

Block grants or transfers are programs bundling previously separate transfers into a single large transfer, often with more general conditions attached.

Conditional grants or transfers are payments made, usually on an annual or quarterly basis, from one government to another for a specified purpose and according to conditions normally established by legislation.

Unconditional grants or transfers are payments made, usually on an annual or quarterly basis, from one government to another for general purposes, without specific conditions.

Cost-shared grants are funds transferred to specific programs on the condition that they be matched by the receiving government according to a specified formula (e.g., 50–50).

Equalization is a federal government program designed to bring the fiscal capacity of the poorer provinces closer to a national average so that they can fully meet their constitutional and program spending obligations. See also **horizontal fiscal balance**.

Fiscal capacity is the ability of a government (federal or provincial) to raise revenues within its jurisdiction. Each government's fiscal capacity depends on the level and nature of economic activity, as well as the amount of wealth and its distribution within its borders.

Horizontal fiscal balance or imbalance refers to the relative fiscal positions among the provinces (states, etc.) in a federation. Imbalances reflect the differing fiscal capacities of these units to carry out similar constitutional and program spending responsibilities. Balance is achieved by redistributing fiscal resources to the poorer provinces. This is done in Canada through the equalization program.

Tax allocation refers to the division of tax revenues among the jurisdictions in which they have been generated.

Tax base refers to the part of the economy that is explicitly covered by the tax in question.

Tax expenditure is spending in the form of forgone government revenues, usually as a specific tax credit or deduction. Tax expenditures are not usually shown in budget documents as expenditures as such.

Tax harmonization refers to the effort to make tax structure and its implementation similar across the provinces, to ensure that individuals and firms can move freely and do business in all parts of the federation (i.e., the economic union). Harmonized tax structures need not be identical, but key features such as tax base will be identical or very similar.

Tax point. See **tax room**.

Tax rate is the percentage of income or business transaction payable as tax. **Tax brackets** divide total incomes in order to tax higher income at a higher rate. For example, federal personal income tax in 1999–2001 had five different income brackets. Bracket creep occurs when inflation, rather than a real salary increase, pushes a taxpayer into a higher tax bracket.

Tax room provides—usually through a transfer of percentage points of tax share— 'room' for the provinces to collect a greater share of a given tax base, while the federal share is correspondingly reduced.

'Tax on tax' is the system in which provincial tax payable is expressed as a percentage of the federal tax payable, levied on the identical tax base, and using the same tax rates and brackets. A separate provincial **'tax on income'** implies separate tax rates and brackets (and possibly tax base) for the provincial share.

Vertical fiscal gap refers to a situation in which the central government's revenues exceed its expenditure needs and the provinces' revenues do not exceed theirs. In most federations the central government reduces the gap by transferring some of its surplus to the provinces.

Vertical fiscal imbalance occurs when the **vertical fiscal gap** is not sufficiently reduced by transfer payments from the federal government, and provinces claim a chronic inability to meet their expenditure responsibilities with their own revenues.

Chapter 5

Parliamentary Canada and Intergovernmental Canada: Exploring the Tensions

Richard Simeon and Amy Nugent

The three principal pillars of Canada's institutional architecture are Westminster-style parliamentary government, federalism, and the Charter of Rights and Freedoms. A fourth pillar, derived from the first two, might be labelled intergovernmental relations. In many ways these four pillars are part of a coherent whole: one that balances majority rule against minority rights, and national interests against interests and identities that are defined by territory and language.

But each of these pillars also embodies values—including fundamental conceptions of democracy and effective government—that may be in deep tension with each other. In this chapter we will explore some of these tensions as they relate to the fundamental purpose of this volume: to understand federalism in terms of 'performance, effectiveness, and legitimacy'. To that end, we will investigate the development of what we might call 'intergovernmental Canada', and the ways in which this conception interacts with what we might call 'parliamentary Canada'. Responsible government, a foundational principle of Canadian parliamentary democracy, is at the heart of this tension. It says that each government (first minister and cabinet) is responsible to its own legislature for legislation, regulation, and the raising and spending of revenue. In a federal system, however, many policy responsibilities are shared; both orders of government have broad taxing powers; there are extensive transfers of funds between orders of government; and much of the intergovernmental relationship is managed through intergovernmental accords and agreements. As a consequence, another level of accountability arises: that of the responsibility of governments to each other for the shared management of the federal system.

So long as Canadian governance remains executive-centred, with the executive fully in control of legislative majorities, it is possible to overcome these difficulties through 'elite accommodation': informal, high-level intergovernmental negotiations that make intergovernmental decision-making possible (Watts, 1989: abstract). Yet measures to further institutionalize 'intergovernmental Canada' through more binding and enforceable intergovernmental agreements may well run afoul of a more robust 'legislative Canada'. We will conclude our discussion by asking whether these two conceptions can be effectively blended, either through greater legislative involvement in intergovernmental relationships or through more flexible mechanisms for transparency, accountability, citizen participation, and deliberation.

From this discussion a reform agenda emerges. Indeed, there are two reform agendas at play here. One is about reforming the institutions and practices of federalism and intergovernmental relations (IGR) in order to make them more open, accountable, transparent, legitimate, and effective. The other is about legislative reform, designed to mitigate the executive dominance—excessive even in comparison with other Westminster-style democracies—that characterizes the Canadian system at both federal and provincial levels.

But readers should not hold their breath. The institutions of Canadian governance, with their built-in incentives and constraints, are remarkably resistant to change. For example, despite the massive changes that have occurred in the Canadian society and economy—globalization, multiculturalism, the mobilization of Aboriginal peoples, and the rise of non-territorially-defined social movements—the dynamics of executive federalism or 'federal diplomacy' today look remarkably like those that existed in the 1960s (Simeon, 2006b: 314–32). There have been important changes in IGR, to be discussed below, but they are limited and incremental. Similarly, in recent years there has been much discussion of parliamentary reform, generally designed to check the dominance of the executive ('First Minister Government') through an enhanced role for backbench MPs (Baier et al., 2005). But the dynamics of 'government from the centre' suggest limited prospects for change. The contrast between the commitment to restoring the role of Parliament in the Conservatives' platform and the reassertion of central control immediately upon their forming the government in early 2006 makes the point (Doyle, 2006). Nevertheless, in the hopes of better policy and more legitimate, democratic relations, it is worth exploring the possibilities for change and innovation.

The Logic of Parliamentary Government

The Westminster model of parliamentary government that Canada inherited from Britain has, as part of its 'unwritten' constitution, a number of central features in both the federal parliament and provincial legislatures. First, responsible government requires that the government (prime minister/premier and cabinet) remain in office only so long as it holds the confidence of the House of Commons or legislature. Accountability in its most fundamental sense, therefore, runs from the government to the elected members of the legislature and from those members to the electorate. As is well known, in all Westminster systems this logic has been turned around as a result of party discipline and many other forces that (at least in times of majority government) strengthen the hand of the executive vis-à-vis ordinary members (White, 2004: 64–101). (Prime Minister Trudeau once famously described MPs as 'nobodies' once they left Parliament Hill.) Except in their party caucus, backbench members have little opportunity to express either their own views or those of their constituents when doing so would challenge the government and party leadership. Second, parliamentary government places virtually all power in the hands of the majority; 'Her Majesty's Loyal Opposition' has little opportunity to influence government policies. Third, Westminster systems are typically (though some changes have been made recently in Australia, New Zealand, and the Scottish Parliament) based on single-member, simple-plurality electoral systems, which have the potential to produce large discrepancies between votes received and seats won.

All these characteristics have recently created their own reform agendas. They include a greater role for backbench members, more free votes in the legislature, stronger committees, and more direct reporting to the legislature by independent agencies like the Auditor-General and the Privacy Commissioner (MacKinnon, 2003; Docherty, 2004; Savoie, 1999). Many commentators also appear to wish that adversarial and combative legislatures could become more collegial, deliberative, and consensus-oriented, though the logic of the institutional design makes such a transformation unlikely. Many also worry about the 'wasted' votes and unfair representation associated with the first-past-the-post system and call for reform of the electoral system to inject a substantial measure of proportionality into the system (Law Commission of Canada, 2004; Kent, 2003).

These characteristics of the parliamentary system also have important implications for federalism and the capacity of the federal legislature to represent fairly all regions of the country. A significant part of the problem is the interaction of Canada's regional society and economy with the electoral system. The result is that parties with regionally concentrated support (such as the Bloc Québécois today) are strongly rewarded while those whose support is distributed across the country (such as the NDP today) are penalized. This effect artificially reinforces the perception of regional division in our national Parliament. Moreover, as Chapter 6, on political parties, demonstrates, the discrepancy between seats and votes has typically meant that one or more parties have often found it impossible to win substantial numbers of seats in some regions, even if they have significant voter support in them. The result is, again, to enhance the perception that regional divisions are insurmountable. When power is concentrated in the hands of a government that has little or no representation from important regions of the country, those regions are likely to feel excluded and marginalized. And this effect is exacerbated by the inability of the appointed Senate to give effective voice to smaller provinces or those not adequately represented in the cabinet. This analysis should not be pushed too far: regional interests are often strongly expressed in party caucuses, and convention demands full regional representation in the cabinet (even if the prime minister needs to reach into the Senate to find suitable representatives). Nevertheless, in addition to a widely perceived 'democratic deficit' in the operations of the national Parliament, there is what we might call a 'federalism deficit'.

The consequence of this federalism deficit in the national government is that the national Parliament is not well equipped to represent all regions of the country effectively, much less to be the primary arena for accommodation among competing regional interests. This failure is perhaps the chief reason intergovernmental relations are so critical in the Canadian system. Citizens who feel excluded from the federal table are likely to turn to their provincial governments, both to take responsibility for issues important to them and to provide them with a stronger voice in dealing with Ottawa. This effect is reinforced by yet another characteristic of the parliamentary system: the concentration of power in the hands of executives who exercise authority not only by virtue of controlling legislative majorities, but also by virtue of the fact that they exercise many of the prerogatives once exercised by the British Crown. This situation is what permits executive federalism: first ministers are able to speak with one voice for their constituents and to make commitments that they will be able to enforce. Contrast this situation with that in the United States, where the separation of powers sharply limits the power of executives. Westminster-style parliamentary government explains why the Canadian pattern of intergovernmental relations leans towards the inter-state rather than the intra-state model.

Tom Kent (2003) sees this failure of effective representation of regional diversity in national institutions as a fundamental reason for the weakening of federal authority and legitimacy. 'The obstacle', he says, is 'not in the provinces' nor in the 'diversities of our regions.' 'It lies in the poverty of democratic involvement in our national politics' (2003: 5).

The Logic of Federalism

In Canada both federal and provincial governments follow the parliamentary model of 'First Minister' government. In principle, therefore, there should be no conflict on this score. In the classical federal model of 'watertight compartments'—in which each order of government has both a clear list of powers and responsibilities, and the financial and bureaucratic resources to carry them out—there is little need to interact or overlap. The federal principle would require only that each government be autonomous within its own jurisdiction, that there be no hierarchy or subordination between them—hence that each order respect the jurisdiction of the others, and that each government be responsible to its own legislators and citizens for its assigned tasks.

But of course hierarchy has never been lacking in Canadian federalism. The Constitution Act of 1867 gave the federal government draconian powers with respect to the (then) major areas of public policy; sweeping responsibility for the 'peace, order and good government' of Canada; the power to 'disallow' any provincial legislation of which it disapproved, to declare provincial 'works and undertakings' national responsibilities, and so on. The result was what the noted British scholar K.C. Wheare called 'quasi-federalism' (1953). By the 1930s a combination of political events and judicial decisions (the relative weight of these factors remains in dispute) had curbed the dominance of the federal government and enhanced provincial autonomy (Simeon and Robinson, 1990). But then the tables turned again. With the Great Depression of the 1930s, which drove several provinces close to bankruptcy, then the need for massive centralization to fight the Second World War, and then the post-war commitment, in Canada and all other western democracies, to the building of the welfare state, the pendulum shifted once again towards federal leadership. The new policy agenda engaged issues—health, education, welfare—that were largely within provincial jurisdiction. But Ottawa had the resources and the public support to take the lead by engineering the transfer of responsibility for employment insurance and pensions to Ottawa through constitutional amendment, and by using its 'spending power' to influence provincial priorities and programs with 'fifty-cent dollars'. In this period commitment to the 'federal principle' mostly took a back seat to 'co-operative federalism': the need to work together on collective goals, whatever the Constitution said. In the modern period, the expansion of the welfare state, together with the increasing political, bureaucratic, and fiscal weight of the provinces, has brought the federal principle back to the forefront. Now provinces are unwilling to defer to federal leadership. They wish to exercise their full autonomy in their assigned areas of jurisdiction; they ask what right entitles the federal piper, whose share of spending in areas like health and welfare has dropped precipitately in recent decades, to call the provincial tune. Hence the pressure to limit the spending power, to oppose federal 'intrusions' into provincial jurisdiction, and to ensure that federal transfers come with minimal conditions attached. Hence the contemporary debate about 'fiscal imbalance', suggesting a mismatch between the responsibilities that governments face and the revenues available to finance them.

In a complex, interdependent, multicultural country like Canada, the very idea of the primacy of the 'federal principle' is problematic. It suggests that federalism is a value in itself, to be sustained even if it contradicts other widely held values. Yet a quick survey of federal systems around the world suggests that there are few common 'federal' values, beyond the classic formulation of Daniel Elazar (1994) that federalism must find the right balance between 'self-rule' and 'shared rule'; between pan-Canadian and provincial identities; and between unity, homogeneity, 'national standards,' and common purposes on the one hand, and autonomy, diversity, and difference on the other. Another way of thinking about federalism is as a set of institutions and practices that should be judged and evaluated in terms of whether they serve or frustrate other, more fundamental values, such as democracy, social justice, national unity, and the meeting of citizen needs and concerns (Simeon, 2006a, 18–43). In this case, questions of 'national standards' versus 'provincial variation' become matters of ongoing debate rather than principled fiats. This is where a more malleable federalism and a stricter parliamentary–legislative accountability diverge.

Indeed, though the Constitution Act, 1867 notes that Canadians are to be 'federally united', it has been up to governments, courts, and citizens to express the changing meaning of federal union over time. For the Supreme Court of Canada, in the 1998 *Reference re: Secession of Quebec*:

> The principle of federalism recognizes the diversity of the component parts of Confederation, and the autonomy of provincial governments to develop their societies within their respective spheres of jurisdiction. The federal structure of our country also facilitates democratic participation by distributing power to the government thought to be most suited to achieving the particular societal objective having regard to this diversity (para. 58).
>
> The relationship between democracy and federalism means, for example, that in Canada there may be different and equally legitimate majorities in different provinces and territories and at the federal level. . . . No one majority is more or less 'legitimate' than the others as an expression of democratic opinion, although, of course, the consequences will vary with the subject matter. A federal system of government enables different provinces to pursue policies responsive to the particular concerns and interests of people in that province (para. 66).

In accordance with the autonomy of governments, the court tells us that each legislature has the authority to enact its own policies. Yet the co-ordinated policy development that takes place between governments in our federal system creates a deep tension between democratic, responsible government, and effective policy-making.

The Logic of Intergovernmental Relations

The classical 'watertight compartments' model of federalism no longer exists, if indeed it ever did in reality. The pattern common to all federal systems, Canada included, is one of interdependence, overlapping, and shared responsibilities. Hence 'Intergovernmental Canada'. Virtually all important problems cut across jurisdictional lines—local, provincial, national, international. This interdependence necessitates intergovernmental machinery to assist in 'multilevel governance' or achieve co-ordination on matters of common concern. As with federalism itself, there is no single model of 'right' intergovernmental relations. In Canada we have seen the shift from federal dominance, in which the disallowance power was wielded aggressively, to a more classical model, to the more paternalistic federally-led model of 'co-operative federalism' in the post-war period. Other federations range from some in which the provinces are subordinate to the central government (South Africa) to some in which the relationship is much more equal (Watts, 1999; Hueglin and Fenna, 2006).[1] These differences appear to be a result of the interaction of federal states and federal societies. Jan Erk (2003, 2006) nicely demonstrates that culturally homogenous federations, such as Germany, tend to centralization; culturally diverse ones tend to decentralization.

There is also a debate about the preferred model of intergovernmental relations. On the one hand is the view that the primary goal is to achieve intergovernmental harmony, accommodation, and consensus: intergovernmental success is intergovernmental agreement and mitigation of conflict. The alternative view holds that one of the primary virtues of federalism is that it creates alternative governments that will compete for citizen support; and that public policy is likely to be more responsive to public needs as a result of this competition (Breton, 1996; Harrison, 1996; Kenyon, 1997).

Intergovernmental relations in Canada today are a complex mixture of collaboration and competition carried out in a wide array of institutions. Some innovations in these institutions and processes have recently been achieved. At the federal–provincial and territorial level (FPT) the apex is the first ministers' conference or meeting. Then there are various ministerial councils covering most of the main areas of public policy. These are backed up by a host of officials' meetings. Informal contacts at all levels play a role in the work of officials and politicians almost every day.

Much intergovernmental discussion consists of debate, argument, persuasion, and information-exchange. But increasingly the results of executive federalism have taken the form of intergovernmental accords and agreements. Many of these—the 1995 Agreement on Internal Trade (AIT), the 1999 Social Union Framework Agreement (SUFA), various health accords and others—are discussed elsewhere in this volume. Typically, these accords contain broad statements of common purposes, commitments to collaboration, co-operation, and information exchange, mechanisms for the resolution of disputes, and commitments to transparency and accountability. It is increasingly common for governments to negotiate a broad multilateral agreement, including common principles and goals and a broad funding structure, supplemented by separate bilateral agreements between the federal government and individual provinces. This development opens the door to more flexibility, and to a greater measure of *de facto* asymmetry. These agreements, particularly at the bilateral level, strongly reflect the language and rhetoric of the New Public Management (Savoie, 1995, 2003). The focus on responsiveness and 'results' in NMP implies a very different idea of accountability than that embedded in the parliamentary system. In a parliamentary sense, accountability means holding the government responsible for actions or decisions: the executive is accountable to the legislature and the legislature to the public. With New Public Management, governments must account to citizens as 'stakeholders' or 'clients' for the responsiveness and efficiency of their actions. Public reports on health-care wait lists, agreed to by first ministers in 2004, are an example of this kind of accountability (Federal, Provincial, and Territorial Communiqué, 2004).

Most agreements also include provisions for financial transfers from Ottawa to the provinces. In the post-war period of federally led 'co-operative federalism', clear and explicit conditions were attached to significant federal payments: the spending power was used to buy federal policy influence. Today, with some important exceptions such as the Canada Health Act, most intergovernmental transfers have very few, and very general, conditions. Agreements contain language that makes funding contingent on parliamentary approval and asserts that nothing in them alters the legislative powers of any government or its rights under the Constitution. The former clause is effectively more significant, allowing Parliament to withdraw funds from intergovernmental programs with little or no notice to provinces.

Despite their format of clauses, sections, subsections, appendices, indemnity provisions, and signature blocks, these intergovernmental agreements exist in a legal limbo. They are not legally enforceable contracts. Nor are they equivalent to statutes. They do not trump the fundamental parliamentary principle that each government should be responsible to its own legislature. In the *Reference re Canada Assistance Plan (B.C.)* (1991) the Supreme Court made it clear that the doctrine of parliamentary sovereignty trumps intergovernmental agreements, and that any 'legitimate expectations' on the part of the provinces that such agreements could not be altered unilaterally had no legal effect. As Gerald Baier concludes: 'the court abdicated any role in the supervision of the federal spending power even if the stability of an intergovernmental compromise was at stake' (2002: 31). Nor do individual citizens have standing to challenge governmental conduct under the agreements. A challenge to the federal government for failing to enforce provisions of the Canada Health Act and report to Parliament on provincial compliance was rejected by the Federal Court of Appeal (*CUPE*, 2004). In sum, commitments made by governments to each other are fundamentally ambiguous, which poses a serious problem for policy planning and delivery.

An increasingly important element of intergovernmental relations is the Provincial–Territorial (PT) network. Annual Premiers' Conferences (APCs) have been held since the 1960s and have played a steadily growing role both in encouraging the sharing of experience in common policy areas, and in shaping provincial strategies for dealing with Ottawa. On a regional level, collaboration also takes place at annual Atlantic and Western Premiers' Conferences.

The most important recent institutional innovation in intergovernmental relations was the transformation of the APC into the Council of the Federation in 2003. Like its predecessor, the Council is made up of the ten premiers and three territorial leaders, with the chair rotating among provincial premiers and the host acting as the lead provincial/territorial spokesperson for the year. It is to meet twice a year, and has a small permanent secretariat based in Ottawa. According to its Founding Agreement, the Council is intended to strengthen provincial–territorial co-operation, 'provide an integrated co-ordinated approach to federal-provincial relations', assess federal actions with a major impact on the provinces, 'develop a common vision of how intergovernmental relations should be conducted in keeping with the fundamental values and principles of federalism', and work with 'the greatest respect for transparency and better communication with Canadians' (Council of the Federation, Founding Agreement, 2006: 2–3). Decisions are to be reached by 'consensus'.

Whether the Council of the Federation will become a more central feature of the intergovernmental landscape is not yet clear. Much will depend on its ability to reconcile differences among a hugely diverse membership: large and small, rich and poor, east, west and north. Much will also depend on provinces' avoiding the temptation to strike individual agreements with Ottawa when it is to their advantage, rather than to act as a group. There is little evidence that provinces are willing to temper their individual interests in favour of interprovincial consensus. For example, Newfoundland and Labrador as well as Nova Scotia abandoned the united interprovincial approach to federal–provincial fiscal relations when offered the chance to sign the 'Atlantic Accord' with Ottawa. Similarly, Ontario Premier McGuinty wasted no time breaking ranks in response to the report of the Council of the Federation's Advisory Council on fiscal imbalance. The capacity of the Council to resolve interprovincial differences, and hence to serve as an independent arena for regional accommodation, is thus mainly unproven. There is no getting around the fundamental structure of incentives: provincial politicians are rewarded or penalized by their own voters, not by voters elsewhere in Canada.

The most expansive possible interpretation of the role of the Council is that it hints at a more 'confederal' Canada, one in which provinces and territories make collective national decisions, at least in those broad areas lying primarily in provincial jurisdiction (Burelle, 2003; Courchene, 1999). This possibility is underlined by the absence of the government of Canada from the Council. Alternatively, the Council of the Federation could become little more than a minor formalization of existing provincial–territorial consultative processes and mechanisms (Brown, 2003).

Complex, elaborate, and pervasive, the institutions and practices of intergovernmental relations nonetheless remain weakly institutionalized. They are awkwardly 'added-on' to our parliamentary system, rather than integrated with it (Papillon and Simeon, 2004). There is no reference to mechanisms of IGR in the Constitution; none of the institutions—FMC, ministerial councils, or Council of the Federation—has a statutory basis. FMCs are called at the discretion of the prime minister, according to the PM's political needs. There is no regular schedule of meetings. Nor are there any voting procedures or binding decisions.

Some change has taken place in recent years. Intergovernmental accords have become more detailed and precise, and, with the use of bilateral agreements, more tailored to the needs of individual provinces. Several ministerial councils have become more formally established, with regular meetings, rotating chairs, and bureaucratic support (Simmons, 2004). In democratic terms, the meetings are largely restricted to ministers and high-level advisers. Although some intergovernmental forums do allow for participation by others—for example, the two meetings of first ministers and Aboriginal leaders in November 2005 that produced the so-called Kelowna Accord—they are infrequent, and the non-governmental involvement in them tends to be ad hoc and informal. Furthermore, the products of such forums may not carry sufficient weight to be respected; this was certainly the case with the Kelowna Accord, as Papillon notes in Chapter 14.

The Council of the Federation represents a deepening of the provincial–territorial relationship and a strengthening of the capacity to co-ordinate action. But even here, a recent comparative analysis of horizontal co-ordinating capacity among states and provinces concludes that, of six modern federations, Canada has the least institutionalized machinery (Bolleyer, 2006). Two factors seem to account for this situation. First is the principle of parliamentary government, which overrides any inclination to establish intergovernmental mechanisms that would make decisions binding on legislatures. Second is the great variation among provinces, and the resulting diversity of their interests and priorities, which strongly inhibits their capacity for collective decision-making.

Assessing Intergovernmental Canada

Performance

As the various policy-oriented chapters in this book demonstrate, there can be no single answer to the question of whether the intergovernmental system generates or facilitates policy choices that meet the needs and preferences of Canadians in either the federal or the provincial context. We see relative harmony, collaboration, healthy competition, and effectiveness in some areas; conflict and paralysis in others. It is possible to tell a good-news story: despite the rigidities of the Constitution, Canadian governments have managed to work out agreements that permit federal and provincial governments, sometimes on their own, sometimes together, to address many issues effectively; for example, specific outcomes in the area of health care. It is also possible to tell a bad-news story about policy overlap, contradictions, and dropped balls; examples here might include climate change or the treatment of urban Aboriginal people.

Such assessments will also vary depending on the perspective of the assessor. Policy activists tend to ask not whether outcomes are consistent with the federal principle or the division of powers in the Constitution, but whether they advance or hinder their particular policy goals. Advocates of a more unitary or centralist vision of Canada will ask whether the system has strengthened or weakened 'national standards' and common policies across the country; provincialists will ask whether the system has blocked or recognized their desire for distinctive provincial variation. Politicians will ask their own questions: have my autonomy, discretion, and ability to win support among my voters been enhanced or constrained? Thus provinces continue to object to federal 'intrusions', and to the fact that, as in the recent termination of carefully constructed agreements on support for child care by a newly elected government (see Chapter 9 by Friendly and White), intergovernmental transfers remain subject to the vagaries of federal policy and therefore lack permanence and predictability.

A few general observations about this process are possible. First, the overall dynamic of intergovernmental relations is competitive and adversarial, despite frequent promises of co-operation. Second, this dynamic tends to emphasize turf protection, the claiming of personal credit, and avoidance of blame. The substance of public policy often takes second place to such considerations; institutional interests often trump substance (although some would argue that this is a false dichotomy). Third, policy debates in the intergovernmental arena quickly become transmuted into questions of fiscal federalism; money trumps policy—just as in an earlier period the Constitution trumped substance. Fourth, the preoccupation of federal and provincial policy-makers with federal–provincial relations diverts their attention from larger questions about Canada's economic and political roles in the world. We are directed inwards rather than outwards. Managing intergovernmental relationships consumes an excessive proportion of the time, attention, and energy of senior politicians and public servants, to the detriment of other considerations. Fifth, all these factors have contributed to a decline in trust among intergovernmental actors, especially between federal and provincial governments.[2] Trust relationships obviously vary between different policy areas and ministries, but at the centre—in the premiers' offices, Privy Council Office (PCO), and Prime Minister's Office (PMO), from which intergovernmental relations are increasingly directed—strategic considerations, institutional protection, and local political calculations (whether federal or provincial) take precedence (Dupré, 1985).

Nothing in this portrait is surprising. These features are built into the political structure of parliamentary federalism, and the incentives and constraints that it provides. Two conditions could overcome these tendencies. The first is a relatively clear hierarchy among governments, as there was in the early years of the federation, before the provinces came to see themselves as equal partners, in no way subordinate to the federal government. The second is a clear national project to which all governments are committed, as with the commitment to building the post-war welfare state. Neither of these conditions holds today.

Nowhere are the difficulties of competitive intergovernmentalism more evident than in fiscal federalism, where the relationships between money and power have been particularly tumultuous since the federal government made dramatic cuts to the Canada Health and Social Transfer in its 1995 budget. (See Chapter 4 by Douglas Brown.) In 2006, after extensive study and consultation, both the federal government and the Council of the Federation released reports on the health of fiscal relations. *Reconciling the Irreconcilable* is the pessimistic title given by the Council of the Federation Advisory Panel on Fiscal Imbalance to its report. The system of fiscal federalism, the panel said, 'has fallen into disrepair' (Council of the Federation, 2006: 9). Intergovernmental relationships are 'corrosive' (17). The panel's interviews with provincial governments identified a 'decline in trust' attributed to 'irregular federal-provincial meetings, called on an ad hoc basis'; 'last minute negotiations on major issues'; 'wedge strategies' used by the federal government to divide and rule; intergovernmental agreements such as the Social Union Framework Agreement ignored at will; and 'squabbling, ad hoc tinkering, and short-term thinking'. Few if any principles or rules govern the process. There is little permanency, predictability, or consistency when intergovernmental agreements, many of which are achieved only with great difficulty, can be cancelled or altered unilaterally. Provincial policy-making is hostage to federal fiscal decisions; federal policy-making hostage to the need for provincial co-operation. A dramatic example, as White and Friendly note in Chapter 9, is the Harper government's cancellation (contingent on parliamentary approval) in 2006 of the agreements on child care negotiated with all provinces by Paul Martin's government. 'We have a governance problem,' said the Council of the Federation Panel; 'the institutions and processes we use to manage the fiscal arrangements of the Canadian federation are inadequate to the task' (89). The same observation could be applied to several other policy areas.

Democracy

Donald Smiley delivered one of the earliest and most devastating critiques of executive federalism in his article 'An Outsider's Observations of Federal-Provincial Relations Among Consenting Adults' (1979: 105–13). First, he wrote, executive federalism

> contributes to undue secrecy in the conduct of the public's business. Second, it contributes to an unduly low level of citizen-participation in public affairs. Third, it weakens and dilutes the accountability of governments to their respective legislatures and the wider public. Fourth, it frustrates a number of matters of crucial public concern from coming on the public agenda. . . . Sixth, it leads to continuous and often unresolved conflicts among governments, conflicts which serve no purpose broader than the political and bureaucratic interests of those involved in them (1979: 105–6).

'My argument, then,' he concluded, 'is that executive federalism contributes to secret, non-participatory and non-accountable processes of government' (107). Smiley's powerful critique still resonates today.

Most intergovernmental relations continue to take place behind closed doors. The language of intergovernmental relations continues to be arcane and obtuse, especially where fiscal issues are involved. Citizens have little access to the process. Popular mobilization led to the defeat of the Meech Lake Accord in 1990 and the Charlottetown Accord in 1992; more recently, however, there has been no popular mobilization against either the Agreement on Internal Trade or the Social Union Framework Agreement, both of which were negotiated in the traditional closed-door way, with little public input. More specific agreements on topics such as environmental assessment have attracted criticism only from the groups immediately affected. The broad lesson here seems to be that when intergovernmental relations touch on issues of fundamental symbolic importance, such as the Constitution, citizens will mobilize to challenge the process. But public opinion surveys also suggest that citizens do not support one level of government over the other or seek any fundamental shift in the division of powers; above all, what they want is for governments to co-operate and collaborate (Centre for Research and Information on Canada, 2005; Leonard et al., 2006: 6).

How well do contemporary intergovernmental relations meet democratic criteria of transparency, accountability, and participation? With respect to transparency, not well. Despite intensive media coverage of high-profile intergovernmental conflicts over issues such as health-care funding, the process is still largely closed. Intergovernmental relations, like national security issues, remain outside the Freedom of Information Act. Sectoral intergovernmental cultures do vary with respect to levels of citizen responsiveness, opportunities for participation, and degrees of transparency and accountability. But in general the record on these counts is weak (DiGiacomo, 2005).

Accountability is a complex matter in a federal system. Multiple accountabilities co-exist. Fundamental, of course, is the accountability of each government to its own legislature. But when there are large intergovernmental transfers, as in Canada, then the complications begin. If the federal government is to be accountable to Parliament for these expenditures, one would expect recipient provinces to be subject to strict reporting requirements, if not strict conditions, as to how the funds are used. But such a requirement conflicts directly with provincial autonomy, since most transfers are directed to areas in which provincial legislatures and governments make the basic policy choices. Similarly, it is reasonable to assume that the federal government should be accountable for stability in its funding commitments. Yet the federal government is reluctant to curtail in any way its spending power, and provinces have long resisted the attachment of conditions to federal payments. Reconciling these multiple and competing accountabilities is no easy task.

Conditionality in federal transfers has diminished over time, to the point that intergovernmental transfers in Canada have fewer conditions attached to them than is the case in most other federations (Lazar, 1999). In recent years provincial governments have committed themselves to sharing information, developing common indicators of success, and the like. Such reporting and monitoring of program outcomes is increasingly framed not as accountability to the federal government, but as accountability to the provinces' own citizens for how the funds are used (Laurent and Vaillancourt, 2004). The Social Union Framework Agreement established this wording, now invariably included in intergovernmental agreements: 'enhancing each government's transparency and accountability to its citizens', by monitoring and measuring outcomes, and 'reporting regularly' to its citizens.

In terms of participation, the intergovernmental arena is not entirely closed to citizen or civil-society influences. As Julie Simmons demonstrates in Chapter 17, some ministerial councils have been highly effective in involving interest groups in conferences, workshops, and round tables. But even here, when the political and financial stakes for governments increase, the doors tend to close. As Jennifer

Smith (2004) concludes: 'The general public, mostly, can only watch from the bleachers.' Only when 'there is sharp, deep conflict between the governments' does the public get 'to see through the cracks' (2004: 108).

Whether all this adds up to a serious democratic deficit is debatable. It might be argued that if each government fully represents its citizens and remains responsible to its legislature for its actions in the intergovernmental arena there is little problem: ours is, after all, a representative democracy. There are three problems with this perspective. First, it neglects the central role played by inter-governmental processes in Canadian policy-making; second, executive domi-nance poses a clear challenge to fully responsible government; and third, recent years have seen calls for a more robust conception of citizen involvement or 'deliberative democracy' than is captured in the traditional model.

Legislative Federalism

The vagaries of electoral and party politics as they play out in federal and provin-cial parliaments do indeed have important consequences for the intergovern-mental agenda, and for the dynamics of intergovernmental relations at any time. The ideology of parties in power, a regionalized federal party system, majority or minority government will all affect the way a government acts, with the immedi-ate pressures and constraints of a domestic political situation weighing more heavily on governments' minds than the one-step-removed intergovernmental arena. The Paul Martin government's pre-election use of its spending power and large surpluses to increase funding in areas of provincial jurisdiction, such as health care and early childhood education, and its 'one-off' deals on equalization with Newfoundland and Labrador and Nova Scotia are examples of intergovern-mental politics driven by political need. (See Brown on fiscal federalism in Chapter 4.) So are the Harper government's promises of 'Open Federalism', an end to 'fiscal imbalance', and other efforts to build support in Quebec for a future majority.[3] Similarly, provincial strategies in intergovernmental relations are shaped by local circumstances and personalities. This is another example of the tension between parliamentary government and federalism.

The tension is clearest with respect to accountability. The parliamentary prin-ciple is that governments are responsible to their own legislatures for laws, regu-lations, and the raising and spending of money. The federal idea is that each gov-ernment is autonomous in its own sphere, not subject to monitoring or control from others. These two ideas clash when there are significant transfers among governments, as in Canada.[4] The parliamentary principle suggests that it is legit-imate for the federal Parliament to attach clear conditions and rules for report-ing to all transfers. If not, how can the legislators hold the government account-able? The more carefully Parliament scrutinizes spending programs such as the Canada Health Transfer or the Canada Social Transfer, the more provincial autonomy is infringed.

Amy Nugent (2006) illustrates this point in her analysis of the role of the

Office of the Auditor General (OAG). It is an agency of Parliament, charged with 'following the money'. Its recent approach has been to move beyond simply counting dollars and investigate more policy-related issues, based on criteria such as 'value for money', effectiveness, and performance. In its 2002 report, *Placing the Public's Money Beyond Parliament's Reach*, the OAG recommended that the Treasury Board Secretariat and the Privy Council Office ensure better reporting, more ministerial oversight, and auditing of a large number of major intergovernmental agreements. Nugent concludes: 'The overwhelming thrust of the OAG's recommendations is to treat duly elected and constitutionally autonomous provincial legislatures and governments as an alternative service delivery agent of the federal government (Nugent, 2006: 9).

The debate here touches not only on appropriate mechanisms of accountability, but also on the potential tension between the conditions necessary for government accountability to legislatures and the need for co-operation and trust between orders of government. Even more broadly, the issue is whether the federation is to be an equal partnership or a more paternalistic, hierarchical, top-down system, and whether the primary gains from a federal system are seen to lie in co-operative or in competitive relationships (Smith, 2004: 127–8).

The public is not the only body largely frozen out of the intergovernmental area: so are legislators. Legislatures have on occasion been arenas for fundamental debates about federalism. One thinks of the parliamentary committee that considered Prime Minister Trudeau's proposed constitutional amendments in 1981, or the Bélanger-Campeau Commission that explored constitutional options for Quebec, or the two federal parliamentary committees that explored constitutional options following the failure of the Meech Lake Accord. In general, however, parliaments have little voice. Typically, governments do not consult the legislature at the stage when intergovernmental strategies are being formed. Nor do they typically report back to Parliament on intergovernmental relations unless legislative or budgetary change is involved. Intergovernmental accords and agreements are not normally ratified or approved by legislatures. No government, federal or provincial, has a standing committee on intergovernmental relations, and intergovernmental issues are seldom discussed in sectoral portfolio committees. And the opposition parties, needless to say, have little influence, even though they may well hold the preponderance of seats from particular regions.

It could be argued that openness, responsiveness, and accountability would be enhanced by giving legislatures a stronger role in monitoring and scrutinizing governments' conduct of intergovernmental affairs. Further, a more conversational and deliberative style of parliamentary debate might improve the national Parliament's capacity to act as an arena for the accommodation of regional differences, thus reducing the accommodative burden that now falls on the intergovernmental process. Such reforms would also be consistent with the larger project, advocated by many observers (and promised by opposition parties, but usually abandoned once they gain office), of restoring influence to Parliament.

But here again the tension arises between parliamentary and intergovernmental Canada, and between popular participation and politics as elite accommodation. Assume, for example, that governments agree on a carefully crafted compromise that balances regional and national concerns and is sensitive to the federal principle. Assume then that it must be ratified by 11 (or 14, including the territories) legislatures. In some of those legislatures it is rejected or amended substantially. It falls apart, and there is no effective mechanism to rescue it. This is what happened to the Victoria Charter of 1971. It was agreed to by Quebec Premier Robert Bourassa in the intergovernmental forum, but was soon repudiated when the premier was unable to win caucus and cabinet support at home. A similar process scuttled the Meech Lake Accord, and a referendum—rather than parliamentary process—did the same to Charlottetown. It can be argued that these agreements failed because they did not deserve to succeed (or 'did not meet a democratic standard of legislative or popular support'). But the larger question is how to reconcile these two quite different patterns of decision-making.

It is impossible to predict how a fundamentally reformed federal government would behave. Much would depend on the specific reforms implemented. A mildly enhanced role for MPs and committees, a more proportional electoral system, Senate reform that did (or did not) approach the Triple-E—all would have major implications. On the one hand, Parliament could become a much more majoritarian body (a worry to smaller provinces and, for different reasons, to Quebec); on the other hand, it could become much more regionally fragmented, with regional parties and MPs cultivating local and regional constituencies through log-rolling and coalition-building.[5]

But such fundamental reform is unlikely. We have seen how visceral is executives' distaste for giving up power. We have a constitutional amendment process that requires broad provincial consent; reforms that would weaken their influence will therefore be blocked. If basic legislative reform is achieved, it is much more likely to be at the provincial level, where there are fewer interests to balance, than at the federal level.

Thus we are likely to see the difficult and complex balance between federal, intergovernmental Canada, and parliamentary Canada continue. Such tension has not served us too badly in the past, and may continue to serve in the future, even if the aspirations of more radical democrats will be frustrated. But a number of more modest reforms might be possible, both at the level of intergovernmental relations and at the level of parliamentary practice. What might such a reform agenda look like?

In terms of the intergovernmental process, the most serious dysfunctions are a result of the perverse incentives of fiscal federalism. The spending power, together with large federal surpluses, creates a constant incentive for Ottawa to intervene in areas of provincial jurisdiction, often in capricious and uninformed ways. The same dynamic places the provinces in the role of *demandeurs*, always asking for more while resisting stronger conditions and reporting requirements. The transfer system also blurs accountability to citizens: if child-care spaces are inadequate, or support for universities and research too low, who is to blame?

Thus there is much to be said for resolving the 'fiscal imbalance', moving towards a closer fit between each government's responsibilities and resources, and reducing the role of federal–provincial transfers outside the Equalization program.

Similarly, while interdependence and overlapping responsibilities (and hence the need for intergovernmentalism) will never disappear, there is much to be said for clarifying as far as possible which level of government is responsible for what. In some ways, the remedy for the dysfunctions of intergovernmentalism is to have less of it (Simeon and Cameron, 2002: 291; DiGiacomo, 2005: 36). This approach resonates in the new Conservative government's 2006 election platform and subsequent budget documents (Finance Canada, 2006b). Here the emphasis is on re-centring federal spending on core responsibilities such as defence, immigration, justice and law enforcement, and Aboriginal peoples. There is some lack of clarity, however, as to what will happen to investments in intergovernmental initiatives already up-and-running in areas such as housing, homelessness, and early childhood development. Good policy will not result from overnight withdrawal of federal funds, as with child-care agreements. Such a shift requires consultation and joint planning, just as new initiatives would.

Even with a degree of clarifying and disentangling, governments will have to work together to effectively manage economic, social, and cultural aspects of the federation. As has often been suggested (most recently by the Council of the Federation's Advisory Council), first ministers' conferences should become a regular part of our institutional landscape. They should not be hostage to the political needs of an incumbent prime minister anxious to cobble together some last-minute compromise over dinner at 24 Sussex Drive. Rather, they should be the forum for general and strategic discussion of the policy agenda that faces Canadians everywhere, held largely in public, with follow-up activities delegated to ministerial councils and to individual governments. After a year in office, Prime Minister Stephen Harper, like his predecessors, has avoided making any commitment to such scheduled meetings.

To move away from public perceptions of bickering and blaming, intergovernmental Canada needs greater levels of trust not just between governments but between governments and the public. A step in this direction would be to address the ambiguous status of intergovernmental agreements. Johanne Poirier (2002: 455) suggests that 'an explicit legal framework governing the conclusion, ratification, modification, publicity and archiving of IGAs' would go some way towards making IGAs more formal and reliable.

More formal change could also provide increased permanence and predictability to intergovernmental agreements so that all governments know what the rules are and can trust that they will not be changed unilaterally. The Social Union Framework Agreement pointed in this direction, but had little effect on future government actions. The more these agreements impinge on the rights and concerns of citizens, however, the more important citizen access to their decision-making procedures and their dispute-settlement processes becomes (as with the Agreement on Internal Trade). Therefore, the more such agreements take on the form and commitments we associate with legislation or with treaties, the more legislative scrutiny and legitimation is required.

Modest recommendations may be made in terms of legislative federalism, including a fuller discussion of intergovernmental issues both before and after major conferences, thus complementing the process as it already works within the bureaucracy and government. Standing committees on intergovernmental relations in federal and provincial legislatures might scrutinize and report to the legislature on the state of intergovernmental relations and agreements in specific policy areas. Meekison, Telford, and Lazar (2004: 11) concluded that 'citizen participation could be effectively channelled through legislative committees in Ottawa and the provincial capitals.' Perhaps legislatures could also ratify major intergovernmental agreements, such as the SUFA (Simeon and Cameron, 2002: 292). The monopoly that executive federalism currently exercises over intergovernmental relations could be somewhat attenuated by the development of forums in which federal, provincial, and indeed local elected members could informally exchange ideas about development needs in each province.

None of this is to deny the desirability of a much more dramatic reform agenda that addresses the role of municipal and local governments (see Sancton in Chapter 15) and Aboriginal governments (see Papillon in Chapter 14) in our federal system. There is also the matter of how our system should be adapted to the reality of a country in which territorially defined differences, privileged in our existing Constitution and political practice, co-exist with other bases of identity and interest. (See Gagnon and Iacovino in Chapter 16.) Adapting federalism to the global imperatives of productivity, competitiveness, and innovation is also critical. Historical legacies and institutional inertia explain why it is so difficult to address these profoundly important questions. Every country carries its inherited burdens. From the beginning, ours has been the need to balance federalism and parliamentarism. We will continue working to figure out how to do so in ways responsive both to democratic participation and to the ever-evolving policy agenda.

Notes

1. Watts (1999) uses several indices to measure the degree of decentralization of a federal system, including the intrastate involvement of sub-national units; scope of jurisdictional and fiscal responsibility and autonomy; and the mobility of people, goods, services, and capital. In aggregate terms, Watts concludes that Canada is one of the world's most decentralized federations.
2. Veterans of intergovernmental relations suggest that in earlier periods, despite occasionally profound policy differences, a network of intergovernmental professionals worked to keep lines of communication open. These links appear to have weakened, partly because of increased control from premiers' offices and the PMO, partly because of more rapid turnover to deputies in intergovernmental affairs units. See Inwood et al. (2004).

3. As explained in the Conservative Party's 2006 federal election platform, 'Open Federalism' will 'facilitate provincial involvement in areas of federal jurisdiction where provincial jurisdiction is affected, and enshrine these practices in a Charter of Open Federalism.' Open Federalism includes inviting Quebec to play a role at UNESCO.
4. However, these transfers are smaller as a proportion of both federal and provincial spending than in most other federations (Courchene, 2004, Watts, 1999, 46–9).
5. This scenario would be similar to the situation in the United States, which comes closer than any other modern federation to full legislative federalism.

References

Arrangement between the Government of Canada and the Government of Nova Scotia on Offshore Revenues. 2005. Available on-line at: <www.fin.gc.ca/FED PROV05/OffshoreResAcc/novascotiaarr-e.html>.

Arrangement between the Government of Canada and the Government of Newfoundland and Labrador on Offshore Revenues. 2005. Available on-line at: <www.fin.gc.ca/FEDPROV05/OffshoreResAcc/nfldarr-e.html>.

Baier, G. 2002. 'Judicial Review and Canadian Federalism'. In *Canadian Federalism: Performance, Effectiveness and Legitimacy*, ed. H. Bakvis and G. Skogstad. Toronto: Oxford University Press.

———, H. Bakvis, and D. Brown. 2005. 'Executive Federalism, the Democratic Deficit and Parliamentary Reform'. In *How Ottawa Spends, 2005–2006: Managing the Minority*, ed. G.B. Doern. Montreal-Kingston: McGill–Queen's University Press.

Breton, A. 1996. *Competitive Governments: An Economic Theory of Politics and Public Finance.* Cambridge: Cambridge University Press.

Brock, K. 'The End of Executive Federalism'. In *New Trends in Canadian Federalism*, ed. F. Rocher and M. Smith. Peterborough: Broadview.

Brown, D.M., ed. 2003. *Constructive and Co-operative Federalism?* A Series of Commentaries on the Council of the Federation, Institute of Intergovernmental Relations, Queen's University, Kingston. Available on-line at: <www. iigr.ca/igr.php/site/browse_publications?Section=39>.

Burelle, A. 2003. *The Council of the Federation: From a Defensive to a Partnership Approach.* A Series of Commentaries on the Council of the Federation, Institute of Intergovernmental Relations, Queen's University, Kingston.

Centre for Research and Information on Canada (CRIC). 2005. 'Portrait of Canada 2005, Priorities, Making the Country Work Better'. Ottawa. Available on-line at: <www.cric.ca/pdf/cric_poll/portraits/portraits_2005/en_prior ities_tb.pdf>.

Cameron, B. 2004. 'The Social Union, Executive Power and Social Rights', *Canadian Woman Studies* 23, 3, 4: 49–56.

Conference Board of Canada. 2006. *Death by a Thousand Paper Cuts: The Effect of Barriers to Competition on Canadian Productivity*. Ottawa.

Council of the Federation, Advisory Council of Fiscal Imbalance. 2006. *Reconciling the Irreconcilable*. Available on-line at: <www.councilofthefeder ation.ca>.

Courchene, T.J. 1996. 'ACCESS: A Convention on the Canadian Economic and Social Systems. Report prepared for the Ontario Ministry of Intergovernmental Affairs'. In *Canadian Business Economics* 4: 3–26.

————. 2004. 'Intergovernmental Transfers and Societal Values'. *Policy Options* 25 6: 83.

DiGiacomo, G. 2005. 'The Democratic Content of Intergovernmental Agreements in Canada'. Public Policy Paper 38. Regina: Saskatchewan Institute of Public Policy.

Docherty, D. 2004. *Legislatures*. Canadian Democratic Audit, Vancouver: University of British Columbia Press.

Doyle, S. 2006. 'Full Cabinet Meeting Irregularly, Every Two Weeks to a Month', *The Hill Times* 26 Jun.: 5.

Dupré, S. 1985. 'Reflections on the Workability of Executive Federalism'. In *Intergovernmental Relations*, ed. R. Simeon. Toronto: University of Toronto Press.

Elazar, D. 2006. *Federal Systems of the World*. Harlow: Longman Group Limited.

Erk, J. 2003. 'Federal Germany and its Non-federal Society: Emergence of an All-German Educational Policy in a System of Exclusive Provincial Jurisdiction', *Canadian Journal of Political Science* 36, 1: 295–317.

————. 2006. 'Uncodified Workings and Unworkable Codes', *Comparative Political Studies* 39, 4: 441–62.

Federal, Provincial, and Territorial Communiqué, 'A Ten-Year Plan to Strengthen Health Care'. 2004. First Ministers' Meeting, Ottawa, 13–16 Sept. Available on-line at: <www.hc-sc.gc.ca/hcs-sss/delivery-prestation/fptcollab/2004-fmm-rpm/index_e.html>

Federal, Provincial, and Territorial Governments (not Quebec), An Agreement to Improve the Social Union for Canadian (Social Union Framework Agreement). 1999. News release, 4 Feb. Available on-line at: <social union.ca/news/020499_e.html>.

Finance Canada. 2006a. *Achieving a National Purpose: Putting Equalization Back on Track*. Ottawa: Department of Finance Canada: 39. Available on-line at: <www.eqtff-pfft.ca/english/EQTreasury/index.asp>.

————. 2006b. 'Restoring Fiscal Balance in Canada: Focusing on Priorities', *Turning a New Leaf, Budget 2006*, Ottawa: Department of Finance. Available on-line at: <www.fin.gc.ca/budtoce/2006/budliste.htm>.

Gibbins, R., L. Youngman, and K. Harmsworth. 2000. *Following the Cash: Exploring the Expanding Role of Canada's Auditor General*. Calgary: Canada West Foundation.

Globe and Mail. 2006. 'The Bedrock Need to Let Ministers Be Ministers'. Editorial. 22 Mar.: A18.

Harrison, K. 1996 *Passing the Buck: Federalism and Canadian Environmental*

Policy. Vancouver: University of British Columbia Press.

Harrison, K. 2004. 'Races to the Bottom? Provincial Interdependence in the Canadian Federation'. Paper presented at the Annual Meeting of the Canadian Political Science Association, Winnipeg.

Hueglin, T., and A. Fenna. 2006. *Comparative Federalism: A Systematic Inquiry*, Peterborough, ON: Broadview Press.

Inwood, G.C., C. Johns and P. O'Reilly. 2004. 'Intergovernmental Officials in Canada'. In *Canada: The State of the Federation 2002, Reconsidering the Institutions of Canadian Federalism*, ed. J.P. Meekison, H. Telford, and H. Lazar. Montreal and Kingston, McGill–Queen's University Press.

Kent, T. 1999. 'How to Renew Canadian Democracy: PR for the Commons, FPTP Elections for the Senate, and Political Financing for Individuals Only'. In *Making Every Vote Count: Reassessing Canada's Electoral System*, ed. H. Milner. Peterborough, ON: Broadview Press.

———. 2003. *A Short Path to Revitalized Federalism*. A Series of Commentaries on the Council of the Federation, Institute of Intergovernmental Relations, Queen's University, Kingston.

Kenyon, D. 1997. 'Theories of Interjurisdictional Competition', *New England Economic Review* Mar./Apr.: 13–35.

Laurent, S., and F. Vaillancourt. 2004. 'Federal-Provincial Transfers for Social Programs in Canada: Their Status in May 2004'. Institute for Research on Public Policy Working Paper Series, no. 2004–07. Montreal: Institute for Research on Public Policy.

Law Commission of Canada. 2004. *Voting Counts: Electoral Reform for Canada*, Ottawa, ON. Available on-line at: <www.lcc.gc.ca/research_project/gr/er/report/ER_Report_en.pdf>.

Lazar, H., ed. 1999. *Canadian Fiscal Arrangements: What Works, What Might Work Better*. Kingston, ON: Institute of Intergovernmental Relations.

Leonard, J., C. Ragan and F. St. Hilaire. 2006. 'The Canadian Priorities Agenda', *Policy Options* 27: 4–11.

MacKinnon, J. 2003. *Minding the Public Purse: The Fiscal Crisis, Political Trade-offs and Canada's Future*. Montreal–Kingston: McGill–Queen's University Press.

Meekison, J.P., H. Telford, and H. Lazar. 2004. 'Introduction', *Canada: The State of the Federation 2002*. Montreal and Kingston: McGill–Queen's University Press.

Nugent, A. 2006. 'Intergovernmental Accountability and the Office of the Auditor General of Canada', unpublished paper, 31 Mar.

Office of the Auditor General of Canada (OAG). 2002. *Placing the Public's Money Beyond the Public's Reach: Report of the Auditor General to the House of Commons*.

Papillon, M., and R. Simeon. 2004. 'The Weakest Link? First Ministers Conferences in Canadian Intergovernmental Relations'. In *Canada: The State of the Federation 2002, Reconsidering the Institutions of Canadian Federalism*, ed. J.P.

Meekison, H. Telford, and H. Lazar. Montreal and Kingston: McGill–Queen's University Press.

Poirier, J. 2004. 'Intergovernmental Agreements in Canada: At the Crossroads Between Law and Politics'. In *Canada: The State of the Federation 2002, Reconsidering the Institutions of Canadian Federalism*, ed. J.P. Meekison, H. Telford, and H. Lazar. Montreal and Kingston: McGill–Queen's University Press.

Savoie, D. 1995. 'What is Wrong with the New Public Management?' Debate in *Canadian Public Administration* 38, 1: 112–21.

————. 1999. *Governing from the Centre: The Concentration of Power in Canadian Politics*, Toronto: University of Toronto Press.

————. 2003. *Breaking the Bargain*. Toronto: University of Toronto Press.

Simeon, Richard. 2006a. 'Federalism and Social Justice: Thinking Through the Tangle'. In *Territory, Democracy and Justice: Regionalism and Federalism in Western Democracies*, ed. S.L. Greer. Basingstoke: Palgrave Macmillan: 18–43.

————. 2006b. 'Postscript'. In *Federal-Provincial Diplomacy: The Making of Recent Policy in Canada*. Re-issued with a new postscript. Toronto: University of Toronto Press.

———— and D. Cameron. 2002. 'Intergovernmental Relations and Democracy: An Oxymoron if Ever There Was One?' In *Canadian Federalism: Performance, Effectiveness, and Legitimacy*, ed. H. Bakvis and G. Skogstad. Toronto: Oxford University Press.

———— and I. Robinson. 1990. *State, Society and the Development of Canadian Federalism*. Toronto: University of Toronto Press.

Simmons, J. 2004. 'Securing the Threads of Cooperation in the Tapestry of Intergovernmental Relations: Does the Institutionalization of Ministerial Conferences Matter?' In *Canada: The State of the Federation 2002: Reconsidering the Institutions of Executive Federalism*, ed. J.P. Meekison, H. Telford, and H. Lazar. Montreal and Kingston: McGill–Queen's University Press.

Smiley, D.V. 1979. 'An Outsider's Observations of Intergovernmental Relations Among Consenting Adults'. In *Confrontation or Collaboration: Intergovernmental Relations in Canada Today*, ed. R. Simeon. Toronto: Institute of Public Administration of Canada.

Smith, J. 2004. *Federalism*. Canadian Democratic Audit. Vancouver: University of British Columbia Press.

Thorlakson, L. 2003. 'Comparing Federal Institutions: Power and Representation in Six Federations', *West European Politics* 26: 1–22.

Watts, R.L. 1989. *Executive Federalism: A Comparative Analysis*, Research Paper No. 26, Institute of Intergovernmental Relations.

————. 1999. *Comparing Federal Systems*, 2nd edn. Kingston, Ont.: Institute of Intergovernmental Relations.

Wheare, K.C. 1953. *Federal Government*, 3rd edn. Oxford University Press.

White, G. 2004. *Cabinets and First Ministers*. Canadian Democratic Audit. Vancouver: University of British Columbia Press.

Cases

CUPE et. al. v. the Minister of Health (2004), F.C. 1334.
Reference Re: Canada Assistance Plan (B.C.) (1991), 2 S.C.R. 525.
Reference Re: Secession of Quebec (1998), 2 S.C.R. 217.

Websites

Canadian Intergovernmental Conference Secretariat: www.scics.gc.ca
Centre for Research and Information on Canada: www.cric.ca
Council of the Federation: www.councilofthefederation.ca
Conference Board of Canada: www.conferenceboard.ca
Conservative Party of Canada: www.conservative.ca
Finance Canada, Budget 2006: www.fin.gc.ca/budtoce/2006/budliste.htm
Finance Canada, Expert Panel on Equalization and Territorial Formula
    Financing: www.eqtff-pfft.ca/english/index.asp
A Framework to Improve the Social Union: www.socialunion.ca
Institute of Intergovernmental Relations: www.iigr.ca
Law Commission of Canada: www.lcc.gc.ca

Chapter 6

Federalism, Political Parties, and the Burden of National Unity: Still Making Federalism Do the Heavy Lifting?

Herman Bakvis and A. Brian Tanguay

It may prove to be the one of more iconic moments of the Harper Conservative government: a picture on the front page of *The Globe and Mail* showing Prime Minister Stephen Harper flanked on one side by his Quebec lieutenant, Lawrence Cannon, and on the other by the regional minister for Alberta, Jim Prentice. Moments earlier, the prime minister had stated, as part of a resolution, that 'the Québécois form a nation within a united Canada.' The political significance of this announcement will no doubt be debated for some time to come. Also significant, and perhaps equally iconic, is the manner in which it was raised and introduced. The statement had been made by a party leader, the prime minister, supported by the leader of the opposition, and in response to an earlier initiative by the leader of another party, the Bloc Québécois, all of which suggests that political parties might still have a role in carrying the burden of national unity. In particular, the presence of ministers Cannon and Prentice in the photograph suggested a more traditional style of brokerage politics, harking back to the days of William Lyon Mackenzie King—an era that most would argue has long passed.

A single snapshot does not establish a trend. Yet the idea of political parties' once again playing a role in reconciling regional differences is intriguing. Political parties perform a number of essential functions in liberal democratic societies: organizing electoral choices for citizens, representing interests, channelling political participation, and recruiting decision-makers for government are among the most important (King, 1969; Covell, 1991). In federal systems, parties are frequently called upon to perform another task, namely to unify or integrate the nation. In Canada, broad-based brokerage parties have long played a crucial nation-building role, constituting what David Smith called the 'sinews of a healthy federalism' (1985: 1). From Confederation right up to the Diefenbaker landslide of 1958, and despite the repeated emergence of regional protest parties from 1921 onward, the two main national parties continued to play this pivotal role. Since the late 1950s the national parties have not been as successful in knitting together the different regions and sectional interests that make up the country. Voters in the western provinces, in particular, have chafed under a series of governments—those of Pierre Trudeau, Brian Mulroney, and Jean Chrétien—seemingly dominated by central Canada. The election in 1993 of a Liberal government with close to two-thirds of its seats drawn from Ontario only served to heighten this perception. The rise of the Bloc Québécois in Quebec and the Reform party in the West were evidence that the party system had become not only regionalized but also fragmented. Furthermore, there was the spectre of an even more fragmented system should the Liberal party, with the bulk of its parliamentary eggs in the Ontario basket, cease to play the role of a significant, if not dominant, centrist party. Not surprisingly, over the past decade there has been little reference to political parties as constituting the 'sinews of a healthy federalism'. A recent work suggests that Canadian political parties are increasingly seen as part of the problem rather than the solution to the unity woes of the Canadian federation (Carty and Wolinetz, 2004).

Yet from the perspective of the latter part of the first decade of the twenty-first century one can argue that the party system is taking a rather different turn. First, despite the discrediting of the Liberals through scandal (quite likely the product of one-party dominance) and the reduction of their government to minority status in 2004, the subsequent minority parliament was more responsive not only to regional but also to other forces. Second, to the surprise of many, in 2004 the Alliance and Progressive Conservative parties were able to consummate a merger. Third, in 2006 the new Conservative party successfully supplanted the Liberal government (though only as a minority government) by obtaining a number of seats in Quebec and Ontario, while maintaining a solid base in Western Canada. Finally, the leadership of the new Conservative party, with its bedrock of support in Western Canada, has nonetheless gotten its mind around the fact that Quebec is unique, as indicated in pre-election speeches in 2005 and Harper's 2006 'Québécois as a nation' statement.

These recent developments give rise to some tantalizing questions. Does the Harper government represent a new point of departure? Could we see important regional and federal issues discussed and perhaps even resolved by the parties in Parliament rather than by the elite of a single traditional brokerage-style party? Would such a pattern be contingent on minority government becoming the norm? There are also questions about what can be reasonably expected of the party system in maintaining the viability of the Canadian federation.

The questions addressed in this chapter, therefore, are threefold. Is there a renewed prospect of parties playing a more active role in carrying the burden of national unity? What can one reasonably expect of political parties in this respect? And, by extension, is the literature on the knitting function of political parties in federal systems, first developed and applied in the 1960s and 1970s, still relevant? The first part of the chapter examines some of the mechanisms through which parties perform some of these 'knitting' functions and where they appear to fall short. From there we move to discussions of how the party system has performed in the past, and in particular its putative decline in the final decades of the last century. In the concluding section we address directly the question of the performance, effectiveness, and legitimacy of the party system in relation to the Canadian federation and its future prospects.

A Parties-Based Theory of Federalism

As Campbell Sharman (1994) notes, there are three aspects to a 'parties-based theory of federalism', beginning with William Riker's concept of 'the federal bargain' (Riker, 1964). Riker argued that the degree of partisan symmetry–asymmetry in a federation determined the nature of the federal bargain and whether the federation was centralized or decentralized. A symmetrical party system, with the same parties operating at the national and state or provincial levels, would lead to a more centralized federation, especially if the link between the state and national parties was strong. A strong federal–provincial/state linkage was indicated if a party had a strong presence at both state and national levels, if the two levels shared many members in common, and if local elected officials typically moved up to the national level through the medium of the party. Most of Riker's work in this area was based on evidence from the United States, where the party system is in many ways more flexible and open than its Canadian counterpart.

The second aspect of parties-based federalism is the intrastate dimension: the representation of local and regional interests directly in national governance. The thinking here is that parties facilitate the representation of local and regional interests in national political institutions by providing conduits not only for communication but for flows of power, influence, and, above all, people: elected officials from the local and provincial/state arenas who move up to the national arena while maintaining their links with the former. This pattern has several advantages. Politicians starting their careers at the state level and aspiring to higher office at the national level know they must not appear too parochial: they must keep broader national perspectives in mind, and national ambitions reduce politicians' inclination to focus purely on local issues. At the same time, politicians at the national level who have local and regional experience under their belts are likely to be more understanding than others of the issues faced by local and regional governments (Barrie and Gibbins, 1989). Finally, although this does not bear directly on federalism, regional governments and parties can help national governments perform better by serving as talent pools from which national parties can recruit candidates for national office who have actual government experience.

Examining the degree of alignment between provincial and federal levels of Canadian parties in partisan support, party ideology, nominating procedures, and financial linkages, Donald Smiley argued that on Riker's integrated versus confederal dimension 'the Canadian party system is significantly more confederal than that of any other federation with which I am familiar' (1987: 117). He concluded that there was a disjunction between the federal and provincial party systems; for all intents and purposes the two party systems operated in two separate realms (see also Dyck, 1996). Nonetheless, Smiley and Ronald Watts (1985) argued that the federal cabinet remains the only significant intrastate institution: that is, the only institution within the government of Canada capable of representing regional interests. Since the parties remain the primary source for the recruitment of cabinet ministers, they remain an important part of the equation, if only by default.

The third dimension of parties consists of the structure of party systems and the norms governing competition between them. William Chandler (1987) identified three types of party system: single party majority; multiparty with one party dominant; and coalition, where no single party has a majority and two or more parties constituting a majority of parliamentary seats form a coalition in order to make government work. The importance of these distinctions, according to Chandler, lies in the type of competition and relations between the parties. In the single party majority system, Chandler claims, highly adversarial relations are often the norm, especially in parliamentary systems. Multiparty with one party dominant systems can also be highly adversarial; the difference is that the dominant party may have a rather narrow base. Coalition-style systems are the least likely to be adversarial. For Chandler, the single-party majority system is the most problematic for federalism in the sense that adversarial norms are likely to undermine the collaborative norms necessary for the smooth functioning of the federation. The parties under this model would likely exacerbate rather than alleviate conflict between the national government and the constituent units. Chandler's point—that the combativeness between parties is essentially transplanted to the federal–provincial arena when 'federal and parliamentary traditions are combined within one regime' (1987: 156)—may go some way towards explaining conflict between federal and provincial governments. Carty and Wolinetz (2004), also focusing on the 'coalition' model, concede that Canadian parties have long eschewed inter-party coalitions of the type typically found in European systems; yet 'their leaders regularly actively engage in bargaining and accommodative coalition-style politics in the federal–provincial decision-making arena' (Carty and Wolinetz, 2004: 67–8). They suggest that competitive behaviour at the level of parties is not necessarily transplanted directly into the federal–provincial arena.

In the following sections we examine not only how the Canadian party system falls short on the three dimensions noted above, but also the ways in which it helps to link regions to the centre and promote collaboration, though not necessarily in ways consistent with the standard theories of parties-based federalism. In the conclusion we consider whether these dimensions are still appropriate in assessing the role played by the party system in helping to carry the burden of national unity, and whether recent examples of collaboration between parties on certain issues, such as the 'Québécois as nation' resolution, may represent a shift away from the traditional arenas of executive federalism, such as first ministers' conferences, for the resolution of federal–provincial differences.

Canada's Party System from 1867 to 2000: The Triumph of Regionalism

Since Canada's birth as a nation, regionalism has played a prominent role in federal politics. Until the middle of the First World War, however, these regional tensions were effectively contained within a competitive two-party system in which the governing party—the Conservatives, largely under John A. Macdonald, from 1867 to 1896 and the Liberals under Wilfrid Laurier from 1896 to 1911—forged a winning electoral coalition based on solid pluralities (often outright majorities) of the vote in the two most populous provinces, Ontario and Quebec. Together these two provinces accounted for between 60 and 75 per cent of the seats in the House of Commons, and no party was able to win national office without attracting the support of a solid core of moderate nationalist voters in Quebec. This pattern was not broken until the election of the pro-conscription Unionist government in 1917.

The compromises and concessions needed to make Canada a viable political and economic entity—fostering industrialization behind high tariff barriers, opening up the west to settlement, and providing the Maritimes with their own railroad and favourable freight rates, for example—succeeded in smoothing over the fundamental divisions within the country. But regional economic grievances, coupled with rapid industrialization and urbanization in the early part of the twentieth century, shattered the two-party system and led to the development of a second national party system (English, 1977; Carty, 1988). Between 1921 and 1925 the balance of power was held by the Progressives, the first in a long line of regional protest parties—including the Co-operative Commonwealth Federation (CCF) and Social Credit in the 1930s—that challenged the dominant parties' monopoly on representation. Although these newer minor parties did not necessarily hold the balance of power, they nonetheless articulated the economic, political, and cultural grievances of particular regions and social classes within Confederation (Gagnon and Tanguay, 1996; Mallory, 1954).

The two most successful prime ministers in this second party system, Mackenzie King and Louis St Laurent, managed to contain the challenge to the established political and economic order posed by the regional protest parties. Both party leaders—but King in particular—were astute practitioners of the art of brokerage politics, the pragmatic cobbling together of party programs designed to appeal to a broad coalition of diverse interests. King, for instance, limited the effectiveness of the Progressives as the voice of agrarian protest by buying off some of the movement's leaders (most notably T.A. Crerar) with cabinet posts and implementing relatively minor reforms of federal tariff and freight rate policies. By the late 1920s the Progressives were a spent force in federal politics.

A second method used by King and St Laurent to moderate regional conflict within the party system was to stock their respective cabinets with influential regional chieftains—men like Jimmy Gardiner (former premier of Saskatchewan), C.D. Howe (Ontario), and Ernest Lapointe (Quebec). In many respects these figures gave direct representation to broader provincial and regional interests in the Canadian cabinet. King frequently paid heed to the views and advice of these ministers on regional matters, and was particularly dependent on Lapointe for counsel on virtually all matters relating to Quebec. This brokerage system of party politics was far from complete, however, since some provinces, such as Alberta, were simply frozen out of the arrangement. The Maritimes were represented in cabinet by figures such as J.-E. Michaud from New Brunswick and J.L. Ilsley and Angus L. Macdonald from Nova Scotia, the latter a former premier of his province. However, these maritime ministers carried very little weight in cabinet; Macdonald, for example, was continually out-manoeuvred by C.D. Howe on matters affecting Nova Scotia (Bakvis, 1991). The system also had its dark side. The minister for British Columbia, Ian Mackenzie, persuaded a reluctant Mackenzie King and an even more reluctant senior public service not only to intern Japanese Canadians but also to strip them of their possessions and citizenship and to continue discriminating against them long after the war had ended (Sunahara, 1981).

Nonetheless, the system worked—in large part because the ministers in question were able to deliver votes and seats at election time. In Saskatchewan Jimmy Gardiner, as former premier, still had a superb party machine at his disposal; Howe controlled a good part of Ontario; and Michaud in New Brunswick received his cabinet position largely because of his talent as a political organizer. Two changes were afoot, however. First, while the patronage system declined following the Civil Service Reform Act of 1918, it was replaced in good part by the pork-barrel in the form of large-scale government contracts awarded to favoured regions (Noel, 2001). The new regional barons allowed the Liberal party's connections with the constituencies to atrophy (Whitaker, 1977). Second, as David Smith (1985) notes, in the post-war period regional brokering was largely displaced by the 'pan-Canadian' approach of John Diefenbaker and, later, Pierre Elliott Trudeau. The arrival of television in the mid-1950s sharpened the focus on national leaders and helped make regional power brokers less critical in the conduct of election campaigns and delivery of the vote.

The electoral defeats suffered by the federal Liberals in 1957 and 1958 laid the groundwork for this third, 'pan-Canadian' system. It was less accommodating of regional interests than its two predecessors. The policies pursued by each successive prime minister were shaped by a centralizing vision of the country, even if some leaders (Diefenbaker) were more sensitive to regional concerns than others (Trudeau). Diefenbaker's concept of 'One Canada', combined with his championing of a Bill of Rights, drew attention to the formal equality of all citizens and 'appealed to Canadians as Canadians regardless of where they lived or what language they spoke' (Smith, 1985: 27). Lester B. Pearson's national medicare program, the Canada Pension Plan, and the Royal Commission on Bilingualism and Biculturalism, along with Trudeau's Official Languages Act, National Energy Program (NEP), and Charter of Rights and Freedoms were even more centralizing in nature. As Kenneth McRoberts (1997) has argued, Trudeau's pan-Canadian policies in many ways failed to unite the country, leaving a significant proportion of Quebec feeling betrayed and creating animosity towards Ottawa in many other regions. Official bilingualism and the National Energy Program antagonized the western provinces, and though Trudeau's constitutional reforms may have struck a responsive chord in some parts of English Canada, they alienated Quebec and provided fertile soil for the later growth of the sovereignist movement.

The pan-Canadian thrust of federal economic and social policy from 1957 to 1984 was paralleled by the development of an increasingly regionalized party system. Each of the two main parties drew the bulk of its electoral support from one or two regional strongholds, as did the CCF–NDP. None of these organizations was actually a national party with solid cross-country support. Except in 1968, the Liberals in this period managed to win elections mainly because of their pre-eminence in Quebec, where they typically won between 75 and 99 per cent of the available seats. However, the Liberals were virtually shut out in the west: in 1980 they won only 2.5 per cent of the region's seats, which accounted for 1.4 per cent of the governing caucus. The Liberals' woes in the west were mirrored by the Conservatives' failure to make any electoral headway in Quebec. In 1979 Joe Clark formed a minority government with only 1.5 per cent of his caucus drawn from Quebec.

This regional fragmentation was exaggerated by the well-known effects of Canada's first-past-the-post electoral system. In each of the four western provinces the Liberals managed to take at least a fifth of the votes in every election between 1968 and 1980. Because of the vagaries of the single-member, simple plurality electoral system, however, these respectable vote totals translated into no more than a handful of seats, except in 1968. Even though the Progressive Conservatives managed to win at least 13 per cent of the popular vote in Quebec in the five elections held between 1968 and 1980, this electoral support consistently translated into 2 or 3 seats at most (Tanguay, 1999). Alan Cairns (1973) described this effect as 'detrimental to national unity'.

The problems created by Canada's first-past-the-post system were compounded by conscious party electoral strategy. Party officials quite rationally tended to direct the bulk of their limited organizational and financial resources to those regions in which they stood the best chance of winning. After the crushing defeat of the Liberals in 1958, when Diefenbaker's Conservatives won the biggest (to that point) landslide in Canadian history, a group of young Liberal reformers recast virtually all aspects of party organization and ideology. The party's structures were centralized; new types of candidates were attracted into the fold; new campaign techniques modelled on American practices were adopted (improved use of television and opinion polling, for example); and the focus of the party's electoral appeal was shifted to the urban ridings in British Columbia, Ontario, and Quebec, rural voters being more or less conceded to the populist Diefenbaker (Wearing, 1981).

Thus it is commonplace to depict the evolution of the Canadian party system in linear fashion—from patronage to brokerage to pan-Canadianism and then into a spiral of ever increasing regionalization—and to see the Mackenzie King period in particular as the heyday of a cohesive Canadian federation brought together through a well-integrated Liberal party. Yet this depiction is not entirely accurate. First, the integration was far from complete. As R.K. Carty (2002) has noted, success in bringing all regions into the fold can be a dangerous thing. In his view all the major crises affecting the Canadian party system 'have typically arisen when an overreaching national party collapsed under the strain of trying to accommodate the conflicting demands of too many interests gathered into a political omnibus' (Carty, 2002: 726). He points to the eventual collapse even of the all encompassing coalitions constructed by Robert Borden, John Diefenbaker, and Brian Mulroney as a warning that 'successful brokerage parties . . . have to be careful not to actually catch all the interests' (ibid.). In many ways the Mackenzie King coalition was successful precisely because it was more limited in scope. In brief, the construction of all-encompassing coalitions *within* national parties was a rare occurrence and when successful was often followed by fatal results.

The Mulroney government also illustrates that change was far from linear. The cabinet formed in 1984 was in many ways a throwback to an earlier era, centred on ministers with a strong presence in key regions: John Crosbie from Newfoundland, who dominated the Atlantic region; Donald Mazankowski from Alberta; and (for a while) Lucien Bouchard as Mulroney's Quebec lieutenant. Furthermore, Mulroney's style was more reminiscent of Mackenzie King than of Diefenbaker or Trudeau. Even during the Trudeau period, however, regional representation in cabinet—the intrastate dimension—was far from absent. Though in many ways mere shadows of the old regional barons under King and St Laurent, regional ministers continued to perform, and arguably still perform, important representational functions. After the Liberals suffered near-defeat in the federal election of 1972, for example, the party resurrected the role of 'political ministers', one for each province, and gave them responsibility for allocating pork-barrel type funding as well as patronage and party organizational matters in their respective provinces. In the 1980s even unelected ministers, such as senators Hazen Argue in Saskatchewan and H.A. (Bud) Olson in Alberta, exercised considerable influence over the disbursement of infrastructure and regional development funds (Bakvis, 1991). Marc Lalonde, as the political minister for Quebec, dominated the allocation process, meeting on a weekly basis with other Quebec ministers to decide on the allocation of projects in that province (Simpson, 1988).

In addition to dealing with party matters, however, these new-style regional ministers served as critical conduits for provincial governments. In the Maritimes, Trudeau-era figures such as Romeo Leblanc and Allan J. McEachen interacted on a regular basis with the premiers of New Brunswick and Nova Scotia respectively. In effect this interaction came through necessity. Many of the projects that political ministers (and their colleagues) would like to see realized— new roads, bridges, educational institutions, and the like—fall under provincial jurisdiction. Persuading a provincial government to construct a new bridge in a regional minister's federal riding, for example, usually involved some kind of quid quo pro, such as federal funding for a project high on the list of provincial priorities.

Prime Minister Chrétien continued the practice of appointing regional ministers; Brian Tobin was an especially adroit and influential minister for Atlantic Canada. And by the fall of 2006 it had become clear that the cabinet system set up by the new Harper government, with the operations committee playing a central role in handling sensitive political issues and political ministers designated for each of the provinces, essentially replicated the Mulroney-era model. In brief, regional ministers are alive and well. Furthermore, coalitions of federal ministers, provincial premiers, local MPs, provincial ministers, MLAs, and municipal politicians help each other through intricate horse-trading and logrolling, largely centred on regional development, infrastructure, and employment creation programs. In many ways the relationships are pecuniary in nature, but they are durable and easily cross party lines.

The regional caucuses of the parties constitute another dimension of intrastate activity. All parties with more than one MP per province or region have a regional caucus, which tends to be dominated by the regional or political minister. Paul Thomas, in a detailed study conducted in the 1980s, noted that these regional parliamentary party caucuses tended to be skewed in the direction of 'allocation responsiveness' (i.e., 'generalized benefits for their constituencies'), as opposed to 'symbolic' or 'policy responsiveness' (Thomas, 1985: 74). Nonetheless, regional caucuses will weigh in on broader issues. The Quebec caucus under the firm grip of Marc Lalonde in the last Trudeau government (1980–4) had a significant influence on government policy in areas such as foreign aid, La Francophonie, and protection of the textile and footwear industries based mainly in Quebec (ibid.: 102). One of the flaws of this kind of regional representation at the centre, many argue, is its focus on the pork barrel. Another is that not only allocational activities but also broader representational activities tend to take place under the cloak of caucus secrecy (Thomas, 1985). As a result—even though it is a fundamental principle of political representation that politicians must be seen to be working in the interests of their constituents—the efforts of MPs and ministers on behalf of their provinces will often not be known or visible to the public. Even so, the strictures of party discipline and caucus secrecy have not prevented either ministers or MPs from publicly voicing concerns if they feel important provincial interests are at stake. John Crosbie, the Atlantic regional minister in the Mulroney cabinet, famously rebuked the prime minister and extracted a public apology from the deputy prime minister over a proposed Canada–France fisheries treaty that, in the eyes of Crosbie and the government of his province, would have compromised the cod stocks and other species off Newfoundland (Crosbie, 1997: 261–6). And in the summer of 2006 the Chair of the Saskatchewan Conservative party caucus publicly warned his leader, Prime Minister Stephen Harper, that the Conservative party would face significant damage if the government did 'not stick to the initial promise to exclude non-renewable resources such as oil and gas from the equalization formula' (*Globe and Mail*, 15 Aug. 2006).

In summary, the basic system of regional ministers and caucuses may have evolved and changed, but it is still very much in place. Even in the present era of 'governing from the centre' (Savoie, 1999), regional representation still has some meaning. When a governing party's regional representation in Parliament is uneven, it will tend be much more balanced in cabinet. Thus while Quebec represents only 8 per cent of the Conservatives' seats in Parliament (10 out of 124), close to 20 per cent of Harper's ministers come from there.

Table 6.1 presents data on regional representation in both Parliament and cabinet from 1867 onward. Note that where regional representation is lacking in Parliament, the difference is almost always compensated for in cabinet. The quality and impact of that representation can vary considerably, of course, depending on the ministers, including the prime minister, in question. However, as we noted earlier, even the supposedly centralized cabinet of Jean Chrétien included some powerful regional personalities. In the Canadian context, cabinet government also means party government, and the political parties are still the primary source of recruits for the cabinet. In short, cabinet and party are inextricably linked.

From Chrétien to Harper: Hyper-Regionalism and the Perfect Storm

The 1993 election was a watershed. The collapse of the Progressive Conservative government was unprecedented in Canadian electoral history. The rise of the Reform party in the West and the Bloc Québécois in Quebec, with both parties vying for the mantle of her majesty's official opposition, and the fact that the Liberals drew the bulk of their seats from Ontario, with only spotty representation from other regions of the country, suggested that the regionalization of the party system had entered a new and dangerous phase. While the Liberals could claim representation from all regions of the country, most of their 19 Quebec seats came from Montreal ridings with heavy concentrations of anglophones and non-francophone minorities; the BQ, overwhelmingly, was the voice of francophone Quebec. As well, the Reform party was clearly the first choice of voters in the two most disaffected western provinces, Alberta and British Columbia. In the words of Alan Cairns, '[A]lthough the Liberals won the election, the election's

Table 6.1   Regional Representation in Government Caucus and Federal Cabinet

General election	Governing party[1]	% of seats from (# of seats)				% of cabinet positions from (# of cabinet positions)				
		West[2]	Ont.	Que.	Atl.	Total[3]	West	Ont.	Que.	Atl.
1867	LIBERAL–CONS	—	47.0 (47)	45.0 (45)	8.0 (8)	13	—	38.5 (5)	30.8 (4)	30.8 (4)
1872	CONSERVATIVE	7.1 (7)	38.4 (38)	39.4 (39)	15.2 (15)	13	7.7 (1)	38.5 (5)	23.1 (3)	30.8 (4)
1874	LIBERAL	1.5 (2)	47.8 (65)	25.7 (35)	25.0 (34)	14	—	35.7 (5)	28.6 (4)	35.7 (5)
1878	CONSERVATIVE	5.1 (7)	44.6 (62)	33.8 (47)	16.5 (23)	14	—	35.7 (5)	28.6 (4)	35.7 (5)
1882	CONSERVATIVE	6.5 (9)	40.3 (56)	36.7 (51)	16.5 (23)	14	—	42.9 (6)	28.6 (4)	28.6 (4)
1887	CONSERVATIVE	10.3 (13)	43.7 (55)	26.2 (33)	19.8 (25)	15	—	33.3 (5)	33.3 (5)	33.3 (5)
1891	CONSERVATIVE	11.1 (13)	38.9 (46)	23.7 (28)	26.3 (31)	14	7.1 (1)	35.7 (5)	28.6 (4)	28.6 (4)
1896	LIBERAL	7.6 (9)	36.9 (44)	41.2 (49)	14.3 (17)	14	7.1 (1)	28.6 (4)	35.7 (5)	28.6 (4)
1900	LIBERAL	7.7 (10)	27.7 (36)	44.6 (58)	20.0 (26)	16	6.3(1)	37.5 (6)	31.3 (5)	25.1 (4)
1904	LIBERAL	14.6 (20)	27.7 (38)	38.7 (53)	19.0 (26)	16	12.5 (2)	37.5 (6)	31.3 (5)	18.8 (3)
1908	LIBERAL	13.5 (18)	27.8 (37)	39.1 (52)	19.6 (26)	14	14.3 (2)	35.7 (5)	28.6 (4)	21.4 (3)
1911	CONSERVATIVE	13.6 (18)	54.6 (72)	19.7 (26)	12.1 (16)	18	22.2 (4)	38.9 (7)	27.8 (5)	11.1 (2)
1917	UNIONIST	36.0 (54)	48.0 (72)	2.0 (3)	14.0 (21)	22	27.3 (6)	40.9 (9)	18.2 (4)	13.6 (3)
1921	Liberal	5.2 (6)	17.2 (20)	56.0 65)	21.6 (25)	19	15.8 (3)	31.6 (6)	31.6 (6)	21.1(4)
1925	Conservative	18.4 (21)	58.8 (67)	2.6 (3)	20.2 (23)	14	21.4 (3)	14.3 (2)	57.1 (8)	7.1 (1)
1926	LIBERAL	21.4 (25)	18.8 (22)	52.1 (61)	7.7 (9)	18	27.8 (5)	22.2 (4)	38.9 (7)	11.1 (2)

Table 6.1   (continued)

General election	Governing party[1]	% of seats from (# of seats)				Total[3]	% of cabinet positions from (# of cabinet positions)			
		West[2]	Ont.	Que.	Atl.		West	Ont.	Que.	Atl.
1930	CONSERVATIVE	22.6 (31)	43.1 (59)	17.5 (24)	16.8 (23)	19	21.1 (4)	36.8 (7)	26.3 (5)	15.8 (3)
1935	LIBERAL	20.3 (35)	32.6 (56)	32.6 (56)	14.5 (25)	16	25.0 (4)	25.0 (4)	31.3 (5)	18.7 (3)
1940	LIBERAL	23.9 (43)	31.1 (56)	34.4 (62)	10.6 (19)	18	27.8 (5)	27.8 (5)	27.8 (5)	16.6 (3)
1945	LIBERAL	15.6 (19)	27.9 (34)	40.9 (50)	15.6 (19)	20	20.0 (4)	35.0 (7)	30.0 (6)	15.0 (3)
1949	LIBERAL	22.0 (42)	28.8 (55)	35.6 (68)	13.6 (26)	21	19.0 (4)	33.3 (7)	28.6 (6)	19.0 (4)
1953	LIBERAL	15.9 (27)	29.4 (50)	38.8 (66)	15.9 (27)	20	25.0 (5)	30.0 (6)	30.0 (6)	15.0 (3)
1957	Progressive Conservative	20.3 (23)	54.0(61)	7.1 (8)	18.6 (21)	22	36.4 (8)	31.8 (7)	13.6 (3)	18.2 (4)
1958	PROGRESSIVE CONSERVATIVE	31.6 (66)	32.5 (68)	23.9 (50)	12.0 (25)	2?	30.4 (7)	30.4 (7)	21.8 (5)	17.4 (4)
1962	Progressive Conservative	42.2 (49)	30.2 (35)	12.1 (14)	15.5 (18)	21	33.3 (7)	33.3 (7)	19.0 (4)	14.3 (3)
1963	Liberal	7.8 (10)	39.8 (51)	36.7 (47)	15.6 (20)	26	15.4 (4)	38.4 (10)	30.8 (8)	15.4 (4)
1965	Liberal	6.9 (9)	38.9 (51)	42.7 (56)	11.5 (15)	26	11.5 (3)	34.6 (9)	34.6 (9)	11.5 (3)
1968	LIBERAL	18.2 (28)	40.9 (63)	36.4 (56)	4.5 (7)	29	20.7 (6)	34.5 (10)	34.5 (10)	10.3 (3)
1972	Liberal	6.4 (7)	33.0 (36)	51.4 (56)	9.2 (10)	30	13.3 (4)	40.0 (12)	33.3 (10)	13.3 (4)
1974	LIBERAL	9.2 (13)	39.0 (55)	42.6 (60)	9.2 (13)	29	13.8 (4)	34.5 (10)	37.9 (11)	13.8 (4)

Table 6.1   (continued)

General election	Governing party[1]	% of seats from (# of seats)				Total[3]	% of cabinet positions from (# of cabinet positions)			
		West[2]	Ont.	Que.	Atl.		West	Ont.	Que.	Atl.
1979	Progressive Conservative	43.4 (59)	41.9 (57)	1.5 (2)	13.2 (18)	30	30.0 (9)	40.0 (12)	13.3 (4)	16.7 (5)
1980	LIBERAL	1.4 (2)	35.4 (52)	50.3 (74)	12.9 (19)	33	12.1 (4)	36.4 (12)	36.4 (12)	15.1 (5)
1984	PROGRESSIVE CONSERVATIVE	28.9 (61)	31.8 (67)	27.5 (58)	11.8 (25)	40	32.5 (13)	27.5 (11)	27.5 (11)	12.5 (5)
1988	PROGRESSIVE CONSERVATIVE	28.4 (48)	27.2 (46)	37.3 (63)	7.1 (12)	33	24.2 (8)	33.3 (11)	30.3 (10)	12.1 (4)
1993	LIBERAL	16.4 (29)	55.4 (98)	10.7 (19)	17.5 (31)	23	21.7 (5)	43.5 (10)	21.7 (5)	13.1 (3)
1997	LIBERAL	11.0 (17)	65.2 (101)	16.7 (26)	7.1 (11)	28	17.6 (5)	42.9 (12)	25.0 (7)	14.3 (4)
2000	LIBERAL	9.4 (16)	58.5 (100)	21.1 (36)	11.1 (19)	28	17.6 (5)	42.9 (12)	25.0 (7)	14.3 (4)
2004	Liberal	11.9 (16)	55.2 (74)	15.6 (21)	17.1 (23)	38	23.6 (9)	39.4 (15)	21.0 (8)	15.7 (6)
2006	Conservative	53.2 (66)	31.4 (39)	8.0 (10)	7.3 (9)	27	40.7 (11)	33.3 (9)	18.5 (5)	11.1 (3)

1. Upper-case = majority government; lower-case = minority government.

2. 'West' includes NWT, Yukon, and Nunavut.

3. Size of cabinet for the year of each general election includes changes occurring up to and including 31 December of that year (i.e., includes the last ministerial shuffles for each portfolio but does not include portfolios terminated in that year).

SOURCE: Guide to Canadian Ministries since Confederation (Canada: Privy Council Office, 2006); Senators and Members – Historical Information (Canada: Library of Parliament, 2006).

overall symbolic message was of an old order tottering, of its possible replacement by one knew not what, and thus that Canadians, haltingly and apprehensively, were beginning a new era' (1994: 226).

The intimation of dangerous times was reinforced by the return to power of the Parti Québécois a year later and the holding of the second referendum in 15 years in the fall of 1995. That was the closest Canada has come to seeing one of its constituent units make a unilateral declaration of sovereignty: the referendum was won by the No side with only the slimmest of margins. After the crisis of the referendum, however, the Chrétien government governed much as previous Liberal governments had: from the centre, finding informal ways to accommodate Quebec's demands. Especially after Chrétien's third victory in 2000, it appeared that Canada's 'government party' had successfully revived its traditional formula and was now poised to extend its benign dictatorship (Simpson, 2001) indefinitely into the twenty-first century (Tanguay, 2003). The government's deficit slashing under Program Review had been largely successfu. Especially in the 2000 election, the Liberals had made gains in Quebec at the expense of the Bloc (Tanguay, 2006).

There were some crucial differences from the past, however. The regional coalitions under King, St Laurent, and Mulroney had had three components: Quebec, Ontario, and the West (usually a single province such as Alberta or Saskatchewan). In the Chrétien era Ontario for the first time became the Liberals' single stronghold. Aside from the fact that the principal voices from Quebec and the West represented not a competing national party but two distinct regional parties (Reform in the West and the nationalist Bloc in Quebec), there were two other features serving to undermine the role of the Liberal party as a broker of regional interests.

First, the Liberals' total dominance in Ontario, and in turn the dominance of the parliamentary party by the Ontario Liberal caucus, proved in many ways a perfect illustration of Chandler's thesis that party competition in a single-party majority (i.e., Westminster) system can exacerbate conflict in a federal system. Essentially, the 100-plus members of the Ontario federal Liberal caucus took it on themselves to do battle with the controversial Conservative provincial government of Mike Harris. Historically, Ontario has never enjoyed a single regional minister; rather, a number of ministers—for the Toronto area, southwestern Ontario, northern Ontario, and so on—have represented different parts of the province in both Liberal and Conservative governments over the years (Bakvis, 1991). In the Chrétien government, ministers such as Sheila Copps at times undermined negotiations between Ottawa and the Ontario government on issues such as labour-market development because they were unwilling to see federal dollars transferred to, and spent by, a provincial government with a reputation for slashing social programs. As a result, Ontario was the only province with which Ottawa was unable to negotiate a labour-market development agreement in 1997 (Bakvis, 2002).

Two other factors that ultimately undermined the Liberal party were directly related to its dominance and the absence of an effective opposition. First, when a single party is so dominant that it represents the only route to political power, eventually factions begin to form within it. In the Liberal party factionalism took the form of a bitter conflict between Chrétien loyalists and supporters of his Finance minister, Paul Martin, who had lost the race for the party leadership to Chrétien in 1990.

Second, a dominant party facing a weak or fragmented opposition is almost certain to develop pockets of corruption. In the Liberal case the corruption manifested itself in what has become known as the sponsorship scandal. In 2002 newspaper reports surfaced on inflated contracts for government advertising, primarily in Quebec, as part of the national unity campaign that Ottawa launched in the aftermath of the 1995 referendum. Further reports indicated that some of the money attached to these contracts was being kicked back to members of the federal Liberal party in Quebec. A subsequent report by the Auditor General and a full-scale judicial inquiry under Justice John Gomery found there was substance to the allegations. The Gomery inquiry was just beginning its work at the time of the 2004 election, but the scandal likely cost the new Liberal leader, Paul Martin, his majority. The crisis only deepened as Quebecers—outraged to learn that the Liberals had thought they could win support for the federalist option with a few Canadian flags—watched the proceedings of the Gomery Inquiry unfold on television. Public opinion polls indicated that Liberal support in Quebec was in free fall.

In this way the stage was set for a perfect storm in the party system. The Bloc, clearly positioning itself to capture the support of previous Liberal voters, stood to obtain its largest seat share ever. And even though the Conservative party was gaining elsewhere in Canada, it appeared unlikely to make significant inroads in Ontario, let alone Quebec, whether because of its Western origins or its social conservatism. Yet its leader—showing a remarkable capacity to distance himself from his party's Reform roots—was willing to promise not only separate Quebec representation in international cultural and educational bodies such as UNESCO but a resolution to the putative federal–provincial fiscal imbalance—an issue that was high on the Quebec government's agenda. The election of January 2006 saw the Conservatives not only break through in Ontario but win 10 seats in Quebec, where there had been none before. Thus the perfect storm was averted: even though the Liberals clearly lost in Quebec, the Bloc failed to make significant gains, falling short of the high-water mark of 54 seats won in 1993. With the Liberals at 102 seats and the Conservatives at 125, Paul Martin, following the peculiarly Canadian convention on minority governments, turned in his mandate to the governor general, who duly invited Stephen Harper to form a minority government. In addition to signifying that one-party dominance was not necessarily a permanent feature of the Canadian party system, the election of 2006 demonstrated that it was still possible for a second national party to gain a significant foothold in the province of Quebec.

There were some other noteworthy features to the new Conservative minority government. No fewer than seven of Harper's 27 ministers had served in provincial cabinets—one of the highest proportions ever, not seen since the days of Macdonald and Laurier. In addition to bringing some of their provincial sensibilities to the cabinet table, they no doubt also brought the new government hands-on and recent experience in elected office—a rare advantage for a party that has been out of office for a while. This feature clearly fits the Riker model of an integrated party system, in which personnel moving from the regional to the national level bring with them a number of positive attributes. It is also a feature that, as Smiley (1987) and Barrie and Gibbins (1989) have argued, has been largely absent from the Canadian party system.

Also notable is the presence in cabinet of no fewer than five representatives from Quebec, including Lawrence Cannon, who had served in the Liberal cabinet of Robert Bourassa, and Josée Verner, who was also closely associated with the Bourassa government as an adviser in the 1980s. Half (14) of Harper's ministers come from Ontario and Quebec, a proportion that no doubt reflects not only the weight that central Canada carries both electorally and in the federal system but also the Conservatives' desire to strengthen their position for the next election in those two provinces.

The seats gained by the Conservatives and the links between provincial and federal governments may inspire hope that at long last the party system will once again be able to carry some of the burden of national unity. This hope may be premature or foolish or both; the perfect storm may yet arise. Individually or collectively, Canada's Afghanistan mission, the social conservatism of the Conservative party, and the politics of the fiscal imbalance (see Chapter 4 by Douglas Brown), could prove to be the Harper government's undoing. The next election may see the Bloc recover seats lost to the Conservative Party in 2006. Nonetheless, even if the Conservatives were to be defeated in the next election, this would not necessarily mean a return to single-party dominance and a fragmented opposition. Particularly if the pattern of minority government continues beyond the next election, we could see new forms of coalition–building develop, directly involving political parties. This would have important implications for federalism.

Performance, Effectiveness, and Legitimacy

Before turning to our three thematic criteria, let us briefly review our conclusions so far. First, the party system of the past may not always, indeed may never, have performed the role attributed to it. The party omnibus was far from all-encompassing, and when all regions of the country have been represented within a single major party, the results are often calamitous, as Carty (2002) has argued. Party government appeared to work best when it took the form of a minimum winning coalition with three anchors in critical regions of the country.

In the absence of an elected or provincially appointed second chamber, in the context of an electoral system that routinely produces wide discrepancies between popular votes and seats, the institution that makes the system work has always been the federal cabinet. Regional representation in cabinet was the critical link in the eras of both Macdonald and King. When a governing party's regional representation in Parliament is uneven, that imbalance can be compensated for in cabinet.

At a minimum it would be unwise to assume there was ever a halcyon period when parties played a more critical role in linking regions to the centre. As we have argued, federal and provincial party systems were already bifurcated in the 1920s and 1930s, ostensibly the heyday of regional brokerage; and parties in general have always been limited in terms of the regional interests they could accommodate at any one time. In short, it may be unrealistic to use the past either as a standard by which to judge the current party system or as a model we might wish to recreate in order to relieve the present system of executive federalism of some of the burden of national unity. A not unreasonable assessment might be that the Canadian party system was never all that critical to the function of federalism; the Canadian federation survived despite the limited integrative capacity of Canadian parties.

National unity or integration is the chief criterion used in discussing the performance and effectiveness of the Canadian party system in relation to federalism. Yet here again one might ask whether our expectations in this respect are not perhaps unrealistic, given the tendency to romanticize earlier times. Second, one can ask whether integration should be the most important criterion for judging performance and effectiveness. Federalism is about more than integration; it is about diversity as well. Divergence between the federal and provincial levels may simply mean that the federation is working as it should: allowing the constituent units to give expression to their local and regional identities and to pursue goals important to them. Furthermore, one of the functions of political parties, and one central to the democratic process, is to compete with other parties for the affections of voters (Elkins, 1991).

There is an accommodative side to political parties. Accommodation takes place both within parties (as evidenced by their efforts to represent a variety of interests, including regional interests), and between parties (most common in systems where coalition government is the norm). In Canada the competitive side of parties may be more pronounced, but it would be naive to think that even in more accommodative systems the competitive dimension of parties is largely absent. The best examples of a totally integrated party system can be found in the old quasi-federations such as the former Soviet Union in the era when the Communist party was the primary instrument of control, or Mexico when the PRI dominated both the state and national governments. These are extreme examples, to be sure, but they underscore the idea that beyond a certain point integration may be too much of a good thing. Yet it would be misleading to suggest that Canadian parties are lacking with respect to inter-party collaboration.

In the event, in applying the assessment criteria of performance, effectiveness, and legitimacy, we should include not only the integrative dimension but also the extent to which parties contribute to diversity in a federation and help foster flexibility and responsiveness. These three elements are related; for instance, integrative capacity may be improved when the party system demonstrates flexibility. In assessing performance, for example, we likely have in mind the capacity of the system to facilitate upward mobility by channelling politicians from the provincial level to the federal, thereby helping to foster informal linkages, trust, and understanding between the two levels.

The Canadian system has never fared very well in this regard. Barrie and Gibbins note 'that career mobility from provincial to national office is the exception rather than the rule' (1989: 138) and that mobility has declined over time. Even during the King era, the number of provincial figures moving to Ottawa was actually quite limited, and some of those moves involved crossing party lines. On the other hand, the crossing of party lines does suggest flexibility. The appointment of figures closely associated with the Liberal government of Robert Bourassa in Quebec to the Harper cabinet was noted earlier. Jean Charest's transformation from leader of the federal Progressive Conservative party to that of the Quebec Liberal party can be seen as a successful move in the other direction. And Paul Martin recruited Ujjal Dosanjh, former NDP premier of British Columbia, as his minister of Health.

Thus the fact that overall mobility between provincial and federal parliaments may be low and the links between federal and provincial parties weak has not prevented close interaction between individual ministers in the federal and provincial governments. Even if their attention is often focused on what Thomas (1985) calls allocational issues, the more astute ministers will take their regional role seriously and use it to convey broader regional concerns directly into cabinet; meanwhile, other ministers and their staffs, as well as the prime minister, will often consult regional ministers to get a sense of the way various issues might play out in their particular regions or provinces. In brief, while it can be argued that the Canadian federation would perform better if the career path of federal politicians were to incorporate a stint in a provincial legislature, and ideally as a member of the same party, the Canadian federation and party system have been able to overcome this obstacle.

At the same time, simply having the same party in power at both the federal and provincial levels is no guarantee that relations will be closer, friendlier, or more effective. The pitched battles between Lester Pearson and Premier Ross Thatcher of Saskatchewan, or Mackenzie King and Mitch Hepburn of Ontario—all of them Liberals—are legendary. Equally famous (or infamous) was the support given by Robert Bourassa, as the Liberal premier of Quebec, to Conservative Prime Minister Brian Mulroney in the 1988 federal election campaign, to the chagrin of federal Liberal leader John Turner. At a minimum, these examples suggest that common partisan ties are not likely to be terribly helpful when it comes to bridging major divisions between governments; conversely, partisan differences are not likely to be a major hindrance when it comes to forging partnerships when there is a common interest.

At this stage it may be useful to recall the coalition model of parties and federalism. Carty and Wolinetz (2004) note that inter-party coalitions in federal systems are much more common in Europe than in Canada. It can argued, however, that Canada has its own unique practice of inter-party coalition-building, though it is not formally labelled as such. It is found primarily in the context of minority government. While there have been no formal agreements between parliamentary parties, extensive consultation and negotiation on an issue-by-issue basis is a hallmark of Canadian-style minority government. Some minority governments have been famously short-lived—notably the Conservative governments of Meighen (1926) and Clark (1979–80) but others, such as the Pearson government of 1963–8, have survived for longer periods. The 1962–8 period coincidently saw the introduction of most of the major federal–provincial social programs, such as medicare and the Canada and Quebec pension plans, as well as a major expansion of the equalization system (see Chapters 4 and 7 by Brown and Banting respectively).

In the most recent period of minority government, beginning in 2004 with Martin and continuing with Harper, we see a familiar pattern emerge: the NDP supporting the Martin government budget in 2005 on the understanding that more money would be devoted to post-secondary education; the Conservatives counting on the support of the NDP when they clamped down on income trusts; and in November 2006, the three federalist parties (and ultimately the Bloc itself) joining together to support the Conservative motion affirming the status of the Québécois as a nation within a united Canada. The Harper motion came about not through intricate federal–provincial bargaining but in the cut and thrust of parliamentary manoeuvring, and ultimately agreement, among the four parties. Thus under conditions of minority government there is greater potential for Canadian parties to contribute to the unity question. Note, however, that this does not necessarily mean an enhanced role for Parliament as an arena for debate or for individual parliamentarians. This kind of inter-party bargaining tends to centre on party leaders. As a consequence there may well be greater centralization within parties and concomitantly greater reliance on instruments such as party discipline. No doubt over time there will be questions raised about the legitimacy of a process so driven by party elites.

A number of the tantalizing questions identified earlier remain: first, whether the pattern of minority government will continue; second, whether substantial issues of a federal–provincial nature will increasingly be raised, discussed, and perhaps even resolved among political parties rather than in the context of executive federalism; and, third, whether the latter is contingent on the former. A further question is whether this pattern can be seen as a positive development. We would argue that it can be, if one assumes or accepts that it may be better for regional voices to express themselves directly and openly through regionally based parties than to be subsumed in traditional brokerage-style national parties—as long as such regional parties are balanced with others offering a national vision. Legitimacy (perhaps the most critical, and the scarcest, commodity of all) is more likely to develop in the context of open debate in Parliament and parliamentary committees than that of traditional elite accommodation either in the federal–provincial arena or within traditional brokerage parties. Among the challenges that lie ahead, therefore, is the need to wrest control of these debates away from the inner party elites and shift it to the broader arena of Parliament.

Note

We would like to acknowledge the research assistance of Shannon Wells in compiling the data in Table 6.1, as well as the financial support provided by the Social Sciences and Humanities Research Council.

References

Bakvis, Herman. 1991. *Regional Ministers: Power and Influence in the Canadian Cabinet*. Toronto: University of Toronto Press.

———. 2002. 'Checkerboard Federalism? Labour Market Development Policy in Canada', in *Canadian Federalism: Performance, Effectiveness, and Legitimacy*. Ed. H. Bakvis and G. Skogstad. Toronto: Oxford University Press.

Barrie, Doreen, and Roger Gibbins. 1989. 'Parliamentary Careers in the Canadian Federal State', *Canadian Journal of Political Science* 22, 1: 137–45.

Cairns, Alan C. 1973 [1968]. 'The Electoral System and the Party System in Canada, 1921–1965'. In *The Canadian Political Process*, ed. O. Kruhlak, R. Schultz, and S. Pobihushchy. Rev. edn. Toronto: Holt, Rinehart and Winston, 133–58. Originally published in the *Canadian Journal of Political Science* 1, 1 (March 1968).

Cairns, Alan C. 1994. 'An Election to Be Remembered: Canada 1993', *Canadian Public Policy* 20, 3: 219–34.

Carty, R. Kenneth. 1988. 'Three Canadian Party Systems: An Interpretation of the Development of National Politics'. In *Party Democracy in Canada*, ed. George Perlin. Scarborough: Prentice-Hall.

———. 2002. 'The Politics of Tecumseh Corners: Canadian Political Parties as Franchise Organizations', *Canadian Journal of Political Science* 35, 4: 723–45.

——— and Stephen Wolinetz. 2004. 'Political Parties and the Canadian Federation's Coalition Politics' In *Canada: The State of the Federation 2002: Reconsidering the Institutions of Canadian Federalism*, ed. J. Peter Meekison, Hamish Telford, and Harvey Lazar. Kingston: Institute of Intergovernmental Relations.

Clarkson, Stephen. 2001. 'The Liberal Threepeat: The Multi-System Party in the Multi-Party System'. In *The Canadian General Election of 2000*, ed. Jon Pammett and Christopher Dornan. Toronto: Dundurn.

Covell, Maureen. 1991. 'Parties as Institutions of National Governance'. In *Representation, Integration and Political Parties in Canada*, ed. Herman Bakvis. Toronto: Dundurn Press.

Crosbie, John. 1997. *No Holds Barred: My Life In Politics*. Toronto: McClelland and Stewart.

Dyck, Rand. 1996. 'Relations Between Federal and Provincial Parties'. In *Canadian Parties in Transition*, ed. A. Brian Tanguay and Alain-G. Gagnon. 2nd edn. Scarborough, Ont.: Nelson.

Elkins, David. 1991. 'Parties as National Institutions: A Comparative Study'. In *Representation, Integration and Political Parties in Canada*, ed. Herman Bakvis. Toronto: Dundurn Press.

English, John. 1977. *The Decline of Politics: The Conservatives and the Party System, 1901–1920*. Toronto: University of Toronto Press.

Gagnon, Alain-G. and A. Brian Tanguay. 1996. 'Minor Parties in the Canadian Political System: Origins, Functions, Impact'. In *Canadian Parties in Transition*, ed. A. Brian Tanguay and Alain-G. Gagnon. 2nd edn. Scarborough, Ont.: Nelson.

King, Anthony. 1969. 'Political Parties in Western Democracies: Some Sceptical Reflections', *Polity* 2, 2: 111–41.

Mallory, J.R. 1954. *Social Credit and the Federal Power in Canada*. Toronto: University of Toronto Press.

McRoberts, Kenneth 1997. *Misconceiving Canada: The Struggle for National Unity*. Toronto: Oxford University Press.

Noel, S.J.R. 1996. 'Patronage and Entourages, Action-Sets, Networks'. In *Canadian Parties in Transition*, ed. A. Brian Tanguay and Alain-G. Gagnon. 2nd edn. Scarborough, Ont.: Nelson.

Riker, William H. 1964. *Federalism: Origin, Operation, Significance*. Boston: Little, Brown.

Savoie, Donald J. 1999. *Governing from the Centre: The Concentration of Power in Canadian Politics*. Toronto: University of Toronto Press.

Sharman, Campbell 1994. 'Discipline and Disharmony: Party and the Operation of the Australian Federal System'. In *Parties and Federalism in Australia and Canada*, ed. C. Sharman. Canberra: Federalism Research Centre, The Australian National University,

Simpson, Jeffrey. 1988. *Spoils of Power: The Politics of Patronage*. Toronto: Collins.

———. 2001. *The Friendly Dictatorship*. Toronto: McClelland and Stewart.

Smiley, D.V. 1987. *The Federal Condition in Canada*. Toronto: McGraw-Hill Ryerson.

Smith, David E. 1985. 'Party Government, Representation and National Integration in Canada'. In *Party Government and Regional Representation in Canada*, ed. Peter Aucoin. Toronto: University of Toronto Press.

Sunahara, Ann Gomer 1981. *The Politics of Racism: The Uprooting of Japanese Canadians During the Second World War*. Toronto: Lorimer.

Tanguay, A. Brian. 1999. 'Canada's Political Parties in the 1990s: The Fraying of the Ties that Bind'. In *Canada: The State of the Federation 1998/99*, ed. Harvey Lazar and Tom McIntosh. Montreal and Kingston: McGill–Queen's University Press, published for the School of Policy Studies, Queens' University.

———. 2003. 'Canada's Quasi-Party System: the Causes and Consequences of

Liberal Hegemony', *Inroads* 12 (Winter/Spring): 136–41.

———. 2006. 'Quebec and the Canadian Federal Election of 2000: Putting the Sovereignty Movement on the Ropes?' In *The Elections of 2000: Politics, Culture and Economics in North America*, ed. Mary K. Kirtz, Mark J. Kasoff, Rick Farmer, and John C. Green. Akron, Ohio: University of Akron Press.

Thomas, Paul G. 1985. 'The Role of National Party Caucuses'. In *Party Government and Regional Representation in Canada*, ed. Peter Aucoin. Toronto: University of Toronto Press.

Wearing, Joseph. 1981. *The L-Shaped Party: The Liberal Party of Canada, 1958–1980*. Toronto: McGraw-Hill Ryerson.

Whitaker, Reginald. 1977. *The Government Party: Organizing and Financing the Liberal Party of Canada, 1930–58*. Toronto: University of Toronto Press.

Part Two

The Social and Economic Union

Chapter 7

The Three Federalisms: Social Policy and Intergovernmental Decision-Making

Keith G. Banting

Canada has never adopted a single approach to federalism. Rather, we have chosen to live with three distinct models of federalism—three federalisms in one country—each with its own decision rules and intergovernmental processes. Social policy reflects all three models particularly well. Throughout the history of the Canadian welfare state, federal and provincial governments have designed different social programs according to different intergovernmental rules and processes. The distinctive incentives and constraints inherent in the different models help explain a number of puzzles about the Canadian welfare state, including the striking contrast between the limited nature of the country's income security programs and the more universalist character of its health care. Moreover, in recent decades, the three models help explain the highly uneven impact of retrenchment on different social programs.

This chapter develops these themes in four sections. The first section describes the federal–provincial division of jurisdiction in social policy and the three models of federalism. The second section examines the impact of the three federalisms on the expansion of the welfare state in the middle decades of the twentieth century, while the third section examines their impact on the politics of retrenchment in recent decades. A final section then pulls together the threads of the argument.

The Three Federalisms and Social Policy

In formal terms, authority over social policy is divided between the federal and provincial governments in ways that make Canada one of the most decentralized federations in the world (Banting, 2006). From the outset, the Constitution Act, 1867 gave the provinces a central role in social policy, with specific sections granting them authority over education, hospitals, and related charitable institutions. In addition, the courts extended the provincial role by subsuming social policy under provincial powers over 'property and civil rights' and 'matters of a local or private nature'. In a key decision in 1937, the courts struck down a federal social insurance program as intruding on these provincial powers.

Despite the centrality of provincial jurisdiction, the federal government also has a significant presence in social policy. Amendments to the Constitution in the middle of the twentieth century gave federal authorities full jurisdiction over unemployment insurance and substantial jurisdiction over contributory pensions. Federal tax powers also constitute a powerful tool of social redistribution, especially with the development of refundable tax credits. However, the cornerstone of the federal role has been implicit rather than explicit in the Constitution. According to constitutional doctrine, 'the federal Parliament may spend or lend its funds to any government or institution or individual it chooses, for any purpose it chooses; and it may attach to any grant or loan any conditions it chooses, including conditions it could not directly legislate' (Hogg, 2001: 6.8a). This convention, known as the doctrine of the spending power, has been challenged both politically and judicially. In the mid-1950s, for example, a Quebec Royal Commission asked: 'What would be the use of a careful description of legislative powers if one of the governments could get around it and, to some extent, annul it by its taxation methods and its fashion of spending?' (Quebec, 1956, vol. 2: 217). Nevertheless, court decisions repeatedly sustained the federal position, and the spending power became the constitutional footing for a number of central pillars of the welfare state. It has helped sustain federal benefits paid directly to citizens, such as Family Allowances; it provides a constitutional basis for shared-cost programs through which the federal government supports provincial social programs; and at the outset it provided authority for equalization grants, which are federal transfers to the poorer provinces designed to enable them to provide average levels of public services without having to resort to above-average levels of taxation.[1]

With federal and provincial governments both engaged in social policy, much depends on the mechanisms through which they manage their interdependence. It is here that the three models of federalism emerge sharply. Each of these models posits a different set of relationships between federal and provincial governments. Each model generates its own decision rules, altering the range of governments in the process, the power of different governments at the table, and the level of intergovernmental consensus required for a decision. And each model has different implications for policy outcomes. The three models can be summarized in simple terms:

- *Classical federalism*: Some programs are delivered by the federal or provincial governments acting independently within their own jurisdiction:

unemployment benefits, child benefits, non-contributory old-age pensions at the federal level; workers' compensation at the provincial level. This model involves unilateral decisions by both levels of government, with minimal efforts at co-ordination even when decisions at one level have a serious impact on programs at the other level.

In the classical model, the federal and provincial governments behave in their own domain much as unitary governments would do. Decisions are more flexible, requiring no elaborate intergovernmental consensus, and policy can shift dramatically with changes in the government in power, interest-group pressures, or public opinion. At the federal level, policy-makers are still sensitive to different regional interests in a program such as unemployment benefits, but provincial governments have no formal role in the decisions.

- *Shared-cost federalism*: Under this model, the federal government offers financial support to social programs operated by provincial governments on specific terms. This instrument underpinned the development of major sectors of the welfare state, including health care, post-secondary education, social assistance, and social services.[2] The shared-cost model generates an intermediate level of constraint on government action. In formal terms, each government makes separate decisions: the federal government decides when, what, and how to support provincial programs; and each provincial government must decide whether to accept the money and the terms. In practice, however, the substance of new programs has tended to be hammered out in intergovernmental negotiations. This process increases the range of governments at the table, and opens more channels for new ideas to be injected into the decision process. But, because there are no formal decision rules for this process, agreements depend on a broad intergovernmental consensus or—in some cases—acquiescence.

Any tendency to consensus is not absolute in this model, however. The shared-cost mechanism retains a potential for unilateral action, as became clear when the federal government began to cut its financial commitments to provincial programs in the 1980s and 1990s. But the political scope for unilateralism is still more constrained than in the classical model. As long as the two levels of government remain committed to the policy sector, they both have stakes in the programs and are held accountable by the electorate. Governments tend to push back politically against unilateralism at the other level, generating pressures over time for a return to consensus decision-making. In their Introduction, the editors of this volume highlight an enduring dynamic of competition and co-operation in Canadian federalism, and the shared-cost model certainly reflects these realities. Over the decades, the pattern has been a fluctuating one of co-operation, unilateralism, and uneasy co-operation, all of which inclines the sector towards a more incremental, evolutionary pattern of policy change than would prevail in the classical model.

- *Joint-decision federalism*: In this model, the formal agreement of both levels of government is required before any action is possible. Unilateralism is not an option here. The major example is the Canada Pension Plan, changes in which legally require an elaborate intergovernmental agreement. The essential feature of this model is that nothing happens unless formal approval is given by both levels of government.

  As in the case of shared-cost federalism, this model increases the range of governments and ideologies at the table. But the formal requirement for a strong intergovernmental majority sets the bar especially high in terms of intergovernmental consensus and reduces the probability of change. In effect, the joint-decision model creates buffers against the shifting currents of democratic politics.

With three distinct models of federalism in operation, the politics of Canadian social policy represent a natural laboratory in which to dissect the impact of institutions on public policy. During the mid-1960s, the same federal government expanded different social programs at the same time and in the same political context, but according to different decision rules. As we shall see, the outcomes differed. Similarly, in the late 1980s and 1990s, the federal government restructured different programs at the same time and in the same political context, but according to different decision rules. Again, the rules mattered to the outcomes. The following two sections highlight these consequences during the development of the welfare state and during its subsequent restructuring in the era of retrenchment.

The Three Federalisms and the Development of the Welfare State

Canada laid down the basic planks of its version of the welfare state between the 1940s and the mid-1970s. As in other countries, the primary pressures for social reform came from changes in the political economy of the country: the emergence of an industrial economy; the steady urbanization of the population; the unionization of the labour force; the mobilization of left-wing political parties in the form of the CCF–NDP; the ideological conversion of policy elites to Keynesian economics; and a widely shared faith in the capacity of state action to solve important economic and social problems.

In Canada, however, reformist pressures were refracted through federal institutions. The early post-war years were a period of unparalleled political dominance by the federal government. The war centralized power dramatically, bequeathing federal authorities with a highly professional bureaucracy and— most importantly—dominance of the primary tax fields. After the war, Ottawa was anxious to retain enough of the tax fields to expand conditional grant programs and equalization payments to poorer provinces. Provincial governments, however, fought to recapture tax room to finance education, health, and social

Figure 7.1   Federal and Provincial/Local Government Shares of Total Public Revenues

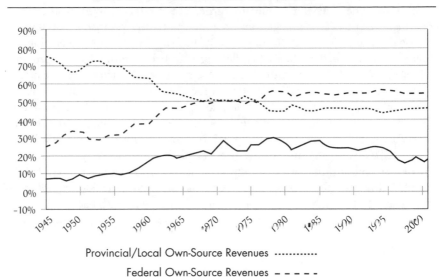

Provincial/Local Own-Source Revenues ··············

Federal Own-Source Revenues – – – – –

Federal Transfers ——————
(as % of Federal Revenues)

SOURCE: Lazar et al. (2004: 171).

services on their own terms. In effect, the struggle was for control over the Canadian welfare state. Federal dominance was to erode over time, as Figure 7.1 indicates, but in the early days Ottawa controlled the purse strings.

In addition, linguistic and regional tensions, while never absent, were at a historic low tide in the 1940s and 1950s. The provinces accepted constitutional amendments to strengthen federal jurisdiction, and many English-speaking provinces lobbied for broader federal engagement. In these early stages, only Quebec complained about federal pre-emption of social policy terrain, but it was not in a strong position to resist. Dominated by a conservative, clerical tradition, the province was not committed to building its own social programs and was therefore vulnerable to federal initiatives that proved popular with the Quebec electorate.

The federal government capitalized on its early strength, introducing several programs during the war years and announcing a sweeping package of proposals as part of post-war reconstruction in a series of Green Books before the 1945 election. The package collapsed at a federal–provincial conference later that year, when the two largest provinces rejected the associated proposals on intergovernmental finances. Nevertheless, the Green Book proposals represented a coherent agenda that the federal government pursued on an incremental basis over the next two decades.

The high tide of federal dominance turned out to be short-lived. By the 1960s, provincial resistance was beginning to grow. With the resurgence of Quebec nationalism and the Quiet Revolution, Quebec was increasingly determined to build a *provincial* welfare state, one reflecting a Québécois sensibility. The province declared an end to new jurisdictional concessions and launched a campaign to recapture ground lost in earlier decades. In 1965, Quebec won the right to 'opt out' of a number of national shared-cost programs, receiving additional tax room from the federal government so that it could operate the programs on its own. The victory was partly symbolic, since the province agreed to meet existing conditions associated with the programs. Nevertheless, symbolic asymmetry signalled that the era of easy centralization was over. In time, other provinces also came to resent the detailed controls and financial tensions implicit in traditional shared-cost programs, and by the mid-1970s provinces generally began to push back.

Beneath these highly visible swings of the pendulum of power, however, federal institutions left their imprint on new social programs in more subtle ways. Much depended on the model of federalism at work.

Classical Federalism and Exclusively Federal Programs

In comparison with the need for consensus among governments of different political ideologies in the other models, decisions about exclusively federal programs reflected the ideological orientation of the governing party. Since the Liberals formed the government continuously from 1935 until the end of the 1970s, with the exception of a short interregnum from 1957 to 1963, the programs were shaped by the centrist orientation of the Liberal Party, which favoured social programs but ones of relatively modest proportions. The more social democratic perspective of the CCF–NDP was articulated by the party's representatives in Parliament, but theirs was only one voice in the political cacophony of the day. The NDP did have more influence when the Liberals were in a minority in Parliament in 1963–8 and 1972–4, but even then the party's influence was indirect, affecting choices made within the Liberal cabinet.

These dynamics proved critical in the field of income security. In contrast to health care, the programs that emerged were relatively modest compared to the programs developed in many other Western democracies. The first step came in 1940 when a constitutional amendment gave the federal government full authority over unemployment insurance. The Unemployment Insurance (UI) program, which followed that same year, was the first major social insurance program in the country. By comparative standards, however, the Liberals' plan was limited. While it covered most of the industrial workforce, it excluded workers in agriculture, fishing, and private domestic service, as well as public employees and high-income earners. Moreover, the benefit replacement rate was only 50 per cent of wages, with a small supplement for married claimants.

Family Allowances came next. In 1944, the federal government introduced a universal, flat-rate benefit funded from general tax revenues. By the standards of similar programs in Europe, the benefits were modest, providing an average monthly payment of $14.18 per family (Guest, 1997: 132). There was little federal–provincial conflict over the program. Quebec did object, and passed a short bill authorizing a provincial plan if the federal government would withdraw. However, the province had no formal role in the process, and its attack 'was launched too late and soon decreased as the political danger of fighting such a popular measure became clear' (Jean, 1992: 403).

Pensions represented the final step. In 1951, another constitutional amendment gave the federal government authority to provide old-age pensions directly to citizens. At the time, the Quebec government was not interested in launching its own program, but it did preserve its options for the future, insisting that the constitutional amendment retain provincial paramountcy by stipulating that no federal pension plan should affect the operation of any future provincial legislation. The Old Age Security (OAS) enacted the next year was a universal, flat-rate pension of $40 per month for elderly citizens funded through general tax revenues. In 1966, the benefit was extended by the Guaranteed Income Supplement (GIS), an income-tested supplement added to the OAS payment for elderly citizens with low and middle incomes.

These exclusively federal programs, unencumbered by intergovernmental constraints, remained responsive to the shifting currents of national politics in the years that followed. During the post-war era, these currents were largely expansionist, and parties entered election campaigns armed with promises to raise benefits. From the 1950s until the 1980s, promises to increase the pensions featured in virtually every federal election. After its introduction in 1965, the GIS emerged as a particular favourite in this process, and the program was repeatedly enriched in real terms, usually just before or after an election.

Similarly, the federal government was free to expand UI on its own terms. In 1971, legislation broadened the program to include all employees, increased the replacement ratio to 66 per cent of wages, introduced extended benefits in regions with high levels of unemployment, and covered unemployment resulting from sickness and temporary disability. The legislation also introduced maternity benefits. All of this came with remarkably little consultation with provincial governments; even the regional features of the plan represented 'the federal government's own policy priorities in regional development', and 'were not pressed upon Ottawa by the provinces' (Pal, 1988: 161).

The freedom to act was perhaps best illustrated by Family Allowances, where Liberal governments zigzagged with abandon. In 1970, the Liberals proposed transforming the universal benefit into an income-tested Family Income Supplement, analogous to the GIS, in order to target resources on low-income families. However, Liberal MPs encountered resistance to the idea of taking the Family Allowance away from middle-income families during the 1972 election and the government promptly changed direction, maintaining the universal program and tripling the payment, thereby restoring most of its original purchasing power. In 1978, however, the Liberals returned to income-testing in an incremental way, introducing a refundable Child Tax Credit, financed in part through a reduction in the universal Family Allowance. All of these shifts had major implications for provincial social assistance programs, but the provinces had no role in the decisions.

Joint-Decision Federalism

Joint-decision federalism represented the other extreme. The introduction of contributory pensions in 1965 and their subsequent evolution were governed by a complex intergovernmental process requiring a high level of consensus for change.

The legal origins of joint decision-making lay in the provincial paramountcy embedded in the 1951 constitutional amendment on pensions. When the issue of a contributory pension plan came to the fore in the mid-1960s, Quebec announced that it would operate its own plan. As a consequence, the Quebec Pension Plan (QPP) operates in that province, and the Canada Pension Plan (CPP) operates generally throughout the rest of the country. Although the other provinces were content with a federally delivered plan, they wanted control over it, and the limitations of the 1951 constitutional amendment gave them leverage. An additional constitutional amendment was required to include survivor and disability benefits in the plan, and the provinces insisted on joint decision-making in return for agreeing to the amendment. As a result, changes in the CPP require the consent of the federal government and two-thirds of the provinces representing two-thirds of the population of the country, a requirement more demanding than the amending formula for most parts of the Canadian Constitution.

Asymmetry and joint decision-making create complex veto points. First, to avoid the administrative and political headaches that would emerge if the two plans diverged sharply, pension planners in Ottawa and Quebec City accept that the Canada and Quebec plans should remain broadly parallel, with neither side making significant changes alone. Second, the formula for provincial consent to changes in the CPP means that Ontario alone, or a variety of possible combinations of other provinces, has a veto. In effect, then, the CPP rules and the pressure for parallelism between CPP and QPP create a system of multiple vetoes: Ottawa, Ontario, Quebec, or several combinations of other provinces can all stop change.

The introduction of the plans illustrates the dynamics well. Federal leadership was critical to catapulting contributory pensions to the top of the national agenda in the 1960s. Had contributory pensions remained an exclusively provincial jurisdiction, 'it is most unlikely that a plan comparable to CPP would have been enacted' (Simeon, 1972: 270). Pensions were not a provincial priority, and many provinces would have followed the private-sector approach advocated by the Conservative government of Ontario, which planned to require employers above a certain size to provide occupational pensions. However, the federal proposal for a public plan was popular with the electorate, and the Ontario government accepted that contributory pensions of some sort were inevitable. But it held out for a limited plan that left ample scope for private pensions and minimized redistribution by relating individual contributions and benefits closely.

Initially, federal officials assumed Ontario was their major obstacle, and trimmed their sails accordingly, for example, reducing the proposed benefits from a replacement rate of 30 per cent to 20 per cent of average wages. But during a 1963 federal–provincial conference, the Quebec government created a sensation by outlining its own plan, which included more generous benefit levels and a more redistributive funding formula. Moreover, Quebec called for a partially funded plan, with the accumulated fund purchasing provincial government bonds, effectively loaning capital to the provincial government on favourable terms, an idea that attracted other provinces as well. At that point, the federal proposal was dead. A final round of secret negotiations between Ontario and Quebec City produced a compromise plan: Ottawa accepted partial funding, and the replacement rate was set at 25 per cent of average monthly earnings, lower than Ottawa's initial preference but higher than its Ontario-focused version. The Ontario government and the insurance industry were not happy and felt that Ottawa 'had used Quebec to turn the tables on them' (Kent, 1988: 286). But Ontario, too, was attracted by the funding model, and in the end accepted the need for parallelism with Quebec.

In subsequent decades, multiple vetoes slowed the pace of expansion and helped deflect electoral promises away from the C/QPP. The 1970s did witness one major effort to expand the C/QPP. In 1975 the Canadian Labour Congress and social groups launched a 'Great Pension Debate', urging a doubling of CPP benefits. The federal Liberals were initially sympathetic to some expansion, and an advisory commission in Quebec was also supportive. Wider provincial support, however, was lacking. As the CPP Advisory Committee noted in 1975, 'the CPP has become the backbone of provincial debt financing', contributing more than 30 per cent of total provincial borrowing and even more in periods of stress in capital markets (Canada, 1975: 7–8). In this situation, provinces had a vested interest in opposing any liberalization of benefits that would erode the size of the fund. The campaign's momentum was slowed and the historic moment passed. By the time an intergovernmental consensus emerged 10 years later, economic recession and an increasingly conservative political climate had shifted the centrist currents of Canadian politics: by then, all governments opposed expansion of the C/QPP and focused instead on encouraging private pension plans and personal retirement savings in tax-sheltered accounts. The 1985 changes in the contributory plans were limited to division of credits on divorce and remarriage, and a schedule of increases in the contribution rates.

These institutional dynamics help explain the relatively limited nature of Canadian pensions. The original contributory pensions were modest, more modest even than the federal government's initial intentions, and subsequent expansions were largely forestalled. In combination, the OAS and the maximum c/QPP benefit replace approximately 40 per cent of earnings for the average wage earner, a low rate by European and even US standards. The average Canadian retiree receives a larger portion of his or her income from private occupational pensions, personal retirement accounts, and other forms of savings than in most other Western countries (Béland and Myles, 2005).

Shared-Cost Federalism

The third model, shared-cost federalism, structured federal–provincial relations in the fields of health care and social assistance. In contrast to exclusively federal programs, the shared-cost model broadens the range of governments and ideologies influencing policies; but in contrast to the joint-decision rules, this model does not give a veto to any particular province. These differences in decision rules reshuffled the opportunities and constraints facing individual governments, with significant implications for the ideological balances struck in the emerging policies.

Health care

In the early days, federalism slowed progress towards public health insurance. As noted earlier, the courts invalidated the federal government's social insurance legislation in 1937 and the provinces rejected the Green Book proposals in 1945, both of which included health insurance. In the wake of paralysis at the federal level, however, federalism created opportunities for innovation at the provincial level, which the political left used to establish a universal system as the leading option for the country as a whole. In 1947, the CCF government of Saskatchewan implemented universal hospital insurance, the first jurisdiction in North America to do so. Two other western provinces—British Columbia and Alberta —followed in quick succession. At that point, the spread across the country stalled, and provinces looked to the federal government to build a national approach. The Liberal prime minister of the day, Louis St Laurent, was initially reluctant to act, insisting that his government would support provincial health insurance programs only when a majority of the provinces representing a majority of the population were ready to join a national scheme. By the mid-1950s, however, this condition was met when Ontario and Newfoundland joined the list of provinces supporting federal action. In 1957, the federal government introduced a universal hospital insurance program, which shared the costs of provincial programs, and all of the provinces had joined within four years.

A similar cycle extended health insurance to physician services. In 1962, the NDP government of Saskatchewan again took the lead, introducing a medicare plan, despite a bitter three-week doctors' strike, the first organized withdrawal of services by medical professionals in North America. Key elements in the settlement that ended the strike—universal and comprehensive coverage, the right of patients to choose their own doctors, and the preservation of fee-for-service payment for physicians—became the starting point for national debate. The Saskatchewan experience demonstrated that a universal approach was feasible in administrative and political terms. Doctors no longer had to provide uncompensated care, and their incomes actually rose in the early years of the program, easing the danger of militant opposition elsewhere. This early success gave ammunition to reformist forces in national politics, and their opportunity came in 1963 with the return to power of the federal Liberal Party. The Liberals were committed to a national program of some sort, and their minority government depended on the support of third parties, including the NDP.

Conservative political forces mounted fierce resistance to the universal model. The Canadian Medical Association and the insurance industry were opposed, and ideological conflict coursed through intergovernmental channels. Conservative governments in Ontario, Alberta, and British Columbia were committed to private coverage for the majority of the population, with public programs limited to the 'hard to insure', such as the elderly and the poor. Without federal action, this position would probably have prevailed in large parts of the country, and health insurance in Canada would have more closely resembled the system emerging at the same time in the US. However, after the Royal Commission on Health Services, chaired by Justice Emmett Hall, recommended in 1964 a universal program, the federal government came down on that side of the debate. The conservative provincial governments were caught in a vice. The federal proposal was popular with their electorates; and if they refused to join, their residents would still have to pay federal taxes to support the program in other provinces. The long-serving health minister in Alberta resigned in protest. The premier of Ontario denounced medicare as 'one of the greatest frauds that has ever been perpetrated on the people of this country' (Taylor, 1987: 375). In this case, however, Ontario lacked the veto that had given it leverage in the pension debate. By 1971, all provinces had medicare programs in place.

Federalism thus played a distinctive role in the politics of health insurance. Although jurisdictional issues delayed action in the early years, federalism created room for a reformist province to implement health insurance on social democratic principles. In the end, federal action was required to transform this regional initiative into a national program. But federal–provincial interaction launched health insurance on a social democratic trajectory that contrasts sharply with the contributory pensions being developed at the same time by the same governments. While the pension reforms carefully left substantial room for private pensions and personal retirement accounts, health insurance displaced the private insurance industry completely from core hospital and medical services. Decision rules were not the only difference between the sectors. But they were critical.

Social assistance

The same dynamics did not shape social assistance. The federal government assumed social assistance would shrink to a residual role after the new income security programs matured, and it never sought to establish a powerful national framework for provincial welfare programs. The result was to deprive the

CCF–NDP provinces of the sort of leverage they were able to exert in health care.

Over the years, the federal government had established a number of small shared-cost programs to support provincial benefits for specific categories of needy people, and in 1966 Ottawa introduced the Canada Assistance Plan (CAP), which consolidated these initiatives into a broader program. Despite the funding, however, the federal policy role in social assistance was tepid. Under CAP, provinces were required to support all persons 'in need', to establish a formal appeal machinery, and to abolish provincial residency requirements for social assistance. Otherwise, they had complete control. The federal government never gave serious thought to establishing national standards for benefit levels, and even a proposal to require provinces to report annually on their policies was squashed within the federal government by the Department of Finance.

Federal financial support did trigger 'a major restructuring of social assistance across Canada on a scale unseen since the Depression' (Struthers, 1994: 190). Spending on social assistance and services rose strongly as a percentage of total provincial expenditures. Although it is impossible to know how much provincial spending would have risen in the absence of federal transfers, the increase was larger in programs eligible for cost-sharing than in non-shareable services; and federal and provincial officials certainly believed the federal transfers were critical, especially in poorer provinces (Canada, 1991).[3] Within this overall pattern, however, the federal approach left lots of room for provincial programs to evolve along distinctive trajectories, and benefits have gone through cycles of convergence and divergence over the years (Boychuk, 1998).

Summary

Three models of federalism thus left their imprint on the new Canadian welfare state. Exclusively federal programs were shaped by centrist politics and emerged on relatively modest premises; joint decision-making constrained the role of contributory pensions in the retirement income system; but the shared-cost model gave opportunities to social-democratic forces in health care, although not in social assistance where the federal government did not try to define a national approach.

The Three Federalisms and the Politics of Restructuring

The mid-1970s represented the high-water mark of the post-war welfare state. A new politics came to dominate during the last quarter of the twentieth century, as governments focused on retrenchment and restructuring. Restructuring in Canada was driven by the same economic and political changes reshaping the welfare state in other countries: the slowing of economic growth, the acceleration of technological innovation, the globalization of international trade, and the growing ascendancy of conservative political parties and philosophies. In the Canadian case, the fiscal problems of governments were particularly acute. As Figure 7.2 indicates, the ratio of public debt to GDP rose steadily from the late

Figure 7.2   Consolidated Public Debt as a Percentage of GDP, All Levels of Government, 1977–2001

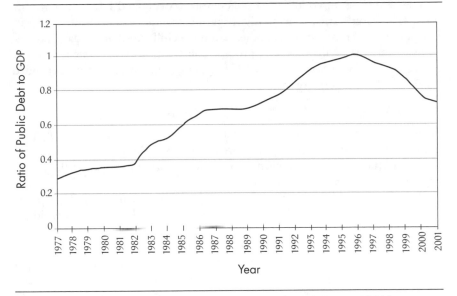

SOURCE: GDP data: Statistics Canada, *Canadian Economic Observer*, Cat. no. 11-210; consolidated debt data: Statistics Canada/CANSIM II, Table No. 385-0017.

1970s until the mid-1990s, by which time 35 per cent of all federal revenues was pre-empted by interest payments on federal debt and several provinces faced problems placing their bonds in financial markets. In this context, public opinion stiffened. Universal programs such as health care and pensions retained strong support, but opinion polls recorded more resistance to unemployment and social assistance benefits and greater support for tax cuts, a pattern that peaked in the mid-1990s.

The new politics of social policy was reinforced by the politics of federalism, which generated increasing challenges to the social role of the federal government. In 1976 the Parti Québécois won power in the province of Quebec, confirming its status as a major political force. In 1980 and 1995, the country was to live through emotionally wrenching referenda on the separation of Quebec, with the separatist option losing in 1995 by less than 1 per cent of the vote. Regional economic conflicts also deepened, with the energy crisis of the 1970s and free trade in the 1980s pitting region against region. These tensions plunged the country into protracted federal–provincial negotiations over constitutional reform. Throughout this constitutional odyssey, Quebec, supported in varying degrees by other provinces, pressed for restrictions on the federal spending power. In the end, the country failed to coalesce around a new constitutional model, and the spending power was not formally limited. But the social role of the federal government was constantly on the defensive.

The result was an era of social policy restructuring and retrenchment. The impact, however, varied enormously from one program to another. Some programs were better insulated than others from the chill winds of the day, and federalism was part of the buffering process, constraining retrenchment where it had constrained expansion in earlier days. Once again, however, much depended on the model of federalism in play.

Classical Federalism and Exclusively Federal Programs

Federal decision-makers were unconstrained by federalism in restructuring programs in their own jurisdiction, and the outcomes faithfully reflected the electoral importance of different client groups, with stark differences in the fate of pensioners, children, and the unemployed.

Pensions escaped virtually unscathed. In 1985, the Conservatives proposed partial deindexation of OAS, but backed down quickly in the face of angry elderly voters. A decade later, the Liberal government sought to replace the OAS and GIS with an integrated income-tested Seniors' Benefit, but abandoned the idea in the face of attacks from the left by women's groups and the NDP and from the right by investment brokers worried about eroding the incentive to save for retirement. The only change that survived was a more stealthy measure to 'claw back' OAS from high-income seniors through the tax system. However, the measure affects barely 5 per cent of the elderly.

Child benefits were restructured more pervasively, in light of the changing ideologies of the day. In a long, tortuous series of moves during the 1980s and 1990s, the universal Family Allowance was slowly eliminated, in favour of the Child Tax Benefit, an income-tested payment delivered to low- and middle-income families with children. During the later 1990s the federal government did depart temporarily from unilateralism in this sector, co-ordinating increases in its benefit with related changes in provincial social assistance and social services. However, co-ordination had largely run its course by the end of the decade, and unilateralism soon reasserted itself. In 2006, the newly elected Conservative government changed course again, reintroducing a universal allowance for all families with young children as part of its child-care strategy. As in times of old, there was no advance consultation with provinces.

It was UI, however, that suffered the largest cuts, which came relentlessly, one slice after another. The replacement rate was reduced from the peak of 66 per cent established in 1971 to 60 per cent in 1978, 57 per cent in 1993, 55 per cent for some workers in 1994, and 50 per cent for repeat beneficiaries in 1996 (although offset in part for some recipients by a slightly increased family supplement). By 1996, the replacement rate resembled that in 1940. In addition, increasingly restrictive eligibility requirements contributed to a dramatic decline in the proportion of beneficiaries actually receiving benefits, as Figure 7.3 indicates.

Figure 7.3   Ratio of UI/EI Beneficiaries to Total Unemployed, Canada, 1976–2002

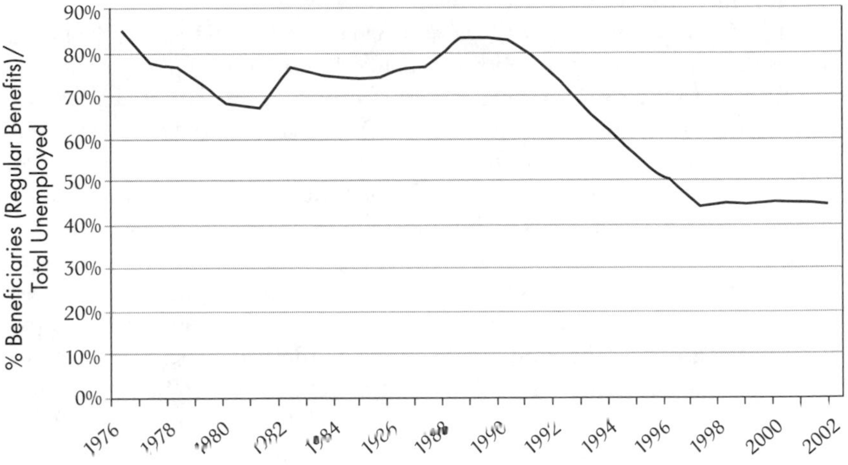

SOURCE: Figure kindly provided by Gerard Boychuk. Reproduced with permission.

The primary constraint on federal discretion over this program was the politics of regionalism. In many countries, proposals to reduce unemployment benefits pit politicians against organized labour; in Canada, the most effective opponents of cutbacks are politicians from poor regions. A ritualized political dance was repeated many times: governments proposed reductions; backbench MPs from Atlantic Canada and Quebec mounted fierce resistance; provincial governments from those regions supported their protests; the government compromised in ways that softened the impact in poor areas. However, the unemployed in more affluent provinces such as Ontario and British Columbia received no such protection. This dance, performed by Liberal and Conservative governments alike, resulted in growing regional variations in both qualification requirements and benefit duration. By 2006, only a quarter of the unemployed in Toronto were receiving unemployment benefits.

Joint-Decision Federalism

At the other extreme, the consensus-driven, incremental logic inherent in joint decision-making helped protect the C/QPP. During the 1990s, actuarial reports raised questions about the long-term financial status of the plans, triggering extensive rhetoric about unsustainability. Yet the final adjustments largely served to stabilize the program. Joint decision-making was not the only factor at work. The electoral sensitivity of pensions, evident in the OAS case, was undoubtedly important here as well. Yet contributory pensions create opportunities for subtle adjustments that are largely invisible to the electorate in the short term but have major effects in the long term. The fact that these opportunities were exploited primarily to reinforce rather than weaken the program was due in part to the need for intergovernmental consensus.

An intergovernmental review was launched in 1996, with the release of a joint discussion paper on reform options (Canada, 1996). From the outset, however, negotiations focused on a narrow range of options, and radical changes were never considered seriously. The province of Quebec announced that it would not consider significant reductions in benefits, a position supported by NDP governments in Saskatchewan and British Columbia. Advocates of privatization or a shift to personalized accounts within the C/QPP found little resonance for their ideas. In the end, the federal and provincial governments agreed to accelerate increases in contribution rates from 5.5 per cent to 9.9 per cent of earnings over a 10-year period, and to invest the enhanced revenues in equities in the hope of further strengthening the long-term funding of the plan. There was a modest trimming of some benefits, and the two NDP governments refused to sign the final agreement. But governments did not even try for more dramatic retrenchment, such as an increase in the retirement age, and the final changes largely stabilized the role of contributory pensions in the retirement income system (Béland and Myles, 2005).

Shared-Cost Federalism

The most intense federal–provincial politics in recent years centred on shared-cost programs; they provided ample opportunity for off-loading, blame avoidance, and mutual recrimination. The overall pattern was one of unilateralism at the federal level, relentless push-back from the provinces, and eventual reinvestment by the federal government. The outcome, at least in the case of health care, was relatively little change in the basic policy model.

The stage for these conflicts was actually set as far back as 1977, when block funding was introduced in response to frustrations with the traditional form of cost-sharing. The federal government became concerned that its open-ended commitment to pay half the cost of expensive provincial programs reduced its control over its own budget. Provincial governments complained that shared-cost programs distorted provincial priorities and locked them into endless arguments about whether specific projects qualified for federal support. After extensive negotiations, the two levels agreed to shift to a block grant for health and post-secondary education. The federal government gained greater control over its finances and provincial governments gained greater freedom. Although the formal conditions attached to the federal health programs remained in place, provinces were able to allocate federal funding as they saw fit. Indeed, there was no explicit requirement that the funding actually be devoted to health and post-secondary education.

Over time, however, provinces were to pay a high price for the additional flexibility, as the federal government was no longer committed to paying half the costs of provincial programs. At the outset, increases in federal support were tied to the rate of growth in the economy as a whole. But as federal deficits grew, Ottawa repeatedly made unilateral cuts: in 1986, indexation of the transfer was limited to the increase in GDP less two percentage points; in 1990, the transfer was frozen in absolute terms for four years; and the 1995 budget folded CAP into a broader block fund known as the Canada Health and Social Transfer (CHST) and cut the cash payment to provinces dramatically. These changes, conceived in secrecy and imposed without warning, provoked a bitter reaction among provinces and seriously eroded the legitimacy of the federal role in their eyes. The impact of this process, however, varied from program to program, depending on the extent to which the federal government remained committed to a policy role in the sector, as the contrast between health care and social assistance once again illustrates.

Health insurance

In the case of health care, federalism helped to buffer the universal model from pressures for change. The federal government, especially when the Liberals were in power, defined itself as the guarantor of equality of access to health care and resisted efforts by conservative provincial governments to introduce user fees or increase the role of the private sector. Poll after poll showed that Canadians strongly supported the existing health-care system, and the federal Liberals could mobilize that opinion in conflicts with the provinces. However, the ability of federal health ministers to play Sir Galahad also reflected the dry realities of inter-governmental finances. Under the block grant system, the federal treasury was not directly affected by changes in provincial health expenditures and, therefore, did not bear the costs associated with the defence of universal health care. As a result, federal health ministers were freer to defend the principles of universality and equality of access. Indeed, they did so even as their colleague, the minister of Finance, was reducing transfers to the provinces.

This drama unfolded in several acts. Just before the 1984 election, the federal Liberals nailed their colours to the mast with the passage of the Canada Health Act (CHA). During the early 1980s, a growing number of doctors began charging patients a supplementary fee in addition to the payment they received from the provincial medical plan, a practice known as 'extra-billing'. At the same time, a number of provinces began to flirt with the idea of hospital fees for patients. The federal Liberals opposed both practices as inhibiting equal access to health care, and the CHA prohibited user fees and all charges at the point of service. The CHA was opposed by all provincial governments. But it was immensely popular with the electorate and passed unanimously in both the House of Commons and Senate.

The federal government proceeded with penalties, withholding a total of $247 million from provinces that allowed charges. However, the financial penalties were not large enough to have induced provincial compliance on their own. The real sanctions were political. Provincial electorates supported the principles of

Table 7.1   Federal Transfers for Health Care as a Percentage of Provincial Health Expenditures, 1975–2000

Year	Cash	Tax	Total
1975	41.3	41.3	
1977	25.2	17.1	42.3
1980	25.3	17.7	43.7
1985	23.8	15.6	39.7
1990	17.9	16.0	33.9
1995	16.4	15.8	32.1
2000	12.8	16.5	29.3

the CHA, and they were upset when their provincial governments were declared to be in violation of its terms. In moving to comply, provinces faced difficult negotiations with the medical profession, which demanded compensation for the banning of extra-billing. Ontario endured a 25-day strike by a majority of doctors, and Saskatchewan doctors held rotating one-day strikes. The doctors made important financial gains in a number of provinces, costs that the provinces alone had to absorb. But by the late 1980s, all provinces were largely in compliance (Tuohy, 1994). The mid-1990s witnessed a repeat of this cycle, this time focused on private clinics providing specialized medical services, such as cataract surgery, and charging a 'facility fee'. The federal Liberal government challenged such fees in 1995, and in the end the provinces grudgingly moved largely into compliance by banning them.

In contrast to this forceful policy role, the federal financial role declined steadily in the 1980s and 1990s. The extent of the erosion depends on how one defines the 'real' federal contribution. At the time of the introduction of block funding in 1977, the federal transfer was split into an annual cash payment and a transfer of tax points (which involved the federal government lowering its taxes and the provinces raising their taxes by the same amount). The result was a bitter dispute over the size of the federal share. Ottawa insisted that its contribution included both the cash payment and the current value of the tax points transferred in 1977. Provinces replied that the tax points were now simply part of the provincial tax base, and the federal contribution was limited to the cash. Table 7.1 demonstrates the dramatic difference: provinces looked only at the first column; Ottawa focused on the final column. On either accounting, however, the federal share of health spending declined in the 1980s and 1990s.

Provincial governments were squeezed between growing health costs and declining federal transfers. They, in turn, squeezed health spending, reducing expenditures by an average of 2 per cent each year between 1992 and 1997 (Fierlbeck, 2001). However, such intense restraint was difficult to sustain. Beginning in the late 1990s, newspaper reports increasingly described a system in decline: the closing of hospital wards; the slow acquisition of new technologies; declining staffing levels; controversy about waiting times for non-emergency surgical procedures; and crowded emergency departments. Moreover, polls suggested that public faith in the health-care system had fallen more rapidly in Canada than in other Western nations (Schoen et al., 2002). The political limits of retrenchment had been reached.

Not surprisingly, the provincial governments pushed back. They mounted protracted public campaigns blaming Ottawa for the erosion of health care and demanding federal reinvestment. With the return of federal fiscal health in the late 1990s, Ottawa did reinvest, significantly increasing its funding in 1999, 2000, 2002, and 2004. In effect, the federal cuts were reversed, slice by slice. These increases did not resolve the intergovernmental tensions, as provinces still faced serious cost pressures. Moreover, the rupture of the mid-1990s delegitimized federal conditionality in the eyes of provincial governments, which rebuffed federal efforts to give priority to specific reforms or attach conditions to the new money. Not until 2004 were provinces prepared to sign a joint plan, and Quebec insisted on a separate agreement. Even then, while the provinces agreed on objectives, their only accountability was to report on progress, not to Ottawa, but to their own citizens.

Despite the tensions, the two levels of government have remained locked in an embrace that has tended to slow the process of change in health care. On the surface, the stability of the basic parameters of the system is striking. The CHA remains unchanged, and health services are still provided primarily by non-profit and community hospitals on one side and doctors working on a fee-for-service basis on the other. There has been some de-insuring of marginal procedures and new reproductive technologies. But there has been nothing like the revolution wrought south of the border by HMOs and for-profit hospital chains, or by experiments with internal markets in the UK.

Such buffering effects are never absolute. There are signs that support for the CHA model of health care is weakening. The role of the private sector re-emerged in 2004 with the opening of private clinics offering MRI diagnostic services in Quebec and elsewhere (Laghi, 2004), and the federal government did not charge into the breach as of old, even before the election of a more decentralist Conservative government in 2006. It is possible that Canada will eventually move to a new mix of the public and private sectors in health care. But federalism suggests that the process will be an evolutionary one and will require a higher level of consensus in the country as a whole than would otherwise be needed.

Social assistance

In contrast with health care, social assistance saw a much more straightforward decentralization and the elimination of the buffering effects of intergovernmentalism. Although CAP was not included in block funding in 1977, full cost-sharing fell victim in the 1990s to the battle against the federal deficit. In 1990, the Conservative federal government unilaterally imposed a 'cap on CAP' for the three richest provinces, limiting growth in the federal contribution to 5 per cent a year. With the onset of a serious recession shortly afterwards, the federal share of welfare costs in these provinces fell sharply; within a few years the Ontario government reported that Ottawa was contributing only 28 per cent of its welfare costs (Courchene with Telmer, 1998). The final step came in 1995, when the subsequent Liberal government abolished CAP altogether, rolling its support for social assistance into the CHST. This change significantly increased provincial discretion, as the federal funding no longer had to be devoted to social assistance. Ottawa also took the opportunity to eliminate the requirements that provincial programs respond to all persons in need and maintain appeals procedures. Only the prohibition on provincial residency requirements remained, and even this modest provision was difficult to enforce.

In contrast with health care, where the federal government accepted a continuing responsibility, the virtually total abandonment of social assistance by the federal government made it harder for provinces to push back. In effect, the sector moved from shared-cost federalism to the classical model. Many social policy advocates predicted that decentralization would trigger a speedy race to the bottom. Although CAP had never set national benefit rates, they argued that cost-sharing had protected social assistance, since provincial treasurers would reap only half of any savings generated by cuts. They also argued that the CAP requirement that provincial programs assist all persons 'in need' precluded the more draconian forms of workfare and term limits that had emerged in the US.

In fact, benefits did decline. In 1996, for example, a newly elected Conservative government in Ontario cut benefits by 20 per cent. As always, it is hard to isolate the impact of decentralization. At the national level, the downward trend in benefits began in 1992, between the cap on CAP and CAP's final elimination, and a careful study of the trends concludes that benefits were 'slouching', not racing, towards a bottom (Boychuk, 2006). The consequences for eligibility for benefits were clearer, however. Beneficiaries were under increasing compulsion to participate in employability programs, and liens on home equity were introduced in Ontario. The harshest step came in 2002, when British Columbia introduced time limits, restricting employable people without children to two years of support in any five-year period. Subsequent revisions reduced the numbers affected significantly. But all of these provisions would have been fully precluded by CAP.

Summary

As in the past, the new politics of social policy had to flow through the three distinctive institutional filters, which help explain the uneven impact of retrenchment on different social programs. Exclusively federal programs were fully exposed to the shifting currents of centrist politics, with the elderly, children, and the unemployed enduring different fates. At the same time, joint-decision federalism helped protect contributory pensions. Shared-cost federalism helped buffer the basic model of health care, but the mild protection afforded social assistance collapsed with the abolition of CAP, exposing recipients more fully to political pressures in the provinces. Interestingly, the cumulative impact of these changes was to deepen a disjunction at the heart of Canadian social policy. Income security shifted more firmly into the limited, selectivist mould, as unemployment benefits and social assistance were weakened and children's benefits shifted towards income testing. In contrast, the universal model of health care has endured, if in somewhat battered form, in hospital and physician services. The two worlds of Canadian welfare moved further apart.

Conclusions

The Canadian federation embraces three distinct models of federalism, each of which alters the range of governments at the table, redistributes power among the governments that get there, and requires different levels of intergovernmental consensus for action. At any point in time, during both the years of expansion and the years of retrenchment, the same federal and provincial governments operating in the same political environment were shaping different programs according to different rules. These models have left their imprint on the Canadian welfare state. Because they act as institutional filters through which wider political and economic pressures flow, it is difficult to isolate precisely their independent influence on policy outcomes. It is, however, possible to identify the set of incentives and constraints embedded in each model and determine the direction of its influence. At a minimum, the three models of federalism remain an essential part of explanations of a number of puzzles about Canadian social policy, including the different ideological trajectories of income security and health care and the uneven impact of restructuring in recent decades.

Evaluating the three federalisms in light of the normative criteria adopted in this volume—performance, effectiveness, and legitimacy—produces a mixed report. The classical model, almost by definition, comes closest to meeting traditional federal principles. The issue has always been whether this model establishes the right balance between the claims of social citizenship—the belief that all Canadians should be entitled to a comparable set of social rights and benefits irrespective of where they live—and the belief that a federation should enhance the scope for regional variation in social benefits. In comparative terms, the Canadian welfare state leans towards giving greater scope to regional variation; virtually all other federal states among advanced democracies give more weight to the equal treatment of citizens (Banting, 2006; Obinger et al., 2005). Greater regional variation results primarily because the federal government plays a smaller role in social policy, and more programs fall into the domain of provincial governments. But it also reflects the tendency for regional variations to creep into the design of some federal programs. The most troublesome failure of the classical model is undoubtedly the federal Employment Insurance program. A basic rationale for central delivery of a program in any federation is to ensure that citizens in similar circumstances are treated similarly, irrespective of where they live. By that standard, the federal unemployment program fails spectacularly.

At the other extreme, the joint-decision model can also be seen as a strong assertion of federalism. As we have seen, the effect has been to buffer the C/QPP from the pressures for change inherent in democratic politics. Defenders of the model might note that over time the frustrations generated by joint decision-making have been visited equally on advocates and opponents of the welfare state. In the post-war decades, advocates of expansion regarded the formula with despair; in the era of retrenchment, advocates of privatization have faced similar disappointments. Defenders of joint decision-making might also argue that privileging stability makes sense in the field of pensions, where policies require long-term horizons. The actual formula is undoubtedly too exacting; there is no reason that contributory pensions should be more difficult to change than most sections of the Constitution. Nevertheless, the model does generate intergovernmental legitimacy, and the plans governed by it enjoy strong public support.

Our greatest difficulties haunt the domain of shared-cost federalism. The legitimacy of this model has been under growing challenge, particularly in health care. Federal intervention in health care is less pervasive and less detailed in Canada than in any other advanced federation, including the United States and Switzerland, yet its intervention generates more intergovernmental resentment (Banting and Corbett, 2002). The country is paying a high price for the lack of agreed federal–provincial decision rules and for the unilateralism and ruptures of the 1990s. In the aftermath of the 1995 budget, the provincial governments pressed for a stronger set of decision rules and a dispute resolution mechanism, an effort in effect to shift closer to a joint-decision model.[4] But the resulting Social Union Framework Agreement failed to meet their concerns, disappointing those who saw it as a mechanism for rebuilding trust between governments. As a result, federal and provincial governments remain locked in an uneasy embrace.

Undoubtedly, the balance among the three models of federalism will evolve in the future, as it has in the past. It is possible that the shared-cost model will play a smaller role in the years to come. But as long as Canadians look to both levels of government to respond to the social problems they confront, it is difficult to envisage any of the three models disappearing completely from the world of social policy. It seems likely that pressures for change in the Canadian welfare state will continue to flow through three distinctive institutional filters, each with its own implications for the future.

Notes

1. With the inclusion of section 36 in the Constitution Act, 1982, equalization grants have specific constitutional footing and no longer depend on the federal spending power.
2. Shared-cost programs were also important in the area of post-secondary edu-

cation and child care. See Chapters 10 (Bakvis) and 9 (Friendly and White).
3. The decline in the proportion of unemployed receiving benefits also reflected changes in forms of employment, which decrease eligibility for the program.
4. Throughout the negotiations over the Social Union Framework Agreement, Quebec took a different position from the other provinces, favouring the autonomy of the classical approach rather than an elaborate system of joint decision-making. It briefly joined the provincial consensus on the condition that any province would have the right to opt out fully from any intergovernmental agreement with full fiscal compensation. When this provision was qualified in the final accord, Quebec declined to sign.

References

Banting, K. 2005. 'Canada: Nation-building in a Federal Welfare State'. In *Federalism and the Welfare State: New World and European Experiences*, ed. H. Obinger, S. Leibfried, and F. Castles. Cambridge: Cambridge University Press.
——— 2006. 'Is a Federal Welfare State a Contradiction in Terms?' In *Democracy and Devolution*, ed. S. Greer. London: Palgrave/Macmillan.
——— and R. Boadway. 2004. 'Defining the Sharing Community: The Federal Role in Health Care'. In *Money, Politics and Health Care: Reconstructing the Federal–Provincial Partnership*, ed. H. Lazar and F. St-Hilaire. Montreal: Institute for Research on Public Policy.
——— and S. Corbett. 2002. 'Health Policy and Federalism: An Introduction'. In *Health Policy and Federalism: A Comparative Perspective on Multi-Level Governance*, ed. K. Banting and S. Corbett. Montreal and Kingston: McGill–Queen's University Press.
Béland, D., and J. Myles. 2005. 'Stasis Amidst Change: Canadian Pension Reform in an Age of Retrenchment'. In *Ageing and Pension Reform Around the World: Evidence from Eleven Countries*, ed. G. Bonoli and T. Shinkawa. Cheltenham: Edward Elgar.
Boychuk, G. 1998. *Patchworks of Purpose: The Development of Provincial Social Assistance Regimes in Canada*. Montreal and Kingston: McGill–Queen's University Press.
———. 2006. 'Slouching Toward the Bottom? Provincial Social Assistance Provision in Canada, 1980–2000'. In *Racing to the Bottom? Provincial Interdependence in the Canadian Federation*, ed. K. Harrison. Vancouver: University of British Columbia Press.
Canada. 1975. Canada Pension Plan Advisory Committee, *The Rate of Return on the Investment Fund of the Canada Pension Plan*. Ottawa: Minister of Supply and Services Canada.
———. 1991. Health and Welfare Canada, Program Audit and Review Directorate, *Evaluation of the Canada Assistance Plan*. Ottawa: Health and Welfare Canada.
———. 1996. *An Information Paper for Consultations on the Canada Pension Plan*

Released by the Federal, Provincial and Territorial Governments. Ottawa: Department of Finance.

Courchene, T., with C. Telmer. 1998. *From Heartland to North American Region State: The Social, Fiscal and Federal Evolution of Ontario.* Toronto: Faculty of Management, University of Toronto.

Fierlbeck, K. 2001. 'Cost Containment in Health Care: The Federalism Context'. In *Federalism, Democracy and Health Policy in Canada*, ed. D. Adams. Montreal and Kingston: McGill–Queen's University Press.

Guest, D. 1997. *Emergence of Social Security in Canada*, 3rd edn. Vancouver: University of British Columbia Press,

Hogg, P. 2001. *Constitutional Law in Canada.* Toronto: Carswell.

Jean, D. 1992. 'Family Allowances and Family Autonomy'. In *Canadian Family History*, ed. B. Bradbury. Toronto: Copp Clark Pitman.

Kent, T. 1988. *A Public Purpose: An Experience of Liberal Opposition and Canadian Government.* Montreal and Kingston: McGill–Queen's University Press.

Langhi, B. 2004. 'Stop Clinics from Billing their Patients, Quebec Told', *Globe and Mail*, 10 Feb.: A4

Lazar, H., F. St-Hilaire and J.-F. Tremblay. 2004. 'Vertical Fiscal Imbalance: Myth or Reality?' In *Money, Politics and Health Care: Reconstructing the Federal–Provincial Partnership*, ed. H. Lazar and F. St-Hilaire. Montreal and Kingston: Institute for Research on Public Policy and Institute for Intergovernmental Relations, Queen's University.

Obinger, H., S. Leibried, and F. Castles, eds. 2005. *Federalism and the Welfare State: New World and European Experiences.* Cambridge: Cambridge University Press.

Pal, L. 1988. *State, Class, and Bureaucracy: Canadian Unemployment Insurance and Public Policy.* Montreal: McGill–Queen's University Press.

Quebec. 1956. Royal Commission of Inquiry on Constitutional Problems in the Province of Quebec, *Report* (The Tremblay Report), 5 vols. Quebec: Province of Quebec.

Schoen, C., R. Blendon, C. DesRoches, and R. Osborn. 2002. *Comparison of Health Care System Views and Experiences in Five Nations, 2001.* New York: Commonwealth Fund.

Simeon, R. 1972. *Federal–Provincial Diplomacy: The Making of Recent Policy in Canada.* Toronto: University of Toronto Press.

Struthers, J. 1994. *Limits of Affluence: Welfare in Ontario, 1920–1970.* Toronto: University of Toronto Press.

Taylor, M. 1987. *Health Insurance and Public Policy in Canada*, 2nd edn Montreal and Kingston: McGill–Queen's University Press.

Tuohy, C. 1994. 'Health Policy and Fiscal Federalism'. In *The Future of Fiscal Federalism*, ed. K. Banting, D. Brown, and T. Courchene. Kingston: Queen's University, School of Policy Studies.

Chapter 8

Health Care

Antonia Maioni

The politics of intergovernmental relations in the health-care arena include familiar squabbles about money and jurisdiction. But today the stakes around issues of health-care financing and the boundaries of policy-making are much higher. The debate over federalism and health care in Canada is about more than funding formulas and dispute resolution mechanisms. It is an open discussion about the future direction of provincial health-care systems and the political sustainability of the Canadian health-care model.

The issue of health reform goes beyond the policy sector. Health care is of central importance to discussions about the future of Canadian federalism. For federal Liberal governments in the past, health care captured the essence of the successful model of Canadian federalism: decentralized jurisdictional responsibility (which allows provinces extensive policy-making capacity) combined with flexible federal intervention (which ensures equity across political boundaries). Whether the Conservative government elected in January 2006 shares this view is not yet clear. For their part, provincial governments have varying degrees of enthusiasm for the existing model of health-care delivery, but all recognize the extent to which disputes about health care involve larger struggles over economic and political space in the federation.

Federalism and Health Policy

Despite the federalist ideal of subnational units as 'laboratories of democracies', modern federal systems are generally considered to harbour tendencies towards fragmentation, decentralization, and discord, making it difficult to achieve consensus and coherence (Wheare, 1951). Federalism facilitates governments' attempts to avoid blame or dodge accountability when cutting back public expenditure or dismantling programs (Weaver, 1986). In the welfare state literature, several cross-national studies have demonstrated a correlation between federal systems (as opposed to unitary systems of government) and lower public social expenditures, showing the 'dampening' effect of federalism on welfare state expansion (Huber et al., 1993).

In the Canadian case, federalism did have a delaying impact on the development of social policy, but it also served as an innovative dynamic. The federal–provincial 'diplomacy' that led to pension reform is a good case in point (Simeon, 2006). Health policy in Canada also represents an example of how federalism can contribute to policy development and the expansion of social protection (Gray, 1991).

Federalism, as a political institution, is a significant element in health policy development. But it must be remembered that 'how it matters depends on the particular structure of federal institutions, and the ways in which they are rooted in the wider political environment' (Banting and Corbett, 2002: 30). The Canadian experience reveals how, under certain conditions, a federal system of government can encourage health policy innovation and diffusion. In Canada, substantial decentralization in terms of the jurisdictional division of powers between the federal government and the provinces coexists with the fusion of executive and legislature in the system of parliamentary government (Watts, 1999). The interplay of federalism and the Westminster parliamentary system has had a profound influence on the development of health insurance. In addition, the 'territorial politics' of Canadian federalism are such that social benefits are seen to contribute to regional equity and the ideal of Canadian citizenship (Banting, 2005).

The division of powers in health care, on paper, makes Canada look like the most decentralized of all federations. Instead of a 'national' health-care system or a single medicare program, Canada has a mosaic of 10 provincial and three territorial health-care systems. In contrast to national health systems, the government of Canada does not administer health insurance plans, nor does it allocate health-care budgets or stipulate how much money should be spent. Under the division of powers, the provinces have primary responsibility for health care. Section 92(7) of the Constitution Act of 1867 gives provincial legislatures exclusive jurisdiction to enact laws for the 'Establishment, Maintenance, and Management of Hospitals, Asylums, Charities, and Eleemosynary Institutions'. Section 92(13) gives provinces legal authority over 'Property and Civil Rights in the Province', and section 92(16) gives them jurisdiction over 'Generally all Matters of a merely local or private Nature in the Province'. The federal government does have constitutional responsibilities in public health matters under section 91(11) and for the general welfare of specific classes of people: 'Indians' and 'aliens', as well as federal inmates and members of the armed forces. However, the federal spending power opened up an important role for the central government to bolster the fiscal capacity of provinces and facilitate the diffusion of health benefits across the country.

The 'Canadian' health-care model can be thought of as a system of 10 provincial and three territorial health insurance plans, bound together by certain norms (Maioni, 1999). Some of these norms are incorporated into reciprocal ententes between the provinces, for example, in interprovincial agreements on medical training or on coverage for out-of-province services. The most important norms, however, are those described in a federal statute, the Canada Health Act (CHA). The CHA includes five principles that the provinces must respect in the functioning of their health-care systems: public administration of health insurance, comprehensiveness of benefits, universality of coverage, portability across provinces, and equal access to services.

The standards derived from these principles that tie provincial health-care systems together are at once more fragile and more robust than in other countries: more fragile because they rest on a federal statute rather than constitutional principles; and more robust because, until now, they have limited experimentation with private market mechanisms. These principles are explicit in banning certain initiatives, such as those that impinge on equal access to care or the private financing of health-care services under provincial plans. These constraints are unique to Canada, which—unlike virtually every other country in the industrialized world with a publicly financed health-care system—forbids the purchase of private insurance for necessary medical services available under provincial health plans. Although supplementary health insurance does exist, it is limited to non-essential care and various forms of diagnostic testing. And Canadians can, and do, purchase out of their own pockets some medical goods and services, such as laser eye surgery.

Some argue that the CHA gives the federal government the moral suasion to ensure that provinces will follow certain rules in the design of their health-care systems. But because the CHA's principles derive from a federal statute (not a formal constitutional requirement), the federal government has been obliged to offer incentives to ensure provincial collaboration. To date, these incentives have been financial: in particular, they include the threat of dollar-by-dollar deductions in the cash portion of federal transfers to the province. As that cash portion fluctuates, so too does provincial willingness to play by the federal government's rules.

The role of federalism as a political institution that gives rise to this innovation/diffusion dynamic in health policy can be considered against the backdrop of two other components of policy change. These two components are the logic of policy feedback and the power of political ideas. Policy legacies, in the form of past policy choices at a critical historical juncture, become part of a self-reinforcing positive feedback that shapes the politics of future policy reform (Pierson, 2000). Embarking on a certain 'path' in health care, therefore, creates preferences and expectations about government involvement. The chosen path also shapes the strategies and interests of political and societal actors in the policy process, and narrows the range of feasible policy alternatives. As Tuohy (1999) argues, the logic of the Canadian health-care model may have been 'accidental' in that it emerged at a particular moment when 'windows of opportunity' for co-operation existed between governments and between the state and health-care providers. The timing and sequence of the chosen path are of obvious importance, particularly since the Canadian health-care model has since then shut out widespread use of the private market alternative. The privileged position of the ideas embedded in the Canadian health-care model does not mean that private market ideas have disappeared. Public health insurance may be something most Canadians want, but at the same time alternative ideas about health-care financing and organization have gathered considerable economic and legal clout and an increasing measure of interest from policy-makers and the public alike. In this sense, these alternative ideas may have a potent future in Canada.

It is important not only to understand institutions in health policy, but also to consider how ideas are embedded in political institutions. Political ideas, when mobilized by influential actors and institutionalized through policy outcomes, can affect political behaviour and perceptions about the boundaries of change. Federal systems by definition should allow innovative ideas to flourish, for such ideas naturally seek out laboratories for experimentation.

The unfolding history of health policy in Canada offers a persuasive example of the connection between ideas and institutions in political life. The presence of a social democratic party, the Co-operative Commonwealth Federation, and its charismatic leader, Tommy Douglas, were profoundly important in transmitting ideas about the need for public health insurance. Likewise, the Saskatchewan government's initiatives in hospital and then medical insurance provided examples for other provinces in setting up their own systems. More recently, the recent Supreme Court of Canada's decision in *Chaoulli v. Québec* (2005) offers a good illustration of this dynamic, but in a different direction. In this controversial case, the Supreme Court ruled that Quebec's ban on private insurance contravened the Quebec Charter of Rights and Freedoms. In a divided ruling penned by Chief Justice Beverley McLachlin on whether the Quebec legislation also contravened the Canadian Charter, ideas about equal access to care in the public system were challenged by alternative ideas about the private provision of insurance and of health care itself. These alternative ideas have found a powerful transmission belt through the legal system as courts have become important actors in health reform (Manfredi and Maioni, 2002).

Federalism and the Development of Health Insurance in Canada

The development of health insurance in Canada, and the pattern of intergovernmental relations that surrounds it, can be divided into three periods. The first period, when provincial health plans were put into place, was an era of federal leadership and co-operative federalism. This period lasted from the late 1940s through to the late 1970s. The second period, which began with the passage of the Canada Health Act in 1984, was marked by greater intergovernmental conflict, principally around federal–provincial shares of health-care costs. This period lasted through to the late 1990s and is characterized by what some have called 'unilateral federalism' as Ottawa cut its contribution to health-care costs. The third era dates from 2000 and is marked by more collaborative intergovernmental relations. The federal government's increase in health-care spending and its longer-term funding commitments have helped to ease some of the intergovernmental tensions.

Co-operative Federalism and Shared-Cost Federalism, 1947–1977

The emergence of public health insurance coincided with what has been termed an era of co-operative federalism (Robinson and Simeon, 1994). This co-operative relationship and the federal spending power led to a pattern of shared-cost federalism (see Chapter 7 by Banting) in health care.

Although there were no formal rules about intergovernmental co-operation in policy making, the 1940 Rowell-Sirois Report interpreted the federal spending power as a necessary instrument in building social programs in Canada but conceded that major funding initiatives would necessitate consultation with the provinces. Throughout his long tenure as Prime Minister, Mackenzie King resisted encroaching on provincial jurisdiction in health-care matters, although Paul Martin Sr did persuade him to support the 1948 National Health Grants Program.

In the absence of federal initiative, Saskatchewan's CCF government, led by Tommy Douglas, chose to 'go it alone' (Taylor, 1987) in setting up the first public hospital insurance plan in North America in 1947. The demonstration effect of Saskatchewan, in tandem with political pressure applied by Ontario (where the government was loath to take on such a large fiscal responsibility), contributed to the passage of the Hospital Insurance and Diagnostic Services Act under the Liberal government of Louis St Laurent in 1957. It set up an open-ended, cost-sharing arrangement, in which the federal government reimbursed about half of the costs of provincial hospital insurance plans, on condition that coverage was comprehensive and universal. By 1961, all the provinces had implemented hospital insurance plans that conformed to this new arrangement.

Federal involvement also provided the diffusion mechanism for provincial innovation in medical insurance. Against the backdrop of a bitter political battle, Saskatchewan introduced public medical insurance in 1962. After extensive study, a federally appointed Royal Commission (the Hall Commission) recommended in 1964 that the federal government develop legislation for public medical insurance (Canada, Royal Commission on Health Services, 1964). At the 1965 federal–provincial conference, Liberal Prime Minister Lester Pearson announced a new open-ended arrangement, in which the federal government would cover half the costs of provincial medical insurance plans. To ensure a measure of uniformity across the country, the Medical Care Insurance Act of 1966 stipulated that provincial programs would have to be comprehensive, universal, portable, and publicly administered. By 1971, every province had such a plan in operation.

Three specific ideas were embedded in these provincial health plans. (1) Health care is a public good and should be subject to extensive regulation. (2)The state must ensure universal coverage and equitable access. (3)The federal (central) government belongs in the health policy arena as a guardian of the 'right' to health care. These ideas are consistent with a social democratic view of the public sector and contributed to the rapid expansion of social protection throughout the industrialized world in the 'Golden Age' of the post-war welfare state (Esping-Andersen, 1996). In Canada, this view was most strongly transmitted by political leaders in the CCF–NDP and was institutionalized through the Saskatchewan experiments in public hospital and medical insurance. Once these innovations captured the health policy agenda, federalism was the vehicle through which they were diffused to other provinces. In some cases, the social democratic impetus was already strengthening (e.g., the Lesage administration in Quebec); in other cases (e.g., Alberta), the federal purse was able to trump contending ideas and alternatives.

With the help of shared funds from the federal government, each province designed its own health-care system to address the specific needs and concerns of its residents. Quebec's health insurance legislation, for example, does not explicitly refer to any federal principles and it was distinctive in several respects. Part of a broader expansion of the role of the state into economic and social affairs begun during the Quiet Revolution in the 1960s, Quebec health policy was designed as part of an integrated system of health and social services, and included such innovations as the network of CLSCs (health and social services clinics) (White, 1999). From the start, Quebec governments demonstrated a more aggressive stance towards professional stakeholders than did the governments in the other provinces. Many reforms that were diffused to the other provinces, such as the ban on extra-billing, salary caps on physicians, wide mandates for regional boards, and a pharmacare program, were first implemented in Quebec.

Although this early era was infused with a spirit of negotiation and compromise, intergovernmental health policy-making in the 1960s was not without conflict. Provincial leaders in Alberta and Ontario objected to the imposition of universal public health insurance. The Social Credit government in Alberta, for example, preferred its 'Manningcare' model of voluntary insurance plus public subsidies for the poor; Conservative premier John Robarts in Ontario referred to the federal policy as 'political fraud' (Taylor, 1987). Successive Quebec governments in the 1960s attempted unsuccessfully to change the funding formula to allow provincial opting out with compensation. Although there was widespread political and popular support for the Castonguay Commission's recommendations for universal insurance, the sticking point for Quebec was the extent to which the federal government could use taxation to fund programs within provincial jurisdiction (Desruisseux and Fortin, 1999).

The rapid expansion of the state into the health-care sector contributed to state-building by both provincial and federal governments and exacerbated conflict in intergovernmental relations to some extent (Young et al., 1984). At the same time, a series of fiscal crises almost immediately placed the two levels of government at loggerheads over health-care financing. By 1977, cost-sharing was replaced by Established Programs Financing (EPF)—block grants to provinces for health and post-secondary education. With the introduction of block grants, decisions that affected health-care funding were no longer in the realm of intergovernmental relations, but rather were tied to calculations about public expenditures in annual budgets. This change in the way the government of Canada contributed to health and post-secondary education allowed the federal Progressive Conservative government to reduce and eventually freeze EPF transfers in the late 1980s.

Federal Unilateralism and Intergovernmental Conflict, 1984–1999

Although the provinces became fully responsible for health-care cost increases after the introduction of the EPF, the federal government continued to exert an influence on health policy through the conditions attached to the cash component of fiscal transfers. In a dramatic gesture, Liberal Prime Minister Pierre Trudeau reinforced the federal government's political stake in health care by passing the CHA in 1984. Ostensibly directed at ensuring equal access to health services by eliminating the practice of extra-billing by physicians, the 1984 Act amalgamated hospital and medical legislation into a single, visible, and highly symbolic federal statute. Although the Liberal party went down to defeat shortly after its passage, the CHA retained its symbolic appeal. After the Progressive Conservative government attempted to scale back social programs with mixed results, Prime Minister Brian Mulroney stated publicly that health care remained a 'sacred trust' of the Canadian government. Following the Liberal party's return to power in Ottawa in 1993, the CHA became a focus of dispute between a federal government with a centralist vision and a tight purse, and provincial governments with increasing financial burdens in health care (Smith and Maioni, 2003). The federal government could more easily disengage itself from the consequences of these cost considerations, while provincial governments remained 'on the "front line" of public displeasure' (Fierlbeck, 1999).

The change in funding with the implementation of the Established Programs Financing arrangement in 1977 meant that federal money to each province included both cash transfers and tax points. The EPF formula was initially calculated on a per capita basis but this formula was replaced with one based on growth in GNP—2 per cent in 1986 and essentially frozen after 1990. As each change in the funding formula led to decreases in federal health transfers to the provinces, critics pointed out that the federal government was 'off-loading' its deficit problems by reducing its health-care funds to the provinces (Boothe and Johnson, 1993).

More precipitous changes were yet to come. In 1995, the Liberal Finance minister, Paul Martin, introduced the Canada Health and Social Transfer to replace the EPF arrangement and the Canada Assistance Plan. The CHST amalgamated federal funds for health, social assistance, and post-secondary education into a single grant and considerably reduced the cash portion of the transfer (Phillips, 1995). The cash transfer to the provinces declined from $18.5 billion to $12.5 billion. The tax-point portion was largely unaffected. In consequence, by the mid-1990s federal transfers represented only one-third of provincial outlays in health as compared to 40 per cent of provincial health expenditures in the mid-1970s (CIHI, 1999).

Intergovernmental relations in health care took a significant turn for the worse with the implementation of the CHST. The provinces responded by launching their own intergovernmental initiative: to create a 'social union' in which provincial governments would set the agenda rather than the federal government (Courchene, 1996). At the centre of the health agenda were attempts to build an effective partnership between the federal and provincial governments that would entail 'adequate, predictable and stable cash transfers' and new, formal mechanisms to ensure more transparency and less ambiguity in dispute resolution. The federal government eventually captured this process with the signature of all provinces but Quebec to the Social Union Framework Agreement (SUFA) in February 1999. Although broad in scope and not specific to health care, the provisions of SUFA were directly relevant to health policy (Choudhry, 2000). The agreement acknowledged the need for more transparency and consultation in intergovernmental policy-making, including dispute resolution. Nevertheless, these initiatives were overshadowed by the pressing issue of the day in intergovernmental politics of social policy: money.

A New Kind of Collaborative Federalism? 1999–Present

Recent years have seen an increase in federal transfers for health care, and with them, improved intergovernmental relations. The 1999 federal budget finally changed the tide. It earmarked additional funds for the CHST (including the injection of $11.5 billion over five years for health transfers to the provinces) and introduced measures to eliminate interprovincial disparities (Canada, Department of Finance, 1999). In 2000, a health-care funding agreement further increased transfers to the provinces, with a guaranteed minimum, but still left provincial leaders concerned about their fiscal capacity to meet increasing health-care costs. In 2003, the Canada Health Transfer (CHT) came into effect. Increased funding was provided through a Health Reform Fund intended to finance targeted initiatives (Primary Health Care, Home Care, Catastrophic Drugs, and Diagnostic/Medical Equipment).

After extensive negotiations at a high-profile first ministers' meeting in 2004, the premiers reached another agreement on health-care funding. The federal government committed to a 10-year plan for increased health-care transfers and a special fund to reduce waiting times, a matter that had become a thorny political issue. In all, the federal government estimated this would inject $41 billion into health care across Canada. The 2004 accord was marked by several 'side deals'. One provided for asymmetrical treatment of Quebec and came after the Quebec government refused to accept certain conditions of federal funding, including participation in the newly formed Health Council of Canada.

Currently, the federal government provides money for provincial health care in several ways. The first, and the largest, is the contribution through the CHT. It consists of a direct cash and tax-point transfer 'tied' to provinces respecting the five principles of the Canada Health Act. Second, the federal government has entered into specific funding arrangements with the provinces for targeted initiatives (for example, the recent Health Reform Transfer, the Diagnostic/Medical Equipment Fund, and the Primary Health Care Transition Fund). Third, the federal government also indirectly contributes to health care through equalization payments to eight provinces. These payments are intended to ensure that provinces can deliver comparable levels of services regardless of their revenue situation. Alberta and Ontario, the richest provinces in Canada, are net contributors to equalization and do not receive these funds. Fourth, the federal government contributes directly for subject matters under federal authority, such as Aboriginal peoples and military personnel. These funds also have an impact on provincial health-care systems and provincial residents. And finally, although the provinces spend money on public health, health promotion and disease prevention, and health research, the federal government invests heavily in all provinces in these areas as well.

Health Care: A Poorly Performing Federal System?

How has the federal system performed in regard to health care in Canada? This question directs us to an examination of whether the institutions and processes of intergovernmental relations have functioned so as to ensure respect for each order's jurisdiction; maintained a federal balance between unity and diversity; and facilitated communication, negotiation, and sometimes agreement across the two orders of government.

By the above measures, the federal system performed poorly in health care over the 1990s. Throughout the decade, provincial governments were locked in a political battle with the federal government over *who pays how much* in health care. The federal government's reduction in its direct transfers to the provinces for health care had an obvious negative impact on provinces' budgets. The Liberal government's zero-sum attitude in dealing with the provinces after 1995 further added to provincial perceptions of Ottawa's perceived intransigence in recognizing provincial concerns in health care. At least part of the resentment on the part of provincial governments had to do with the sense of the ground shifting under their feet. Provinces long ago had agreed to set up and live with health insurance systems that conformed to federal principles, only to have a latter-day federal government change the rules of the game. To the provinces, the federal government seemed content to occupy the high ground on health-care reform while leaving the provinces with the political fallout over the details of cost containment and access to care. Tensions between provincial and federal governments, from first ministers down through officials in health-care bureaucracies, were palpable.

In this rocky intergovernmental landscape, the provinces and the government of Canada acted independently to search for new policy directions in health care. Beginning in the early 1990s, almost every province commissioned reports and studies that could address the political concerns and fiscal pressures of health reform (Angus, 1992). The federal government was also conscious of the political repercussions of a perceived lack of leadership in health care and launched the National Forum on Health in 1994. This initiative met with provincial reluctance and, in some cases, hostility; provinces perceived it to be an instance of federal involvement in a sector of provincial responsibility. However, there was some room for common ground. Both the report of the National Forum on Health (1997) and the report of the Conference of Provincial/Territorial Ministers of Health (1997) concluded that predictable funding was essential for the functioning of provincial health systems and that the federal government should guarantee a minimum cash transfer to the provinces to ensure this outcome.

In a healthier financial state by the end of the decade, the federal government was able to respond to the political fallout from its cost-control initiatives by increasing contributions to the provinces for health care. And, as health care intensified as a political issue and became increasingly salient in general elections, Prime Minister Jean Chrétien set up a Commission on the Future of Health Care in Canada in 2000. Like the Hall Commission established in 1961, it was led by a prominent figure from Saskatchewan; unlike Justice Emmett Hall, however, Roy Romanow had served as the provincial premier in an NDP government that had been faced with major cost-cutting in health care.

The Romanow Commission was an extraordinary exercise in participatory democracy. While Hall had heard the reasons why public health insurance was needed, Romanow instead was faced with the challenge of reconciling Canadians' evident support for this outcome with preoccupations about the quality of care and the sustainability of health-care financing. His report, issued in 2002, was intended to shore up confidence in the public system. But it also included important insights about intergovernmental relations. Romanow said that the 'long-distance hollering' between premiers and the prime minister had to stop and that the federal government had to reinvest serious money in health care (including in specific targeted areas) (Commission on the Future of Health Care, 2002). Even though several of the Romanow Commission recommendations regarding where to target funds (such as for primary care) were high on provincial reform agendas, the very recommendation to target funds, rather than increase direct transfers, did not sit well with some of the premiers. And some provinces interpreted the Commission's recommendation to set up a Health Council, as a mechanism to ensure accountability in health-care spending, as jeopardizing provincial autonomy in health care.

Although the recommendations in the Romanow report have had an impact on federal funding of health care, the real contours of health reform in the provinces have been set by provincial health-care commissions, many of which were highly critical of the federal government. The fact that provinces have been at the forefront of health-care restructuring reflects the character of the health-care system; that is, it is not one national system but rather 10 provincial and three territorial health insurance plans that are united only by overarching norms.

Subsequent political changes have also affected intergovernmental relations in the health-care arena. For example, the transfer of power to Paul Martin Jr as prime minister served to mute, at least temporarily, the mutual bashing, and led to a more amicable, although not entirely consensual, first ministers' meeting and health-care accord in 2004. Health-care issues remained salient in the 2006 election, with the major federal political parties reaffirming the importance of public health insurance and emphasizing the need to reduce waiting lists and restore confidence. The arrival in power of a Conservative government may also affect intergovernmental relations, since the new prime minister, Stephen Harper, is known to be a staunch supporter of provincial autonomy in areas of jurisdiction such as health care. In addition, the changing of the guard in many provinces also changed the political playing field. A good case in point is Quebec, where Jean Charest's Liberal government came to office in 2003 and provided much of the leadership in building a Council of the Federation designed to forge a more constructive political voice for the provinces.

Federalism and Health-Care Policy: Effectiveness and Legitimacy

Evaluations of the impacts of federalism and intergovernmental relations on the effectiveness of health-care policies vary depending on the observer. Four criteria are used here with respect to the impact of intergovernmental relations on health care: (1) its contribution to equitable treatment of all Canadians regardless of their province/economic circumstances and consistent with shared membership in a social union; (2) its impact on cost-effective delivery of health care; (3) its capacity to facilitate adjustment of health-care policies consistent with the fiscal capacities of governments; (4) its capacity to respond effectively when new health-care issues and crises arise.

In regard to the first indicator of policy effectiveness, goals of equity constituted the rationale from the outset for the federal involvement in health care. In using its spending power to assist provinces in financing health care, the federal government attempted to ensure that all Canadians, regardless of province of residence, could enjoy comparable levels of health care. Reliance on federal transfers plus the use of equalization payments has tended to put provinces on an equal footing in terms of money spent. Today, health-care costs show some variation among the provinces but the existence of federal transfers and equalization payments tends to minimize these differences. More significant differences in levels of care have to do with regional and economic disparities, both within and between provinces.

A second indicator of policy effectiveness is whether Canadians get good value for money spent on health care. Health care has become an expensive proposition for governments. Overall, Canada is considered a 'big spender' among industrialized countries. In 1975, relatively soon after the full implementation of hospital and medical insurance, health-care spending accounted for 7 per cent of the gross domestic product (GDP). That figure grew to 10 per cent by the early 1990s, but declined somewhat over the decade as spending cuts were implemented. By 2005, however, health-care spending represented 10.4 per cent of GDP, or almost $142 billion dollars; about 70 per cent of that total was spent through the public sector (CIHI, 2006b).

Per capita health-care spending has also increased substantially, and now averages about $4,400 across Canada, a significant increase since the late 1990s. This figure is fairly similar across the provinces, although there is nonetheless a considerable difference between Alberta, the highest spender at $4,800 per capita, and Quebec, the lowest spender at $3,900 per capita. And health-care costs are substantially higher in the three territories, where spending averages over $7,000 per capita. Richer provinces tend to spend more per capita on health care, although spending also has to do with a government's political priorities as well as the organizational details of the health-care system. In Quebec, for example, costs are lower in part because of the distinct organizational features of the system, including the presence of community clinics and lower physician reimbursement rates. The percentage of provincial GDP devoted to health care also varies from one province to another, with about 7 per cent of a province's total wealth now devoted to health care. More stark, for provincial budget planners, is the fact that for some provinces and territories health care has become the largest single item of program expenditure, and this figure is growing apace. In 1975, on average, health care accounted for about 28 per cent of a province's program spending; today that average is almost 40 per cent (CIHI, 2006b).

A third indicator of policy effectiveness is the capacity to adjust policies as circumstances warrant. Have intergovernmental relations in health care facilitated the search for cost-containment strategies? Even while it reduced transfers to the provinces, the federal government insisted that the principles of the CHA be respected. In contrast to private insurance plans and most public health insurance systems in other countries, the Canadian provinces must provide services without co-payments or any kind of user fees. And, unlike the situation in many other countries, equal access provisions became a rampart against the development of a 'two-tier' system in which public and private services coexist, usually to the detriment of the public system. Essentially, equal access provisions prevented the channelling of 'excess' demand for health care towards a parallel private system in which ability (or willingness) to pay could override the need for care. Up to now, by insisting on equal access and uniform terms and conditions in the delivery of health care to individual patients, the federal government has upheld the ideal that all Canadians should receive the same benefits regardless of where they live or their economic situation.

This stance, combined with financial incentives in the form of fiscal transfers, served as a brake on widespread provincial experimentation with other forms of health insurance. But it left the provinces, as the 'single-payers' in the health-care system, with the brunt of responsibility—and blame from patients and providers—for cost control. To some extent, the federal system helped provinces learn from one another about how to contain costs. Following the release of the Barer-Stoddart report in 1990, most provinces attempted to reduce costs by reducing the numbers of foreign physicians and medical school enrolments (Sullivan et al., 1996). Other measures to deal with inflationary costs were diffused across the provinces through demonstration effects. Quebec was the first province to regulate physicians directly, imposing income ceilings, regulating the ratio of generalists to specialists, and assigning physician quotas by region (Demers, 1994). British Columbia was the first to attempt to control the number of physicians in the province through differential fees for new physicians, although these measures subsequently came under legal challenge in that province (Barer, 1988; Manfredi and Maioni, 2002).

In the 1990s, provincial governments reduced beds and closed hospitals—a development that would have seemed unthinkable a decade earlier. Although many hospital closures were bitterly opposed by local communities (and several were challenged in courts), this practice did not attract a response from the federal government (except in the case of Jean Chrétien's protest against the closure of the Montfort Hospital in Ottawa, on the basis of minority-language rights). As cost-containment strategies multiplied, however, public and provider discontent fuelled concerns that the reduction of services was jeopardizing access to care, particularly through longer waiting lists for certain procedures and overcrowding in emergency rooms.

Indeed, the very success of provincial health-care systems impeded their reform. Canadians consider timely access to expensive, sophisticated, and high-quality health services as a right, making provincial attempts at reining in costs and reorganizing delivery politically unpopular. Still, within the explicit constraints of the Canada Health Act and the policy grooves set by past experience, and with some interprovincial borrowing of tools and instruments, most provinces attempted to rationalize their health-care systems. Rationalization meant extensively restructuring the hospital sector and attempting to impose limits on health-care providers (Deber et al., 1994). Restructuring was facilitated by regionalization. Newly created regional health boards (some elected, others appointed) were made responsible for decisions about the allocation of global budgets to health institutions. Regionalization rationalized budget-making to some extent, but it raised the problem of passing the burden of accountability from provincial health ministries. In Ontario, the approach was more direct: the Conservative government passed legislation to empower it to close or merge hospitals through the auspices of a temporary Health Services Restructuring Commission (Tuohy, 1999).

In Alberta health-care reform throughout the 1990s was directed primarily at cutting public expenditures rapidly and eliminating the budget deficit. Following the 1994 Deficit Reduction Act, major hospital cuts were made in Edmonton and Calgary, salary rollbacks were imposed on public-sector employees (including hospital workers), and health insurance premiums were raised (Fierlbeck, 1999). By the end of the decade, Alberta had one of the lowest rates of growth in public health-care expenditures across the provinces, while private spending was among the highest in Canada. But the constraints of the federal conditions imposed on provincial health plans by the CHA frustrated the Klein government's efforts to encourage the expansion of private clinics. In 1996, the Alberta government finally backed down on facility fees after the federal government docked its transfers to the province. Another federal–provincial standoff emerged with the passage of legislation (Bill 11) in early 2000 to allow regional health authorities to contract with private clinics for surgical facilities as a way to deal with excess demand (Choudhry, 2000). The Mazankowski report (Alberta, 2001), highly critical of the federal government and of the 'public monopoly' imposed by the Canada Health Act, provided an alternative road map for health reform in Alberta and pushed the boundaries of the debate about private financing in health care. In 2005, the government proposed a plan for reform 'that follows neither the American nor the purely Canadian systems of health care' (Alberta, 2005). In 2006, however, reacting to public opinion within the province, the government retreated from some of the more controversial aspects of its 'third way' plan, such as allowing for physicians to be compensated both through the public sector and through private-sector arrangements.

A final way to measure the effectiveness of intergovernmental relations in health care is the capacity of governments to co-ordinate their actions when crises make it necessary. Intergovernmental co-ordination and collaboration are required in areas in which health has no borders—public health, infectious disease, and pandemics. During the spring of 2003, the SARS flu, a highly contagious viral illness, spread quickly through Toronto-area hospitals. Attempts to track and contain it had a ripple effect throughout the provinces and led to calls for a more co-ordinated approach to planning for and dealing with such problems. The task force set up to investigate the epidemic zeroed in on the need for better intergovernmental co-ordination and a 'truly collaborative framework and ethos among different levels of government'; it concluded that 'Canada's ability to contain an outbreak is only as strong as the weakest jurisdiction in the chain of P/T (provincial–territorial) public health systems' (Naylor, 2003). The Canadian Public Health Agency was put into place by the federal government in 2004, and part of its mandate was to ensure federal leadership in this area.

In summary, the record above indicates that the pattern of intergovernmental relations in health care—with the federal government unilaterally reducing funding but continuing to determine how the reduced funds will be spent—has narrowed provinces' scope for reform. At the same time, the high value that Canadians put on the existing system has discouraged the development of innovative cost-containment strategies. That said, the challenge of controlling public spending in health care and intergovernmental discord over health-care costs have clearly undermined the legitimacy of health-care systems. The three ideas underpinning the original Canadian model—state regulation, equitable access, and a federal role in health care—are all under question today. A window of opportunity has opened for political and social actors who believe in less state intervention. They have been able to question the legitimacy of federal standards and argue for the need to explore other options for financing health care, including private market alternatives.

Although the attachment of Canadians to the principles of universal health care remains robust across the provinces, there are some regional differences in openness to privatization options (Mendelsohn, 2002). Since the 1990s, however, a more generalized unease has developed among Canadians about the long-term sustainability of the existing public model, fuelled by growing concerns about cost and timely access to specific services (Blendon et al., 2002). Changes in ambulatory practice and controls on providers have increased the length of waiting lists and times for some elective procedures and for access to specialist care in some provinces. Waiting lists are also a form of implicit rationing of services in order to contain health-care costs. (Unlike user fees or extra-billing, which require patients to contribute directly to the cost of health care, waiting lists are compatible with the principle of equal access in the sense that they ensure that services are dispensed according to medical need rather than ability to pay.) For consumers of health care, the availability of physicians, the ratio of generalists to specialists, and the distribution of generalists/specialists across urban and rural/remote areas all are matters that affect perceptions of the legitimacy of existing health-care systems (CIHI, 2006a).

Ideas that support privatization in health care are not new in Canada. What is new is the way in which such ideas are pushing the frontiers of public debate about health reform. Although Canadian federalism has so far prevented the widespread implementation of private alternatives, conflicts over what level of government is responsible for cost control and the extent to which provincial health policy choices can be constrained by federal government preferences have created political room for these alternatives to gather political momentum.

The basic challenges that affect provincial health-care systems directly impact on the role the federal government has carved out for itself in health care. What should be covered by a provincial health plan? Who should pay for services? When can equal access be provided? How can the provinces address demographic and technological pressures? And, as the recent court battles over health care suggest, constitutional debates in health care are not only about the division of powers, but also about rights of Canadians under the Charter. For example, in *Auton v. British Columbia*, a group of BC parents claimed a specific treatment for their autistic children under the equality rights provisions (s. 15) of the Canadian Charter of Rights and Freedoms. They had won their case at the provincial court level, but the Supreme Court of Canada overturned the BC rulings, arguing that the contents of the health-care basket were a 'matter for Parliament and the legislature' (Manfredi and Maioni, 2005).

In 2005, the Supreme Court of Canada invalidated prohibitions against private insurance for core medical services provided through Quebec's public health-care system (Manfredi and Maioni, 2006). This decision in *Chaoulli v. Québec* was a divided and controversial one involving three separate judgments. The majority decision overturned rulings by provincial courts, and found Quebec's hospital and health insurance legislation to be in violation of the Quebec Charter of Rights and Freedoms (the right to life and inviolability of the person). After requesting a stay of one year, the Quebec government finally drafted a legislative response in June 2006 (Quebec, 2006). Bill 33 opens the provision of core services in the Quebec health-care system to private insurance, but only in three specific areas: hip, knee, and cataract surgery. It also goes further and opens the door to the eventual extension of private insurance to other procedures, and introduces a new instrument for the provision of services through the establishment of 'affiliated medical clinics' through public–private partnerships, a central theme of the Liberal government's attempts to 're-engineer' the Quebec state. At the same time, however, the proposal retains the 'wall' between physicians who remain in the public system and those who opt out of it. It thus differs from Alberta's ill-fated proposals, and introduces a wait-time guarantee akin to what the federal Conservative party had promised in the January 2006 election.

The *Chaoulli* court case involved the federal government and five other provinces as intervenors on behalf of Quebec. Interestingly, the plaintiffs had the support of a group of senators who had signed a 2002 Senate committee report claiming that waiting times for certain medical services were unacceptable and suggesting a better mix of private and public delivery. Regardless of this interest at the federal level, the case has driven home the fact that health care is governed primarily by provincial laws rather than federal regulations. Because the majority decision was reached on the basis of the Quebec Charter, there was no direct or immediate impact on other provincial health-care legislation. But other provinces are facing pressures similar to the ones that led to this legal saga. The case had been making its way through the Quebec courts since the 1990s, when the brunt of health-care cuts was taking effect, and involved an elderly patient (George Zeliotis) who waited over a year for hip replacement surgery and a maverick physician (Chaoulli) who had been trying for over a decade to pressure the Quebec government to allow more private medicine in the health-care system.

Perceptions of legitimacy clearly differ depending on whether one is a recipient of health care or a provider. At times, physicians have had a turbulent relationship with Canada's health-care system. At the outset of publicly funded health insurance, medical interests came into conflict with the provinces over issues of financial and professional autonomy (Evans et al., 1989). Physicians opposed the introduction of medical insurance legislation in Saskatchewan in 1962; Quebec specialists went on strike in 1970; Ontario doctors opposed the ban on extra-billing in Ontario in 1986; and, more recently, there were limited work stoppages in Ontario to protest funding cuts. Doctors have accepted the bargain of the state monopoly on health care: that is, fee schedules in return for the freedom to practise on a fee-for-service basis. The majority of doctors are reimbursed for their services on a fee schedule negotiated between provincial governments (or their public agency) and the provincial medical association. (In Quebec, there are separate negotiations for specialists, general practitioners, and residents.) These fee schedules are roughly similar across the provinces, although they are set separately in each province—there is some variation in the definition of billing codes and reimbursement rates tend to be lower in Quebec. Across the provinces, most doctors continue to be paid on a fee-for-service basis, but salaried doctors who staff community clinics and hospitals are more common in Quebec, Manitoba, and New Brunswick.

Conclusion

The politics of intergovernmental relations in the health sector point to the strength of federalism in helping to build a coherent health-care model across the provinces. Health care has long been touted as a success story of what federalism can achieve, and provincial health-care systems are vaunted as the success story of public-sector involvement in the health sector. Since the passage of initial health legislation, the health-care system has occupied an influential symbolic role in Canadian federalism, and federalism continues to exert a significant influence on health policy. The scope for provincial experimentation in health reform is considerably narrowed by the institutional levers of intergovernmental relations and policy legacies that characterize the health-care system in Canada. Health 'reformers' have had to work within the relatively limited boundaries of provincial health statutes and the stipulations of the CHA. In this sense, policy legacies have had powerful resonance in maintaining the logic of a single-payer model.

But this model has hardly survived unscathed by the economic and political turbulence of the past decade. Sustained cost controls, limits on providers, and extensive hospital restructuring have put enormous pressure on provincial systems and frayed public confidence in the public sector. Meanwhile, federal–provincial relations in the health-policy sector deteriorated, as health ministers and first ministers skirmished publicly over money and rules. And the emergence of the courts as a player in health care has further muddied the policy playing field. The CHA, which insists that the principle of equal access be maintained by provinces receiving federal monies for health care, is seen by its supporters as a firewall against private health-care services. The Act cannot, however, impel provinces to prohibit such services and it is unclear how the federal government will respond in its application of the statute in the wake of the *Chaoulli* ruling.

Today, the federal government is in a position of surplus rather than deficit, and most of the provinces are doing better financially as well. Not surprisingly, the conflicts over money have not abated with the return of better economic scenarios. If anything, the politics of surplus budgets have exacerbated tensions about money and jurisdiction, and about regional disparities, and have empowered provinces to 'push the envelope' in some areas of health reform. The enduring debate over the fiscal imbalance is directly related to health care, since the questions of costs and responsibility remain at the heart of fiscal federalism.

Besides representing a growing share of fiscal resources, health care is seen by many as the most important service funded by government. The Liberal Party of Canada, in its recent tenure in Ottawa, seized upon its historical role in promoting and diffusing the public model and carving a political space in the health sector despite a limited jurisdictional role. Ottawa's role in health care has been both symbolic and practical. In symbolic terms, the federal government claimed to have 'nationalized' health care, promoted 'equal citizenship' among Canadians, and guaranteed health benefits to all. This discourse is of enormous significance in debates about provincial autonomy, national unity, or constitutional renewal. It allows the federal government to defend the 'integrity' of the features that reflect 'Canadian values' without the headache of administering and budgeting for health-care services. In practical terms, the federal government was able to use the CHA as a way to minimize asymmetry in health provision among the provinces and to contribute towards regional equity. In doing so, federalism served as an instrument for narrowing reform alternatives, and ironically constrained the principle of policy diversity inherent in the Canadian federal principle.

The 2006 federal election of a Conservative government may change the perception and appreciation of federal roles and responsibilities in health care. Provincial autonomy and innovation are central principles in Prime Minister Stephen Harper's world view. It remains to be seen whether these principles will conflict with existing federal statutes, such as the CHA, and how the intergovernmental relations in health care will be played out in a new era of institutional change and against a changing backdrop of political ideas in Canada.

References

Alberta. 2001. Report of the Premier's Advisory Council on Health for Albertans (The Mazankowski Report). Edmonton. Available at: <www.health.gov.ab.ca /resources/publications/PACH_report_final.pdf>.

———, Health and Wellness. 2005. *Getting On With Better Health Care*. Edmonton. Available at: <www.health.gov.ab.ca/key/AHW_WebFinal_REV.pdf>.

Angus, D.E. 1992. 'A Great Canadian Prescription: Take Two Commissioned Studies and Call Me in the Morning'. In *Restructuring Canada's Health*

System: How Do We Get There From Here?, ed. R. Deber and G. Thompson. Toronto: University of Toronto Press.

Banting, K. 2005. 'Canada: Nation-Building in a Federal Welfare State'. In *Federalism and the Welfare State: New World and European Experiences*, ed. H. Obinger, S. Leibfried, and F.G. Castles. Cambridge: Cambridge University Press.

———— and S. Corbett. 2002. 'Health Policy and Federalism: An Introduction'. In *Health Policy and Federalism: A Comparative Perspective on Multi-Level Governance*, ed. Keith Banting and Stan Corbett. Montreal and Kingston: McGill-Queen's University Press.

Barer, M.L. 1988. 'Regulating Physician Supply: The Evolution of British Columbia's Bill 41', *Journal of Health Politics, Policy and Law* 13: 1–25.

Blendon, R.J., et al. 2002. 'Inequalities in Health Care: A Five-Country Study', *Health Affairs* 21, 3: 182–91.

Boothe, P., and B. Johnston. 1993. 'Stealing the Emperor's Clothes: Deficit Offloading and National Standards in Health Care', *Commentary*, C.D. Howe Institute, 41 (Mar.).

Canada, Department of Finance. 1999. *Federal Transfers to Provinces and Territories*, Oct.

————, National Forum on Health. 1997. *Canada Health Action: Building on the Legacy*. Ottawa: Minister of Public Works and Government Services.

————, Royal Commission on Health Services. 1964. *Final Report: Volume I.* Ottawa: Queen's Printer.

Canadian Institute for Health Information (CIHI). 1999. *National Health Expenditure Trends, 1975–1998*. Ottawa.

————. 2006a. *Geographic Distribution of Physicians in Canada: Beyond How Many and Where*. Ottawa.

————. 2006b. *Health Care in Canada*. Ottawa.

Choudhry, S. 2000. 'Bill 11, the *Canada Health Act* and the Social Union: The Need for Institutions', *Osgoode Hall Law Journal* 38: 40–99.

Commission on the Future of Health Care. 2002. *Building on Values: The Future of Health Care in Canada*. Final Report of the Commission. Ottawa.

Conference of Provincial/Territorial Ministers of Health. 1997. *A Renewed Vision for Canada's Health System*.

Courchene, T.J. 1996. 'ACCESS: A Convention on the Canadian Economic and Social Systems'. Working paper prepared for the Ministry of Intergovernmental Affairs, Government of Ontario.

Deber, R., B. Sharmila, L. Mhatre, and G.R. Baker. 1994. 'A Review of Provincial Initiatives'. In *Limits to Care: Reforming Canada's Health System in an Age of Restraint*, ed. A. Blomqvist and D.M. Brown. Toronto: C.D. Howe.

Demers, Louis.1994. 'La profession médicale.' In *Le système de santé québécois: organisations, acteurs et enjeux*, ed. Vincent Lemieux et al. Québec: Presses de l'Université Laval.

Desruisseaux, A., and S. Fortin. 1999. 'The Making of the Welfare State'. In *As I*

Recall/Si je me souviens bien, ed. Institute for Research in Public Policy. Montreal: IRPP.

Esping-Andersen, G. 1996. 'After the Golden Age? Welfare State Dilemmas in a Global Economy'. In *Welfare States in Transition: National Adaptations in Global Economies*, ed. G. Esping-Andersen. London: Sage.

Evans, Robert G., et al. 1989. 'Controlling Health Expenditures—The Canadian Reality', *New England Journal of Medicine* 320, 9: 571–7.

Fierlbeck, K. 1999. 'Cost Containment in Health Care: The Federal Context'. In *The Canadian Social Union: Case Studies from the Health Sector*, ed. H. Lazar and D. Adams. Montreal and Kingston: McGill-Queen's University Press.

Gray, G. 1991. *Federalism and Health Policy: The Development of Health Systems in Canada and Australia*. Toronto: University of Toronto Press.

Huber, E., C. Ragin, and J.D. Stephens. 1993. 'Social Democracy, Christian Democracy, Constitutional Structure and the Welfare State', *American Journal of Sociology* 99, 3: 711–49.

———. 1999. 'Les normes centrales et les politiques de la santé'. In *Le Système de santé québécois: Un modèle en transformation*, ed. C. Bégin et al. Montréal: Presses de l'Université de Montréal.

Manfredi, C.P., and A. Maioni. 2002. 'Courts and Health Policy: Judicial Policy Making and Publicly Funded Health Care in Canada', *Journal of Health Politics, Policy and Law* 27: 213–40.

——— and ———. 2005. 'Reversal of Fortune: Litigating Health Care Reform in *Auton v. British Columbia*', *Supreme Court Law Review (2d)* 29: 111–36.

——— and ———. 2006. 'The Last Line of Defence for Citizens: Litigating Private Health Insurance in *Chaoulli v. Quebec*', *Osgoode Hall Law Journal* 44, 1.

Mendelsohn, M. 2002. 'Canadians' Thoughts on their Health Care System: Preserving the Canadian Model through Innovation'. *Royal Commission on the Future of Health Care*. Ottawa: Government of Canada.

Naylor, D.C. 2003. *Learning from SARS—Renewal of Public Health in Canada*. A report of the National Advisory Committee on SARS and Public Health. Ottawa: Health Canada.

Pierson, Paul. 2000. 'Not Just What, but When: Timing and Sequence in Political Processes', *Studies in American Political Development* 14: 72–92.

Phillips, S.D. 1995. 'The Canada Health and Social Transfer: Fiscal Federalism in Search of a Vision'. In *Canada: The State of the Federation 1995*, ed. D.M. Brown and J. Rose. Kingston: Institute of Intergovernmental Affairs, Queen's University.

Québec, Assemblée nationale. 2006. *Projet de loi n 33: Loi modifiant la Loi sur les services de santé et les services sociaux et d'autres dispositions législatives*. Québec: Éditeur officiel du Québec.

Robinson, I., and R. Simeon. 1994. 'The Dynamics of Canadian Federalism'. In *Canadian Politics*, 2nd edn, ed. J. Bickerton and A.-G. Gagnon. Peterborough, Ont.: Broadview Press.

Simeon, R. 2006. *Federal–Provincial Diplomacy: The Making of Recent Policy in Canada, with a new preface and postscript.* Toronto: University of Toronto Press.

Smith, M., and A. Maioni. 2003. 'Health Care and Canadian Federalism'. In *New Trends in Canadian Federalism,* 2nd edn., ed. F. Rocher and M. Smith. Peterborough, Ont.: Broadview Press.

Sullivan, R.B., et al. 1996. 'The Evolution of Divergences in Physician Supply Policy in Canada and the United States', *Journal of the American Medical Association* 276, 9: 704–9.

Taylor, M.G. 1987. *Health Insurance and Canadian Public Policy: The Seven Decisions That Created the Canadian Health Insurance System and Their Outcomes,* 2nd edn. Montreal and Kingston: McGill-Queen's University Press.

Tuohy, C.H. 1999. *Accidental Logics: The Dynamics of Change in the Health Care Arena in the United States, Britain and Canada.* New York: Oxford University Press.

Watts, R.L. 1999. *Comparing Federal Systems,* 2nd edn. Kingston. Institute of Intergovernmental Relations, Queen's University.

Weaver, R.K. 1986. 'The Politics of Blame Avoidance', *Journal of Public Policy* 6: 371–98.

Wheare, K.C. 1951. *Federal Government,* 2nd edn. London: Oxford University Press.

White, D. 1999. 'La santé et les services sociaux: réforme et remise en question'. In *Le Québec en jeu: comprendre les grands défis,* ed. G. Daigle and G. Rocher. Montréal: Les presses de l'Université de Montréal.

Young, R.A., P. Faucher, and A. Blais. 1984. 'The Concept of Province-Building: A Critique', *Canadian Journal of Political Science* 17, 4: 783–818.

Cases

Auton (Guardian ad litem of) v. British Columbia (Attorney General) (2004), 3 S.C.R. 657.

Chaoulli v. Quebec (Attorney General) (2005), 1 S.C.R. 791.

Websites

Canadian Institute for Health Information: www.cihi.ca

Health Canada: www.hc-sc.gc.ca

Canadian Policy Research Network: www.cprn.com

Chapter 9

From Multilateralism to Bilateralism to Unilateralism in Three Short Years: Child Care in Canadian Federalism, 2003–2006

Martha Friendly and Linda A. White

For an 18-month period in 2004–5, federal and provincial/territorial governments seemed poised to establish the foundations of a new national early learning and child-care (ELCC) system.[1] The federal Social Development minister at the time, Ken Dryden, compared this social program initiative to the establishment of national health care in the 1960s (Rollason, 2004). This initiative came to an end, however, when the Martin Liberal government was defeated by the Conservative party in January 2006. The new minority Conservative government, with a very different philosophy of social and family policy, immediately served notice that it would terminate the intergovernmental ELCC agreements signed by the Martin government and all the provinces. In place of the nascent national program that focused on developing an ELCC system, the Harper government opted for a straight cash transfer to parents, as well as a capital fund to build new child-care spaces (Conservative Party of Canada, 2006: 31).

In the first edition of this book, White (2002) argued that fiscal and ideological factors that had helped prevent the emergence of universal child care in previous decades appeared to be playing diminishing roles. By the late 1990s, the federal government had budget surpluses and appeared willing to commit funds to some kind of national early childhood development program (Canada, House of Commons, 1999; Canada, Department of Finance, 2000). Public and expert opinion was shifting towards greater support for high-quality early childhood education programs for improving human development and helping reconcile work and family life (Cleveland and Krashinsky, 1998; McCain and Mustard, 1999; Michalski, 1999). At the same time, the collaborative federalism regime under the Social Union Framework Agreement (SUFA) (Government of Canada and Governments of the Provinces and Territories, 1999) seemed to render policy-making increasingly complicated. In 2002, however, it was unclear whether SUFA's requirement of collaborative intergovernmental relations would help or hinder in achieving substantive child-care policy outcomes.

In this second edition, we argue that—in the end—SUFA did not matter much. Indeed, we note explicit movement away from the collaborative federalism regime established under SUFA. In the child-care policy area, Canada has moved from multilateralism to bilateralism to unilateralism in three short years.

More important in explaining recent developments have been the shifts from a majority Liberal federal government under Jean Chrétien, to Paul Martin's minority Liberal government, to a minority Conservative government under Stephen Harper. The prediction in the first edition of this book that ideological factors were fading in importance has proved to be wrong. Regime change—shifts among governments with very different, even opposing views about the value of early learning and child care—has played a major role in the policies of federal governments over the past three years.

The child-care case thus provides a graphic example of the centrality of political executives—in particular, their interests and their ideological beliefs—to the development of social policy in intergovernmental Canada.[2] These partisan political factors have interacted with the structures and processes of federalism to affect federalism's performance, effectiveness, and legitimacy in the area of child care.

In evaluating the performance, effectiveness, and legitimacy of federalism over the past three years, we examine four assumptions held in the policy community about the nature of federalism and intergovernmental relations in the area of child care. While political actors often act on the basis of these assumptions, the assumptions have not held true in recent years in the child-care policy area, suggesting that they should be re-evaluated.

The first assumption concerns the ideas held by the government of Canada. In the post-SUFA era, the federal government purported to be constrained in its ability to exercise leadership on child care such that it would not even initiate discussions about it without the consent of all provinces/territories. We argue, consistent with a more general argument made by Choudhry (2002), that institutional and constitutional impediments did not prevent the federal government from taking leadership when the political will existed (see also Boismenu and Graefe, 2004). But they did provide a convenient rationale for why the federal government could not do more when faced by challenges from advocacy groups.

The second assumption, asserted by certain federalism scholars as well as by some provincial governments, is that subnational governments in a federal system can serve as laboratories of policy innovation (see, e.g., Mintrom, 1997; Noël, 1998). We argue that, outside the government of Quebec's demonstrated leadership on ELCC and family policy,[3] provincial and territorial governments in the rest of Canada have generally not proven to be major laboratories of innovation.

The third assumption, held by some (but not all) provincial officials interviewed for this chapter, is that a bilateral process reflects a failure of a multilateral process or a movement away from the principle of collaborative federalism. We disagree, and argue that although the process of the 2005 ELCC bilateral negotiations may have reflected (as provincial officials suggested) failure to communicate adequately across levels of government and party lines, multilateral agreements are not necessarily a superior way to make social policy while maintaining the principle of collaborative federalism.

A fourth and final assumption, espoused mainly by the federal Conservative government, is that the Conservatives' style of 'open federalism' signals a respect for provincial autonomy (PMO, 2006). In fact, the Harper government's plan for disbursing capital funding directly to child-care operators has quite far-ranging implications vis-à-vis provincial jurisdiction and—as it will leave responsibility for ongoing funding in provincial/territorial hands—for provincial coffers.

In examining the interaction of the three evaluative criteria—performance, effectiveness, and legitimacy—performance concerns such as getting agreement per se continue to trump concerns with substantive policy effectiveness; and attention on the part of one level of government to appeasing demands of political executives at another level of government means that less attention is paid to issues of democratic legitimacy.

The chapter begins with a brief overview of the state of early learning and child-care policies and programs in Canada. It then documents the emergence of three federalism regimes—multilateral, bilateral, and unilateral—over the past three years. It concludes with a discussion of lessons from child care regarding the performance, effectiveness, and legitimacy of these three federalism regimes.

The State of Canadian Early Learning and Child Care

It is now more than 20 years since the federal Task Force on Child Care concluded that 'sound child care and parental leave programs can no longer be considered a frill but are, rather, fundamental support services needed by all families in Canada today' (Cooke et al., 1986: iii). But Canada has made little or no progress towards this system either at the national level or—outside Quebec—provincially.

In its review of Canada undertaken as part of a 20-nation comparative study, the Organization for Economic Co-operation and Development (OECD) commented that 'national and provincial policy for the early education and care of young children in Canada is still in its initial stages. Care and education are still treated separately and coverage is low compared to other OECD countries' (OECD, 2004a: 6). Canada is a laggard compared not only to Western Europe but even to the Anglo-American nations and some developing countries (OECD, 2006; UNESCO, 2006). Government spending on early learning and child care remains low in Canada. As the OECD's comparative analysis showed, Canada was the lowest spender in the OECD at 0.25 per cent of GDP (compared to Denmark, the highest spender, at 2 per cent of GDP) (OECD, 2006).

Each province/territory has its own approach to ELCC; there is no national approach as there is to health care under the Canada Health Act—also under provincial jurisdiction. Each province/territory has regulated child-care centres, part-day nursery schools, regulated family daycare (in private homes), and public kindergarten. The range, quality, and access to ELCC programs vary considerably by region and circumstance but generally 'care' and early childhood education for children younger than five years is a private family responsibility. The funding model of all provinces except Quebec—and, to some extent, Manitoba—relies heavily on fee subsidies for eligible low-income families (and by no means do all eligible families receive subsidized places). This welfare (rather than universal) approach means that high user fees for regulated child care—required to support most of the cost of program operations—are a major barrier to access for parents of modest and middle income. The supply of child-care spaces covers only a minority of children, and public kindergarten schedules do not meet the needs of working parents. Research shows that across Canada even regulated child-care programs are more likely to be mediocre than excellent (Goelman et al., 2000).

No province/territory has a system of high-quality ELCC programs that serves a majority of children. Yet the proportion of Canadian mothers in the paid labour force who have young children has continuously increased over the last three decades. Between 1995 and 2003, mothers' labour force participation rates had risen from 61 per cent to 66 per cent for mothers whose youngest child was 0–3 years, 75 per cent for those whose youngest was 3–5 years, and 82 per cent for those women with a child 6–15 years (Friendly and Beach, 2005).

Well-organized systems of early learning and child care are now the norm in most industrialized countries. In most OECD countries, many more 0–6-year-olds attend ELCC programs than do so in Canada (OECD, 2006). In Western Europe, most 3–6-year-olds attend ELCC programs that are primarily publicly delivered (usually under educational auspices) and publicly funded—although parents often pay some fees (ibid.). The main purpose is usually 'early childhood education', broadly construed, although in most European countries there are provisions—albeit not always adequate—to meet parents' needs for child care while in the paid labour force.[4] The quality of programs for 3–6-year-olds in most countries would be considered at least reasonably high (or at least acceptable) by most standards, with educational goals, early childhood teacher training, and curriculum statements in place in most countries (ibid.).

In past decades, there has been growing recognition—based on child development research—that learning begins at birth, young children learn through play, development in the early years forms a foundation for the future, and early childhood education programs play an important role both in how young children develop and in their quality of life (ibid.). Abundant child development research has reinforced the importance of the early years to children's subsequent developmental, social, and economic success, and the cutting-edge discourse in early learning and child care has moved beyond 'care' for children of working mothers to holistic early childhood education for all young children (Shonkoff and Phillips, 2000; Moss, 2006). Although these ideas have been widely accepted in countries such as France and Sweden for some years, they are relatively new to Canada.

Current public opinion reflects growing acceptance of these views in Canada, too. An Angus Reid/*Globe and Mail* poll found that 68 per cent of 2,499 Canadians polled agreed that daycare is good for children, with agreement highest in Quebec (78 per cent) and the Atlantic provinces (72 per cent) (Angus Reid/*Globe and Mail*, 1999: 6). A 2002 poll found that 90 per cent of the 1,200 Canadians polled agreed that child care is very important (64 per cent) or somewhat important (26 per cent) in furthering a child's education and development (Espey and Good Co., 2003: 10). A survey of public attitudes towards education in Ontario found that 75 per cent of 1,002 Ontarians polled agreed strongly (37 per cent) or somewhat (38 per cent) that 'licensed daycare programs should share information and co-ordinate programs with public kindergartens' (Livingstone and Hart, 2005: 7). These data demonstrate a growing acceptance of the idea that child-care services should be integrated with early childhood education. Most recently, an Environics report found that 81 per cent of the 2,005 Canadians polled felt that child care prepares children for school and 79 per cent felt that it promotes early learning and child development (Environics Research Group, 2006: 9).

Public support for building a national and universally accessible child-care *system* is also quite strong. The 1999 Angus Reid/*Globe and Mail* survey found that 78 per cent of Canadians polled supported (48 per cent strongly and 30 per cent somewhat) the federal government 'setting up an inexpensive day care system to all families who want it' (Angus Reid/*Globe and Mail*, 1999: 6). The 2006 Environics report found that 77 per cent believed that 'lack of affordable child care is a very (34 per cent) or somewhat (42 per cent) serious problem in Canada today' (Environics Research Group, 2006: 4). Eighty-two per cent felt 'that government should play a very (47 per cent) or somewhat (35 per cent) important role' in helping parents meet their child-care needs (ibid., 5). Seventy-five per cent of those polled believed strongly (43 per cent) or somewhat (33 per cent) in the national child-care program proposed in 2004 (ibid.). Fifty per cent of those polled favoured funding new child-care spaces over the Conservative government's $1,200 taxable allowance, with 15 per cent stating no preference or preferring both approaches (ibid., 7).

Use of non-parental child care continues to grow. Between the 1980s and 2006, the proportion of children aged six months to five years who were in child-care arrangements outside the nuclear family increased significantly (from 42 per cent of children in 1994–5 in non-parental care while one or both parents worked for pay or studied, to 54 per cent in 2002–3) (Bushnik, 2006). Most of the 1.2 million children aged 0–5 years with mothers in the paid labour force were assumed to be in unregulated[5] child care (a relative, an unregulated family child-care provider or in-home caregiver).[6] There are few concrete data about unregulated child-care arrangements.

Progress in Child Care: An Overview of Three Federalism Regimes

Before 2003

From the 1970s to 1995, the Canada Assistance Plan (CAP) provided provinces and territories with cost-shared funds to support the cost of child care for eligible low-income families. Eligibility was defined by a set of federal conditions that applied to both service providers and parents. Under CAP, child care was conceptualized as part of employment support for low-income families, not as an early learning program.

A national child-care program was first addressed at the federal level in 1984, when the Trudeau Liberal government appointed the ministerial-level Task Force on Child Care. After the 1984 federal election, the Mulroney Conservative government set up a special parliamentary committee that held cross-Canada hearings on child care, issued recommendations and tabled Bill C-144, the Canada Child Care Act (Canada, House of Commons, 1988).[7] Bill C-144 died when the 1988 federal election was called and was not revived.

In 1993, the federal Liberal party under Jean Chrétien campaigned to spend $720 million on child care over three years in order to create up to 50,000 new regulated spaces per year for three years. The pledge came with two caveats, however: first, the spaces would be created only in a year following a year of 3 per cent economic growth; second, the expansion would occur only with the agreement of the provinces (Liberal Party of Canada, 1993: 38–40). Although a number of provinces signified their willingness to participate, the Chrétien government failed to fulfill this promise (Timpson, 2001; Friendly, 2001). Instead, in the 1995 federal budget, CAP, the sole federal child-care funding scheme, was amalgamated into the Canada Health and Social Transfer (CHST), a block fund that replaced more specific transfer payment mechanisms for social welfare, post-secondary education, and health while massively reducing federal program expenditures. As Cameron and Simeon argue (2002: 54), the net effect of the experience of these federal cuts in the mid-1990s was 'to invest the provincial governments with a stronger sense of their autonomy, their responsibility and their right to judge, within their spheres of jurisdiction, what the national, as well as the provincial interest requires.'

By the late 1990s, the federal government looked to be getting out of the business of funding service delivery, instead providing income supplements such as the 1997 National Child Benefit (Cameron, 2005). SUFA formalized a more collaborative provincial/executive decision-making model that would preclude unilateral federal action in areas of provincial jurisdiction without provincial consent. Specifically, under SUFA (section 5), the federal government agreed that its 'federal' spending power would effectively become a 'national' spending power. The change from 'federal' to 'national' signified that the government of Canada would cede its authority to use social transfers for new initiatives without provincial consent. Any new federal transfer programs would require the agreement of a majority of the provinces.

The Multilateral Phase

Under the SUFA regime, the federal government could not direct the specific program spending requirements in federal transfers to the provinces without substantial provincial consent. Yet that did not stop it from venturing into social-policy waters. In its later years, the Chrétien government brought about the Federal–Provincial–Territorial Agreement on Early Childhood Development (ECDA). Signed by all provinces except Quebec in September 2000, it provided federal transfer funds in program areas deemed to be part of a 'child development' agenda. The government of Canada agreed to provide $2.2 billion over five years, beginning in 2001–2, to help provincial and territorial governments improve and expand early childhood development programs and services in four priority areas: healthy pregnancy, birth, and infancy; parenting and family supports; early childhood development, learning, and care; and community supports (CICS, 2000; Canada, Social Union, 2006).

ELCC was one of the ECDA's four identified areas even though, throughout this period, child care was not high on most government policy agendas and, indeed, lost ground in some provinces such as Ontario and Alberta (Friendly et al., 2002). Under the ECDA, some provinces chose to spend money on child care or early childhood education, and other provinces focused on more parent-based programs. Analysis of provincial/territorial spending on regulated child care in 2001–2 under the ECDA found vast variation among provinces and territories (CRRU, 2001); while some provinces spent a considerable proportion of their allocation on regulated child care (Newfoundland and Labrador spent $2.2 million of $5.2 million and Nova Scotia spent $6 million of $9.1 million, approximately two-thirds of its allocation), Ontario spent nothing on regulated child care.

In an effort to direct monies more explicitly to child-care programs, the federal Human Resources minister, Jane Stewart, reached an agreement with provincial and territorial ministers responsible for social services (except Quebec) in March 2003 on the Multilateral Framework Agreement on Early Learning and Child Care (MFA). Under the MFA, the federal government agreed to provide $900 million over five years, beginning in 2003, to support specific provincial and territorial government investments in early learning and child care (CICS, 2003; Canada, Treasury Board Secretariat, 2006). The programs could be delivered in a variety of regulated settings such as child-care centres, family child-care homes, preschools, and nursery schools. The list of allowed investments was quite broad: capital and operating funding, subsidies for parents, wage enhancements for workers, training, professional development, and parent information and referral services.

This multilateral agreement was noteworthy. It had the signed support of all the provinces (except Quebec, which even so declared support for the principles of both the MFA and ECDA); even the Ontario government of Mike Harris, which had been cutting child-care expenditures (CRRU, 2002), signed on. The MFA specified that the federal funds would be used for regulated ELCC programs only (outside school systems); it set out principles for child care (available and accessible, affordable, quality, inclusive, parental choice); and it committed governments to annual reporting to Canadians on 'descriptive and expenditure information', specifying indicators of availability, affordability, and quality (CICS, 2003).

The Bilateral Phase

Paul Martin was elected leader of the federal Liberal Party in December 2003. A brief weakening of neo-liberal ideas in the early twenty-first century ushered in a short period of policy expansionism with major increases in federal social program spending. Prior to winning the 2004 election with a minority government, Martin made ELCC a major part of his 2004 election platform, pledging to spend $5 billion over five years (beyond funds already committed through the MFA) to build a national system, based on four principles referred to as 'QUAD': quality, universality, accessibility, and developmentally focused programming (Liberal Party of Canada, 2004: 29).

Getting agreement from the provinces to spend the $5 billion on building a national early learning and child-care system became one of the defining issues of the Martin minority government. The extended negotiation process, which began shortly after Ken Dryden became the Social Development minister in July 2004 and lasted almost until the time the Martin government fell in a non-confidence vote in the House of Commons in December 2005, was very different from that of the MFA negotiations only two years earlier—and had a very different outcome.

This time all the provinces, *including* Quebec, entered into agreements to spend the federal government's funds.[8] However, although the provinces had previously agreed to the similar (and quite limited) conditions in the MFA process and to the QUAD principles at a social services ministers' meeting in November 2004, a public attempt to showcase a multilateral agreement in February 2005 was unsuccessful. The Alberta government resisted the requirement that the federal funds be spent only on regulated child care (CBC News, 2005a); the PEI and territorial governments campaigned for an enriched funding formula for smaller jurisdictions (CBC News, 2005b; Laghi, 2005); and the Quebec government, as usual, was reluctant to accept any conditions at all from the federal government in an area of contested responsibility (De Souza, 2005).

Turning away from a multilateral approach, Dryden managed to execute arrangements with all provinces including Quebec through a series of bilateral agreements. The final agreement was signed in November 2005 with the New Brunswick government, just before the Liberal government's defeat on a non-confidence motion. The protocols and overarching scheme for the bilateral agreements fell under a national umbrella of the QUAD principles and a common national format for each bilateral agreement (except Quebec's).

In each instance, the federal government and the province signed an agreement-in-principle (AIP) that included a general outline of how the funds were to be used (CRRU, 2006). According to a time frame specified in each AIP, each province was to develop a more specific Action Plan for the five-year phase. Following development of the Action Plan, a five-year bilateral funding agreement was expected. However, when the government fell at the end of 2005, only two provinces, Manitoba and Ontario, had finished the process. Three five-year funding agreements (the third was with Quebec) and seven AIPs were in various stages of progress.

By the time of the 2006 federal election, Canada was—for those who had advocated for child care for more than three decades—achingly close to achieving at least the foundations of a national system.[9] While the Liberal program may not have been all that some had hoped it would be, the 2006 Liberal election platform contained a pledge to make the federal commitment to the ELCC program permanent (Liberal Party of Canada, 2006). A switch in government, however, ended the federal–provincial agreements and the provincial development plans that accompanied them.

The Unilateral Phase

The Conservative Party had ignored the issue of child care in the 2004 federal election campaign, pledging instead to provide, if elected, a $2,000 per child income tax deduction for all families with dependent children under age 16 (Conservative Party of Canada, 2004: 18). However, in the 2006 election campaign, the Conservatives took a different approach. They pledged to end the bilateral ELCC agreements after one year, to introduce a $1,200 taxable allowance for each child under age six, and to provide $250 million in tax credits to employers and non-profit associations to create 125,000 child-care spaces (Conservative Party of Canada, 2006: 31).

The Conservative party explicitly countered the idea of a national early learning and child-care system in its election platform by calling its proposal a 'Choice in Child Care Allowance'. The platform stated:

> The Liberals and the NDP believe that the only answer to expanding childcare in Canada is their one-size-fits-all plan to build a massive childcare bureaucracy which will benefit only a small percentage of Canadians. Only the Conservatives believe in freedom of choice in child care. The best role for government is to let parents choose what's best for their children, and provide parents with the resources to balance work and family life as they see fit—whether that means formal child care, informal care through neighbours or relatives, or a parent staying at home (ibid., 31).

After it took office in January 2006, the Conservative government quickly announced—and then notified the provinces—that it was cancelling the ELCC agreements and providing one year of funding in all provinces/territories (whether they had an AIP, a five-year funding agreement, or no agreement at all). The child allowance was included in the May 2006 budget (Canada, Department of Finance, 2006: 99–103) and cheques to parents began to flow in July. The second part of the Conservative platform, the Child Care Spaces Initiative, was scheduled to begin during the 2007–8 fiscal year.

While the Conservatives' cancellation of the bilateral agreements was at the top of the agenda in a May 2006 meeting of social services ministers (Brown, 2006), by the time of the July meeting of the Council of the Federation, any mention of child care had disappeared from the agenda (Urquhart, 2006).

Rating the Performance, Effectiveness, and Legitimacy of Federalism

Analyzing the performance, effectiveness, and legitimacy of Canadian federalism in the area of early learning and child care requires an appreciation of the workings of federalism, both as the actors *perceive* their working relations and as they exist in practice. We have identified four assumptions—some made in the academic literature and some reported to us in interviews—about these relations. The workings of federalism over the past three years, however, provide little evidence to support these assumptions.

Assumption 1: Since the signing of SUFA, *institutional and constitutional impediments have prevented the federal government from taking the lead in policymaking.*

Under the Constitution Act, 1867, substantive jurisdictional authority over child care has been deemed to lie with provincial governments. Child care is not among the items specifically assigned to either s. 91 or s. 92 of the Constitution Act. Rather, it has generally been classified as a matter of social policy and therefore considered to fall under provincial jurisdiction under s. 92(13), as a matter of 'property and civil rights.' Even if child care is treated as an educational matter, the constitutional jurisdiction still lies with provincial governments under s. 93.

Traditionally, the federal spending power has allowed the federal government to shape social policy indirectly through the use of financial incentives, something it chose to do quite extensively until the 1990s. By the mid-1990s, and more specifically, with the watershed 1995 federal budget, the use of the federal spending power as an instrument of federal policy leadership became increasingly contested as a result of federal spending cutbacks and a near-victory for Quebec separatists in the 1995 sovereignty referendum (Boismenu and Graefe, 2004: 72–3; Doherty et al., 1998).

SUFA formalized a more collaborative federalism regime that required the co-operation of the provinces in the launch of any new federal social policy initiatives. Scholars such as Noël (2000) have pointed out, however, that the federal government had not shaken its habit of unilaterally involving itself in social programs. (See also Chapter 10 by Bakvis.)

With respect to child care, for some years the federal government had been extricating itself from shared-cost initiatives, culminating in the elimination in 1996 of CAP, the last shared-cost program. However, it continued to use the income tax system to offer working families some tax relief for child-care expenses through the Child Care Expense Deduction (CCED), funds for Aboriginal early learning and child care, military family resource centres, child-minding services through Citizenship and Immigration Canada, and services for at-risk children through the Community Action Program for Children (CAPC) (Friendly and Beach, 2005: xxi–xxii).

SUFA did little to iron out these jurisdictional disputes. As documented above, the federal government in the latter years of Jean Chrétien, and then under Paul Martin, strongly encouraged the provinces and territories to expand their spending on child-care programs by offering the carrot of federal funding. Paul Martin made achieving a 'national system of early learning and child care' with the provinces and territories a central focus of his minority government (Canada, 2004: 8).

Thus, while the federal government continued to use SUFA to justify its failure to take more prescriptive action—for example, by introducing national standards similar to those found in the Canada Health Act (author interview)—the experience of the past three years suggests that Ottawa can work with the provinces to forge national programs—if it has the political will to do so.

Assumption 2: A strength of federalism as it is practised in Canada is that, even in the absence of federal leadership, provincial governments act as laboratories of innovation.

According to some of the federalism literature (e.g., Noël, 1998), substantive jurisdictional capacity allows provinces to innovate in social policy areas, as the province of Saskatchewan did with regard to health care in the 1960s and as the Quebec government has done regarding child care and maternity/parental leave. We are less optimistic, however, about how many provincial and territorial actors in the rest of Canada see Quebec as a replicable model. Instead, Quebec is regarded by other provincial and territorial government officials as exceptional, driven to provide these services for its own policy purposes and for reasons that do not exist in the rest of Canada.

Overall, the record of provincial and territorial policy innovation with regard to child care is not outstanding. Even in the CAP era, when the federal government provided open-ended matching funds to provinces to develop social assistance programs, including money for child care for low-income families, provinces were remarkably uncreative and uninspired in developing comprehensive programs such as those found in Europe. Certainly, none of the provinces moved decisively to develop policy and funding schemes to support national objectives (as per the National Children's Agenda), such as promoting the development of all children.

One or two provinces have demonstrated some leadership, however, within this decentralized and relatively uncreative system. In addition to Quebec, Manitoba stands out as a have-not province that has still been in the forefront in committing to a children's agenda, putting child care on its own list of social policy priorities and committing to delivering services in a not-for-profit manner, which is seen by child-care advocates as the 'gold standard' in terms of best policy practices. Such policy leadership is important, since policy officials and political executives may find an example set by another province more compelling than one set by a different country. In that sense, intergovernmental processes can help both to diffuse knowledge of one province's practices to others and to push recalcitrant provinces to consider policies that other provinces have adopted.

The fact that no other province or territory has followed either Quebec's or indeed Manitoba's lead, however, suggests that diffusion of innovative ideas and policies is difficult, even with the added leverage of intergovernmental forums. Recent explanations for that lack of innovativeness have focused on what provincial premiers and pundits are calling the 'fiscal imbalance'; that is, the provinces may have the jurisdictional capacity but not the fiscal capacity, given their more limited taxing authority (see Chapter 4 by Brown). But, given that the Quebec government was able to implement its program, and given Alberta's shrinking child-care spending even while its provincial coffers are full (Friendly and Beach, 2005), the claim of fiscal incapacity rings hollow.

Assumption 3: Multilateral policy-making is better, stronger, and more national than bilateral approaches; a bilateral approach is less desirable, even a failure.
Many assumed that the signing of SUFA in 1999 ushered in a new period, one in which the intergovernmental process would have legitimacy only if all provinces participated and agreed to outcomes. Indeed, some provincial officials argued that the bilateral agreements the federal government ultimately employed—after the multilateral child-care process failed in 2004–5—were a second-best route.

We argue, however, that the bilateral process the federal government initiated was neither a major departure from past intergovernmental practice in Canada nor necessarily an inferior approach. The bilateral phase occurred after federal, provincial, and territorial governments (save Quebec) had agreed to a number of principles and conditions both under the MFA and through negotiations in 2004 with Ken Dryden, the federal Social Development minister. The MFA and the QUAD principles provided at least the foundation of an overarching 'national' policy platform. Analysis shows that the differences among the provincial AIPs and more detailed plans/agreements developed as part of the bilateral process are not substantial (Mahon, 2006).

Bilateral agreements are not unknown in Canada, although McRoberts (1985: 73) notes that they have often been achieved when an issue involves or affects only one or two provinces or where one or two provinces seek 'distinct arrangements with the federal government'. Sometimes, though, the federal government may negotiate specific agreements with provinces under a general agreement or policy approach. For example, in the late 1990s, the federal government negotiated a series of bilateral labour market development agreements (LMDAs) with the provinces and territories (Bakvis, 2002). Even under the Canada Assistance Plan Act, each province had its own agreement with the federal government, although they were not substantially different from one another.

Indeed, one senior provincial official, in an interview with the authors in August 2006, described bilateral negotiations as more useful and realistic both procedurally and substantially. He noted that 'The de facto political requirement of unanimity amongst the provinces and territories and the federal government in order to launch new federal spending makes it very difficult to achieve agreement, especially on ideologically polarized issues.' While a pan-Canadian master agreement may be necessary and/or desirable, bilateral agreements allow for greater flexibility in working out complex specifics. Furthermore, bilateral agreements can respond substantively to the different circumstances of each jurisdiction. Indeed, one interviewee noted that some child-care policy experts advised the federal government that moving to bilateral agreements could make the process slower, but it could also strengthen the resulting agreements.

While the federal government may choose the bilateral approach for functional reasons, McRoberts (1985: 74) argues that a government will be heavily influenced by its calculations 'as to which approach is to its strategic advantage, helping it to secure the maximum impact on a given policy sector or to maximize political credit among its citizens and so on.' The switch to bilateral negotiations, we argue, occurred in large part because the federal government realized that it was not possible to accommodate provincial and territorial demands under a multilateral collaborative process, especially since it was in the interest of some governments to stymie the negotiations for political gain. One interviewee suggested that some provinces, such as New Brunswick under a Conservative government, had an interest in being recalcitrant in order to help the electoral fortunes of its federal counterpart.

We find some evidence of this political explanation for the end of the multilateral process. Federal Human Resources Minister Jane Stewart was able to achieve a multilateral agreement in 2003 with similar principles while facing provincial resistance, but Social Development Minister Ken Dryden could not in February 2005. One observer suggested to the authors that, with the minority government situation and the perception that a federal election was looming, Dryden needed a successful outcome and so was not in a strong position to thrust something onto the provinces.

Another official noted that the dynamics of the two periods were very different. With regard to the funding cuts of the late 1990s, all provincial governments lost a great deal of the money used to support existing social programs. In the early 2000s, not all provincial governments had begun to implement their child-care funding schemes. Furthermore, provincial governments were genuinely divided as to how to react to the announcement and whether monies would still be delivered by other means.

Several interviewees suggested that the intergovernmental *processes* may have been problematic. One provincial official said that the switch to the bilateral route meant that some provinces—believing they had been bargaining in good faith and not expecting the federal government to abandon the multilateral process—felt betrayed. As a consequence, the process of reaching the three funding agreements (with Ontario, Quebec, and Manitoba) and the agreements-in-principle took a long time and expended a lot of political capital. In the end, it may have helped the newly elected Conservatives that the provinces (which were already divided by ideology and approaches to ELCC) had been dealt with in a bilateral manner, for when the Harper government announced cancellation of the agreements, there was no collective statement by the premiers condemning the move. Indeed, provincial leaders' response to the cancellation of the agreements demonstrated little provincial solidarity (Séguin and Laghi, 2006: A1, A4) compared to the solidarity witnessed in the late 1990s when the premiers were united against Ottawa's funding cuts. Thus, the Harper government received fewer complaints from the provinces than might have been expected in the face of a unilateral termination of a federal–provincial program.

One provincial official described the switch to bilateralism as a failure in process management by the federal government because it unilaterally reframed the process without getting prior agreement from the provinces and territories. The lesson may well be, then, that a transparent negotiation process based on mutual trust is as important as the end product.

Assumption 4: The Conservatives' 'universal child care' initiative means less federal intrusion on provincial jurisdiction.

As we pointed out earlier, there is an argument to the effect that, since signing SUFA, the federal government is hamstrung in exercising social policy leadership in areas of provincial jurisdiction. In any case, the federal government must employ more-or-less conventional federal powers that are more-or-less intrusive jurisdictionally. In the first edition, White (2002: 115) wrote:

> Provincial transfers, either in a shared-cost or block-funded way, may be the more efficient and effective way to deliver monies for child care. However, it will be difficult for all governments to agree on Canada-wide priorities and objectives. . . . Thus, it is possible that the federal government . . . could provide more child care funds via direct transfers to individuals. . . . It would be ironic were ministers to search out ways to 'get around' the SUFA in order to deliver child care monies. If this occurs, it will provide further evidence of the limitations of the collaborative federalism regime.

The Harper government's 'universal child care' policy appears to reflect exactly those sentiments. To pull back from the morass of federal–provincial–territorial negotiations, the Harper government chose instead to step away from providing transfers to provinces and territories by delivering direct cash benefits to families (Canada, 2006: 103). This tactic allows the federal government to spend money without encountering jurisdictional problems.

However, the second part of the Conservative policy—offering financial incentives directly to employers and non-profit organizations to encourage them to create child-care spaces—interferes with provincial jurisdiction. Leaving aside the question of whether providing capital incentives in the absence of funds to operate programs will have an impact on accessibility or quality for families (CCAAC, 2006b), there are serious jurisdictional implications in this initiative. The plan to give money directly (through tax credits, grants, or some other method) to employers and non-profit organizations to cover capital costs has the potential to intrude on provincial jurisdiction. The money committed—$250 million per year, beginning in 2007–8—is for capital funding only. Ongoing program operating funds and subsidies for low-income families will remain the provinces' responsibility, as they have been in the past.

Thus one provincial official described the Conservative government's 'space creation' plan as 'bad federalism' and went so far as to say that its decision to provide funds for infrastructure but not operating costs 'makes me shake my head and wonder if we have not learned anything over the past 30 years . . . . It is one thing to say to provincial governments, we plan to add to provincial coffers in order to create spaces. But if the feds approach a local YMCA, for example, with capital money, it is an entirely different matter and contrary to getting out of the provinces' faces.'

As federalism legal scholar Sujit Choudhry (2000) points out, in cases where the federal government has signed contracts with non-governmental recipients of federal funds:

> On the continuum of coercive state power, with spending at one end, and legislation at the other, contracts lie closer to the latter than the former, because they are legally enforceable. . . . If sufficiently detailed, contract terms could be used for standard-setting, etc. in the same way as provincial regulations. The availability of this out for the federal government deserves to be recognized, because it affects the relative bargaining power of the federal and provincial governments.

In the federal budget of 2007, the Conservative government followed through on its pledge to encourage employers and non-profit community organizations to create child-care spaces, introducing a 25 per cent investment tax credit to a maximum of $10,000 per space created. However, it also agreed to provide $250 million to provinces and territories to support the creation of child-care spaces (Canada, 2007: 124–5). This move marked a significant change for a government that had earlier refused to provide any money to provinces and territories for child care. But the amount is far less than what the Liberal government had promised. Furthermore, unlike the Liberal proposal, the Conservative plan does not make any commitment to conditions or reporting (Greenaway, 2007: A4). Nor does it offer funding for Aboriginal communities or provide for federal–provincial collaboration on data and accountability.

Conclusions

This chapter highlights some of the unique lessons generated by the case of early learning and child care both for Canadian federalism and for policy-making. Partisan political interests have interacted with the structures and processes of federalism to affect federalism's performance, effectiveness, and legitimacy in the area of child care. Not only institutions but also interests and underlying political ideologies explain developments regarding early learning and child care over the past three years.

Three years of intergovernmental negotiations using three different federalism regimes have left us exactly where we were before: with no national early learning and child-care system and with little progress in most regions. This policy outcome reflects a failure of the way federalism is practised in Canada.

The child-care case reveals that the flexibility of the intergovernmental process—for example, its ability to shift from multilateral to bilateral negotiations—enhances its performance. At the same time, however, that flexibility can detract from the legitimacy of the process unless the switch from one process to another is mutually agreed upon by all affected parties to the negotiation. Successful negotiations, therefore, require attention to issues of process as well as to substance.

The requirement of unanimity and joint agreement to act can detract from the effectiveness of the process. It can allow the strategic interests of ideologically driven political executives opposed to ELCC policy development to act as veto players. Conversely, political actors supportive of ELCC policy developments must bargain with these veto players, and, therefore, progressive policy-makers cannot make too many demands on recalcitrant players. At worst, this leads to policy inertia; at best, to lowest-common-denominator policies. At the same time, the child-care case demonstrates that opportunities for agreement do occur when one level of government possesses substantial fiscal resources to leverage agreements with recalcitrant provinces and territories.

The federal cancellation of previously negotiated agreements also raises real concerns regarding the legitimacy of the process of intergovernmental bargaining and intergovernmental relations generally. While cancellation clauses are pro forma in intergovernmental agreements, we raise the question of what cancellation does to the spirit of federalism. As Premier Dalton McGuinty of Ontario stated, 'We entered into an agreement with the Government of Canada, not with the Paul Martin Liberals' (Livingston, 2006). The unilateral decision of the Harper government to cancel the bilateral funding agreements and agreements-in-principle could thus damage trust ties between federal and provincial governments for years to come, and add fuel to sovereignists' claims that federalism cannot accommodate the diversity of those bilateral agreements. As one senior provincial official from a small province argued in an interview, the governing principle of intergovernmental bargaining should be that 'when one order of government signs an agreement with another order, rescinding of those agreements ought to be done by both parties.'

In the short term, the future of substantive child-care policy development at the national level is bleak under these damaged trust ties. After the Harper government announced the cancellation, provinces were left to figure out once again how to fund their long-term policy commitments. There have been some suggestions that some of the federal money could be returned in the form of tax points—the most sterile and least creative of policy instruments—or through some resolution of the so-called 'fiscal imbalance'. This alternative points to a very different kind of intergovernmental bargaining than that witnessed under the Chrétien and Martin governments, though with no guarantee of success.

In terms of the interaction among the evaluative criteria of performance, effectiveness, and legitimacy, then, attention to issues of process can lead to less effective substantive policies; but lack of attention to issues of process can hinder the legitimacy of the agreements reached. Performance criteria raise questions about whether agreements reached respect federal principles and sustain the balance between unity and diversity in the federation; allow for discussion and negotiation of issues arising between governments; and facilitate agreement or at least understanding on major issues so as to respect the positions of both levels of government. We argue that these performance criteria can trump considerations of policy effectiveness. They can result in agreements that do not resolve the problems that occasioned intergovernmental bargaining in the first place; that do not follow recognized best practices in policy; or that do not allow governments to meet international commitments. As one interviewee stated about the Early Childhood Development Agreement of 2000, 'It was well done', while another asserted, 'but it's bad policy regarding program development because anything goes'; to which the first interviewee responded, 'Yes, but it's good politics.' That is to say, Fritz Scharpf (1988) is right: federalism can create joint-decision traps that take us very far from substantive policy-making. The fact that intergovernmental agreements are not legally enforceable and therefore non-binding on future governments also detracts from the effectiveness of the process to deliver substantive policy commitments. In terms of federalism, then, and in terms of early learning and child care, we continue to live in interesting times.

Notes

1. Some interviewees requested that their comments not be specifically attributed to them or to their position. Thus material gleaned from interviews has been incorporated into the text without attribution unless the interviewee has explicitly granted consent to be quoted.
2. The 2006 election campaign, in particular, sparked a maelstrom of public debate and newspaper commentary regarding the desirability of non-parental care. See, for example, Geddes (2005), Leblanc (2005), Sokoloff (2005), and MacCharles (2006) for articles documenting the public debate.

See also the websites of Kids First Parents Association of Canada: <www.kidsfirstcanada.org>; Prairie Advocates for Childcare Choices: <p.a.c.c.tripod.com>; and compare with the Child Care Advocacy Association of Canada's federal election campaign 2006 website: <www.childcareadvocacy.ca/action/election2006/resources.html>; and the Code Blue for Child Care campaign: <www.buildchildcare.ca>.

3. In 1997, Quebec began to phase in $5-a-day child care (raised to $7 in 2003) for all 0–four-year-olds together with full-day kindergarten for all five-year-olds. See Friendly and Beach (2005: 64–5). In 2006, the Quebec government expanded its maternity and parental leave program to include between 70 and 75 per cent wage replacement for 15 weeks of maternity leave and three weeks of paternity leave, followed by 32 weeks at a wage replacement rate of between 55 and 75 per cent (Canada, House of Commons, Standing Committee on the Status of Women, 2005: 17).

4. Continental European countries vary considerably in policy goals and program models. Child care in Sweden, for example, began as 'care' so mothers could participate in the workforce. Although the program was shifted to the National Department of Education in 1996, children with working mothers still had priority until very recently. In France, public early childhood education programs date back to the 1800s. While virtually all children attend from the age of three years or younger and the full school-day programs are supplemented by after-school and summer programs, coverage for children with working mothers and for children under three is less than perfect (OECD, 2004b).

5. 'Regulated care' refers to facilities and homes that fall under provincial/territorial regulations with respect to such matters as physical, health, and safety requirements; child/staff ratios; and staff training.

6. This number is 'assumed' based on the gap between the number of children 0–5 years with a mother in the paid labour force and the number of regulated child-care spaces; more specific data are unavailable.

7. These federal recommendations were quite intrusive by today's post-SUFA standards. They specified that the financing be based on 'Operating grants for all spaces in the amount of $3 per day for infants, $2 per day for children age 3–5, $.50 per day for children aged 6–12' (Canada, House of Commons, 1988: 87). The tabled (but not passed) Canada Child Care Act specified maintenance of financial and other records 'by the province and by child care agencies' and that the Minister of National Health and Welfare would carry out 'examination and audit' (ibid., 4).

8. Quebec and the federal government never signed an agreement-in-principle but went right to a five-year funding agreement, the rationale being that Quebec was already much more advanced in developing its ELCC program than any other Canadian jurisdiction.

9. See the statement of the Child Care Advocacy Association of Canada (CCAAC) regarding the federal government's budget announcement (CCAAC,

2006a) and the Canadian Child Care Federation's (CCCF) statement after the election of the Harper government (CCCF, 2006).

References

Angus Reid/*Globe and Mail*. 1999. *Family Matters: A Look at Issues Concerning Families and Raising Children in Canada Today*. Toronto: Angus Reid Group.

Bakvis, H. 2002. 'Checkerboard Federalism? Labour Market Development Policy in Canada'. In *Canadian Federalism: Performance, Effectiveness, and Legitimacy*, ed. H. Bakvis and G. Skogstad. Toronto: Oxford University Press, 197–219.

Boismenu, G., and P. Graefe. 2004. 'The New Federal Tool Belt: Attempts to Rebuild Social Policy Leadership', *Canadian Public Policy* 30, 1: 71–89.

Brown, J. 2006. 'Child Care Funding Heads Agenda as Federal, Provincial Ministers Meet', *Canadian Press*, 29 May.

Bushnik, T. 2006. *Child Care in Canada*. Cat. no. 89-599-MIE2006003. Ottawa: Statistics Canada.

Cameron, B. 2005. Personal interview, Ottawa, 1 Apr.

Cameron, D., and R. Simeon. 2002. `Intergovernmental Relations in Canada: The Emergence of Collaborative Federalism', *Publius* 32, 2: 49–71.

Canada. 2006. *Canada's Universal Child Care Plan: Choice, Support, Spaces*. At: <www.universalchildcare.ca/>.

———, Department of Finance. 2000. *Budget 2000*. Ottawa: Department of Finance.

———. 2006. *The Budget Plan 2006: Focusing on Priorities: Canada's New Government Turning a New Leaf*. Ottawa: Department of Finance.

———, House of Commons. 1988. Bill C-144. An Act to authorize payments by Canada toward the provision of child care services, and to amend the Canada Assistance Plan in consequence thereof. Second Session, Thirty-Third Parliament. Ottawa: Minister of National Health and Welfare.

———. 1999. Speech from the Throne to Open the Second Session, Thirty-Sixth Parliament of Canada. *Debates of the House of Commons of Canada* (Hansard), 12 Oct.

———. 2004. *Speech From the Throne to Open the First Session of the Thirty-Eighth Parliament of Canada* (5 Oct.). Ottawa: Government of Canada.

———, Standing Committee on the Status of Women. 2005. *Interim Report on the Maternity and Parental Benefits under Employment Insurance: The Exclusion of Self-Employed Workers*. Ottawa: Communication Canada.

———, Social Union. 2006. *Early Childhood Development*. At: <www.socialunion.ca>.

———, Treasury Board Secretariat. 2006. *Federal/Provincial/Territorial Multilateral Framework on Early Learning and Child Care*. At: <www.tbs-sct.gc.ca>.

Canadian Child Care Federation (CCCF). 2006. 'CCCF Urges New Government to

Work Together to Solve Child Care Crisis in Canada' (24 Jan.). At: <www.cccf-fcsge.ca/pressroom/pr_32_en.htm>.

Canadian Intergovernmental Conference Secretariat (CICS). 2000. 'First Ministers' Meeting Communiqué on Early Childhood Development', Ref. 800-038/005 (11 Sep.). At: <www.scics.gc.ca>.

———. 2003. *Multilateral Framework on Early Learning and Child Care*. Ref. 830-779/005 (13 Mar.). At: <www.scics.gc.ca>.

CBC News. 2005a. 'Alberta Says It Won't Participate in National Day-care Program', CBC news website (7 Feb.). At: <action.web.ca/home/crru/rsrcs_crru_full.shtml?x=72081>.

———. 2005b. 'Northern Territories Looking for Extra Child Care Funding', CBC news website (5 Nov.). At: <action.web.ca/home/crru/rsrcs_crru_full.shtml?x=83071>.

Child Care Advocacy Association of Canada (CCAAC). 2006a. 'No Child Care in Today's Budget' (2 May). At: <action.web.ca/home/ccaac/alerts.shtml?x=87322&AA_EX _Session=4ae4a55a585d54d2bc268edb060999a9>.

———. 2006b. *The Community Child Care Investment Program: Does the Evidence Support the Claims?* Ottawa: CCAAC.

Childcare Resource and Research Unit (CRRU). 2001. *The Early Childhood Development Agreement: Provincial Initiatives and Spending Allocations, 2001–2002*. At: <circ.web.ca/resources/CRRUpubs/factsheets/ecd_chart/>.

———. 2002. 'Ontario's Spending for Regulated Child Care, 1942–2001', CRRU briefing note. Toronto.

———. 2006. 'The State of the National Child Care Program and Provincial/Territorial Contexts', CRRU briefing note (Mar.). At: <www.child-carecanada.org/pubs/bn/statenatprogram.html>.

Choudhry, Sujit. 2000. Comment. 'The Child Care Agenda and the Social Union', Canadian Federalism: Performance, Effectiveness, and Legitimacy Workshop, 5 May

———. 2002. 'Recasting Social Canada: A Reconsideration of Federal Jurisdiction over Social Policy', *University of Toronto Law Journal* 52: 163–252.

Cleveland, G., and M. Krashinsky. 1998. *The Benefits and Costs of Good Child Care: The Economic Rationale for Public Investment in Young Children*. Toronto: University of Toronto Centre for Urban and Community Studies, Childcare Resource and Research Unit.

Conservative Party of Canada. 2004. *Demanding Better: Federal Election Platform, 2004*. Ottawa: Conservative Party of Canada.

———. 2006. *Stand Up for Canada: Federal Election Platform, 2006*. Ottawa: Conservative Party of Canada.

Cooke, K., J. London, R. Edwards, and R. Rose-Lizée. 1986. *Report of the Task Force on Child Care*. Ottawa: Status of Women Canada.

De Souza, M. 2005. 'Quebec Isn't Rushing into Day-care Talks', *Montreal Gazette*, 27 Apr. At: <action.web.ca/home/crru/rsrcs_crru_full.shtml?x=75910>.

Doherty, G., M. Friendly, and M. Oloman. 1998. *Women's Support, Women's*

Work. Child Care in an Era of Deficit Reduction, Devolution, Downsizing, and Deregulation. Ottawa: Status of Women Canada.

Environics Research Group. 2006. *Canadians' Attitudes toward National Child Care Policy.* Ottawa: Environics Research Group.

Espey and Good Company. 2003. Perceptions *of Quality Child Care Final Report.* Ottawa: Canadian Child Care Federation and Child Care Advocacy Association of Canada.

Friendly, M. 2001. 'Child Care and Canadian Federalism in the 1990s: Canary in a Coal Mine'. In *Our Children's Future: Child Care Policy in Canada,* ed. G. Cleveland and M. Krashinsky. Toronto: University of Toronto Press.

————— and Jane Beach. 2005. *Early Childhood Education and Care in Canada 2004.* Toronto: Childcare Resource and Research Unit, University of Toronto.

—————, —————, and Michelle Turiano. 2002. *Early Childhood Education and Care in Canada 2001.* Toronto: Childcare Resource and Research Unit, University of Toronto.

Geddes, J. 2005. 'The Gathering Storm', *Maclean's* 118, 27/28: 16–17.

Goelman, H., G. Doherty, D. Lero, A. LaGrange, and J. Tougas. 2000. *Caring and Learning Environments: Quality in Child Care Centres across Canada.* Guelph, Ont.: Centre for Families, Work and Well-Being, University of Guelph.

Government of Canada and Governments of the Provinces and Territories. 1999. *A Framework to Improve the Social Union for Canadians* (4 Feb.). At: <www.socialunion.ca/news/020499_e.html>.

Laghi, B. 2005. 'East Coast Premiers Lobby for New Deal on Daycare Dollars', *Globe and Mail,* 29 Oct. At: action.web.ca/home/crru/rsrcs_crru_full.shtml?x =82724.

Leblanc, D. 2005. 'Whoa, Baby! Chew on These Child-Care Plans', *Globe and Mail,* 6 Dec., A4.

Liberal Party of Canada. 1993. *Creating Opportunity: The Liberal Plan for Canada* (Red Book). Ottawa: Liberal Party of Canada.

—————. 2004. *Moving Canada Forward: The Paul Martin Plan for Getting Things Done.* Ottawa: Liberal Party of Canada.

—————. 2006. *Securing Canada's Success.* Ottawa: Liberal Party of Canada.

Livingston, G. 2006. 'McGuinty Hopes Harper Will Be "Flexible" on Day Care Deals', *Ottawa Citizen,* 8 Feb.

Livingstone, D.W., and D. Hart. 2005. *Public Attitudes towards Education in Ontario 2004: The 15th OISE/UT Survey.* Toronto: Ontario Institute for Studies in Education.

MacCharles, T. 2006. 'Child-care Battle Rages', *Toronto Star,* 4 May, A8.

McCain, M., and F. Mustard. 1999. *Reversing the Real Brain Drain: Early Years Study Final Report.* Toronto: Children's Secretariat of Ontario.

McRoberts, K. 1985. 'Unilateralism, Bilateralism and Multilateralism: Approaches to Canadian Federalism'. In *Intergovernmental Relations,* ed. R. Simeon. Toronto: University of Toronto Press.

Mahon, R. 2006. 'Main Features of the Early Learning and Child Care Bilateral

Agreements'. At: b2c2.org/resources/index.php.

Michalski, J. 1999. *Values and Preferences for the "Best Policy Mix" for Canadian Children*. CPRN Discussion Paper No. F/05. Ottawa: Canadian Policy Research Networks.

Mintrom, M. 1997. 'Policy Entrepreneurs and the Diffusion of Innovation', *American Journal of Political Science* 41: 738–70.

Moss, P. 2006. 'Farewell to Child Care', *National Institute Economic Review* no. 195 (Jan.): 70–84.

Noël, A. 1998. 'Is Decentralization Conservative? Federalism and the Contemporary Debate on the Canadian Welfare State'. In *Stretching the Federation: The Art of the State in Canada*, ed. R. Young. Kingston: Queen's Institute of Intergovernmental Relations.

——— 'General Study of the Framework Agreement'. In *The Canadian Social Union without Quebec: 8 Critical Analyses*, ed. A. Gagnon and H. Segal. Montreal: Institute for Research on Public Policy.

Organization for Economic Co-operation and Development (OECD). 2004a ODEC *Thematic Review of Early Childhood Education and Care: Canada Country Note*. Paris.

———. 2004b. OECD *Thematic Review of Early Childhood Education and Care: France Country Note*. Paris.

———. 2006. *Starting Strong II: Early Childhood Education and Care*. Paris.

Prime Minister's Office (PMO). 2006. 'Prime Minister Harper Outlines His Government's Priorities and Open Federalism Approach', speech to the Montreal Board of Trade, 20 Apr. At: <www.pm.gc.ca/eng/media.asp?id= 1119>.

Rollason, K. 2004. 'New Child-Care System Just a Matter of When: Dryden Minister Hopes January Meeting Will Lead to National Program', *Winnipeg Free Press*, 13 Nov., B6.

Scharpf, F.W. 1988. 'The Joint-Decision Trap: Lessons from German Federalism and European Integration', *Public Administration* 66: 239–78.

Séguin, R., and B. Laghi. 2006. 'Harper Reaches Out to Quebec on Daycare', *Globe and Mail*, 8 Feb., A1, A4.

Shonkoff, J.P., and D.A. Phillips, eds. 2000. *From Neurons to Neighborhoods: The Science of Early Childhood Development*. Washington: National Academy Press.

Sokoloff, H. 2005. 'Gulf between Parties Is Size of a Small Child: Liberals, Tories Differ Distinctly on Daycare Options', *National Post*, 5 Dec., A8.

Timpson, A.M. 2001. *Driven Apart: Women's Employment Equality and Child Care in Canadian Public Policy*. Vancouver: University of British Columbia Press.

United Nations Educational, Scientific, and Cultural Organization (UNESCO). 2006. *Strong Foundations: Early Childhood Care and Education*. Education for All Global Monitoring Report 2007. Paris.

Urquhart, I. 2006. 'Premiers Rebuff Child-care Advocates', *Toronto Star*, 4 Aug.

White, L. 2002. 'The Child Care Agenda and the Social Union'. In *Canadian Federalism: Performance, Effectiveness, and Legitimacy*, ed. H. Bakvis and G. Skogstad. Toronto: Oxford University Press.

Websites

Childcare Resource and Research Unit, University of Toronto: www.childcare canada.org

Dr Gordon Cleveland, University of Toronto (economic analyses of early childhood education): www.earlylearning.ubc.ca/CHILD/research_child_child care.htm

Centre for Families, Work & Wellbeing at the University of Guelph: www.work lifecanada.ca/

OECD, Thematic Review of Early Childhood Education and Care: www.oecd. org/dataoecd/41/36/33852192.pdf

Chapter 10

The Knowledge Economy and Post-Secondary Education: Federalism in Search of a Metaphor

Herman Bakvis

Few sectors have changed as dramatically over the past decade as post-secondary education. The transformation of Canada's university system, a development described as Jean Chrétien's 'greatest legacy' by Jeffrey Simpson (2002) and as Ottawa's 'Quiet Revolution' by Allan Tupper (2003), came about largely through the effort of the federal government alone. It represents an excellent example of uncontested independent action by the federal government. That is, it is a case where one order of government proceeds unilaterally, even where its actions may have repercussions for the other order, but where these actions are largely uncontested by that other order.

Three points are worth noting at the outset. First, examples of this sort of federalism have been relatively rare in recent decades. Second, Ottawa's forays into post-secondary education (PSE), a system involving institutions exclusively under provincial jurisdiction, went virtually uncontested by the provinces, including Quebec. Their silence stands in sharp contrast to the bitter wrangling that characterizes the health-care field and fiscal federalism more generally. And third, the PSE initiatives undertaken by Ottawa, although in good part a product of particular circumstances and path dependencies, can be described as constituting a coherent set of policies with largely positive outcomes. It is a description many would be reluctant to apply to a number of Ottawa's other policies and programs. These policy outcomes include a university system with a considerably enhanced capacity for both pure and applied research, and a capacity on the part of the federal government to impart to universities a sense of national purpose and to give more specific direction to them through a variety of mechanisms. At the same time, this development is coupled with a much more distinctive hierarchy among universities, and students are now bearing a larger share of the direct costs of their education.

The case of PSE poses a number of interesting questions for the study of federalism and intergovernmental relations. First, what transpired in the period in question, roughly beginning in 1996 up to the present? That is, what new priorities were launched and how was funding reallocated? Second, beyond what Keith Banting describes as the 'classical' model, what particular explanations, lenses, or metaphors can be used to understand the nature of the relations between Ottawa and the provinces in this area? Notions such as checkerboard federalism or the 'marble cake' analogy do not really capture the interesting fact that in many respects the provinces acted as bystanders and simply accepted the understandings worked out between the presidents of some of the major universities and a number of key public servants in Ottawa. Third, why were the provinces so acquiescent? Why, in particular, was Quebec, headed as it was for most of the period in question by a Parti Québécois government? And fourth and finally, what does the PSE case say about the effectiveness and performance of executive federalism? And if we agree that federalism performed well and that the policies were effective (a conclusion with which some would disagree), can we say that the process and outcomes were legitimate in the eyes of the different constituencies—small as well as large universities, students and their families, and the different regions—that were affected by these changes?

Ottawa's Quiet Revolution

In 1995 it appeared as if Ottawa was on the cusp of reducing further its already attenuated role in the post-secondary sector (Bakvis and Cameron, 2002). Its primary vehicle for supporting PSE up to that point had been the Established Programs Financing (EPF) arrangement, which saw Ottawa transfer block grants to the provinces for the financing of health care and PSE. For the last year of EPF, 1995–6, the amount of the transfer was $21.734 billion in the form of cash and tax points. EPF, introduced in 1977, had ended a period of conditional funding, which imposed certain, albeit very limited, requirements on the recipient provinces as to how the money was to be spent. With respect to health care under EPF, these requirements were replaced with the broad principles of universality, accessibility, public administration, comprehensiveness, and portability. These principles applied explicitly only to health care, not to PSE.

In 1984 the Canada Health Act allowed Ottawa to penalize provinces that permitted extra-billing by doctors. No comparable conditions were imposed with respect to PSE. Furthermore, with block funding the provinces were not obliged to devote a fixed amount to either health or PSE. As long as the basic principles were respected in regard to health care, the provinces could shift funding from one area to the other. Indeed, under EPF the block funding could be spent in other areas, such as highways, should a province so choose. In practice, virtually all provincial governments decided that health was by far a greater priority and apportioned the transfer accordingly. At a certain point in the transition from EPF to CHST (the Canada Health and Social Transfer), Ottawa indicated its understandings of the nominal health and PSE proportions for the EPF grant—in 1995–6, for example, $6.251 billion of the $21.734 billion, or 28.8 per cent, was supposedly for PSE. But this notional breakdown did not require provinces to allocate the sum in question to PSE. And, in reality, far less was so allocated.[1]

As discussed in the chapters on health care, social policy, and fiscal federalism, effective in 1996–7 Ottawa replaced EPF with the CHST, which cleverly combined EPF with the Canada Assistance Plan (CAP) to create a single block grant that was greater than the cash portion in the old EPF but smaller than the combined EPF-CAP—to be precise, 9.38 per cent less than the combined EPF-CAP figure for 1995–6. Since the old CAP was composed of cash, adding this transfer to the block grant meant that more cash was now being transferred than under the old EPF.

However, the cut to PSE was likely considerably greater than 9.38 per cent (Advisory Panel, 2006: 75). Both PSE and welfare programs bore the brunt of the cuts, given the politically much more difficult task of cutting back on the health-care sector. The fiscal year 1997–8 saw a further reduction in block grant payments as the new CHST was reduced from $26.9 billion to $25.8 billion. The direct consequences were well documented, and publicized, as university students saw their tuition fees more than double over a five-year period. Federal support for students through the Canada Student Loans Program (CSLP), delivered through the provinces, was increased slightly, and students were permitted to carry more debt; but on the whole there did not appear to be any immediate prospect of Ottawa putting more money back into PSE. Not to put too fine a point on it, it appeared that Ottawa was on the cusp of withdrawing its physical presence almost completely from the PSE field. And while provinces lamented the reduction in transfers, their focus was on health care, and for many provinces allowing universities to raise their tuition fees proved to be a convenient financial safety valve. Some provinces, such as British Columbia and Quebec, froze tuition fees, which, while beneficial to students in the short run, put the universities in those provinces under even greater strain.

By 1999–2000 the CHST was roughly back to the level of the combined amount of CAP-EPF in 1995–6. At the same time, the actual cash flowing from Ottawa to the provinces under the CHST was less. Since the CHST (like the old EPF) was a combination of cash and tax points, Ottawa had allowed the tax point part of the CHST to grow more quickly than the cash part. Thus in 1995–6 the combined EPF-CAP amount consisted of 60 per cent cash (at that time the entire amount of CAP was in cash); in 1999–2000 only about 45 per cent of the CHST was in cash. Focusing simply on the cash transfers, provinces proclaimed that Ottawa was no longer carrying its fair share of social programs under the CHST.

However, the amounts under the CHST as an indicator of Ottawa's role in PSE proved to be misleading. Beginning with the Speech from the Throne in 1997 and then as part of the Canadian Opportunity Strategy (COS), announced as part of the 1998 federal budget (Canada, 1998), Ottawa was quietly redrafting its strategy for PSE. Thus, under COS, Ottawa provided a measure of tax relief on student loan interest and created the Canadian Education Savings Grants, allowing parents to receive grants for money placed in Registered Education Savings Plans (RESP) for their offspring, as well as tax sheltering for income earned on these savings. To be sure, these new programs were delivered in the form of tax expenditures to individuals rather than actual cash either directly or through provincial governments for PSE institutions.

The COS, however, addressed another area of federal transfers and expenditure outside the CHST and the CSLP. These transfers bore directly on PSE institutions, almost exclusively universities, an area that generally had attracted little attention. In addition to transfers through EPF and, later, the CHST, Ottawa had also been transferring money directly to the universities, primarily through the granting councils, such as the Social Sciences and Humanities Research Council (SSHRC), Natural Sciences and Engineering Research Council (NSERC), and Medical Research Council (MRC). These entities, and precedents for using them as conduits for federal funding, date back to the 1950s; the origins of SSHRC and NSERC, for example, can be traced back to the Massey Commission on the Arts, Letters and Sciences of 1951. Although some of the premises of the Massey Commission, and the actions undertaken by Ottawa following the Commission's report, were challenged by Quebec in particular—indeed, it led the Duplessis government to strike the landmark Tremblay Commission (Kwavnick, 1973) on the constitutionality of Ottawa's intrusions—Ottawa subsequently was reasonably successful in establishing its presence in this area. It did so primarily by arguing that areas such as research, both pure and applied, and labour market development were of legitimate concern to the federal government and well within its jurisdictional authority. Over the years, Ottawa certainly has been by far the largest financial supporter of university-based scientific research.

In 1995–6, transfers from the three councils totalled $804.716 million. In 1998 Ottawa signalled in the COS budget document that it intended to increase these transfers so that by 2003–4, they totalled $1,292.276 million, a 60 per cent increase. More significantly, from 1997 onward, under the rubric of 'innovation' introduced in the Speech from the Throne that year, and then as part of the COS, Ottawa added to this mix two wholly new programs: the Canada Foundation for Innovation (CFI) and the Canada Research Chairs (CRC) programs. By 2003–4 the amount allocated just for that year under the CFI and CRC programs totalled $2,547.951 million, more than twice as much as allocated by the three granting councils. One of the existing councils, the Medical Research Council, was transformed into the Canadian Institutes of Health Research (CIHR) and given more resources and an expanded mandate (more than half of the 60 per cent increase noted above went to the CIHR). By 2004, provinces noted that the transfers from these programs (granting councils plus the CFI and CRC) were roughly one-and-a-half times as much as the actual cash that provinces receive as the PSE portion under what is now the Canada Social Transfer (which was separated out from the

CHST when it was split in 2004 into the Canada Health Transfer and the Canada Social Transfer).

Furthermore, it is worth underscoring the nature of this funding. Not only were the grants made directly to universities, but they came with a variety of strings attached, including, in the case of the CFI, for example, matching require-ments. The CFI requires the successful applicant to cover 60 per cent of costs from other sources, from industry for example. In practice, this often means funding from provincial governments, especially in provinces with a relatively weak industrial base, such as those in the Atlantic region. In the case of the CRC program, universities are required to submit a detailed strategic plan for their institution to show what innovative research programs these research chairs would support and, more broadly, how these would contribute to the university's overall mission. Nominations from the universities for these chairs, that is, the candidates to whom they planned to offer the chairs, undergo a peer review process conducted by the granting councils.

Both the CFI and the CRCs were targeted towards the fostering of innovative research and the creation of knowledge. The goal of the CFI has been to support infrastructure needs to help universities rebuild or strengthen their research capacities. Infrastructure needs were broadly defined to include not only bricks and mortar but also software and other elements of the research environment. The CRCs represented an effort to recruit the brightest younger scholars as well as more senior researchers and to repatriate Canadian researchers who had gone abroad. The CRCs are allocated largely on the basis of an institution's past record in attracting granting council funding. The more funding in previous years, the larger the quota of CRCs allocated to that institution. To ensure that smaller insti-tutions were not unduly disadvantaged, a basic floor was established with smaller institutions receiving a minimum of 6 per cent of the 2,000 chairs. The CIHR, created in 2000 to replace the Medical Research Council, was modelled after the US National Institutes of Health Research. With an organizational structure cen-tred on 13 'virtual' institutes, it now encompasses a much wider array of less tra-ditional topics, such as population health and health determinants.

Some innovative, albeit controversial, financing techniques were used as well. The legislation that established the Canada Foundation for Innovation, for example, provides for an independent foundation governed by a 15-person board and 15 foundation members. Only six of each group are appointed by the Minister of Industry; the remainder are appointed by the chair of the board and the original appointees. One stipulation is that half of the foundation and board members must be from the research community and the rest from industry and the non-profit sector. The most controversial aspect is the endowment, initially $800 million (up to $3.5 billion as of 2004), to be spent over a multi-year period and not subject to the annual appropriations process. In part the objective was to allow the federal government to commit its burgeoning surplus—in effect, to park it—for future, long-term needs. The aim was also to create, as much as pos-sible, an arm's-length agency that would be well insulated from political pressures. Some critics (e.g., Aucoin, 2003) have argued that foundations such as the CFI and the Millennium Foundation succeeded all too well in this respect, since they are for all intents and purposes beyond the control of ministers and Parliament itself.

Channelling money through foundations can also be seen as a way of easing relations with provinces, since it reduces the need for direct government-to-government interaction.. As well, the granting councils have close and long-standing relationships with their constituencies. Members of the governing bodies are in good part drawn from the universities, and the research community more generally, and the adjudication committees, which are at the heart of the decision-making process for allocating funds to researchers and individual projects, are drawn primarily from the university community. As will be noted in the following sections, there are ample reasons to account for the positive relationship between the granting agencies and foundations and the recipient institutions. Any tensions arising between the federal and provincial governments would not arise because of pressures from universities, for example. The only exception to the tacit acceptance of the federal role by provinces was with respect to the Millennium Foundation.

The Prime Minister's Office (PMO) had been persuaded of the merits of the CFI and CRC. Indeed, the prime minister himself and Eddie Goldenberg, his principal adviser, became eager supporters. But the PMO was keen to do something that would have an impact beyond the research community and connect more directly with ordinary Canadians, especially young Canadians. Thus was born the Millennium Scholarship program. In effect, it represented an effort by Prime Minister Chrétien to leave a visible legacy of his tenure for younger generations. However, insofar as it involved direct transfers to individuals in support of their education—an area where the provinces had long been the primary sources of financial support—the announcement of this program in 1999 sparked an immediate response from provincial governments, not least the government of Quebec. The program also appeared to run against the grain of the Social Union Framework Agreement (SUFA), which stipulated that provinces be consulted on any new federal initiatives in areas involving provincial jurisdiction, even when Ottawa relies solely on its spending power. The Millennium Foundation, provided with a sizable endowment and a governance structure that made it, like the CFI, impervious to direction from ministers or Parliament, was responsible for direct negotiations with the provinces.

It soon became a classic example of fractious federalism, coupled with outcomes that were far from optimal. The goal of the program was ostensibly to improve student access to post-secondary education. However, the dilemma facing all such federal direct-to-citizen transfers in areas where the provinces already have programs is to find mechanisms to ensure that the new federal money becomes additional money in the hands of the recipients. The danger, from a federal perspective, has always been that 'new' federal money simply displaces money already being handed out by provincial governments, which then reallocates this 'old' money to other provincial programs. The Millennium Foundation ultimately negotiated agreements with the provinces that addressed the displacement problem, but with only limited success. (Provinces committed themselves to using the additional money in areas related to PSE but not necessarily student aid.)

Only in provinces such as New Brunswick, with traditionally low levels of student support, did the Millennium Scholarships represent additional funding in the hands of students. Furthermore, negotiations with Quebec were handled directly by Ottawa (specifically, Human Resources Development Canada [HRDC] and the Privy Council Office) when the Quebec government refused to deal with the Millennium Foundation. One of the key issues here was the symbolic one of 'federal cheques with the maple leaf on them'. The controversy was ultimately resolved by using the electronic transfer system for transmitting funds to recipients rather than paper cheques. When the program was actually in operation, the warm praise that the federal government expected from grateful recipients and their families was to a large extent undermined as stories appeared in the press of students receiving letters congratulating them on receiving a Millennium Scholarship, followed a few days later by another letter, this time from their provincial government, informing them that the Millennium Scholarship would be treated as income and the amount in question deducted from their provincial grant. All in all, this specific program would likely rank poorly on the three criteria of performance, effectiveness, and legitimacy. Yet for the period in question, the Millennium Scholarship experience stands as an exception. In the area of overall support for post-secondary education institutions, Ottawa succeeded in providing new money to universities *and* in leveraging provincial resources through programs such as the CFI.

The CFI, CRC, and Millennium Foundation are not the only federal initiatives in PSE. Beginning in 2001 the federal government began paying universities a portion of indirect costs of university research, an area of long-standing concern for universities. In 2006 the amount stood at $225 million a year. Other federal agencies and programs have been used to transfer additional funding to universities, such as the Atlantic Canada Opportunities Agency (ACOA). It is responsible for the $300 million Atlantic Innovation Fund launched in 2000, much of which is targeted towards universities, and for serving as a substitute for private-sector or provincial government money to meet the matching requirements of the CFI program.

Overall, Ottawa succeeded in transforming the manner in which funding was delivered, from a regime based primarily on block transfers to provinces consisting of money and tax points to one with much more reliance on direct transfers to universities coupled with specific conditions. And this transformation came about with little protest from the provinces.

Federal Initiative, Provincial Acquiescence

The study of federalism is rich in metaphor: Canada's Constitution as a ship of state with watertight compartments versus a living tree capable of growth (Hogg,

2005: 415); checkerboard federalism, denoting a series of separate and distinct deals struck between Ottawa and the provinces (Bakvis, 2002); and federalism as marble cake (Grodzins, 1966), denoting the tightly interwoven strands of federal and provincial activities typically found in most policy areas and the difficult task of disentangling them. Benoît Pelletier, Quebec's minister of Intergovernmental Relations, has used the analogy of a backyard swimming pool to illustrate Ottawa's putative illegitimate use of its spending power (Pelletier, 2004). According to Pelletier, Ottawa is like the neighbour who jumps uninvited into your jurisdictional 'pool'. In the case of federal–provincial relations in the PSE field, two researchers from Industry Canada invoke both 'triangle' and 'sandwich' analogies (Farina and Hart, 2004, cited in Cameron, 2004). In the dialogue between federal and provincial governments, the universities constitute the meat in a sandwich in danger of being squeezed. David M. Cameron (2004), in turn, argues that the meat in this case is very much 'a dog's breakfast', with universities in fact representing a variety of conflicting interests, including students, faculty associations, and administrators.

A triangle analogy, suggesting three main actors—the universities and the two orders of government—is probably more accurate, although this, too, may be misleading insofar as one order of government (the provinces) has been a distinctly passive player. The idea of an open-faced sandwich, though perhaps not the most appetizing analogy (at least not in comparison to Grodzins's marble cake), likely comes closest. In effect, the universities can be seen as providing the underlay for a number of attractive toppings, such as CRCs. But there are also elements of marble cake insofar as these 'toppings' have a definite link to other parts of the post-secondary system. Funding of CRCs has a definite impact on teaching, for example, in that within universities priorities are set and resources reallocated from some fields to others. Jeffrey Simpson (2006), for example, has argued that the CRCs have contributed to a clear decline in the resources that universities devote to the teaching function, with many professors seeking to escape the burden of growing student–faculty ratios by searching out opportunities for teaching release time in their research grant applications.

Even the combined marble cake/open-faced sandwich model, however, fails to capture the active role that universities, and key figures in particular universities, have played in getting the federal funding to flow and the close symbiotic relationships between these individuals and senior officials in certain key departments in Ottawa. In brief, in probing this relationship further, what one finds is an 'epistemic community' (Haas, 1992) consisting of highly entrepreneurial university presidents from a number of Canada's leading universities. These university presidents, supported by the Association of Universities and Colleges of Canada, on the one side, and the Department of Industry with deputy minister Kevin Lynch and his minister, John Manley, and the Department of Finance and the deputy, David Dodge and his minister, on the other side, struck a series of understandings and specific deals to put more resources into university-based research and development. The Department of Industry—Industry Canada—

was particularly critical since the granting councils and the CRC program were part of its portfolio. Subsequent to program review in the mid-1990s, which saw programs and agencies slashed and transfers under the CHST reduced, federal officials began looking at issues such as the productivity gap and the long-term capacity of the Canadian economy to generate growth.

Beginning in the 1997 Speech from the Throne under the heading of 'Investing in Knowledge and Creativity', the Canadian government emphasized the importance of the 'knowledge-based economy' and the need 'to provide public support for research done in our universities'. This initiative came to be centred almost exclusively within Industry Canada, a department that was well-positioned to move this file forward. First, Industry Canada, a product of the 1993 government reorganization, which also saw the creation of HRDC, had responsibility for a wide variety of programs and regulatory instruments. They included the aforementioned granting councils, the National Research Council, the Canadian Space Agency, and the regional economic development agencies. Many of these agencies and organizations, prior to 1993, had been housed in other departments or constituted self-standing departments. Most of the tools and programs, therefore, were housed in Industry Canada, allowing a small coterie of officials to use a top-down approach in pushing their agenda without having to worry about cumbersome interdepartmental working groups and competing agendas. Second, Industry Canada had an excellent working relationship with the one department that mattered, the Department of Finance. Kevin Lynch had previously been in Finance, and he and the deputy minister, David Dodge, saw eye to eye on the issues of productivity and innovation and their connection with the knowledge-based economy. What is important to note is that the budgetary process became the primary vehicle for announcing the specific initiatives stemming from the vision summarily articulated in the 1997 Throne Speech. Finance became a willing partner, conspirator even, not only in securing funding for initiatives such as the CFI but in creating foundations as independent corporations that would allow the government to commit funding for several years into the future. Third, Industry Canada is responsible for providing direct support to the body that advises the cabinet and prime minister on science matters, the Advisory Council on Science and Technology (ACST). In various ways the department had the direct ear of cabinet ministers and the prime minister.

Universities, in part through the AUCC, had been pestering the federal government for years to bolster its support for post-secondary education. At the same time, David M. Cameron (2002) notes that the years of retrenchment and cutbacks had left universities ossified, resistant to change, and not well-positioned to request funding for new initiatives when receding deficits put Ottawa in the mood to spend. Nonetheless, as a result in part of developments abroad, the 1990s also saw the arrival of a new breed of university official: the president and vice-chancellor as entrepreneur. According to Jeffrey Simpson (2002), Robert Lacroix of the University of Montreal, Martha Piper of UBC, and Robert Prichard of the University of Toronto were the key figures in successfully lobbying the federal government. Paul Davenport of Western and David Strangway, Piper's predecessor at UBC, also figure in accounts of those who successfully articulated a vision of the university's critical role in the knowledge economy and the kinds of federal programs that would serve the purposes of the federal government, the private sector, and industry. These university presidents were also fully cognizant that the federal surpluses beginning to appear in the late 1990s represented a significant opportunity.

They found a receptive audience in Ottawa in the hallways of Industry and Finance and played a significant role in the creation of the first of the new programs, the Canada Foundation for Innovation. Cameron (2002) has documented these developments in some detail and I will not recount them here. What is interesting to note is that David Strangway became president and CEO of the CFI, while another former university president, John Evans of the University of Toronto, became chair. Martha Piper, president of UBC, became a member of the CFI as well as a member of the ACST. Robert Giroux, president and CEO of the AUCC and a former senior federal public servant, became a member of the CFI. Overall, members of the university community were very well represented on the CFI and its board. Again, the CFI was created as an independent corporation with an endowment that totalled $3.5 billion by 2004, allowing it to operate outside the constraints imposed on most government agencies. Coupled with increased funding to the granting councils and the Canada Research Chairs program, the creation of the CFI stands as a remarkable coup on the part of a lobby group.

Where were the provinces in all of this? There were, to be sure, some signs of involvement, if only because many of the provinces, including Quebec, were willing to step up to the plate and fulfill the CFI matching requirements. There were grumblings from Atlantic Canada, given that its relatively weak industrial base limited opportunities for obtaining matching contributions from the private sector. However, the Atlantic Innovation Fund established in 2000 helped alleviate these concerns. The 1997 Throne Speech made reference to the federal government working in partnership with the provinces as well as the universities and private sector in promoting the innovation agenda. Although meetings of federal, provincial, and territorial deputy ministers of Industry, Trade, Science and Technology did take place on a fairly regular basis, once or twice a year, and presumably some of the issues related to the innovation agenda were discussed at them, it was not until September 2001 that a full-scale ministerial meeting on the theme of innovation and the knowledge-based economy took place, in Quebec City. Co-hosted by the federal minister at the time, Brian Tobin, and, significantly, Pauline Marois—the Quebec minister responsible not only for the Economy and Finance but for Research and Science and Technology—the meeting generated an 'Agreement on Principles of Action to Speed Up the Transition to an Innovation and Knowledge Based Economy'. One of the three 'Principles for Action' affirmed the crucial role of universities in creating new knowledge and identifying a 'sustainable university research environment', and encouraged 'partnerships between universities, government laboratories and private sector R&D

facilities' (Canadian Intergovernmental Conference Secretariat, 2001). Overall, the three principles appear quite consistent with Ottawa's innovation strategy as originally formulated in 1997. There was a subsequent meeting of ministers in 2002, and deputy ministerial meetings 2003 and 2004, but there has been no discernible intergovernmental activity at that level since then. Nonetheless, the adoption of the Principles for Action in 2001 by both orders of government strongly suggests that the provinces bought into the federal agenda.

At other levels activities also appear limited. Thus, a statement from the Advisory Council on Science and Technology, that 'during the second half of 2004, the ACST initiated contact with provincial and territorial external advisory councils to identify the potential and willingness to collaborate on mutual priorities and projects' (Council of Science and Technology Advisors, 2004), suggests that collaboration between federal and provincial governments at the level below the ministerial and deputy level was not extensive. At the same time, judging from the announcements from both universities and provincial governments, there is plenty of evidence that provincial governments were more than happy to support the applications made by universities, primarily in the form of matching grants. In Quebec, applications from universities for CFI infrastructure grants, for example, are submitted first to the provincial Fonds québécois de la recherche sur la nature et les technologies, which, after reviewing the applications, forwards those it finds acceptable to Ottawa. In its special arrangement with the Quebec government, the CFI has agreed to accept, as part of its peer review process, the reports solicited by the Fonds in connection with the latter's assessment of proposals. In effect, Quebec takes the lead in deciding which projects to select and support, technically leaving it to Ottawa to concur with decisions initially made by Quebec. In all other provinces applications are submitted directly to the CFI, and provinces make their decisions only after that body has decided whether or not to support a given project. Overall, therefore, it appears that, while not active collaborators, provinces have been quiet supporters nonetheless. What explains this blissful state?

Passive Collaboration: An Explanation

The explanation of passive provincial collaboration includes a number of immediate factors. They include the replacement of budget deficits with surpluses, the willingness of Ottawa to spend money on its innovation and productivity agenda and to have universities play an important part in implementing this agenda, and astute lobbying by the leadership of Canada's main universities. Further, the federal agenda in large part coincided with provincial agendas, and those provinces without an explicit agenda very quickly developed one. In Ontario, for example, the Conservative government under Mike Harris launched its SuperBuild Growth fund in 2000 with 75 per cent of funding targeted towards capital projects in applied technology, health sciences, and general sciences (Trick, 2005). It may very well have reflected Harris's jaundiced view of the humanities and social sciences, but it happily dovetailed with the federal government's innovation agenda. Newfoundland and Labrador, in turn, announced in its 2003 budget speech the creation of a new Research and Innovation Fund, with an explicit goal 'to leverage significant new R&D investments from federal institutions, including the Canadian Foundation for Innovation' (Newfoundland and Labrador, 2003). Other provinces created similar bodies with similar purposes in mind.

One development worth noting is the acceptance of distinct roles and responsibilities. The provinces appeared to accept the legitimacy of federal support for universities as long as it was cast as support for research and development. When Ottawa went against the grain and launched the Millennium Scholarship program, provincial feathers, especially Quebec's, were immediately ruffled. Student financial support was seen by provinces as being in their domain. Furthermore, the provinces had all the necessary data and delivery infrastructure, which meant that the Millennium Foundation, and the federal government, was in a weak bargaining position. When restricting itself to the traditional paths of funding for research, albeit with some interesting innovations, Ottawa gained tacit if not active approval.

With respect to longer-term factors, there is also a certain amount of path dependency at work. Ottawa has been involved in post-secondary education in various ways since the early part of the nineteenth century. More than 40 years ago, however, Ottawa began withdrawing from direct support of universities, or at least universities as educational institutions. It first introduced opting-out arrangements, then turned over delivery of the student loans program to the provinces, and later introduced EPF and then the CHST. On the research side, however, the government of Canada continued and expanded its presence, hiving off SSHRC and NSERC from the Canada Council, for example. These agencies developed close links not just with universities but with the individual scholars working within them who frequently were both recipients and adjudicators of SSHRC and NSERC programs, as well as with students who worked on council-funded projects or were awarded council scholarships. The Centres of Excellence program of the 1980s was a precursor to the later virtual institutes and networks currently supported by the councils and especially by the CIHR.

Certain provinces, most notably Quebec, also set up their own research funding agencies with the view to maximizing the likelihood of obtaining funds from Ottawa. Thus, the Fonds was set up by Quebec in 1981 in part to help researchers obtain federal funding as well. In some respects the Fonds was a pioneer in promoting the ideal of large-scale team projects, in an era when a lot of SSHRC funding, for example, was still largely construed in terms of individual scholars working on single projects. In essence, the pathways were both established and well accepted by both orders of government.

A further consideration that deserves attention is the *intra*governmental dimension. *Within* the federal government the design and implementation of its innovation agenda was essentially a closed, top-down process. Industry and Finance were not just the main players, they were the sole players. Only the elites of the university research community and certain private-sector interests gained access to and became part of this magic circle. It is interesting to note that the only time the innovation strategy started to falter was after the Throne Speech in 2001, when most of the major pieces crafted by Industry Canada were already in place. In 2001, however, cabinet and PCO decided that an innovation agenda by definition was also a skills and learning agenda and instructed Industry Canada to work with HRDC to develop a joint white paper on learning and innovation and to consult with other departments. The end result was a near shambles. Instead of a single white paper, there were two separate green papers, implying that these were simply consultation documents rather than policy planning documents or proposals (presented separately to cabinet in two back-to-back sessions) and two separate consultative processes where participants were sometimes confused as to whether they should be attending the HRDC session or the Industry Canada session (Bakvis and Juillet, 2004). Various events, such as the terrorist attacks on the United States in September that year, contributed to the chaos; but in terms of laying the groundwork for the next phase of the innovation agenda, it was a very poor start. Had something similar transpired back in 1997—for example, had Industry Canada been required to work with several other departments at that time—the end result might have been quite different with respect to initiatives such as the CFI.

At the provincial level, there were also some *intra*governmental issues at play, though here it was more an issue of lack of capacity. Only Quebec with the Fonds was really well-positioned to take full advantage of initiatives such as the CFI. Other provinces still had infrastructural research capacity in the form of cancer agencies, research facilities, and the like that were linked to various research networks and thus were capable of understanding the programs in question and how to apply to them. But these research bodies were relatively independent of provincial governments. Their autonomy was not necessarily a bad thing from a federal perspective because it allowed the government of Canada to work quietly and effectively with the provincial agencies in question. Furthermore, because the money was new and because there was an important constituency eager to take advantage of these programs (university researchers and administrators and private-sector interests), provincial governments were happy to see the money flow.

The university community itself, and specifically university presidents, likely also played an important role in acting as both a buffer and intermediary between provincial and federal authorities. Both Prichard and Piper were enormously popular and charismatic figures, and not just within their own institutions. Their networking skills were not only applied to working the federal government connection; much of their time was also spent cultivating good relations with provincial officials and politicians as well as with the private sector and the community at large within their respective provinces. They were also able to demonstrate a capacity for raising money from private and corporate donors, a skill that helped establish their credentials in the eyes of provincial governments. One suspects that a good part of these presidents' work involved explaining the benefits of the federal programs and how the provinces could help universities take advantage of them.

A final consideration worth noting is raised by Harvey Lazar (2006) regarding the intergovernmental dimension of the Social Union. Lazar observes that 'hierarchical federalism', as found in the health-care sector, with all its attendant conflicts resulting from Ottawa's unilaterally invading provincial jurisdiction and imposing conditions, is the exception rather than the norm. The implication is that if governments stick to their traditional roles and pathways, conflict is less likely. Furthermore, one suspects that governments, and especially provincial governments, can fight only so many battles on so many fronts. The case of Ottawa's transformational role in post-secondary education, therefore, may simply be one of the unexceptional cases identified by Lazar.

Performance, Effectiveness, Legitimacy

Performance

In this instance it appears that executive federalism functioned like a well-oiled machine. But it was an odd kind of executive federalism, since one set of executives—those from provincial governments—was largely absent. The best-oiled part of the machine was the strategic alliance forged among key officials from Industry and Finance and the CEOs from top universities. The near-absence of provincial government actors may well explain why things went so smoothly. However, the fact that Ottawa was able to use a very tightly controlled and orchestrated strategy—one that limited the number of actors involved both inside and outside Ottawa—in implementing its innovation agenda goes some way towards explaining the success of the process. Certainly there are lessons here on how to manage the *intra*governmental dimension of an intergovernmental strategy. But the success resulted in good part from the provinces deciding not to challenge or contest Ottawa's presence in this field, which, as noted below, was not necessarily an unmixed blessing.

Effectiveness

If effectiveness means substantive outcomes, then one can point to the additional money that flowed to universities, a revitalized research infrastructure, and new research capacity in the form of Canada Research Chairs. For the most part it also represented new money added to the bottom lines of universities; further, in the case of the CFI, the program was structured so as to leverage additional monies from both the private sector and provincial governments. At the same time, the new resources and the manner in which they were allocated worked to the benefit of the major research-oriented medical-doctoral universities. The result is what some would call a two-tier or perhaps even a three-tier system. The top tier, concentrated in what is referred to as the G-10, a group of universities whose presidents meet on a regular basis, is located exclusively in central and western Canada. There are no G-10 members from Atlantic Canada. Thus, the federal PSE transformation has likely exacerbated already existing differences in resources within the PSE community.

Effectiveness is somewhat in the eyes of the beholder. Some view the 'tiering' of universities as a positive sign: the concentration of resources allows Canada, at long last, to aspire to creating two or three world-class universities. In Atlantic Canada, and especially in Nova Scotia, where government expenditures on universities on a per capita basis are among the highest but spending per student among the lowest because of the net inflow of out-of-province students, this concentration on the G-10 is seen in a much less positive light.

Similarly, the off-loading of the cuts in the post-secondary education portion of the CHST directly onto students and their families means that students now pay substantially more of the direct costs of their university education than was the case before 1995. Again, some see this as a positive development, arguing that since a university degree confers considerable financial benefits later in life, those who receive one should pay a good portion of the upfront costs. On the other hand, there are worries about access and increasing student debt loads, despite considerable debate as to how tuition fees actually affect access to higher education (Finnie et al., 2004). Many within universities would agree that the arrival of CRCs and CFI money has been positive. Even those who have benefited the least—individuals in the humanities and social sciences—have acknowledged a frisson of excitement as deans announced opportunities to hire new scholars, often at a senior level, in areas such Elizabethan drama or oriental archaeology, depending on the priorities selected for the CRC strategic plan by their institution.

Legitimacy

The PSE transformation, if one can use that label, may well score high on performance and effectiveness. It is not certain whether the same thing can be said about the legitimacy of either the process or the outcome. It was a very closed process. There may have been extensive consultation with important elements of the research community, but very little was done with other constituencies within the more broadly defined post-secondary education sector. Certainly students were not consulted as to whether they would prefer to see federal funding redirected towards research at the expense of support for operational costs. In brief, there was little or no debate over the changes that were about to be unleashed in the mid-1990s. Defenders of the process would likely argue that a more open process would have ended badly. Indeed, there had been a wide-ranging open process in 1994–5 when Lloyd Axworthy, at the time the minister of HRDC, launched his Social Security Review (SSR) of all federal social policy programs, including student support. Although the review process had its merits (Lindquist, 2005), it ultimately ended in failure when the various parties concerned—provincial governments, universities, students—failed to come to any consensus. The failure to reach consensus on any of the issues addressed by the SSR contributed to the much more active role subsequently played by Finance in managing the program review process (Bakvis, 1996).

As noted, the CRC and CFI programs built upon Ottawa's previous experience with the granting councils and innovations such as the Centres/Networks of Excellence of the 1980s. The university community, by virtue of its extensive participation in adjudication processes and memberships on committees and the councils themselves, sees the relationship between itself and the councils, now including the CFI, as a strong one and has conferred considerable legitimacy on it. Ottawa, although it may not fully realize it, has reaped considerable benefit from this relationship: it enjoys the loyalty of a significant element of the Canadian community, one responsible for shaping, literally, the minds of many young Canadians. In many respects, therefore, post-secondary education can be seen as a successful, and legitimate, example of executive federalism, with Ottawa operating largely in its own sphere and its role largely uncontested by the provinces.

Yet, on another level, the role played by Ottawa and its tacit acceptance by the provinces can be seen as a federal failure. It assumes that federal and provincial spheres are distinct and separate. Is this really the case with post-secondary education? One can argue that there are, in fact, all kinds of interdependencies among research, teaching, and community service, and that they as difficult to separate as the marbling in Grodzins's cake analogy. If there are indeed these sorts of interdependencies, then one can further argue that the provinces had a responsibility to represent the interests of students and other constituencies involved in what David M. Cameron (2004: 26) has labelled the 'social contract': that is, 'an accord that embraces the interests of students, faculty, administration, and the general public'. The failure thus lies not so much in the unilateral actions of the federal government as in the fact that the provinces failed to contest those actions, to recognize for themselves the 'primary constitutional roles of the provinces' (Cameron, 2004: 27), and to signal to Ottawa the importance of those interests the provincial governments have an obligation to represent.

In its March 2007 budget the federal Conservative government stated its intention to increase the PSE component of the CST by $800 million a year, effective in 2008–9, and to continue raising it by three per cent a year thereafter, subject to 'discussions with provinces and territories on how best to make use of this new investment and ensure appropriate reporting and accountability to Canadians' (Canada, 2007). No doubt the provinces, Quebec in particular, will contest the conditionality of the proposed increase. Nevertheless, such intergovernmental 'discussions' can also be seen as opportunities if the provinces prepare for them properly: by re-engaging the aforementioned constituencies in conversation about how this new money can be most effectively allocated to meet the hitherto neglected needs of universities and their students.

Notes

The author would like to thank Harvey Lazar, Ron Manzer, Peter Meekison, and a reader for Oxford University Press for detailed and most helpful comments on an earlier draft. All errors remain my own.

1. Data on transfers and expenditures presented here are drawn from the following sources: Advisory Panel (2006), Association of Universities and Colleges and Canada (2005), Canada (1996a, 1996b, 1996c, 1997, 2004), and Canada Foundation for Innovation (2005).

References

Advisory Panel on Fiscal Imbalance. 2006. *Reconciling the Irreconcilable: Addressing Canada's Fiscal Imbalance.* Ottawa: Council of the Federation, 31 Mar.

Association of Universities and Colleges and Canada. 2005. *Momentum: The 2005 Report on University Research and Knowledge Transfer.* Ottawa: Publications and Communications Division.

Aucoin, P. 2003. 'Independent Foundations, Public Money and Public Accountability: Whither Ministerial Accountability as Democratic Governance?', *Canadian Public Administration* 46, 1: 1–26.

Bakvis, H. 2002. 'Checkerboard Federalism? Labour Market Development Policy in Canada'. In *Canadian Federalism: Performance, Effectiveness, and Legitimacy*, ed. H. Bakvis and G. Skogstad. Toronto: Oxford University Press.

———. 1996. 'Shrinking the House of "HRIF": Program Review and the Department of Human Resources Development'. In *How Ottawa Spends, 1996–97*, ed. Gene Swimmer. Ottawa: Carleton University Press.

——— and D.M. Cameron. 2002. 'Old Wine in New Bottles: Post-Secondary Education and the Social Union'. In *Building the Social Union: Perspectives, Directions and Challenges*, ed. I. Peach. Regina: Saskatchewan Institute of Public Policy.

——— and L. Juillet. 2004. *The Horizontal Challenge: Line Departments, Central Agencies and Leadership.* Ottawa: Canada School of Public Service.

Cameron, D.M. 2002. 'The Challenge of Change: Canadian Universities in the 21st Century', *Canadian Public Administration* 45, 2: 145–74.

———. 2004. 'Collaborative Federalism and Post-Secondary Education: Be Careful What You Wish For', paper presented at the John Deutsch Institute for the Study of Economic Policy, Queen's University, Kingston, 13 Feb.

Canada. 1996a. *1996–97 Estimates: Part II.* Ottawa: Treasury Board Secretariat.

———. 1996b. *Budget 1996.* Ottawa: Department of Finance, 6 Mar.

———. 1996c. *Program Expenditure Detail: A Profile of Departmental Spending.* Ottawa: Treasury Board Secretariat, 7 Mar.

———. 1997. Speech from the Throne to Open the First Session Thirty-Sixth Parliament of Canada. Ottawa: Privy Council Office. At: <www.pco-bcp.gc.ca/default.asp?Language=E&Page=sftddt&doc=sftddt1997_e.htm>.

———. 1998. *Budget 1998.* Ottawa: Department of Finance, Feb.

———. 2001. Speech from the Throne to Open the First Session Thirty-Seventh Parliament of Canada. Ottawa: Privy Council Office. At: <www.pco-bcp.gc.ca/default.asp?Language=E&Page=sftddt&doc=sftddt2001_e.htm>.

————. 2004a. *Budget 2002*. Ottawa: Department of Finance, 23 Mar.

————. 2004b. CSTA *Update Fall/Winter 2004*. Ottawa: Council of Science and Technology Advisors.

Canada. 2007. *Budget 2007*. Ottawa: Department of Finance, 19 Mar. At: <www.budget.gc.ca/2007/bp/bpc5de.html#post>.

Canada Foundation for Innovation. 2005. *Annual Report, 2004–05*. Ottawa. At: <www.innovation.ca/publications/annual/annual05_e.pdf>.

Canadian Intergovernmental Conference Secretariat. 2001. 'Research, Science and Technology Ministers Agree on Principles of Action to Speed Up the Transition to an Innovation and Knowledge-Based Economy'. Quebec City, 20–1 Sept.

Finnie, R., A. Usher, and H. Vossensteyn. 2004. 'Meeting the Need: A New Architecture for Canada's Student Financial Aid System', *Policy Matters* 5, 7: 1–48.

Haas, P. 1992. 'Introduction: Epistemic Communities and International Policy Coordination', *International Organization* 46, 1: 1–35.

Hogg, P.W. 2005. *Constitutional Law of Canada*, student edn. Toronto: Thomson Carswell.

Kwavnick, D., ed. 1973. *The Tremblay Report: Report of the Royal Commission of Inquiry on Constitutional Problems*. Toronto: McClelland & Stewart.

Lazar, H. 2006. 'The Intergovernmental Dimensions of the Social Union', *Canadian Public Administration* 49, 1: 23–45.

Lindquist, E.A. 2005. 'Organizing for Mega-Consultation: HRDC and the Social Security Reform', *Canadian Public Administration* 48, 3: 348–85.

Newfoundland and Labrador. 2003. *Budget Speech: Budget 2003*. St John's: Government of Newfoundland and Labrador.

Pelletier, B. 2004 'The State of Our Federation: A Québec Perspective', speech to Canada West Foundation, Calgary, 24 Mar.

Simpson, J. 2002. 'UBC's Remarkable President', *Globe and Mail*, 2 Feb., A19.

————. 2006 'The "Flight from the Classroom" Leaves Undergrads Behind', *Globe and Mail*, 28 June, A23.

Trick, D.W. 2005. 'Continuity, Retrenchment and Renewal: The Politics of Government–University Relations in Ontario', Ph.D. thesis, University of Toronto.

Tupper, A. 2003. 'The Chrétien Governments and Higher Education: A Quiet Revolution in Canadian Public Policy'. In *How Ottawa Spends, 2003–2004*, ed. G.B. Doern. Toronto: Oxford University Press.

Chapter 11

Canadian Federalism, International Trade, and Regional Market Integration in an Era of Complex Sovereignty

Grace Skogstad

Developments in the international political economy, argue Grande and Pauly (2005), are giving rise to a world of 'complex sovereignty'. In such a world, a country like Canada no longer has a monopoly on the exercise of political authority—the right to make binding rules—within its territory. International trade agreements, like the North American Free Trade Agreement (NAFTA; see glossary, p. 245) and the World Trade Organization (WTO), have done much to create a world of complex sovereignty. The provisions of these commercial treaties 'rub against various aspects of domestic politics, ultimately posing challenges to the independence and autonomy of national and subnational jurisdictions' (Hocking, 2004: 5).

The international institutions of rule-making and rule adjudication that arise with trade agreements are examples of international co-operation, of countries pooling their sovereignty to realize mutual gains. A world of complex sovereignty is also then a world of 'transnational governance', that is, one wherein state actors (and sometimes private actors) interact with foreign counterparts at the regional and global levels to make binding decisions. In this situation of complex sovereignty (pooled sovereignty and transnational governance), territorial states remain central actors. However, they can only accomplish their objectives in co-operation with other states and non-state actors in the domestic, regional, and global arenas.

What challenges does complex sovereignty pose for Canadian federalism? The notion of states pooling or sharing their sovereignty is compatible in some important respects with practices of Canadian federalism. Even though most legal authority in Canada is divided between the two orders of government, with only three matters being shared (pensions, agriculture, and immigration), federal and provincial governments in practice have long pooled their authority to accomplish mutual objectives. The language of 'co-operative' and 'collaborative' federalism captures this practice. A world of complex sovereignty, even if it suggests more, not less, collaboration and power-sharing across governments, is consistent with this long-standing pattern in Canadian federalism.

Some features of complex sovereignty are nonetheless potentially destabilizing for Canadian federalism. First, transnational governance would appear to privilege the government of Canada at the expense of the provinces. Canada's Constitution gives the government of Canada alone the legal authority to engage in international relations, including the signing of international treaties that could cause a diminution in the political authority of national and provincial/territorial governments. The government of Canada also has exclusive constitutional authority to represent the country in international institutions and other forums of transnational governance. Via such routes, there is a possibility for the political authority of the provinces and their exercise of sovereignty within their constitutionally assigned domain to be undermined (Robinson, 1993). Were this to occur, the federal principle that neither order of government can unilaterally alter the political authority of the other would be ignored. To ensure it is not, the pattern of collaboration will have to continue on matters of transnational governance.

Second, a world of complex sovereignty puts a premium on internal co-ordination within the Canadian state. Effective and legitimate participation in transnational governance requires a 'co-operation state': one that is not only willing and able to co-operate with other states but also able to garner a domestic consensus across subnational governments and engaged 'stakeholders' or organizations representing civil society (Grande and Pauly, 2005). Doing so requires keeping the dynamic of co-operation across federal and provincial/territorial governments uppermost and curbing the competitive dynamic that is also ever-present. It also requires bringing into the networks of intergovernmental negotiation the non-state actors whose knowledge and compliance are normally essential to effective strategies to deal with market integration and supranational governance.

This chapter examines the reciprocal relationship between Canadian federalism and 'complex sovereignty' in international trade policy, focusing on the negotiation of international trade agreements and the management of trade disputes and tensions in the North American region. It addresses a number of questions. How do the principles and practices of Canadian federalism affect the ability of Canadian governments to embrace a world of complex sovereignty by entering into liberalizing international trade agreements? As complex sovereignty has taken hold with Canadian–American economic integration and global regulation via the World Trade Organization, what changes are we witnessing in Canadian federalism? Is the transnational governance implied by both developments causing a blurring in the boundaries of the sovereignty of each order of government, one consistent with national governments pooling their sovereignty, be it with one another, subnational governments, and/or non-state actors? What do the patterns we see here tell us about Canada's ability to play the role of the co-operation state that Grande and Pauly (2005) suggest is needed to meet the challenges and reap the opportunities of regional economic integration and international regulatory governance? And finally, what are the implications of the way Canada approaches complex sovereignty for the performance, effectiveness, and legitimacy of governing in Canada's federal system?

The chapter proceeds in six parts. The first part situates international trade policy within the context of Canada's political economy, examining how it gives federal state actors strong incentives to embrace complex sovereignty—at home and abroad—on matters of international trade. The second section examines how complex sovereignty has taken shape in the negotiation of international trade agreements. It discusses the formal and informal structures that facilitate close collaboration across the two orders of government, but importantly, as well, those by which non-state actors are incorporated into policy formulation. The third section considers how Canada approaches transnational governance, focusing on the resolution of trade disputes over softwood lumber, agricultural commodities, and matters on which the government of Canada enjoys exclusive legal authority. The fourth part looks at the performance of intergovernmental relations in trade policy and considers proposals to formalize and extend provinces' role. Part five addresses the legitimacy of trade policy processes and substance from the perspective of non-governmental actors. The final section appraises the impact of federalism on international trade policy and addresses why the transition to complex sovereignty in international trade policy has been relatively uncontroversial to date.

Canada's Political Economy and International Trade

Two features of Canada's political economy give rise to close collaboration across the two orders of government on matters of international trade. First, the economic well-being of Canada depends significantly on international trade and the capacity of Canadian exporters to access foreign markets. In the mid-1980s, in advance of the regional and multilateral trade agreements, exports accounted for about 25 per cent of Canada's GDP; today they account for around 40 per cent.[1] Initiatives to open foreign markets, through liberal trade agreements, can thus be expected to benefit the country as a whole. But the stakes of market opening are especially important for some provinces/regions whose economic well-being is closely tied to one or two commodities or sectors. Examples include oil and gas for Alberta, grain and oilseeds for Saskatchewan, forestry for British Columbia, and auto manufacturing for Ontario. This external market dependence gives provinces the justification to demand input into Canadian international trade policy.

Second, the federal system, by dividing jurisdiction over the implementation of international treaties, guarantees the legal right of provincial input when international trade policy directly implicates provincial constitutional authority. The 1937 judicial ruling in *Attorney General for Canada v. Attorney General for Ontario* decreed that the federal government's right to negotiate and ratify international treaties does not extend to implementing provisions of international agreements whose subject matter falls within provincial jurisdiction.

Until the late twentieth century, the terms of international trade agreements fell virtually exclusively within federal legal authority. After 1947, the General Agreement on Tariffs and Trade (GATT) promoted international trade by lowering tariffs and establishing rules for the conduct of trade. As long as the GATT negotiations stuck to tariff reductions, as they did prior to the Tokyo Round of GATT (1973–9), the government of Canada had little incentive to involve provinces in international trade policy discussions. Nor were the provinces involved in these discussions.

Negotiating trade agreements became more complex, however, once tariffs were largely eliminated and GATT negotiations turned to potentially trade-distorting 'inside-the-border' regulatory and expenditure policies. Such measures were just as likely to be provincial as federal. The legal obligation of the government of Canada to implement the provisions of an international treaty, even when those provisions lie within provincial jurisdiction, presents it with essentially four options to secure treaty compliance.

Option I is to secure provinces' acceptance of the terms of an agreement that intrude into their areas of jurisdiction. Doing so necessitates, at a minimum, extensive consultation with the provinces throughout a treaty negotiation and their a priori agreement with any terms that impact on their jurisdiction. Provincial agreement could be solidified by giving provinces the right of formal ratification or veto over Canada's negotiating position.

Option II is consistent with a classical or watertight compartments model of federalism. Under this option, the government of Canada negotiates only international agreements whose terms fall within federal authority, excluding matters that require provincial compliance. Even then, provincial consultation and an effort to accommodate their concerns may be desirable; the economic well-being of the provinces is invariably affected indirectly by trade accords that curtail national powers and policy instruments. Ottawa has used both Options I and II in devising international trade policy.

Under Option III, the Canadian government concludes international agreements that impact on both federal and provincial spheres of authority, but obligates only itself to enforce the agreement, leaving provinces the latitude to bind themselves or not. This option has not been used for trade agreements, but it was used for the two parallel agreements to NAFTA: the North American Agreement on Environmental Co-operation (NAAEC) and the North American Agreement on Labour Co-operation (NAALC). The rights and obligations of the two agreements are similar. Taking the NAAEC as an example, only the government of Canada is initially bound by its enforcement obligations, and it is not responsi-

ble for any provincial breach of the NAAEC enforcement rules. Only when a sufficient number of provinces agreed to be bound by the terms of the NAAEC do
the full range of its obligations and rights apply to Canada.[2] Because the two
agreements impacted far more on provincial jurisdiction than they did on federal, provinces were 'completely involved in the drafting of the Canadian proposals' and had access to all the Mexican and American position papers on the
NAAEC and NAALC. They were also 'invited to the final stages of the negotiations
in Washington in August 1993' (Kukucha, 1994: 31).

Under Option IV, the government of Canada uses its international treaty
obligations to force domestic compliance, overruling provinces if need be.
Recourse to this option might be expected, since the FTA/NAFTA regime obligates
the Canadian government to take 'all necessary measures' to give effect to the
provisions of the agreement and the WTO requires it to take all 'reasonable measures'. Indeed, it could be argued that the Supreme Court of Canada would sanc-
tion federal intrusions into provincial areas of jurisdiction in order to implement
international treaties, as consistent with federal legal authority with respect to
'peace, order, and good government' (R. v. Crown Zellerbach, 1984) or 'the general regulation of trade' (*General Motors v. City National Leasing*, 1989).

Contrary to predictions (Robinson, 1993), Option IV has not been used.
Ottawa apparently considered and then rejected this option with regard to the
Free Trade Agreement ('Issues of Constitutional Jurisdiction', 1988: 45). Since
then, the federal government has relied on provinces to implement those provisions of trade agreements that fall within their territory and it has worked in
partnership with provinces to formulate Canada's trade policy. What Brown
(1991: 12) describes as a situation of de facto shared jurisdiction over international trade can also be seen as one that verges on 'complex sovereignty'.

Negotiating International Trade Agreements:
The Role of the Provinces

Since the negotiation of the Canada–US Free Trade Agreement (FTA, effective
January 1989), provinces have had institutionalized input into international
trade negotiations. So have stakeholder representatives from business, labour,
and civil society groups. The fact that these mechanisms exist, however, does not
mean that Ottawa shares its trade-negotiating with provinces and private-sector
actors to the degree needed to warrant the term 'complex sovereignty'.

The Conservative government's decision to negotiate the FTA in the mid-
1980s was highly contentious, with many Canadians apprehensive that free trade
would reduce Canadian sovereignty vis-à-vis the United States. The FTA figured
prominently in the 1988 federal election campaign and met with opposition in
Prince Edward Island, Manitoba, and Canada's largest provincial economy,
Ontario. Given the high stakes of free trade for their economies, provincial input
was vital and it was provided through the Continuing Committee for Trade
Negotiations (CCTN) and, in the latter stages of the bilateral negotiations, via first

ministers' meetings. Although Ottawa recognized the necessity of consulting and briefing the provinces, it resisted a more extensive role for the provinces. It rejected a provincial proposal to establish an oversight committee of trade ministers co-chaired by a province and the federal government, and did not accede to provinces' request that they name a representative to participate directly in the negotiations (Ritchie, 1997: 142–8; Doern and Tomlin, 1991: ch. 6). Despite appreciable provincial consultation, the provinces were left out of the final, crucial stage of the bilateral negotiations. Prime Minister Mulroney never formally asked premiers for their concurrence with the negotiated package and the provinces thus never formally approved or rejected the FTA (Doern and Tomlin, 1991, Ritchie, 1997).

The precedent of provincial consultation and briefing established during the FTA negotiations is now an institutionalized feature of international trade negotiations. The primary mechanism is the Federal–Provincial–Territorial Committee on Trade, known as C-Trade. This committee is chaired by a senior federal official in the Department of Foreign Affairs and International Trade but its agenda must be accepted by all members. Through quarterly meetings of C-Trade, and more frequently as negotiating circumstances dictate, provincial officials are briefed frequently and information is exchanged confidentially over a protected website. Provincial officials vary in their views of C-Trade as an effective vehicle of two-way communication, but the pre-meeting circulation of the agenda and release of federal documents to provinces are steps to improving C-Trade's efficacy (Kukucha, 2004: 122). Federal and provincial ministers responsible for trade meet much less frequently (Dymond and Dawson, 2002: 8).

These structures have provided for extensive provincial input into negotiations subsequent to the FTA, including NAFTA, the Uruguay Round of GATT and Doha meetings of the WTO, the OECD-led Multilateral Agreement on Investment (MAI), and the Free Trade Area of the Americas (de Boer, 2002; Hale, 2004; Hocking, 2004; Kukucha, 2004). Their functioning is consistent with the Canadian government's pursuit of Options I and II in order to avoid subsequent difficulties in enforcing treaties. Ottawa obtained provinces' agreement for provisions in NAFTA and the 1995 WTO agreements that affected their jurisdiction, and managed to exclude matters from the terms of WTO agreements on which provincial consensus and consent were not forthcoming. While the eventually aborted MAI negotiations were underway, provinces were 'consulted frequently and consistently', debriefed after every negotiating session, and copied in on all reports, and they had access to all negotiating documents (DFAIT, 1998). This coordination was viewed as necessary because the MAI would have increased the exposure of provincial governments to challenges by foreign investors and governments.

Paralleling the processes of provincial/territorial consultation are those that engage non-governmental actors: not only industry/business but also those representing civil society (including those opposed to trade liberalization and international regulatory governance). Fifteen Sectoral Advisory Groups on

International Trade (SAGITS) were created during the FTA negotiations to consult with non-governmental actors. Since the early 2000s, the SAGITS have been supplemented with multi-stakeholder information and consultation sessions. I will return to these forums for wider societal participation later in the chapter.

Complex Sovereignty and Transnational Governance: Resolving Trade Disputes

Subsequent to the 1989 FTA and the 1994 NAFTA agreements, the Canadian and American markets have become closely integrated as north–south trade has accelerated and east–west trade has become relatively less important. Fully 84 per cent of domestic exports are to the United States, up from 73 per cent in 1989 (Industry Canada, 2006). The Canadian economy has become extraordinarily dependent on the American market. It absorbs by far the greatest proportion of exported goods and services of all provinces, including those of the largest provincial economies of Ontario, Quebec, and Alberta. With the sole exception of Manitoba, the value of provincial exports to the United States exceeds that to other provinces (Courchene, 2006: Table 1).

Along with market liberalization and integration have come trade disputes and the need for mechanisms to resolve them. Disputes arise when a trading partner's policies are believed to give an 'unfair' advantage to its producers/industry. Both the NAFTA and WTO agreements provide for mechanisms and procedures to resolve trade disputes among members. These dispute settlement procedures are a means to enforce trade agreements and ensure that their rules, rather than the economic or political power of a dominant trading partner, determine terms of trade. Impartial dispute settlement bodies were a major objective of Canada during the FTA negotiations (and were carried forward to NAFTA). Binding dispute settlement powers are also a prominent feature of the WTO, and again Canada played an important role in their creation. Although dispute settlement bodies are a crucial feature of managing commercial relations, they do not replace interstate diplomacy at the official and highest ministerial levels.

By virtue of their composition and mandate, the NAFTA and WTO dispute settlement bodies are properly regarded as a form of transnational governance. NAFTA dispute settlement bodies include individuals (often but not always lawyers) named by each of the disputing states; those selected for WTO dispute panels are not named by disputing states but must have their approval. In both cases, the decisions of dispute panels are supposed to be authoritative—that is, binding—but the WTO panels realize this objective far better than do the NAFTA dispute panels. In this dimension of transnational governance, the government of Canada has a legally privileged position vis-à-vis the provinces. Although private firms can initiate disputes under NAFTA's Chapter 11 on Investment, provincial governments cannot. Among governments, only the government of Canada can initiate dispute settlement procedures and name Canada's members to

NAFTA panels. It also has the exclusive right to initiate a formal WTO complaint.

The government of Canada has *not* chosen to use its exclusive legal authority with respect to transnational governance of trade disputes to attempt to centralize trade policy. The reasons are obvious. Most trade disputes have appreciable economic stakes for one or more provinces. As well, when a provincial policy is targeted by a trade action, provinces will possess the information needed to rebut an unfair trade charge. Both factors rule out any unilateral federal approach to trade dispute resolution where provincial instruments are implicated. Perhaps surprisingly, consultation with provinces also occurs when federal policies are in dispute, as illustrated below.

The pattern of intergovernmentalism around international trade disputes thus approximates 'pooled' authority. That is, the two orders of government work closely to avoid disputes with trading partners and to settle trading tensions in advance of formal complaints. When such disputes escalate to formal complaints, the interaction across federal and provincial officials is continuous. Provinces also participate as members of the Canadian delegation in international meetings and forums to resolve trade disputes that are of interest to them (Dymond and Dawson, 2002: 8).

This extensive role for provinces in dispute settlement proceedings is paralleled by an equally appreciable role for representatives of the affected industry. As with the provinces, industry groups' involvement in formulating a trade challenge response is closely tied to their possession of expertise and acknowledges that industry groups bear the economic costs of borders closing to their products. Sometimes, as well, industry consultation and agreement are prerequisites to implementing an international agreement.

The imperative of a domestic consensus-building process creates the potential for a joint decision-making trap (Scharpf, 1988). Where unanimity is sought prior to decisions being taken, decisions may be prolonged and/or may represent the outcome that the most recalcitrant party is willing to accept. Because the Canadian government is unable to 'dictate terms to the provinces' or 'create consensus where it does not exist' (Brown, 1991: 122), Canada's response to external trade challenges may be both delayed and weakened if provinces are at odds with one another or inclined to promote their own interests unilaterally.

The extent to which federalism results in suboptimal outcomes in handling trade disputes is now examined by looking at three different trade disputes: those around softwood lumber where provincial measures and jurisdiction are overwhelmingly involved; those around agriculture where both orders of government exercise legal authority; and those around periodicals and regional aircraft carriers where only the federal government's measures are under attack.

Softwood Lumber

Disputes over Canadian exports of softwood lumber to the United States constitute the largest by value and the longest-running of Canada's trade disputes with the United States. They originate in differences in Canadian provincial and

American forest management practices, including their timber pricing policies. With the softwood lumber industries on either side of the border competing for the same—American—market, a rise in the Canadian share of the American market meets with quick opposition from the American lumber coalition. The US Coalition for Fair Lumber Imports alleges that provincial forest management practices in BC, Ontario, Alberta, and Quebec regarding stumpage rates (the fees forest companies pay to log on Crown land) and restrictions on raw log exports are unfair subsidies that cause material harm to American lumber interests. The coalition has successfully petitioned the American government to levy counter-vail duties on Canadian softwood lumber imports on four separate occasions since 1982. Under NAFTA and the WTO rules, countries are allowed to levy countervail duties on imports when they can demonstrate that (1) the enterprise or industry exporting the product has received a government financial contribution that confers a benefit (a subsidy), and (2) the subsidized import is causing material injury to an industry in the importing country.

Canadian trade officials and ministers, with the concurrence of the provinces, the largest forestry industry companies, and most groups representing them, have pursued a two-pronged approach to ward off American protectionist challenges. The first is to use existing legal remedies to get the US complaints dismissed. This strategy worked with the first softwood lumber dispute in 1982. It has proven to be much less effective since bilateral dispute settlement bodies were established under NAFTA. In 2001, the US imposed unprecedentedly large duties, initially amounting to over 27 per cent on Canadian softwood lumber imports, on the grounds that the Canadian products were not only subsidized by federal and provincial policies but also being 'dumped'; that is, sold below the cost of production or at prices lower than in Canada. The Canadian government, with the support of the provinces/territories and industry associations in BC, Ontario, and Quebec, challenged these duties under NAFTA and the WTO as inconsistent with US law and therefore illegal. Despite dispute settlement rulings in Canada's favour, the US government refused to remove the duties, although it did lower them.

The second prong of Canadian attempts to combat American protectionism and secure access for Canadian softwood lumber exports is to negotiate an outcome of 'managed trade'. Between 1986 and 1991, a Memorandum of Understanding (MOU) between the governments of Canada and the United States governed bilateral trade in softwood lumber. The MOU required Canada to impose a 15 per cent export tax on softwood lumber exports to the US. In 1996, Canada again agreed to restrict its access to the US softwood lumber market in order to stave off an American legal challenge to provincial forest management practices. A specified amount of Canadian softwood lumber exports entered the US tax-free for a five-year period; exports above this level were subject to an export tax. The most recent instance of a negotiated outcome to bilateral disputes occurred in 2006 when the Harper Conservative government agreed to conditions on Canadian access to the US market. Under the 2006 agreement, the US lifted its remaining duties on Canadian softwood lumber imports and, in return, Canadian provinces agreed to levy an export tax and/or quotas on softwood lumber products when their price fell below a stipulated amount.

The involvement of provinces in negotiations towards managed trade does not ensure their unanimous support for the terms of such agreements. Negotiated access agreements require provinces and forest companies to agree on a formula (ordinarily, historic market share) by which to share the US market, as well as a means of curtailing exports—with an export tax or quotas—when the export ceiling is reached. Although Alberta, Quebec, and Ontario are all affected by American market access limitations, British Columbia has the most at stake. With about half of Canadian softwood lumber exports to the US, and with the sector significant to the provincial economy, BC's government and forestry companies have an effective veto over a negotiated agreement. On occasion, BC political leaders have acted unilaterally, and arguably in excess of their provincial authority, to press their interests directly to US trade officials.

Negotiated access agreements in 1986, 1996, and 2006 accommodated the demands of the British Columbia government and its dominant forest companies and forestry business and labour organizations. The dissatisfaction of the BC forestry sector with the 1986 MOU led the Canadian government to exercise the option to terminate it in 1991. The 1996 negotiated quota on Canadian exports to the US was proposed by the British Columbia forestry industry, and was not the option preferred by the Canadian government (Cashore, 1998: 27). The allocation of the export quota among the provinces was highly divisive, with British Columbia Premier Glen Clark complaining that Ottawa was favouring Ontario and Quebec at BC's expense. Over the duration of the agreement, the BC premier criticized its costs to the province's economy. The 2006 negotiated outcome again reflects the preferred position of British Columbia's government and lumber industry, which had earlier blocked an outcome negotiated by the federal Liberal government (LeGras, 2006). Still, the politics of domestic consensus-building span more than one province and more than one provincial forestry company and organization. The governments and forest companies and groups in Ontario and Quebec have to be on board as well (Howlett et al., 2006: A10).

Difficulties in securing agreement for the 2006 negotiated settlement reveal the important role that not only provinces but private actors themselves play in trade disputes. The 2006 accord required that forestry companies agree not to bring any further legal action against the US over softwood lumber exports. For several months after the accord was struck, and despite persistent industry opposition, the Harper government and its International Trade minister, David Emerson, formerly a Liberal minister of Industry who jumped to the Conservatives immediately after the 2006 election, departed from their Liberal predecessors in adopting a 'take or it leave it' attitude, even threatening to treat a vote on its implementing legislation as a vote of confidence in the government. By late summer, as the largest forest companies continued to indicate their disapproval with the deal, Emerson was forced to acknowledge the need for further modifications to the accord to ensure 'sufficient buy-in from industry' (Vieira, 2006). The agreement implemented in October 2006 contained other inducements to bring recalcitrant industry players on side. Even so, the Harper government's actions suggested that it was much more inclined than previous Liberal governments to use its unilateral authority over international trade policy to press industry and provincial governments to accept its preferred outcome to this long-running bilateral trade irritant.

Agriculture

Agriculture represents the second arena of trade policy where bilateral disputes over access of Canadian agricultural products to the US market have been rife and prolonged. Unlike softwood lumber, agriculture is an area in which both federal and provincial/territorial governments have legal authority. Thus even though international trade of any kind is a federal responsibility, the two orders of government effectively share the policy-making authority in disputes involving agricultural trade. Provincial agricultural ministers and officials have been closely consulted, through a committee parallel to C-Trade, on disputes that have entailed American threats to close the American market to Canadian agricultural products, including wheat (Skogstad, 1995), beef, cattle, hogs, and pork. Provincial officials were included on the team of Canadian officials that defended Canada's dairy pricing system when the US and New Zealand jointly, and successfully, challenged it at the WTO. Representatives of dairy producers and processors were also regularly debriefed.

The closing of the American border to Canadian cattle and beef in May 2003, after BSE (bovine spongiform encephalopathy or 'mad cow' disease) was found in an Alberta cow, provides a recent illustration of intergovernmental and government–industry collaboration on agricultural trade policy. At the time the American border closed, the Canadian livestock sector depended on the US market for 80 per cent of Canadian beef exports and almost 100 per cent of live cattle exports. The cattle industry is concentrated in Alberta, but virtually all provinces suffered economic losses as a result of export markets closing to Canadian beef and live cattle.

Reopening foreign markets, including the American market, required demonstrating to foreign consumers that Canada had put in place measures to mitigate the risk of BSE in the Canadian cattle herd and BSE-infected meat entering the food supply chain. The task of ensuring the safety of Canadian animal and food products for international trade falls to the government of Canada. However, the effective implementation of measures to mitigate BSE risks required that provincial governments and the cattle and beef industry agree to new (and more costly) rules for such things as cattle surveillance, meat inspection, and disposal of materials associated with BSE. The federal government (more precisely, the responsible agency, the Canadian Food Inspection Agency) worked closely and cooperatively with provincial governments and the industry to get their agreement for new BSE risk mitigation measures (Canadian Food Inspection Agency, 2004).

Recognition of 'complex sovereignty' was equally important both inside Canada, in building the internal consensus needed for regulatory reform, and outside, in transnational governance forums. Transnational networks of NAFTA government officials—chief veterinarians and those responsible for food safety—worked to harmonize BSE risk mitigation measures in the NAFTA region and in the international body that sets safety standards for traded animals. Within NAFTA, working groups of technical officials were supplemented by transborder networks of industry groups (representing cattle, meat-packing, meat-processing, and export trade interests). They also promoted consensus-building around both regulatory harmonization and the eventual reopening of markets. Borders around the world had been closed to Canadian cattle and beef exports after the discovery of BSE, and reopening them depended ultimately on the US administration satisfying its own legal authorities that Canadian products were safe. Notwithstanding the dependence of Canadian authorities on regulatory actions of foreign countries, the BSE dispute illustrates the capacity and willingness of Canadian federal and provincial governments to work co-operatively in pursuit of a shared interest in eliminating barriers to trade for export-oriented industries.

Disputes over Federal Measures

Intergovernmental and industry–federal government co-operation also prevails with respect to dealing with trade disputes that involve solely federal measures. Among the WTO cases where solely federal measures have been the substance of international trade disputes are the 1999 ruling that found Canadian export subsidies to the regional jet producer, Bombardier, to be illegal; the ruling against (insufficient) Canadian patent protection for pharmaceutical drugs; the successful challenge by Honda and Toyota car manufacturers that the 1965 Autopact provision allowing US auto manufacturers Ford, General Motors, and Chrysler to import cars duty-free from outside North America while the Japanese automakers faced a 6.1 per cent tariff on such imports was discriminatory; and the ruling in the *Sports Illustrated* case that excise taxes and tariffs on split-run magazines[3] were illegal. In seeking responses to these negative rulings that minimize their costs to the affected Canadian industries, Ottawa has consulted closely with the affected private interests and provinces. Their information and analyses have improved the legitimacy of the eventual policy responses.

This picture of regular input of provincial governments into Canadian international trade policy needs qualification. Not all provinces participate in international trade policy discussions to the same degree. Larger and economically dominant provinces are more consistently involved than smaller provinces that lack the resources of personnel and finances required to follow international trade policy matters closely. Even for those provinces most involved, their degree of involvement in international trade policy varies by issue. The four largest provinces—Ontario, Quebec, Alberta, and, to a lesser extent, British Columbia—have the greatest policy capacity on trade issues (Kukucha, 2004: 122–4). However, even their resources of expertise and personnel pale in comparison with those of the Canadian government. Thus, provincial attention is selective. Even with its appreciable trade bureaucracy, Alberta concentrates on those trade issues of highest economic significance: energy resources and agriculture.[4] Quebec was closely involved with the federal government in seeking a solution to the dispute over *Sports Illustrated*, which had clear implications for cultural sovereignty. Other issues with economic importance, like trade in services, engage the attention of several provinces. Even then, smaller and poorer provinces, such as those in Atlantic Canada, lack the resources to follow trade issues closely, although they are sometimes able to piggyback on the research and advocacy of larger provinces whose interests overlap with their own.

Performance and Effectiveness: Provinces' Role in International Trade Policy

Two questions arise. First, does this pattern of intergovernmental relations pass the tests of a well-performing federal system, where performance is gauged by respect for core federal principles as well as the provision of forums in which governments can discuss, negotiate, and agree on policy outcomes? Is this pattern of intergovernmental relations also conducive to an *effective* international trade policy that allows Canada to meet international trade commitments and bargain hard for optimal outcomes?

A core federal principle is that governments at each level respect one another's authority and not act in a way that reduces it. Some provinces worry that this principle will be violated because the federal government is obliged by NAFTA to take 'all necessary measures' to implement the agreement. Even if Ottawa has not to date trespassed into provincial jurisdiction to meet its treaty enforcement obligations, provinces seek greater formalization of their role in international trade policy to protect their jurisdiction. Aside from cycling their concerns through the Canadian government, provinces have no other way to influence the contours of international trade. The cross-border networks that provinces have cultivated, such as the Pacific Northwest Economic Region[5] and the New England governors-eastern premiers meeting, lack status in the context of NAFTA. The infrastructure of the European Union allows subnational governments to have input into EU-level policy-making, but NAFTA has no similar political structures to enable the independent influence of provinces on trade and policy developments under NAFTA (Keating, 1999: 20).

Accordingly, many provinces seek greater clarification and formalization of their role in international trade matters and treaties that impact on them. The Parti Québécois has long argued that provinces should not only be a part of the Canadian negotiating team, but also be at the negotiating table and able to intervene directly on issues of importance to a local industry. To date, provincial representatives have been present at international consultations to resolve trade disputes, but have intervened only when asked to do so by the (federal) head of the Canadian delegation.

In addition, provinces such as British Columbia and Quebec have proposed that trade agreements that impact on provincial jurisdiction should require the formal approval of provincial legislatures (British Columbia, 2000; Quebec, 2002). At the national level, Bloc Québécois members of Parliament have introduced private members' bills on three occasions that would require the government of Canada to consult provincial governments before negotiating or concluding a treaty in an area under provincial legislative authority or affecting provincial legislative authority. These bills, including Bill C-260, introduced in November 2004 in the Thirty-Eighth Parliament, seem to be motivated primarily by the desire to protect provincial, i.e., Quebec, rights in the areas of education and culture. In somewhat more ambiguous language, Canada's premiers, through the Council of Federation (2005), have collectively proposed that provinces be given 'a significant and clear role in the development of Canada's international position on areas within provincial and territorial responsibility'. The Council has requested 'a formal agreement' with the federal government 'to provide clarity, certainty and continuity' in their relationship with Ottawa regarding 'Canada's international activities that affect provincial and territorial jurisdictions, responsibilities and interests'.

In the past, Liberal governments in Ottawa responded to such requests by pointing out that provinces already have significant participation in international treaties, with the federal government consulting them when treaties affect areas of provincial jurisdiction. Since current mechanisms to ensure provincial participation were working well, they argued there was no need to formalize them. The Harper Conservative government, which took office in January 2006, has proposed 'establishing a formal mechanism for provincial input into the development of the Canadian position in international negotiations or organizations where provincial jurisdiction is affected'. This position is essentially the status quo. Prime Minister Harper has been silent on whether or not provincial governments should have the right to ratify international treaties that affect their jurisdiction. He did depart from his Liberal predecessors, however, in inviting the province of Quebec to represent itself at UNESCO (Office of the Prime Minister, 2006).

The workability of the current arrangements for formulating international trade policy constitutes a powerful argument for the status quo. Existing mechanisms that leave the federal government with the sole authority to sign and ratify international treaties avoid the joint decision-making trap that a formal provincial veto over international treaties would create. Instead, the ample venues for consulting provincial governments (and affected industry groups) are proving fairly effective in building the domestic consensus on trade policy issues, and this consensus manages conflict over sometimes difficult internal trade-offs. The intergovernmental conflict that surrounded Canada's entry into the FTA and that lingered with NAFTA has essentially dissipated. But it would be unrealistic to think that future multilateral trade negotiations—a resumed WTO Doha Round, for example—could not yet engender appreciable interprovincial and provincial–federal discord.

To this point, however, the reigning logic of pragmatism, with governments working to circumvent the division of treaty implementation powers and all parties recognizing that the provinces have both 'offensive' (market-opening) as well as 'defensive' (protectionist) trade interests, appears to be effective. In contrast to American states, Canadian provinces are adhering to provisions in international trade agreements and decisions of international regulatory bodies that affect their legislative authority (de Boer, 2002). Accordingly, there seems little reason to bind governments to less flexible rules and procedures for making trade policy. Canada has approximated—as best as one could expect in a country of regional diversity and strong subnational governments—the 'co-operation state' that Grande and Pauly (2005) suggest is necessary for a world of complex sovereignty.

Legitimizing International Trade Policy: Multi-Stakeholder Consultations and Legislatures

However legitimate Canadian provincial *governments* find current procedures with respect to devising a Canadian strategy towards market-opening trade and investment agreements, these procedures and the move to international regulatory governance must still be perceived as legitimate by Canadian *citizens*. From the outset, the federal government was concerned that industry and sectoral groups directly affected by recent market liberalizing agreements regard them as legitimate. To this end, it developed the SAGIT structures and more informal consultations with industry/sectoral interests to provide them with information and receive their input into trade policy. These sectoral linkages are broader and more formalized at the federal level than at the provincial level, where they tend to be 'ad hoc', 'limited to specific sectoral disputes and international negotiations', and 'politicized' (Kukucha, 2004: 125).

However, developments towards complex sovereignty have lacked legitimacy in the eyes of representatives of broader public interests, especially those opposed to liberalizing trade and financial flows. Organized through such vehicles as the Council of Canadians, Canadians helped to block the Multilateral Agreement on Investment and, by virtue of their protests in Seattle in late 1999, to delay the launch of the Doha Round of the WTO.

Several initiatives have been undertaken by the government of Canada to enhance the legitimacy of its international trade policy.[6] An important one is the multi-stakeholder model of consultations and information briefings organized since 1998 by the Department of Foreign Affairs and International Trade (DFAIT) (Hocking, 2004: 18). Multi-stakeholder conferences organized by DFAIT have been used, for example, to provide information and consultations on the currently stalled Free Trade Area of the Americas (FTAA). These conferences have been supplemented by a dedicated multimedia Internet site and parliamentary hearings (ibid., 16)

This strategy to build legitimacy within mobilized publics for Canada's international trade policy receives high marks for 'process' and 'transparency' from observers and surpasses efforts of provinces (Kukucha, 2004). Dymond and Dawson (2002: 15) describe as 'exemplary' the formal and informal mechanisms for consultation, education, and information dissemination. Still, they worry that this broad consultative strategy emphasizes 'process over content', and many of the civil society groups that participate lack 'legitimate representative authority'. Hocking (2004: 26) raises additional concerns, suggesting that expanding older models of consultation that were relatively closed—the SAGITs, bilateral consultations between industry and trade officials—into a multi-stakeholder model creates a strong likelihood for 'a clash of expectations regarding what can be realistically achieved'. Whereas business and trade officials share the goal of trade liberalization, NGOs often do not, and therefore they attempt to use multi-stakeholder processes to redefine the political agenda away from trade liberalization to embrace other goals. Still, Hocking recognizes that governments have little option but to move to broader and more inclusive consultative strategies to build legitimacy for their policies.

Parliamentary standing committees responsible for international trade have provided an opportunity for groups representing economic and social interests to present their views on Canada's trade policies (the FTA, NAFTA, the Uruguay and Doha Rounds of GATT/WTO, and the FTAA). These committees, however, have only as much influence as cabinet ministers and first ministers (premiers, prime ministers) are prepared to give them. The negotiation and ratification of international agreements are prerogative rights of the Crown, vested in the cabinet and prime minister. There is no requirement for Parliament to give its prior approval to treaties, although its agreement must be sought for any changes to domestic law that are needed to implement treaty provisions.

Some seek a role for the Canadian Parliament in ratifying international treaties. Following the passage of Bill 56 in 2002, requiring the Quebec National Assembly to ratify any federal treaty that affects Quebec's areas of jurisdiction, the Bloc Québécois proposed a similar ratification process for the Canadian Parliament. The private member's bill introduced by a Bloc Québécois MP in the Thirty-Eighth Parliament, which called for provincial consultation in advance of negotiating or concluding a treaty affecting provincial legislative authority, would also have required the House of Commons to give its prior approval to ratification of an 'important' treaty. The sponsoring MP argued that treaties have a discernible impact on Canadians' lives but they are 'negotiated in secret'. Accordingly, the bill was needed both 'to ensure real transparency' in treaty-making and to make it 'more democratic' (Roy, 2005). Both arguments were rebutted by the Liberal government as not reflecting the 'reality' of ample opportunities for consultation of non-state interests in Canadian treaty-making.

Survey data suggest the public views Canadian trade policy initiatives—or at least their outcomes—as legitimate. These data reveal that Canadians believe they have reaped economic rewards from trade agreements and that Canadian governments have protected 'national interests' in negotiating trade deals with other countries (DFAIT, 2002). However, Canadians' support for international trade agreements does not extend to support for deep integration of the Canadian–American political economies or to 'globalization' (Mendelsohn et al., 2002). This finding suggests that Canadians may not fully appreciate the link between regional trade agreements, regional economic integration, and 'complex sovereignty'.

Conclusion

Federalism has a discernible impact on the *processes* of formulating Canadian international trade policy. Because Canada's Constitution divides authority to implement the provisions of international trade agreements and denies the government of Canada the right to implement treaty provisions within provincial jurisdiction, the federal government has deemed it necessary to engage in extensive consultation and consensus-building with provincial governments on its trade strategy. It also has several mechanisms to elicit the views of industry groups and, of late, individuals and groups representing broader social interests. The question thus arises: Is the *substance* of Canadian trade policy also different as a result of federalism? If provinces were not there to promote their interests as subnational governments and those of their constituent economic and social actors, would the content of Canadian trade policy differ?

Some light can be cast on this question by considering the two cases of softwood lumber and agriculture. In the first case, where provincial policy instruments are the source of bilateral contention, forest industry firms and groups clearly consider their provincial governments to be their primary interlocutor with the federal government. The BC Lumber Trade Council describes itself as 'joined at the hip with the BC government'; the Ontario Lumber Manufacturers Association says it relies on the Ontario government 'to put in our remarks as their own', and the Quebec Forest Industry Council works closely with its provincial government.[7] That said, forestry companies and their trade associations have been powerful actors in their own right, and given their high economic stakes in the outcome of the dispute, it is not unreasonable to conclude that they would have exercised significant influence on international trade policy even were there no provincial governments to champion their cause. On agricultural trade policy matters, industry groups interact directly with federal trade negotiators, both at home and at WTO sites of international trade negotiations. The direct lobbying of federal officials by agricultural industry groups does not obviate the importance of provincial governments as intermediaries on industry's behalf. Supply management groups, in particular, have counted on the support of provincial governments (especially those in Quebec and Ontario) in the past to defend their interests. In the case of supply management, larger strategic questions—most notably the concentration of the dairy sector in a province where federalism chronically battles sovereignty—have undoubtedly also played a role in the (protectionist) substance of Canadian international trade policy. Federalism probably exacerbates the incoherence of Canadian agricultural trade policy; that is, it leads to a trade policy that is simultaneously liberal and protectionist in advocating that other countries open their markets for our export-oriented commodities even while Canada maintains restrictions on imports of supply-managed commodities. However, this position is not unique to Canada; the United States and the European Union have analogous incoherent trade-negotiating strategies.

If federalism has shaped the processes and substance of international trade policy, what about the reverse? How have international trade and investment agreements and regional market integration shaped Canadian federalism? Scholars divide on this question. Canada's leading federalism scholar concludes that the impacts of globalization on the institutions and practices of intergovernmental relations have been 'minimal' (Simeon, 2003: 128). Others disagree, arguing that these developments have had major sovereignty-constraining effects on both orders of government (Clarkson, 2002; McBride, 2003).

The theme advanced here sits in between these two poles. It is that the institutions and practices of Canadian federalism are being reconfigured in a way consistent with a complex sharing of sovereignty, both domestically and transnationally. Developments pursuant to international trade have led federal and provincial governments to share and pool their authority with one another and with representatives of industry. The incorporation of non-state actors into the formulation of international trade policy suggests caution in assuming that federal–provincial diplomacy freezes out non-governmental actors. The domestic pooling of governing authority runs parallel to the emergence of transnational governance in the management of trade disputes and to states pooling their sovereignty in international regulatory institutions like the WTO.

Given the intergovernmental conflict that is so apparent in other policy areas, why have intergovernmental relations in trade policy been relatively free of conflict? One reason is the legal and political interdependence of the two orders of government. Neither order of government can realize its trade policy objectives without the co-operation and collaboration of the other. Moreover, the technical nature of trade policy means that interactions occur primarily at the bureaucratic rather than the political level, and at this level 'trust ties' and a logic of problem-solving around often highly technical issues tend to prevail (Dupré, 1985).

A second reason for the relatively harmonious pooling of political authority across governments is a shared interest in a liberal, rules-based trade strategy. All provincial economies depend on trade, even if some rely more than others on foreign markets to absorb surplus goods and services. This dependence helps to explain why all provinces tend to support rules-based trade liberalization and international regulatory governance. At the same time, Canadian trade negotiators have been able to secure a measure of protection for our most sensitive sectors, at least at a level that one could reasonably expect given the country's middle-sized status and asymmetrical trading relationship with the United States. Thus, realism and economic self-interest help to explain the limited amount of provincial 'second-guessing' of Canadian international trade policy even when the federal government has limited carrots or sticks to nudge the provinces along. This harmony is fragile, however, and could well turn to greater intergovernmental conflict as international trade developments take larger bites out of the policy autonomy of federal and provincial governments.

The pooling of political authority on matters of trade policy across the two orders of government is not complete. Even while provincial governments have considerable input into and influence on Canada's international trade policy, Ottawa has not consented to a formal sharing of its exclusive powers to negotiate and sign international treaties with the provinces and territories. A full pooling of internal sovereignty would give provinces direct representation in international trade negotiations as well as the right of formal a priori approval of trade agreements that impact on provincial spheres of authority.

From the perspective of this observer, a more formal and extended role for the provinces in international trade policy is not desirable. Existing procedures are working fairly effectively to create a 'co-operation state', so why change them? Were a majority or all provinces to have a veto over Canada's international trade policy, the result would likely be greater intergovernmental competition and a joint decision-making trap of policy-making. With a veto over Canada's negotiating position, larger provincial governments would have increased incentives to engage in unilateral efforts to secure the best possible outcomes for themselves at the expense of a national trade strategy that tries to balance interests across provinces and regions.

In conclusion, Canadians are likely to continue to debate whether our governments have oriented us correctly in sending us further down the path of regional market integration and international regulatory governance. At least some Canadians will argue for a more judicious balancing of trade and social policy goals in both initiatives. It will be harder to fault the Canadian government for not having tried to build domestic consensus for Canadian trade policies.

Notes

The author gratefully acknowledges the research assistance of Rick Russo, Ph.D. candidate in the Department of Political Science, University of Toronto, and the comments of John Kirton on an earlier version of this chapter.

1. Exports as a percentage of GDP peaked in 2000 at 45 per cent. They have since levelled off to comprise 38 per cent of GDP in 2005. See Department of Foreign Affairs and International Trade, 'Pocket Facts: Canada—Economic Indicators at a Glance', at: <www.dfait-maeci.gc.ca/eet/tradeneg/pfacts_his torical_2006en.asp>.
2. Canada's obligations kick in when provinces representing 55 per cent of Canadian GDP signify their willingness to be bound by the NAAEC. To date, only three provinces (Alberta, Quebec, and Manitoba) have done so.

3. A split-run magazine is one produced in the US and sold in Canada with virtually unaltered editorial content. Ottawa's initiatives, in the form of tax deductions and postal subsidies, have been designed to prevent Canadian advertising from being drained off to these magazines, which sell advertising space at low rates.
4. Alberta has its own counsel in Washington to assist with the chronic American threats and actions against Canadian cattle exports.
5. This co-operative economic association includes BC, Alberta, Yukon, and the five northwest states of Alaska, Idaho, Montana, Oregon, and Washington.
6. DFAIT also lists consultations with municipalities, advisory groups, and round tables, the posting of regulations on the Internet *Canada Gazette*, and public opinion research as mechanisms to elicit public views on trade policy. See: <www.dfait-maeci.gc.ca/tna-nac/IYT/why-consult-en.asp>.
7. See testimony of these groups to the House of Commons Standing Committee on International Trade, 31 May 2006, at: <parl.gc.ca/cmte/ CommitteePublication.aspx?SourceId=146839>.

References

British Columbia, Ministry of Employment and Investment. 2000. International Trade Policy. At: <www.ei.gov.bc.ca/Trade&Export/FTAA-WTO/provincial. htm>.

Brown, D.M. 1991. 'The Evolving Role of the Provinces in Canadian Trade Policy'. In *Canadian Federalism: Meeting Global Economic Challenges*, ed. Douglas M. Brown and Murray G. Smith. Kingston, Ont.: Institute of Intergovernmental Affairs, Queen's University.

Canadian Food Inspection Agency. 2004. 'Regulatory Impact Analysis Statement', 10 Dec. At: <www.inspection.gc.ca/english/reg/consultation/20098ria_e. shtml>.

Cashore, B. 1998. *An Examination of Why a Long-Term Resolution to the Canada– US Softwood Lumber Dispute Eludes Policy Makers*. Victoria: Canadian Forest Service, Pacific Forestry Centre. At: <www.pfc.cfs.nrcan.gc.ca>.

Clarkson, S. 2002. *Uncle Sam and Us: Globalization, Neoconservatism, and the Canadian State*. Toronto: University of Toronto Press.

Council of Federation. 2005. 'Council of the Federation Seeks Views of Federal Party Leaders', 19 Dec. At: <www.councilofthefederation.ca/newsroom/seek views_dec19_05.html>.

Courchene, T.J. 2006. 'The North American Free Trade Agreement and Canadian Federalism'. In *Continuity and Change in Canadian Politics: Essays in Honour of David E. Smith*, ed. H.J. Michelmann and C. de Clercy. Toronto: University of Toronto Press.

de Boer, S. 2002. 'Canadian Provinces, US States and North American Integration: Bench Warmers or Key Players?', *Choices* 8, 4. Montreal: Institute for Research on Public Policy.

Department of Foreign Affairs and International Trade (DFAIT). 1998. 'Back-grounder: Highlights of the Government Response to the Sub-Committee on International Trade, Trade Disputes and Investment of the Standing Committee on Foreign Affairs and International Trade (SCFAIT)', 23 Apr. At: <www.dfait-maeci.gc.ca/english/news/press_releases98_press/98_097e.htm>.

———. 2002. 'Canadian Attitudes Toward International Trade'. At: <www.dfait-maeci.gc.ca/tna-nac/documents/DFAIT_2002_en.pdf>.

Doern, G.B., and B.W. Tomlin. 1991. *Faith and Fear: The Free Trade Story.* Toronto: Stoddart.

Dupré, J.S. 1985. 'Reflections on the Workability of Executive Federalism'. In *Intergovernmental Relations*, ed. Richard Simeon. Toronto: University of Toronto Press.

Dymond, W.A. 1999. 'The MAI: A Sad and Melancholy Tale'. In *Canada Among Nations 1999: A Big League Player?*, ed. F.O. Hampson, M. Hart, and M. Rudner. Toronto: Oxford University Press.

——— and L.R. Dawson. 2002. *The Consultation Process and Trade Policy Creation: Political Necessity or Bureaucratic Rent-Seeking.* Ottawa: Centre for Trade Policy and Law, Carleton University.

Grande, E., and L.W. Pauly. 2005. 'Reconstituting Political Authority: Sovereignty, Effectiveness, and Legitimacy in a Transnational Order'. In *Complex Sovereignty: Reconstituting Political Authority in the Twenty-first Century*, ed. Edgar Grande and Louis W. Pauly. Toronto: University of Toronto Press.

Hale, G.E. 2004. 'Canadian Federalism and the Challenge of North American Integration', *Canadian Public Administration* 47, 4: 497–522.

——— and C. Kukucha. 2004. 'Investment, Trade and Growth: Multi-level Regulatory Regimes in Canada', paper presented for CRUISE conference, Rules, Rules, Rules, Rules: Multi-level Regulatory Governance in Canada. Ottawa, Carleton University, 27–8 Oct.

Hocking, Brian. 2004. 'Changing the Terms of Trade Policy Making: From the "Club" to the "Multistakeholder" Model', *World Trade Review* 3: 3–26.

House of Commons of Canada. 2004. Bill C-260. *An Act respecting the negotiation, approval, tabling and publication of treaties.* First reading, 3 Nov., First Session, Thirty-Eighth Parliament.

Howlett, K., R. Seguin, and P. Fong. 2006. 'Ontario–B.C. Alliance Influenced Outcome', *Globe and Mail*, 28 Apr., A10.

Industry Canada. 2006. 'Trade Data Online', At: <strategis.ic.gc./sc_mrkti/tdst/tdo/tdo.php#tag>.

'Issues of Constitutional Jurisdiction'. 1988. In *Canada: The State of the Federation 1987–88*, ed. P.M. Leslie and R.L. Watts. Kingston, Ont.: Institute of Intergovernmental Relations, Queen's University.

Keating, M. 1999. 'Challenges to Federalism: Territory, Function, and Power in a Globalizing World'. In *Stretching the Federation: The Art of the State in Canada*, ed. Robert Young. Kingston, Ont.: Institute of Intergovernmental

Relations, Queen's University.

Kukucha, C. 1994. 'International Economic Regimes, Canadian Federalism and the NAFTA Side Deals—The Role of Provinces', paper presented at the annual meeting of the Canadian Political Science Association, 14 June, Calgary.

————. 2004. 'The Role of Provinces in Canadian Foreign Trade Policy: Multi-Level Governance and Sub-National Interests in the Twenty-first Century', *Policy and Society* 23, 3: 113–34.

Le Gras, G. 'Canada Provinces Still Split on Softwood: Minister', *Washington Post*, 28 Feb. At: <www.washingtonpost.com/wp-dyn/content/article/2006/02/28/AR2006022801147_pf.html>.

McBride, S. 2003. 'Quiet Constitutionalism in Canada: The International Political Economy of Domestic Institutional Change', *Canadian Journal of Political Science* 36: 251–73.

Mendelsohn, M., R. Wolfe, and A. Parkin. 2002. 'Globalization, Trade Policy and the Permissive Consensus in Canada', *Canadian Public Policy* 28, 3: 351–71.

Office of the Prime Minister. 2006. 'Open Federalism', 21 Apr. At: <pm.gc.ca/eng/media.asp?id=1123>.

Quebec, National Assembly. 2002. *Bill 52: An Act to amend the Act respecting the Ministere des Relations internationales and other legislative provisions.* Assented to 8 June. National Assembly, Second Session, Thirty-Sixth Legislature.

Ritchie, G. 1997. *Wrestling with the Elephant: The Inside Story of the Canada–U.S. Trade Wars.* Toronto: Macfarlane, Walter & Ross.

Robinson, I. 1993. 'NAFTA, the Side-Deals and Canadian Federalism: Constitutional Reform by Other Means?' In *Canada: The State of the Federation, 1993*, ed. R.L. Watts and D.M. Brown. Kingston, Ont.: Institute of Intergovernmental Relations.

Roy, J.-Y. 2005. 'Private Members' Business: Hansard', House of Commons, 18 May. At: <www.parl.gc.ca/38/1/parlbus/chambus/house/debates/101_2005-05-18/han101_1800-e.htm>.

Scharpf, F. 1988. 'The Joint-Decision Trap: Lessons from German Federalism and European Integration', *Public Administration* 66, 3: 239–78.

Simeon, Richard. 2003. 'Important? Yes. Transformative? No. North American Integration and Canadian Federalism'. In *The Impact of Global and Regional Integration of Federal Systems: A Comparative Analysis*, ed. H. Lazar, H. Telford, and R.L. Watts. Montreal and Kingston: McGill-Queen's University Press for the School of Policy Studies, Queen's University.

Skogstad, Grace. 1995. 'Warring over Wheat: Managing Bilateral Trading Tensions'. In *How Ottawa Spends 1995–96*, ed. Susan Phillips. Ottawa: Carleton University Press.

Standing Committee on Foreign Affairs and International Trade. 1999. *Report: Implementation of the WTO Agreements and Dispute Settlement.* At: <www.parl.gc.ca/InfoComDoc/36/1/FAIT/Studies/Reports/faigtrp09-e.htm>.

Statistics Canada. 1998. *Interprovincial Trade in Canada 1994–1996.* Catalogue no. 15-546-XIE. Ottawa: Statistics Canada.

Vieira, Paul. 2006. 'Lumber Deal Near Collapse. Support Lacking: Ottawa. Emerson Warns Lumber Leaders of "Consequences", *Financial Post*, 1 Aug.

Cases

Attorney General for Canada v. Attorney General for Ontario (1937), A.C. 326.
General Motors v. City National Leasing (1989), 1 S.C.R. 641.
R. v. Crown Zellerbach (1984), 1 S.C.R. 401.

Websites

Department of Foreign Affairs and International Trade: www.dfait-maeci.gc.ca

Glossary

GATT: General Agreement on Tariffs and Trade, created in 1947 as a set of trading rules that promoted fairer and freer trade across countries.

market liberalization: The opening of domestic borders to competition from foreign goods and services by reducing or removing tariffs and other measures that restrict imports.

NAFTA: North American Free Trade Agreement, effective January 1994, an agreement among Canada, Mexico, and the United States designed to foster trade and investment by progressively eliminating tariffs and reducing other barriers to trade and investment. (More information about NAFTA can be found at: <www.dfait-maeci.gc.ca/nafta-alena/over-e.asp>.)

WTO: World Trade Organization, which replaced the GATT in 1995 as a forum for the negotiation and enforcement of multilateral trade agreements to liberalize trade. (See its website: <www.wto.org>.)

Chapter 12

Federalism and Economic Adjustment: Skills and Economic Development in the Face of Globalization

Rodney Haddow

Much recent discussion of the relationship between federalism and economic performance in Canada focuses on the role of interprovincial trade barriers in impeding the free flow of goods and services within the country. The two levels of government devoted considerable attention a decade ago to an Agreement on Internal Trade (AIT). It was designed to reduce interprovincial obstacles judged especially unacceptable when international trade agreements already had attenuated their use beyond our national borders (MacDonald, 2002). Of potentially significant value in creating a more efficient internal market, the AIT nevertheless addressed only one aspect of the broader nexus of federalism and economic life in Canada. Moreover, interprovincial measures reflect only one limited respect in which political institutions affect economic outcomes, or, to use terminology deployed in this discussion, of how governmental *hierarchies* affect *markets*. In this view, governmental hierarchies often burden or impede markets so that the best solution is for hierarchies to 'get out of the way', allowing markets, unshackled, to create prosperity.

The relationship between Canadian federalism and the nation's internal economic life is cast in a broader conceptual framework in this chapter, which addresses the positive role federal and provincial governments—distinctive hierarchies, acting within the same territory, whose actions may conflict, cohere, or interact in some other way—seek to play in stimulating markets. Consistent with a growing literature on the prerequisites of economic vitality, the chapter also examines how much these governmental activities foster local and regional *networks* among economic actors, and whether the emergence of the networks concept as a possible middle term between hierarchies and markets has affected what both levels of government do and the interaction between them. The chapter examines the interplay of hierarchies, markets, and networks in Canadian economic adjustment policy. It focuses on two dimensions of economic adjustment by which governments attempt to improve the supply of capital and labour: economic development and active labour market (or skills) policy. ('Economic adjustment' will be used here as a generic term to refer to both economic development and labour market training.) The chapter concentrates on the contemporary period but pays attention to two earlier eras: from 1867 until World War II, and between the 1960s and the 1980s. For each of these three eras, the nature of the federal–provincial relationship is examined. For reasons of space, the discussion of provincial policy concentrates on four jurisdictions: Ontario, Quebec, and one province each from the West (Alberta) and Atlantic Canada (Nova Scotia).

Throughout Canada's history, the intergovernmental relationship in economic development and labour market policy has been largely unco-ordinated and conflictual. Each level of government is now active in the field, but there is little effort to co-ordinate policies in broad terms. The model of federalism in economic development and labour market policy is one of independent governments. Both levels of government are now very active in fostering economic adjustment, and the specific responsibilities of each level are often constitutionally ambiguous. Despite the somewhat anarchic style of federal–provincial interaction in this field, conflict nevertheless has abated in recent years. This trajectory is summarized in Table 12.1 (p. 251).

The concluding section relates this chapter's findings to the three federalism themes that are the focus of this volume: performance, effectiveness, and legitimacy. It argues that throughout the country's history, the federal–provincial relationship in the economic adjustment area has been less than ideal in each of these respects. Nevertheless, this relationship arguably has improved on each count during the contemporary era. There is little reason to conclude that Canada's economy would now be better served by alternative federalism arrangements.

Hierarchies, Markets, and Federal Policy in Canadian Economic History

It is now common to distinguish hierarchy from markets as a way of co-ordinating social activities (Williamson, 1987). Hierarchy relies on vertical control of subordinates by those assigned responsibility to direct their activities; markets involve horizontal relations between actors, whose interaction reflects self-interest and is regulated by price signals. Much activity in the private economy clearly involves both kinds of co-ordination, as is the case, for example, with large corporations. The distinction nevertheless is frequently used to characterize the difference between *governments*, the most comprehensive and authoritative hierarchies in modern societies, and *private-sector economic actors* as a whole, whose interactions can often usefully be seen as driven by market incentives. Some market-oriented classical liberals envisage the possibility of markets operating in a relatively 'pure' form, largely unaffected by public hierarchies, or they conceive of this, at minimum, as an ideal to be striven for (Hayek, 1944). Scholarship on the history of market economies since the emergence of capitalism suggests, in contrast, that market activity is always supplemented and directed in important ways by hierarchy, and, indeed, that markets require the judicious use of public authority to be viable (Polanyi, 1944). Some governmental roles, termed *infrastructural*, are generic to all market economies. They include the protection of property through policing and the maintenance of a legal framework, provision of physical infrastructure, discouragement of market-inhibiting behaviour, and the dispensing of at least a minimal level of social protection. But comparative historical research has revealed that the precise nexus of hierarchy and markets varies considerably among capitalist societies. These differences reflect the distinctive conditions under which different nations began to develop capitalist economies, resulting in a variety that persists, even if in significantly altered forms, to this day (Gerschenkron, 1962; Hall and Soskice, 2001). In late developing industrial societies, governments play important roles, termed *interventions*, in addition to those listed above, by fostering indigenous business interests in the face of more advanced foreign rivals, assuring them access to cheap and reliable finance, subsidizing the acquisition of new technologies, protecting domestic markets at an early stage of development as a prelude to a later export-oriented approach to growth, and encouraging the acquisition of advanced technical skills in industry.

In the United Kingdom, the first industrializer, governments used these interventionist tools much less than did governments in the later industrializers of Continental Europe and East Asia. In important respects, the state's role in Canada's early economic development reflected the pattern in its colonial mother country: neither federal nor provincial governments in the nineteenth century developed effective tools for intervention, that is, for funnelling financial resources to industry, or encouraging technological advancement in domestic industries with a view to positioning them favourably in international markets. The one exception was in the area of tariff protection. Using its jurisdiction over this domain, and over transportation and immigration, more typically infrastructural tools, the federal government nevertheless sought to foster an industrial economy in Canada after Confederation. In the wake of the 1879 National Policy, an industrial economy did emerge, but it was disproportionately concentrated in southern Ontario; technologically dependent on foreign, usually American, parent firms; and, as a result of the latter, largely confined to local markets, with the result that Canadian exports remained dominated by the raw materials sector. Consistent with the typical pattern in the Anglo democracies, labour market training was not yet identified as an appropriate focus for significant government intervention. The provinces played a more modest role in fostering economic development during the nineteenth century and, indeed, until after World War II. In both the Atlantic provinces (Bickerton, 1990) and the West (Fowke, 1957), the National Policy and subsequent federal initiatives occasioned considerable resentment; Ottawa's policies were seen there largely as tools to promote central

Canadian interests. Yet it was in Ontario, paradoxically, that a provincial government launched significant economic development initiatives designed to correct for the perceived failings of federal policy (Nelles, 1974). For the most part, however, Ottawa was the dominant actor in the economic development field until World War II and during the first two or three post-war decades. The complex interplay of federal and provincial authority that emerged later, and that rendered the relationship between federalism and economic adjustment particularly problematical during the post-war years, was then less pronounced.

New Concerns, New Tools, and New Actors: Economic Adjustment in Post-War Canada

Canada experienced satisfactory rates of economic and employment growth during the quarter-century between the end of World War II and the early 1970s. In the context of General Agreement on Tariffs and Trade (GATT) agreements, elements of the old tariff-focused system of industrial protection in Canada eroded during these years. By the 1960s, a widespread concern nevertheless emerged that Keynesian macroeconomic policy, now Ottawa's preferred tool for economic management, had left some problems unaddressed. Observers advocated more interventionist measures to address deficiencies in the supply of capital and labour in Canada. At the national level, attention was drawn to the continued technological backwardness and lack of export competitiveness of Canadian industries. Conjoined to nationalist objections to the predominance of foreign ownership in the manufacturing and resource sectors, this lack of competitiveness of Canadian industry resulted in demands that Ottawa use more robust tools to foster domestic industry, including grants and loans to leading indigenous firms, the provision of research and development (R&D) assistance, restrictions on foreign ownership in strategic sectors, and the use of public enterprise in pivotal sectors (Laux and Molot, 1988: 59). By the early 1980s, Ottawa had responded to these concerns with a broad array of industrial interventions. However, these measures were never as comprehensive or as integrated as those that had emerged earlier in the late industrializing nations (Howlett and Ramesh, 1992: 237–52). In view of persistent regional imbalances in the distribution of industry, there were also demands that a particular effort be made to support industrial development outside of central Canada (termed *regional development* below). Ottawa's modest efforts to sponsor higher levels of industrial skills, a field until then largely left to the provinces, also came under attack, and proposals emerged to provide more public support for technical training in community colleges as well as on-the-job training. Consistent with its broadly Anglo-Saxon economic model, Canada had made limited use of such interventionist instruments to this point (Laux and Molot, 1988: 15).

Along with new concerns and new tools came new actors: the provinces became more consistently involved in economic adjustment (Leslie, 1987: 173–5). And they did so to rectify the perceived injustices and imbalances they experienced under the old National Policy framework. In part, their enhanced standing reflected the nature of the new instruments themselves: unlike the tariff, transportation, and immigration powers that formed the core of Ottawa's post-Confederation National Policy, these new interventionist tools were within provincial as well as federal jurisdiction. The Constitution Act, 1867 is frequently judged to have granted the main economic powers to Ottawa. The government of Canada did have the main economic role, as it was understood in 1867, but it was mostly a negative role. Reflecting the broadly classical liberal assumptions of the Constitution's drafters, government represented a potential burden on the economy and should restrict itself to those infrastructural activities needed to allow markets to function effectively: regulating banking and commerce, providing infrastructure, and, in the Canadian case, encouraging and regulating immigration. (The option of using tariffs, hopefully in keeping with British economic interests, was an exception to this liberal orthodoxy; Ottawa both acquired and used this power.) Consequently, the Constitution Act, 1867 was silent regarding the provision of industrial assistance, support for scientific research and R&D, and labour market training. Ottawa could claim a presence in each of these domains based on its extensive economic powers. But the provinces could do the same, based on specific enumerated responsibilities in section 92 of the Constitution Act: their jurisdiction over property and civil rights as well as education; their ownership of Crown land and the associated rights to manage natural resources and receive royalties; and their power to collect direct taxes, today the most important source of government revenue, and to incorporate companies. In effect, the Constitution granted both levels of government the right to use the new tools of economic intervention extensively. Table 12.1 outlines the historical patterns of this governmental intervention.

The new prominence of the provinces in economic development also had other causes. Construction of the post-war welfare state rapidly expanded their administrative and fiscal capacity, especially for the larger and more affluent provinces; post-war social and cultural change ignited, or rekindled, much stronger regional political identities in the West and, above all, in Quebec than had existed during the highly centralist 1940s and 1950s; the concentration of much post-war growth in the resource sector enhanced provincial power; and ownership of their natural resources was an enormous source of revenues and authority for provinces. Regionally based and provincially oriented elites also came to prominence in parts of the country in the post-war period. They stood in contradistinction to the federally oriented financial, commercial, and transportation interests based in central Canada that had supported and benefited from the National Policy economy (Stevenson, 2004).

The Variable Geometry of Post-War Federal–Provincial Economic Relations

Canada's Constitution therefore did little to specify the role of either jurisdiction or the relationship between them. Ottawa and the provinces entertained dis-

Table 12.1   Nexus of Federalism and Economic Adjustment in Canada: Historical Patterns

Era	Most Distinctive Adjustment Tools for Market	Dominant Form of State Support	Jurisdiction	Intergovernmental Relationship
Pre-World War II	Tariffs; transport infrastructure; immigration	Infrastructure	Federal predominance	Federally led, with limited/ occasional interaction of Ottawa and provinces
1960s–1980s	Grants & loans; state enterprise; ownership restrictions	Intervention	Federal and provincial	Unco-ordinated; strategic conflict
Post-1990	Science policy; R&D finance; agglomeration support	Facilitation via network enhancement	Federal and provincial	Unco-ordinated; less/ reconfigured conflict

parate views of the merits of pre-existing (federal) development policy, and represented distinctive identities and interests. Interventionist policies, by their very nature, presupposed an enhanced role for the state and for its definition of 'national' economic interests. They also fostered interstate (federal–provincial, provincial–provincial) conflict when more than one government used interventionist measures separately, within the same territory. In view of these parameters, it is not surprising that little effective co-ordination emerged between federal and provincial economic development and skills policies. Ottawa's relationship to the provinces in these fields also varied considerably across the country, reflecting the distinctive resource endowments of provinces and how much provincial objectives diverged from federal ones. Among the wealthier provinces, Ontario stood out as an exceptional case: until the late 1980s, it took only modest steps towards fostering indigenous industrial activity. It was content, observers argued, with the National Policy framework that had usually served its interests in the past and that continued to sustain its uniquely strong industrial base well into the 1980s (Courchene and Telmer, 1998: 11–12).

Beginning with the Quiet Revolution of the 1960s, Quebec developed an extensive set of tools for economic intervention—including public ownership and expansion of the strategic hydroelectric power sector and the use of state-guided investment funds to sponsor indigenous firms—that exceeded anything to be found elsewhere in Canada (Coleman, 1984: 91–129). Quebec's interventions represented a significant break with the Anglo-Saxon model of economic development and a partial step in the direction of the more directive and co-ordinated kinds of industrial development that typified late industrializers in Europe.[1] In the other three provinces discussed here, the core elements of this model were never threatened, and have reasserted their predominance in recent years (see below). Quebec firms frequently benefited from federal development assistance, and the two levels of government often co-operated on such measures. But the broader objectives and competing nationalisms informing each government's efforts meant that no strategic co-ordination was possible. In relation to regional development spending, Ottawa quickly established itself as a significant dispenser of subsidies to economic activities in poorer regions of Quebec. As the province developed its own policies for its less favoured regions, these typically operated as competitive rivals to those introduced by Ottawa.

Alberta's challenge to federal adjustment policy was equally pronounced, though based on different objections to federal policy and a distinctive vision of the state's economic role. Convinced that the post-1973 rise in energy prices would be of little long-term value unless the resulting bounty was used to diversify its economy, Alberta pursued economic diversification ambitiously and expensively during the next decade. It declined, however, to take on the kind of state-led developmental mentality with which Quebec's government felt more comfortable (Richards and Pratt, 1979). When world oil prices collapsed in the early 1980s, the diversification strategy, which had borne limited fruit, was substantially curtailed. The province nevertheless has subsequently remained the leader among the provinces, on a per capita basis, in the amount of financial assistance that it provides for industrial development.[2] Conflict with federal policy was particularly palpable in Alberta, where federal energy policy was seen as favouring the short-term goal of providing cheap energy to central Canada and enhancing that region's National Policy-derived advantages at the expense of Alberta's long-term economic interests. This tension reached its climax in the early 1980s when the Trudeau Liberals implemented the National Energy Program (NEP). The NEP was the last of the major federal industrial policy initiatives launched two decades earlier. (Clarkson, 2002, reviews these earlier initiatives).

Other provinces had equally strong objections to Ottawa's economic policies, but were less able to challenge them. In Nova Scotia, for instance, the province's ability to finance industrial interventions was far exceeded by Ottawa's funds for regional development measures for poorer regions. Provincial officials complained, to no avail, about Ottawa's failure to consult the province meaningfully before spending these sums, and about the expenditures' frequently fragmented and changeable objectives. Federal officials responded that provincial industrial spending also appeared to lack an underlying logic, was changeable, and seemingly shaped by short-term political expediency. In Nova Scotia, as in all other provinces that received federal regional development funds (available, eventually, in every region except southern Ontario), federal–provincial agreements have existed since the mid-1970s to co-ordinate development spending. But there is little evidence that these agreements have ever attained this objective, as opposed to simply enumerating lists of goals and initiatives by the co-signing governments (Haddow, 2000).

Federal–provincial co-ordination was more extensive in the labour market training field than in economic development. But between the 1960s, when Ottawa first began to spend substantial funds on labour market training, and the mid-1980s, intergovernmental co-ordination reflected the fact that the federal government largely conceded the right to provinces to decide how Ottawa's training money would be spent. The provinces typically used this authority to stabilize the financing of their community college networks; provinces were much less successful, however, in ensuring that federal funds benefited the intended recipients or the provincial economy. When provincial failure in this regard led Ottawa to break with existing federal–provincial agreements in the mid-1980s, a protracted period of federal–provincial conflict followed. It was resolved only when Ottawa effectively transferred control over a large part of its training budget to the provinces in the mid-1990s (see below). Here, too, as with economic development spending, the prevailing pattern was one of poor co-ordination and competing strategic designs.

New Challenges and New Concepts: Globalization and the Network Economy

Canada's economy entered a period of rapid change in the 1980s. It experienced a combination of rapidly increasing openness to international trade and investment flows, abetted by the implementation of major new bilateral and multilateral trade agreements in 1989, 1994, and 1995, slower economic growth, and chronic budgetary deficits for both federal and provincial governments. The new conjuncture was widely understood as an entirely new challenge for the Canadian economy, quite different from those identified by post-war policymakers. The new task was to survive economically in an environment where low-skill manufacturing jobs were threatened by competition from developing nations, investors had the opportunity and inclination to move funds more rapidly from one country to another in search of the highest return, and governments had less capacity to finance interventionist economic development and training policies. Such policies, moreover, increasingly ran afoul of international trade rules that prohibited governments from granting preferences to domestic firms over foreign ones, impeding foreign ownership, or subsidizing exports—tools used extensively during the post-war era.

By no means have interventionist tools been abandoned. Restrictions on foreign ownership are now less extensive, mostly confined to the airline, telecommunications, and media sectors; tariff protection of domestic industries, the old National Policy standby, has largely ended; and the Autopact, a managed trade

Table 12.2   Per Capita Spending in Constant (1992) Dollars on Resource Conservation and Industrial Development

	Federal	Provincial/Local	Total
1990	$274.50	$347.63	$622.13
1995	$277.01	$260.22	$537.23
2000	$165.39	$273.69	$439.08
2005	$194.76	$298.72	$493.48

SOURCE: Statistics Canada. CANSIM II Series, table 3850001, vectors V156381 and V632456.

arrangement in the automotive sector, the backbone of Ontario's industrial economy, contravened the new trade regime and was eliminated. Industrial grants and subsidies also frequently run afoul of trade agreements; they are less available than in the past, and cannot be offered on a preferential basis to domestic firms. As Table 12.2 indicates, such grants and subsidies nevertheless have by no means disappeared. Their use by Ottawa stagnated under the Mulroney Conservative administration between 1984 and 1993, and was curtailed severely by the subsequent Chrétien Liberal administration in its draconian deficit-reducing 1995 budget. Per capita federal spending on what Statistics Canada terms 'Resource Conservation and Industrial Development', our best available measure of industrial grants and loans, therefore declined precipitously in the late 1990s, following a trajectory established by the provinces in the first half of the decade. For both levels of government, however, the relatively economically buoyant and deficit-free years since 2000 saw a modest resurgence of spending. In 2005, it reached almost 80 per cent of its 1990 level in per capita, inflation-adjusted terms.

This new era of globalization, like its predecessor, nevertheless saw the emergence of new concepts about how to promote economic growth. These new ideas suggested a need to depart from a primary reliance on the old interventionist tools. The new 'endogenous' growth theory argued, contrary to classical economics, that a nation's long-term growth potential depended on its inherent capacity to generate innovative ways to improve productivity, a capacity that might vary considerably among economies at similar levels of development and possessing comparable technologies (Gilpin, 2001: 112–17). Economists also now speculate that the proximity of economic actors and the density of relationships among them play an important role in stimulating productivity-enhancing innovations in advanced economies (Krugman, 1995). In this view, networks are a crucial construct that fall between hierarchies and markets in understanding how economic life is organized (Frances et al., 1991). Like markets, networks involve horizontal relations between voluntarily interacting actors; unlike markets, they rely on 'untraded interdependencies', based on trust, shared knowledge, and face-to-face contact, without which their market-based interactions would be impoverished.

The implications of these new ideas for government's role are not straightforward. The network concept confirmed the belief of market-oriented liberals that dynamic economies rely on unplanned, horizontal relationships, not the use of government hierarchy. From this perspective, governments have even more reason than in the past to leave markets alone. But for others, the network concept justified renewed state involvement, though of a different kind than had been practised earlier. It legitimized government activities to facilitate networking dynamics that can enhance innovation. Such measures include an enhanced commitment to scientific research and its transfer to industry, more R&D assistance, especially for firms in high-technology sectors, and efforts to encourage the development and deepening of networks among firms, their suppliers and customers, research institutions, and potential sources of finance and advanced skills. While some argue that positive agglomeration effects can occur on a nationwide basis (in what are termed 'national systems of innovation'), the more common view is that geographic proximity is key: networks emerge in 'clusters', consisting of actors in a particular sector and locale (Porter, 1991) or, more broadly, thrive in 'regional innovation systems' that include a number of distinct but potentially interacting sectors within larger cities or sub-regions of a nation (Cooke, 1998).

The policy instruments of use in fostering networks are available to both levels of government, like the interventionist tools of the previous era, and both employ them. Both jurisdictions can, if they wish, fund research on new technologies, subsidize R&D in firms, and encourage collaboration among proximate economic actors. Nevertheless, Ottawa has traditionally been more active than the provinces in sponsoring science research and its industrial dissemination in Canada (Niosi, 2000: 42–4). In recent years, moreover, the government of Canada appears to have expanded this commitment and refocused its economic adjustment spending initiatives to favour science and innovation-enhancing measures, partly at the expense of the older style of industrial subsidies. A glimpse, though partial and imperfect, of the extent of this shift, and of Ottawa's leadership in this domain, is provided by Table 12.3, which reports government spending on scientific research organizations and on R&D assistance to non-governmental actors. Federal spending rose significantly during the early 1990s, weathered the late 1990s period of restraint relatively unscathed, and surged again after 2000. Provincial spending in this area, always much lower than Ottawa's, nevertheless took off after 2000. In 2005, combined inflation-adjusted per capita federal and provincial spending was 63 per cent higher than it was 15 years earlier.

Federalism and the 'Network Economy' in the Twenty-first Century

Intergovernmental relations in the area of economic adjustment are no more co-ordinated today than they were in the past. There is still no forum within which

Table 12.3   Per Capita Spending in Constant (1992) Dollars on Research Establishments and Grants

	Federal	Provincial/Local	Total
1990	$43.54	$10.07	$53.61
1995	$57.49	$13.64	$71.13
2000	$53.56	$ 6.98	$60.54
2005	$68.01	$16.59	$85.60

SOURCE: Statistics Canada. CANSIM II Series, table 3850001, vectors V156359 and V631839.

Canadian governments can plan development measures jointly. Most initiatives are conceived with little prior intergovernmental discussion, although consultation is more common on implementation. Yet there is also less overt conflict between Ottawa and the provinces about the country's economic future, and the federal government's role in shaping it, than occurred between the 1960s and 1980s. Federal–provincial friction is greater in some regions than in others. But here, too, there has been change. In the post-NEP, free trade era, friction is much less pronounced with Alberta. It is greater with Ontario, which has belatedly discovered a need to husband its own economic fortunes and to query the value of federal policies in achieving this goal.

The perceptible reduction in federal–provincial tension can be attributed partly to the simple fact that Ottawa is the dominant player in fostering the new economy. The provinces have expanded their research spending; for instance, they all now offer tax subsidies for R&D, although the extent of this generosity varies considerably across provinces (McKenzie, 2005). But, as Table 12.3 illustrates, they still spend considerably less than Ottawa does in this area. The Chrétien Liberal administration did little to promote innovation during its first term in power, but in its second, having conquered the deficit, it took significant steps in this direction. New measures included the launching of a Canada Foundation for Innovation, Genome Canada, and the Canada Research Chairs. Federal spending for existing arrangements, including the National Research Council, the Networks of Excellence, Technology Partnerships Canada, the Canadian Space Agency, and research in medicine, the natural sciences, and engineering, expanded considerably (Wolfe, 2002). Much of the new federal research funding went to the country's universities. As Bakvis points out in Chapter 10 of this volume, Ottawa has shifted the focus of its spending on post-secondary education significantly since the mid-1990s. Broad block-grant transfers to the provinces to help them finance university operating expenses have been curtailed, while direct transfers to universities to bolster research have expanded considerably. As the data reported in Table 12.3 suggest, these initiatives continued to bolster federal research spending a number of years after their launch in the late 1990s. The new spending was designed to increase Canada's perpetually low R&D levels and appeared to have some success, although Canadian firms remain R&D laggards compared to their competitors in most other affluent nations (De la Monthe, 2003: 177). Yet, according to critics, the additional funding did little to advance other aspects of the network concept, such as fostering stronger relationships among actors within innovative regions and clusters. Similarly, Ottawa failed to take the provincial governments into consideration as important partners in stimulating network-based innovation (Wolfe, 2002: 152). Ottawa's championing of the new network-based growth agenda consequently has not been matched by any greater willingness to work co-operatively with the provinces.

If the federal government's pursuit of its new agenda has occasioned less provincial resistance than did the preceding interventionist agenda, it is probably also partly because of distinctive intrinsic features of these two agendas, not because Ottawa has involved the provinces more in its new one. During the interventionist years, the federal government and several provinces pursued equally ambitious, but fundamentally incompatible, interventionist development strategies (Leslie, 1987: 8–22), This interventionist policy style led to conflict during the post-war high tide of interventionism. There is now much less room for states to see themselves as strategic 'players' pursuing comprehensive visions for the economies over which they exercise authority. Interventionist development tools are still very much in use, but globalization and the new growth concepts ensure that they are no longer deployed in pursuit of such comprehensive strategies. The new, network-focused growth agenda, by contrast, privileges localized dynamics, the strength of which is supposed to depend on their internal vitality, not on their location in relation to broader national or provincial development goals. Political considerations nevertheless still influence greatly where Ottawa chooses to foster local activity. Observers frequently allege that within and between provinces a desire to 'spread around' the opportunities created by the new economy often distorts Ottawa's selection of favoured projects.

Thus, Ottawa abandoned the pursuit of a strategic, national economic development policy (anchored, as it always was, on a determination to bolster a manufacturing economy concentrated in southern Ontario) after the Conservatives came to power in 1984 (Clarkson, 2002: 233–6). The subsequent 1989 Free Trade Agreement (FTA) provisions that effectively ruled out the regime of regulated exports, differential prices, and ownership restrictions, which had formed the core of the NEP, alleviated Alberta's main concerns about federal policy. The early 1980s collapse of Premier Lougheed's strategy of diversifying the province's economy by expanding its manufacturing base also meant that Alberta's own policies were less likely to be perceived in central Canada as a direct challenge to its established strength in manufacturing. Alberta has since turned its attention to encouraging the same kinds of science-based and innovative networks that have become the objective of federal policy (Taft, 1997:112). To the extent that federal policy is now premised on facilitating place-specific innovation in a manner that no longer effectively privileges one region over others, it is no longer, in principle, incompatible with the policies of any province, such as Alberta, that wishes to foster networks within its own borders.

During the 1980s, Quebec's development policies also departed somewhat from the particularly strategic interventionism that typified those of the Quiet Revolution, though they remain distinctive (Bernier and Garon, 2004: 210–15). In the late 1980s its Liberal government adopted the 'clusters' concept and the notion that localized networks are crucial for the province's future. An industrial policy designed to facilitate cluster development was launched in 1991 and continued by the Parti Québécois government that came to power in 1994 (Bourque, 2000: 136–40). This policy involves much more government-sponsored formal co-ordination among actors than has ever succeeded in English Canada, and it is still complemented by more extensive use of state-sponsored investment funds, though these have become less active in pursuing nationalist goals. Its conception of how growth occurs nevertheless is relatively localized and disaggregated. This local focus represents a departure, albeit partial in Quebec's case, from the earlier disposition to conceive of the provincial economy as a strategic whole, in need of 'planning and thus an increased role for the provincial government', in order to achieve the key (Quebec) nationalist objectives of fostering a francophone-owned manufacturing base (Coleman, 1984: 116). Such a strategic stance is more likely to occasion conflict when it encounters on its own ground distinctive strategies designed elsewhere.

Network economy thinking also underlies much recent development policy in Ontario. Rather than alleviating older conflicts, its influence has coincided with a discernible deterioration of the province's relationship with federal authorities regarding economic adjustment. In Ontario, unlike Alberta and Quebec, network economy thinking did not partly displace an earlier interventionist stance, but instead represented the province's first concerted engagement with development issues after several decades of relative quiescence. It also coincided with the emergence of serious doubts about whether federal policy is consistent with the province's economic interests. Ontario complains that it is unique in receiving virtually no federal funding for regional development (the exception being a minuscule initiative for northern Ontario). The province also opposed the FTA, and in the late 1980s formed private-sector panels to study how to sustain its manufacturing base, now perceived as threatened by economic globalization. The NDP administration of the early 1990s initiated programs designed to encourage innovation and collaboration among economic actors in various sectors. Unlike their Quebec counterparts, however, Ontario's network-promoting policies did not benefit from support across the partisan spectrum; most NDP measures were terminated by the Harris Conservative government that came to power in 1995 (Wolfe and Gertler, 2001). The province has continued to look for ways to promote innovation, but more tentatively than under the NDP. Ontario governments since the late 1980s, including the Liberal administration that came to power in 2003, also complain bitterly that Ontario does not receive what they consider to be its fair share of spending under many federal programs, including the rapidly expanding outlays for innovation discussed above.

Among the provinces examined here, Nova Scotia has experienced the least noticeable change. It is still disproportionately reliant on federal regional development funds, which have been reduced since the early 1990s (Haddow, 2001a: 254). Nova Scotia has adopted network economy concepts to the extent of launching a series of Regional Development Authorities (RDAs) across the province. Consisting of business and other leaders from the same locale, the RDAs are designed to foster potentially innovative interaction among these actors. However, the RDAs have almost no resources of their own, and rely on a shrinking supply of funds from existing provincial and federal programs to finance initiatives. The economic and demographic stagnation that characterizes much of Nova Scotia outside of Halifax presents RDAs with a Herculean task. As with other rural and thinly populated parts of Canada, most of these areas do not benefit from the creative dynamics that, according to network theorizing, occur in more densely populated and diverse cities and regions.

The federal–provincial relationship regarding skills training has evolved considerably since the mid-1990s, but there is little evidence that the skills imparted in training programs are becoming more relevant for current economic needs, including those associated with the 'new economy'. In the 1980s Ottawa had, in fact, taken steps to enhance the quality of skills purchased with its training dollars. To do this, it effectively disengaged itself from provincial decision-making in determining how to allocate its funds, even when the monies were being expended in provincial colleges. But in the wake of the narrow victory of the 'no' option in the 1995 Quebec sovereignty referendum, and of its own substantial deficit, Ottawa offered to devolve the administration of part of its training expenditures (the share that is funded from the Employment Insurance [EI] fund) to the provinces. Six provinces, including Quebec, Alberta, and Ontario (agreement with the latter was delayed until 2005), signed Labour Market Development Agreements (LMDAs) with Ottawa that accepted the 'full' federal offer. Called 'devolution', this allowed them to take over the administration of EI-financed programs previously delivered by Ottawa. The provinces would still have to meet certain federal conditions in spending the money, but these have little direct bearing on the content of the skills provided: provinces must ensure that a certain proportion of funded training recipients are, or recently were, EI recipients; and they commit themselves to meeting difficult-to-enforce targets regarding the proportion of trainees who return to work. The four other provinces signed more modest LMDAs. These either allow the province to jointly manage the funds with Ottawa, which continues to administer them (called 'co-management'); or, uniquely in the case of Nova Scotia, left federal authorities largely in control of EI-funded training in the province. In all provinces, the federal government nevertheless continues to administer non-EI-financed training programs of its own for three categories of people who have particular difficulties entering the labour force: youth, Aboriginal people, and the disabled. These changes shifted an important number of training recipients from federal to provincial administration, although in an uneven pattern that has been termed 'checkerboard federalism' (Bakvis, 2002). With respect to the substance of skills provided, however, federal and provincial programs remain largely disengaged, subject to policy objectives defined separately by each jurisdiction.

Moreover, the panoply of innovation-oriented economic development initiatives launched by Ottawa in the late 1990s has not been complemented by major steps to ensure that its remaining training measures address specific skill needs in innovative sectors. Indeed, the targeting of its main programs at the three 'at-risk' groups mentioned above suggests that the centrepiece of federal skills policy today is equity rather than efficiency. In November 2005 Paul Martin's Liberal administration did promise to expand federal spending on vocational skills by $3.5 billion over five years, allegedly a 30 per cent increase (Leblanc, 2005). But the minority government was on its deathbed at that time, and it expired before it was able to proceed with this idea.

Ottawa's lethargy in extending its innovation agenda to the skills area is partly explained by hesitation to reassert itself aggressively in a policy domain where it had so recently made significant concessions to the provinces. But it may also reflect a feature of the network economy perspective that has guided recent federal adjustment policy. Network thinking certainly assigns an important role to the supply of 'talent' in the success of innovative locales. Particular attention is paid to the attraction and retention of a 'creative class', i.e., professionals with advanced technology and entrepreneurial skills. In a labour market perceived to be increasingly global for this category of people, there is a concern to attract the creative class as immigrants (Florida, 2004). Although Canadian immigration policy was adjusted in the mid-1990s to enhance the entry prospects of skilled workers and the well-educated (Green and Green, 2004: 127–8), some observers in high-technology industries argue that Canada must do more to attract this exclusive category of migrant (Haddow, 2001b: 15–16). By contrast, exponents of the network economy devote less attention to workers with less to offer to the 'new economy', and to the possibility that network-based growth may not be advantageous for them (Donald and Morrow, 2003). And it is such less sought-after workers who are most likely to benefit from the more 'ordinary' vocational skills, provided in colleges or on the job, that are funded by the federal and provincial training measures discussed above.

Does Federalism Impede Economic Adjustment in Canada?

After 1945, the provinces became much more active in pursuing economic adjustment policies. The federal–provincial relationship in this area has subsequently manifested important continuities. It is mostly unco-ordinated, with each level of government typically pursuing its preferred policies after little meaningful consultation with the other level of government; these policies are strongly influenced by prevailing ideas about how best to accomplish economic growth; and, in the context of a diverse federation, such unco-ordinated policies occasion intergovernmental friction. The style of federalism in this domain comes closest to one of independent governments because of the very limited and inconsistent pattern of intergovernmental co-ordination. Jurisdiction is not 'watertight', however; neither government can confidently exclude the other from the policy domain.

The nexus of federalism and adjustment policy nevertheless also experienced important discontinuities between the post-war period and the years since 1980. First, the ideas that now prevail about how to foster growth differ from those that typified the post-war era. During the latter, strategic and interventionist approaches to economic development and skills became popular, though (with the partial exception of Quebec) always within the comparatively limited scope permitted for these in the Anglo-Saxon economic model. Current policy is instead animated by a desire to facilitate innovative networks, which are likely to be found in the most urbanized, educated, and economically diverse locales and regions of the country. Variations in the pattern of policy change—for instance, the fact that Ottawa has altered the content of its economic development policies much more than its training ones—reflect the fact that the new growth agenda has distinctive implications for these different areas. While some of the instruments favoured in the earlier period are still deployed today (especially industrial assistance), these have been curtailed, and others eclipsed, victims of a more globalized economy and of trade policy. Second, in this new context, there is less friction between federal policies and those pursued in the more assertive provinces than there once was. The retreat from policies centred on strategic 'grand designs' has reduced the potential for conflict between such designs. The regional focus of federal–provincial tension, moreover, has changed.

How should this pattern be evaluated in relation to the three federalism norms—performance, effectiveness, and legitimacy—employed in this volume? Regarding performance, intergovernmental relations in the economic adjustment field have never been fully consistent with federalism principles. The ambiguity of jurisdictional responsibilities in this area makes it difficult to assert that post-Confederation federal policies did not properly respect the jurisdictional autonomy of the provinces, because the written Constitution is of only limited help in identifying the provinces' responsibilities here. The National Policy, and much post-World War II federal policy after it, nevertheless was widely rejected outside central Canada as not reflecting the distinctive adjustment needs of the different regions. The relative absence of forums for intergovernmental bargaining meant that disaffected provincial governments lacked effective avenues for representing these concerns. In light of this earlier pattern, the performance of the federal system arguably has improved in the contemporary era, when federal adjustment policies are less subject to the accusation of regional bias, and when the dearth of formal mechanisms of federal–provincial co-ordination consequently is less important. As will be suggested below, more elaborate intergovernmental machinery would probably generate more conflict, not less, in view of the highly distinctive economic development needs of different Canadian regions. Canadian federalism is likely to perform best, regarding economic adjustment, when the need for formal intergovernmental negotiation and agreement is kept to a minimum.

To what extent does this intergovernmental pattern impede the effectiveness of economic adjustment in Canada, our second criterion? Would Canadians be better off economically, for instance, (1) if they lived in a unitary state, (2) if the provinces controlled all adjustment policies, or (3) if there were more extensive federal–provincial co-operation in this area? Quite likely, they would not be. A substantial academic literature in the field of comparative political economy (CPE) now seeks to ascertain whether some of the institutional arrangements found in developed capitalist economies are better than others for promoting growth. But this scholarship gives us no reason for concluding that Canada would be better off with a fully centralized, decentralized, or co-ordinated policy regime. A standard distinction in the CPE literature, broached at the beginning of this chapter, is between the more market-oriented political economies that are typical of Anglo-Saxon nations, and an alternative model in Continental Europe and East Asia that involves more non-market formal co-ordination among economic actors or more state intervention. Each model has distinctive strengths and weaknesses: the Anglo economies resolve adjustment problems best in an unco-ordinated, unplanned way, allowing market forces to take their 'natural' course; co-ordinative economies are better at solving economic problems through co-operative interaction among the major economic interests. But neither model is clearly superior to the other in its long-term capacity to sustain economic growth (Hall and Soskice, 2001). Nevertheless, individual countries are much more dynamic economically than are others that conform to the same model; in effect, some countries do a better job of exploiting a model's particular strengths than do other countries that reflect the same model.

Canada's political economy more closely approximates the market-oriented model, and is best suited to non-planned economic adjustment. But, as we have seen, its institutions feature idiosyncrasies that distinguish it from the Anglo-Saxon norm. A comparatively small population and extensive geography mean that the Canadian (federal and/or provincial) state has always been significantly involved in economic adjustment; Canada's federal Constitution ensures that these activities are divided between two jurisdictions; and the country's internal diversity entails that these multiple governmental actors face distinct challenges and favour different policies. The question, then, is the following. Is the style of policy-making described in this chapter the most effective, in light of an institutional endowment that creates a propensity for market-based adjustment, but that also has charged multiple and heterogeneous governments with a larger adjustment task than is typical in market-oriented settings?

A case can be made that it is, indeed, most suited to these parameters. Ottawa and the provinces are sufficiently heterogeneous in their interests and goals that it is hard to argue that the country would be well served by centralizing adjustment policies controlled by Ottawa. The history of the post-Confederation National Policy suggests that centralized adjustment policy would likely be perceived as benefiting one region at the expense of others. What about full devolution of adjustment policy to the provinces? This scenario may hold some appeal for the larger and more affluent provinces, but not elsewhere. Even in richer provinces, moreover, governments continue to support a federal role in adjustment, presumably in recognition of the closeness of economic links between the provinces and the resulting value of sharing some important adjustment policies among them.[3]

In closing, it is worth noting that Canada's adjustment style may have two specific advantages with respect to policy effectiveness and legitimacy in the current globalization era. If network theorists are correct, growth now occurs in a more localized, decentralized manner than it has in the past. A disaggregated, even relatively anarchic, approach to adjustment policy may be well suited to such an environment, presenting local economic actors with the opportunity to exploit links with multiple and diverse government programs—an interactive style that is entirely consistent with the norm in dynamic economic networks. Further, federal–provincial conflict over adjustment, while probably a perennial feature of Canadian politics, has attenuated somewhat since the end of the post-war era of strategic intervention. Rather than representing a mortal challenge to its national integrity, as is often argued, globalization—or, more specifically, the changes in federal and provincial adjustment policy styles that it encouraged—may reduce some of the political-economic tensions that have plagued Canada's internal politics since its early history. In the past, these tensions often called into question the very legitimacy of our federal institutions for citizens and governments in many Canadian provinces.

Notes

1. This argument about Quebec's political economy is developed in Chapter 2 of Haddow and Klassen (2006).
2. See data reported by Statistics Canada for provincial spending on 'resource conservation and industrial development' since the 1980s; Statistics Canada, CANSIM II data series, table 3850001.
3. Some economists argue that the extent of trade among Canadian provinces is much greater than is reflected in official trade statistics; see Helliwell (2002). For a recent example of provincial premiers publicly endorsing a continued federal role in adjustment policy, in this case training, see Cordozo (2006).

References

Bakvis, H. 2002. 'Checkerboard Federalism? Labour Market Development Policy in Canada'. In *Canadian Federalism: Performance, Effectiveness, and*

Legitimacy, ed. H. Bakvis and G. Skogstad. Toronto: Oxford University Press.

Bernier, L., and F. Garon. 2004. 'State-Owned Enterprises in Quebec.' In *Quebec: State and Society*, ed. A.-G. Gagnon. Peterborough, Ont.: Broadview.

Bickerton, J. 1990. *Nova Scotia, Ottawa, and the Politics of Regional Development.* Toronto: University of Toronto Press.

Bourque, G. 2000. *Le modèle québécois de développement.* Sainte-Foy, Que.: Presses de l'Université du Québec.

Clarkson, S. 2002. *Uncle Sam and Us.* Toronto: University of Toronto Press.

Coleman, W. 1984. *The Independence Movement in Quebec, 1945–1980.* Toronto: University of Toronto Press.

Cooke, P. 1998. 'Introduction: Origins of the Concept'. In *Regional Innovation Systems*, ed. H.J. Braczyk, P. Cooke, and M. Heidenreich. London: UCL Press.

Cordozo, A. 2006. 'Premiers Want a National Skills Strategy to Address Future Skills Needs', *The Hill Times*, 6 Mar.

Courchene, T., with C. Telmer. 1998. *From Heartland to North American Region State.* Toronto: Faculty of Management, University of Toronto.

De la Monthe, J. 2003. 'Ottawa's Imaginary Innovation Strategy: Progress or Drift?' In *How Ottawa Spends, 2003–2004*, ed. G.B. Doern. Toronto: Oxford University Press.

Donald, B., and D. Morrow. 2003. *Competing for Talent: Implications for Social and Cultural Policy in Canadian City-Regions.* Ottawa: Department of Canadian Heritage.

Florida, R. 2004. *The Flight of the Creative Class.* New York: Harper Business.

Fowke, V. 1957. *The National Policy and the Wheat Economy.* Toronto: University of Toronto Press.

Frances, J., R. Levacic, J. Mitchell, and G. Thompson. 1991. 'Introduction'. In *Markets, Hierarchies and Networks*, ed. G. Thompson, J. Frances, R. Levacic, and J. Mitchell. London: Sage.

Gerschenkron, A. 1962. *Economic Backwardness in Historical Perspective.* Cambridge, Mass.: Harvard University Press.

Gilpin, R. 2001. *Global Political Economy.* Princeton, NJ: Princeton University Press.

Green, A., and D. Green. 2004. 'The Goals of Canadian Immigration Policy: An Historical Perspective', *Canadian Journal of Urban Research* 13, 1: 102–40.

Haddow, R. 2000. 'Economic Development Policy: In Search of a Strategy'. In *The Savage Years: The Perils of Reinventing Government in Nova Scotia*, ed. P. Clancy, J. Bickerton, R. Haddow, and I. Stewart. Halifax: Formac.

———. 2001a. 'Regional Development Policy: A Nexus of Policy and Politics'. In *How Ottawa Spends, 2001–2002*, ed. L. Pal. Toronto: Oxford University Press.

———. 2001b. 'Report on the CSLS Roundtable on Creating a More Efficient Labour Market'. In *Reports and Proceedings from the CSLS Roundtable on Creating a More Efficient Labour Market.* Ottawa: Centre for the Study of Living Standards.

——— and T. Klassen. 2006. *Partisanship, Globalization and Canadian Labour*

Market Policy. Toronto: University of Toronto Press.

Hall, P., and D. Soskice. 2001. 'An Introduction to Varieties of Capitalism'. In *Varieties of Capitalism*, ed. P. Hall and D. Soskice. Oxford: Oxford University Press.

Hayak, F. 1944. *The Road to Serfdom*. Chicago: University of Chicago Press.

Helliwell, J. 2002. *Globalization and Well Being*. Vancouver: University of British Columbia Press.

Howlett, M., and M. Ramesh. 1992. *The Political Economy of Canada*. Toronto: McClelland & Stewart.

Krugman, P. 1995. *Development, Geography, and Economic Theory*. Cambridge, Mass.: MIT Press.

Laux, J.K., and M. Mollot. 1988. *State Capitalism: Public Enterprise in Canada*. Ithaca, NY: Cornell University Press.

Leblanc, D. 2005. 'Billions Set Aside for Schooling, Skills', *Globe and Mail*, 15 Nov., A7.

Leslie, P. 1987. *Federal State, National Economy*. Toronto: University of Toronto Press.

MacDonald, M.R. 2002. 'The Agreement on Internal Trade: Trade-offs for Economic Union and Federalism'. In *Canadian Federalism: Performance, Effectiveness, and Legitimacy*, ed. H. Bakvis and G. Skogstad. Toronto: Oxford University Press.

McKenzie, K. 2005. 'Tax Subsidies for R&D in Canadian Provinces', *Canadian Public Policy* 31, 1: 29–44.

Nelles, H.V. 1974. *The Politics of Development: Forests, Mines & Hydro-electric Power in Ontario, 1849–1941*. Toronto: MacMillan.

Niosi, J. 2000. *Canada's National System of Integration*. Montreal and Kingston: McGill–Queen's University Press.

Polanyi, K. 1944. *The Great Transformation*. Boston: Beacon Press.

Porter, M. 1991. *The Competitive Advantage of Nations*. New York: Free Press.

Richards, J., and L. Pratt. 1979. *Prairie Capitalism*. Toronto: McClelland & Stewart.

Stevenson, G. 2004. *Unfulfilled Union*, 4th edn. Montreal and Kingston: McGill–Queen's University Press.

Taft, K. 1997. *Shredding the Public Interest*. Edmonton: University of Alberta Press.

Williamson, O. 1987. *The Economic Institutions of Capitalism*. Oxford: Blackwell.

Wolfe, D. 2002. 'Innovation Policy for the Knowledge-Based Economy: From the Red Book to the White Paper'. In *How Ottawa Spends, 2002–2003*, ed. G.B. Doern. Toronto: Oxford University Press.

——— and M. Gertler. 2001. 'Globalization and Economic Restructuring in Ontario: From Industrial Heartland to Learning Region?', *European Planning Studies* 9, 5: 575–92.

Chapter 13

The Harmonization Accord and Climate Change Policy: Two Case Studies in Federal–Provincial Environmental Policy

Mark Winfield and Douglas Macdonald

The efficient and effective co-ordination of federal and provincial government activity is essential in the field of environmental policy. Pollution crosses borders, and Canadian courts have established that the regulation of harmful emissions lies within the jurisdictional competence of both levels of government. In this chapter we examine the processes by which the two levels of government co-ordinate their environmental policy-making. We consider both the formal institutional mechanisms and the 'politics of co-ordination', that is, the process whereby federal and provincial governments (and, to some extent, relevant non-state actors such as business and environmentalists) bargain and negotiate to develop and implement national environmental policy. In particular, we look at the two most significant examples of efforts to co-ordinate federal and provincial environmental policy since the early 1990s: the negotiation and implementation of the 1998 Environmental Harmonization Accord, and the ongoing challenge of developing the domestic policies necessary to meet Canada's commitments under the 1992 United Nations Framework Agreement on Climate Change and the 1997 Kyoto Protocol to that agreement.

A comparison of the harmonization and climate processes helps identify the principal factors influencing efforts to co-ordinate national policy. The harmonization initiative led to agreement on a stronger, codified institutional framework for co-ordinating provincial and federal actions. The climate processes, however, witnessed a complete breakdown and abandonment of the multilateral institutional framework at the time of Kyoto ratification in 2002. This was followed by unilateral federal action and individual bilateral federal–provincial agreements. At the time of writing, in 2007, the Harper government seems to be returning to a multilateral approach.

How do we explain the very different results of the two cases of harmonization and climate change, and what do they tell us about joint federal–provincial policy-making? Further, what do they tell us about the capacity of intergovernmentalism to yield outcomes that meet the tests of institutional performance, policy effectiveness, and governing legitimacy?

We begin the chapter with a historical overview, beginning in the 1970s, of the mandates of the two levels of government, the institutional mechanisms used to achieve federal–provincial co-ordination on environmental policy, and the politics of co-ordination. We then examine, in the two sections that follow, the harmonization and the climate change cases, assessing their outputs and outcomes against the criteria of performance, effectiveness, and legitimacy. Finally, we compare the two cases and, in the conclusion, discuss environmental policy co-ordination in general and evaluate its capacity for generating effective and legitimate policy outcomes.

National Environmental Policy-Making

National policy is defined here as policy that stems from collaboration between provinces and the federal government. It is required to ensure at least some uniformity of regulatory standards across the country and to implement bilateral or international environmental agreements to which Canada is a party.

Jurisdiction over environmental protection in Canada is shared between the provinces and the federal government. The 'environment' per se is assigned to either order of government in the written Constitution. The provinces have taken primary responsibility for environmental protection, acting on their jurisdiction over natural resources, municipal institutions and services, and 'matters of a local and private nature' within a province. However, there are several avenues through which the federal government is constitutionally empowered to intervene, including its responsibilities in the areas of sea coasts and fisheries, interprovincial and international trade and commerce, and criminal law; in addition, the federal Parliament has the general power to legislate for the 'Peace, Order and Good Government of Canada' (Valiante, 2002: 4).

Since the 1960s, efforts have been made to co-ordinate federal and provincial environmental policy by means of two different sets of institutional arrangements. The first set involves multilateral processes, usually organized around committees or 'councils' of the federal and provincial ministers, supported by a small body of staff, which in turn co-ordinates federal–provincial staff-level committees. Examples include the Canadian Council of Ministers of the Environment (CCME) and the Council of Energy Ministers (CEM).

The second formal co-ordinating mechanism has been bilateral federal–provincial agreements that set out the terms negotiated between a given province and the federal government. During the 1970s, the federal government signed a series of bilateral agreements with provinces. As discussed below, after the break-down of the process of joint meetings of environment and energy ministers (referred to as Joint Meetings of Ministers, or JMM) in 2002, the federal government began working to develop national climate policy through a series of bilateral agreements.

The two processes are very different. In the multilateral system, the federal government is only one among equals and decisions are made on the basis of consensus. Although this approach implies acceptance of decisions by all parties, it also grants each party a veto, which raises the risks of deadlock or a 'lowest-common-denominator' decision. In other words, policy directions can tend to appease all of the participating governments and, therefore, deviate only marginally from the status quo. Bilateral agreements, on the other hand, result from active federal leadership and, since they are negotiated separately, avoid the problems of veto and the lowest common denominator. However, they can result in variations or inconsistencies between agreements and the absence of a single national policy.

Political calculations by federal and provincial governments have always influenced the environmental policy-making process. The federal government and most of the provinces began to establish departments of the environment and enact new legislation to deal with environmental protection in response to the first wave of public concern for the environment during the late 1960s and early 1970s. The creation of Environment Canada in 1970 was followed by a brief period of federal activism. Regulations controlling water discharges from six industrial sectors were implemented under the Fisheries Act and air pollution from four sectors was regulated under the Clean Air Act in the mid-1970s. Major amendments were also made to the Fisheries Act to strengthen the protection of marine and freshwater fish habitat.

The federal government's activism, however, prompted adverse responses from a number of provinces. That pressure, and the declining public concern for the environment that reduced the political rewards associated with action, meant the federal government became much less active in environmental matters in the late 1970s and early 1980s (Harrison, 1996a).

When public concern for environmental protection was rekindled in the late 1980s, the federal government assumed a more active role. The government of Canada was emboldened by rulings of the Supreme Court of Canada in *R. v. Crown Zellerbach* (1988) and *Friends of the Oldman River Society v. Canada* (1992), which expanded its jurisdictional claims. A national Green Plan was announced in 1990 and new legislation, including the Canadian Environmental Protection Act (CEPA) and the Canadian Environmental Assessment Act, was enacted. At the same time, growing awareness of the global dimensions of environmental issues culminated in the 1992 World Conference on Environment and Development in Rio de Janeiro and translated into new international environmental commitments that Canada had to implement.

Yet, by the mid-1990s the federal government had retreated from its activist role and showed a renewed willingness to see the provinces take the lead, prompted in part by major deficit-reduction cuts to Environment Canada funding. Moreover, badly shaken by the close call of the 1995 referendum, the Chrétien government was eager to promote federal–provincial coordination and to show that federalism could be renewed without constitutional change. These considerations were major forces behind the federal interest in the Harmonization Accord.

In summary, from the 1970s to the present, three patterns are evident. First, the federal government's role in environmental policy has oscillated. Spurred by perceived electoral advantage, it has twice moved to play an activist, leadership role, only to retreat from the policy field and defer to provincial wishes. The degree and nature of federal government motivation are thus among the most important factors shaping the process of co-ordination.

Second, historically federal and provincial jurisdictions competed with one another to raise environmental standards. During the period of high public concern for the environment in the 1980s, many provinces also began to modernize their existing legislation and adopt new standards. The result was upward competition between the federal government and the provinces, and among the provinces themselves in terms of environmental initiatives and standards. These competitive dynamics were particularly evident with respect to the control of water pollution from the pulp and paper industry (Harrison, 1996b).

Third, and finally, non-state actors have not played a significant role in national processes. By and large, industry prefers provincial regulation, while environmentalists have traditionally called for an expanded federal role. With the exception of the harmonization process, which was the subject of significant environmental non-governmental organization (ENGO) challenges, both industry and the ENGOs have largely focused their lobbying efforts on influencing the policies of individual governments, rather than the national process per se.

The Canada-Wide Accord on Harmonization and Sub-Agreements

The environmental harmonization initiative began during the brief 1993 government of Prime Minister Kim Campbell under the auspices of the CCME (Harrison, 1996a: 158). The Canada-Wide Accord on Environmental Harmonization and sub-agreements on Canada-wide standards, inspections, and environmental assessment were signed on 29 January 1998, by the federal minister of the Environment and the provincial and territorial environment ministers. Only Quebec's minister did not sign, stating that his government would not do so until its principles were incorporated into federal legislation, specifically CEPA (Québec, 1998).

The Canada-Wide Accord set out the goals of the harmonization initiative and included a framework for the contents of the substantive sub-agreements. Decisions pursuant to the Accord must be 'consensus-based' and 'driven by the commitment to achieve the highest level of environmental quality within the context of sustainable development' (CCME, 1998a: principles, article 8).

The Accord and the sub-agreements all placed a strong emphasis on 'one-window' delivery of environmental protection services by a single order of government. There was an explicit bar on action ('shall not act in the role') by the level of government not charged with service delivery. The government 'best-situated' to deliver a service is the one-window delivery mechanism. The criteria for 'best situation', such as physical proximity and ability to address client and local needs, appeared to favour the provinces in most cases. The Accord, and each of the sub-agreements, can be amended only with the unanimous consent of the parties, although parties may withdraw on six months' notice. The inspections sub-agreement specifically targeted situations where more than one level of government had the potential to act. Inspection activities related to industrial and municipal facilities and discharges were to be assigned to the provinces. The sub-agreement on Canada-wide standards required the development of standards on a case-by-case basis that would be endorsed by the ministers prior to adoption. Once a government accepts responsibility for the implementation of a standard, the other order of government 'shall not act' in that role. An individual government had considerable flexibility on whether to implement an adopted standard dealing with a problem whose effects were limited to its own territory. The federal government was limited to implementing measures at international borders, on federal lands, and in cases where regulation of a product or substance (as opposed to emissions) was required. The provinces and territories, on the other hand, are to implement measures requiring action from industrial, municipal, and other sectors.

Like the previous two sub-agreements, the environmental assessment sub-agreement also reflected the themes of 'one-window delivery'. The sub-agreement provided for the identification of 'lead parties' for environmental assessments, and for the use of the assessment process of the 'lead party'—i.e., a province or Ottawa—for individual assessments. The federal government can act as a lead party only for projects on federal lands. Provinces must be the lead parties for all other assessments, except where an environmental assessment exists pursuant to an Aboriginal land claim or self-government agreement.

Throughout its development, the harmonization initiative was subject to intense challenges of its likely performance, effectiveness, and legitimacy from ENGOs (Canadian Environmental Network, 1998), Parliament's Standing Committee on Environment and Sustainable Development (Standing Committee, 1997), and members of the academic community. These criticisms focused on how well the proposed arrangements would work, particularly the potential decision traps associated with the CCME's consensus-based decision-making process, the lack of transparency and accountability mechanisms, and the apparent abandonment of federal responsibility for leadership in national environmental policy-making and backstopping of the efforts of provinces, particularly during a period of major budgetary reductions among provincial environmental agencies. The affected industries, on the other hand, were generally supportive of the initiative (Fafard, 2000).

Nearly a decade after the signing of the Canada-Wide Accord, we can evaluate its performance, effectiveness, and legitimacy. In many ways the Accord defined the federal government's approach to environmental policy, and provisions reflecting the co-operative federalism theme underlying the Accord were incorporated into the 1999 Canadian Environmental Protection Act, the 2002 federal Species At Risk Act, and the 2003 amendments to the Canadian Environmental Assessment Act.

With respect to 'performance', the decade following the signing of the Canada-Wide Accord has seen relatively little federal–provincial conflict in the areas covered by the Accord and its sub-agreements, particularly those regarding national standard-setting and environmental assessment. The absence of conflict is largely a result of federal deference to the provinces with respect to environmental assessment and the regulation of industrial pollution.

The Canada-Wide Standards (cws)-setting processes were established under the auspices of the sub-agreement on various pollutants of high concern, including dioxins and furans, benzene, mercury, ground-level ozone and particulate matter, and petroleum hydrocarbons in soil. In practice, these processes were extremely diverse. Each standard-setting exercise was led by a different jurisdiction. Some of the processes, such as those related to dioxins and furans, involved extensive consultative processes with non-governmental (e.g., industry and environmental and public health) interests. With others, such as hydrocarbons in soil, the consultative processes were more limited.

In some cases the results were unexpectedly strong. Provinces put pressure on Newfoundland and Labrador to ban the use of conical waste burners, a primitive form of municipal waste incinerator (CCME, 2003). In the emissions inventory developed in support of the standard-setting process, conical burners had been identified as the largest source of atmospheric emissions of dioxins and furans in Canada. Their use was virtually unique to Newfoundland and Labrador and their phase-out was unlikely without external pressures.

There have also been some very clear illustrations of the pitfalls of the cws process, including the availability of multiple veto points and the potential for deadlock and lowest-common-denominator outcomes, identified by critics of the initiative at the outset. Coal-fired electricity generating plants, for example, were identified early on as a leading source of atmospheric emissions of mercury, a persistent toxic pollutant targeted by a number of international agreements to which Canada is a party. However, a cws for mercury emissions from coal-fired power plants was not proposed until January 2005 (CCME, 2005), seven years after the initiation of the standards development project. In June 2006, Ontario blocked the adoption of the standard by the CCME on the basis of the province's decision to defer the phase-out of its coal-fired electricity generation facilities, originally scheduled for 2007 (Benzie, 2006).

Turning to the criterion of 'effectiveness', assessing the environmental quality of policy outputs from the processes set in motion through the Canada-Wide Accord is complex. Outcomes are mixed at best. The environmental assessment sub-agreement has been implemented through a series of bilateral agreements between the federal government and individual provinces. The result has been that aside from projects on federal lands, where a federal assessment is triggered, meaningful federal environmental assessment of other projects is increasingly a dead letter. Federal environmental assessment requirements have either been folded into provincial processes through provisions for process substitution established through the federal–provincial agreements and the 2003 amendments of the Canadian Environmental Assessment Act, or the absolute minimal federal requirements are applied.

'Screening-level assessments', the lowest possible level of federal scrutiny, or very narrowly 'scoped' assessments have been required even for very large projects, such as oil sands developments in northern Alberta, with significant environmental implications (Pembina Institute, 2006). In other cases, such as the York–Durham sewer system (the 'Big Pipe'), which supports sprawling urban development north of the City of Toronto, the federal government has sought to avoid triggering federal environmental assessments altogether. It issues 'letters of advice' rather than federal approvals under the Fisheries Act (Environmental Defence, 2005). Compared to the period prior to the signing of the Accord, when the federal government applied its environmental assessment requirements more assertively (for example, in the cases of the Alberta Pacific pulp mill in northern Alberta and the Great Whale hydroelectric project in northern Quebec in the early 1990s), there has been less scrutiny of major undertakings with significant environmental implications.

The situation with respect to the CWS is more mixed. On the whole, with the exception of the phase-out of conical waste burners in Newfoundland, the standards that have emerged from the CCME process are neither especially aggressive nor groundbreaking relative to existing requirements or international initiatives. Indeed, some, such as the ground-level ozone standards for ambient air quality, were less stringent than existing federal guidelines. Others, such as the Canada-Wide Acid Rain Strategy (CCME, 2000), fell well short of what had been identified in the scientific literature as necessary to protect human health and the environment. The relatively unambitious character of the standards may reflect underlying weaknesses in the CCME's consensus-based decision-making processes, particularly the tendency towards lowest-common-denominator outcomes.

In addition to the issue of the adequacy of the standards adopted, the question of their actual implementation by the federal government and provinces has to be considered. Agreement on a standard is meaningless if it is not then fully implemented by the participating jurisdictions. Each of the agreed-upon standards included an implementation plan, outlining the actions to be taken by governments to implement the standard. However, no systemic review of the implementation of the CWS has been completed. The CCME's own evaluations in the reviews mandated by the Accord did not examine CWS implementation in any detail.

The federal government appears to have been quite diligent in the fulfillment of its implementation commitments under the CWS sub-agreement. Smog and acid rain precursors and other targeted pollutants, such as mercury and dioxins and furans, have been added to the National Pollutant Release Inventory (NPRI), as per the implementation plans. The federal government also moved forward on other implementation commitments, such as the establishment of emission standards for diesel engines and small engines in relation to the ground-level ozone and particulate matter standards. However, the bulk of standards implementation is concerned with the application of standards to individual facilities. Consistent with the direction of the Accord, this aspect of implementation has been entirely in the hands of provinces.

In fact, Ontario is the only province in which such tracking is possible (through the electronic registry established under the province's 1992 Environmental Bill of Rights). In that province, the CWS for dioxins, furans, and mercury had been incorporated into the approval of one commercial hazardous waste incineration facility, but had not been applied to the other two commercial facilities. In addition, no amendments had been made to approvals to any of the private (i.e., company-only waste) hazardous waste incineration facilities operating in the province.

With respect to actual environmental outcomes, the addition of the substances targeted through the CWS to the NPRI provides a mechanism through which actual levels of emissions of pollutants from industrial facilities can be tracked. However, the reporting requirements for the CWS substances came into place only for the 2002 reporting year and a meaningful assessment is not yet possible.

What about the 'legitimacy' of the harmonization initiative? Virtually all of Canada's major national and regional ENGOs and some parliamentarians (Standing Committee on Environmental and Sustainable Development, 1997) opposed the accord because they believed it was the federal government's responsibility to act as a backstop for provincial efforts, to establish and ensure the maintenance of minimum national environmental standards for all Canadians, and to prevent the emergence of pollution havens among provinces seeking to attract investment. Significant accountability problems also trouble the CCME process. Provinces' reporting on their implementation of the CWS remains incomplete and inconsistent. The two- and five-year reviews of the effectiveness of the Canada-Wide Accord conducted by the CCME provided no meaningful evaluation of the quality of outputs, functionality of processes, or implementation of the CWS. Transparency also remains a substantial problem. It is apparent, for example, that vetoes have been exercised in the CWS processes, but there are no formal mechanisms through which such behaviour can be attributed to specific governments.

With respect to engagement and acceptance as indicators of legitimacy in the eyes of key actors and the public, government officials themselves invested considerable effort in the CCME standards development process. Officials have seen the intergovernmental commitments resulting from the CWS as useful in advancing policy change within their own governments. There was also a genuine belief among some officials that the processes were useful ways to pool resources in the context of a period of extreme budgetary restraint.

Although ministers endorsed the standards emerging from the CWS exercise, the level of political engagement prompted by the process is uncertain. In fact, some governments reduced their budgetary commitments to the CWS processes at crucial points, albeit usually as a result of their own budgetary pressures. The long-term commitment at the political level is unclear. A draft 'Commitment Statement on Environmental Sustainability', largely reaffirming the original direction of the Accord and sub-agreements, was released by the CCME in June 2005. However, no new agenda has emerged as the process has worked its way through the initial round of CWS proposed in the original 1998 Accord. As capacity to develop policy and standards has been rebuilt in some jurisdictions, particularly at the federal level and in Ontario, governments have begun to embark on their own standards development processes independently of the CCME. The impacts of the CWS and other outputs of the Accord have been largely invisible to the public. Public attention regarding environmental issues at the national level, however, has been focused on the question of climate change during the implementation period of the Canada-Wide Accord and its sub-agreements.

ENGO and other non-governmental actors involved in environmental policy development accept rather than endorse the co-operative approaches established through the Accord. Non-governmental stakeholders participated in the CCME process of setting standards as this was the only available national policy-making forum in relation to the targeted substances. But the ENGO community in particular has continued to harbour serious doubts about the effectiveness and legitimacy of the process.

In the fall of 2006, the new Conservative government of Prime Minister Stephen Harper introduced legislation to create a Clean Air Act. The proposed legislation is to deal with both greenhouse gas (GHG) emissions and other forms of air pollution, including substances covered by the Canada-wide standards. A closer analysis of the legislation and the accompanying notice of intent to regulate reveals that the federal government expects the provinces to play a central role, both through consultation in the development of standards and through the development of 'equivalency' and 'administrative' agreements for their implementation. Thus the Clean Air Act may represent far less of a departure from the multilateral approach than it might have seemed when it was introduced.

Climate Change

We now review the four periods of intergovernmental climate change policy-making from 1990 to the present.

1990–1995

The government of Brian Mulroney adopted the goal of stabilizing Canadian greenhouse gas emissions in 1990, two years before that same goal was agreed to by the international community in the United Nations Framework Convention on Climate Change (UNFCCC) at the Rio Conference in 1992. Whether the

Mulroney government had consulted the provinces before adopting that objective is not clear. Provinces were drawn into the picture, however, once Canada ratified the UNFCCC and began to develop a domestic plan to implement its commitments.

In 1993, two committees were created to deal with air pollution: the National Air Issues Coordinating Committee—Climate Change deals with climate change and reports to two secretariats, CCME and the Council of Energy Ministers (CEM); the National Air Issues Coordinating Committee deals with other air pollution issues and reports only to the CCME. Starting in 1993, these joint meetings of environment and energy ministers (JMM) became the major institutional vehicles for federal–provincial co-ordination of climate policy. Unlike the CCME, the JMM lacked a permanent office and dedicated staff. These were provided by the CCME. The CEM itself had neither offices nor staff. In 1995, the federal and provincial governments released the first Canadian national program, the National Action Program for Climate Change (NAPCC). Development of this policy output was given impetus by Canada's obligation under the UNFCCC to report to the Conference of Parties that year on its actions to stabilize emissions. The primary policy instrument to be used was the Voluntary Challenge and Registry. Not long before the October 1995 referendum, Quebec withdrew from all federal–provincial bodies, including the JMM, and prepared its own 'national' plan for climate action. It presented this plan, ÉcoGESte, to the UNFCCC. Like the Canadian program, it relied primarily on voluntary action.

Thus during the first five-year period, federal–provincial co-ordinating mechanisms were strong enough to generate a national plan. They were not strong enough, however, to ensure that this plan was anything more than a lowest-common-denominator description of what provinces were willing to commit to—essentially, nothing more than asking the sources within their borders to reduce emissions voluntarily; no provisions were made for either legal penalties or financial incentives.

1995–1997

Between 1995 and 1997, the provincial and Canadian governments worked amicably to implement the NAPCC. That co-operative spirit began to unravel, however, in the months leading up to the December 1997 third conference of UNFCCC parties in Kyoto, Japan. By the summer of 1997, it had become apparent that an international consensus existed on the need to significantly strengthen the UNFCCC regime. All involved knew that the Kyoto meeting was likely to result in replacement of the general goal of stabilization with more specific targets for each party, albeit with an extension of the deadline by 10 years or more.

Using the JMM process, although still without formal Quebec participation, the federal and provincial environment and energy ministers agreed at their 12 November 1997 meeting that the Canadian international position should retain the goal of stabilization, with a new deadline of 2010 instead of 2000. Shortly afterwards, Prime Minister Chrétien responded to external pressure from other heads of state (Bernstein, 2002) and personally intervened in the policy process. On 3 December, the opening day of the Kyoto meeting, Canadian representatives were instructed to state that Canada would commit to a target 3 per cent below 1990 levels (at the end of the Kyoto meeting, that target had been changed to a 6 per cent reduction commitment). The JMM mechanism had not been strong enough to prevent the federal government from breaking ranks—the same basic weakness that was to reappear five years later. Determining the Canadian policy target under the Kyoto Protocol marked the first time the prime minister and his office had been more than nominally engaged with the climate issue. As was the case with 2002 ratification, direct engagement of the PMO coincided with federal government abandonment of the multilateral, consensus-based system of national policy development. The possible relationship between degree of federal government interest in a given issue and the national co-ordination process is discussed below.

1997–2002

In February 1998, the federal government created the Climate Change Secretariat, a body intended to improve co-ordination among the 10 or more federal departments involved with the issue. (The two lead departments were Environment and Natural Resources.) A few years later, horizontal co-ordination within the federal government was strengthened by creation of an ad hoc cabinet committee, made up of ministers from all relevant departments (Bakvis and Juillet, 2004). In April 1998, the JMM augmented its staff resources by creating the National Climate Change Secretariat. That mechanism was then used to provide organizational support for two years' worth of multi-stakeholder consultations, this time involving a much greater number of participants than the previous 1993–4 consultations.

The output of this consultative effort was the October 2000 National Implementation Strategy and Business Plan. By this time Quebec was again a participant in the JMM process, but Ontario, to protest what it called ineffective action, refused to sign the final communiqué (Bjorn et al., 2002: 82.) Like its 1995 successor, the plan set out no specific targets for each province or for any given economic sector and continued to rely primarily on appeals for voluntary action. At the federal level, voluntary action was induced by government spending for technological development and implementation of specific emission-reduction projects.

In early 2001, the newly elected Bush administration announced that the United States would not ratify Kyoto and that it was replacing the goal of an absolute cap on GHG emissions with an 'intensity' target. The term refers to the ratio of emissions to total activity of any given source, and thus eliminates any risk that climate policy might hinder economic growth. Following Kyoto, Canada had supported the US-led movement to delay and weaken the UNFCCC regime, and—given the importance of Canadian export sales to the US (and therefore Canadian industrial competitiveness with the US)—most analysts expected that

Canada, too, would pull out. Instead, Canada managed to convince the other parties to the Kyoto agreement that a significant part of its international commitment could be met simply on the basis of its 'carbon sinks'—areas where the soil and vegetation already serve to remove carbon from the atmosphere. As a result, Canada's target for cutting emissions was reduced by approximately 25 per cent. By the fall of 2001 it had become clear that the Chrétien government planned to ratify Kyoto on the basis of this lower target.

The new international commitments triggered new domestic tensions. The Quebec National Assembly passed a resolution in April 2001 calling on Canada to ratify and Manitoba was equally supportive. Ontario stayed mute, and Alberta and British Columbia led the fight to prevent ratification, joined by a vocal coalition of business interests. By the 21 May 2002 meeting, the JMM was close to the point of rupture. Alberta pressed for endorsement of its much softer approach but did not receive support from other provinces. In consequence, Alberta refused to sign the final communiqué and the Alberta Environment Minister withdrew as co-chair of the National Air Issues Coordinating Committee—Climate Change (NAICC—CC). At the other end of the spectrum, the federal government failed to gain approval for the approach set out in its discussion paper launched that month. For the first time, it discussed sector-specific targets and the use of more coercive instruments, as opposed to staying the course with a voluntary regime. By that time, it had become clear to federal representatives that there was no chance of working with the provinces to develop a national plan with specific targets for allocating the overall Canadian reduction objective (Manson, 2006).

The federal government then started down the path of unilateral regulation. Following consultations on its May 2002 discussion paper, it released its own plan in November (Canada, 2002). The provinces had not provided any formal input. The plan provided specific targets for different forms of emitting activity and stated that the federal government was working to develop legally binding regulatory controls for industry. A few weeks earlier, at the 28 October 2002 joint meeting of environment and energy ministers, all the provinces, including Quebec, had called on the Chrétien government to discuss the issue at a first ministers' meeting prior to ratification. As it had five years earlier, the Chrétien government ignored this plea and held a ratification vote in the House of Commons on 10 December. Five days later, the federal minister of Natural Resources released an open letter to the Canadian Association of Petroleum Producers, setting out commitments made during secret federal–industry negotiations that fall. The oil and gas sector was limited to reducing emissions by no more than 15 per cent, measured on an intensity basis, and all industrial sectors would be subsidized for all reduction costs greater than $15 per tonne of carbon dioxide equivalent (Natural Resources Canada, 2002). The two most important policy developments of this period, ratification and the establishment of industry targets, had taken place completely outside the JMM institutional process.

2003–2006

By 2003 there were no longer any institutional mechanisms in place for the multilateral co-ordination of climate policy. The National Climate Secretariat and the NAICC—CC had been disbanded. The joint meetings of energy and environment ministers, although not formally discontinued (they had never been formally instituted), had come to an end. The CCME secretariat, actively pursuing CWS for other air pollutants, did not address greenhouse gas emissions.

Canadian policy had lost whatever coherence it might once have had. Alberta, the only province to have enacted climate change legislation, adopted a policy goal completely at odds with the Kyoto objective. While Canada as a whole was committed, at least on paper, to capping and then reducing total emissions, Alberta had passed legislation committing itself to the same goal adopted by the Bush administration: working to reduce emissions as measured in proportion to total industrial production of a given source (Macdonald et al., 2004). This 'intensity-based' approach discards any notion of an overall cap on greenhouse gas emissions.

While no other province had broken so dramatically with national policy, none was working actively and effectively to cap and reduce emissions within their borders. The most successful, Quebec, had seen its emissions grow by 7 per cent between 1990 and 2003, compared with increases in Alberta of 34 per cent and Saskatchewan of 45 per cent (Tremblay, 2005). Emissions for Canada as a whole had risen by 27 per cent by 2006 (Gélinas, 2006: 8). Ontario, the other major source of emissions besides Alberta (the two provinces account for close to 60 per cent of the Canadian total), had not adopted a policy objective, had taken no legislative action, and had created no new administrative bodies to administer climate policy. It did, however, point to climate as an important rationale for both land-use policy reform and the planned elimination of coal-fired electricity generation. In comparison with the US states, despite the recalcitrance of the Bush administration, the record of provincial inaction is dispiriting (Rabe, 2005: 5).

The institutional form of co-ordination between 2003 and 2006, after the breakdown of multilateralism, has been the federal effort to negotiate bilateral agreements with the provinces and territories. This effort is backed with offers of substantial federal funding. As of the spring of 2006, the government of Canada had entered into six such agreements: Nunavut, 2003; PEI, 2003; Manitoba, 2004; Newfoundland, 2004; Ontario, 2004; and Saskatchewan, 2005 (Manson, 2006).

As written, the agreements contain virtually no specific commitments for either party. The Canada–Manitoba Memorandum of Understanding, for instance, states the parties have agreed to 'pursue co-operation' and 'ensure consistency among their respective actions and initiatives to avoid duplication and to maximize synergies' (Canada–Manitoba, 2004: 2). It lists in very general terms priorities for action, such as renewable energy development and energy efficiency. The agreements do, however, provide the framework for shared-cost funding of specific projects, something that has become more tangible and attractive for provinces since the commitment of $3 billion to a Climate Change Partnerships Fund in the 2005 federal budget. Putting that federal money on the table 'strengthened and enhanced' the ability of the federal government to reach agreements with the provinces (Manson, 2006). Provinces were consulted during development of the 2003 federal program under the Martin government to regulate directly large industrial emitters (Clare, 2005). Such consultations never, however, constituted formal three-way or multilateral negotiations, as was the norm prior to 2002 (Manson, 2006). Although never finally implemented, the serious intent of the Martin government is shown by the fact that official notice of pending regulations had been issued prior to the fall of the government in December 2005 (Canada, 2005).

By late fall 2006, the newly elected Harper government had taken two significant actions. It had first significantly reduced climate policy funding, but then restored a number of the Martin government's climate-related expenditure programs. Second, as noted above, it had introduced new legislation, the Clean Air Act, to address both GHG emissions and other forms of air pollution. The latter bill was widely seen as an attempt to shift the focus from climate change to air quality issues. On the surface, the Clean Air Act seems to indicate a continuation of the Martin government's unilateral federal approach, based on regulation, albeit with extended timelines and reduced targets. In fact, however, it seems clear that the Harper government expects the provinces to play a major role in developing and implementing targets, particularly since it has restored the federal funding carrot.

How does intergovernmental co-ordination on climate change policy stack up in terms of the three criteria of institutional performance, policy effectiveness, and governing legitimacy? Beginning with institutional performance, the national climate change process had failed by early 2006 to accommodate major conflicts between provinces with very different economic interests and, since 2001, between the oil-producing provinces and Ottawa. The JMM secretariats process, supported at the staff level by the NAICC—CC and National Secretariat, was ineffective in reaching agreements respected by all parties. At various times, Alberta, Ontario, and Quebec all refused to endorse JMM agreements. The process was not strong enough to prevent the federal government from striking out on an independent path in 1997 and 2002. Nor did those agreements or plans ever constitute anything more than a simple collection of actions taken independently in various jurisdictions—actions that might well have been taken even if the JMM had never been brought into existence. Finally, the multilateral process broke down completely in the fall of 2002, and it has not functioned since. The process that replaced it, led by the federal government, was leading towards viable policy outcomes, but it was cut short by the fall of the Martin government.

Nor have policy outputs and policy outcomes been effective. Prior to its breakdown in 2002, the intergovernmental process around climate change initially showed some capacity to generate policy outputs (the 1995 National Action Plan and 2000 National Implementation Strategy and Business Plan). However, these outputs tended to be reiterations of existing initiatives, containing no new actions or commitments, particularly at the provincial level. In terms of actual policy outcomes, Canada committed to stabilization by 2000 in 1990 and then, in 1997, to a 6 per cent reduction by 2012. As noted, by 2006 emissions have increased by something like 27 per cent. No estimates are available of the extent to which emissions would have risen had governments taken no policy action at all. However, the refusal by all governments to use effective policy instruments, such as legislation or a carbon tax, means that climate change policy to date has had virtually no impact on emissions.

It is difficult to assess the effectiveness of the independent federal policy that followed from 2002 onward. The key initiatives—particularly legally binding emission limits for large industrial sources of GHGs, the 2005 partnership fund, and bilateral federal–provincial and territorial agreements—remained works in progress with the change in government in January 2006.

The process around climate change scores better in terms of its legitimacy, although the JMM secretariat process up to 2002 was not marked by a high degree of accountability. While it generated extensive shopping lists of actions promised by all participating governments, it never resulted in the basic accountability mechanism of specific reduction targets either for individual provinces or for industrial sectors or other groups of emitters. Accountability increased with the move to unilateral federal action in 2002, since the federal action plan did specify targets for different sources of emissions (although the overall Canadian target was never publicly broken down to allocate specific sub-targets to each province).

Given the secrecy that accompanies all forms of federal–provincial diplomacy, the JMM process was probably as transparent as possible. Certainly it relied heavily on multi-stakeholder engagement. By its nature, however, the federal–provincial process was not transparent. The policy positions of the different actors for the most part were only made public at the point of rupture, when a given province would refuse to sign a JMM communiqué and then issue its own press notice, explaining its reasons.

The federal government, when it acted alone, was also reasonably transparent, in terms of both supporting analysis and development of policy through discussion documents in 2002. Its negotiations with industry, however, both in the fall of 2002 as agreement was reached on the reduction and spending caps outlined above, and since, have been done completely in private.

What of legitimacy in the eyes of governments, as indicated by their willingness to participate in the process? All governments participated up to 2002, since the process did not require that they take actions they would not have taken independently. None, however, made any effort to revive the process after its collapse. Six provinces and territories have considered the post-ratification approach sufficiently legitimate, with the added incentive of federal funding, to sign bilateral agreements. Quebec is likely to do so in the near future, if the Harper government continues with that approach.

Comparing the Harmonization and Climate Change Cases

Assessments of the performance, effectiveness, and legitimacy of the intergovernmental policy processes followed in the climate change and harmonization case studies are summarized in Table 13.1. The climate change case emerges as a failure on all fronts, while the harmonization case is more complex.

How can the two different outcomes be explained? The influence of non-state actors, although different in the two cases, can be ruled out. Business was mildly supportive of harmonization (Fafard, 2000) but mounted a major campaign to block Kyoto ratification (Macdonald, 2003). With the exception of that outburst, however, by and large business has learned to live with national climate policy, presumably because it has gained major concessions from federal regulators during the regulatory negotiating process since the fall of 2002. ENGOs tried to block harmonization in the same way that business had tried to block ratification, and with the same lack of success. In each case the lobbying influence of business was—to some extent at least—cancelled out by environmental groups. For that reason, we set aside the role of non-state actors and do not include it in our explanation of the different outcomes.

Rather, the different outcomes can be attributed to, first, differences in the nature of the two issues addressed (in terms of both physical reality and public salience), and second, the difference between an almost purely domestic process and one embedded in an international process. The physical nature of the two issues is significant. Harmonization focused on specific pollutants from very discrete sources. The implementation of Canada-wide standards may impose costs on specific sectors, but it does not imply structural economic change. Action on climate change, on the other hand, has significant implications for the production and consumption of fossil fuels and therefore has the potential for structural economic impacts, concentrated in particular sectors and regions. Harmonization focused on an unwanted by-product—pollution—that firms have always been able to manage for less than 5 per cent of total operating costs. Climate policy, in contrast, seeks to cap total use of a widely used product, potentially imposing much higher costs on both specific industrial sectors and specific regions of the country.

As a result of the different costs involved, provinces had very different interests and played different roles in the two processes. Provincial approaches to the harmonization initiative did not differ greatly. Some provinces were enthusiastic, some simply accepting, but none sought to block it. The climate case was completely different. Alberta, with its overwhelming economic dependence on fossil fuel production and exports, actively worked against the process. It co-operated as long as participation was voluntary, but balked when ratification came on the agenda. It did what it could to prevent ratification, and when that failed, the province simply abandoned the system, concentrating instead on putting in place its own climate policy. Nor was Alberta's opposition offset by strong leadership

Table 13.1   Comparison of the Climate Change and Harmonization Processes

Criteria	Climate Change	Harmonization
Performance	Intergovernmental co-operation not conflict: *failure*. Ability to produce outputs/functionality: *mixed* (some initial outputs, but then complete breakdown post-2002).	Intergovernmental co-operation not conflict: *success*. Ability to produce outputs/functionality: *mixed*. Some successes, but also cases of deadlock on key standards.
Effectiveness	Quality of policy outputs: *failure*. Heavy reliance on ineffective instruments (e.g., voluntarism). Substantive outcomes: *failure*. Emissions continue to rise.	Quality of policy outputs: *mixed*. Tendency towards lowest common denominator on CWS; meaningful federal environmental assessment increasingly a dead letter off federal lands. Substantive outcomes of policy: *incomplete*. Provincial implementation inconsistent and incomplete, environmental results difficult to measure due to data gaps.
Legitimacy	Accountability: increased with move from JMM to unilateral federal action. Transparency: JMM limited, marginally better in federal process. Engagement and acceptance: • Governmental: ultimately a *failure*, although some governments re-engaged via bilateral agreements with federal government. • Stakeholder: *substantial engagement* in multilateral and federally led processes. • Public: blocking provincial behaviour may have laid groundwork for *acceptance* of federally led as opposed to multilateral approach.	Accountability: *weak*. Transparency: *weak*. Engagement and acceptance: • Governmental: *good* (at official level) to *mixed* (at political level). • Stakeholder: *reluctant acceptance*. • Public: subject matter too arcane to draw public attention.

from either of the natural candidates, Manitoba or Quebec. The former lacked sufficient economic power, and the latter was preoccupied by other issues. Ontario, the usual federal ally in federal–provincial matters, sat on the sidelines.

The two issues of harmonization and climate change also differed in terms of salience. Harmonization largely involved technical issues that never caught public attention. Even the highest-profile target of the CWS exercise, smog, has high public salience only in the regions of the country heavily affected by air quality problems, such as the lower mainland of British Columbia, southern Ontario, and New Brunswick. In addition, given its regionally concentrated impacts, public expectations of action on smog have tended to focus on the relevant provincial governments. Climate change, on the other hand, was the most visible national environmental issue of the decade, with consequent public expectations of federal action and the possibility of public reward to the federal government for taking such action.

The international character of the climate change issue further focused attention on the role and responsibilities of the federal government. Federal activism on the climate file coincided with international events. The international climate negotiations at times compelled the federal government to take firm public positions on Canada's intentions and commitments. Prime Minister Chrétien's intervention in 1997 was motivated by international pressure from other heads of state. Similarly, his decision to ratify was only taken after Canada had gained agreement from other parties to the Convention for a reduction in the policy objective, through the sinks credit. More important, had climate change been a purely domestic process, there would have been no need for the high-profile commitment that ratification represented.

The high public profile of events such as the original 1992 Rio Conference, 1997 Kyoto agreement, 2002 ratification, and 2005 Montreal Conference of the Parties to the UNFCCC also offered the potential for considerable domestic political benefits. The federal government's 2002 public break with the Bush administration on ratification, like the refusal to send troops to Iraq, was good domestic politics. It also provided a means for the Chrétien government to establish a more positive environmental 'legacy' than its record to that point might have warranted.

There was far less external influence on the harmonization initiative. Although some of the substances targeted through the CWS processes were subject to international agreements, the driving factor was the interest of the federal government, after 1995, in non-constitutional changes that would be well received by Quebec.

In summary, then, two factors are important in explaining the differing outcomes of the harmonization and climate change issues: first, the interests of state actors, and in particular the intensity of their interest; and second, the degree to which environmental policy is enmeshed in a larger international process. Federal government interest includes both the desire to gain electoral advantage from action on salient issues and the desire for effective policy. While provincial

governments undoubtedly have similar motivations, most provinces are motivated by economic interests. The desire to avoid the economic costs of environmental agreements will lead a province either to play a blocking role or to opt out
of the national process. The fact that both options are available to provinces illustrates the weakness of the co-ordination mechanisms.

Conclusion

What do the two cases of harmonization and climate change policy tell us about
federal–provincial co-ordination? Three lessons can be drawn. First, federal government interest is a key variable that affects the institutional form used for co-
ordination. In the harmonization case, improved co-ordination was sought as an
end in itself in the post-1995 referendum national unity strategy. The federal
government stayed in the multilateral arena and worked to strengthen that
process regardless of the quality of the resulting policy outputs or outcomes. In
the climate change case, the federal government set aside the Canadian negotiating position arrived at prior to the Kyoto meeting and substituted its own. In the
2002 ratification process, Ottawa again abandoned the JMM process in favour of
unilateral action towards a more effective policy.

The broader lesson is that when the federal government is motivated to play a
leadership role on a particular environmental issue, it pursues one of two
options. Either it seeks to move policy development from the institutional forum
of multilateral consensus-based structures to bilateral agreements forged separately and sequentially with individual provinces or, alternatively, it resorts to
unilateralism. Bilateralism may be a way to avoid the decision-trap risks of deadlock or weak policy outputs posed by consensus-based multilateralism. Indeed,
there are other instances of this pattern. In the early 1970s, the federal government unilaterally regulated and negotiated bilateral agreements. During negotiation of the 1985 acid rain program it privately threatened to regulate unilaterally, as a means of inducing provincial action. In the late 1980s the Mulroney
government unilaterally introduced the Green Plan (although that initiative, in
the face of provincial resistance, relied on spending instruments rather than
direct regulation). We conclude, then, that the format used for federal–provincial
co-ordination largely depends on the degree of federal motivation. Further evidence in support of this conclusion is provided by the Harper government's air
pollution and climate policy with its emphasis on federal–provincial co-operation. Although it is too early to judge the former, with respect to climate such
things as the explicit abandonment of the goal of achieving Canada's Kyoto commitment and relaxation of the policy objective by changing the base year from
1990 to 2003 leave no doubt the Harper government is seeking the appearance of
action rather than the substance. Such governments prefer multilateralism over
unilateral or bilateral action.

Second, regardless of whether the approach is multilateral or bilateral, climate
change is the exceptional issue that shows the limits of co-ordination. The co-

operative federalism of the Canada-Wide Accord, the 1999 Canadian Environmental Protection Act, the 2002 Species At Risk Act, and 2003 amendments to the Canadian Environmental Assessment Act does not prevail on climate change, where the same federal government opted for unilateral policy. The federal government really had no choice but to act alone, since strongly motivated state actors such as Alberta were blocking any meaningful progress in the multilateral forum. Finally, the case studies demonstrate the critical importance of the external, international context within which national policy is developed and implemented. External pressure brought to bear by other heads of state may stiffen the resolve of the Canadian prime minister. International environmental agreements include provisions for regular reporting on progress to periodic conferences of parties and include periodic decision-making points, as agreements are strengthened and when countries face the basic issue of deciding yes or no on ratification. Both aspects work to increase visibility of the policy process and, therefore, accountability. Insofar as it is the government of Canada that signs these international agreements, it is Ottawa, rather than the provinces, that the public tends to hold accountable for their outcomes.

The number of international environmental agreements to which Canada is party has increased dramatically over the past 20 years, and that trend will undoubtedly continue. Thus the federal government will always be a player in national processes, spurred by external pressure and the periodic reporting requirements of international agreements. It will also be encouraged to enter the environmental field because of the domestic political rewards associated with participation in highly visible international issues. Intergovernmental relations in this context are less likely to involve multilateral processes co-ordinated by secretariats and more likely to focus on reaching bilateral agreements.

In conclusion, federalism has had mixed results in terms of performance since the 1970s. Intergovernmental conflict has been largely avoided because of the willingness of the federal government to retreat in the face of provincial resistance, to seek co-ordination as an end in itself, or to simply ignore problems. The intergovernmental process has shown that it can produce policy outcomes, but both the climate and harmonization cases have shown the limits of that capacity. The process has been marginally effective, simply because policy has often been generated by provinces acting in a fairly autonomous manner. Even the 1985 acid rain initiative, the most successful national program to date, was more a collection of individual provincial actions than a truly co-operative effort.

As measured by the democratic criteria of accountability and transparency, the legitimacy of the intergovernmental record on environmental policy is also uneven. While federal–provincial staff committees work in secret, the broad outlines of national processes have always been visible. Governments have given non-state actors the right to be consulted during policy formulation, but their inclusion does not always garner environmental groups' support for the CCME process or its outcomes.

These limitations to the effectiveness, legitimacy, and performance of the national environmental policy process will need to be overcome if Canada is to adhere to its international commitments and secure an environmentally sustainable future.

References

Bakvis, H., and L. Juillet. 2004. *The Horizontal Challenge: Line Departments, Central Agencies and Leadership*. Ottawa. Canada School of Public Service.

Benzie, R. 2006. 'Mercury Pledge Broken', *Toronto Star*, 19 June, A8.

Bernstein, S. 2002. 'International Institutions and the Framing of Domestic Policies: The Kyoto Protocol and Canada's Response to Climate Change', *Policy Sciences* 35: 203–36.

Bjorn, A., et al. 2002. *Ratification of the Kyoto Protocol: A Citizen's Guide to the Canadian Climate Change Policy Process*. Toronto: Sustainable Toronto. At: <www.utoronto.ca/envstudy/sustainabletoronto/publications/kyotocitizens-guide.pdf>.

Boyd, D.R. 2003. *Unnatural Law: Rethinking Canadian Environmental Law and Policy*. Vancouver: University of British Columbia Press.

Canada. 2002. *Climate Change Plan for Canada: Achieving Our Commitments Together*. Ottawa: Government of Canada.

———. 2005. 'Notice of Intent to Regulate Greenhouse Gas Emissions by Large Final Emitters', *Canada Gazette* 139, 29.

———. Canada–Manitoba Memorandum of Understanding, 19 Mar. 2004. At: <www.ec.gc.ca>.

Canadian Environmental Network. 1998. 'Letter to the Rt. Hon. Jean Chrétien, regarding the CCME Environmental "Harmonization" Initiative'.

CCME. 1998. *Canada Wide Accord on Environmental Harmonization*. At: <www.ccme.ca/assets/pdf/final_phc_method_rvsd_e.pdf>.

———. 2000. *Canada-Wide Accord on Environmental Harmonization Two-Year Review: Consultation Paper*. Winnipeg.

———. 2003. *Canada Wide Standards for Dioxins and Furans: Conical Waste Combustion of Municipal Waste*. At: <www.ccme.ca/assets/pdf/d_f_conical-waste_cws_e.pdf>.

———. 2005. *Canada-wide Standard for Mercury Emissions from Coal-Fired Power Plants*. At: <www.ccme.ca/assets/pdf/canada_wide_standards_hgepg.pdf>.

Clare, J. 2005. Senior Policy Advisor, Large Final Emitters Group, NRCan, personal communication to Kara Lefevre, 29 Mar.

Doern, G.B., and T. Conway. 1994. *The Greening of Canada: Federal Institutions and Decisions*. Toronto: University of Toronto Press.

Environmental Defence. 2005. 'Federal Government Dismisses Big Pipe Court Action', 18 Nov. At: <www.environmentaldefence.ca/pressroom/releases/20051118.htm>.

Fafard, P.C. 2000. 'Groups, Governments and the Environment: Some Evidence from the Harmonization Initiative'. In *Managing the Environmental Union: Intergovernmental Relations and Environmental Policy in Canada*, ed. P.C. Fafard and K. Harrison. Kingston, Ont.: Queen's University School of Policy Studies.

Gélinas, Johanne. 2006. *Report of the Commissioner of the Environment and Sustainable Development to the House of Commons*. Ottawa: Office of the Auditor General of Canada.

Harrison, K. 1996a. *Passing the Buck: Federalism and Canadian Environmental Policy*. Vancouver: University of British Columbia Press.

———. 1996b. 'The Regulator's Dilemma: Regulation of Pulp Mill Effluents in the Canadian Federal State', *Canadian Journal of Political Science* 29, 3: 469–96.

———. 1999. 'Retreat from Regulation: The Evolution of the Canadian Environmental Regulatory Regime'. In *Changing the Rules: Canadian Regulatory Regimes and Institutions*, ed. G.B. Doern, M.M. Hill, M.J. Prince, and R.J. Schultz. Toronto: University of Toronto Press.

Macdonald, Douglas. 2003. 'The Business Campaign to Prevent Kyoto Ratification', paper delivered at the annual meeting of the Canadian Political Science Association, 31 May.

———, A. Bjorn, and D. VanNijnatten. 2004. Implementing Kyoto: When Spending Is Not Enough'. In *How Ottawa Spends: 2004–05*, ed. G.B. Doern. Montreal and Kingston: McGill–Queen's University Press.

Manson, A. 2006. Director General, Domestic Climate Change Policy, Environment Canada, personal communication with Doug Macdonald, 31 Jan.

Natural Resources Canada. 2002. 'Government of Canada Responds to Industry Concerns about Climate Change', accompanying release of letter from the Honourable Herb Dhaliwal, Minister, to Mr John Dielwart, Chairman, Canadian Association of Petroleum Producers, 18 Dec.

Pembina Institute. 2006. 'Alberta Tar Sands Project May Face Supreme Court Challenge', 27 Mar. At: <www.pembina.org/media/media-release.php?id=1227>.

Québec. 1998. Communiqué: 'Le Québec surcroît à la signature de l'entente d'harmonization environnementale du conseil canadien des ministeres de l'environnement', 29 Jan. Gouvernement du Québec.

Rabe, B. 2005. 'Moral Super-Power or Policy Laggard? Translating Kyoto Protocol Ratification into Federal and Provincial Climate Policy in Canada', paper delivered at the annual meeting of the Canadian Political Science Association, London, Ont.

Standing Committee on Environmental and Sustainable Development. 1995. *It's About Our Health! Towards Pollution Prevention*. Ottawa: House of Commons.

———. 1997. *Harmonization and Environmental Protection: An Analysis of the Harmonization Initiative of the Canadian Council of Ministers of the Environment*. Ottawa: House of Commons.

Tremblay, A. 2005. Ministère de l'Environnement, Presentation at Université Laval, 16 Nov.

Valiante, M. 2002. 'Legal Foundations of Environmental Policy: Underlining Our Values in a Shifting Landscape'. In *Canadian Environmental Policy: Context and Cases*, 2nd edn, ed. D. VanNijnatten and R. Boardman. Toronto: Oxford University Press.

VanNijnatten, D.L., and W.H. Lambright. 2002. 'Canadian Smog Policy in a Continental Context: Looking South for Stringency'. In *Canadian Environmental Policy: Context and Cases*, 2nd edn, ed. D.L. VanNijnatten and R. Boardman. Toronto: Oxford University Press.

Winfield, M. 1994. 'The Ultimate Horizontal Issue: The Environmental Policy Experiences of Alberta and Ontario, 1971–1993', *Canadian Journal of Political Science* 27, 1: 129–52.

———. 2002. 'Environmental Policy and Federalism'. In *Canadian Federalism: Performance, Effectiveness, and Legitimacy*, ed. H. Bakvis and G. Skogstad. Toronto: Oxford University Press.

Cases

R. v. Crown Zellerbach Canada Ltd. (1988), 1 S.C.R. 401.

Friends of the Oldman River Society v. Canada (1992), 1 S.C.R. 3.

Websites

Canadian Council of Ministers of the Environment: www.ccme.ca

Environment Canada: www.ec.gc.ca

House of Commons Standing Committee on Environment and Sustainable Development: www.parl.gc.ca

Office of the Commissioner for Environment and Sustainable Development: www.oag-bvg.gc.ca/domino/cesd_cedd.nsf/html/menu_e.html

Canadian Environmental Law Association: www.Cela.ca

The Pembina Institute: www.pembina.org

The David Suzuki Foundation: www.davidsuzuki.org

Environment Canada, Climate Change: www.ec.gc.ca/climate/home-e.html

United Nations Framework Convention on Climate Change: unfccc.int/2860.php

Part Three

Persistent and New Challenges to the Federation

Chapter 14

Canadian Federalism and the Emerging Mosaic of Aboriginal Multilevel Governance

Martin Papillon

In the past thirty-five years, Aboriginal peoples[1] have mounted a fundamental challenge to the institutions of Canadian federalism. They have adopted the language of recognition and national self-determination to reassert their political status and to question the legitimacy and authority of Canadian governments over their lands and communities. Following the analytical framework proposed in this volume, this chapter discusses and assesses the performance, effectiveness, and legitimacy of Canadian federalism in light of these challenges. How, and to what extent, have the institutions and processes of Canadian federalism responded to Aboriginal claims for greater recognition and political autonomy? Ten years ago the Royal Commission on Aboriginal Peoples (RCAP) proposed a fundamental reconfiguration of Aboriginal–state relations in which Aboriginal governments would form a third order of government in the federation. Are current dynamics conducive to the development of such a relationship?

There are significant obstacles to the recognition of Aboriginal governing institutions as coequal partners in the federation. Deeply embedded assumptions about state sovereignty, as well as institutions and practices inherited from colonial policies, have proven highly resistant to change. Moreover, the diversity in socio-economic and demographic conditions of Aboriginal communities, not to mention the particularities of each nation's historical relationship with the Canadian state, complicates the picture for advocates of an Aboriginal order of government.

That being said, significant changes have taken place over the past few decades in the dynamics of Aboriginal, federal, provincial, and territorial relations. In addition to the constitutional recognition of Aboriginal and treaty rights, new treaties and self-government agreements have proven to be a significant platform from which some Aboriginal nations and communities have rebuilt their governing capacities. As Frances Abele and Michael Prince argued in the previous edition of *Canadian Federalism* (2002: 228), less visible but nonetheless significant changes have also taken place in the dynamics of policy-making and policy implementation between Aboriginal organizations and governments and their federal, provincial, and territorial counterparts. These changes have led to the development of a complex and highly diverse mosaic of multilevel governance relations. It is increasingly through such multilevel exercises that Aboriginal organizations and governments are asserting their authority and legitimacy, and reconfiguring the landscape of Canadian federalism. The extent to which this process of incremental changes is conducive to larger shifts in the structure of Canadian federalism over the long run is, however, a matter of debate.

Aboriginal Peoples and Canadian Federalism: Facing the Legacy of Colonialism

Aboriginal peoples are the descendents of the populations that lived in what is now North America prior to the arrival of European settlers. Like all colonized societies, Aboriginal peoples in Canada are facing a state that was imposed upon them by external powers. As elsewhere, the dominant society simply imposed its conception of sovereignty and claimed exclusive jurisdiction over the territory. In the process, Aboriginal peoples, who initially engaged in nation-to-nation treaty relations with the Crown, were absorbed into the dominant political order without their consent. This process of 'internal colonization' is now well documented (RCAP, 1996, vol. 1), from the initial stage of diplomatic alliances and treaty making to the processes of land confiscation, cultural assimilation, and dismantlement of traditional forms of government. Indigenous societies became 'domesticated' and 'dependent' nations, as Chief Justice John Marshall of the United States Supreme Court famously stated. Aboriginal peoples now seek to liberate themselves from this process, reassert their status as distinct political entities, and redefine their relationship with the Canadian federation accordingly.[2] There are, however, a number of challenges in addressing the legacy of colonialism.

A Multi-faced Reality

Aboriginal people represent approximately 3.4 per cent of the Canadian population. They are highly diverse: of the 1,066,500 individuals who identified with an Aboriginal group in the 2001 census, 63 per cent identified as North American Indians (First Nations), 31 per cent as Métis, and 6 per cent as Inuit.[3] In addition, there are between 40 and 60 distinct Aboriginal nations in Canada today, according to the Royal Commission on Aboriginal Peoples (RCAP, 1996, vol. 2), each with its own traditions, history, language, and sense of collective identity. To further complicate things, 50 per cent of the Aboriginal population now lives in urban centres.[4] As Figure 14.1 suggests, Aboriginal people form a significant

Figure 14.1 Geographic Distribution of the Aboriginal Population

Legend:
- ■ Aboriginal population as % of provincial population
- ■ Distribution of Aboriginal population across Canada

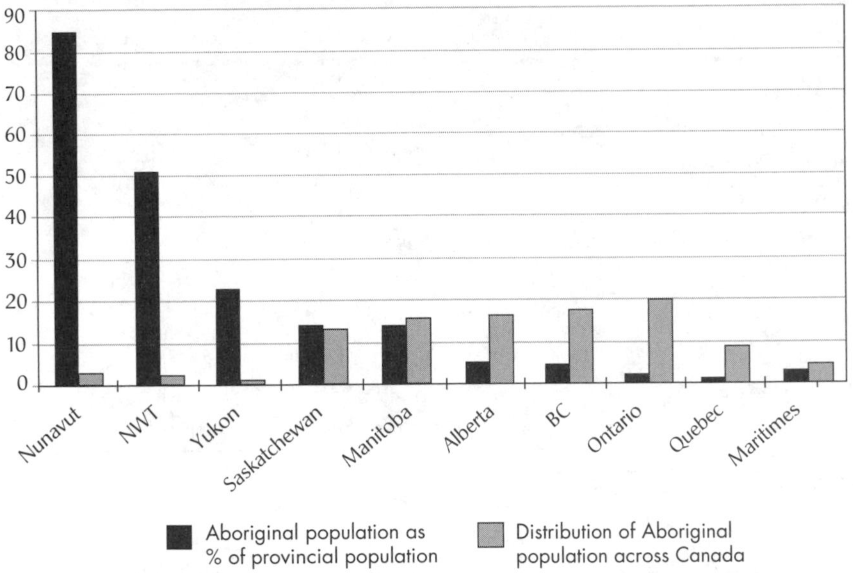

SOURCE: Statistics Canada (2003)

proportion of the population only in the northern territories, Saskatchewan, and Manitoba.

Aboriginal people also face important social and economic challenges, largely as a result of past policies designed to accelerate their assimilation into the Canadian mainstream. As the comparative data in Table 14.1 indicate, while improving in certain areas, the Aboriginal population's socio-economic conditions are still significantly worse than those of the average Canadian.[5] The average income of Aboriginal families is 28 per cent lower than that of non-Aboriginal Canadians. Fifty-five per cent of Aboriginal individuals living in cities live in poverty, compared to 24 per cent for all Canadians. These conditions are compounded by demographic trends; the Aboriginal population is younger and growing faster than the Canadian average. A chronic housing crisis and a lack of basic infrastructure, such as sewage and drinking water, also negatively affect the living conditions of the Aboriginal population in many remote areas.

Aboriginal peoples also vary considerably in their status and institutional relationships with the Canadian state. For one, while all Aboriginal peoples were recognized as having the same rights under the Constitution Act, 1982, it is important to recognize that not all have a treaty-based relationship with the Crown. The result is significant variations in the land and governance regime of each nation. In addition, while most First Nations come under the regime of the federal Indian

Table 14.1 Socio-Economic Conditions of the Aboriginal Population of Canada

	Aboriginal Population	Canadian Population
Median age	24.7	37.7
Population growth (annual rate)	1.8%	.7%
Average household income	$21,296	$29,769
Low-income families	31.2%	12.9%
Secondary diploma (15 & over)	55%	70%
University degree	6%	15%
Single-parent families	32% on reserve 46% in urban areas	17%
Life expectancy at birth	Men: 68.9 Women: 76.3	Men: 76.3 Women: 81.5

SOURCES: Statistics Canada (2003); Indian and Northern Affairs Canada (2004)

Act, Inuit and Métis do not. The federal government also distinguishes between First Nations who are considered 'status' Indians, and thus entitled to certain benefits under the Act, and non-status Indians, who fall outside the Act and live mostly in urban areas. These legal distinctions, despite their somewhat arbitrary nature, tend to reinforce political divisions amongst Aboriginal peoples.

These differences in conditions, status, and entitlements have significant repercussions for Aboriginal peoples and their relationship with Canadian federalism. Clearly, there is not one single Aboriginal reality to be addressed with a single set of solutions. This reality is further compounded by the fact that Aboriginal peoples do not necessarily all share the same conception of their relationship with the Canadian state. While some simply reject Canadian sovereignty over their traditional lands, others, especially the Inuit and Métis, have historically been less reluctant to accept the authority of the Canadian Constitution. Aboriginal populations living in urban settings also often have very different viewpoints and interests than those living in remote areas, where control over the land and natural resources is a key element of ongoing conflicts with the state. Within each community there are also often conflicting views between 'traditionalists', who seek to reassert traditional lifestyle, values, and governing practices, and those who focus on the modernization of socio-economic and political structures as a key element of the project of autonomy.

The Constraining Nature of Canadian Federalism

In addition to their diverse realities, Aboriginal people also face significant challenges related to the institutions of Canadian federalism. Although the Royal

Proclamation of 1763 recognized the status of Aboriginal nations as distinct political entities, no Aboriginal representatives were invited to the Charlottetown and Quebec conferences of 1864, where the foundations of the Canadian federation were established. As a result, they never consented, explicitly or implicitly, to the division of authority over the land and peoples that resulted from the Constitution Act, 1867. Instead, they effectively became an object of federal jurisdiction according to section 91(24) of the Act, which confers on the federal Parliament the power to legislate over 'Indians and Land reserved for Indians'. The institutions of Canadian federalism thus have very little, if any, legitimacy from an Aboriginal perspective. The initial exclusion of Aboriginal peoples from those institutions created a number of constraints that still limit their political aspirations in the Canadian context.

Most significantly, while authority in a federation is divided between orders of governments, the doctrine of state sovereignty is still deeply entrenched in the British-inspired Canadian parliamentary system. There is no space in the Canadian federation for the expression of political authority outside the two constitutionally recognized orders of government.[6] As a result, from a strictly positivist constitutional perspective, Aboriginal governments' authority can only be delegated from the federal and provincial Parliaments. Aboriginal peoples, supported by many legal scholars and Aboriginal rights advocates, reject this conception of sovereignty and argue instead that they have an *inherent* right to self-government, that is a right that emanates not from the Constitution, but from their historical presence—as politically organized peoples—on the land (Macklem, 2001; RCAP, 1996, vol. 2). As we will see in the second part of this chapter, the principle of an inherent Aboriginal right to self-government has been accepted by the federal government and most provinces, but its implementation in practice still faces significant institutional resistance.

Without formal status as federal partners, Aboriginal peoples and their governments[7] also have no statutory voice in the shared institutions of 'intrastate federalism', such as the federal Parliament, the Cabinet, or the Supreme Court, other than what their demographic weight calls for. They also have had historically only limited access to the important mechanisms of 'interstate federalism' associated with the growing web of intergovernmental processes and institutions that characterize the Canadian federation. This lack of access to key institutions and processes of Canadian federalism reinforces their weak legitimacy and certainly affects their performance and effectiveness in addressing Aboriginal claims.

The division of powers in the Canadian federation has also contributed to what are often tense relations between Aboriginal peoples and provinces (Long and Boldt 1988). Especially relevant in the Canadian context is provincial authority over public lands and natural resources. Provinces have naturally sought to maximize local economic development, mainly through natural resource extraction, often without much regard for Aboriginal rights and interests. Highly visible conflicts over hydroelectric developments, forestry and fisheries, or over developments on public lands for which the title is still contested by an Aboriginal group, regularly make headlines in Canadian media and contribute to divisions and a high degree of mistrust between the Aboriginal population and non-Aboriginal Canadians.[8]

Finally, Aboriginal people have also long been, and continue to be, victims of the competitive nature of Canadian federalism, especially with regards to the provision of social programs and services. Paradoxically, the issue here is not so much who *can*, but rather who *must* exercise its legislative authority. Again, the conflict revolves around the interpretation of section 91(24) of the Constitution Act, 1867. As we have seen, the federal government initially interpreted its responsibilities restrictively and excluded Inuit, Métis, and non-status Indians from the Indian Act regime. But even for those covered by the Indian Act, the federal government has on numerous occasions sought to transfer its responsibilities for the provision of services to provinces.[9] The latter, though reluctant to allow federal interventions in their areas of jurisdiction, have always insisted on the federal government's responsibility for the provision of social programs to the Aboriginal population. As a result, a significant number of Aboriginal individuals, especially off-reserve Indians and Métis, have fallen into a jurisdictional gap and for a long time were simply ignored by both orders of government. Even today federal and provincial authorities tend to interpret their respective responsibilities in relation to Aboriginal people more or less liberally depending on the interests at stake. Jurisdictional uncertainties add to an already complex policy challenge in developing long-term, co-ordinated solutions to Aboriginal socioeconomic conditions.

We can thus conclude that in addition to lacking legitimacy as a result of Aboriginal people's exclusion at the time of the creation of the federation, Canadian federalism has not been a particularly effective conduit for addressing the legacy of colonialism. Nor has it historically performed well as a unifying system of governance. In fact, the institutions and processes of Canadian federalism have exacerbated conflicts with Aboriginal people and have contributed significantly to the reproduction of the system of exclusion inherited from the colonial period. Reconciling the Canadian federal system with Aboriginal claims to self-determination is thus not a simple task.

A Renewed Federal Partnership?

Although the institutions of Canadian federalism in many ways constitute an obstacle for Aboriginal people, Canada's 'federal condition' can also open the door to significant opportunities. Canadians are familiar with the idea of coexistence in a diverse, even divided, political community. The ongoing debate over the accommodation of Quebec nationalism has opened avenues for Aboriginal people towards a greater recognition of their political status, as the definition of what constitutes Canada as a political community is constantly questioned in public discourse as well as in intellectual circles.

The redefinition of Canadian federalism in order to recognize the political status of Aboriginal nations has been the object of many theoretical reflections in recent years. While some have argued that Aboriginal peoples could form a province, the small size, territorial dispersion, and diversity of Aboriginal communities make such a proposal impractical.[10] The most widely discussed model consists instead of recognizing Aboriginal governments as a third order of government, with a distinct sphere of authority within the existing federation. This is the model proposed by the Royal Commission on Aboriginal Peoples (RCAP). According to the Commission, the foundation of this third order rests on the recognition of the inherent right to self-government as an existing right under section 35(1) of the Constitution Act, 1982. As a previously self-governing political community, each Aboriginal nation should be entitled to control a series of 'core' jurisdictions and to negotiate a new division of responsibilities with the federal and provincial governments through treaties or other forms of agreement (RCAP, 1996, vol.2: 215).

As an alternative to incorporating Aboriginal governments *within* the existing federation as a third order, some argue in favour of a treaty-based relationship *outside* the institutions of Canadian federalism. In this perspective, Aboriginal nations would be considered sovereign entities on their own, independent of the Canadian Constitution, and treaties would establish bilateral confederal relations with Canada in the same way that international treaties are the constitutive basis of the European Union. Proponents of this alternative argue that early treaties between Aboriginal nations and the Crown, which are still valid today, created a bilateral relationship of self-rule and shared rule between co-existing and coequal partners. According to Sakej Henderson (1994), this 'treaty federalism' should be reinstated as the basis of a renewed, postcolonial partnership between Aboriginal nations and the Canadian state. Building on a similar perspective, James Tully (1995) argues that Canada should be conceived as a double confederation: the treaty-based partnership between Aboriginal peoples and the Crown, and the newer federal–provincial federation.[11]

While the RCAP and treaty federalism models offer inspiring theoretical models for reconfiguring Canadian federalism in light of Aboriginal claims, they nonetheless pose numerous practical challenges. Most significantly, it is not clear how Aboriginal peoples would be represented in the shared institutions of a two-level federal system, or even in a third-order model. Should all nations, no matter their size, have equal representation, or should representation be more proportional? How would shared decisions be made? Moreover, as Alan Cairns (2000: 191) argues in his critique of the RCAP model, it is not self-evident how one can reconcile a treaty-based, nation-to-nation association with a substantive conception of shared citizenship, a necessary condition to foster a sense of solidarity and co-operation across communities that are bound to live together in a common territory. Finally, these models, which both assume some degree of fiscal autonomy for Aboriginal governments, may not be suitable for all Aboriginal nations or communities, as most are highly dependent on fiscal transfers from the federal government, especially those with limited land bases or access to resources. As history shows, equality in principle means little without some balance in resources. These obstacles are not insurmountable, but they illustrate the challenges of moving from theoretical constructs to more concrete institutional reforms.

The Changing Relationship between Aboriginal Peoples and Canadian Federalism

So, where are we today? Moving away from theoretical considerations and look-ing at recent developments, it is safe to say that the relationship between Abori-ginal peoples and the institutions of Canadian federalism has changed in the last few decades. From the now infamous 1969 White Paper on Indian Policy, which sought to do away with the differentiated status of Aboriginal peoples, to the con-stitutional recognition of Aboriginal and treaty rights and the negotiation of treaties and self-government agreements in Quebec, Yukon, British Columbia, and elsewhere, the shifts are remarkable. That being said, the existing framework of Canadian federalism continues to be more of a constraint on than a vehicle for Aboriginal aspirations. The recognition of Aboriginal governments as a third order of government, or of a parallel treaty-based federal structure, remains more theoretical than real, and the representation of Aboriginal peoples in shared federal institutions remains problematic. Interestingly, it is perhaps out-side the traditional institutions of the federation, in emerging dynamics of mul-tilevel governance between Aboriginal, federal, and provincial governments, that the changes with the greatest significance for Canadian federalism are taking place.

Recognition through the Courts

With only limited access to the traditional institutions of Canadian federalism, Aboriginal peoples, like other minorities in Canada, have used the courts and the language of rights to assert their claims for recognition. As a result, the courts have played a central role in redefining the legal framework of Aboriginal peo-ples' relationship with the Canadian federation. The 1973 Calder decision, in which the Supreme Court recognized for the first time the possibility that an Aboriginal title resulting from prior occupation of the land could have legal force in contemporary Canada, created a significant hole in the doctrine of unmedi-ated Crown sovereignty. It opened the constitutional door for one of the most significant developments in Aboriginal–state relations since Confederation: the recognition of Aboriginal and treaty rights in section 35(1) of the Constitution Act, 1982.

A significant Aboriginal rights jurisprudence has developed since 1982 in which the Supreme Court confirmed the substantial nature of Aboriginal consti-tutional rights and limited the power of governments to infringe on these rights without a compelling reason.[12] The Court effectively created a legal space, albeit a limited one, for Aboriginal peoples to assert their presence in the political land-scape of the Canadian federation. Although the Supreme Court never said so explicitly, it is increasingly accepted that section 35 rights include the inherent right to self-government. The failed Charlottetown Accord of 1992, to which all first ministers agreed, contained a disposition to that effect, and the federal government reiterated its support for such interpretation of section 35 in a policy statement in 1995.[13]

The Supreme Court, however, in the few decisions where governance rights under section 35 have been discussed, has adhered to a relatively restrictive interpretation. As for other Aboriginal rights, the Court has limited governance rights to activities, customs, or traditions 'integral to the distinctive culture of Aboriginal peoples' and has insisted on the need to reconcile these rights with federal and provincial constitutional authority. This interpretation has prompted commentators to suggest that the Aboriginal rights recognized under section 35 are 'frozen in time', as they concern traditional practices and do not constitute a basis for the development of modern governance structure and a renewed political relationship with the state (Asch 2002; Borrows, 2002).

Beyond questions of definition, there are inherent limits to what the courts can do in redefining the status and role of Aboriginal governments. The interpretation of Aboriginal rights by the Supreme Court, however liberal it may be, will remain constrained by the parameters of the Canadian Constitution, from which it derives its own authority. Though important in establishing a more level playing field and interpreting negotiated agreements, tribunals can neither create new institutions of governance nor completely replace the political process in redefining the constitutional foundations of our relationships. In fact, the Supreme Court has recognized its limited role in this respect a number of times.[14] Given the lack of legitimacy of existing institutions, the redefinition of the relationship between Aboriginal peoples and the Canadian federation should ideally stem from negotiations between mutually consenting parties. The federal government and, increasingly, the provinces have started to recognize the need for a negotiated response, at least in principle.

Modern Treaties

The re-emergence of treaties as a key institutional mechanism for negotiating and redefining the relationship between Aboriginal peoples and the Canadian federation is certainly one of the most significant constitutional developments of the past thirty years in Canada. There are, however, many disagreements regarding the meaning of 'modern treaties'. For the federal government, as well as for the provinces involved in negotiations, the objective of treaties is not to renegotiate the configuration of state sovereignty but rather to confirm its legality and legitimacy in light of the Canadian Constitution. The stated objective of the federal land claims policy, under which modern treaties are negotiated, is 'to obtain certainty respecting ownership and use of lands and resources' (Canada, INAC, 2003: 3). To ensure certainty, the federal government requires the surrender of all existing and possibly existing land rights on the territory covered by the agreement in exchange for the rights and benefits defined in the settlement. This approach, under which Aboriginal rights outside those defined in the agreement are 'extinguished', has been the object of criticism from numerous quarters, including the United Nations.[15] Not surprisingly, the understanding of treaties that informs this process is fundamentally at odds with Aboriginal conceptions of the treaty process as establishing a political relationship between coequal partners, sharing responsibility for stewardship of the land (Tully, 2001).

Despite these important limits, and the extremely slow and frustrating nature of the process, land claim negotiations have been an important vehicle for Aboriginal peoples to redefine their relationship with the federal and provincial governments. Following its 'inherent right' policy of 1995, the federal government now accepts the negotiation of self-government arrangements as an integral part of land claim settlements, thus creating constitutionally protected and distinct governance structures for a growing number of Aboriginal nations and communities.[16]

The Nisga'a Final Agreement, signed in 1998 after 25 years of mobilization and negotiations, is worth noting in this context. The agreement provides for ownership and self-governing control of approximately 2,000 km² of land in the Nass Valley in British Columbia, including surface and subsurface resources. The agreement establishes law-making authority—within the limits of the Canadian Constitution—for the Nisga'a Lisims Government and four Village Governments, as well as three urban locals, which provide a voice for Nisga'a citizens who do not live in the Nass Valley. The Nisga'a Lisims Government has paramount legislative authority over the management of community lands, citizenship, and local matters. However, the treaty includes important limitations on Nisga'a authority even in areas where Nisga'a laws are paramount. The Nisga'a government cannot make laws that run contrary to the general interests of the federal and provincial governments, and must operate within the framework of the Canadian Constitution, including the Charter of Rights. In a number of other areas, such as education, transport, and environmental regulation, Nisga'a authority is concurrent with federal and provincial jurisdictions. In most cases, Nisga'a laws prevail only if they meet or exceed federal and provincial requirements.[17] A similar system of paramount and concurrent jurisdictions was established under the Council of Yukon Indians Umbrella Agreement of 1993, under which Yukon First Nations have been negotiating specific self-government agreements.

Another important milestone was achieved with the Nunavut Land Claims Agreement. Signed in 1992, it led to the creation of the Nunavut territory in 1999 and the establishment of a public government controlled by a majority of Inuit. The new territory covers almost 2 million km². The Inuit themselves are recognized as having collective title to 351,000 km² of land (of which about 10 per cent include sub-surface mineral rights), as well as a share of resource royalties and participation in co-management bodies in a number of areas involving land development and environmental issues.[18] The Government of Nunavut is a public government and follows the Canadian parliamentary model. It is formed by a cabinet of nine ministers, responsible to a legislature of 19 members elected by the population of the territory. Like the other two territories, Nunavut does not have the constitutional status of a province. Its authority is delegated though federal legislation and, most significantly, unlike a province it does not have jurisdiction over Crown lands and resources. Its authority is nevertheless significant in most areas where provinces normally have jurisdiction, and, like the other territories, it has full status in the various federal–provincial intergovernmental mechanisms. Although it is a public government, the Nunavut government promotes the interests, culture, and traditions of Inuit. It has also tried since its creation to adopt a working philosophy that corresponds to Inuit approaches to governance, through a policy known as Inuit Qaujimajatuaqangit, aimed at shaping the public service according to Inuit values.

Modern treaties and self-government agreements constitute an important development in Canada's constitutional landscape. Aboriginal nations like the Nisga'a or the Inuit in Nunavut are recognized as legitimate political entities, sharing in practice some governmental authority with the federal and provincial orders of governments. On the other hand, treaty-based self-government agreements certainly do not constitute a radical realignment of the distribution of sovereignty and democratic legitimacy in the federation. Self-governing Aboriginal nations still struggle to have their status and place properly recognized in the institutions and processes of Canadian federalism. In many ways, these developments seem to take place in spite of our federal system rather than in conjunction with it.

Participation in the Intrastate and Interstate Institutions of Canadian Federalism

As was noted earlier, a central element compounding the lack of legitimacy of Canadian federalism for Aboriginal peoples has been their exclusion, as political entities, from its institutions and processes. Although there have been many discussions of reforming the institutions of 'intrastate' and 'interstate' federalism so as to make them more inclusive for Aboriginal peoples, success has been limited. For now, proposals to reform the electoral system and the structure of representation in the federal Parliament to increase Aboriginal representation remain only theoretical. Although there are Aboriginal members of Parliament and senators, their influence on the overall balance of power is limited to their demographic weight, which is minimal. The Royal Commission on Electoral Reform and Party Financing proposed the establishment of special Aboriginal electoral districts to enhance Aboriginal representation in the House of Commons (RCER, 1991). The RCAP (1996, vol. 2) also proposed the creation of an additional Aboriginal House of Representatives, and the Charlottetown Accord contained guaranties for enhanced Aboriginal representation in a reformed Senate. Not surprisingly, such reforms have met with skepticism amongst advocates of individual equality and status-blind representation in parliamentary institutions, but they are also perceived with suspicion by some Aboriginal peoples themselves, especially those defending a treaty-based, nation-to-nation conception of the relationship (Schouls, 1996). From that perspective, greater participation of Aboriginal citizens as individuals in Canadian institutions is associated with institutional assimilation, and helps to legitimize unilateral Canadian sovereignty (Alfred, 1998: 110).

Interestingly, it is perhaps in the institutions and processes of interstate federalism that Aboriginal peoples have made the most significant headway. National Aboriginal organizations have gained access to the various intergovernmental forums through which Canadian governments co-ordinate their policies. The main national Aboriginal organizations are the Assembly of First Nations (AFN), which represents mostly on-reserve First Nations; the Congress of Aboriginal Peoples (CAP), representing non-status Indians; the Métis National Council (MNC); the Inuit Tapiriit Kanatami (ITK); the Native Women's Association of Canada (NWAC); and two more organizations representing Inuit and Métis women respectively. The participation of Aboriginal organizations in the mechanisms of Canadian intergovernmental relations is a legacy of the constitutional negotiations of the 1980s and early 1990s. Between 1983 and 1987, these national organizations were directly involved in the intergovernmental negotiations dedicated to the definition of Aboriginal rights under section 35(2) of the Constitution Act, 1982. Despite its ultimate failure, this process allowed the organizations involved to gain legitimacy and significant experience in dealing with the intricacies of intergovernmental negotiations (Brock, 1991). The outcry produced by their exclusion from the Quebec-driven Meech Lake process contributed to their return as full, and high-profile, participants during the 'Canada round' that led to the Charlottetown Accord in 1992.[19]

Many assumed that Aboriginal leaders' inclusion in constitutional talks created a precedent that would be difficult to reverse. With the demise of mega-constitutional negotiations, however, Aboriginal organizations lost their leverage and today their participation in the various mechanisms of intergovernmental relations—at the first minister, ministerial, or administrative level—remains contingent on the nature of the issues being debated and the discretion of federal and provincial governments. For example, despite intense lobbying by the Assembly of First Nations, Aboriginal organizations were excluded from the Social Union Framework Agreement negotiations in the late 1990s. They were, however, included in the implementation process following the Agreement though consultations at the administrative level (Dacks, 2001). More recently, in November 2005, Aboriginal organizations were invited to the first ministers' table for an intergovernmental meeting specifically dedicated to Aboriginal matters. The Kelowna meeting resulted in a federal–provincial–Aboriginal accord on a five-year plan to foster socio-economic development in Aboriginal communities.[20] In a succession of events indicative of the limited institutional and political weight associated with such agreements, the newly elected Conservative government of Stephen Harper promptly withdrew federal support for the Kelowna Accord. It did not feel bound to an agreement negotiated under the previous Liberal government.

Recent developments may suggest a growing involvement of Aboriginal orga-nizations in the institutions of executive federalism, but as the demise of the Kelowna Accord suggests, their status in such processes remains largely ad hoc and contingent on the federal–provincial agenda. Except for Nunavut, the Aboriginal presence in intergovernmental forums is thus unlikely to become institutionalized. There are very few incentives for the federal and provincial gov-ernments to encourage greater Aboriginal participation in a process that is already complex and difficult to manage with fourteen governments. The prospect of further institutionalization also raises the question of who would determine which organizations, or Aboriginal governing institutions, have the legitimacy to take part in intergovernmental processes.

Beyond the Existing Institutions of Federalism: Changing Relations of Governance

The developments discussed thus far concern fairly high-profile aspects of the changing dynamics between Aboriginal peoples and Canadian federalism. In parallel with constitutional debates and the negotiation of treaties and self-gov ernment agreements, some fundamental, though less visible, changes in the rela-tionship between Aboriginal organizations and governments (band councils and others) and their federal and provincial counterparts are also taking place in the dynamics of everyday governance. In the past twenty years, the federal govern-ment and its provincial counterparts have undertaken a significant decentraliza-tion of programs and services to Aboriginal governments and organizations. The process of decentralization started as early as the 1960s, with the transfer of school administration to some First Nations. But it was only in the 1980s that it became a systematic element of federal policy, as Aboriginal claims for greater autonomy coincided with the rise of the neo-liberal agenda promoting a scaled-down, more flexible state and a greater role for communities in their socio-economic development.

As Figure 14.2 suggests, the transfer of budget for program management to Aboriginal governing authorities rapidly increased in the mid-1980s. The result was a significant shift in the role of both Aboriginal governments and Indian and Northern Affairs Canada (INAC), the main federal department responsible for Aboriginal programs. In 1983, INAC directly managed close to 50 per cent of pro-grams directed towards Aboriginal peoples. This proportion is now reduced to 8 per cent. In addition to local infrastructures, First Nations band councils and tribal councils, as well as local and regional Inuit governments, are now largely responsible for the administration of social services, education, training, eco-nomic development, and housing services in communities.

This redefinition of the federal approach to Aboriginal governance is largely consistent with broader changes in the dynamics of governance in most indus-trialized countries (Pierre and Peters, 2000). As in many other service-oriented policy areas, instead of running programs directly, the federal government increasingly works in partnership with Aboriginal organizations and govern-

Figure 14.2 Who Administers Federal Funds Directed towards Aboriginal Peoples? (%)

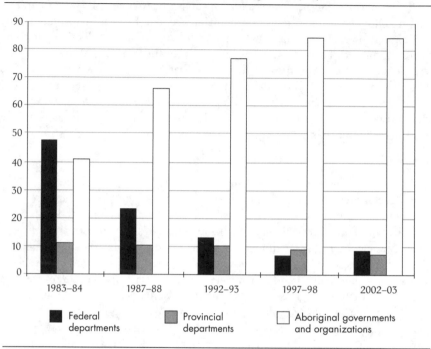

SOURCE: Indian and Northern Affairs Canada (2004).

ments in the regulation, management, and delivery of services. A number of government programs developed in the wake of *Gathering Strength*, the 1998 federal action plan designed in response to the report of the Royal Commission on Aboriginal Peoples, follow this 'partnership' approach (Canada, DIAND, 1997). For example, under the federal Aboriginal Human Resource Development Strategy, launched in 1999, instead of running training programs directly in communities, the federal government funds initiatives developed by Aboriginal governments and organizations related to labour-market integration. A number of bilateral and trilateral agreements in specific policy fields are also reshaping Aboriginal governance. For example, in July 2006 a trilateral agreement between the federal government, the government of British Columbia, and the First Nations Education Steering Committee of that province proposed the transfer of some legislative authority to First Nations in education matters.[21]

What is the impact of administrative decentralization and governance through partnerships? While this new approach increases the role of Aboriginal governments in the administration of programs, it does not change their legal and constitutional status, nor does it change the division of powers and authority in the federation. With some exceptions, notably the recent British Columbia agreement on education, these decentralization agreements are mostly administrative in nature. Very few are enacted through legislation. They can thus be revoked unilaterally, or drastically reduced, without much warning. Administrative decentralization may in fact increase the dependent and hierarchical relationship between Aboriginal authorities and federal and provincial governments, since the capacity of Aboriginal governments to deliver services to their communities is entirely dependent on such programs. Moreover, the minister of Indian Affairs is still responsible to Parliament for the funds allocated through those agreements. As a result, the transfer of responsibilities is accompanied by an increased emphasis on accounting and reporting mechanisms, which, as the Auditor General noted in a recent report, has become a significant administrative burden for Aboriginal governments.[22] In sum, critics of decentralization may well be correct when they argue that it represents little more than a new way for Canadian governments to maintain a form of 'control at distance' on Aboriginal communities (Neu and Therrien, 2003).

That being said, one should not underestimate the long-term political impact of administrative transfers on the role and legitimacy of Aboriginal governments. For one, even if they do not formally transfer any jurisdiction, these agreements considerably increase the relevance of Aboriginal governments in the daily life of communities. They are, in effect, becoming the sole governmental presence in those communities. Second, despite tight fiscal controls, administrative decentralization leaves a certain leeway for Aboriginal governments in the implementation of programs. In a de-centralized governance context, the relationship between the policy objectives defined at one level and the implementation process at another needs to be relatively loose, so that the agents responsible for implementation can adapt programs to their specific context (Pierre and Peters, 2000). The administration of decentralized programs targeted at Aboriginal economic development or training, for example, involves a substantial degree of policy choice in defining priorities at the community level. In addition to the development of policy capacity, this margin of autonomy for Aboriginal governments can also reinforce their democratic legitimacy in communities where they have long been considered little more than state agents. Decentralized program administration fosters political debates and deliberation in communities that, for most of the last century, have been governed from above and shut out of any substantial democratic debates regarding their own development. In other words, it may well force Aboriginal governments to be more responsive to the priorities, values and culture of their communities.

This decentralized approach to governance is also significantly altering the nature of the relationship between Aboriginal governments and their federal and provincial counterparts. Administrative decentralization, just like formal self-government arrangements, increases the need for co-ordination and consultation between governments. Ongoing discussions are necessary in order to negotiate the various administrative agreements, establish financial needs, and evaluate services, but also to co-ordinate federal or provincial objectives with Aboriginal ones, and define future priorities. For example, the transfer of federal education responsibilities to band councils or Aboriginal-led school boards creates a need to co-ordinate with provincial governments in order to ensure the recognition of diplomas and facilitate Aboriginal students' access to postsecondary education. The transfer of responsibilities over public security involves similar trilateral relations to ensure co-ordination and co-operation between Aboriginal, federal, and provincial police corps. Intergovernmental relations are thus increasingly becoming part of the Aboriginal policy landscape. As a result, Aboriginal governments, just like their federal and provincial counterparts, have significantly developed their intergovernmental capacities in the past decade. Many Aboriginal governments now have a team of professional civil servants whose expertise is not in running programs but in policy analysis, fiscal relations, and the negotiation of intergovernmental agreements.

To be sure, Aboriginal governments are not on an equal footing with their federal and provincial counterparts in such intergovernmental negotiations, as the latter have the jurisdictional upper hand and control the purse strings. But intergovernmental meetings and negotiation processes are political spaces through which Aboriginal governments can assert their authority and legitimacy as governments, representing self-determining nations or communities.

Finally, the capacity of Aboriginal governments to influence the outcome of intergovernmental negotiations over administrative agreements varies considerably depending on their demographic and geographic situation, their resources, and, of course, the nature of their institutions of governance. Aboriginal nations with a treaty-based self-government agreement have significantly more leverage and resources to engage in government-to-government relations. Even within the Indian Act framework, not all Aboriginal governments are equal in their capacity to engage in intergovernmental relations. Those with a strong tradition of political affirmation and an effective governmental structure logically fare better. The Kahnawake Mohawks, for example, have unilaterally asserted their authority in a number of policy areas, such as education, policing, gambling, and other commercial activities, as well as trade of good and services, and then used intergovernmental forums with the federal and Quebec governments to negotiate the recognition of their authority in exchange for a greater co-ordination and harmonization in the implementation of policies.

Conclusion: An Emerging Mosaic of Multilevel Governance Relations

The relationship between Aboriginal peoples and Canadian federalism remains uncertain and tentative. The initial exclusion of Aboriginal peoples from the federal compact still looms large today, affecting not only the legitimacy but also the performance and effectiveness of the institutions and processes of Canadian federalism as they try to address the difficult colonial legacy. Although Canadians are often perceived to be more supportive of Aboriginal rights than their Australian or American counterparts, this support has not lead to a radical reconfiguration of Canadian federalism along the lines proposed by the RCAP and proponents of treaty federalism. Multiple factors work against such a significant reform of Canadian federalism, most significantly the institutional resilience of existing practices and conceptions of state sovereignty and governmental authority. The profound diversity, demographic situation, and socio-economic conditions of Aboriginal peoples also compound these difficulties. So does the fiscal dependency of Aboriginal governments on their federal and provincial counterparts.

That being said, significant shifts have taken place in the constitutional framework and institutions of Canadian federalism. As we have seen, these shifts remain very much a work in progress. The extent and meaning of Aboriginal rights are still being defined though the courts as well as through public and academic debates. Despite the recent developments in treaty negotiations, federal and provincial authorities still impose significant limits on both the process and the substance of agreements. The status of the self-governing structures slowly emerging from such processes varies considerably from one agreement to the other, and their viability largely depends on the willingness of both federal and provincial authorities to put resources and goodwill into implementing each agreement. In this respect, Canadian federalism has performed rather poorly, as the specific responsibilities and obligations of the federal and provincial governments often remain unclear. The participation of Aboriginal organizations in mechanisms of executive federalism raises a new set of issues in terms of legitimacy and accountability, as their status in such processes remains largely ad hoc and uncertain. The rejection of the Kelowna Accord by the newly elected Conservative government also raises concerns regarding the effectiveness of intergovernmental mechanisms in addressing pressing social and economic issues in Aboriginal communities that cut across the boundaries of federal and provincial jurisdictions.

As I have suggested, it is perhaps in the emerging dynamics of multilevel governance in the negotiation of policy implementation that Aboriginal, federal, and provincial relations have changed most significantly. This change may not affect the constitutional status of Aboriginal peoples, but Aboriginal governments now play a growing role in the development and implementation of policies, and as a result consolidate their capacity and legitimacy both within the communities and in their relations with federal and provincial authorities. Aboriginal governance is now increasingly being played out in multiple venues. If the federal government has kept the upper hand with its constitutional authority and fiscal capacity, provinces now play an increasing role as a result of their involvement in treaty negotiations and in the process of administrative devolution to Aboriginal governments and organizations. Aboriginal governments have been increasingly proactive in developing their intergovernmental capacity, and engage with their federal and provincial counterparts in policy negotiations. In other words,

Aboriginal governance is less and less a unidirectional, top-down affair and is increasingly becoming a multilevel, trilateral reality.

This emerging trilateral, multilevel governance regime is far from uniform, as the context, status, needs, and expectations, as well as political clout of Aboriginal nations vary considerably. Different self-government agreements, land bases, and provincial positions in relation to Aboriginal peoples also affect the nature and dynamics of multilevel governance. It is perhaps more accurate to talk of a mosaic of multilevel governance relations between Aboriginal nations and their federal and provincial counterparts, each with its own institutional framework and evolving dynamics. While it does not create a formal third order of governments or a parallel treaty-based federal structure, this emerging multilevel mosaic offers what can, in effect, be defined as an alternative way for Aboriginal peoples to reshape their relationship with Canadian federalism. In this perspective, change is not coming from above, through formal constitutional processes, but rather from below, through the consolidation of Aboriginal governments' capacity and legitimacy in exercises of governance. Only time will tell whether this changing dynamic can eventually lead to a more efficient and legitimate relationship between the Canadian federation and Aboriginal peoples.

Notes

The author would like to acknowledge the helpful comments of Peter Russell and the editors of this volume on earlier drafts of this chapter. Some sections were also inspired by an earlier text by the author, 'Vers un fédéralisme postcolonial? La difficile redéfinition des rapports entre l'État canadien et les peuples autochtones', published in *Le Fédéralisme canadien contemporain. Fondements, traditions, institutions*, ed. Alain-G. Gagnon (Montreal: Presses de l'Université de Montréal).

1. Following the practice in the Canadian literature, the term 'Aboriginal peoples' in this text refers to Métis and Inuit peoples as well as First Nations (still often referred to as Indians). Distinctions among the three are made when necessary.
2. There is no space here to discuss the normative foundations and various conceptions of Aboriginal self-determination. For a more detailed analysis, see for example Tully (2000) and Macklem (2001).
3. The data in this section are from Statistics Canada (2003) and Indian and Northern Affairs Canada (2004).
4. Of major Canadian cities, Winnipeg has the largest Aboriginal population, with 56,000 persons, accounting for 8 per cent of its population.
5. A 2004 report of the United Nations Human Rights Commission suggests that while Canada was 7th on the UN Human Development Index for that year, Aboriginal peoples living in Canada would rank 48th on the list of 174 countries.

6. According to the oft-repeated doctrine established by the Judicial Committee of the Privy Council, 'whatever belongs to self-government in Canada belongs either to the Dominion or to the provinces, within the limits of the British North America Act' *A.G. Ontario* (1912).

7. Aboriginal governments vary considerably in form and size, as well as in degree of responsibility and legitimacy within communities. Elected band councils are the most common form of government for First Nations. Formally, they exercise delegated administrative authority under the Indian Act, although many play a much greater political role. Bands have also aggregated themselves into national or regional tribal councils. Other Aboriginal governments were created though federal or provincial legislation pursuant to self-government agreements and exercise powers accordingly. In some cases, self-governing structures reproduce the ethnic-based council system, but Inuit in Nunavut and elsewhere, for example, have opted for public forms of local and regional governments.

8. There is no space here for an exhaustive list of recent conflicts, but one can think of the 1990 Oka crisis in Quebec, the 1995 standoff at Ipperwash Provincial Park and the 2006 land dispute in Caledonia, Ontario, as examples of land disputes that turned sour. The recent conflicts over the fisheries in the Maritimes and British Columbia are examples of disputes over natural resources.

9. The infamous *White Paper on Indian Policy* of 1969 notably proposed such transfer.

10. The obvious exception here is Nunavut, where Inuit form a majority on a significant territory that could well become self-sustainable given its extensive natural resources.

11. Ladner (2003) discusses in greater details the conceptual foundations of treaty federalism and the differences with the model proposed by the RCAP.

12. Landmark decisions, such as *Sparrow* (1990), *Van der Peet* (1996), *Delgamuukw* (1997) and *Marshall* (1999), amongst others, have defined the extent and content of Aboriginal and treaty rights. For critical analyses, see amongst others Borrows (2002) and Macklem (2001).

13. Both the Charlottetown Accord and the 1995 policy statement made it clear, however, that such a right was to be exercised within the existing boundaries of the Canadian Constitution.

14. This definition was developed in *Van der Peet* (1996). In *Pamajewon* (1996) 2 S.R.C. 164, the Court suggested a similar criteria should be applied to governance rights.

15. For example, in *Delgamuukw* (1997), former Chief Justice Lamer called for a negotiated solution to conflicts over resource extraction and land development.

16. See *Concluding Observations of the Human Rights Committee: Canada*. United Nations, CPR/C/CAN/CO/5, November 2005. In response to criticisms, the federal government has sought an 'alternative mechanism to pro-

vide certainty' (Canada, INAC, 2003: 3). For example, the Nisga'a Final Agreement states that Nisga'a rights continue to exist *as modified* by the treaty. Despite this change in wording, the objective remains to contain Aboriginal rights to what is explicitly stated in the treaty. More recently, the Quebec and federal governments agreed with four Innu communities to negotiate a settlement based on the continuity of Aboriginal rights, as defined in the treaty but also in future agreements. For a discussion of this slightly different approach, see Maclure (2005).

17. At the time of writing, 18 final agreements had been ratified since the first 'modern treaty', the *James Bay and Northern Quebec Agreement* in 1975. This includes ten specific agreements with Yukon First Nations negotiated under the *Council for Yukon Indians Umbrella Agreement* of 1993. All agreements are available at: <www.ainc-inac.gc.ca/pr/agr/index_e.html> (accessed 30 April 2006).

18. For various viewpoints on the *Nisga'a Final Agreement*, see the special issue of *BC Studies* (no. 120, Winter 1998–9). The agreement is also discussed in Raynard (1999).

19. For a discussion of the Agreement and its impact on Inuit governance, see Hicks and White (2001).

20. The Native Women's Association of Canada was excluded and vehemently opposed the Accord during the ensuing referendum. See Turpel (1993).

21. The five major national organizations were directly involved in defining the agenda of the meeting and in the administrative process that laid the ground for the agreement. For more details on the Kelowna summit, see <www.scics. gc.ca/cinfo05/800044004_e.pdf> (accessed 29 April 2006).

22. At the time of writing, the agreement had just been ratified. See <www.ainc-inac.gc.ca/nr/prs/m-a2006/2-02773_e.html> (accessed 7 July 2006).

23. The Auditor General (2002) estimates that band councils are required to produce an average of 202 reports to various federal agencies each year under the most common of existing funding arrangements.

References

Abele, F., and M. Prince. 2003. 'Alternative Futures: Aboriginal Peoples and Canadian Federalism'. In *Canadian Federalism: Performance, Effectiveness and Legitimacy*, ed. H. Bakvis and G. Skogstad. Toronto: Oxford University Press.

Alfred, T. 1998. *Peace, Power and Righteousness: An Indigenous Manifesto*. Toronto: Oxford University Press.

Asch, M. 2002. 'From Tierra Nullius to Affirmation: Reconciling Aboriginal Rights with the Canadian Constitution', *Canadian Journal of Law and Society* 17, 2: 23–39.

Borrows, J. 2002. *Recovering Canada: the Resurgence of Indigenous Law*. Toronto: University of Toronto Press.

Brock, K. 1991. 'The Politics of Aboriginal Self-Government: A Canadian

Paradox', *Canadian Public Administration* 34, 2: 272–85.

Cairns, A. 2000. *Citizens Plus: Aboriginal Peoples and the State*. Vancouver: University of British Columbia Press.

Canada, Auditor General. 2002. *Streamlining First Nations Reporting to Federal Organizations, Auditor General's December 2002 Report, Chapter 1*. Ottawa: Minister of Supply and Services.

———, Department of Indian Affairs and Northern Development. 1997. *Gathering Strength: Canada's Aboriginal Action Plan*. Ottawa: Minister of Supply and Services. Available online at: <www.ainc-inac.gc.ca/gs/chg_e.html>.

———, Indian and Northern Affairs Canada. 2003. *Comprehensive Land Claim Policy and Status of Claims*. Ottawa: Comprehensive Claims Branch, Indian and Northern Affairs Canada. Available online at: <www.ainc-inac.gc.ca/ps/clm/brieft_e.html>.

———, Indian and Northern Affairs Canada. 2004. *Basic Departmental Data 2003*. Ottawa: Minister of Public Works and Government Services Canada. Available online at: <www.ainc-inac.gc.ca/pr/sts/bdd03/bdd03_e.html>.

———, Statistics Canada. 2003. *Aboriginal Peoples of Canada. A Demographic Profile (2001 Census Analysis Series)*. Cat. No. 96F0030XIE2001007. Ottawa: Statistics Canada.

Dacks, G. 2001. 'The Social Union Framework Agreement and the Role of Aboriginal Peoples in Canadian Federalism', *The American Review of Canadian Studies* 31, 2: 301–15.

Henderson, S. 1994. 'Empowering Treaty Federalism', *Saskatchewan Law Review* 58, 2: 242–71.

Hicks, J. and G. White. 2001. 'Nunavut : Inuit Self-Determination through a Land Claim and Public Government?' In *The Provincial State in Canada*, ed. K. Brownsey and M. Howlett. Peterborough, Ont.: Broadview Press.

Ladner, K. 2003. 'Treaty Federalism: An Indigenous Vision of Canadian Federalisms'. In *New Trends in Canadian Federalism*, 2nd edn, ed. F. Rocher and M. Smith. Peterborough: Broadview Press.

Long, J., and M. Boldt. 1988. *Governments in Conflict? Provinces and Indian Nations in Canada*. Toronto: University of Toronto Press.

Macklem, P. 2001. *Indigenous difference and the Constitution of Canada*. Toronto: University of Toronto Press.

Maclure, J. 2005. 'Définir les droits constitutionnels des peuples autochtones. Une évaluation normative de la "nouvelle" approche du Québec', *Éthique publique* 17, 1: 35–62.

Neu, D., and R. Therrien. 2003. *Accounting for Genocide: Canada's Bureaucratic Assault on Aboriginal People*. London: Zed Press.

Pierre J. and G. Peters. 2000. *Governance, Politics and the State*. New York: Oxford University Press.

Raynard, P. 1999. 'Welcome In, but Check Your Rights at the Door: The James Bay and Nisga'a Agreements in Canada', *Canadian Journal of Political Science* 33, 2: 211–43.

Royal Commission on Aboriginal Peoples (RCAP). 1996. *Report of the Royal Commission on Aboriginal Peoples*, 5 vols. Ottawa: Communication Group Publishing.

Royal Commission on Electoral Reform and Party Financing (RCER). 1991. *Reforming Electoral Democracy*. Ottawa: Supply and Services Canada.

Schouls, T. 1996. 'Aboriginal Peoples and Electoral Reform in Canada: Differentiated Representation versus Voter Equality', *Canadian Journal of Political Science* 29, 4: 729–49.

Tully, J. 1995. *Strange Multiplicity. Constitutionalism in an Age of Diversity*. Cambridge: Cambridge University Press.

———. 2000. 'The Struggles of Indigenous Peoples for and of Freedom'. In *Political Theory and the Rights of Indigenous Peoples*, ed. D. Ivison, P. Patton, and W. Sanders. Cambridge: Cambridge University Press.

———. 2001. 'Reconsidering the BC Treaty Process'. In *Speaking Truth to Power: A Treaty Forum*, ed. Law Commission of Canada. Ottawa: Minister of Public Works and Government Services Canada.

Turpel, M. E. 1993. 'The Charlottetown Discord and Aboriginal Peoples' Struggle for Fundamental Political Change'. In *The Charlottetown Accord, the Referendum, and the Future of Canada*, ed. K. McRoberts and P. Monahan. Toronto: University of Toronto Press.

Cases

A.G. Ontario v. A.G. Canada (1912), A.C. 571
Delgamuukw v. British Columbia (1997), 3 S.C.R. 1010.
Pamajewon (1996), 2 S.C.R. 164.
R. v. Marshall (1999), 3 S.C.R. 456.
R. v. Sparrow (1990), 1 S.C.R. 1075.
R. v. Van der Peet (1996), 2 S.C.R. 507.

Websites

Aboriginal News Network: www.aborinews.com
Assembly of First Nations (AFN): www.afn.ca
Congress of Aboriginal Peoples: www.abo-peoples.org
Indian and Northern Affairs Canada (INAC): www.inac.gc.ca
Indigenous Peoples and Governance Research Project: www.pag-ipg.com/en/index.htm
Inuit Tapiriit Kanatami: www.itk.ca
Métis National Council: www.metisnation.ca
Treaties and Agreements in Canada: www.ainc-inac.gc.ca/pr/agr/index_e.html

Glossary

First Nations: The majority of Aboriginal peoples in Canada. There are approximately 40 to 60 historic nations in Canada, divided into nearly 700 bands. They are still sometimes referred to as 'Indians'.

Inherent right to self-government: The right of Aboriginal peoples to govern themselves, based on their historical presence as distinctly constituted nations prior to the establishment of Crown sovereignty in what is now Canada.

Inuit: Aboriginal people living in the Circumpolar North. In Canada, they mostly live in Nunavut, where they form a majority, in Nunavik (northern Quebec), and in Labrador. Inuit were excluded from the Indian Act.

Métis: The descendants of early unions between Europeans settlers (mostly French) and First Nations people. They also are not governed under the Indian Act.

Non-status Indians: Members of First Nations communities, often living in urban areas, who are not covered by the Indian Act.

Treaty federalism: Federal association between sovereign Aboriginal nations and the Canadian state based on the negotiation of agreements amongst equal partners that have a status equivalent to international treaties.

Third order of government: The recognition of Aboriginal governing authorities as a legally distinct order of government within the Canadian Constitution.

Chapter 15

The Urban Agenda

Andrew Sancton

All three levels of government have been profoundly important to Canadian cities for many decades. This situation is unlikely to change anytime soon. Our cities, this chapter will argue, would be better served if our elected politicians at all three levels focused their attention on working together within their own spheres of jurisdiction to tackle the real urban problems, rather than involving themselves excessively in attempts to rearrange their various roles and responsibilities.

Municipalities have not often been thought of as being part of the Canadian federal system. The first section of this chapter, by contrasting the role of municipalities in American and Canadian federalism, explains why this has been so. Although recently there has been much discussion about why municipalities merit more attention from the federal government, the second section of this chapter demonstrates that federal involvement with municipalities is nothing new. The third section outlines Paul Martin's 'new deal for cities' and the next briefly outlines how the Harper government is approaching cities. The concluding section addresses some of the underlying reasons why, despite the growing importance of cities in Canada, their municipal governments are unlikely ever to become full partners in the Canadian federation. The conclusion also links the urban agenda to the themes of this book: the performance, effectiveness, and legitimacy of the Canadian federal system.

Municipalities and the Canadian Federation

Municipalities, together with local special-purpose bodies, comprise the Canadian system of local government. The words 'local' and 'government' are both crucial to understanding the nature of municipalities. In the Canadian context, 'local' means any specified territory that is smaller than that of the province in which it is located. In most cases, the territories of local governments are much smaller, often including only the built-up areas of small villages.

The term 'government' is more problematic. Everyone accepts that such central institutions as parliaments and ministries are part of 'government'. But what about incorporated companies that are similar to privately owned companies in all respects except that they are owned by the government? This question is answered in different countries—and often even within the same country—in different ways. If such definitional issues are difficult at the central level, they are even more so at the local level, in part because, for English-language countries at least, the historical origins of what we now know as 'local government' are just as closely connected to private corporations as to government.

In English constitutional theory, the government always acts in the name of the monarch. The institutions that today we label as 'local governments' began as municipal corporations. Such corporations were essentially private: Parliament vested a self-perpetuating governing body with the authority to establish certain public institutions (such as marketplaces), to pay for them through specified levies, and to make appropriate regulations to facilitate their operation. Whatever authority they possessed derived from Parliament, but they did not act in the name of the monarch. To this day in Britain (and Canada), the central government is Her Majesty's government and all its actions are carried out in her name. Local governments in Britain are now very much public, governmental institutions, but they still possess a corporate legal form and they still do not act on behalf of the monarch. Local governments in North America have followed a similar evolutionary pattern (Hartog, 1983).

Even when municipal corporations and their successors are clearly defined in law as public and democratic institutions, it is still sometimes difficult to know what aspects of their operations form part of the government. This problem of defining what municipal governments do has become especially obvious in recent years as the tenets of New Public Management have become more popular and local governments have become increasingly involved in various forms of partnerships with each other and with private enterprise. Some observers have labelled such arrangements as 'governance' because they are much looser and more flexible than the rigid hierarchies and defined accountabilities usually associated with traditional departments of government. Governance arrangements are often extremely difficult to classify as either public or private.

Nevertheless, bearing in mind the definition of 'local' that has already been discussed, it is possible to list the following core characteristics of local governments:

- They are distinct legal entities rather than administrative subdivisions of some other entity.
- They are controlled by a governing body most of whose members are local citizens.

- They have some form of legally defined access to public funds or to publicly regulated fees.
- They have some degree of decision-making autonomy with respect to at least one aspect of public policy within their defined territory.
- Apart from the governing body itself, they have no other forms of membership; all eligible residents of the defined territory are automatically under their jurisdiction with respect to their defined responsibility.

This is a broad approach to the definition of 'local government'. It allows us to include institutions that are much more specialized than municipalities, whose distinguishing characteristics are that the members of their governing bodies are usually popularly elected and that they are at least partially responsible for a wide range of public services, everything from garbage collection to recreational programs for children. Special-purpose bodies, on the other hand, often have appointed governing bodies and are always responsible only for a particular public function or set of closely related functions.

Among all the world's liberal democracies, one could probably find that almost any conceivable function of government is somewhere carried out, at least in part, by a local government. There can be no theory about which level of government is—or should be—involved in any particular function. There are, however, theories about which level of government—central or local—is likely to be more effective in setting broad, enforceable policies with respect to particular functions. For example, it is generally acknowledged that income-support policies are best set at the federal or provincial level (Peterson, 1981). Doing so forces upper-income residents of rich municipalities to contribute to the cost of such policies even if their own areas contain few poor people. Similarly, it makes sense that central governments would create rules about environmental protection. Otherwise, particular municipalities could simply pass on their pollution to their neighbours through prevailing winds and river flows. But there is no strong reason why, subject to central control, local governments could not be responsible for delivering or enforcing such centrally made policies.

At the other end of the spectrum are government functions that seem especially amenable to autonomous local decision-making. An example might be the provision of public open spaces (often the site of civic ceremonies and outside special events) and decorative urban parks. It is hard to imagine any reason why a central (provincial) government would have any interest in such matters. Nevertheless, chances are that somewhere, sometime, there has been a central-government program that, under certain conditions, has provided funds to local authorities to help improve the quality of urban life or promote local economic development by subsidizing the cost of providing urban public spaces.

A vast range of public services and regulatory regimes are often the responsibility of local governments. Disputes about which level of government should do what with respect to a particular function are common and are part of the everyday give-and-take of democratic politics. Sometimes proponents of a particular view can advance good technical reasons for their position. Usually, however, participants in these debates are trying to promote a particular policy outcome rather than being concerned in the abstract about what government is better suited to the task at hand. In any event, there appears to be a strong view among Canadians that municipal governments are and should be especially concerned with matters relating to the regulation and servicing of property: zoning, local roads, sewers, water supply, and parks, for example (Lorimer, 1972).

Under both the American and Canadian federal constitutions, municipal institutions come under the formal jurisdiction of states and provinces. But in the United States the federal system is commonly conceptualized as a partnership between the federal government, on the one hand, and 'state and local' governments, on the other. There are at least two interconnected reasons why 'provincial and local' is not a common term in Canadian political discourse.

First, unlike American states, Canadian provinces do not have their own distinct written constitutions (Cameron, 1980). In the constitutions of the various American states, local government receives at least some form of constitutional recognition and protection. In many states, the municipal governments of the larger cities are guaranteed a form of 'home rule', which prevents the state legislature from changing local municipal boundaries, functions, and structures without some form of local consent. In this context, the term 'state and local' makes perfect sense: in any particular state, the basic structures of both the state government and the various local governments are established under the authority of the same state constitution. In Canada, on the other hand, the provincial legislatures established by the Constitution of Canada can alter all aspects of a province's governmental structure except for the office of lieutenant-governor. Canadian municipalities thus have no established form of constitutional protection whatever. They have not been recognized as being in any sense equal to provincial governments.

The second reason why we seldom use the term 'provincial and local' in Canada is that our federation is in part held together by the notion that provincial governments collectively possess at least equal political status with the federal government. This notion is itself closely connected to the recognition that the Quebec National Assembly has a special responsibility to advance and protect Quebec's distinct French-speaking character. Anyone in Canada who in any way equates a municipal council with the Quebec National Assembly is, at a minimum, using highly controversial political language. If Quebec's legislature cannot be considered in any way like a municipal council, neither can the legislature of any other province.

Previous Urban Agendas

Canada's first 'urban agenda' was advanced by the Unionist government of Sir Robert Borden in the aftermath of World War I. In late 1918, following the return of Canadian soldiers, housing became a major national issue. Under the authority of the War Measures Act, the federal government loaned $25 million to the provinces for 25 years at 5 per cent interest. The money was to be granted mainly to municipalities willing to construct new housing for sale at cost, but limited-dividend housing societies and lot-owners building houses for their own personal occupancy could also benefit. Other relevant federal restrictions were that land should be purchased 'without regard to speculative value'; not more than 10 per cent of the cost of any house should derive from the cost of the land; 10 per cent of all land purchased should be reserved for playgrounds; water and sewage should be supplied before construction; and all houses should meet specified minimum standards of construction (Canada, 1919: 55). Ontario responded in April 1919 with the passage of the Ontario Housing Act, which outlined the conditions under which municipalities could gain access to the federal funds (Sancton and Montgomery, 1994: 765). Significantly, the federal conditions laid down in 1918 for providing funds to municipalities were tougher and more detailed than any conditions in place today. In this sense there was more federal involvement in urban policy then than there is today.

The next federal initiative did not emerge until the Great Depression. In 1935 Parliament approved the Dominion Housing Act authorizing the federal government to share up to a quarter of the value of individual mortgage loans with approved lenders and to set housing standards as a condition for federal involvement. In 1937 amendments were approved to allow for federal participation in loans for home improvements and in 1938 the Act was replaced by the National Housing Act, which also provided for federal loans to builders of low-rental family housing. Such loans were never taken up because they required that provinces or municipalities limit taxes on such properties and guarantee operating losses (Axworthy, 1972: 30).

In another attempt to ease unemployment, Parliament in 1938 approved the Municipal Improvements Assistance Act, which provided low-interest loans to municipalities to reinvest in their physical infrastructure. Writing about this legislation in 1975, David Bettison commented that

> The constitutional problem of financial responsibility for local authorities was met by having the provincial governments approve each local authority's project and also guarantee to the Dominion the repayment of the loan and amortization charges to the municipality. . . . The maximum limit of federal funds was fixed at $30 million and the distribution among municipalities was to be determined by the ratio of a municipality's 1931 census population to the population of the dominion at that date (Bettison, 1975: 67–8).

During World War II, the federal government allocated space, administered rent controls, and directly provided housing to employees of war-related industries. Such obvious involvement in matters under direct provincial jurisdiction could not survive the end of the war. Parliament approved more housing legislation in both 1944 and 1945. The 1944 Act provided that the federal government could pay 50 per cent of municipal costs of what was soon to be called 'slum clearance'. The 1945 Act established the Central Mortgage and Housing Corporation (CMHC) as a Crown corporation to administer the federal government's involvement in housing. Its expenses were covered by its income from loans and from the provision of mortgage insurance to private lenders.

After 1949 amendments allowed the federal government to cover up to 75 per cent of the costs of low-rental public housing. Demands that the federal government use its superior financial resources to end the shame of urban slums and overcrowding were similar to today's claims that only the federal government is able to finance the massive expenditures to solve our cities' infrastructure deficits. Perhaps the major difference is that large-scale public housing projects were more controversial. Nevertheless, the federal Liberals under Prime Ministers King and St Laurent were clearly supportive. Together with Premier Duplessis of Quebec, they built during the mid-1950s the massive Habitations Jeanne-Mance in downtown Montreal over the strong objections of first-term mayor Jean Drapeau (Black, 1977: 401–2), who did not believe that any level of government should own housing, especially large apartment buildings that he felt were unsuitable for families. Sponsorship of 'urban renewal' placed the federal government at the heart of some of the great urban conflicts of the late 1950s and 1960s (Fraser, 1972).

At the same time the federal government, after provincial approval, continued to make direct loans to municipalities for infrastructure improvement. This practice was further institutionalized and expanded in 1963 when the Pearson government sponsored the Municipal Development and Loan Board Act. Premier Lesage of Quebec objected strenuously but the federal government proceeded anyway. The Act stayed in force until 1968 (Bettison, 1975: 150–2).

Opposition to urban renewal was sparked more by displaced residents than by the kind of ideological or moral concerns advanced by Mayor Drapeau in Montreal. In any event, by the mid-1960s urban issues were squarely on the national agenda, in part because American cities were literally being torched by urban protestors but also because no one knew how middle-class Canadian adult baby boomers were going to be housed. Shortly after taking office as prime minister in 1968, Pierre Elliott Trudeau agreed to let his deputy prime minister, Paul Hellyer, chair a federal Task Force on Housing and Urban Development. The Hellyer Task Force is surely the high-water mark for apparent federal interest in urban affairs. Its members toured the country (shepherded by Hellyer's executive assistant, Lloyd Axworthy) hearing deputations from all kinds of groups about issues deeply within provincial and municipal jurisdiction. The Task Force did not hesitate to make recommendations that directly intruded into spheres of provincial jurisdiction. Some examples are:

- Municipalities or regional governments, as a matter of continuing policy, should acquire, service, and sell all or a substantial portion of the land required for urban growth within their boundaries.

- The federal government should make direct loans to municipalities or regional governments to assist in assembling and servicing land for urban growth (Canada, 1969: 43).
- The federal government should make loans to municipalities to acquire dispersed existing housing for use by low-income groups (ibid., 57).
- Since urban planning can be done effectively only on a regional basis, the provinces should establish a system of regional governments, equipped with adequate powers for each major area (ibid., 63).
- The federal government, in co-operation with a provincial government, should seriously consider the construction of a 'new city' as a pilot project where proposed urban solutions could be tested in an actual environment (ibid., 75).

The report was made public in late January 1969. In late April Hellyer resigned from the cabinet because Prime Minister Trudeau refused to take any action on it, even on recommendations that were clearly within federal jurisdiction (Axworthy, 1972: 240). Instead, in 1971 the federal government created the Ministry of State for Urban Affairs, an agency with no direct administrative responsibilities but with a mandate to co-ordinate federal government activities in Canada's cities. The various problems of the Urban Affairs ministry have been well documented (Cameron, 1974; Feldman and Milch, 1981). A sympathetic account by a former senior official listed the following well-known urban projects as having been 'studied, proposed, and shepherded' by the ministry:

- the Waterfront Development in Halifax
- the Civic Centre and City Square in St John's, Newfoundland
- the Vieux-Port in Montreal
- Harbourfront in Toronto
- the cancellation of Transport Canada's plan for an international airport in Pickering
- the Trizec complex in Winnipeg
- the Rideau Canal waterway in Ontario
- Granville Island in Vancouver
- the Lachine Canal redevelopment in Quebec
- the railroad relocation projects in Regina (Saumier, 1987: 44).

Even allowing for some self-congratulatory hyperbole and recognizing that most of these projects took place on federally owned lands, this is remarkable evidence of direct federal involvement in the shaping of Canadian cities. Nevertheless, the ministry was abolished as a symbolic cost-cutting measure. By this time, it had many enemies, but no friends (Feldman and Milch, 1981: 259).

One of the ministry's major innovations—not seen before or since—was its sponsorship of national tri-level conferences. Ironically, the very creation of the ministry probably slowed a planning process for such conferences that had been underway for some time. The ministry's existence caused provincial politicians to hesitate, fearing new federal jurisdictional incursions. National tri-level conferences were held in 1972 and 1973. A third was scheduled for 1976 but was cancelled by provincial ministers of municipal affairs. Then, as now, municipalities were pushing for new tax sources and saw the tri-level conference as the ideal forum to make their case. They were not successful. Regional and local tri-level conferences were also held and led to some real results, Winnipeg probably being the best example (Feldman and Graham, 1979: 29–58).

Urban issues did not reappear on the federal agenda until the 1990s. However, on the basis of apparently unrelated federal initiatives involving urban land and infrastructure, housing, and security, Caroline Andrew wrote in the early 1990s that 'one could claim' federal influence on major urban centres 'was more profound in the 1980s than in previous periods' (Andrew, 1994: 430). The famous 'Red Book', containing the Liberal platform for the federal election of 1993, committed a government led by Jean Chrétien to spend $6 billion over two years, in co-operation with provinces and municipalities, to upgrade transportation and local services. The promise was the culmination of 10 years of lobbying by the Federation of Canadian Municipalities (FCM) to obtain federal funding for the municipal 'infrastructure deficit' (Andrew and Morrison, 1995: 108). After winning office, the new government quickly negotiated infrastructure agreements with each of the provinces and territories, specifying how much was to be spent and on what kinds of projects. The FCM was mildly concerned that in some provinces not all the money went to municipal projects and some media outlets focused on a few seemingly frivolous expenditures (ibid., 133). Generally, however, the program was a political success for the government and was consequently renewed in one form or another until the end of Chrétien's prime ministership in 2003.

Paul Martin's New Deal for Cities and Communities

In the same way that the FCM lobbied for tri-level conferences in the 1970s and infrastructure funds in the late 1980s and early 1990s, for the past 10 years it has been lobbying for a much broader 'urban agenda'. In responding to the FCM's agenda, Paul Martin found one way to distinguish his policies for Canada from those of his Liberal rival, Jean Chrétien. The campaign for infrastructure funds involved a relatively specialized and technical set of issues that was mainly restricted to political insiders. But the campaign for a new urban agenda was designed to capture public attention in a much more dramatic and politically effective way. Cities featured on the national political agenda in the late 1960s and early 1970s because there was a real fear that they would be subject to the same cycles of decay, violence, and territorial inequalities that American cities had been experiencing. Now the concern is that cities are crucial for global economic competitiveness and that Canadian cities might not have whatever it takes to be successful, especially in relation to American cities. In the 1960s American cities were the horrible example; now their economic dynamism is threatening Canadian complacency.

Concern about the state of Canadian cities has come from banks (TD Bank Financial Group, 2002), think-tanks (especially the Canadian Policy Research Networks, e.g., Bradford, 2005), academics (Young and Leuprecht, 2006), consultants (Berridge, 2002), and from research sponsored directly by the FCM itself (Federation of Canadian Municipalities, 2005). Most of the concern is about money. There are at least four different variants of this concern:

1. There has been insufficient societal investment in urban infrastructure, including infrastructure associated with such vital urban institutions as hospitals, universities, research institutes, museums, and other cultural facilities.
2. The Canadian tax system extracts more than is appropriate from urban areas to redistribute and invest in small towns and rural areas.
3. Compared with other advanced industrialized countries, the national government makes very limited contributions to the capital and operating budgets of urban municipalities.
4. Urban municipalities have insufficient capacity to raise money themselves because they are generally restricted to taxes on real property and user charges.

The federal government, even if it wanted to, cannot fix all of these problems because of the important role of the provinces. In particular, it can do nothing about the fourth concern. What follows is a discussion of some of the issues that have been raised about potential federal involvement.

Infrastructure

The FCM has experienced continued success in pressing the case for increased federal funding of municipal infrastructure. Its claim that there is a $60 billion 'infrastructure deficit' is often cited as justification for such funding. Infrastructure Canada states that there is now about $7.65 billion available in federal funds for four distinct programs funding various kinds of local infrastructure (Canada, 2006a). All such funding requires provincial approval for each individual project.

Such funding is rarely criticized (but see Mintz and Roberts, 2004). At least one particular infrastructure issue, however, merits further consideration: federal spending on water purification plants. Such spending subsidizes the provision of drinking water. But almost all policy analysts, representing a wide spectrum of ideological views, seem to agree that individual consumers should be paying the full cost of the water they consume. In his *Report of the Walkerton Inquiry*, Mr Justice O'Connor wrote: 'As a general principle, municipalities should plan to raise adequate resources for their local water systems, barring exceptional circumstances.' O'Connor discusses briefly how such 'exceptional circumstances' might be defined, and it is clear that the availability of federal infrastructure funds is not one of them (Ontario, 2002: 312). Even if one were to argue that some small communities can only survive with capital subsidies for updated water purification facilities, it is obvious that such an argument does not apply, for example, to the City of Montreal. Nevertheless, the Canadian Strategic Infrastructure Fund has committed $58.5 million to Montreal's Atwater and Charles-J. Des Baillets water treatment plants (Canada, 2006a). The problem in Montreal is not that consumers cannot afford to pay for water. Rather, most of them do not have water meters. If the federal government is going to subsidize the water-supply system in Montreal, surely it could begin by subsidizing the installation of meters.

Urban vs Rural

The original argument here—most articulately advanced by Joe Berridge (2002: 15–17)—was that Canada's federal and provincial legislatures pay far more attention to rural issues than is warranted by the size of the rural population. He presented data showing that more big cities are under-represented in the House of Commons and that there are more references in debate to rural problems than to urban ones. The argument is that an 'urban agenda' is needed to counteract the inherent anti-urban bias within the normal political process. Whatever one thinks about this argument, it is clear that the Martin government ultimately did not accept it. The original idea of a 'New Deal for Cities' emerged from the policy process as the 'New Deal for Communities', a notable semantic shift, and there is no evidence that the federal government is in any way requiring provinces to privilege urban municipalities over rural ones.

Berridge's concern about urban representation in the House of Commons is justified. The main problem is that the less populous provinces and territories—which almost by definition are more rural—are overrepresented in the House of Commons. There is still a bias *within* each province's membership in the House of Commons in favour of rural areas, but this has decreased markedly over the last few decades (Courtney, 2001). A constitutional amendment would be necessary to remove the special protection of smaller provinces and open the door to fairer representation of urban voters. Significantly, the Conservatives have promised to 'Restore representation by population for Ontario, British Columbia, and Alberta in the House of Commons while protecting the seat count of smaller provinces' (Conservative Party, 2005: 44). The federal Parliament can act alone to make this change, as long as it does not produce a scheme in which a province ends up with fewer MPs than senators. However, the inevitable result will be a significantly larger House of Commons. Despite their alleged attachment to cities, the Liberal Party in government never addressed this issue of urban under-representation. If the Conservatives follow through on their promise, they could well end up doing more for the political strength of voters in the city-regions of Toronto, Vancouver, Calgary, Edmonton, and Ottawa than anything accomplished by the Liberals.

Federal Financial Support

As we have seen, a significant level of federal support has come through the various infrastructure programs. In 2004, the federal government decided to refund to municipalities all of the money they spend on GST for the purchase of goods and services. Over 10 years, this is supposed to provide Canadian municipalities with $7 billion that they otherwise would not have had (Canada, 2005).

In its 2005 budget, the Liberal government promised that municipalities would begin receiving a share of the federal tax on gasoline, such that by 2010 they would be receiving five cents per litre (the federal tax, exclusive of the GST, is 10 cents per litre). The money is being channelled to the municipalities in accordance with the terms of federal–provincial agreements and is allocated to provinces on a per capita basis. The Ontario government allowed the federal government to negotiate directly with the Association of Municipalities of Ontario and the City of Toronto; Ontario is the only province that is not a party to one of the agreements. The funds are to be used 'to support environmentally sustainable infrastructure projects such as public transit, water and wastewater treatment, community energy systems and the handling of solid waste' (ibid.). For municipalities under 500,000 in population, the funds could also be used for roads.

Finally, the 2005 budget added $300 million to the $200 million already committed to Green Municipal Funds administered by the FCM. These funds 'provide grants, low-interest loans and innovative financing to increase investment in infrastructure projects that deliver cleaner air, water, and soil, and climate protection' (ibid.).

Apart from the GST relief, the new federal funding does not have an immediate impact on municipal operating budgets. In theory, most of the funding is supposed to be for capital expenditures that municipalities would not otherwise have incurred. It is highly unlikely, however, that the federal government will be able to enforce such a requirement. In reality, the federal money will simply substitute for at least some planned municipal capital expenditure. In other cases, it will cause municipal plans to be accelerated. Such funding is aimed at improving the quality of life in Canadian communities, not at reducing municipal tax rates. To some extent, however, the new funding will reduce total borrowing in the future and therefore will eventually serve to reduce borrowing costs that otherwise would have had to be absorbed through the local property tax. But federal funding of this kind does not solve the municipal fiscal problems about which big-city mayors have long been complaining.

New Sources of Revenue

The concern of big-city mayors has been that they are excessively reliant on the property tax. Unlike many of their American counterparts, Canadian central-city municipalities receive no income tax revenues from suburban commuters and no sales tax revenue from tourists. In comprehensive visions of a 'new deal' for Canadian cities, this problem would be addressed. There is no shortage of consultants' reports calling for wide-ranging changes in the fiscal system such that Canadian city governments would be net gainers (Slack, 2004). The fact is, however, that the federal government can do little or nothing to grant cities new taxation authority. In theory, Ottawa could share more tax revenue with municipalities, following the model worked out with the gasoline tax. Or it could lower the rates for certain taxes after extracting ironclad guarantees from provinces that they would legislate to allow municipalities to move into the fiscal territory from which the federal government withdrew. But neither prospect is very likely. The provinces inevitably will claim, with considerable justification, that fixing their 'fiscal imbalance' with Ottawa is the immediate priority, not some elaborate scheme to have the federal government come to the aid of municipalities. The road to new sources of revenue for Canadian municipalities runs through provincial capitals, not Ottawa.

In addition to lobbying for money, the FCM and big-city mayors have been arguing that they deserve 'a voice at the national table'. In its 2005 budget, the Liberal government responded with soothing words:

> The government is consistently seeking new ways to involve Canada's municipal governments in the decision-making process on national issues that directly affect their interests. The proposed new Department of Infrastructure and Communities will be the Government of Canada's primary contact for municipal issues. In addition, the Minister of Finance has formally met with municipal decision-makers as part of his pre-budget consultations and is committed to do so again for future budgets. The Government will continue to seek further opportunities for dialogue with municipal leaders, while respecting provincial and territorial jurisdiction (Canada, 2005).

Such words were hardly a clarion call for a new form of tri-level Canadian federalism. But Canadians were never to learn what, if anything, they meant. Within a few months, the government lost the confidence of the House of Commons, and early in 2006 it lost the ensuing election.

'Open Federalism' and the Urban Agenda

In *Stand Up for Canada*, its platform for the 2006 election, the Conservative Party of Canada included a separate section entitled 'Stand Up for Our Communities'. Under 'Improving Canada's National Infrastructure' the Conservatives stated:

> Infrastructure is a crucial investment in our economic productivity and quality of life. Suburban commuters should not have to sit on gridlocked highways. Truckers carrying cargo vital to Canada's economy should not have to dodge potholes for much of the year. The Liberals have committed to funding municipal infrastructure, but roads, highways, and border crossings never seem to keep up. A Conservative government will have a better approach to fixing Canada's infrastructure deficit (Conservative Party, 2005: 36).

The Conservatives went on to promise that they would maintain municipal funding committed to by the Liberals and that they would 'Expand the New Deal to allow all cities and communities, including cities with more than 500,000 people, to use gas transfer dollars to build and repair roads and bridges to improve road safety and fight traffic congestion' (ibid., 38). Although the Conservatives also promised to 'Give public transit riders a federal tax credit to cover the cost of their monthly transit passes' (ibid., 39), it is clear that the main thrust of their infrastructure policy was to make it easier for municipalities to use federal funds for roads, a policy aimed obviously more at their suburban political supporters than at residents of the inner cities. The Conservatives' political connection to suburbia has important implications for analyzing the role of cities in Canadian federalism, a subject to be addressed in the next and concluding section of this chapter.

More important than the Conservatives' particular promise about communities is their general approach to relations with the provinces. In their election platform the Conservatives referred to their approach as 'Open Federalism' (ibid., 42). Once elected, Prime Minister Harper developed the concept in somewhat greater detail during a speech in Montreal in April 2006. Although not referring to anything related to the 'urban agenda', he stated that

> Open federalism means respecting areas of provincial jurisdiction. Open federalism means limiting the use of the federal spending power, which the federal Liberals abused—much to the dismay of all hard-working, tax-paying Canadians (Canada, 2006b).

This is one piece of evidence that the Conservatives will not be expanding 'the urban agenda'. Another is that Harper did not appoint a separate minister for infrastructure and communities. Instead, the minister of Transport adds these responsibilities to an already large portfolio.

As with all federal governments, many policies and actions of the Harper government can be expected to have profound impacts on the quality of life in Canadian cities in general, and certain decisions will have a particularly strong impact on particular cities, either by design or by accident. To the extent that the government is genuinely concerned about the fate of cities, it will attempt to filter its policy analysis through an 'urban lens' such that unanticipated negative consequences for cities of particular policies are minimized and potential positive urban effects are maximized. What the Harper government surely will not do is to proclaim its own distinct 'urban agenda'. Federal involvement in Canadian cities will inevitably continue and evolve but, for all practical purposes, the days of the federal 'urban agenda' are over.

Cities and Federalism

The important issues about the relevance of cities for Canadian federalism do not relate to the details of federal funding for particular municipal projects or exactly how the federal government organizes itself to manage its involvement in city issues. What is important is the possibility that the increasing significance of cities for our economic and social life will lead to profound changes in the structure of our federation. Anyone reading the work of such varied authors as Jane Jacobs (1984), Kenichi Ohmae (1995), Neal Peirce (1993), and Tom Courchene (2005) might think it will. Even the well-known Canadian historian Michael Bliss has recently wondered about the country evolving 'into a league of provinces, and perhaps a sprinkling of city-states, some of these jurisdictions effectively independent' (Bliss, 2006).

Speculating in this way has its value. But it is time to subject such thinking to some serious analysis before we all get carried away with futuristic fantasies—or romantic nostalgia for the Italian city-states of the fifteenth century. Can cities somehow become as important as provinces? Will some even secede from provinces and effectively become provinces themselves? If not, then we need not be concerned that the growing economic importance of cities will somehow change the nature of Canadian federalism.

My argument is that, in Canada and other Western liberal democracies, cities will not become like provinces; they will not become independent units of government. In short, they will generally *not* become city-states. This kind of self-government requires a territory delimited by official boundaries. For cities, unlike sovereign states and provinces, the boundaries will never be static, will never be acceptable to all, and will always be contested. Boundaries fatally limit the capacity of cities to be self-governing.

It should be apparent already that, in using the word 'cities', I am *not* referring to central-city municipalities that carry the name of their 'city-region'. This distinction is the source of much confusion and difficulty. There *are* examples of populous city-regions comprising only one municipality but, for fast-growing city-regions at least, the boundaries of such a municipality will always be problematic. The much more common pattern, especially in North America, is for city-regions to comprise dozens, or even hundreds, of municipalities. Making central-city municipalities—and perhaps also their surrounding suburbs—more autonomous does nothing except reify existing boundaries that are invariably seen as arbitrary, outdated, discriminatory, and irrelevant; but to focus on the economic and social reality of a city means focusing on the city-region as a whole—and determining its territorial extent for the purposes of self-government is not a practical proposition.

Arguing that cities cannot be self-governing might seem unnecessary. A much more common concern is that cities are hardly self-governing at all, and need release from the dead hand of central regulation. I am highly sympathetic to such a concern, but have become worried about the implications—and confusions— relating to many of the arguments (and inflated rhetoric) about more autonomy for cities. They take us down a path that, in my view, can ultimately be damaging for cities, if for no other reason than that they divert valuable resources to fruitless undertakings, much like searching for the end of a rainbow.

Residents of some Canadian cities (Calgary, Winnipeg, Regina, Saskatoon, and Halifax, for example) can point out that their municipalities actually do include almost all the residents of their respective city-regions, as such regions are defined by Statistics Canada. But the fastest growing of these cities is Calgary and it is clearly facing territorial problems. For decades it has continually annexed contiguous land so as to ensure a steady stream of new developable land. But the City of Calgary is also surrounded by non-contiguous *urban* municipalities. Such places as Airdrie, Crossfield, Cochrane, Chestermere, and Okotoks are growing even faster than Calgary itself. The more Calgary grows, the more these places will grow and the more they will become integrated into the urban area focused on Calgary as the central city. The strategic choice that the City of Calgary faces is whether it will work co-operatively with these urban governments or whether its ultimate objective will be to absorb them as part of a continuing commitment to a rigid model of continuing annexation.

All the great, growing cities of the world eventually expand in such a way that their influence starts to impinge on neighbouring communities that were once quite distinct. But no central governments in the Western world, as a matter of consistent, ongoing policy, provide for central cities to absorb systematically their urban-based municipal neighbours. Even Ontario, one of the most interventionist jurisdictions with respect to municipal boundaries and structures, has not followed such a policy for Toronto; hence the continued existence of Mississauga, with a current population of close to 700,000.

Toronto is Canada's most likely candidate for city-state status. Precisely because the city does have a large territory, a substantial population, and significant fiscal resources, it is at least possible to imagine a disgruntled, charismatic mayor convincing his or her constituents that secession from Ontario would be a good idea. In financial terms, city taxpayers would probably be better off than they are now. The city's population would make it the third largest province in Canada, behind the rest of Ontario and Quebec.

The main problem with such a plan is that it would bifurcate the Toronto city-region. The city's boundaries run through densely populated areas. Turning them into provincial boundaries would surely create more problems than it would solve. Deciding on the 'real' boundaries of the Toronto city-region is a nightmare. Even Statistics Canada (Canada, 2006c) is unsure. It now refers to an area it calls the 'Extended Golden Horseshoe', which includes 6.7 million people (59 per cent of Ontario's population), stretching from Barrie to Niagara Falls and from Kitchener to Clarington.

In Alberta, Statistics Canada uses a similar area it calls the 'Calgary–Edmonton Corridor', with a population of 2.15 million that constitutes 72 per cent of the province's population. In British Columbia there is the 'Lower Mainland and Southern Vancouver Island', with a population of 2.7 million or 69 per cent of the province's population.

Rather than wasting time worrying about the emergence of city-states, it is time to recognize that the provinces containing our largest city-regions have in fact become dependent on these urban centres. These provinces contain vast, sparsely populated territories, but their political centres of gravity are increasingly located in Canada's largest cities. Large or small, these provinces require within them multi-functional units of local government to make decisions about local issues and services. The municipalities that include the territories of our central cities especially merit our careful attention and scrutiny because the cumulative impact of their many seemingly small decisions will determine much about the quality of our urban life. Meanwhile, the federal government will continue to make crucial decisions about such matters as fiscal policy, immigration, and criminal law that will have much to do with the general pattern of our urban lives. Provincial governments will continue to make big decisions about health, education, and social services—as well as strategic infrastructure investments for city-regions and their hinterlands.

The 'urban agenda' of the late 1990s and early 2000s began as a concern about the state of our largest city-regions. But these places contain dozens of municipalities, even after the controversial municipal amalgamations in Toronto and Montreal. Many of the toughest policy choices for the future relate not to our central-city municipalities but to the municipalities on the edges of our city-regions. The mayors of our central cities should have a voice in these decisions, but they cannot claim to represent people who do not elect them. No one argues that only our largest central-city municipalities should have a place at the table in Canadian federalism. Such an arrangement would not be fair to the majority of Canadians who live outside these municipalities. But to argue that our city-regions should have such a place leads to even more problems. In this case no one even knows how such an objective would be accomplished. Such is the dilemma of attempting to integrate our city governments into the decision-making processes of Canadian federalism.

Assessing how the Canadian federal system responds to urban problems and issues is a complicated task. The complications arise primarily from the fact that, for politicians at least, 'urban problems' are either defined primarily by municipalities or are seen as being mainly within their jurisdiction. As we have seen in the first section of this chapter, however, municipalities are not formally part of the federal system, even though municipal leaders have been conducting a sustained campaign over many years to gain some form of enhanced recognition. Big-city mayors would no doubt argue that the Canadian federal system cannot possibly be rated highly on criteria relating to performance, effectiveness, and legitimacy unless they are fully included as part of the process. In short, some of them are just as interested in changing the definition of federalism (with respect to cities at least) as they are with making traditional two-level federalism work better in addressing urban problems. Others are less interested in formal definitional issues but still insist that urban problems cannot be effectively addressed by the federal system unless mayors are 'at the table' and able to participate in decision-making as political equals to representatives of the federal and provincial governments.

But all such demands cause problems for most provincial governments—

especially the government of Quebec—because they open the possibility that a province will not be seen as speaking with one voice. The provinces' worst fear is that on some issues the federal government will be able to ignore them altogether as it makes direct deals with their municipalities. If provinces resist municipal demands for more direct involvement with the federal government and if the federal government accepts this provincial resistance, how are we to assess the result? From a traditional perspective, the system appears to be performing well because the federal government is respecting provincial jurisdiction. But from the perspective of big-city mayors, such an outcome would be an illustration of everything that is wrong with Canadian federalism. I have already argued that adjusting the processes of Canadian federalism to include formally the municipal representatives of large cities is not as easy as some the proponents suggest. But, by any conceivable measure, we have not gone far down that road, and are unlikely even to continue the journey while the Harper government is in office.

So let us assume instead, with respect to urban problems, that Canadian federalism involves only the federal and provincial levels of government, with each having an obligation at least to take account of the expressed wishes of municipal representatives, especially of big-city mayors who are directly elected by more voters than any leader in federal and provincial politics. Even with this assumption, assessments remain difficult, primarily because the nature of the most acute urban problems varies from place to place. Even within the same city, there can be wide disagreement about the nature of the most pressing issues. For example, in Toronto some might point to homelessness, others to the appalling way in which the downtown is cut off from the lakefront, the city's most desirable natural asset. Both issues involve the federal and provincial governments, but the relevant governmental programs and actors are dramatically different in each case.

Even allowing for all these qualifications, there can be little doubt that Canadian cities, relative at least to American cities, have experienced hard times in recent years. This, after all, was one of the main reasons why the 'urban agenda' of the 1990s emerged in the first place. Accustomed to seeing their cities as safer, cleaner, and more vibrant, Canadians who travelled to American cities and who observed what was happening to them gradually became aware that, as conditions in American cities were improving, they seemed to be declining in many Canadian ones, most notably Toronto. At least some of the difference seemed to be accounted for by the injection of massive amounts of American federal dollars for new urban infrastructure, funds that were simply not available in Canada. These funds flowed in the United States without any significant debate about which level of government should be doing what.

On the basis of apparent popular perceptions about the health of Canadian cities in recent years, Canadian federalism cannot be ranked highly in terms of performance, effectiveness, or legitimacy. Perhaps attitudes will soon change, however, as Canadians begin to experience the results of the recent increased federal funding for urban infrastructure. But cities need more than new capital investment. Improvements in the day-to-day public services so important for the quality of urban life will depend at least partly on efforts to improve the fiscal balance between the federal governments and the provinces. The needs of cities for better public facilities and services must be kept on the Canadian political agenda. But these needs can be met without restructuring the Canadian federal system.

References

Andrew, C. 1994. 'Federal Urban Activity: Intergovernmental Relations in an Age of Restraint'. In *The Changing Canadian Metropolis: A Public Policy Perspective*, vol. 2, ed. F. Frisken. Toronto: Canadian Urban Institute.

————— and J. Morrison. 1995. 'Canada Infrastructure Works: Between Picks and Shovels and the Information Highway'. In *How Ottawa Spends 1995–96: Mid-Life Crises*, ed. S.D. Phillips. Ottawa: Carleton University Press.

Axworthy, N.L. 1972. 'The Task Force on Housing and Urban Development: A Study in Democratic Decision-Making', Ph.D. thesis, Princeton University.

Berridge, J. 2002. *Cities in the New Canada*. TD Forum on Canada's Standard of Living. Oct.

Bettison, D. 1975. *The Politics of Canadian Urban Development*. Edmonton: University of Alberta Press.

Black, C. 1977. *Duplessis*. Toronto: McClelland & Stewart.

Bliss, M. 2006. 'Has Canada Failed?', *Literary Review of Canada* 14, 2: 3–5.

Bradford, N. 2005. *Place-Based Public Policy: Towards a New Urban and Community Agenda for Canada*. Research Report F/51. Ottawa: Canadian Policy Research Networks, Mar.

Cameron, D.M. 1974. 'Urban Policy'. In *Issues in Canadian Public Policy*, ed. G.B. Doern and V.S. Wilson. Toronto: Macmillan of Canada.

—————. 1980. 'Provincial Responsibilities for Municipal Government', *Canadian Public Administration* 23, 2: 222–35.

Canada. 1919. Commission of Conservation. *Conservation of Life* 5–1 (Jan.). Ottawa: King's Printer.

—————. 1969. *Report of the Task Force on Housing and Urban Development*. Ottawa: Queen's Printer.

—————, Department of Finance. 2005. *Budget 2005: A New Deal for Canada's Communities*. 23 Feb.

—————. 2006a. 'Infrastructure Programs'. Infrastructure Canada, at: <www.infra-structure.gc.ca/funding/index_e.shtml>.

—————. 2006b. Office of the Prime Minister. 'Prime Minister Harper Outlines His Government's Priorities and Open Federalism Approach'. At: <www.pm.gc.ca/eng/media.asp?category='2&id=1119>.

—————. 2006c. 'Thematic Maps'. Statistics Canada. At: <geodepot.statcan.ca/Diss/Maps/ThematicMaps/index_e.cfm>.

Conservative Party of Canada. 2005. *Stand Up for Canada: Conservative Party of Canada Federal Election Platform 2006*. At: <www.conservative.ca/media/

20060113-Platform.pdf>.

Courchene, T.J. 2005. *Citistates and the State of Cities: Political-Economy and Fiscal-Federalism Dimensions*. IRPP Working Paper Series, 2005-03. Montreal: Institute for Research on Public Policy, June.

Courtney, J.C. 2001. *Commissioned Ridings: Designing Canada's Electoral Districts*. Montreal and Kingston: McGill–Queen's University Press.

Federation of Canadian Municipalities. 2005. Big City Mayors' Caucus. *Cities: Partners in National Prosperity*, 2 June.

Feldman, E.J., and J. Milch. 1981. 'Co-ordination or Control: The Life and Death of the Ministry of State for Urban Affairs'. In *Politics and Government of Urban Canada: Selected Readings*, 4th edn, ed. L.D. Feldman. Toronto: Methuen.

Feldman, L.D., and K.A. Graham. 1979. *Bargaining for Cities: Municipalities and Intergovernmental Relations, An Assessment*. Montreal: Institute for Research on Public Policy.

Fraser, G. 1972. *Fighting Back: Urban Renewal in Trefann Court*. Toronto: Hakkert.

Hartog, H. 1983. *Public Property and Private Power: The Corporation of the City of New York in American Law, 1730–1870*. Chapel Hill: University of North Carolina Press

Jacobs, J. 1984. *Cities and the Wealth of Nations: Principles of Economic Life*. New York: Random House.

Lorimer, J. 1972. *A Citizen's Guide to City Politics*. Toronto: Lorimer.

Mintz, J.M., and T. Roberts. 2004. 'Holes in the Road to Consensus: The Infrastructure Deficit—How Much and Why?' C.D. Howe Institute e-brief, 13 Dec.

Ohmae, K. 1995. *The End of the Nation State: The Rise of Regional Economies*. New York: Free Press.

Ontario. 2002. *Report of the Walkerton Inquiry. Part Two: A Strategy for Safe Drinking Water*. Toronto: Queen's Printer.

Peirce, N.R., and C.W. Johnson, with J.S. Hall. 1993. *Citistates: How Urban America Can Prosper in a Competitive World*. Washington: Seven Locks Press.

Peterson, P.E. 1981. *City Limits*. Chicago: University of Chicago Press.

Sancton, A., and B. Montgomery. 1994. 'Municipal Government and Residential Land Development: A Comparative Study of London, Ontario in the 1920s and 1980s'. In *The Changing Canadian Metropolis: A Public Policy Perspective*, vol. 2, ed. F. Frisken. Toronto: Canadian Urban Institute, 777–98.

Saumier, A. 1987. 'MSUA and the Regionalization of Federal Urban Programs'. In *The Ministry of State for Urban Affairs: A Courageous Experiment in Public Administration*, ed. H.P. Oberlander and A.L. Fallick. Vancouver: Centre for Human Settlements, University of British Columbia.

Slack, E. 2004. *Revenue Sharing Options for Canada's Hub Cities*. A Report prepared for the Meeting of the Hub City Mayors, 17–18 Sept.\

TD Bank Financial Group. 2002. TD Economics. *A Choice between Investing in*

Canada's Cities or Disinvesting in Canada's Future. Special Report. 22 Apr.

Young, R., and C. Leuprecht, eds. 2006. *Canada: The State of the Federation 2004: Municipal–Federal–Provincial Relations in Canada.* Montreal and Kingston: Institute of Intergovernmental Relations and McGill–Queen's University Press.

Websites

Federation of Canadian Muncipalities: www.fcm.ca

International City Management Association: www.icma.org

United Cities and Local Governments. www.cities-localgovernments.org/uclg/index.asp

Canadian Federalism and Multinational Democracy: 'Pressures' from Quebec on the Federation

Alain-G. Gagnon and Raffaele Iacovino

Evaluating the performance of a federation composed of two or more nations requires, first, an understanding of the purposes of particular institutional configurations in specific historical contexts. In other words, federalism is a normative and thus contested category that cannot be evaluated outside of the particular socio-political identities that have constituted the polity and the extent to which they have consented to institutional outcomes. Questions of performance in multinational democracies that have adopted a federal form are thus overwhelmingly about legitimacy and are ultimately constitutional questions. If the political community is not constituted democratically, it is not perceived as legitimate. Without legitimacy, a federation cannot be politically stable, and without stability, it is harder for it to address problems effectively. The purposes of states built on federal principles must always be aimed towards legitimacy if democracy is a foundational principle of the polity.

This chapter discusses how the Canadian federation continues to sidestep the question of legitimacy as a result of its ongoing efforts to define itself in opposition to principles of multinational democracy. James Tully, one of the foremost thinkers on multinational democracy, argues that it is a unique political association with distinct constitutional challenges. He defines a multinational democracy on the basis of four main principles. First, these polities consist of two or more nations that seek not only group rights, but actual self-rule and self-determination as it is understood in international law. Self-rule does not necessarily imply outright secession, but it does involve compromises that at a minimum link relative degrees of political sovereignty with a group's status as an internal nation. Second, multinational democracies are not to be viewed as confedera-

tions of independent nation-states. They are characterized by an overlap of jurisdictions, modes of representation and participation, and national identities of
citizens that are open to negotiation. Third, the nations and the larger association, or the 'multination', are constitutional democracies. Finally, multinational
democracies are also culturally plural in the broad sense of the term, consisting
of a diversity of socio-cultural minority groups that seek recognition of their particular identities. Struggles over minority and multinational diversity typically
compete and are subjects of democratic negotiation (Tully, 2001).

In Canada, one of the fundamental issues of legitimacy that the federation has
continued to sidestep is what is often referred to as the 'Quebec question'. As long
as the Quebec question continues to be seen as an irritant, or as 'pressure' on
Canadian federalism, Canada will continue to fail in its quest to consolidate itself
as a political community worth federalizing along the lines associated with
multinationalism. If it cannot constitute itself as a multinational federation,
Canada will ultimately not be effective because it will lack the legitimacy to
remain intact. Quebec insists that federalism be the foremost value underpinning
the Canadian federation. Moreover, since adhering to federal principles is ultimately about the boundaries of democratic contestation among political communities, no discussion of federalism and legitimacy can be complete without
wading into questions about the institution of citizenship in a multinational setting. The socio-political variable of multinationalism in Canada touches both
how one perceives legitimate institutional arrangements related to federalism
and the crucial variable of how state–citizen (vertical) and citizen–citizen (horizontal) relations are structured by the relevant orders of government. In short, in
evaluating Quebec's contribution to the performance of Canadian federalism,
one cannot stop at a linear reading of its interests, or its demands, as though the
Quebec government of the day merely represents an additional input into the
Canadian policy process. Quebec's contribution to Canadian federalism is a constitutional question in the broad sense of the term and adds to the enrichment of
political life in the country.

As a final note, our emphasis on Quebec is not meant to undercut the past and
potential contributions of Aboriginal peoples to the normative foundations of
the country. Indeed, we take for granted that Aboriginal peoples are fully self-
governing and have the same right to self-determination as do other minority
nations. A redefinition of Canadian citizenship and federalism along multinational principles must include First Nations as well; however, there is not sufficient room in this chapter to address their history, relations with the federal government, place in federal institutions, and citizenship status.

Understanding the Federal Idea: Multinational Democracy, Asymmetrical Federalism, and Legitimacy

In the foundations and historical evolution of Canadian constitutionalism, the
one consistent strand that has survived the test of time is the fact that Quebecers

consider themselves a 'people'. They are not a province like the others, with similar interests and demands on the central government. Nor are Quebecers either an ethnocultural group among many or a language group in a bilingual state. Quebec is not a mere administrative unit, subordinate to the central government. It is a political nation within a multinational state, a founding member state with its own legitimate representative institutions, legal traditions, and claims on framing citizenship status. In short, Quebec constitutes what Will Kymlicka has termed a *societal culture*, defined as a 'culture which provides its members with meaningful ways of life across the full range of human activities' (Kymlicka, 1995). A societal culture stands in contrast to polyethnic identities, which may not be institutionally complete, are usually the direct result of immigration, do not inhabit a concentrated territorial mass, and are more likely to require public policies relating to fair terms of integration and inclusion than they are to seek self-government rights. For Quebec, Canada as a political unit is legitimate to the extent that it recognizes the principle of dualism as a structuring guide for representative institutions. The country, in this view, was created as a compact between two founding peoples, each occupying majoritarian political space in their agreed-upon jurisdictions. Constitutionally, Quebec representatives across partisan lines have exhibited remarkable consistency in maintaining this position.

How best to represent French and English Canadians in constitutionally self-governing institutions? Until patriation of the Canadian Constitution in 1982, this question was the fundamental starting point of constitutional debates in the country, and it remains largely so in Quebec today. Debates surrounding relevant majorities in particular areas of governance informed the initial distribution of powers in 1867. Subsequent constitutional negotiations and judicial decisions regarding sovereignty over given policy areas have all been guided by principles that have less to do with efficacy from a functional standpoint and more to do with the legitimacy and recognition of territorial political communities. In this sense, Canada has always been a 'work in progress', lacking a founding myth shared by all citizens, since the citizenry itself has never perceived itself as a monolithic national group. Describing the outcome of 1982, Peter Russell observed that 'patriation was complete but the patria had not defined itself' (Russell, 1993). Indeed, if a country's amending formula represents the ultimate expression of where constitutional sovereignty is situated (citizens, social groups, provincial or federal governments, the judiciary, national constituents, etc.), then the mere fact that Canada has never had a formal amendment procedure acceptable to Quebec reveals the unfinished and questionable nature of the Canadian federal project. Even the development of a rights consciousness, culminating in the entrenchment of a Charter of Rights and Freedoms in 1982, and seemingly concerned with shielding citizens from governments in a neutral, liberal tradition, in effect recognizes some groups and individuals to the detriment of others. The Charter gives rights and freedoms a marked 'national' quality on a pan-Canadian level by strengthening the ties of citizens to Canadian institutions and emphasizing symmetry rather than entrenching federal identity as the primary normative principle upon which citizens relate to central institutions and to each other across the federation (Cairns, 1995; LaSelva, 1996). The symmetry inherent in the present configuration of Canadian political institutions in effect became a 'powerful new focus of Canadian nationalism' (McRoberts, 1993), undermining political negotiations between constituent units that have distinct needs within the federation and limiting the constitutional potential for justice and stability in the specific context of a multinational democracy.

Like most federal societies, Canada will always experience conflicts, tensions, and—perhaps most important— ambiguity with respect to legal arrangements, regardless of the form the federation takes. Many observers believe that a federal state is therefore a 'soft' state that must constantly work to strengthen the centre, rather than allow the various political identities to negotiate the parameters of representation and sovereignty in a spirit of mutual trust and accommodation. The various conceptions of federalism that have been in conflict over time reveal inherent disagreement over how Canadians of myriad interests and identities ought to be represented in the polity. This chapter does not purport to introduce a panacea. Indeed, federalism relies on faith, loyalty, and trust as much as it does on a written legal text, and faith, loyalty, and trust cannot be so easily assessed empirically. One conclusion that cannot be avoided, however, is that no dominant political identity ought to unilaterally impose a particular 'vision' of representation in order to keep the country together—much less so if this involves forging a national project to achieve such ends at the expense of a national minority.

Tully provides an important normative framework with which to evaluate the legitimacy of constitutional outcomes in states constituted of two or more nations. In *Strange Multiplicity*, he argues that the modern age has shaped political discourse around the negation of identities, through the elevation of the independent self-governing nation-state and the equality of individual citizens. In his view, constitutional theory in the face of diversity ought to embody the idea of an open-ended series of contracts and agreements between adherents. Constitutions ought not to be imposed on self-determining groups, as fixed and unchanging guides for social and political behaviour. Moreover, in response to fears that this approach may render the constitution susceptible to constantly changing political currents, Tully believes such processes can take place without hindering harmonious relations in daily sub-constitutional politics (Tully, 1995).

The normative backdrop employed by Tully rests on the liberal ideal of freedom from constraints, of being able to choose the direction of one's own life. Yet Tully notes that contemporary liberals have also conceded the importance of belonging to a culture and a place—of being 'at home'. This language is reminiscent of Kymlicka's (1995, 1998) reference to a 'liberal-culturalist consensus' in which the diverse societal cultures within multinational states ought to be accommodated and recognized, not wiped away by nationalizing forces of the majority nation. Tully develops three fundamental pillars of constitutionalism—continuity, consent, and mutual recognition—as conducive to the twin goals of liberalism that simultaneously avoid the imposition of extreme expressions of the universal and the particular.

The common thread among these three pillars of constitutionalism is that while a modern constitution seeks to constitute, an 'ancient' constitution, according to Tully, builds on what is already constituted. The basic division is between (a) the imposition of a structure within which individuals can be self-determining, where people are said to be free insofar as they forgo customs and historical associations, and (b) custom-based recognition, which builds on long-held principles that a free people, through deliberation and contestation over time, have come to accept as binding and that manifests itself as a consensually based association. Moreover, this view holds that constitutions need not be legally uniform. Rather, in reflecting a combination of freely formed associations, they are by nature multiform—an assemblage of jurisdictions—and are more likely to result in asymmetrical federalism in multinational settings.

Most modern constitutionalist theorists see the differential structure inherent in such an approach to diverse polities as a challenge to equality. Yet Tully notes that this view assumes that constitutions are a precondition to democracy. His contention is that constitutions ought to follow from democratic practices. Hence the emphasis on due process in his three pillars. The example of Quebec is fundamental here. Quebec is not a mere cultural grouping that requires substantive protections in the Canadian Constitution, as though the Constitution were there to act as its guardian. Treating the question of Quebec's constitutional status as though it were a matter of cultural policy implicitly misconstrues the idea that Quebec is a partner in the determination of constitutional outcomes, not a target for policy. The question *what does Quebec want?* is in itself indicative of the modern conception of constitutionalism in Canada. In contrast, viewed through the prism of the three pillars, the approach would assume that Quebec exists as a historically self-determining entity, already constituted, and the Constitution would be the result of an evolving set of agreements that are acceptable to all parties.

Managing Diversity in Canada: A Denial of the Federal Idea

Adding to the challenges posed by the political sociology of multinationalism is the fact that Canada faces diversity on two fronts. Canada must navigate through questions surrounding a plurality of nation-based forms of representation and sovereignty while simultaneously addressing issues related to self-understanding, belonging, and, more generally, citizenship in a setting characterized by diverse social and cultural identities. In Canada's multinational democracy, debates surrounding diversity often stop short of sorting out the various layers of diversity (national, ethnocultural, social groups) without actually taking a step further to find solutions for the management of diversity (Kymlicka, 1995, 1998). Moreover, these distinct layers of diversity are frequently pitted against one another, and political projects or solutions made in their names are employed to undermine other legitimate expressions of diversity.

On the one hand, Canada must manage the question of 'national' diversity, a challenge that most other liberal nation-states do not have to grapple with to the same extent. In the language of Kymlicka's (1991) theory of multiculturalism, Canada contains separate 'contexts of choice': that is, national identities that are instrumental to individuals' well-being. On the other hand, Canada is also involved in crafting the boundaries of citizenship; it must address questions related to integration of immigrants, cultural pluralism, and more broadly ethnocultural diversity. Kymlicka's conceptual categorization relating to the distinct policy implications of national minorities and ethnocultural groups makes an important contribution to the way we comprehend citizenship. Yet as this discussion emphasizes, addressing one problem in a multinational state invariably limits the options available in dealing with the other. Indeed, Kymlicka concedes that self-government rights for national minorities pose a theoretical problem for liberal citizenship, as opposed to what he considers the more straightforward task, within a liberal framework, of recognizing culture as a primary good for citizens. In the latter approach, members of ethnocultural group are integrated on the basis that, first, they seek integration and, second, they must be allowed to flourish as members of their particular cultures.

This reconciliation of diversity with citizenship is the fundamental challenge confronting Canada today. Conceptually, the question of diversity itself must be disaggregated to reflect distinct political and social projects. A multinational democracy is the ideal case for evaluating such projects, since the term 'diversity' means different things to different social and political actors.

Canada's formal attempts to manage diversity have defined the country in terms that emphasize homogeneity at the expense of national diversity. The Charter defines the country in terms of individual rights, while recognizing certain rights for socio-cultural groups with the aim of addressing discrimination and regional economic disparities. With regard to cultural pluralism, Canada has entrenched official multiculturalism as an interpretive clause in the Charter. This reconciliation of individual and group rights has endured over many years, and reflects the impact of Pierre Elliott Trudeau, considered by many to be the architect of this approach to diversity in Canada (Ignatieff, 2000).

Trudeau promoted the ideals of individual liberty, autonomy, justice, and equality: values that did not limit themselves to particular communities but applied universally, to all individuals, regardless of spatio-temporal contingencies. Trudeau rejected the nation-state model, preferring the foundations of the modern state to be based on universalizing and individualist liberalism. He thus contrasted the 'sociological nation'—which he associated with reactionary and emotive politics—with the 'juridical nation', based on universalism and reason. National identity was depicted as an outdated loyalty, which narrowed interests and undermined the progression of civilization. Quebec neo-nationalism was deemed to constitute a threat to progressive politics and certain to lead to a cycle of never-ending conflicts that would hinder reconciliation and unity. For

Trudeau, a federal state was most conducive to the development of the juridical nation and the exercise of reason in politics (Bickerton et al., 2003). However, Trudeau himself, several years earlier, had defended the principle of Canada as a multinational state (Trudeau, 1962).

The pillars of Trudeau's thought culminated in the formal construction of pan-Canadian nationalism based on multiculturalism, official bilingualism, and, above all, the primacy of individual rights as entrenched in a Charter of Rights and Freedoms. Although culture is recognized as constituting individuals through formal multiculturalism, the vision sought by Trudeau did not allow for any particular collective status based on historical, cultural, linguistic, or territorial claims as defining political markers of attachment to Canada. Indeed, the pan-Canadian treatment of diversity through multiculturalism, official bilingualism, and individual rights serves as a counterforce to Quebec's aspirations for national status. This vision of Canada has endured and, since 1982, has left a mark on Canada's self-understanding that makes innovative approaches to the management of diversity extremely difficult, particularly a constitutional formula that acknowledges socio-cultural diversity simultaneously with national diversity.

The Canadian approach to the management of diversity, although pluralist and post-national in rhetoric, paradoxically undermines the substantive aspirations of distinct societal cultures. It does so by misinterpreting the meaning of 'equal status'. Through the central institution of formal citizenship, Canada has successfully carved out the *national* parameters of the country—from coast to coast—based on a rights regime that has not undergone a historical 'process' of acceptance and consensus necessary for any political community to thrive. The fundamental question for the management of diversity in Canada is not *What is Canada's position on pluralism?* Rather, a commitment to diversity that accounts for its multi-layered character would ask: *How does Canada accommodate demands by distinct national groupings that constitute the country to determine the boundaries of diversity within their respective polities?* This approach would go a long way towards constructing the country on legitimate bases around the federal idea as it is understood in Quebec. In other words, at the pan-Canadian level, the central state and its use of the institution of citizenship would exhibit a stronger commitment and effort to manage the challenges associated with diverse modes of belonging as well as acknowledging its formal limits as an arbiter of citizenship status through constitutional adjustments. Short of such measures, diversity in the Canadian context, defined by multiculturalism in a bilingual framework, formal equality of provinces, and a Charter of Rights and Freedoms, is not post-national or cosmopolitan or universal in orientation, but filling in for a national void.

The next section will examine the distinct societal cultures at work in Canada by briefly contrasting the policy of multiculturalism with Quebec's own response to cultural diversity—'interculturalism'. In the present conception of Canadian federalism, however, multiculturalism and interculturalism are not independent policy areas. Multiculturalism is a nation-building device, meant to circumscribe citizenship status in Canada, and it does not account for the multinational condition. Indeed, it is meant to trump Quebec's aspirations to play a part in defining belonging in Canada for its citizens.

Multiculturalism, Interculturalism, and Symmetrical Federalism: Concurrent Nation-Building Strategies

Policy-makers at the federal level charged with defining the bases of belonging in Canada have faced the challenges associated with incorporating diverse cultural identities, as well as a national minority in Quebec with established political institutions, within a well-circumscribed territory. The adoption of multiculturalism as a pan-Canadian nation-building strategy was related to goals of unity and fostering citizen dignity through the recognition of particular cultural affiliations. The strategy emphasizes the primacy of individual rights in a constitutionally entrenched Charter of Rights and Freedoms, and a choice of language use— French or English—applied across the country. Superimposed on individual rights is the official recognition of all constituent cultures as equal. Such recognition, however, is largely a symbolic concession and is the fabrication of an identity marker based on the voluntary adherence to particular cultural allegiances. Indeed, cutbacks in fiscal transfers to ethnocultural groups suggest a withdrawal from the commitment to multiculturalism (Abu-Laban and Gabriel, 2002). Moreover, a genuine commitment to cultural pluralism, at a minimum, requires more than a mere 'sponsorship' of diverse ethnocultural groups (see also Pal, 1993.) Current multiculturalism policies hardly qualify as examples of fostering citizen dignity through recognition of a diversity of contributions to the country's self-understanding. First, qualitative citizenship through participation and deliberation and interchange is hardly furthered by the federal government simply throwing money at the issue. When a policy is made or broken by spending and cutbacks, then a government's commitment to deep philosophical principles needs to be questioned. Second, paying for allegiance in a top-down state–citizen framework is not what those promoting institutional recognition and accommodation had in mind. Canadian multiculturalism works only on a rhetorical level; people believe they need not assimilate and shed their cultural sources of meaning. This symbolic function does have its virtues in terms of conditions for belonging.

However, there is no real substance to multiculturalism policy other than the familiar pattern of groups being at the whim of federal spending. Moreover, as Abu-Laban and Gabriel (2002) illustrate, the new direction of the policy does not move to a more firm commitment for 'national inclusion and belonging' based on 'recognition and respect', the original rationale for the policy, but on national and global competitiveness. Multiculturalism has become a commercially defined comparative advantage in a global economy. Indeed, the policy may be taking a more direct turn towards an instrumental application; the strengthening of national sovereignty, symbolically, in the face of global pressures, is Canada's very own 'niche'.

By forging a common identity throughout the country based on the 'sum of its parts', it was hoped that the identity marker for unity could be universal: the equal recognition of all cultures, within a regime governed by individual rights and bilingualism. In this way, adherence to particular cultural attachments could be voluntary for all *individuals*. At the same time, claiming to empower citizens of minority cultures through reductionist means signified that Canada's symbolic order was to be based on the negation of any particular cultural definition. The Canadian political community in this sense is predicated on the judicialization of social interactions, to the detriment of the deliberative aspects of representative democracy. The idea of public space for citizen participation, reflection, and deliberation within the political community is reduced to a narrow forum of rights-bearers. Deliberative assemblies give way to the 'legalization' of social relations (Mandel, 1989), preventing parliaments from being responsible for organizing social life and, ultimately, preventing citizens from identifying with others in the larger society (Bourque and Duchastel, 2000). To be sure, there are alternative views (see Chapter 3 in this volume, in which James Kelly argues that legislatures continue to be important forums in determining citizens' rights), but in our view these are misplaced because of the enduring symbolic impact of the Charter on citizenship in Canada.

According to Kymlicka (1995, 1998), Canadian multiculturalism as a symbol for identification fails to differentiate between national minorities and polyethnic communities. Multiculturalism elevates the status of cultural groups to the same level as that of national minorities. It fails in any significant way to recognize territorially defined group-differentiated rights as a federal principle and was not predicated on a genuine commitment to the ideology of multiculturalism as a pillar upon which to frame citizenship status. The goal was unity in the face of a national minority challenge. Quebec's national identity was placed, constitutionally, alongside every other minority culture as a basis for identification. In Charles Taylor's (1991) terms, multiculturalism as such fails to appreciate 'deep diversity' in Canada. Deep diversity recognizes tiers of difference in particular groupings' political aspirations and historical/territorial/linguistic realities. Deep diversity would recognize that national minorities, as opposed to polyethnic communities, seek to provide a 'centre' for identification, their own pole of allegiance necessary for unity and common purpose.

The Canadian model operates alongside the primacy of individual rights in a constitutional bill of rights, with an interpretive clause for the recognition of diverse cultural affiliations. There is no democratic imperative for the recognition of diverse minority cultures besides a legal/procedural provision that may be invoked if the minority group in question chooses to do so. This is a key conceptual distinction between the Canadian and Quebec models of integration and it stems from the nature of the expectations of democracy itself. The fact that Canadian identity—the way citizens relate to each other and to the state in determining societal preferences—is based on such terms implies that we have no public culture on which minority cultures can make their mark. Again, multiculturalism in Canada does not reflect a recognition of minority cultures; rather, it rests on the denial of culture altogether in defining the limits and confines of public space. Public space is based on individual participation via a bill of rights.

Quebec's model of interculturalism strikes a balance between the requirements of unity—an identity basis—and the recognition of minority cultures. Recognition is not limited to viewing a diversity of cultures as a 'problem' and treating them as static, essentialized, and separate groups that require a slice of the public purse and therefore must be 'budgeted for', and who in turn will be vulnerable to cutbacks. Quebec's model of integration is not assimilationist, nor does it conceptually fall into cultural relativism and fragmentation in its commitment to cultural pluralism. Integration is viewed as a necessary prerequisite to full participation in the construction of a common public culture as an identity centre. Identification with and participation through a variety of cultures is not ruled out as a basis for citizenship status, yet the possibility of enclosure and ghettoization is discouraged because the recognition of particular cultural identities is de facto the *recognition of the right and obligation to participate* in the polity. It is not the recognition of culture as existing in self-contained communities that are pre-political, in a vacuum of space and time. Recognition is an *outcome* of participation. It is the result of contributing to the development of a common public culture and to larger consensual bases of allegiance and identification, without rejecting the established symbolic order offered by Quebec society as it has evolved historically. It recognizes that members of minority cultures can make a difference regarding their status as citizens.

In this sense, the unity and solidarity sought by any model of citizenship are viewed as a process, to be constructed by the various parties involved through exchange and dialogue, rather than a model that offers a pre-existing blueprint of recognition. While majority cultural groups may internalize the fact that members of minority cultures warrant certain cultural rights, through recognition, they may fail to appreciate the value of cultural diversity. Awareness of cultural contrasts also endows individuals with a deeper understanding of their own cultures and allows for reflection about larger questions of coexistence between people.

Interculturalism as a model for addressing polyethnicity represents a forum for citizen empowerment, not retrenchment. From the initial premise that a national culture consists of a 'daily plebiscite', to draw from Renan's (1882) conceptualization, the Quebec model stresses the idea that the common public culture is inclusive of all groups in its changing and evolutionary fabric. Webber (1994) has located this dynamic aspect of a national identity in the idea that communities are fostered through public debates in a common language through time. Shared values in themselves do not provide the sense of allegiance necessary for a national community to thrive. Indeed, disagreements about the major orientations of society are perhaps emblematic of a healthy political community because they demonstrate that citizens are concerned with the state of the community. The democratic quality of a constantly changing political community lies precisely in the idea that citizens are able to identify with and make an impact on the current streams of public debate in society. Doing so requires that citizens interact within the framework of a common vernacular (Webber, 1994).

Quebec's model contends that the incorporation of immigrants or minority cultures into the larger political community is a reciprocal endeavour—a 'moral contract'[1] between the host society and the particular cultural group aimed at establishing a forum for the empowerment of all citizens—a 'common public culture' (Harvey, 1991; Caldwell, 1988, 2001). This moral contract defines 'Quebec society' as follows:

- a society in which French is the common language of public life;
- a democratic society in which everyone is expected and encouraged to participate and make a contribution;
- a pluralist society open to multiple contributions within the limits imposed by respect for fundamental democratic values and the necessity of intercommunity exchange (Government of Quebec, 1990).

The common public culture in this view does not consist solely in the juridical sphere; it is not a procedural model based on formal individual rights. Instead, the basic tenets of the moral contract are such that established 'modes of being' in economic, political, and socio-cultural realms are to be respected as markers of identification and citizenship status, with the institutions of democratic participation acting as points of convergence for groups of specific collective identities in order that all may share equally in democratic life.

In establishing a model based on convergence of collective identity, the French language is to serve as the common language of public life. The French language is seen as an essential condition for the cohesion of Quebec society and constitutes the basis for Quebec's self-definition as a distinct political community. In this view, language is not conceptualized as an individual right. Rocher, Rocher, and Labelle (1995) elaborate: 'In Quebec, . . . the French language is presented as a "centre of convergence" for diverse groups, yet at the same time these groups can maintain and let flourish their specificity. While the Canadian policy privileges an individualist approach to culture, Quebec's policy states clearly the need to recognize French as a collective good that requires protection and encouragement.'

The Quebec model is unique because it is part of a larger project for national affirmation. Quebec intellectuals, in formulating the boundaries of the national project, have been engaged in a rich debate about the meaning of belonging in Quebec society. In Canada, this debate is silenced, since no institutional accommodation in the present federal structure allows for a diversity of policies or an asymmetrical approach to integration. Multiculturalism is but another instrument to deny the existence of national pluralism in Canada.

A move away from the formal nation-state model need not imply a retreat from the national bases of belonging to democratic political communities as the foundation for citizenship. Quebec remains mired in debates about the character of its national sentiments. It does not have the option of offering a radically post-national basis of belonging. Given the institutions of a nation-state, Quebec as a societal culture could then choose to manage diversity in whatever fashion it sees fit in a liberal democratic setting. Its present initiatives, even in the face of such glaring obstacles, have demonstrated that Quebec's commitment to cultural pluralism is beyond reproach. Short of self-determination, the ambiguous nature of belonging and self-understanding in Quebec—and the constant confusion with regard to its place in Canada—will persist to the detriment of Quebec citizens vis-à-vis those of other political communities. Even in a post-national age, the 'national' form lends legitimacy to liberal citizenship; it provides the foundational elements of popular sovereignty, accountability, empowerment, representation, and the institutional capacity for decision-making that, at the very least, lend depth and a finite element to public deliberation. Short of this equation, citizenship becomes impoverished.

While many attributes, both institutional and sociological, define federal states, mapping the conditions for the legitimacy of federal polities is inherently a normative exercise. In Canada, the federal idea itself is conceptually contested, with some preferring to define the country along territorial lines and others viewing the federation as a multinational democracy. A uninational view of Canada, in line with the national vision of Pierre Trudeau that remains in place to this day, is embodied in a socio-cultural pluralism that is indifferent to federalism as a normative value that underlies democratic institutions. Federal institutions come to be territorially organized for purposes of expediency, and the central government takes on a role as arbiter of a plurality of interests and identities and is seen as the guarantor of an overarching national sentiment. In Canada, this vision is cemented through the core ideas of multiculturalism, equality of provinces, a constitutionally-entrenched Charter of Rights and Freedoms, official bilingualism, and national standards in social programs.

In contrast to this 'territorial' vision of federalism, most intellectuals in Quebec view the country's history and promise through the lens of a multinational conception of federalism. It paves the way for various constitutional and political asymmetries, and structures the most salient socio-political cleavages around national groupings as the very raison d'être of federalism. Indeed, this fundamental distinction, identified by Will Kymlicka (1998) in terms of 'multinational versus territorial' federations, demarcates the great divide over the relative legitimacy of constitutional possibilities in Canada. Canada continues to structure federalism around monistic conceptions of citizenship and services rather than around representative governments and constituent nations.

This persistent contestation has led some to hail the discursive character of the Canadian 'conversation' (Webber, 1994; Kernerman, 2005) as an ongoing exercise in soul-searching that contributes to thoughtful and productive citizenship. However, for Quebec, certain normative and institutional boundaries related to the federal idea have always served to provide a contextual limitation to the constitutional potential of the country: a socio-political 'grounding' of sorts. For Quebec, Canada has always represented a political arrangement that is conducive to the exercise of Quebec's own national sovereignty, where liberal-democratic majorities are made and remade around clearly defined jurisdictions and representative democracy is delimited by an understanding of multinational democracy as a basis for federalism. In other words, the sovereignty of the Quebec state as an expression of a national grouping, or a 'people', is inviolable. This federal practice requires constitutional entrenchment. It is not open to negotiation across Canada. It is a point of departure for negotiations as a consensus position in Quebec that cannot be altered by Canada-wide majorities.

Quebec's representative institutions continue to adhere to this understanding. Its constitutional position on Canada as a multinational federation has always remained firm. In 1998, the Supreme Court of Canada affirmed the legitimacy of this position in a reference case regarding Quebec secession (*Reference re Secession of Quebec*, [August 20, 1998]). Quebec cannot consent to a federated state that is constructed by a single majority. The legitimacy of the Canadian federation depends on this understanding of Canada.

Constitutionalism in multinational democracies, for purposes of legitimacy, must account not only for questions of justice, but for identity and stability as well. These considerations must be addressed together in the management of diversity. In balancing collective and individual rights, constitutions also recognize social categories, based on gender, sexual orientation, ethnicity, disabilities, and so on. The idea of recognizing constituent national minorities as but another social category—taken together as 'constitutional actors' in a broad sense—confuses the purpose of constitutionalism in multinational settings on two fronts.

First, it fails to make explicit the distinction between the *interests* of social groups, who *channel demands* through state institutions, and the political *identities* of national minorities, who desire to form the *basis* of territorial representative institutions and a democratic polity in their own right—in other words, self-determination. By reducing collective demands to interests and using the constitutional arena to accommodate them, proponents of a uniform conception of nationhood can frame the debate in terms of justice and claim that factors associated with social co-operation, unity, and functionality are the only criteria by which to judge the merits of constitutional outcomes are achieved. In doing so, they can neglect the process through which such outcomes are achieved. Appropriate constitutional actors thus come to be formed not by political communities with mechanisms for democratic accountability, who had been party to the original compromise, but by any social group with sufficient resources to mobilize and with effective access to central government institutions, since this is the social and territorial space deemed essential in carving out a constitutional niche for themselves. The larger federation in this case ceases to be a multinational ensemble, since it is constituted by collective entities that are formed out of political and social mobilization in *opposition* to the federal state, engaging in the normal business of politics yet in the constitutional arena. In a multinational democracy, a constitution cannot be neutral if it disregards its constitutive partners in the name of a 'higher procedural standard', from which to adjudicate political conflict. In multinational democracies, constitutions should privilege political communities and their legitimately elected governments (Ajzenstat, 1995).

Second, and related to the first issue, to recognize constituent national minorities as but another social category is to misconstrue the criteria for evaluating justice in constitutions. In this construct, power rather than democracy determines constitutional accommodation, and getting into the constitutional game is like enjoying the privilege of entering some exclusive club that renders your particular cause invulnerable to the political process. We saw this in the early 1980s in the intense efforts of various identity groups for specific inclusion in the Charter of Rights and Freedoms. A national minority must confront not only a centralist government at the federal level, with its own project for nation-building, but also a set of social groups whose primary allegiance lies at the centre. When this occurs, the Constitution no longer represents a meeting ground for the country's founding constituents, with all of their historical legitimacy. Once constitutional talks are mentioned, citizens have a 'right' to get involved, and political and social mobilization ensues, at a pan-Canadian level, as an act of citizenship itself. Constitutions in themselves are not democratic institutions; if they were, referendums would be the only legitimate institutions for amending them. Constitutions are not meant to compensate for failed representative institutions and a flawed federal structure, and they are *just* when they follow from procedures that privilege negotiations, deliberations, and decisions by elected governments.

In Canada, the debate is taking place between two sets of actors. One set believes the Constitution is an appropriate tool with which to re-engineer society outside of its social bases. The other set believes that the Constitution represents a meeting ground in which the rules of association are to flow from sovereign constituents; in other words, the communities recognized as nations both by international convention and by custom in the Canadian context, as the Supreme Court of Canada maintained in 1998. Ironically, and in apparent contradiction of basic liberal premises, constitutions in multinational states must overtly entrench principles of exclusion as well as inclusion with regard to representation. Social identities can be constantly made and remade, depending on a myriad of factors including power dynamics, material conditions, and ideology. If constitutional actors are defined as such, then it is no wonder that Canadian constitutionalism is perceived to be an impossible game. Indeed, a limited constitution is not incompatible with multinational accommodation. By demanding constitutional affirmation as a founding member, with the full use of majoritarian democratic institutions in its jurisdictional fields, Quebec is in effect trying to limit the set of constitutional actors in Canada. The recognition of minority nations in multinational constitutions in this sense may be conceptualized as *substantive in process* and *procedural in application.* The constitutional game proceeds through negotiations about the substance of jurisdictional conflicts, but once settled and accepted by all, a dualist vision of Canada that may or may not imply asymmetry is not incompatible with a limited, procedural constitution (Simeon, 1988).

Can Canadians be a sovereign people (Russell, 1993)? As argued above, a constitution, by itself, cannot simply create sovereign institutions out of nothing. Linkages between the nation-state and sovereignty, however, are so inextricably tied that it is inconceivable to argue that Canada has never been founded on the notion of popular sovereignty, even though it has attempted in vain to *forge* a constitution that implicitly embodies this principle. Canadians do not constitute a sovereign 'people'; they are a plurality of sovereign *peoples*. This assertion is difficult to make with our common understanding of nation-states, equality of individuals, and constitutional supremacy, but constitutions precede legal imposition. They are not 'made up' out of abstract universal principles. Nor can they be politically motivated, as nation-building tools, meant to negate previously existing self-governing entities or peoples, if they are to be deemed legitimate.

Conclusion: Asymmetrical Federalism and Legitimacy in a Multinational Democracy

Cultural-ideological disagreements with regard to Quebec's specificity, the strong sense of territorial identity expressed by Aboriginal peoples, the consolidated individual rights-based national identity in Canada outside Quebec, and the persistence of regional tensions over the representative institutions of the central government continue to dominate the landscape of diverging visions of Canadian federalism. Moreover, inherent stresses and strains associated with division of powers continue, particularly relating to encroachment by the federal government into provincial areas of responsibility. Much work remains in order to federalize the federation. The endurance of competing visions demonstrates that the defining aspects of the Canadian political community have yet to be accommodated. Indeed, the urgency of persisting with the affirmation of various conceptions of 'political space' in Canada becomes evident when we recognize that territory remains one of the rare areas within liberal democracies where it is still possible to maintain representation and to demand accountability from political actors.

The diverging federal visions in Canada, far from threatening the country, are a positive tribute to the idea of federalism itself. Federalism represents more than an institutional arrangement. It is not reducible to political solutions than can be imposed by any one particular government or prevailing idea of political community, or to ad hoc deals that keep members in line. The Canadian experiment with federalism, rather than being threatened by the political conflicts spawned by diverging visions, has been shaped and indeed defined by the negotiation of distinct visions over time. This negotiation of identity is the essence of the federal spirit. In the interests of federalism, Canada should embrace its diversity of views about political community and take solace in the idea that this debate, like politics more generally, cannot be resolved. The goal is to recognize this fundamental and unchanging condition of Canada's existence. However, democracy ought to be organized around territorial representation. We cannot lump subnational movements together with other group-based movements. If we do, the polity will truly resemble a postmodern assortment that lacks accountability and is responsible to no one but the prime minister, who may pick and choose which groups he deems to be relevant.

This current period of so-called constitutional peace is an aberration and a low point for democracy in Canada. A dominant nation-building view that looks to the intervention of the federal government as the guarantor of Canadian unity has no legitimate competitor in the rest of Canada for the foreseeable future. As long as this situation continues, Quebec will be left out and Canada will, de facto, have no central government that legitimately speaks for all Canadians, short of an instrumental body that serves its citizens as clients of the central state. This is the price to pay for dismissing federalism in Canada's national project—its self-understanding—and the principles upon which citizens identify with each other.

For the Canadian multination to flourish, two developments need to occur. First, it must be understood that Quebec is a constituted society—a societal culture—to use the familiar designation. Second, and related to the first, Quebec citizenship must be allowed to develop independently of Canadian measures that serve only to undercut its development.

In 2003, the election of a Liberal government in Quebec and the replacement of Jean Chrétien by Paul Martin, perceived as more conciliatory to Quebec, led observers to believe that a new era in Ottawa–Quebec collaboration had arrived. But the main dividing lines of Canadian federalism have not been addressed. The question of fiscal imbalance remains unresolved, the federal government continues to play an aggressive role in the area of health, and the initial Martin focus on a 'new deal' for cities had the federal government once again treading into provincial jurisdictions. The general orientation remains: the provinces are considered junior partners, to be consulted in a system of agenda-setting directed by Ottawa. The Liberal party's election platform of 2004 equated social programs to Canadian values, defining the very essence of the Canadian nation (Liberal Party of Canada, 2004). Even the election of a minority Conservative government in early 2006, in which Prime Minister Stephen Harper promised a more 'open federalism' with some special status for Quebec, such as representation at UNESCO and a greater respect for provincial jurisdictions, remain mired at the level of minor administrative deals that do not signal a willingness to constitute the country along asymmetrical lines. While 'open federalism' does signal a positive step, it is a long way from even a mention of the reopening of the constitutional dossier by the federal government.

Another significant development has been the establishment of a formal institution embodying pan-Canadian provincialism: the Council of the Federation. It was spearheaded by the Quebec Liberal government of Jean Charest and established formally in December 2003, in part to tackle the issue of vertical fiscal imbalance. In the short term, the agenda of the Council of the Federation is the improvement of the health-care system and the strengthening of the economic union. The Council of the Federation does not, however, signal a new approach based on partnership (Rocher, 2005). Rather, it simply institutionalizes existing practices among the provinces. It also goes against the grain of traditional Quebec objectives over the last four decades of recognition and autonomy (ibid.). In this sense, while short-term goals may be achieved, nothing is undertaken to resolve the root of the problem as Quebec has always perceived it: a centralizing agenda from Ottawa.

In September 2004, optimism for the merits of collaboration once again emerged with the signing of a bilateral health agreement between Ottawa and Quebec. (See Chapter 8 on health care by Maioni.) The agreement contained a clause that exempted Quebec from accountability provisions imposed on other provinces. While the agreement does signal a moderate move away from the inflexible approach pursued under Jean Chrétien, it still remains a mere administrative response to a much larger phenomenon. Indeed, Quebec managed only to secure full control over a field of policy that lies within its jurisdiction in the first place. In a situation of a priori constitutional asymmetry, Quebec would not have to strike a deal to govern in its area of constitutional competence.

Indeed, federal asymmetries can be concretely summarized in two forms. First, there are asymmetries of a constitutional and juridical nature (de jure), emphasizing the division of powers, and second, there are asymmetries of an administrative nature (de facto), which are more easily reversible. The latter correspond to agreements stemming from practical considerations or as the result of negotiated mutual agreements between representatives of the two orders of government. Quebec has demanded changes that are guaranteed into the future by proposing de jure modifications, yet has been forced to be content with agreements that could be modified according to current power relations, which are invariably unfavourable to Quebec. It has signed de facto agreements without any formal guarantees for the long term (Gagnon and Garcea, 1988).

In the Canadian context, if we exclude the sections of an asymmetrical nature already included in the Constitution Act of 1867 (e.g., sections 93A, 94, 98, and 133) and in the Constitution Act of 1982 (e.g., sections 23[1] and 59) (Beaudoin, 2002), the scope of asymmetrical federalism has been essentially limited to agreements of a non-constitutional nature. They include, for example, the Quebec Pension Plan (1964), the agreements on immigration (Cloutier and Lang Agreement, 1971; Bienvenue and Andras Agreement, 1975; Cullen and Couture Agreement, 1978; Gagnon-Tremblay and McDougall Agreement, 1991),[2] manpower training (1997), and the more recent health agreement (2004).

From a Quebec sovereignist perspective, asymmetrical federalism has been seen as a strategy to demobilize nationalist forces and as paltry compensation for frequent central intrusions in the fields of jurisdiction exclusive to Quebec. The main argument can be summed up as follows: Why be satisfied with piecemeal powers when Quebec could have a single state capable of administering all of its responsibilities? From the Quebec federalist view, asymmetrical federalism is presented as a last hope, allowing for a revival of Quebecers' confidence by pointing to the flexibility that can characterize federalism. In the absence of permanent gains by way of constitutional modifications, these federal forces still believe in the possibility of finding a formula that is tailor-made for Quebec within the Canadian federation. However, it will remain far from an accomplished reality as long as opposition to asymmetrical federalism continues to be ensconced.

Canada is often presented abroad as a multinational federation and a multi-cultural state. It is neither (McRoberts, 2001). It may be so rhetorically, perhaps even sociologically, and perhaps many Canadians believe this to be an apt description of the country. However, its institutions of federalism and citizenship do not reflect these principles. If the notion of difference as the defining feature of the Canadian model is the subject of consensus in the hallways of academia in this country, it is not replicated in our political institutions. The defining aspect of Canadian political life, as it stands now, is an aggressive nation-building pro-ject that does little to address some of the underlying challenges associated with diversity and self-determination (Seymour, 2001). From the perspective of Quebec, two points merit consideration. First, Quebec's predominant position with regard to its place in Canada is not the result of new circumstances like globalization or a greater awareness of justice. Many of the demands for some measure of self-determination in Quebec have persisted since the country's founding and have been supported across partisan lines as a 'Quebec consensus' position. Second, the trend in Quebec and Canada contradicts claims that recent exogenous developments (like globalization) are inimical to the nation form as the focal point for political mobilization, representation, sovereignty, and gener-ally, citizenship. The story of this country is one of competing nationalisms, and it remains the plot to this day, regardless of powerful ideational trends that either revert back to the neutral liberal model or attempt to reconstruct the place of identity in the Canadian polity altogether.

The top-down 'forging' of homogeneity through disassociated rights, as a matter of legitimacy in the contemporary era, can no longer take hold in a vac-uum. National minorities in the contemporary period simply will not allow this to take place. Processes of national integration proceeded in most European cases prior to the consolidation of liberal democracy. Generating a satisfactory model that accommodates diversity in a multinational state can only achieve the stature of a 'procedural' basis of belonging (or patriotism) if the process itself has been adhered to by all parties. The final 'product' that reflects this model of diversity and defines the basic laws, the configuration of political relations, the acknowl-edgement and recognition of national groupings, and the system of representa-tion must, in the end, be a point of pride and consensus for all parties involved.

Some might argue that this vision of the multinational state is simply seces-sion under another name. This contention is mistaken. Rather, the vision rests on a classical notion of the nation-state as the result of an immutable progression. Multinational democracies must live with the prospect of potential secession because of the imperative of self-government rights (self-determination), the dictates of popular sovereignty and democracy, and the fact that citizens are enti-tled to debate the boundaries of their political communities. A multinational democracy must endow active citizens with the freedom to choose their existen-tial futures as political agents. If the will to stay together is strong, as a majority of nationalists in Canada seem to imply in their quest for national unity, then this choice should not be an issue. Multinational citizenship is precisely the arrangement in which this will is allowed to be revealed, while avoiding a domineering and constraining constitution or the constant prospect of zero-sum referendums. Citizenship implies willing participants as members, not as subjects.

Notes

This chapter builds on our book entitled *Federalism, Citizenship and Quebec: Debating Multinationalism* (Toronto: University of Toronto Press, 2007). The authors would like to thank Grace Skogstad and Herman Bakvis, as well as the anonymous reviewers of this article, for their helpful criticisms and suggestions.

1. On 1 November 1999, the Quebec Minister of Citizen Relations and Immigration, Robert Perreault, attempted to recast the model by announcing a new course of action that would emphasize a 'civic contract', more broadly defined. This new approach was designed to focus less on integration as a specific policy field and more on the 'needs of Quebec society in its entirety'. The reciprocity implied by the moral contract was not significantly altered, yet concretely, the policy resulted in a decentralization of services of integration to more local geographical centres. Conceptually, the policy did not significantly alter the notion that integration is a reciprocal endeavour that involves obligations and entitlements for both the host society and minorities and immigrants. See Perreault (1999).
2. The website of the Ministry of Citizenship and Immigration Canada has a short description of all Canada–Quebec agreements. See: <www.cic.gc.ca/english/policy/fed-prov/can-que-guide.html>.

References

Abu-Laban, Y., and C. Gabriel. 2002. *Selling Diversity: Immigration, Multiculturalism, Employment Equity and Globalization*. Peterborough, Ont.: Broadview Press.

Ajzenstat, J. 1995. 'Decline of Procedural Liberalism: The Slippery Slope to Secession'. In *Is Quebec Nationalism Just?*, ed. J.H. Carens. Montreal and Kingston: McGill–Queen's University Press.

Beaudoin, G. 2002. 'La philosophie constitutionnelle du rapport Pepin-Robarts'. In *Le débat qui n'a pas eu lieu. La commission Pepin-Robarts, quelque vingt ans après*, ed. J.-P. Wallot. Ottawa: University of Ottawa Press.

Bickerton, J., S. Brooks, and A.-G. Gagnon. 2003. *Six penseurs en quête de liberté, d'égalité et de communauté*. Sainte-Foy, Que.: Presses de l'Université Laval.

Bourque, G., and J. Duchastel. 2000. 'Multiculturalisme, pluralisme et communauté politique: le Canada et le Québec'. In *Mondialisation, citoyenneté et multiculturalisme*, ed. M. Elbaz and D. Helly. Sainte-Foy, Que.: Presses de l'Université Laval.

Cairns, A.C. 1995. 'The Case for Charter Federalism', in *Reconfigurations:*

Canadian Citizenship and Constitutional Change, Selected Essays by Alan C. Cairns, ed. D.E. Williams. Toronto: McClelland & Stewart.

Caldwell, G. 1988. 'Immigration et la nécessité d'une culture publique commune', *L'Action Nationale* 78, 8: 705–11.

———. 2001. *La culture publique commune.* Québec: Editions Nota Bene.

Gagnon, A.-G., and J. Garcea. 1988. 'Quebec and the Pursuit of Special Status'. In *Perspectives on Canadian Federalism*, ed. R.D. Olling and M.W. Westmacott. Scarborough, Ont.: Prentice-Hall Canada.

——— and R. Iacovino. 2007. *Federalism, Citizenship and Quebec: Debating Multinationalism.* Toronto: University of Toronto Press.

——— and J. Tully. 2001. *Multinational Democracies.* Cambridge: Cambridge University Press.

Harvey, J. 1991. 'Culture publique, intégration et pluralisme', *Relations* (Oct.): 239–341.

Ignatieff, M. 2000. *The Rights Revolution.* Toronto: Anansi.

Kernerman, G. 2005. *Multicultural Nationalism: Civilizing Difference, Constituting Community.* Vancouver: University of British Columbia Press.

Kymlicka, W. 1991. *Liberalism, Community and Culture.* Oxford: Clarendon Press.

———. 1995. *Multicultural Citizenship: A Liberal Theory of Minority Rights.* Oxford: Oxford University Press.

———. 1998. *Finding Our Way: Rethinking Ethnocultural Relations in Canada.* Toronto: Oxford University Press.

LaSelva, S. 1996. *The Moral Foundations of Canadian Federalism: Paradoxes, Achievements and Tragedies of Nationhood.* Montreal and Kingston: McGill–Queen's University Press.

Liberal Party of Canada. 2004. *Moving Canada Forward: The Paul Martin Plan for Getting Things Done.* Ottawa.

Mandel, M. 1989. *The Charter of Rights and the Legalization of Politics in Canada.* Toronto: Wall and Thompson.

McRoberts, K. 1993. 'English Canadian Perceptions of Quebec'. In *Quebec: State and Society*, 2nd edn, ed. A.-G. Gagnon. Scarborough, Ont.: Nelson Canada.

———. 2001. 'Canada and the Multinational State', *Canadian Journal of Political Science* 34, 4: 683–713.

Pal, L. 1993. *Interests of State: The Politics of Language, Multiculturalism and Feminism in Canada.* Montreal and Kingston: McGill–Queen's University Press.

Perreault, R. 1999. 'Notes pour une allocution de Monsieur Robert Perreault sur la réforme des services d'intégration et de francisation', Quebec: Ministère des Relations avec les citoyens et de l'Immigration. At: <www.mrci.gouv. qc.ca/775_2.asp>.

Québec. 1990. *Au Québec pour bâtir ensemble. Énoncé de politique en matière d'immigration et d'intégration.* Québec: Gouvernement du Québec, Ministère des communautés culturelles et de l'immigration du Québec, Direction des communications.

Reference re Secession of Quebec [20 Aug. 1998], <www.justice.gc.ca/en/index.html>.

Renan, E. 1887 [1882]. 'Qu'est-ce qu'une nation?', *Discours et conférences*. Paris: Calmann-Lévy.

Rocher, F. 2005. 'Les relations fédérales-provinciales à l'ère Martin'. In *L'annuaire du Québec, 2005*, ed. M. Venne. Montreal: Fides.

———, G. Rocher, and M. Labelle. 1995. 'Pluriethnicité, citoyenneté et intégration: de la souveraineté pour lever les obstacles et les ambiguïtés', *Cahiers de recherche sociologique* 25: 213–45.

Russell, P. 1993. 'Can the Canadians Be a Sovereign People?' In *The Canadian Political Tradition*, ed. R.S. Blair and J.T. McLeod. Toronto: Nelson Canada.

Seymour, M. 2001. *Le pari de la démesure: l'intransigeance canadienne face au Québec*. Montreal: L'Hexagone.

Simeon, R. 1988. 'Meech Lake and Visions of Canada'. In *Competing Constitutional Visions: The Meech Lake Accord*, ed. K.E. Swinton and C.J. Rogerson. Toronto: Carswell.

Taylor, Charles. 1991. 'Shared and Divergent Values'. In *Options for a New Canada*, ed. R.L. Watts and D.M. Brown. Toronto: University of Toronto Press.

Trudeau, P.E. 1962. 'The Multinational State in Canada: The Interaction of Nationalism in Canada', *Canadian Forum* (June): 51.

Tully, J. 1995. *Strange Multiplicity: Constitutionalism in an Age of Diversity*. Cambridge: Cambridge University Press.

———. 'Introduction'. In *Multinational Democracies*, ed. A.-G. Gagnon and J. Tully. Cambridge: Cambridge University Press.

———. Forthcoming. *Understanding Imperialism Today: From Colonial Imperialism through Decolonization to Post-Colonial Imperialism*. Cambridge: Cambridge University Press.

Webber, J. 1994. *Reimagining Canada: Language, Culture, Community and the Canadian Constitution*. Montreal and Kingston: McGill–Queen's University Press.

Websites

Canada Research Chair in Quebec and Canadian Studies: www.creqc.uqam.ca
Interdisciplinary Research Centre on Diversity in Quebec: www.cridaq.uqam.ca
Ethnicity and Democratic Governance: www.edg-gde.ca

Democratizing Executive Federalism: The Role of Non-Governmental Actors in Intergovernmental Agreements

Julie M. Simmons

In early 2005, then Prime Minister Paul Martin brokered two high-profile intergovernmental deals involving two different regions of the country. In February, Martin made five-year agreements on offshore resource revenues with the premiers of Nova Scotia and Newfoundland and Labrador worth $830 million and $2.6 billion respectively. Four months later, he responded to Ontario Premier Dalton McGuinty's campaign for Ontario's 'Fair Share', announcing that an additional $5.75 billion in federal dollars would be transferred to that province over five years. In both instances, the agreements were the result of a series of exchanges dating back several months, if not years, between high-level officials and first ministers of the two orders of government. But in watching the televised signing ceremony in Newfoundland in February, or the press conference following the nine-hour meeting between Prime Minister Martin and Premier McGuinty in May, one could not but be struck by the discretionary power enjoyed by prime ministers and premiers in the Canadian institutions of government.

Although the prime minister and the premiers are heads of democratically elected governments, the democratic legitimacy of this pattern of decision-making can be disputed. In each case the prime minister, together with his provincial counterpart, celebrated the commitment of billions of federal tax dollars to specific programs in specific provinces without any discussion of or agreement to these commitments in the House of Commons or any provincial legislature. Adjectives one might use to describe intergovernmental negotiations in Canada include tedious and cumbersome. But the prime minister's ability to commit in one private meeting to more federal funding for Ontario than his government had earmarked for sharing among 10 provinces in the development of a national child-care program (for example) reminds us once again of executive federalism's breathtaking efficiency.[1]

Executive federalism can perform well as a forum for negotiating and reaching agreement between two equal orders of government. But the better executive federalism performs in this regard, the more closely its effectiveness at resolving policy problems should be scrutinized. As with most intergovernmental agreements, the Atlantic Accords and the Ontario Fair Share deal themselves do not have legal status.[2] Accordingly, when the Stephen Harper Conservative minority government replaced the Martin Liberal minority government in January of 2006, fiscal federalism resurfaced in these provinces as a matter of federal–provincial debate. While the above agreements may have alleviated some tensions in the federation, they have also created many new ones. The 2005 Ontario deal has not brought an end to the 'fair share' campaign of the Ontario government, and the deals with Ontario, Newfoundland, and New Brunswick led to calls in Saskatchewan and other provinces for the fiscal attention of Ottawa. The fissures between petroleum–producing provinces and the others and among 'have', 'almost have', and 'have-not' provinces are now more perceptible in negotiations on fiscal imbalance and equalization. As in many of the other cases examined in this volume, whether executive federalism performed well in the above cases is contingent upon the preferred policy outcomes of the evaluator.

The more substantive the policy outcomes of intergovernmental agreements are, the more immediate is the question of executive federalism's legitimacy. When Prime Minister Martin and his provincial counterparts reached compromises behind closed doors, they drew attention to executive federalism's imperfect fit with the idea that policy should result from transparent and public deliberation in elected forums of decision-making. Whether this tension between intergovernmental relations and the role of legislatures constitutes a democratic deficit is open to debate, as Richard Simeon notes elsewhere in this volume. Adding to the complexity of the debate is the role of citizens and advocacy groups in intergovernmental policy-making.

This chapter explores why this debate about the democratic character of executive federalism is unresolved, identifying the storylines about democracy, effective governance, and identity that currently underlie arguments about the role of non-governmental actors in intergovernmental deliberations.[3] It investigates the complex relationship between representative democracy and participatory democracy: the former, a system in which elected representatives and their officials alone make decisions; the latter, a system in which citizens deliberate with elected and unelected government actors. The chapter identifies three models of democracy— representative, consultative, and deliberative participatory—that differ in terms of the role that non-governmental actors (unelected individual citizens, or representatives of groups whose members share an interest or identity) have in policy-making with an intergovernmental dimension. The chapter provides examples of these three models drawn from recent intergovernmental negotiations and agreements. Finally, the chapter explores what might account for the variation in different models of democracy at work in intergovernmental relations. It concludes that the principles and rationales guiding interaction with non-governmental actors in particular policy sectors have a tendency to spill over into intergovernmental decision-making. Nevertheless, non-governmental participation in intergovernmental relations tends to be mitigated by the principles of representative democracy. These principles underpin executive federalism and the forces of elite accommodation found there. It is challenging to reconcile participatory democracy with representative democracy in policy-making in general. It is even more challenging in an intergovernmental decision-making process.

The Debatable Democratic Deficit of Intergovernmental Relations

Concerns about a democratic deficit stem from questions about (a) the impact of intergovernmental relations on responsible government and (b) who can best represent the interests of Canadians—elected representatives, citizens, 'stakeholders', or 'policy experts'. Executives of majority governments can enter into intergovernmental agreements assured, by virtue of party discipline, that their home legislature will have confidence in their actions. Further, intergovernmental agreements rarely require legislative change, and thus rarely become the subject of debate in any legislative forum. One consequence is low public awareness of policy developments. When intergovernmental meetings take place, they may or may not result in carefully crafted communiqués, and even these may leave rather unclear what headway ministers have made. Even when such communiqués are decipherable, they are unlikely to garner the same degree of media attention as would a debate within a legislature. Survey data suggest that Canadians continue to find it difficult to trace which elected executives—federal or provincial—are responsible for which policy developments (Cutler and Mendelsohn, 2005).

During the constitutional negotiations of the 1980s and 1990s, the legitimacy of executive federalism became intertwined with broader concerns about representative government itself. On matters of constitutional change, considerable consensus suggests that, in a post-Charter era, rights-bearing Canadians will not accept the idea of democracy being reduced to indirect representation through their elected premier and prime minister meeting behind closed doors (Banting, 1997; Stein, 1993; Brock, 1995; Simeon and Cameron, 2002). The Meech Lake Accord, a carefully crafted consensus among first ministers, failed to be ratified in every provincial legislature, in part because groups of citizens sharing common identities or interests were critical of its content and the closed process through which it had been negotiated. The results of the federal government's 1991 Citizens' Forum on Canada's Future (the Spicer Commission) confirmed that these views were widespread among Canadians. In a marked departure from traditional executive federalism, first ministers involved citizens in the ratification of the Charlottetown Accord through a referendum. What the failure of the Charlottetown Accord suggested about the possibilities for citizen involvement in future constitutional change has been open to debate. For Atkinson (1994), the lesson was that the 'aggregative' process of bargaining and coalition-building among grassroots interests was as vulnerable to stalemate as the 'integrative' process of achieving consensus through deliberation and debate among elites. Similarly, Lusztig (1994) forecast that constitutional change would ultimately fail if the masses in a divided society were part of the legitimization process. More optimistic accounts have suggested that the problem lay not in the fact that non-governmental actors were included in the Charlottetown process, but in the manner of their inclusion (Chambers, 1998). The key is to create spaces for deliberation for non-elites that are integrative (non-majoritarian) (Mendelsohn, 2000). Regardless of the variation in these interpretations, the last two episodes of mega-constitutional politics revealed that, at least when it comes to constitutional change, representative government is insufficiently democratic to meet citizen expectations.

There are other storylines in the contemporary debate about the adequacy of representative democracy that affect the debate about the legitimacy of executive federalism. A disturbing number of Canadians perceive government to be unresponsive to them, and their trust in those they elect is low. Mebs Kanji (2002: 74) warns that if the public's confidence in governmental institutions declines further or their mistrust in politics rises, it 'may eventually detract from the public's overall support for the system of representative government'. Voting rates in Canadian national elections are low, even by international standards. At the same time, Canadians' participation in protest politics—for example, signing a petition, boycotting a product, or attending a lawful demonstration—is higher than ever, and stands out in an international comparison of advanced industrialized democracies (Gidengil et al., 2004).[4]

This citizen interest in alternative participation in the political process has led many theorists to focus on the policy-making process itself, rather than its outcomes, as a measure of democratic legitimacy.[5] The most common storyline maintains that providing citizens with a formalized role in the policy-making process would be beneficial for democracy. Public participation is thought to allow individuals to share views (something the act of voting does not accommodate); enable participants to explore a wider option of alternatives; produce decisions that are more likely to be in the public interest; create the perception of the final decision as legitimate; and enhance citizen understanding through the consideration of others' views (Abelson et al., 2003: 241–2). Proponents of this kind of citizen involvement in public policy argue that, if representative democracy were supplemented with public deliberation, individual citizens might be more likely to revise their opinions in the light of discussion with others (Chambers, 2003). Of particular importance to some advocates of deliberative democracy is its link to the recognition of difference. Democratic processes must accommodate the participation of self-named communities of identities and interests, thereby giving voice to and empowering minority or marginalized groups that otherwise would not be heard or have a means of participation

(Patten, 2001). Indeed, local, provincial, and federal governments have experimented with these forms of public participation. However, resources of time and finances are required to facilitate the participation of a wide array of interests and identities in a policy-making process, and sometimes such a process is incompatible with government timelines and expectations of efficiency. Moreover, the greater the number of participants and the diversity of the perspectives they share, the more challenging it is to make the process meaningful for the participants.

Always present in any discussion of intergovernmental relations in Canada are two alternative conceptions of who best represents Canadians: the federal government or provincial governments as a whole. The question of who represents Canadians is all the more complex when non-governmental actors, representing themselves or a particular identity or interest, or policy 'experts' outside the public service are part of the process. Should only those with something at 'stake' be involved in a policy process? If so, who determines whether an individual is a 'stakeholder'? Grace Skogstad reminds us that so-called 'expert' advice is not a democratic source of legitimacy (Skogstad, 2003) When expert opinion is at variance with the views and interests of citizens affected by a policy, how should governments respond?

Given the resources needed for meaningful citizen involvement, many view elected representatives as the most legitimate actors to represent Canadians in policy-making. Reflecting on the role of non-governmental actors in intergovernmental relations, Hugh Thorburn (1989: 177) cautions that democracy is not necessarily enhanced by a decision-making process in which there is no guarantee that 'all groups' or even 'groups representing all' can or will participate. Similarly, Jennifer Smith (2004: 105) reminds us that interest group lobbying of ministers and government officials involved in intergovernmental deliberations 'has a behind the scenes quality that precludes widespread and informed public debate about whatever is at issue'.

In addition, some scholars have raised questions about how governments use non-governmental input. Éric Montpetit (2006) worries that the federal government might engage stakeholders or citizens as a way of making decision-making processes that exclude provincial governments appear more legitimate. Especially in the case of executive federalism, where the legitimacy of executives making extra-parliamentary decisions has traditionally hinged on their accountability to their respective elected legislatures, grafting opportunities for non-governmental participation onto intergovernmental forums may do less to strengthen democracy than would a focus on revitalizing deliberation among elected representatives within individual legislatures. As Hartley and Skogstad (2005: 324) argue, 'where accountability of public officials to their citizens is at a premium, retaining this democratic value turns one in the direction of reforms to strengthen the representational and deliberative character of parliamentary institutions.'

Another storyline contributing to the contemporary debate about the legitimacy of executive federalism stems from the paradigm of the New Public Management. Beginning in the 1980s, the adequacy of the expertise within the public sector was contested. Public servants were encouraged to see themselves as service providers whose mandate was to be more responsive to citizen needs. Based on a market model of customer satisfaction, better public policy is thought to result from consultation with those—variously referred to as customers, clients, or stakeholders—who will use the policy or service that government seeks to develop.[6] Donald Savoie (2003: 105) explains that in the 1990s 'the ability to arrive at a stable consensus over which problems to address, to secure an understanding with the relevant sectors of the public over actions to take, and to bring a "horizontal perspective" to all issues of public policy became as important as the substance of the policy itself.' The same considerations arise in the context of intergovernmental relations. For example, Harvey Lazar (2006: 42) argues that adjustments to the 'intergovernmental dimension of the social union' require the involvement of 'people found in the sector ministries of provincial and federal governments and among the interest and stakeholder groups whose members are most affected'.

In the 1990s management reform also included reducing the overall size of the public sector. One result was a blurring of the boundary between the public sector and the voluntary sector by advocating their partnership and collaboration in the creation and delivery of services. According to this storyline, non-governmental actors function not simply as passive gauges of public opinion, but as active partners.[7] The role of public servants changes as well. Previously anonymous public servants are now 'legitimate policy actors outside government circles' (Savoie, 2003: 109).

Whether the new administrative practices of responsiveness to and partnership with clients/citizens actually strengthen democracy or lead to better policies is a matter of debate (Pierre, 1998). Encouraging public servants to be accountable to the interests they serve seems to undermine the idea that public servants are accountable to the Crown. The more the nature of government interaction with non-governmental actors shifts from responsiveness to collaboration, with non-governmental actors playing a role as decision-makers and deliverers of services alongside the elected and permanent executive, the more important it becomes to ask whom non-governmental actors represent and to whom they are accountable. However, the important point here is that the goals of responsiveness and collaboration are the current reality for public servants. Together with the distinctly Canadian experience of popular sovereignty and constitutional reform, these storylines about the adequacy of representative government and what constitutes a legitimate process of decision-making in general inform the current debate about the legitimacy of executive federalism in particular. They are also reflected in the varying approaches to the inclusion of non-governmental actors in intergovernmental relations. Before examining these varying approaches, the next section identifies dimensions of participation that correspond to each storyline.

Dimensions of Participation

In order to distinguish different forms of non-governmental participation in intergovernmental relations, it is useful to think of three models of democracy. Each is inspired by one of the storylines described above. There are two separate sites at which intergovernmental actors can be part of intergovernmental relations. The first is at the level of individual governments, whether federal or provincial; the second is within intergovernmental forums. The models of democracy differ according to the activity in which government and non-governmental actors partake, the nature of the non-governmental actors involved, and who ultimately makes the policy decision. Although the models of democracy may share some characteristics, they differ from one another in at least one regard.

Underlying the first model, *representative democracy*, is the idea that elected representatives have sufficient legitimacy to represent the views of citizens. Accordingly, there is no *formal* role for non-governmental actors. Although various interests in society may organize in groups to lobby federal or provincial governments, or even an intergovernmental forum, government actors do not seek to engage non-governmental actors, and ultimately decision-making authority resides with elected officials.

By contrast, *consultative democracy* is likely inspired by the New Public Management's emphasis on government responsiveness to citizens. Government actors deliberately seek advice from the group of citizens who will be most affected by a government decision, or seek to explain to that group why the government's plan is the best possible course of action. The non-governmental participants are commonly referred to as clients or stakeholders. Although government actors may meet repeatedly with non-governmental actors, iterative consultation does not necessarily occur. Interaction may also take the form of one-way consultation, with government actors listening to the views of clients or stakeholders, or, alternatively, governments telling clients and stakeholders why a particular decision has been made. Governments may engage in two-way consultation, asking for input from non-governmental actors but also sharing information with them as well. Governments may also conduct three-way consultation, exchanging information and ideas with non-governmental actors, but also facilitating a dialogue among the non-governmental actors. The significant point is that government actors remain the final decision-makers in the consultative democracy model. However, because responsiveness to citizens, or at least its appearance, is a primary goal, consultative democracy often involves governments 'reporting back' on how non-governmental actors' participation affected the final policy outcome. Explaining this link to participants enhances the latter's sense of how they affected the real process of decision-making.

Sandra Burt (2002: 234) describes this sense as one of 'expressive involvement'. The participation exercise is not oriented towards non-governmental actors learning from one another; there is little attention paid to providing an opportunity for non-governmental actors to engage in a process of self-reflection after having heard the perspectives of others.

Participatory deliberative democracy is distinguished from representative and consultative democracy in several ways.[8] This form of democracy involves citizens as participants in deliberation with government actors.[9] The purpose of the exercise is not to pursue one's own interests, at the expense of the accommodation of others, or even to achieve an outcome that accommodates all interests. Rather, it is to explore why interests differ.[10] With this purpose in mind, interaction is necessarily multidirectional: participants have multiple opportunities to meet with one another, ideally without time limitations on the exercise, and particular care is taken to ensure that members of identity groups who might not otherwise have the means to mobilize are given the resources they need to be informed participants in the process. This last measure is more substantial than governments issuing an open invitation for the public to comment on an ongoing development. It is also different from government actors choosing groups that they perceive to represent the spectrum of stakeholders affected by a policy decision, or, alternatively, that they believe to be sufficiently informed to participate, as often occurs with consultative democracy. Although participatory deliberative democracy includes the possibility for elected officials to share the authority to make decisions with non-governmental actors, the more likely outcome is for the process of engagement to inform the final decision of governments in a way that is clear to the participants. It is unrealistic for all participants to assume that policy outcomes will accommodate their specific perspectives; however, non-governmental participation that parallels real decision-making, as opposed to being part of it, runs the risk of feeding public cynicism.

In mapping the existence of representative, consultative, and participatory deliberative democracy, this chapter distinguishes between activities that individual governments initiate and those attached to specific intergovernmental forums of ministers. This distinction is important because there are longstanding arguments about how the site of participation impacts on the effectiveness and legitimacy of intergovernmental decision-making. On the one hand, excluding non-governmental actors from the intergovernmental site of decision-making is thought to limit the influence of non-governmental actors on the decision-making process and outcome. It can be disillusioning to be part of a meaningful process of public participation with one's provincial government or with the federal government, only to be informed that the results of that public deliberation just couldn't be accommodated at the intergovernmental table. As Richard Simeon (1972: 282) observes, when the concerns that non-governmental groups have brought to individual governments are 'less central than status or ideological goals of governments, they will be the first to be jettisoned in the conference room'. At the same time, however, engaging non-governmental actors in intergovernmental forums may reduce the effectiveness of those forums in terms of their ability to produce new or revised policy.

With these models of democracy and sites of participation in mind, it is possible to distinguish among different roles for non-governmental actors in select cases of intergovernmental activity.[11] These differences are summarized in Table 17.1 and discussed in regard to the fiscal imbalance, the Social Union Framework Agreement, the Canada-Wide Accord on Environmental Harmonization, and the Canada Forest Accord and National Forest Strategy.

Social Union Framework Agreement

The defeat of the Meech Lake Accord demonstrated the necessity of supplementing representative democracy with direct democracy, and the failure of the Charlottetown Accord made clear the complexity of this task. The Social Union Framework Agreement (SUFA) of 1999 provides a compelling contrast with the Charlottetown Accord process. The SUFA was the culmination of an initiative that began among the provinces in 1995 to bring greater predictability to the use of the federal spending power, to provide a larger role for provinces in establishing principles to guide social policy, and to manage disagreements over both. More than a year of formal negotiations between the two orders of government concluded in January 1999 with a first ministers' meeting in Ottawa. It was marked by the same kind of brinkmanship as earlier rounds of constitutional negotiations. Provincial delegations received the draft agreement shortly before Prime Minister Chrétien met with the premiers in a closed meeting. Nine of the 10 premiers agreed to the deal with an offer of $2.5 billion for health care on the dinner table.

This case followed the representative democracy model. Throughout the negotiations, provincial representatives focused on reaching and maintaining consensus among themselves, rather than on developing ways to involve citizens or groups in the deliberations. As a less than enthusiastic participant in the talks, the federal government was not interested in publicizing them further. While public awareness of the process was limited, pressure to open the process came from a spectrum of social policy groups, major labour unions, and social policy think-tanks. Some social policy institutions, such as the Canadian Centre for Policy Alternatives (see Leduc Browne, 1998), even conducted their own round tables on what the subject matter of the framework should be and how the public might be integrated into the process. The secrecy of the social union negotiations led some groups to make assumptions about the nature of the discussions, which further fuelled their campaign for inclusion. While for many public servants SUFA was an administrative agreement, social activists were more concerned with its potential longer-term consequences for the process and substance of social policy. To the extent that non-governmental actors participated in deliberation on the social union negotiations, their participation was not formally linked to the state apparatus and the intergovernmental decision-making process.

The Fiscal Imbalance Debate

Subsequent to the election of a new federal government in 2006, the debate about the federal spending power and 'fiscal imbalance' has again grown louder. By mid-2006, non-governmental actors had been incorporated into discussions around the fiscal imbalance in at least three different ways.

Table 17.1   Roles for Non-Governmental Actors in Select Intergovernmental Relations

Site of Participation	Representative	Consultative	Participatory Deliberative
Intergovernmental	• Social Union Framework Agreement	• Fiscal imbalance (interprovincial) • Canada-Wide Accord on Environmental Harmonization	• Canada Forest Accord and National Forest Strategy
Individual Government	• Social Union Framework Agreement	• Fiscal imbalance (federal–provincial) • Canada-Wide Accord on Environmental Harmonization (federal) • National Child Benefit (federal)	

(1) The premiers collectively agreed, through the Council of the Federation, to establish an 'independent panel' to investigate vertical and fiscal balance and make recommendations to the premiers on how to address any imbalances. Although the panel consisted of just five people with academic, public-sector and business expertise, the panel's engagement of individual citizens reflects some of the characteristics of participatory deliberative democracy. The panel asked Canadian Policy Research Networks, a think-tank, to lead a dialogue with Canadians. A total of 93 randomly selected Canadians participated in five day-long regional sessions held in major city centres. Twenty-one of the regional participants 'reflecting a diversity of backgrounds and perspectives' then participated in a national dialogue process (Advisory Panel on Fiscal Imbalance, 2006: 109). At the regional conferences, participants discussed four different alternative federal–provincial fiscal arrangements.

The executive summary of the citizens' dialogue reveals that it was oriented to exploring differences among participants, having them reflect on each others' views, and attempting to establish a set of shared understandings. These features are hallmarks of the participatory deliberative democracy model:

> participants discussed the four approaches to sharing funds, identifying what they liked and disliked about each approach and why. They agreed on their common

ground and differences, probed tensions among competing values and determined the tradeoffs that they were prepared to make. Through this process they identified the values and principles that they want to see guide the sharing of funds in Canada (ibid., 109–10).

The resulting advice to decision-makers is apparent in the recommendations of the report of the Advisory Panel. In addition to citizens, the panel engaged 20 'experts'—former elected and unelected public servants, academics, and individuals affiliated with several think-tanks—in a three-day round table. However, because the results of this round table are not part of the report, how the round table informed the report is less clear. Two important observations can made about this process. Government officials—elected or unelected—were several degrees removed from this engagement with citizens. Second, given the premiers' very different perspectives on how to resolve the issue of fiscal imbalance, the influence of the Advisory Panel on the premiers' positions is difficult to trace. Accordingly, at this stage it is prudent to characterize this example as one of consultative democracy.

(2) The federal government also engaged non-governmental actors in establishing its position on fiscal imbalance. In March 2005, the Martin Liberal government created a five-person Expert Panel on Equalization and Territorial Formula Financing (2006a). Like the Council of the Federation's Advisory Panel, this Expert Panel did not work in isolation. It invited e-mail submissions in reaction to a 'Key Issues' paper posted on its website. The Expert Panel also held five regional round tables and a round table of academics. Unlike the Advisory Panel's engagement of *citizens*, these round tables provided 'additional opportunities for academics, government officials, business representatives, and other interested parties to meet with the Expert Panel' (Expert Panel, 2006b). Although the summaries of the round-table discussions imply some variation in their format, they also suggest that the emphasis was on participants stating their views with rapporteurs submitting their impressions of the key themes and areas of disagreement among participants. This process differs from one in which participants engage in self-reflection and identify shared principles and points of disagreement. One summary of a regional round table states that:

> The roundtable did not drive for consensus, and thus some caution must be exercised in applying the conclusions that follow to the entire group of participants; no votes were called and opposing points of view may not always have been expressed. It should also be noted that the opinions that were expressed were, in many cases, just that—opinions (Gibbins, 2005).

Unlike the participation process associated with the provincial advisory panel, in which regional exercises informed a national exercise, with some repeat participants, the participation process associated with the federal government's Expert Panel provided snapshots of regional opinions at one point in time. Of the three forms of democracy, this process most closely resembles consultative democracy. It is important to note, however, that—as with the Premiers' Advisory Report— it is not yet clear how this Expert Panel Report will affect the position of the federal Conservative government in future negotiations on fiscal imbalance.

(3) A similar form of consultative democracy is evident in the actions of the Ontario government on the issue of fiscal imbalance.[11] In this case, the government of Ontario hosted a one-day summit on 'strengthening Ontario's future and our country's fiscal arrangement' for over 200 'leaders, stakeholders, and citizens to share their views'. The participants 'represented all of the province's regions, political orientations, and sectors, including business, healthcare, education, agriculture, municipal governments, community groups and the academic world' (Ontario, 2006b). This inclusiveness was consistent with a model of participatory deliberative democracy. However, the day's activities were more reminiscent of the consultative democracy model. After Premier McGuinty outlined his vision for fiscal arrangements and participants heard from a 'panel of experts', participants, guided by a discussion paper, engaged in small discussion group activities. The summary of the discussions was supposed to 'help shape Ontario's position as we proceed with discussion with the federal government and other provinces and territories in the months ahead' (Bountrogianni, 2006). Once again, however, it remained unclear to what extent the results of this one-day summit would be reflected in the position of the government of Ontario. Although the process resembled consultative democracy, the discussion paper and the resulting report on outcomes both stressed that the summit was part of an ongoing dialogue (Ontario, 2006a, 2006b).

These three examples of governmental efforts to bring non-governmental actors into the fiscal imbalance debate suggest three important observations. First, these exercises took place in the early stages of negotiations on concrete options between the two orders of government. Much of the federal–provincial activity still lay ahead. Second, the consultations were nevertheless a departure from the approach of first ministers to the social union in the late 1990s. In the case of SUFA, the debate was public only inasmuch as it was reported by the media. Even though the fiscal balance is among the more difficult policy topics for citizens to comprehend, more Canadians became aware of equalization as a result of these processes of engagement (and the published reports that followed) than would otherwise have been the case. More Canadians could contemplate the merits of various federal–provincial fiscal arrangements than in the past. Third, the three fiscal imbalance exercises reflected, to varying degrees, appeals to popular and expert authority to legitimize the substance of the reports. The extent to which appealing to expert authority, as opposed to popular authority, is democratic is discussed further in the conclusion of this chapter.

National Child Benefit

Moving away from the high politics of first ministers' intergovernmental relations, we can see that government actors, either alone or in concert with their colleagues in other jurisdictions, engage non-governmental actors in various ways. These forms of participation echo the patterns and principles that guide interaction with non-governmental actors in specific sectors. Within social policy circles the language of 'the voluntary sector' is relatively common. Intergovernmental developments reveal traces of these undercurrents as well. The 1997 National Child Benefit is arguably the most significant social policy development in the Chrétien era. This initiative consolidates income support measures for children in families with lower incomes. It emerged in an era following the 1995 Quebec referendum on sovereignty in which the federal government was keen to demonstrate the flexibility of federal–provincial arrangements possible in the federation. It is all the more remarkable because, at the time, relations between provincial social services ministers and their federal counterpart were strained because of major cuts to federal fiscal transfers to the provinces.

In the case of the National Child Benefit, the federal government drew upon the expertise and initiative of individuals with ties to social policy think-tanks. The Caledon Institute of Social Policy had published proposals for an integrated benefit, and Ken Battle, president of the Caledon Institute, became an adviser to the Minister of Human Resources and Development, participating in the initial discussion of the working group of federal and provincial officials seeking to establish a new, integrated policy. There was also a very limited role for a reference group of nine hand-picked representatives of anti-poverty associations, children's policy advocates, or more general social policy institutes or organizations. The federal minister and/or his officials met with this reference group on five occasions. This form of non-governmental participation was consultative, however, with federal officials listening to the concerns of the reference group members, and in turn briefing participants on the details of the new scheme. While some provincial officials and ministers accepted invitations to meet with the minister's reference group, the latter did not adopt an intergovernmental character. The reference group was established after governments had agreed to the general design of the benefit and had collectively established a shared understanding of its rationale. Accordingly, the opportunity for meaningful debate with non-governmental actors about broader strategies to alleviate poverty was limited.

Canada-Wide Accord on Environmental Harmonization

In environmental policy-making, the voices of stakeholders are commonly heard, and again, these voices carry over into the intergovernmental decision-making forum. The Canadian Council of Ministers of the Environment (CCME) is the most transparent and systematic of intergovernmental forums in routinely integrating non-governmental actors into its policy development. As well, this forum is perhaps the most institutionalized of all intergovernmental bodies, with its full-time secretariat located in Winnipeg, established core operating principles, multi-year business plan, formalized task groups, and even an on-line bookstore for its publications (Simmons, 2004). The CCME maintains a consultation calendar of upcoming multi-stakeholder workshops and an extensive database of interested actors who are contacted for such purposes. Since 1998 much of the work of the CCME is governed by the 1998 Canada-Wide Accord on Environmental Harmonization, signed by all ministers except Quebec's. The process by which this Accord was established reveals how embedded the concept of multistakeholder consultation is in the environmental policy sector; and, at the same time, the complexity of practising multistakeholder consultation in the realm of intergovernmental decision-making.

Through the process between 1993 and 1998 of developing the Accord, both individual governments and the CCME initiated consultation with non-governmental actors (Fafard, 1997). The CCME created a 16-person National Advisory Group of 'stakeholders' from 'key sectors' to receive 'ongoing advice and feedback', particularly on how to involve non-governmental actors in the broader process (CCME, 1994). In addition, the CCME sponsored a two-day national workshop of 40 non-governmental actors consisting of individuals and representatives of environmental organizations, industry associations, individual businesses, and First Nations. Some provinces further consulted within their borders, and Environment Canada created and consulted a small Harmonization Advisory Group of academics and interest group leaders. Federal and provincial officials also met with local actors when they travelled throughout the country to working group meetings. The well-organized community of environmental groups across Canada expressed fundamental reservations about the harmonization initiative at every opportunity, and also voiced their criticism of the process by which it was devised.

When compared to other sectors' intergovernmental relations, these measures to incorporate non-governmental actors are significant. Environmental actors' criticisms of the process resonated with the CCME. Even for the government officials involved in the process, the utility of the meetings with the national advisory group was compromised by the pace of policy development, and the result was consultation that was rather ad hoc in nature (Simmons, 2005). When ministers pushed aside their first-draft agreement to start negotiations anew, they paid much closer attention to the role of non-governmental actors in the policy development process and attempted to be more systematic and transparent in posting draft documents on-line for written comment, in hosting multistakeholder workshops, and again in creating an advisory group. However, the resolve of governments to push ahead with the harmonization initiative, with the encouragement of first ministers, was met by the determination of environmentalists to impede it. As a result, the CCME constructed opportunities to listen to non-governmental actors' concerns, rather than opportunities for multidirectional dialogue and learning across the various 'camps'. From the perspective of environmentalists, the consultation had little effect on the predetermined agenda of environmental ministers to 'rationalize' environmental policy (ibid.).

The Accord notes governments' agreement that 'openness, transparency, accountability and the effective participation of stakeholders and the public in environmental decision-making [are] necessary for an effective environmental management regime' and that 'working cooperatively with Aboriginal people in their structures of governance is necessary' (CCME, 1998a). However, criticism of the process the Accord engendered led to further reflection on the appropriate role of non-governmental interests in decision-making within the CCME. The ministerial council ultimately approved an Annex to the Accord in September of 1998 that aimed specifically to clarify issues of accountability and stakeholder participation in decisions made under the Accord (CCME, 1998b). This Annex implies that some form of non-governmental participation will be integrated into all decisions made under the Accord. Although the CCME retains discretion over the design of what it calls 'stakeholder participation', it acknowledges that meaningful participation requires many of the features of participatory deliberative democracy described above. These include giving those with an interest in an issue 'the opportunity to identify themselves and to participate in the process, including the development of the stakeholder participation process itself', ensuring timely stakeholder access 'to relevant information on issues, process and decisions taken', and clarifying for participants 'how their input will be used by governments'. The Annex even alludes to developing shared understandings. It notes that 'while remaining accountable to the constituencies they represent, participants should be willing to consider a broader perspective.' At the same time, the Annex notes that stakeholder participation should 'follow a realistic schedule with clear deadlines, and be cost-effective', making less likely the resource-intensive participatory deliberative democracy (ibid.).

Since the Accord was struck, the record of stakeholder participation in the CCME has been mixed. As discussed in the Chapter 13 by Winfield and Macdonald, there has been no consistent process for developing standards for toxic substances. That representatives of environmental groups declined to participate in the two-year review of the Accord is further evidence of significant variation in the approach of the CCME to non-governmental actors.

Canada Forest Accord and National Forest Strategy

An example of intergovernmental decision-making that further resembles participatory deliberative democracy is the activity of the National Forest Strategy Coalition (NFSC), under the rubric of the Canadian Council of Forest Ministers (CCFM). Since the CCFM was established in 1985 it has overseen three National Forest Strategies, each of which establishes a vision for a sustainable forest in Canada. The 1998–2003 strategy listed strategic priorities for guiding the policies and actions of Canada's forest community and over 100 separate 'commitments to action' reflecting these priorities. The National Forest Strategy for 2003–8 resulted from a process initiated by the NFSC, composed of the 42 signatories to the Canada Forest Accord, a companion document to the 1998–2003 strategy.[12] These 42 signatories included the federal Minister of Natural Resources and the ministers from each of the provinces and the territories (with the exception of Quebec), as well as industry organizations, conservation and Aboriginal groups, and professional associations. The 2003–8 strategy has the backing of 63 signatories to the Canada Forest Accord for 2003–8.[13] These agreements are distinctive from other intergovernmental agreements not just because non-governmental actors are signatories to them but also because of the scope of the deliberative processes used to establish them.

The 2003–8 strategy was the result of a development process that began in 2001 with an NFSC working group establishing and evaluating six different approaches to involving the 'forest community' in developing a new strategy. Ultimately the Coalition settled on an approach whereby it widely distributed copies of a Consultation Workbook in anticipation of six regional workshops held across the country in 2002. Completed workbooks and an independent evaluation of the previous National Forest Strategy informed the discussion at these regional workshops. Out of the feedback at the regional workshops and the completed workbooks, the Coalition created a 'What You Said' document, and a Vision and Issues paper that informed the first draft of the new strategy. 'Engaged Canadians' were then invited to comment on this draft. In early 2003 a national workshop, which brought 'a limited group of forest experts and leaders representing a wide array of Canadians at the national level' to review the draft in detail, resulted in a second draft of the strategy. It was posted on the Coalition's website for public comment and also distributed to 'engaged Canadians' (NFSC and CCFM, 2002). The final draft of the strategy was presented at the Ninth National Forest Congress in May 2003.

The strategy is described as a consensus document (NFSC, 2006), which, rather than 'satisfying everyone on all matters . . . focus[es] on a compelling vision and strong objectives to face priorities across our nation's forest' (NFSC and CCFM, 2002). As such, together with the broadly inclusive and deliberative process by which it was created, it is closer to participatory deliberative democracy than consultative democracy. Inasmuch as the signatories include non-governmental actors, it is certainly a departure from representative democracy. But like its 1992 and 1998 predecessors, the 2003–8 National Forest Strategy is a voluntary agreement. Each of the eight strategic themes outlined in the Strategy is to be supported by a team of governments and forest community organizations. Each team has a 'champion', in the form of one government or organization, whose task it is to 'invite the NFSC members, and enlist new members, to come forward to be part of one or more of the eight strategic theme teams' (NFSC, 2004: 7). Every member of each team is then asked to identify one or more actions pertaining to its particular strategic themes that he or she is prepared to work towards achieving. To date, five provincial departments and Natural Resources Canada have identified some action items to which they are committed, and there is clearly a link between the role of non-governmental actors and substantive policy outcomes. However, it is difficult to say whether the National Forest Strategy is pushing any of these departments in directions they would not otherwise have gone. Moreover, with the 2003–8 Accord, Quebec was joined by Alberta and Manitoba as provinces declining to sign the document.

Conclusions

This review of some of the ways in which non-governmental actors participate in intergovernmental relations reveals how the narratives of stakeholder participation, responsiveness to citizens/clients, and citizen deliberation that surface in policy-making circles are also apparent in the intergovernmental realm. Of the cases examined here, the most developed forms of non-governmental participation are within policy sectors (forestry and the environment). However, even first ministers are initiating round-table discussions and indirectly engaging citizens through the activities of the advisory or expert panels they establish (for example, discussions around the fiscal imbalance). Whether these initiatives enhance the legitimacy of intergovernmental relations depends on one's view of ideal democratic practices and whether there is indeed a democratic deficit to be addressed. But assessment also depends on the performance and effectiveness of executives. Are governments or intergovernmental forums that choose to engage non-governmental actors making headway on the policy issues around which non-governmental participation has been centred? If the answer is no, then even those in favour of participatory democracy would be disappointed.

The cases examined here reveal just how complex it is to marry non-governmental participation with intergovernmental decision-making. When attempting to reconcile forms of non-governmental participation common at the sectoral level with intergovernmental forums premised on the responsible government model, patterns of elite accommodation are difficult to avoid. In the National Child Benefit case, the performance and effectiveness of executive federalism appear to be at a high level. Federal and provincial governments jointly devised a new scheme benefiting the working poor in an era when governments were cutting programs. Yet there was a very limited role for non-governmental actors. In the case of the Canada-Wide Accord on Environmental Harmonization, the performance of executive federalism was high, but its effectiveness at addressing concerns expressed by environmentalists involved in the multistakeholder consultation was low. At the same time as government officials attempted to make interaction with stakeholders more systematic with the second attempt at drafting an Accord, the resolve of ministers to push ahead, as directed by first ministers, strengthened, irrespective of the outcomes of the stakeholder exercises. With the Canada Forest Accord and National Forest Strategy, the role for non-governmental actors is the most substantial, and resembles participatory deliberative democracy. However, despite high performance (the successful creation of an agreement), the effectiveness of this voluntary agreement in modifying existing forestry practices is questionable at best. It may be the case that with further experimentation, the current apparent trade-off between enhancing legitimacy through non-governmental participation and performance and effectiveness will diminish.

Should individual governments engage non-governmental actors, or should engagement take place at the intergovernmental level? On the one hand, engagement at the intergovernmental level carries the risk of further hampering effective outcomes. The intergovernmental decision-making process is already cumbersome, and mutual agreement on solutions by executives is difficult. On the other hand, if non-governmental actors are not engaged within intergovernmental forums, their concerns may be more easily sacrificed, intentionally or unintentionally, by governments in quest of a solution that meets their own preferences. The cases examined here reveal that the activity of elite accommodation—which is deeply embedded in intergovernmental relations—can reduce non-governmental actors' sense of political efficacy, irrespective of where the opportunity for participation is located. Both the federal government and the CCME engaged non-governmental actors in developing the Canada-Wide Accord on Environmental Harmonization. Yet in the end governments moved in a policy direction that dissatisfied the environmental community. This outcome suggests that even when non-governmental participation is attached to intergovernmental machinery, some constituencies will inevitably be dissatisfied with the policy outcomes. However, the National Child Benefit case suggests that when an individual government facilitates non-governmental participation apart from the intergovernmental process, non-governmental actors can also be disengaged from the active intergovernmental policy-making process.

The cases considered here do not settle the debate as to who most legitimately represents Canadians, or which site of non-governmental participation (intergovernmental or individual governments) is more democratic. In his study of transportation policy in Canada in the 1970s, Richard Schultz (1976) stressed that in federal–provincial relations, one or more governments might publicly engage a constituency of interests to bolster the legitimacy of its position vis-à-vis other sides in the negotiation. More recently, Éric Montpetit has argued that the federal government can use citizen engagement to justify bypassing negotiations with provincial governments altogether. 'Resorting to a democratic rhetoric, federal officials can stress the impossibility of betraying the engaged public in the face of provincial demands' (Montpetit, 2006: 98). At the core of these observations is the question of who—the federal government, non-governmental groups and individual citizens, or provincial governments—can best speak for Canadians. When elected executives, federal or provincial, invite non-governmental actors to participate in intergovernmental forums, they are in effect conceding their own inability to adequately represent the interests of Canadians.

The cases examined here reveal that individual governments' decisions to engage non-governmental actors in their own jurisdiction or invite non-governmental actors to participate in intergovernmental forums are not informed exclusively by their answer to the question 'Who best represents Canadians?' but are also guided by a variety of practical and strategic considerations. In the case of the National Child Benefit, there was a limited role for non-governmental actors in part because their involvement risked disturbing the emerging and still fragile federal–provincial co-operation among social services ministers. The reason why SUFA negotiations did not involve non-governmental actors to a significant extent may have been the difficulty of the two orders of government in establishing a starting point for the negotiations (Simmons, 2005). But it also seems that even when there is a chasm between federal government policy preferences and those of one or more provincial governments, a government—particularly the federal government—is unlikely to adopt a strategy of engaging non-governmental actors to enhance its legitimacy unless it is prepared to act on the collective preferences that emerge from a participatory process. In an era when public trust in politicians is low, governments cannot risk creating false expectations among citizens. Thus, although in the SUFA negotiations the federal government could have appealed to citizen preferences and adopted the position of social policy advocates to counter provincial government preferences for predictability and even containment of the federal use of its spending power, it did not initiate engagement with non-governmental actors. Provinces also did not engage citizens specifically on the social union issue. With much of the time and energy of intergovernmental actors necessarily devoted to maintaining the inter-provincial consensus, non-governmental participation became secondary. When one premier speaking to the media out of turn can destabilize a provincial consensus, the full-scale participation of non-governmental actors is indeed unlikely.

The strategic use of non-governmental actors by individual governments may become a reality in the current fiscal imbalance debate. Should governments use non-governmental participation to advance their strategic interests on the issue, one beneficial outcome would be that more citizens would be informed about the nature of fiscal imbalance and options for equalization reform. The potential downside, however, is that just as scenes involving some actors in a film end up on the editing room floor for reasons other than the quality of the actors' work, the perspectives of non-governmental actors may not be reflected in a final federal–provincial agreement. When non-governmental participation is used strategically, the sense of political efficacy of non-governmental actors is most threatened—and likely, as well, their trust in public officials.

These cases also point to the uneasy relationship between expert advice and citizen advice as well as the difference between collaborating with non-governmental actors in service delivery and participatory deliberative democracy. It is not surprising that with an issue as complex as fiscal imbalance, executives are finding ways to combine expert authority with citizen participation. But how to reconcile conflicts between these sources and the preferences of executives remains a challenge. Finally, the case of the Canada Forest Accord and National Forest Strategy demonstrates that impulses towards participatory deliberative democracy are not the same as impulses towards collaboration with non-governmental actors in the delivery of service or the realization of policy outcomes. Participatory deliberative democracy is seemingly a good fit for the development a voluntary agreement. But when the non-governmental actors involved in the process seek to influence the actions of governments, the policy outcome of a voluntary agreement again threatens citizens' sense of political efficacy.

Is executive federalism incompatible with meaningful non-governmental participation? It is true that in intergovernmental forums, the legitimacy of ministers and first ministers has traditionally been derived from their status as elected representatives responsible to a legislature for their actions. It is also true that intergovernmental forums have a long history of trade-offs made in order to reach a mutually accommodating outcome. Even so, it is too soon to draw any conclusions. The only way to answer the question definitively is to continue experimenting with roles for non-governmental actors in future intergovernmental deliberations.

Notes

The author wishes to thank the editors and the anonymous reviewers for their helpful comments on earlier versions of this chapter. The financial support of the Social Sciences and Humanities Research Council of Canada is gratefully acknowledged. This chapter is informed by interviews with government officials and non-governmental actors. Information from these interviews is incorporated into the text without attribution.

1. The Martin government had committed $5 billion over five years to early learning and child care, and in February 2005 federal, provincial, and territorial ministers responsible for social services were discussing 'a national vision and principles for early learning and child care systems in each province and territory' (Federal–Provincial–Territorial Ministers Responsible for Social Services, 2005).

2. However, the federal government did amend the Canada–Newfoundland Atlantic Accord Implementation Act (1987, c. 3) and the Canada–Nova Scotia Offshore Petroleum Resources Accord Implementation Act (1988, c.28) to reflect the content of the new Atlantic Accords. In contrast, there is no single written document detailing the agreement between the federal government and the government of Ontario.

3. I use the term 'storylines' drawing on Carolyn M. Hendricks's concept of participatory storylines, which she defines as the 'narratives on public participation that surround and shape the functioning and legitimacy of a deliberative forum' (2005: 2).

4. It should be noted, however, that Gidengil et al. (2004: 142) have also determined that individuals who are engaged in conventional forms of political participation are also most likely to partake in non-traditional forms of participation. They suggest a participation gap between affluent and highly educated Canadians and poorer, less educated Canadians.

5. Alternatively, this distinction is characterized by Scharpf (2000) as 'input' legitimacy and 'output' legitimacy. His framework is applied to the Canadian context in Skogstad (2003) and Montpetit (2006). Steve Patten's analysis of Canada's institutions of policy-making reflects the shift to input legitimacy. Patten (2001: 225) takes as a starting point the idea that 'in public affairs and policy-making, democratic legitimacy depends on the nature and quality of public deliberation and the decision processes associated with such deliberation.' Similarly, Lorne Sossin (2002: 88) calls for 'democratic administra-

tion' in Canada, asserting that 'democracy is ultimately not about outcomes but about the process of reaching outcomes.'

6. Two analyses where this storyline is particular apparent are Bryson (2004) and Walters et al. (2000).

7. The paradox of these roles is explored in Vigoda (2002).

8. I am intentionally using the term 'participatory deliberative democracy' rather than 'deliberative democracy' or 'participatory democracy'. While the literature on deliberative democracy generally assumes a role for citizens, representatives elected by citizens can themselves deliberate, engaging in conversation that allows them to reflect on the positions of others. Similarly, participatory democracy involving non-governmental participants is not necessarily deliberative, as was the case with the Charlottetown Accord referendum. 'Participatory deliberative democracy' refers to engagement that both involves non-governmental actors and is deliberative.

9. Some who advocate deliberative practices involving non-governmental actors suggest that government actors may not necessarily convene such processes (Phillips and Orsini, 2002; Stein et al., 1999). However, in their consideration of the contribution of the National Action Committee on the Status of Women to the debate on assisted reproductive technology in Canada, Montpetit et al. find that deliberation in autonomous public spheres can have limited effect on policy-making. They rightly point out that 'deliberation among citizens, in an inclusive public sphere distinctive from the state, makes discourses, not decisions' (Montpetit et al., 2004: 138).

10. This description is similar to that of citizen engagement found in Abele et al. (1998). Stein (1993) explores consultation geared to mutual accommodation.

11. The list of cases of non-governmental participation examined here is not exhaustive; rather, the cases have been selected to demonstrate a spectrum of approaches.

12. Ontario is one of the provinces to engage citizens on this topic.

13. This number grew to 52 throughout the life of the strategy. See NFSC and CCFM (2002).

14. The governments of Manitoba, Alberta, and Quebec did not sign the Canada Forest Accord of 2003–8.

References

Abele, F., K. Graham, A. Kerr, A. Maioni, and S. Phillips. 1998. *Talking with Canadians: Citizen Engagement and the Social Union*. Ottawa: Canadian Council on Social Development.

Abelson, J., P.-G. Forest, J. Eyles, P. Smith, E. Martin, and F.-P. Gauvin. 2003. 'Deliberations about Deliberative Methods: Issues in the Design and Evaluation of Public Participation Processes', *Social Science and Medicine* 57: 240–51.

Advisory Panel on Fiscal Imbalance. 2006. *Reconciling the Irreconcilable: Addressing Canada's Fiscal Imbalance*. Ottawa: Council of the Federation.

Atkinson, M. 1994. 'What Kind of Democracy Do Canadians Want?', *Canadian Journal of Political Science* 27, 4: 717–45.

Banting, K. 1997. 'The Past Speaks to the Future: Lessons from the Postwar Social Union'. In *Canada: the State of the Federation 1997: Non-Constitutional Renewal*, ed. H. Lazar. Montreal and Kingston: McGill–Queen's University Press.

Bountrogianni, M. 2006. Preface to the print version of Ontario, *Report on Outcomes: A Strong Ontario for a Strong Canada: A Summit On Strengthening Ontario's Future and Our Country's Fiscal Arrangements*. Toronto: Government of Ontario.

Brock, K.L. 1995. 'The End of Executive Federalism?', In *New Trends in Canadian Federalism*, ed. F. Rocher and M. Smith. Peterborough, Ont.: Broadview Press.

Bryson, J.M. 2004. 'What To Do When Stakeholders Matter: Stakeholder Identification and Analysis Techniques', *Public Management Review*, 6, 1: 21–53.

Burt, S. 2002. 'The Concept of Political Participation'. In *Citizen Politics: Research and Theory in Canadian Political Behaviour*, ed. J. Everitt and B. O'Neil. Toronto: Oxford University Press.

Canadian Council of Ministers of the Environment. 1994. 'CCME Makes Progress on Harmonization', Communiqué, 8 Nov.

———. 1998a. *Canada-Wide Accord on Environmental Harmonization*. At: <www.ccme.ca/assets/pdf/cws_accord_env_harmonization.pdf>.

———.1998b. *An Annex to the Accord on Accountability and Stakeholder Participation*. At: <www.ccme.ca/assets/pdf/annex_to_accord_e.pdf>.

Chambers, S. 1998. 'Contract or Conversation? Theoretical Lessons from the Canadian Constitutional Crisis', *Politics and Society* 26, 1: 143–72.

———. 2003. 'Deliberative Democratic Theory', *Annual Review of Political Science* 6: 307–26.

Cutler, F., and M. Mendelsohn. 2005. 'Unnatural Loyalties or Native Collaborationists? The Governance and Citizens of Canadian Federalism'. In *Insiders and Outsiders: Alan Cairns and the Reshaping of Canadian Citizenship*, ed. G. Kernerman and P. Resnick. Vancouver: University of British Columbia Press.

Expert Panel on Equalization and Territorial Formula Financing. 2006a. *Achieving a National Purpose: Putting Equalization Back on Track*. Ottawa: Department of Finance. At: <www.eqtff-pfft.ca/epreports/EQ_Report_e.pdf>.

———. 2006b. Consultation Activity Report. At: <www.eqtff-pfft.ca/english/consultationcalendar.asp>.

Fafard, P.C. 1997. 'Green Harmonization: The Success and Failure of Recent Environmental Intergovernmental Relations'. In *Canada: The State of the Federation 1997: Non-Constitutional Renewal*, ed. H. Lazar. Kingston: Institute of Intergovernmental Relations.

Federal–Provincial–Territorial Ministers Responsible for Social Services. 2005. 'Federal–Provincial–Territorial Social Services Ministers Reach Consensus on Early Learning and Child Care', News Release, 11 Feb.

Gibbins, R. 2005. 'Roundtable on Equalization and Territorial Formula Financing', *Summary Report*. At: <www.eqtff-pfft.ca/english/documents/Final Report-Calgary.pdf>.

Gidengil, E., A. Blais, N. Nevitte, and R. Nadeau. 2004. *Citizens*. Vancouver: University of British Columbia Press.

Hartley, S., and G. Skogstad. 2005. 'Regulating Genetically Modified Crops and Foods in Canada and the United Kingdom: Democratising Risk Regulation', *Canadian Public Administration* 48, 3: 305–27.

Hendricks, C.M. 2005. 'Participatory Storylines and Their Influence on Deliberative Forums', *Policy Sciences* 38, 1: 1–20.

Kanji, M. 2002. 'Political Discontent, Human Capital and Representative Governance in Canada'. In *Value Change and Governance in Canada*, ed. N. Nevitte. Toronto: University of Toronto Press.

Lazar, H. 2006. 'The Intergovernmental Dimensions of the Social Union: A Sectoral Analysis', *Canadian Public Administration* 49, 1: 23–15.

Leduc Browne, P. 1998. *Finding Our Collective Voice: Options for a New Social Union*. Ottawa: Canadian Centre for Policy Alternatives.

Lusztig, M. 1994. 'Constitutional Paralysis: Why Canadian Constitutional Initiatives Are Doomed to Fail', *Canadian Journal of Political Science* 27, 4: 747–71.

Mendelsohn, M. 2000. 'Public Brokerage: Constitutional Reform and the Accommodation of Mass Publics', *Canadian Journal of Political Science* 33, 2: 245–72.

Monpetit, É. 2006. 'Declining Legitimacy and Canadian Federalism: An Examination of Policy-Making in Agriculture and Biomedicine'. In *Continuity and Change in Canadian Politics: Essays in Honour of David E. Smith*, ed. H.M. Michelmann and C. de Clercy. Toronto: University of Toronto Press.

———, F. Scala, and I. Fortier. 2004. 'The Paradox of Deliberative Democracy: The National Action Committee on the Status of Women and Canada's Policy on Reproductive Technology', *Policy Sciences* 37: 137–57.

National Forest Strategy Coalition (NFSC). 2004. *Implementing the National Forest Strategy. A Sustainable Forest: The Canadian Commitment*. Implementation Approach for the National Forest Strategy (2003–2008). At: <nfsc.forest.ca/background/implementation2003_e.html#implementation>.

———. 2006. National Forest Strategy. At: <nfsc.forest.ca/strategy_e.htm>.

——— and Canadian Council of Forest Ministers (NSFC and CCFM). 2002. *Consultation Workbook To Help Define a Vision and Identify Key Issues for the Next National Forest Strategy 2003–2008 for All Canadians*. At: <nfsc.forest.ca/background/workbook.html>.

Ontario. 2006a. *Discussion Paper for: A Strong Ontario for a Strong Canada: A Summit on Strengthening Ontario's Future and Our Country's Fiscal Arrangements*. At: <www.strongontario.ca/english/summit/DiscussionPaper.pdf>.

———. 2006b. *Report on Outcomes: A Strong Ontario for a Strong Canada: A*

Summit on Strengthening Ontario's Future and Our Country's Fiscal Arrangements. At: <www.strongontario.ca/english/summit/Outcomes.pdf>.

Patten, S. 2001. 'Democratizing the Institutions of Policy-making: Democratic Consultation and Participatory Administration', *Journal of Canadian Studies* 35, 4: 221–39.

Phillips, S.D., and M. Orsini. 2002. 'Mapping the Links: Citizen Involvement in Policy Processes', *CPRN Discussion Paper* F(21).

Pierre, J. 1998. 'Public Consultation and Citizen Participation: Dilemmas of Policy Advice'. In *Taking Stock: Assessing Public Sector Reforms*, ed. B.G. Peters and D.M. Savoie. Montreal and Kingston: McGill–Queen's University Press.

Savoie, D.J. 2003. *Breaking the Bargain: Public Servants, Ministers and Parliament*. Toronto: University of Toronto Press.

Scharpf, F.W. 1988. 'The Joint-Decision Trap: Lessons from German Federalism and European Integration', *Public Administration* 66, 3: 239–78.

———. 2000. 'Interdependence and Democratic Legitimation'. In *Disaffected Democracies: What's Troubling the Trilateral Countries?*, ed. S.J. Pharr and R.D. Putnam. Princeton, NJ: Princeton University Press.

Schultz, R. 1977. 'Interest Groups and Intergovernmental Negotiations: Caught in the Vise of Federalism'. In *Federalism and Political Community: Essays in Honour of Donald Smiley*, ed. D.P. Shugarman and R. Whitaker. Peterborough, Ont.: Broadview Press.

Simeon, R. 1972. *Federal–Provincial Diplomacy: The Making of Recent Policy in Canada*. Toronto: University of Toronto Press.

——— and D. Cameron, 2002. 'Intergovernmental Relations and Democracy: An Oxymoron If There Ever Was One?' In *Canadian Federalism: Performance, Effectiveness, and Legitimacy*, ed. H. Bakvis and G. Skogstad. Toronto: Oxford University Press.

Simmons, J.M. 2004. 'Securing the Threads of Cooperation in the Tapestry of Intergovernmental Relations: Does the Institutionalization of Federal–Provincial–Territorial Ministerial Conferences Matter?' In *Canada: The State of the Federation 2001–2002: Managing Tensions: Evaluating the Institutions of the Federation*, ed. J.P. Meekison, H. Telford, and H. Lazar. Montreal and Kingston: McGill–Queen's University Press.

———. 2005. 'Executive Federalism after Charlottetown: Understanding the Role of Non-Governmental Actors', Ph.D. thesis, University of Toronto.

Skogstad, G. 2003. 'Who Governs? Who Should Govern? Political Authority and Legitimacy in Canada in the Twenty-First Century', *Canadian Journal of Political Science* 36, 5: 955–73.

Smith, J. 2004. *Federalism*. Vancouver: University of British Columbia Press.

Sossin, L. 2002. 'Democratic Administration'. In *The Handbook of Canadian Public Administration*, ed. C. Dunn. Toronto: Oxford University Press.

Stein, M. 1993. 'Tensions in the Canadian Constitutional Process: Elite Negotiations, Referendums and Interest Group Consultation, 1980–1992'. In *Canada: The State of the Federation 1993*, ed. R.L. Watts and D.M. Brown.

Kingston: Institute of Intergovernmental Relations.

Stein, Janice Gross, David R. Cameron, and Richard Simeon, with Alan Alexandroff. 1999. 'Citizen Engagement in Conflict Resolution: Lessons for Canada in International Experience'. In *The Referendum Papers: Essays on Secession and National Unity*, ed. David R. Cameron. Toronto: University of Toronto Press.

Thorburn, H.G. 1989. 'Federalism, Pluralism and the Canadian Community'. In *Federalism and Political Community: Essays in Honour of Donald Smiley*, ed. D.P. Shugarman and R. Whitaker. Peterborough, Ont.: Broadview Press.

Vigoda, E. 2002. 'From Responsiveness to Collaboration: Governance, Citizens, and the Next Generation of Public Administration', *Public Administration Review* 62, 5: 527–40.

Walters, L.C., J. Aydelotte, and J. Miller. 2000. 'Putting More Public in Policy Analysis', *Public Administration Review* 60, 4: 349–59.

Websites

Canadian Council of Forest Ministers: www.ccfm.org

Canadian Council of Ministers of the Environment: www.ccme.ca

Canadian Council on Social Development: www.ccsd.ca

Canadian Intergovernmental Conference Secretariat: www.scics.gc.ca

Canadian Policy Research Networks: www.cprn.org

Council of the Federation: www.councilofthefederation.ca

Expert Panel on Equalization and Territorial Formula Financing: www.eqtff-pfft. ca/english/index.asp

National Child Benefit: www.nationalchildbenefit.ca/home_e.html

National Forest Strategy Coalition: nfsc.forest.ca

Chapter 18

Conclusion: Taking Stock of Canadian Federalism

Herman Bakvis and Grace Skogstad

Together, the essays in this volume paint a contradictory yet fascinating portrait of Canadian federalism. In this concluding chapter we take stock of our contributors' analyses and explore some possible future paths.

The Face of Contemporary Federalism

How can we describe the contemporary face of Canadian federalism? Is there a balance between shared and self-rule—between vesting the central government with sufficient power to unite the country on common purposes and entrusting provincial leaders with the authority to express the values of their distinct political communities? What is the prevailing pattern of relationships between the two orders of government? Is it competitive and adversarial to the point of being dysfunctional? Or is competition tempered by a reasonable degree of collaboration? Are governments going about their business independently, in a fashion consistent with the classical model of federalism, or are they interlocked, their behaviour circumscribed by norms and rules that require co-ordinated and joint action?

On the question of balance between self- and shared rule, one perspective shows federalism to be in robust good health, with strong governments at both levels, neither of them about to be subordinated to the other. The Constitution Act 1867 created the foundations for such a system, while the courts and fiscal federalism have helped to sustain it. Gerald Baier (Chapter 2) observes that although the Constitution and the judicial review process no longer figure as prominently as they once did in determining the jurisdictional balance, both continue to serve as important buttresses of the federal system. Judicial review, he says, 'reinforces the constitutional character of the federal order, reminding governments that the Constitution is meant to be supreme.' James Kelly (Chapter 3) is even more emphatic in his conclusion that the courts have upheld the federal system. Focusing on judicial review of the Charter of Rights and Freedoms, he argues that the Supreme Court of Canada has shown 'sensitivity to federalist concerns' and that its 'balanced jurisprudence' has prevented the Charter from becoming an instrument of centralization. Fiscal federalism has also played an important part in upholding the federal system by helping to mitigate the fiscal inequalities between provinces. Douglas Brown (Chapter 4) singles out equalization payments as 'the key to maintaining autonomy and equality under the Constitution for all provinces'.

This image of a federal system that is performing well, slipping into neither a confederal nor a unitary mode, is not shared by all our contributors, however. Voicing what they argue to be the dominant view in Quebec, Alain-G. Gagnon and Raffaele Iacovino (Chapter 16) state that Ottawa's formal efforts to promote national unity have emphasized homogeneity at the expense of diversity, with the result that federalism has been discredited in Quebec. In their view, the pillars of Trudeau's pan-Canadian nationalism—official bilingualism, multiculturalism, the Charter of Rights and Freedoms—represent a 'counterforce' to Quebec's vision of Canada as a multinational democracy. They warn that a federal system that does not heed Canada's multinational character can have little legitimacy in Quebec.

The federal system appears in a similarly negative light to Aboriginal Canadians. As Martin Papillon (Chapter 14) observes, Aboriginal peoples were not parties to Confederation; they have 'no statutory voice' in the institutions of intrastate federalism (Parliament); and they have only limited access to the institutions of executive federalism. Federal and provincial governments accept in principle the inherent right of Aboriginal peoples to self-government, but they resist it in practice. Yet Papillon is more optimistic than Gagnon and Iacovino: in his view, progress is being made away from colonialism and towards a new relationship between Aboriginal people and the federal system.

The picture becomes more complex when we come to describe contemporary Canadian federalism and the practices of executive federalism. The dominant image has two aspects: competitive *and* co-operative. It is the competitive aspect that Richard Simeon and Amy Nugent emphasize in Chapter 5: 'the overall dynamic of intergovernmental relations,' they say, 'is competitive and adversarial, despite the frequent promises of co-operation.' At the same time, Simeon and Nugent acknowledge the reality of policy interdependence: overlapping responsibilities and programs create both a need and an incentive for co-operation and co-ordination between the two orders of government.

Many more faces of federalism become evident when the point of view shifts from one policy domain to another. In various fields of social and economic policy, the contributors to this text have mapped the pattern of relations between orders of government by assessing the extent to which they are independent/ interdependent, their propensity for co-operation or conflict, and the decision-making norms and rules at play as officials and ministers interact to make and implement policies. These analyses clarify the different models of intergovernmental relations at work in Canada. They include an independent governments model (two orders working independently on policy matters within their assigned jurisdictions); a collaborative model (intergovernmental consultation and co-ordination, normally in a context of policy interdependence); and a joint-decision model (the only one subject to formal rules requiring a super-majority, or even unanimity, for a decision to be taken).

Other variations include asymmetrical federalism, in which one constituent unit (province) has a different status than others in the federal system, either constitutionally or by virtue of special administrative arrangements, and shared-cost federalism, in which both orders of government contribute to the costs of social programs. The latter may take either of two forms: unilateral shared-cost federalism and collaborative shared-cost federalism. This sub-distinction follows from Lazar's (2006) use of 'unilateral federalism' to designate a pattern in which the autonomous activity of one order of government (invariably the government of Canada) imposes conditions on the other and/or distorts its priorities.

Table 18.1 identifies some of the programs and policy areas in which different models of intergovernmental relations have applied. It illustrates the variation that can be observed not only across policy spheres at a given time, but also within a single policy sphere over time. In the case of intergovernmental co-ordination, it differentiates between shared-cost collaboration (centred on fiscal instruments such as transfer payments or tax points) and regulatory collaboration (centred on regulatory policy instruments such as rules about how markets can function). It must be emphasized that this table is by no means comprehensive; the examples it presents are only some of the policy arenas examined in this text. Among the additional policy areas that could be entered in the 'independent governments' column, for example, are defence and international diplomacy at the federal level and education (primary through secondary) at the provincial level. Similarly, the asymmetrical federalism column could also include immigration policy, labour-market training, the participation of Quebec and New Brunswick in La Francophonie, and the Harper government's promise to allow Quebec to represent itself at UNESCO.

Table 18.1 highlights at least three features of intergovernmental relations in Canada. First is the prevalence of collaborative federalism, a model whose emergence was noted in the first edition of *Canadian Federalism* (2002). The range of policy areas in the 'collaborative' column extends from health (Chapter 8) and child care (Chapter 9) after 2004, to the environment (Chapter 12) and international trade (Chapter 11). Second, the table makes it clear that the arm's-length 'independent governments' model is more persistent than one might have thought. In the areas of post-secondary education financing (Chapter 10), economic development (Chapter 12), and (to some degree) climate change after

Table 18.1   Models of Federalism and Programs/Policy Fields

Independent Governments	Collaborative Shared-cost	Unilateral Shared-cost	Collaborative Regulatory	Joint-Decision	Asymmetrical
Unemployment insurance	Health care (1960s–mid-1980s; 2004–)	Health care (1986–late 1990s)	Environmental Harmonization Accord	Contributory pension plans (CPP/QPP)	CPP/QPP
Old-age income security (OAS/GIS)	Social assistance (1966 CAP)	Social assistance (since 1995)	International trade policy		Health care (2004)
Post-secondary education (late 1990s–)	Child benefits (late 1990s)**		Income tax collection*		Post-secondary Education
	Post-secondary education (as part of EPF)				Income tax collection
Economic development					Revenue-resource sharing (2004)
Climate change (2002–)			Climate change (1992–2002)		
Equalization					
Cities					
Aboriginal peoples					

* Except for corporate income taxes in Quebec, Ontario, and Alberta, and personal income taxes in Quebec
** Early Childhood Development Agreement, Multilateral Framework Agreement

2002, federal and provincial activities continue to be largely unco-ordinated.

It is something of a surprise to find both collaborative federalism and independent governments in policy areas affected by the internationalization of the Canadian political economy. One might have expected that the integration of Canada's economy into regional and global markets, and the country's membership in international organizations, would encourage greater intergovernmental collaboration to deal with realities of policy interdependence and the exigencies of fostering domestic and international economic competitiveness. And yet while this presupposition holds for international trade, it does not for economic development, post-secondary education, or (since 2002) climate change. Rather, the independent governments model prevails in both economic development and post-secondary education, with little apparent damage to effective policy-making (see Table 18.2). In the case of climate change, Winfield and Macdonald suggest that internationalization, in the form of participation in international environmental accords, can give the federal government strong incentives to act unilaterally when efforts at collaboration break down.

Finally, a third point that the table emphasizes is the importance of asymmetrical federalism. Quebec politicians have long championed asymmetry as an essential feature of a well-performing federation. Although *de jure* recognition of Quebec's special status is the ultimate goal, Quebec's federalist premiers have also pressed hard for *de facto* asymmetry in intergovernmental administrative arrangements. Table 18.1 shows that Quebec continues to benefit from the success of that effort with respect to the federal government's spending power in the province. The Health Care Accord signed in September 2004, as Antonia Maioni has observed, explicitly recognized asymmetrical federalism as 'an essential part of the fundamental logic of federalism'. But *de facto* asymmetry is not confined to Quebec. Nova Scotia and Newfoundland and Labrador bargained successfully in 2004 for their natural resource revenues to be excluded from calculation of their equalization payments. More generally, when efforts at establishing multilateral agreements including all provincial/territorial governments break down, the alternative of bilateral agreements (in climate change and child care under the Martin government) is likely to widen the scope for asymmetrical federalism.

What determines the form that intergovernmental relations take in a given policy area? Unilateral federalism and the 'independent governments' model have a natural appeal for governments with the legal, fiscal, and political resources to cater to the competitive instincts and electoral calculations of their executives. Collaborative federalism, on the other hand, tends to be the favoured approach in contexts of policy interdependence, where each level of government must work with the other in order to further its own goals and interests. Building on these explanations, we suggest that the reason one model of intergovernmental relations prevails rather than another usually lies in a combination of factors, including the nature of constitutional jurisdiction; the history of intergovernmental relations in the sector concerned; and the ideas and interests of the executives at both levels. Of these three factors, the last is likely the most central.

It is important not to make too much of constitutional jurisdiction. It *is* consequential to the pattern of intergovernmental relations that arises in a policy sector, but it is not an accurate guide to who does what. Consider the following situations. First, the Constitution may be silent or ambiguous in its assignment of legal authority or responsibility in a particular area. Nowhere is 'the environment' mentioned in the Constitution Act, for example. Thus some aspects of environmental policy, such as harmonization of pollution standards, involve collaborative federalism (what Winfield and Macdonald call the multilateral approach); but responses to climate change show evidence of both collaboration and unilateral federalism. Second, the Constitution can unambiguously assign exclusive jurisdiction to one order of government. This situation is usually reflected in an 'independent governments' approach to policy-making. Third, the Constitution can assign both orders (shared) jurisdiction: thus areas such as agriculture and pensions are usually associated with collaborative federalism. Fourth and finally, the Constitution can divide jurisdiction. A case in point is international treaty-making: the government of Canada has the exclusive legal authority to negotiate and ratify international treaties, but the provinces alone have the legal authority to implement the provisions in those treaties that fall under the matters assigned to them.

For this reason, divided jurisdiction would seem to favour co-operation and co-ordinated action, since neither order of government is in a legal position to take unilateral action. In the case of international agreements, if the government of Canada failed to elicit provincial support for those provisions that fall under provincial jurisdiction, its subsequent ability to honour those agreements would be seriously impaired. The prospect of such deleterious consequences has helped to promote a collaborative model in international trade policy. And for a while it looked as though the need for internal co-ordination as a condition for effective participation in international negotiations and agreements would have a similar effect in environmental policy regarding climate change. The Chrétien government did consult the provinces and secure a consensus on appropriate targets for the reduction of greenhouse gas emissions prior to attending the meeting in Kyoto, Japan, in 1997. Once in Kyoto, however, the representatives of the Canadian government abandoned the negotiated targets and agreed to higher emission targets. Subsequent efforts to obtain nation-wide consensus on how to meet these targets have failed, and with the largest energy-producing provinces (Alberta and BC) refusing to commit to the changes needed to honour Canada's commitments under the Kyoto Protocol, Canada is in breach of this international treaty.

Arguably the most important feature of Canada's Constitution is yet another characteristic of federal systems; that is, their potential to create imbalances in the assignment of responsibilities and fiscal capacity. Many of the problems attending intergovernmental relations in Canada reflect the lack of congruence between jurisdictional powers and the financial resources needed to act on them. Besides justifying fiscal federalism, the misallocation of legal powers and fiscal capacities is also the best explanation for shared-cost federalism, both unilateral and collaborative. These jurisdictional imbalances have played a major role in the emergence of the federal spending power and the subsequent transformation of virtually every area of social policy into a potential case of shared-cost jurisdiction.

Although there is flux over time in the model of intergovernmental relations prevailing in a given policy sector (health is a good example)—so that the model at time t2 varies from that at time t1—there is also little doubt that some models are products of historical patterns. The joint-decision model associated with the Canada and Quebec pension plans is a good example. These plans were implemented in the mid-1960s with rules requiring substantial agreement but not complete unanimity for any program changes. In other policy areas, where intergovernmental co-ordination has not been institutionally embedded, patterns of intergovernmental relations are likely to be more susceptible to the shifting interests and ideas of government executives. Indeed, as Richard Simeon and Amy Nugent have pointed out in Chapter 5, it is because intergovernmental relations in Canada have not been well institutionalized that government elites have had the latitude to abandon past models (for example, co-ordinated shared-cost federalism) and pursue their own strategies and preferences, whether in the unilateral-federalism or the independent-governments mode.

How Is Canadian Federalism Faring?

What do the essays in this volume tell us about how Canadian federalism is doing? Is it functioning in such a way that problems can be addressed in a timely, effective, and efficient fashion? Do the governing arrangements and outcomes associated with the various models of federalism pass the test of legitimacy (appropriateness and acceptability) in the eyes of Canadian citizens and policy stakeholders?

Assessing federalism's performance, effectiveness, and legitimacy is admittedly a subjective exercise. As Simeon and Nugent correctly observe, 'there can be no single answer to the question of whether the intergovernmental system generates or facilitates policy choices that meet the needs and preferences of Canadians, in either the federal or provincial context.' 'Such assessments,' they caution, 'vary depending on the perspective of the assessor'.

Consider, for example, two contrasting assessments of fiscal federalism. The expert advisory panel to the Council of the Federation on the Fiscal Imbalance delivered a damning critique in 2006. It said the system had 'fallen into disrepair' and described intergovernmental relationships as 'corrosive', characterized by 'squabbling, ad hoc tinkering, and short-term thinking' (Council of the Federation, 2006: 9, 17). The panel judged the processes of fiscal federalism to be deeply flawed: lacking principles or rules, and with agreements subject to change or termination by Ottawa. Yet Douglas Brown (Chapter 4) does not entirely agree with this indictment, which drew on provincial governments' assessments of fiscal federalism. He agrees with the Council of Federation's advisory panel that there has been 'an erosion of mutual trust among the governments', with the provinces viewing many federal actions as lacking legitimacy. And though he credits fiscal federalism's 'remarkable flexibility' for contributing to more effective policy-making in the federation, he concludes that 'fiscal federalism has also stood in the way of policy effectiveness rather than enabled it.' Still, Brown's assessment of fiscal federalism's performance, especially over the longer term, is more positive: 'The transfer of tax points, the removal of conditions on grant programs, and the maintenance of equalization payments have enabled Canada to sustain an emphasis on provincial autonomy that most other federal systems have abandoned.'

In short, different experts will appraise the performance, effectiveness, and legitimacy of Canada's federal system in different ways. Recognizing that disparate perspectives can lead to disparate judgments, most of our authors have taken note of different constituencies' opinions. In judging policy effectiveness, for example, they have been careful to distinguish between the appraisals of those who prefer national standards and common policies across the country and those who put a premium on policy outcomes that allow for interprovincial variation. As Kelly observes in Chapter 3, the Supreme Court's sensitivity to federalism in its application of the Charter of Rights and Freedoms—its 'federalizing of rights'—enhances the legitimacy of the Charter for provincialists, but undermines it for those who believe that all Canadians should have the same rights, no matter their province of residence. And in the case of cities, Sancton (Chapter 15) notes that big-city mayors tend to judge the federal system, from which they are largely excluded, more negatively than do provinces, whose judgment of Ottawa depends primarily on its respect for provincial jurisdiction.

Another reality that makes assessing the health of federalism difficult is the fact that federal institutions and processes are not the only influences affecting the processes and outcomes of policy debates. It is extremely difficult, perhaps impossible, to isolate the effects attributable solely to federalism. In their overview of the logics of parliament, federalism, and intergovernmental relations, Simeon and Nugent have shown how deeply the democratic deficit in intergovernmental relations is rooted in the executive dominance of parliamentary government. The scores in Table 18.2 on *process legitimacy* may be as much an indictment of the executive dominance inherent in the Westminster parliamentary system as they are of patterns of intergovernmental relations.

In effect, the table is a report card based on the various assessments presented by our authors. The scores—'good', 'fair', and 'poor'—summarize the performance, effectiveness, and legitimacy of federalism and intergovernmental relations in Canada to date. There is clearly a subjective element in the assignment of any score. It also bears repeating that a snapshot taken at a different time could well produce different scores. Nevertheless, efforts have been made to produce systematic ratings.

In terms of performance, a score of 'good' indicates that constitutional jurisdiction and the federal balance are respected, and that intergovernmental processes have succeeded in their purpose of facilitating the consultation, nego-

Table 18.2 Policy Areas: Performance, Effectiveness, and Legitimacy

Policy Area	Performance	Effectiveness	Process Legitimacy	Output Legitimacy
Fiscal federalism	Fair	Good	Fair	Fair
Canada Pension Plan	Good	Good	Good	Good
Social assistance	Fair	Fair	Fair	Fair
Health care	Poor/Fair	Fair	Fair	Fair
Child care	Poor	Poor	Poor	Poor
Post-secondary education	Good	Fair	Fair	Fair
International trade	Good	Good	Good	Good
Economic development	Good	Good	Fair	Good
Climate change	Poor	Poor	Poor	Poor
Environmental regulatory harmonization	Good	Fair	Fair	Fair
Cities	Good	Fair	Poor	Fair
Aboriginal peoples	Fair	Poor	Fair	Poor

tiation, and co-ordination necessary to produce results over time. A score of 'fair' is awarded when some, but not all, of these conditions are met. A score of 'poor' is recorded where intergovernmental relations tend to break down or be riddled with acrimony and distrust.

In terms of policy effectiveness, a score of 'good' means that the policies produced through intergovernmental institutions and processes generally do address substantive problems in a timely and cost-effective fashion; allow for asymmetry as warranted; provide scope for policy innovation and adjustment to changing circumstances; and allow Canada to meet its international commitments. A score of 'fair' means that only a minority of these goals is achieved. A score of 'poor' indicates both policy failure and failure to meet most of the above criteria.

Output legitimacy scores are closely related to policy effectiveness scores with one important difference: output legitimacy gets at *perceptions* of the appropriateness of outcomes. It is possible for policy effectiveness and output legitimacy scores to diverge because policies can be effective in addressing problems or meeting international commitments but still not reflect the preferences and values of some political communities. A score of 'good' on output legitimacy indicates that the policy outcomes of intergovernmental relations receive the approbation of a broad constituency; 'fair' means that some but not all stakeholders/ citizens view policy outcomes as appropriate; and 'poor' means that the outcomes are opposed by virtually all significant members of the policy/political community.

Finally, ratings on process legitimacy reflect the degree to which policy-making processes conform to citizens' expectations. (Expectations at the governmental level are captured by the performance dimension.) A single score on process legitimacy is exceedingly difficult to arrive at; once again, perceptions of what constitute desirable policy-making processes may well vary across the range of citizens, stakeholders, and governments. In Table 18.2 a 'good' ranking indicates respect for democratic norms of accountability to citizens, transparency to public scrutiny, and opportunities for citizen input. A score of 'fair' means that some but not all of these democratic criteria are met; for example, there may have been some opportunities for citizen/stakeholder input, but processes have generally been non-transparent and accountability weak. A 'poor' rating on procedural legitimacy means that none of these democratic criteria has been met. The two cases of environmental policy—responses to climate change and harmonization of environmental standards—may help to clarify the difference between 'fair' and 'poor' ratings. In both cases, the intergovernmental processes at play have lacked accountability and transparency. But there was substantial involvement of stakeholders in the multilateral process that led to the harmonization accord, whereas climate-change policy-making has involved non-state actors working through individual governments rather than intergovernmental forums. This last difference produces a 'fair' rating for the harmonization accord, but a 'poor' grade for responses to climate change.

Looking down the columns and focusing first on 'performance', we note that while responses range from poor to good, the most frequent rating is 'good'. For 'effectiveness' and the two 'legitimacy' categories, there is a similar range, but with more 'fair' ratings than 'good'. In short, the scores with respect to the federation's performance—in terms of generating trust, facilitating collaboration, and producing agreements—are more positive than the scores on either its effectiveness in addressing problems or the perceived legitimacy of its procedures/institutions and their outputs.

If we look along the rows of the table, the most frequent score is 'fair'. Perhaps the most revealing domains are the outliers: the categories where the entries are largely 'good' or uniformly 'poor'. Two domains that stand out as systematically good are trade policy and the Canada/Quebec Pension Plan. Climate change is the only policy area to earn 'poor' scores across the board.

Turning to the 'good' outliers first, the consultative processes used in international trade appear to work well and in conformity with jurisdictional assignments. In most instances, the positions taken by Canada in international trade forums have had the support of provincial governments. And the end results appear to enjoy legitimacy in the eyes of both levels of government as well as among non-government stakeholders. Furthermore, most of the non-government stakeholders are closely involved in the process as well. The Canada/Quebec Pension Plan (C/QPP) also gets a good rating across the board. As we noted earlier, the joint-decision model scores high on both performance and legitimacy. Surprisingly, and in contradiction to Scharpf (1988), who associated this model with policy sclerosis and rigidity, Banting gives it high scores on policy effectiveness. Even though the threshold for agreement was high, the requisite number of provincial governments was eventually able to agree with the federal government on a change in the plan's investment strategy in order to ensure sufficient funds to accommodate growing numbers of pensioners in the future.

In summary, if lessons can be drawn from these two cases, performance, effectiveness, and legitimacy are most closely related when three conditions apply. First, the federal government is not in a position to engage in unilateral action; second, the collaborative model is dominant, preferably underpinned by decision rules that require consensus though not outright unanimity; and, third, failure to reach a consensus is clearly likely to have negative consequences for both governments and their respective bases of electoral support.

The cases in which federalism is performing at a sub-optimal level are almost the mirror image of those for trade policy and the C/QPP. The sorry state of intergovernmental relations in the area of climate change has been described above. In the case of international trade, the government of Canada is on strong jurisdictional ground, but this is not true of the environment. Rather, the provinces own and control the natural resources (oil, gas, coal) implicated in global warming. Furthermore, the international and domestic pressures to honour the Kyoto Protocol have been weaker than those with respect to the WTO or NAFTA. The US has not ratified the Kyoto Protocol, and, unlike the Chrétien Liberal government, few provincial governments have seen their response to Kyoto as a major determinant of votes to be won or lost. Public opinion surveys in early 2007 that showed growing public concern about the state of the environment and climate change, however, may increase the incentive for governments to act on the environment, and to do so collaboratively.

If unilateral action is likely to produce less effective and legitimate outcomes, collaboration does not necessarily correct these sub-optimal outcomes. The environmental harmonization accord of 1999, discussed in Chapters 13 and 17, was in many respects a superb example of collaboration between the two orders of government. Yet the accord was strongly opposed by the parliamentary Standing Committee on Environment and Sustainable Development, as well as environmental organizations, and environmental standards have deteriorated since its implementation.

Health care is another policy area that shows the complicated relationship between performance, effectiveness, and legitimacy. Health care is the policy area most likely to be described as dysfunctional, having been characterized for several years by tension between governments, blame avoidance, and absence of innovation. Ottawa's extensive use of its spending power has come with conditions that have limited provinces' ability to restructure their health-care plans to incorporate private as well as public care. Still, for many Canadians this outcome is a measure of policy effectiveness that adds to the legitimacy of government actions in the policy sphere. They place a high value on a publicly funded single-payer system that provides reasonably high-quality care with a very high level of accessibility at costs far below those of the US system and comparable to costs in other countries.

In important ways, the situation with respect to social assistance and post-secondary education has been the reverse. In reducing its transfers under the Canada Health and Social Transfer, Ottawa allowed the provinces to reduce their support for social assistance programs; the provinces, in turn, gave Ottawa latitude to effectively reshape the post-secondary system. Post-secondary education saw some innovative programming, primarily in the area of research, funded mainly by Ottawa. Overall, though, it is difficult to assess the performance of intergovernmental relations in the post-secondary area because there was relatively little interaction between the two levels of government. Following the 'independent governments' model, Ottawa acted on its own and the provinces, including Quebec, largely acquiesced. Only the Millennium Scholarship program produced sharp conflict and a less than optimal outcome—largely because the provinces saw this program as a unilateral initiative on the part of the federal government that trenched on their jurisdiction.

In the area of child care, 2005 saw the negotiation of several bilateral agreements between Ottawa and the provinces. This success was the product of multilateral sessions and discussions going back to the 1980s, and appeared to represent an important example of well-performing and effective federalism. Then in 2006 the Harper Conservatives were elected and promptly cancelled the agreements. If this sudden turn-around illustrates anything, it is how the partisan element and short-term electoral interests can work against the careful, long-term dialogue and negotiations that characterize most successful federal–provincial processes.

Overall, the number of domains where federalism performs very well, where the policies are generally coherent and effective, and where both the processes and the outcomes are regarded as legitimate by governments and the affected stakeholders, is quite limited. In these areas, trust ties and shared goals are strong enough to trump short-term political and electoral considerations. In some areas, such as health care, there is considerable acrimony, but the impact on policy effectiveness is less obviously negative, even if the legitimacy of the current model appears to have suffered. In other areas—the setting of environmental standards, for example—the effectiveness of the policies may be questionable even when the intergovernmental process works well. Then there are areas such as post-secondary education where the 'independent governments' model of federalism means there is little intergovernmental interaction, but the overall record is fair to good.

Before leaving this discussion of how federalism is working, it may be helpful to reflect further on the role of non-state actors in intergovernmental processes and the degree to which their involvement affects the functioning of federalism on our three main dimensions. One of the prevailing themes in the literature on Canadian federalism is the limited involvement of citizens/non-state actors in interstate federalism. Richard Simeon (1972, 2006), in his classic study of the negotiations surrounding the Canada/Quebec Pension Plan, refers to the 'freezing out' of organized interests when governments perceive the stakes to be high. From one perspective, the exclusion of organized interests in such cases is not necessarily 'anti-democratic': as Simeon and Nugent, as well as Julie Simmons (Chapter 17) remind us, executive federalism is still rooted in representative democracy. As long as the executives who are party to intergovernmentalism represent the best interests of their citizens and answer to them regularly through their elected legislatures and periodically via elections, then one could argue that democracy is served.

And yet it is clear that citizens, especially those with a clear stake in a particular policy outcome, seek something more: their own participation in intergovernmental processes, greater transparency in intergovernmental negotiations and deal-making, and more reporting back on the agreements so brokered. Governments appear to agree—to some extent. The preponderance of 'fair' and 'good' entries in the 'process legitimacy' column of Table 18.2 suggests that federalism and intergovernmental relations are doing better than critics like Simeon would suggest. Citizens, at least in organized groups, are not uniformly excluded from intergovernmental processes. In certain domains, organized interests are much more intimately involved in the intergovernmental process than many might have thought. International trade policy and environmental policy both offer examples of how non-state actors can be included in the collaborative federalism model.

Advocacy groups have certainly taken part in policy formulation under the independent governments model. Chapter 10 documents extensive involvement and extraordinary influence on the part of advocacy groups, primarily representing the university sector, especially the research-intensive component within that sector, in the crafting of federal policy in this area. Furthermore, the university sector appears to have provided an informal bridge between federal and provincial governments. Economic development (Chapter 12) is another example; current thinking emphasizes 'networks' of state and non-state economic actors as essential to economic growth.

More generally, the competitive dynamic in federalism gives governments incentives to engage in what Simmons calls 'consultative democracy'. In health care, one of the most rancorous of federal–provincial arenas, Maioni observes that the creation of the Romanow commission provided an opportunity for 'an extraordinary exercise in participatory democracy'.

The above examples notwithstanding, Simmons is surely correct in her conclusion: that Canada's pattern of interstate federalism offers few opportunities for citizens to engage in deliberative and repeated exchanges with state actors in intergovernmental forums. Her single instance of deliberative participatory democracy is a voluntary intergovernmental agreement. Yet consultative democracy can and does operate alongside representative democracy. Further, although the evidence amassed in this collection is preliminary, the consequences of consultative democracy for the performance, effectiveness, and legitimacy of federalism appear at a minimum benign and may well be beneficial. How modes of interaction with non-state actors affect the working of federalism/intergovernmental relations, and the extent to which patterns of state–society interaction may be changing, are clearly important research questions.

Looking Ahead

Where is Canadian federalism headed? Will it continue to follow its current path? What are the prospects for a change in direction? In the first edition of *Canadian Federalism* (2002), we sketched three possible scenarios regarding the evolution of Canada's federal system. The first two scenarios were predicated on incremental adjustments to existing administrative and political arrangements; the third entailed major restructuring of the federal system through constitutional reform. Before reviewing each scenario more closely and considering its prospects, it is helpful to reflect on the context in which we sketched these scenarios in the early twenty-first century and how that context has changed over the past half-decade.

Some things have not changed. Canadian federalism continues to operate in the context of an internationalized political economy. Likewise, the dominant political culture remains skeptical regarding governing elites, and citizens continue to demand greater input and responsiveness. The same factors that promoted either co-operation or independent action in the past continue in force today. Other contextual features have changed, however. We can identify three significant events since 2002.

First, the election of the provincial Liberals in Quebec in 2003 signalled an important change in that province's strategy with respect to collaborative federalism. Unlike his Parti Québécois predecessor, Premier Jean Charest decided to work with his provincial counterparts to secure recognition of Quebec's asymmetrical status within the federation. He took the lead in the creation of the Council of the Federation. Essentially a more institutionalized version of the annual premiers' conference, the Council of the Federation has a permanent secretariat, a commitment to meet more frequently, and a more ambitious agenda; and it is supported by a number of ministerial councils. With Quebec's backing, indeed leadership, the Council of the Federation makes it easier for the 10 provincial premiers and three territorial leaders to develop a common bargaining position vis-à-vis the government of Canada. With his government reduced to minority status following the March 2007 election, Premier Charest will likely continue to work co-operatively with the other premiers, even though the official opposition in the National Assembly, the Action démocratique du Québec (ADQ), seeks greater 'autonomy' for Quebec within Canada.

The second new element in the context of intergovernmental relations in recent years is the discourse of fiscal imbalance that has emerged as the budgetary situations of the federal and most provincial governments have improved and the gap between a wealthy, energy-rich province like Alberta and the others has widened. The Charest government in Quebec made correcting the 'fiscal imbalance' a high priority. When the provinces failed to present a united front on the issue, the Harper government devised its own solution to the fiscal imbalance. As Douglas Brown noted in Chapter 4, the Flaherty budget of March 2007 went a considerable distance towards fiscal balance by broadening the standard for equalization and increasing funding for the CHST. Yet the issue remained unsettled, as the highly public campaign of Premier Danny Williams against the treatment of Newfoundland and Labrador in the new equalization formula attested. Nova Scotia and Saskatchewan were also unhappy with the new regime.

The third important development since 2002, which has implications for each of the three scenarios, is the election of two successive minority governments in Ottawa. Minority government status, in combination with a healthy federal fiscal surplus, led the Martin Liberals in search of votes and into new expenditure initiatives. Many of these initiatives trespassed on provincial areas of jurisdiction (cities, child and health care), but at the same time they lent momentum to collaborative federalism. The replacement of a Liberal minority government with a Conservative minority in January 2006 keeps alive the same imperative to garner votes in vote-rich provinces. For the Conservatives, the target has been Quebec, virtually ensuring that the priorities of the Charest government—correcting the fiscal imbalance and promoting asymmetrical federalism—loom large. As Bakvis and Tanguay suggest in Chapter 6, minority government may also give greater scope to political parties in helping carry some of the burden of national unity.

The first two of the three scenarios we sketched in 2002 both presumed continuity in Canada's Constitution and political institutions: that is, no formal changes in the division of powers; no constitutional recognition of Quebec's specificity; and no changes in the role, composition, or function of the Senate. Under the first scenario, incremental adjustments do not appreciably alter the existing balance of power between the two orders of government. Both the government of Canada and the provincial governments continue to be important actors in their own right. Competitive and co-operative elements co-exist and the informal pattern of asymmetry continues. In response to the imbalances in federal–provincial and interprovincial revenues, the government of Canada adjusts the equalization formula but not in a significant way. It continues to provide transfer payments, which are extended into new areas such as post-secondary education. The dominant model is collaborative federalism, with some limited rules-based adjudication or conciliation processes for resolving intergovernmental disputes.

This first scenario was exemplified by the last two Liberal governments, under Jean Chrétien and Paul Martin. The latter government in particular appeared eager to use federal largesse to ameliorate conditions in the weaker provinces and at the same time provide for asymmetry in Quebec's administrative arrangements with the federation, and in the resource-revenue sharing agreements with Nova Scotia and Newfoundland and Labrador. Neither prime minister opened up the constitutional agenda. Had the Martin government been re-elected in 2006 with a majority, this first scenario would likely have prevailed through to the end of the decade. It still remains a distinct possibility as long as there is a minority government in Ottawa.

The second scenario envisioned considerably more devolution, with the federal government playing a much more restricted role in Canadians' lives. When disputes arise from heightened competition between Ottawa and the provinces (particularly the larger and better-off provinces), Ottawa resolves them by acceding to provincial demands. The gap between richer and poorer provinces becomes especially pronounced, as Ottawa does nothing to fill it beyond meeting its constitutional requirements for equalization payments. In 2002 we stated that this scenario was most likely under a neo-conservative national government wedded both to smaller government and to the equality-of-provinces principle. Committed to lower levels of taxation, it would also divest itself of any spending responsibilities for social policies like health care.

The 2006 election of the Harper Conservative government, albeit with minority status, has made this scenario more likely. The Conservative party and its leader have their roots in the old Reform/Alliance party, whose platform promised both provincial equality and a smaller role for Ottawa, including letting provinces carry out their primary responsibilities in areas such health care with minimal federal interference. Still, in his first year in office Mr Harper took a number of decisions that contradicted the principle of provincial equality. His government recognized Quebec's unique identity in the form of direct Quebec representation at UNESCO and endorsed a parliamentary motion to recognize the Québécois 'as a nation within Canada'. Both actions pointed towards a more decentralized federation. So did the March 2007 budget of Conservative Finance Minister Jim Flaherty. Its initiatives to rectify the 'fiscal imbalance' have put more money in the hands of provinces. Federal transfers for social programs under the CST are guaranteed on a longer-term basis. The budget did not introduce new federal spending initiatives in areas of provincial jurisdiction. Should the Conservatives succeed in transforming their minority into a majority at the next general election, they would have a freer hand to reduce permanently the federal role in the federation. However, one sign that they might not wish to remove themselves completely from all provincial jurisdiction was the stipulation that payment of the additional $800 million for post-secondary education would not start until fiscal 2008–9, following 'discussions with provinces and territories on how best to make use of this new investment and ensure appropriate reporting and accountability to Canadians'.

In short, the second scenario—decentralization—appears to be the most credible in the late spring of 2007. Some elements of the first scenario are also evident: both orders of government are important, co-operation and conflict co-exist, informal asymmetry persists. Nor, consistent with scenario one, are there formal constitutional changes. But there have been important informal changes to the functioning of the parliamentary and federal systems that have the potential to reshape the balance in the federation. In addition to the changes to fiscal federalism outlined above and the parliamentary recognition of the Québécois as a nation within Canada, there is the as yet unknown impact of Prime Minister Harper's seeming determination to move forward on an elected Senate, beginning with the appointment of an elected senator from Alberta and the introduction of Bill C-43, 'An Act to provide for consultations with electors on their preferences for appointments to the Senate'.

Under the third scenario, as originally described in 2002, the federal system is restructured through major constitutional reform. This scenario is triggered by a serious crisis, possibly in the form of a 'yes' vote in a Quebec sovereignty referendum. Such constitutional reform would undoubtedly entail a major devolution of powers, and, as the Supreme Court of Canada's reference in the *Quebec Secession* case made clear, lengthy constitutional negotiations would be required, involving both orders of government, Aboriginal peoples, and Canadian citizens themselves. This scenario assumes that Canada's governments and a majority of its citizens see the need for compromise and collaboration to preserve the Canadian federation.

The outcome of the March 2007 Quebec election, in which the Parti Québécois was reduced to third-party status and replaced as the Official Opposition by the Action démocratique du Québec, appears to have decreased the likelihood of this scenario. However, the leader of the ADQ, Mario Dumont, has argued that constitutional reforms are needed to enhance Quebec's autonomy within Quebec. Should he and his party replace the Liberals as the province's government, constitutional reform could well become a political issue requiring a response from whatever party holds office in Ottawa.

Constitutional recognition of Quebec's special status remains an important challenge. The parliamentary resolution of November 2006 recognizing 'the Québécois as a nation within Canada' is merely a statement of one parliament at one moment in time; future parliaments could choose to ignore it. There are also two other outstanding constitutional issues: recognition of First Nations as a third order of government, and the status of cities in the constitutional order. To respond fully to these challenges would require more than a 'muddling through' approach. But efficacious action on the last two matters—Aboriginal self-government and 'a better deal for cities'—might not require major institutional restructuring. Papillon in Chapter 14 has documented 'remarkable' movement in the direction of self-government within existing federal structures (though he cautions that the autonomy of most Aboriginal governments will be limited by their dependence on fiscal transfers from the federal government). And Sancton believes that the two senior orders of government could address the problems facing cities simply by working together within their own spheres of jurisdiction. In short, the most significant cost that a government would face under this 'muddling through' scenario would be a further weakening of the federation's legitimacy in the eyes of Aboriginal people and Quebec nationalists.

If something more than the status quo seems necessary to improve the performance, effectiveness, and legitimacy of the federal system, what can be done short of constitutional and major structural changes in the federation? Two reforms could be made within the existing institutional framework. One is to institutionalize the rules of the game of intergovernmental relations. Simeon and Nugent (Chapter 5) believe that the absence of rules and norms regarding matters such as the convening of first ministers' conferences, voting procedures, and alterations to intergovernmental agreements exacerbates conflict in the system. Federalism appears to work better where agreements incorporate explicit rules for amendments to programs as circumstances change. In the interest of enhancing the standing of the federal system on the three dimensions, governments could—and should—make a much greater effort to incorporate decision rules governing amendments to federal–provincial agreements, whether in the area of fiscal federalism or of climate change. Such rules would ideally go beyond the simple right of a government to terminate an agreement after giving notice. As an example of the institutionalization of intergovernmental relations, the Council of the Federation represents a step in the right direction, particularly if, as originally advocated, it evolves to include the Government of Canada.

A second change would be to embrace more fully various mechanisms of consultative democracy: that is, to bring non-state actors into intergovernmental discussions. As Simmons observes in Chapter 17, such linkages have the potential to improve both governments' and non-governmental actors' understanding of issues, and thereby to enhance both the legitimacy and effectiveness of policy outcomes.

The full weight of effective and legitimate governing should *not* be put on the institutions and processes of Canadian federalism. Indeed, if it is democratic government that Canadians seek, then analysts suggest that there are other institutions besides federalism on which we might more profitably focus our attention (Lane and Ersson, 2005; Norris, 2005). A prime example is the electoral system, which could be reformed to secure a fairer translation of votes into seats (Norris, 2005). The issue of electoral system reform has been on the agenda of several provincial governments in recent years. Were one or more provinces to serve as laboratories for innovation in the electoral system, the consequences for representative democracy—and by extension, for Canadian federalism—would be significant.

To conclude, there is room within the existing constitutional framework to reform the practices and norms of executive federalism as well as those of the parliamentary system whose functioning bears so significantly on intergovernmental relations. Whether the political will exists, either among the elites who inhabit the world of executive federalism or within civil society, and what conditions might help foster such political will, are important questions. They deserve the consideration of Canadians, their political leaders, and, not least, those who study the country's federal system.

References

Council of the Federation, Advisory Panel on Fiscal Imbalance. 2006. *Reconciling the Irreconcilable.* Available on-line at: <www.councilofthefederation.ca>.

Lane, Jan-Erik, and Svante Ersson. 2005. 'The Riddle of Federalism: Does Federalism Impact on Democracy?' *Democratization* 12, 2: 163–82.

Lazar, H. 2006. 'The Intergovernmental Dimensions of the Social Union: A Sectoral Analysis', *Canadian Public Administration* 49, 1: 23–45.

Norris, P. 2005. 'Stable Democracy and Good Governance in Divided Societies: Do Powersharing Institutions Work?' Faculty Research Working Paper RWP05-014. John F. Kennedy School of Government, Harvard University.

Scharpf, F. 1988. 'The Joint-Decision Trap: Lessons from German Federalism and European Integration', *Public Administration* 66, 3: 239–78.

Simeon, R. 1972, 2006. *Federal–Provincial Diplomacy: The Making of Recent Policy in Canada.* Toronto: University of Toronto Press.

Index